# CRITICAL QUESTIONS

## Invention, Creativity, and the Criticism of Discourse and Media

# CRITICAL QUESTIONS

## Invention, Creativity, and the Criticism of Discourse and Media

Edited by

**WILLIAM L. NOTHSTINE**

**CAROLE BLAIR**
University of California, Davis

**GARY A. COPELAND**
University of Alabama

**ST. MARTIN'S PRESS**
New York

*Editor:* Nancy Lyman
*Managing editor:* Patricia Mansfield-Phelan
*Associate project editor:* Nicholas Webb
*Production supervisor:* Elizabeth Mosimann
*Art director:* Sheree Goodman
*Text design:* Lee Goldstein
*Cover design:* Marek Antoniak

Library of Congress Catalog Card Number: 92-62794
8 7 6 5 4
f e d c b a

For information, write:
St. Martin's Press, Inc.
175 Fifth Avenue
New York, NY 10010

ISBN: 0-312-08971-6 (paperback)
      0-312-09140-0 (cloth)

# PREFACE

This anthology of original commentaries and reprinted essays on criticism of discourse and media focuses on the most fundamental questions of criticism: those of invention. How do critical questions arise? How do critics arrive at the selection of critical stance and critical object? How do the central questions of criticism evolve and change during the process of researching and writing the critical essay? Our belief in writing this book is that these questions are essential both to writing good criticism and to reading criticism well, and they have been neglected for too long.

The two goals of *Critical Questions* result from this belief. Our first goal in this anthology is to introduce the student critic to crucial but concealed problems of critical invention. Fifteen original commentaries invite beginning critics to read the reflections of critics on their own creative and inventional processes as critics.

Our second, broader goal is to initiate a discussion extending beyond this book on the significance of critical invention. In Chapter 2 we place the prevailing norms of critical invention and practice in their institutional and ideological context, in the hope that we might enable practicing critics and scholars of criticism to question these norms, and to investigate the possibilities of writing and teaching criticism differently.

Thus we have designed this anthology to be of interest and use to two audiences: to provide an introduction to criticism of media and rhetoric for beginning critics, and to raise philosophical and methodological issues relevant to practicing critics. It is intended to be useful as a stand-alone or supplemental text for upper division and graduate courses in rhetorical/media criticism.

As a textbook, this anthology points the way toward the possibility of a uniquely undergraduate-oriented approach to criticism. The traditional approach by criticism texts simply takes many of the professionally oriented assumptions and assignments of a graduate-oriented course and dilutes them for undergraduate readers. True, at the graduate level, and for students with some experience at writing criticism, the traditional approach, driven by method and theory, can be employed with some success. But the curiosity impelling beginning critics to write criticism is rarely fueled by the desire to explore theory, test the virtuosity of method, or develop a professionalized critical voice. By exploring the many and varied reasons and paths by which critics undertake their work, the anthology can help beginning critics to find a rationale for their own criticism other than the values of professional academic criticism.

*Critical Questions* has two distinctive features, arising from the pursuit of these goals. First, it downplays the traditional starting points for learning about criticism—method and theory—in favor of a focus on critical invention, which we consider to be prior to questions of method or theory. Note, however, that we remain sensitive to the range of theoretical and methodological stances popular in contemporary criticism: For those instructors who want their students to examine a variety of critical objects from the broad range of discourse and media, we have included essays examining documentary film, television sitcoms, social movements, classical orations, medical reports, religious broadcasting, government propaganda campaigns, science fiction films, and public memorials. Similarly, the essays also represent a variety of critical stances, such as genre criticism, feminist criticism, analysis of metaphor, Burkean criticism, and several other approaches for which no handy label exists. But our purpose is to place invention, not method, in the foreground.

Second, this book provides a colloquy with no ready counterpart: commentaries by over a dozen critics, candidly discussing the inventional processes behind their own finished criticism. These commentaries display that which is virtually invisible in finished critical essays: how personal choices, moral commitments, blind alleys, institutional forces, and sheer chance shape the choices we make in our role as critics, and—before that—the choices that define even our decision to take up that role. Paired with each of these commentaries is the finished critical work, the research and composition of which have been described by its author(s).

The book is divided into two main sections. Part I begins with an introductory chapter by the editors, intended primarily for the beginning critic who may have little experience with reading or writing criticism. This chapter discusses basic characteristics of criticism, and of media and rhetorical criticism in particular. It places particular emphasis on critical invention, the process by which critics make choices on critical text, critical approach, and so on. Appended to Chapter 1 is an annotated bibliography of essays on critical invention, as a guide to further reading by the beginning critic.

Chapter 2, also by the editors, investigates how and why these important questions, related to invention, have come to be neglected in contemporary criticism. It is written for the beginning critic, but may be of even greater interest to the more experienced critic, whether advanced student or practicing professional.

Chapters 3 and 4 are original essays by two well-known critics—Roderick P. Hart and Michael M. Osborn—discussing the process of critical invention with respect to the body of criticism each has produced in his career.

Part II of the book includes thirteen paired essays by practicing critics: Thomas W. Benson, Carole Blair, Barry Brummett, Maurice Charland, Bonnie J. Dow, Robert L. Ivie, Michael C. Leff, Elizabeth Walker Mechling and Jay Mechling, William L. Nothstine, Janice Hocker Rushing and Thomas S. Frentz, Martha Solomon, Bryan C. Taylor, and Philip Wander. Each pair of essays contains a commentary commissioned for this volume, in which the critics reflect upon the process of critical invention with respect to a particular critical essay of their own. Each of these contributing critics addresses a set of questions designed to encourage discussion of such heretofore slighted subjects as: (1) the selection of text or object and critical approach, (2) the source of the initial critical question, (3) the changing scope of the project, (4) obstacles, blind alleys, and detours in writing, and their consequences, (5) possible ethical issues in the questioning or writing, (6) the influence of manuscript readers, and (7) the resemblance of the finished essay to the original idea. Following each of these commentaries is the finished critical essay whose inventional processes it discusses.

We express thanks, first of all, to our many students in criticism and research methods classes, whose comments and questions have helped us develop ideas found in this book. Thanks also go to the critics and scholars who participated in this anthology, sharing their own inventional practices and processes with colleagues and students. Julie R. Brown, Anthony O. Edmonds, Kent A. Ono, Mary Rose Williams, and Dennis Jaehne and other members of the Ryde Group read and offered valuable comments on early portions of this manuscript. Rosemary McMahill, graduate research assistant, helped with important background research. The provocative contributions of the participants in the 1991 Seminar on the Undergraduate Rhetorical Criticism Course at the Western States Communication Association Convention, codirected by Harry Sharp, Jr., provided the impetus that finally moved this project off the drawing board and onto editorial desks as a proposal. We would like to thank the following reviewers: Jeffery L. Bineham, St. Cloud University; Thomas A. Hollihan, University of Southern California; Ronald E. Lee, University of Nebraska; William F. Lewis, Drake University; Janice E. Schuetz, University of New Mexico; and Craig R. Smith, California State University, Long Beach.

One of the most rewarding parts of this project has been our work with Jane Lambert, acquisitions editor at St. Martin's Press. From the first day, Jane saw the possibilities for this project as clearly as we did—perhaps more so. We owe Jane a tremendous debt of gratitude for helping us realize those possibilities, not only by bringing to bear the considerable resources of St. Martin's, but by her wit, humor, and shrewd editorial eye. Jane Lambert's successor, Nancy Lyman, who came on board the project as we entered production, deserves much of the credit for the look of the finished book, including the cover art. We also thank our project editor, Nick Webb, for the latitude he allowed us in our efforts to give the contributors to this volume their own voices. After consultation with Nick, we have chosen to interpret our permission to reprint materials for this book in the narrowest manner. As a result, the few apparent typos or misprints we found in the original journal articles reprinted in Part II have been left as is. For all other errors and ommisions we accept responsibility.

Finally, we extend special thanks to Margaret Seawell, acquisitions editor at Houghton-Mifflin. Although her press was unable to pursue the project with us, Margaret enthusiastically encouraged the first conversations between the three of us and Jane Lambert, her colleague and counterpart at St. Martin's. Such grace and generosity are too rare, and should not go unrecognized. We have therefore asked Margaret, and she has kindly consented, to stand as godmother to this book.

> William L. Nothstine
> Carole Blair
> Gary A. Copeland

# CONTENTS

# PART II

## CRITICAL INVENTION: MAXIMS, COMMENTARIES, AND CASES

■ MAXIM 1

# PART I

## CRITICAL INVENTION: A GENERAL ORIENTATION

# CHAPTER 1

# INVENTION IN MEDIA AND RHETORICAL CRITICISM: A GENERAL ORIENTATION

**William L. Nothstine, Carole Blair, and Gary A. Copeland**

The aim of this book is to explore the fundamental choices made by rhetorical and media critics when they choose to write or speak *as* critics. For experienced critics, we hope this will offer a productive reexamination of practices with which they are already familiar. But for the beginning critic, some background discussion of these practices and assumptions is in order. What is rhetorical or media criticism? What are its goals? And what part does invention—the fundamental choices of subject matter and approach—play in such criticism? These topics are the focus of this chapter.

This book is motivated by the conviction that rhetorical and media criticism can and should be worthwhile activities, for two reasons. First, rhetoric and its formative media are themselves important things to study, and are, at base, what rhetorical and media critics do study. The study of rhetoric considers talk and mediated discourse (including photographs, advertisements, musical compositions, paintings, situation comedies, films, novels, and so on) to be *consequential,* to have effect in the world. Not just everything that could be said or done actually is said or done, and as a result those things that *are* said and done are marks and measures of the culture, the speaker, and the language that generates them. Moreover, what is said or done has effect—sometimes easily seen, large and notable consequence, and sometimes fleeting, even negligible, perhaps almost undetectable effect. In any case, instances of language use *do* things. And rhetorical and media criticism, at least in our view, ought to be concerned with what rhetorical and mediated texts do and can do.

Second, when people act as rhetorical and media critics, they engage in rhetoric themselves. To act as a critic is to speak or to write, and that action is itself, like other instances of rhetoric, consequential. It is an investment in studying and writing (or speaking) about something that has already been said or done by someone else. It takes up a text and re-circulates it, that is, "says" or "does" that text differently, and asks the listener or reader to re-understand and re-evaluate the text, to see and judge it in new ways suggested by the critic. Criticism of media and rhetoric, conceived in this way, is a profoundly worthwhile activity, for it commits the critic to reflect upon important choices: whether to speak, what to speak about, how to speak, and to whom to speak. And it commits the critic to reflect upon the consequences of these choices for the critic and a community.

To act as a rhetorical or media critic is to act in relation to a text of the past (one already said or done), in the present, with or to an audience. It is therefore a *social* act in every sense. It is invested in living in a particular community, in a culture, and in the world. Moreover, to act as a critic is to act from a particular stance that is constructed socially, since who we are at any given moment is a matter of our *being with* others—our families, friends, acquaintances, genders, races, nationalities—both now and in our pasts. All of those connections affect what we will speak about, how we will speak, and what we have to say. Not only does criticism address events that occur within these arenas, but it also uses the principal resource—language—belonging to and defining those settings. Because language is a socially shared phenomenon, belonging not to one individual but to many, when one uses it, one always is in social territory.

In addition, the critic speaks or writes *to address others,* for the primary purpose of having an effect on the thinking or acting of an audience. Even the critic who speaks or writes as a beginning critic, perhaps for the purpose of fulfilling an obligatory course assignment, is still addressing someone else (an instructor), and asking that individual to accept or accord with the critic's choice of text and way of speaking about it.

One might assume, thus, that because all attempts at criticism have consequences or because they are all connected to one community or another, they are all equally important or worthwhile. But this would ignore the thoroughly social character of criticism: Just as our various communities and cultures value particular events differentially, the community of rhetorical and media critics must select what it values most. What kind of criticism should be most highly valued? Our view is one we believe at least some other critics share: that rhetorical or media criticism should be considered most valuable and worthwhile when it provokes its audience to think or act differently and in socially responsible ways.

How can rhetorical and media criticism manage such provocation? We think that criticism should be most highly valued when it acknowledges, acts upon, and is reflective of its own character as social. That is, we believe that criticism can provoke most effectively when it takes account of these three themes: criticism's investedness in community, its residence in language, and its commitment to an audience.

## ■ Criticism Is Invested in Community

When critics set out to do criticism, they make socially directed and motivated choices. First, critics decide what to write about. Every critic is different, of course, and the choice of texts to study is a critic's personal decision. However, suggesting that the choice is personal is simply another way of saying that it is socially situated. That is, a critic occupies a particular location within and among various social-cultural networks, simply by virtue of being human. It is the case, also, because the alternatives a critic has available—the plethora of texts from among which the critic may choose—are socially generated. They too are located within communities and other, larger social collectives.

Furthermore, the critic chooses to single out an event from an enormous constellation of such events. All critics must attend to this implication: Every time a critic chooses a text to study, that choice already implies that a community the critic occupies or addresses should pay special attention to that text because that text was chosen at the expense of countless others. Thus the critic implies, by the choice of texts, that the chosen text is more significant than others for some reason. This does *not* mean that critics always must choose the most recent, obvious, newsworthy, prominent, historically influential, artful, famous, or infamous text to study. It does mean, however, that the choice of a text should be made on the belief that a critical analysis of that particular text has something to offer—a different way of understanding or acting—to the community the critic addresses.

The relationship of criticism to community (or communities) suggests that critics might pose questions like the following to help clarify their choices of texts for study: With what communities do I identify myself? What might critical study of this text have to say about what is worth doing or worth knowing, in the values of these communities? Whose interests does this text appear to serve? To whom does it speak? To whom does it not speak? What are the consequences for individuals and/or the community if they embrace this text?

Questions such as these do not have to be posed exclusively in an isolated self-dialogue. In fact, the critic can learn a great deal by discussing a text with others, perhaps many others. In this way the critical essay becomes an extension of conversations the critic has already begun with others of similar (or perhaps very different) interests.

## ▉ Criticism Resides in Language

To act critically is to have a voice, and to speak or write about an event. Acting critically, thus, is to use language. However, critics, just like all other speakers, are caught between *using* language and being *used by* it. Because language is social, each of us speaks the language of our communities or cultures. How well we speak it may determine how effectual our criticism will be. This means, in part, that good criticism should fulfill the demands of all language use—it should be clear, interesting, appropriate, and forceful. It also means that the practices of criticism involve rewriting, editing, amending what one has set out to say as a critic. This process is never neutral or "right," like correcting the multiplication in an algebraic proof. Criticism grows and transforms as it is revised and changed. Criticism, even in the earliest stages of thinking through questions, involves unexpected turns, changes of mind, and reversals. This is not a flaw in the process or a sign of error. Such moments simply are part of the critical act. They arguably are even a positive aspect of criticism, for while they may appear to slow the process, a critic's "mistakes" and turns are part of learning what is worth doing and worth understanding, and perhaps will indicate how better to proceed the next time.

The demands on criticism go further than writing or speaking well, however. To speak well *as a critic* is to use not just one's native tongue but the language of criticism as well. To speak as a critic about a text is to single oneself out as capable of talking about a text in interesting and worthwhile ways. Rhetorical and media criticism demand some experience with and understanding of rhetorical and media texts at large as well as of the particular text the critic has chosen to study. One source—one of several—for this experience and understanding is the extensive body of scholarship already accumulated by critics of media and rhetoric. Study of this scholarship is one way to gain familiarity with the ways in which other critics speak, including the theoretical metaphors they employ, and the ways they support their assertions, qualify their findings, and display their reasoning. But this does not mean that a critic should merely emulate or model other critics' talk or ways of thinking about texts—it means that one should become sufficiently competent and familiar with the language of criticism, as with any language, so that one may effectively express *one's own* ideas and judgments.

The language of criticism is extraordinarily nuanced and complex, so much so that few critics ever master all of its many "theoretical dialects." But this nuance and complexity allow a critic a broad variety of ways to interpret or judge a text, according to the interests of the critic and the possibilities of the text itself. The language of criticism allows and often encourages certain kinds of questions on a critic's part, of which these are only some of the most general: What about this text makes it similar to or different from others? What is the significance, if any, of those similarities or differences? What are the components or constituent aspects of the text? How do they relate to one another or to the whole text? Is there a part or aspect of the text that stands out, and if so, why? What makes it convincing or unconvincing to a given audience? What do others see in this text that I do not, and how can they see it this way? What can I say about it that it does not say already? What do I see in the text that might not be so obvious to someone else? How can I make my case for what I see to someone who does not understand the text the way I do?

Such exploratory questions can be asked by critics as they begin to investigate texts. Most of these exploratory questions are derived from some general, theoretical view of rhetoric or media, and competent pursuit of such questions will require some familiarity with these theoretical bases. However, questions like these frequently lead to other, more specific, more interesting, or more arresting issues that the critic may wish to pursue— often, but by no means always, articulating them in the special language of rhetorical or media theory.

The questions we have suggested here are by no means intended to be used as a procedural checklist. They are simply suggestions, guides to ways in which critics can consider what sorts of texts are worth studying, and what approaches seem most likely to be profitable in this study. And although frustrating, it is also true that no text immediately reveals itself to the critic as a satisfactory one for that person to study and write about, and no question will be equally productive when asked of every possible text. Even a critic who has found satisfying answers to the sorts of questions we suggest may still decide that some other text, or some other question about that text, might be more worthy of her/his and the reader's time and energy.

## ▇ Criticism Is Committed to an Audience

The moments of choosing, studying, and speaking or writing about texts most certainly provide critics themselves with opportunities for learning and deliberation. But criticism is a public act, not a private one; it addresses an audience, making a case for re-understanding or re-valuing, and making that case *to* someone. Considerations of who that audience is should have an important constructive influence on critical speaking or writing. This is, in one respect, no more than a reiteration of the two previous points: that criticism is invested in community and that it resides in language. However, it does demand one further consideration. Because criticism itself is rhetorical, critics must be willing to place their speaking or writing into a public arena, where it may be judged and responded to like any other text.

We have suggested that rhetorical and media criticism should provoke socially responsible thinking and acting. "Responsible," in this context, frequently does *not* mean "orthodox." It means instead that criticism should be responsive to the concerns and well being of the communities in which it resides and to which it is addressed. It means that critics should be willing to speak to and within those communities in informed and thoughtful ways. And it means that critics should be prepared for both disagreement with and criticism of their work. Criticism is judged, we argue, by the degree to which it is provocative and worthwhile. This judgment will be rendered in the communities it enters.

Critics acknowledge their commitment to an audience when they ask questions such as the following: What benefit, beyond satisfying my own curiosity, will be gained by critical discussion of this text? What can be said about this text that should be said in the context of my community? What should my understanding or evaluation of it suggest in terms of the ways in which others in my community think or act? Is it worthy of the time and attention I will have to give it in speaking and writing about it? Will it be worth my reader's time and attention to grasp my understanding or evaluation of it?

Such questions, of course, will not all be equally useful in finding initial direction for a critical essay. Nor are they the only questions with which a critic may begin. Criticism that is provocative, that convinces an audience to think or act differently and in socially responsible ways, may arise from unusual or even idiosyncratic questions. "Speaking the language" of rhetorical and media criticism, therefore, does not mean repeating a few orthodox phrases. It means finding a way of understanding or judging a text, and building a case for it in the most thorough, compelling, and convincing way possible using the resources of the language of criticism.

## ▓ Reclaiming the Question of Critical Invention

This book is somewhat unusual among texts on media and rhetorical criticism because it focuses discussion on critical invention, rather than critical method or critical object. For reasons that we discuss in detail in Chapter 2, the available scholarly literature provides innumerable examples of the final *product* of criticism, the finished essay, but very few illustrations of the *process* of criticism—the practices of constructing, refining, and exploring one's critical question or thesis, which are the domain of invention. In Chapter 2, we shall examine trends in media and rhetorical criticism that have led critics often to be insensitive to and unaware of their own inventional practices. Specifically, we argue that attention has been drawn away from critical invention by the culture of "professionalism," which has (among other consequences) caused critics to be preoccupied with generating or contributing to theory rather than participating in civic life, and to adopt as a goal an image of the objectivity of science and technology that even scientists themselves would reject. Reclaiming inventional practices, we firmly believe, is crucial for the critic, whether beginning or experienced, and for the communities in which the critic resides.

Critical invention, we believe, is highly resistant to formalized, methodological prescriptions. Rather than some monolithic system imposed upon critics from above or outside, critical invention instead exists as a diversity of practices, as varied as the kinds of individuals who become critics and as disparate as the situations and communities in which they practice.

Since these inventional practices are rarely discussed explicitly, if at all, we have chosen to return to critical invention by the most direct route: by *asking* critics to describe their own inventional practices. The last two chapters of Part I are original position pieces by Roderick P. Hart and Michael M. Osborn, addressing the general themes of critical invention with regard to these critics' own body of work. Hart identifies his own critical concerns with matters of policy, and describes the political and procedural framework from which his writing emerges. Osborn reflects on his greater concern for the artistic dimension of discourse, rather than the policy dimension.

Following these, in Part II of this book, the inventional moments behind individual critical essays are recounted in thirteen original commentaries contributed by practicing critics. We have invited these critics to reflect upon the following moments in the inventional process, with respect to the critical essay that accompanies their commentary:

1. the selection of text or object and critical approach
2. the source of the initial critical question
3. the changing scope of the project
4. obstacles, blind alleys, and detours in writing, and their consequences
5. possible ethical issues in the questioning or writing
6. the influence of manuscript readers
7. the resemblance of the finished essay to the original idea

Each commentary describing critical invention, from the individual critic's point of view, is paired with the finished essay so that the reader can compare the product of criticism to the author's description of the inventional practices. To be sure, these commentaries detail markedly different approaches to doing criticism, but they also describe practices that are admirably motivated by the urge to write provocative and worthwhile criticism.

The choices these authors describe make up the operations by which critics truly and originally *show themselves to be critics.* While these choices are always, finally, individual in nature, they do display the themes we have associated in this chapter with provocative and worthwhile criticism.

## ■ Four Maxims to Guide Critical Invention

We dislike universal, abstract, methodological strictures and formulae for critics. We are interested instead in the specific and varied practices and motivations that guide critics' work. So we have organized our collection of commentaries on critical invention in Part II around four maxims—practical and moral advice on critical invention. Like all maxims, these express "truths" grounded in what is general rather than what is universal, and they are derived more from practical experience than from abstract principle. The four maxims we offer have a mixed lineage: They are shaped partly by truisms of rhetorical practice, partly by themes emerging from our examination of the commentaries by our contributors, and partly by our own convictions about the role of invention in criticism. In Part II we have grouped together the commentaries we felt threw the practical implications of each maxim into sharpest relief, either by directly addressing those implications, or by indirectly addressing them through contrast with the other commentaries in the same section.

## Maxim 1: Criticism Requires Understanding and Pursuing One's Own Interests

Critics should begin the search for things worth writing about as critic by reflecting on their own experiences, curiosity, and commitments—with what they care about, and think would be worth understanding. Critics should judge finished criticism, in part, by the extent to which its conclusions are useful or insightful for them, and relevant to their own experiences, curiosity, and commitments.

The commentaries in this section of Part II recount how critical projects get started when critics begin to examine important aspects of their experience: Bonnie J. Dow explores the connection of her study of hegemony and feminism to her enjoyment of the adventures of an early television role model of the feminist woman, the character Mary Richards. Similarly, Elizabeth Walker Mechling and Jay Mechling found that their study of the 1950s civil defense campaign was fueled by powerful images and memories of growing up during the early years of the Cold War. And Thomas S. Frentz and Janice Hocker Rushing report that their own study of images of technology in popular media began with their own apprehension about the role technology was beginning to play in their own lives.

## Maxim 2: Criticism Is Written to and for an Audience

Careful consideration of the audience(s) should offer critics direction in many important initial choices, from choices of subject and critical questions to determining the value of the conclusion(s) they expect to draw. Critics should remember that the value of their finished criticism will be judged, in part, by the extent to which it "speaks the language" of their readers and to which its conclusions are useful or insightful for them.

The commentaries in this section of Part II show different ways that consideration of audience can shape criticism: Thomas W. Benson describes how commitment to his professional audience shaped his decision to write for that audience about the documentaries of Fredrick Wiseman. Maurice Charland describes his choice to study Quebec nationalism as that of a critic who wants to write for a professional audience to which he is something of a newcomer, and who must therefore rethink his approach in terms of the context in which his desired audience will likely read the criticism. In the third commentary in this section, William L. Nothstine traces the changes in a manuscript on the PTL Ministry scandal as it was rewritten for three audiences: readers of a weekly magazine of political opinion, participants at a professional conference, and readers of a scholarly journal.

## Maxim 3: Criticism Is Both Served and Confined by Theory and Method

Theoretical abstractions and methodological dictates can function to limit and direct the critic's formative choices about what texts to examine and what to say about or ask of them. This limiting and directing function can help focus the critic's concentration on potentially interesting things to write about, but it can also make it more difficult for the critic to exercise individual imagination, judgment, and intuition in making those same choices.

The four commentaries in this section of Part II describe different ways that critics have relied on theory and method to serve their critical purposes: Robert L. Ivie explains how the rigors of his approach to criticism gave him the distance he felt he needed to study American war rhetoric. Barry Brummett, by comparison, describes theory as balanced and kept in check by his own curiosity about the rhetoric of apocalyptic fundamentalists. Martha Solomon describes the circular movement, between her reading of the Tuskegee Syphilis Reports and her reexamination of theoretical texts on rhetoric, that shaped the questions she asked of those reports. In the last commentary of this section, Michael C. Leff recounts the methodological choices he made in one of his early essays, and speculates on the ways his study of Ciceronian orations might have been improved if he had viewed the role of theory and method differently.

## Maxim 4: Criticism Rarely Travels a Straight Line to Its End

A variety of factors and forces can intervene to redirect the path criticism takes while the critic is still writing it. As a result critics often have to search for new ways to reach their original goals in writing, or for ways to redefine the goals themselves. Remember that the early formulations of critical questions or goals must be regarded as provisional.

The commentaries in this section of Part II all reflect upon the capacity of criticism to take unexpected turns as it is being written: Carole Blair describes how she and her coauthors felt obstructed by the seeming complexity of responses to the Vietnam Veterans Memorial, until they considered the possibility that this complexity itself offered the key to understanding the Memorial. Philip Wander traces the transformation of his essay about American foreign policy from a partisan cry against the Vietnam War to "historical scholarship" published some years after the end of that war. In the final essay of this section, Bryan C. Taylor compares his own attempts to reconstruct his inventional practices in his commentary for this book with the various attempts to tell the "story" of Los Alamos, and concludes that all such self-understanding will be partial at best.

# ▇ Conclusion

Critical invention is a region the boundaries of which are marked off by the distance between a critic's first entanglement with an issue or text and the culmination of that involvement in a provocative and worthwhile critical essay. We have dedicated this chapter, and indeed this book, to the exploration of that region after a long period of professional neglect.

Although this book is a first step toward retrieving the question of critical invention and its place in criticism, we have by no means resolved the matter here. Were critics required to postpone raising the question of invention until they had discovered a "solution," the question would never be raised, to the loss of all concerned. But the vigor, imagination, and commitment contained in the following essays reaffirm for us the value of beginning, and the importance of asking questions, even—and perhaps especially—when the answers are not yet obvious.

# ▇ Additional Readings

The following essays address various aspects of the processes and practices of invention in media and rhetorical criticism. They do not always agree with one another, nor are they always in complete harmony with our own position in this chapter. But this is in part why we recommend them, especially to the beginning critic, as further investigations of the varied practices by which critics begin their criticism. Other commentaries on critical invention are discussed in the text and notes of Chapter 2, "Professionalization and the Eclipse of Critical Invention."

Benson, Thomas W. "The Senses of Rhetoric: A Topical System for Critics." *Central States Speech Journal* 29 (1978): 237–50.

Benson discusses nine broad standpoints from which critics may examine texts, whether oratorical or non-oratorical, including: the investigation of the author's intentions to the persuasive possibilities of the text; the examination of a text's capacity to have unintended social consequences; and the evaluation of the extent to which a text displays ethical commitment, as well as artistic merit or pragmatic consequences.

Campbell, Karlyn Kohrs. "Criticism: Ephemeral and Enduring." *Speech Teacher* 23 (1974): 9–14.

Campbell identifies two important issues: *what* should be studied by the critic, and *to what purpose?* Her answer divides criticism into two broad types: social criticism, concerned with understanding the practical consequences of discourse for the formulation of issues and the justification of policy in particular cases; and academic or professional criticism, directed toward general theoretical understanding rather than response to individual situations.

Crowley, Sharon. "Reflections on an Argument That Won't Go Away: Or, A Turn of the Ideological Screw." *Quarterly Journal of Speech* 78 (1992): 450–65.

The "argument that won't go away," which Crowley examines, is the debate among critics about the connection of ideology and criticism: Do all critics write from some ideological position, however clearly articulated, and hence have responsibilities to clarify and account for their own interests? Or is "ideological criticism" a way for critics of a particular political bias to "find" in a text only what they already expected to see there?

Foss, Sonja K. "Rhetorical Criticism as the Asking of Questions." *Communication Education* 38 (1989): 191–96.

Foss describes the benefits for the beginning critic of focusing on general questions that characterize "thinking rhetorically." She describes three broad categories of such questions: questions about the relationship of a text to its context; questions about the ability of a text to construct a particular reality for its author and audience; and questions about the text as an expression of its creator.

Gronbeck, Bruce E. "Rhetorical Criticism in the Liberal Arts Curriculum." *Communication Education* 38 (1989): 184–90.

Gronbeck describes three talents the beginning critic should acquire and develop: facility with the language of rhetorical criticism; proper understanding of the various contexts within which texts may be examined and interpreted; and preparation for the making of aesthetic, moral, and pragmatic judgments about the uses and abuses of texts. He shows how these talents are directly related to the goals of liberal arts education, "the development of the mental facilities necessary for leading a mature life in society."

Hart, Roderick P. "Contemporary Scholarship in Public Address: A Research Editorial." *Western Journal of Speech Communication* 50 (1986): 283–95.

Hart argues that criticism of public address should be directed toward the conceptual or theoretical implications of individual cases, rather than preoccupied with the case itself. Given this starting point, he identifies several patterns of criticism that undermine movement in this direction, including: fixation on details of occasion or personality; and allowing the jargon of technical criticism to substitute for clear critical insight.

Hillbruner, Anthony. "The Moral Imperative of Criticism." *Southern States Communication Journal* 40 (1975): 228–47.

Hillbruner argues that, while criticism should attend to the aesthetic judgment of the "means" (that is, to the theoretical explanation of how a text functions), critics cannot ignore their responsibility to assess the "ends" of rhetoric as well—to judge and respond to the social and moral consequences of texts. To this end, Hillbruner identifies the moral imperatives for the critic: to seek the truth, to tell the truth, and to expose lies.

Klumpp, James F., and Thomas A. Hollihan. "Rhetorical Criticism as Moral Action." *Quarterly Journal of Speech* 75 (1989): 84–97.

Klumpp and Hollihan identify the role of the critic as part interpreter of events, part teacher, part social actor. They explore the possibilities and demands of this role by offering their own examination of an instance of popular discourse. They conclude that the basis of the critic's link to matters of social consequence is "the creative energy of criticism—the inventional power."

Nilson, Thomas R. "Criticism and Social Consequences." *Quarterly Journal of Speech* 42 (1956): 173–78.

Nilson begins with a point of disagreement among critics: Should criticism concern itself with rendering ethical, practical, or artistic judgments on discourse? Or are such judgments practically impossible and theoretically irrelevant? He lists several grounds for judgment of effects, all consistent with the general principle that such judgments should encompass the influences a text has on the society upon which it has impact, not simply its influence on an immediate audience.

Rosenfield, Lawrence W. "The Anatomy of Critical Discourse." *Speech Monographs* 35 (1968): 50–69.

Rosenfield identifies the role of critic as that of the expert commentator who offers reasoned judgments about texts. He further explores a variety of critical foci, starting points for criticism defined by differing degrees of emphasis laid upon author, text, context, and the critic's own interests within that criticism.

Scott, Robert L. "Focusing Rhetorical Criticism." *Communication Education* 33 (1984): 89–96.

Scott suggests questions that critics may find useful in selecting texts and critical approach: Does the text being considered fit comfortably into conventional rhetorical categories, or it a comparatively unconventional instance? Is the preliminary intention of the critic to focus on the message itself, or its underlying value premises, or the strategies it seems to evidence? He argues that criticism will often be more productive and useful when it recognizes that the answers to these two questions interact to shape the value of the conclusions the critic may draw.

Wander, Philip, and Steven Jenkins. "Rhetoric, Society, and the Critical Response." *Quarterly Journal of Speech* 58 (1972): 441–50.

Wander and Jenkins consider criticism to be "coming to terms with an object in terms of one's values." These values show themselves in what one chooses to study as a critic, how one forms an interpretation of it, and how one attempts to communicate this interpretive response to others. They argue against approaches to criticism that construe the ideal of "objectivity" so as to resist or deny the association of criticism with the critic's commitments and values.

# CHAPTER 2

# PROFESSIONALIZATION AND THE ECLIPSE OF CRITICAL INVENTION

William L. Nothstine, Carole Blair, and Gary A. Copeland

H*ow are the fundamental questions that guide critical research developed, refined, and justified?* The implications of this question, sometimes misunderstood but more often flatly ignored by modern critical researchers, provide the focus for this anthology. In this chapter we investigate the background of the question, tracing how political, historical, and ideological considerations have shaped discussion of critical invention. This investigation will require examination of the grounds for a number of interrelated critical practices and assumptions and a reexamination of contemporary criticism's relationships to philosophy, science, pedagogy, and politics. Our particular focus will be upon professional rhetorical and media criticism, but the concerns raised here are relevant to literary criticism as well as to historical and interpretive research.[1]

Although we believe that the question—how are critical questions developed, refined, and justified?—has been systematically slighted, our goal in this chapter is not to provide a systematic answer to it.[2] Instead, the principal goal for this essay is to explore how the question of critical invention has come to be slighted, why, and at what cost.[3]

By "critical invention," we mean the formative acts preceding and prefiguring the completed critical essay. Critical invention, in this sense, is approximately equivalent to inquiry, "the creation of what is new in any discipline or endeavor" (LeFevre 2). Invention is an active process involving discovery and production. In criticism, it includes the choices animating the decision to write about a particular text, the constructing and choosing of things to say about that text, and decisions about how to say them. It is not just a process of individual reflection; it is, as Karen Burke LeFevre points out, a social process:

> Invention may first of all be seen as social in that the self that invents is, according to many modern theorists, not merely socially influenced but even socially constituted. Furthermore, one invents largely by means of language and

other symbol systems, which are socially created and shared. Invention often occurs through the socially learned process of an internal dialogue with an imagined other, and the invention process is enabled by an internal social construct of audience, which supplies premises and structures of belief that guide the writer. Invention becomes explicitly social when writers involve other people as collaborators, or as reviewers whose comments aid invention, or as "resonators" who nourish the development of ideas. . . . Finally, invention is powerfully influenced by social collectives, such as institutions, bureaucracies, and governments, which transmit expectations and prohibitions, encouraging certain ideas and discouraging others. (2)

We are interested in making critics' inventional practices explicit for two reasons. First, we believe that the far-reaching consequences of the culture and ideology of "professionalism," as it has been construed in academia, have included profoundly negative repercussions for criticism, including blinding critics to their own inventional practices. To acknowledge the problems and issues of critical invention may be a first step in loosening the hold of the institutional ideology of professionalism on criticism. Second, and equally important, students who are called upon to produce critical essays are all too often left with nowhere to begin, because the formative practices of thinking and writing critically are almost never articulated or specified in textbooks or in published professional criticism. We believe that neither practicing critics nor students of criticism can afford to leave these practices unarticulated or unacknowledged.

We acknowledge willingly that the issues regarding critical invention, such as those raised in this anthology, are not usually considered worthy of discussion; that is precisely our point in raising them. The most "trivial" or "obvious" assumptions frequently become more important and less apparent when discussed openly and evaluated carefully. The very fact that critics' inventional acts are taken for granted is what entices us to examine them. We believe that our own scholarship, and that of our colleagues in rhetorical and media criticism, is itself rhetorical and thus subject to questioning and critique at the level of its own rhetorical assumptions and practices.

The initial encounter of a critic with a text is an essential and formative constituent of the critical act.[4] Equally significant are the critic's grounds for the decision to write about that text, as well as decisions made in probing its possibilities, making interpretive and evaluative choices, and finding the words to re-present the text to readers of a critical essay. These are the inventional moments of criticism, the practical acts that constitute it and that lead to its culmination as a "finished" critical essay. Their significance to the critical act is undeniable. Yet, critics who work within the confines of a *professional* critical role generally treat their own inventional acts as the unspeakable, or at least as the unspoken.[5] Readers of critical essays witness the product of these actions but are rarely granted access to practices behind the process.[6]

It would be unusual, for instance, to read a critical essay in which any of the author's personal or political reasons for initial interest in the critical text addressed in that essay were revealed. More typically, the author would argue that the text is (or should be) interesting because of its capacity to illustrate a theoretical point. Also unusual would be a critic's acknowledgment or discussion of having had a change of mind or heart while grappling with the text. Such a change and the thoughtful reflections that engendered it would be considered dubious inclusions in a critical essay. So too would any real focus on the critic's enthusiasm or distaste for a text or any mention of attempts to account for the critic's own reactions. Likewise, critics are unlikely to discuss the obstacles they have encountered, the points at which they "got stuck" in the process, the aspects of the text that resisted their interpretive focus, or the ways in which editorially demanded revision may have pulled their essay in directions they felt were inconsistent with their original interests. Such content is considered irrelevant, trivial, idiosyncratic, or—heaven forbid—subjective, and therefore "inappropriate" to critical writing. These absences in scholarly critical discourse are symptomatic of the larger issue we intend to pursue in this chapter.

The "cover-up" of these issues of critical invention is not the result of individual or conspiratorial directive. The problem, instead, arises from community norms and historical practices. Practicing critics form a professional community that maintains and is maintained by particular, regularized norms. One of these norms is the concealment of the critic's inventional acts. Beginning critics, observing that no one else reports these acts, and having been taught that such material is inappropriate material for inclusion in a critical essay, will understandably be inclined to pass over such matters themselves. As critics gain more experience, these acts are taken for granted more and more, receiving little, if any, reflection, and considered not worth discussing in the precious space they would occupy in a journal article. Since, presumably, an even more experienced critic serves as a gatekeeper (a journal editor or referee) for other critics, any attempts to incorporate reports of the inventional process would commonly be turned back at the gate. It is unlikely that gatekeepers have to do much blocking of this sort, though, because the pedagogical arm of criticism commonly censors these "obvious or trivial" aspects of a critical work prior to a manuscript's submission for publication.

Thus critics refuse discussion of their inventional practices, because they have learned to, because they have imitated the practices of others who do so, or because the gatekeeping function has forced them to do so. But the teachers, role models, and gatekeepers are not the *causes* of the problem. They too are its *symptoms,* having themselves been caught up in the same historical, normative practices as all other critics. We all speak the discourse of our community. Professional critics speak the discourse unique to their critical community, a discourse of product at the expense of process; of theory at the cost of practice; and of knowledge, gallantly if unsuccessfully guarded from the intrusion of interest.[7]

The norms of the contemporary critical community are the product of academic professionalism. By "professionalism" we mean a culture in which individuals practice socially valued skills in exchange for the exclusive right to practice those skills, the right to impart the knowledge necessary to the skills, and prestige. Professionalism in academia is also a historically identifiable ideological edifice held together by three interlocking supports: disciplinarity, the creation and enforcement of academic disciplines, which divide knowledge into separate territories, each with its own proper methods of investigation; scientism, the reduction of all "knowledge" to a somewhat limited interpretation of the assumptions and techniques of modern science; and pressures toward civic and experiential disengagement on the part of the academic professional. (Each of these central terms—*professionalism, disciplinarity, scientism,* and *civic disengagement*—will receive further discussion later in this chapter.) Professionalism, as it is currently practiced in academia, causes criticism to be transformed—or, more precisely, reduced—from a process to a product. Since invention and creativity are aspects of the process of criticism, rather than of the final written product, our understanding of them has become a casualty of this reductive movement. In the next section of this essay we shall present an investigation of professionalism and its institutional supports as a general ideology within which virtually all scholarship, including criticism, operates. Following that, this chapter will trace the implications of this analysis of professionalism for media and rhetorical criticism in the speech communication field.

## ■ Professionalism and Its Institutional Supports

An adequate discussion of the eclipse of critical invention cannot go far without acknowledging the tremendous shaping influence of professionalism on academic institutions and workers. The ideology of professionalism is founded upon the demarcation of a body of expert knowledge to which the professional is heir and guardian, based on extended formal study and often formal or informal apprenticeship (Wilshire 48).

Professionalism has been a fundamental part of the American middle-class experience of the past 150 years. The emergence of professionalism, with its social influence and mystique, has been a potent force toward upward mobility for its practitioners in the many fields influenced by it,[8] but it has had a broader social function as well. The professions took on the role of an aristocracy in a putatively classless society and offered authority in a putatively democratic society. As Gerald Graff suggests, "Faith in professional expertise gave a measure of reassurance to Americans who had always lacked traditional authorities and now, after the Civil War, found themselves confronted by bewildering industrial and social changes. But in exchange for this reassurance, these Americans were obliged to surrender their independence of judgment to experts" (*Professing Literature* 64).

The rise of professionalism in American education is typically linked to the ascendancy of the German university model in the late nineteenth century.[9] The professionalization of the American university, marking a replacement of the old college ideal of reinforcing liberal culture, involved the establishment of disciplinary departments and majors as well as graduate programs for in-depth study. Like their German forerunners, American universities took as their directive the advancement of knowledge rather than the transmission of culture. Thus, research became the keystone of the institution. Professional researchers, that is, professors, would be judged by their accomplishments in "discovering" and publishing original contributions to knowledge. Because advancement of knowledge, not culture, was the aim, these researchers would be "freed" to pursue their research with the detachment and neutrality becoming a professional.[10] The universities would serve society principally by supporting the development and publication of new areas of knowledge, and secondarily by instructing students in these areas of knowledge and by advising decision makers in the public realm. The new ideology supported, and in turn was supported by, the disciplinizing of higher education, disengagement of professionals from civic and cultural experience, and a stance of scientism.

## Disciplinarity

The knowledge and unified research practices that generate knowledge in a field constitute a discipline, the *sine qua non* of professionalism.[11] The founding canons of a discipline not only define the intellectual area proper to it, but they also serve as a powerful, authoritative force for screening out claims and claimants not of the discipline.[12] The functions of the divisions and norms created by disciplinarity are thus profoundly self-interested and conservative. As Edward Said writes:

> It is patently true that, even within the atomized order of disciplines and fields, methodological investigations can and indeed do occur. But the prevailing mode of intellectual discourse is militantly antimethodological, if by methodological we mean a questioning of the structure of fields and discourses themselves. A principle of silent exclusion operates within and at the boundaries of discourse; this has now become so internalized that fields, disciplines, and their discourses have taken on the status of immutable durability. Licensed members of the field, which has all the trappings of a social institution, are identifiable as belonging to a guild, and for them words like "expert" and "objective" have an important resonance. To acquire a position of authority within the field is, however, to be involved internally in the formation of a canon, which usually

turns out to be a blocking device for methodological and disciplinary self-questioning. (22)

Disciplines create both the accepted categories of knowledge and a mystique to separate these categories from one another. In doing so, they also segregate the professionals of one discipline from the professionals of another. In academia, of course, this is accomplished primarily through the bureaucratic logic of the department structure. The existence and legitimation of disciplines largely eliminate the need as well as the opportunity to discuss the possible network of relationships between and among disciplines, the rationale for disciplines, or even what constitutes a discipline.

Disciplines are, by definition, autonomous, self-contained, and self-regulating (Weber x). That is, they are restrictive in character. But as Michel Foucault has suggested, they are also productive. They "have their own discourse," and they "engender . . . apparatuses of knowledge *(savoir)* and a multiplicity of new domains of understanding. They are extraordinarily inventive. . . ." ("Two Lectures" 106). Even these productive characteristics of disciplines, their discourses and apparatuses, work to differentiate and exclude, however. Even "colleagues" at the same university frequently are unable to communicate across their disciplinary divisions, for their discourses and apparatuses allow for no common language in which to converse.[13] Members of a discipline, thus, serve as the almost exclusive audience of another member's discourse. Scholarly discourses address primarily other professionals of the same field.

This restriction of audience also means that the nature of the relationship scholars have to their students has had to be redefined. A few generations ago, the justification of a university education—and of public support for it—was that it prepared students to participate fully and actively in civic and cultural life. But as Bruce Wilshire notes, contemporary undergraduates, through the disciplinary major designed by their professionalized faculty, "are treated as if they were preparing to become graduate students, specialists, young professional academics" (79). In some disciplines, such as accountancy or advertising, the basis for this assumption is evident and plausible; yet this assumption is held with equal firmness in areas such as history, anthropology, literature, or sociology, where far less support exists for such an expectation. By indoctrinating these students in disciplinary discourses and practices, however diluted for ease of learning, their major courses prepare them for careers that the overwhelming majority of them do not seek and even more will not attain. Terry Eagleton's ironic description of students in literary criticism probably is not atypical: the "content of their education was almost wholly beside the point; few of them were likely to find an acquaintance with Baudelaire indispensable for personnel management" (91). The point is that disciplinary discourse *seeks* to confine its audience only to specialists and to students it holds hostage against the grant of a degree.

## Civic and Experiential Disengagement

One of the clearest marks of professionalization is the impulse to unify a discipline. This is an obvious corollary to professionalization, because it is unity that presumably gives a discipline its identity. But if it is to demarcate its boundaries, a discipline must actively separate itself from other realms of knowledge and experience, chiefly through a clearly differentiated subject matter and set of practices. Its population, the professionals who comprise the discipline, must respect and guard those boundaries. A discipline also appears, thus, to require organization of those who belong to it in a guild or professional society, the group that names, contains, and legitimizes the existence and maintenance of the professional.[14] Disciplines thus quarantine academic experience from contamination by knowledge, practice, and experience from outside the discipline and the university.

The professional association tends to usurp from the university the primary loyalties of academic workers as well as the power to set standards for judging their work, particularly at "graduate institutions."[15] In return, the association and its members offer the service of judging the quality of individual faculty members' research. The university (and any culture at large beyond the edge of campus) is excused from much of the responsibility of evaluating the results of a faculty member's scholarly work by the availability of "outside reviewers," who are members of the profession, and who serve as gatekeepers for professional publications and/or evaluators in tenure and promotion cases.[16]

The power of the professional association, to offer judgments or to provide a reservoir of other professionals who may offer judgments, can be maintained only under two conditions. First, the association must represent a specific—that is, unified—expertise. It cannot, after all, offer judgments of scholarly work falling outside a narrow specialty. So its domain must *be* relatively narrow, explicit, and unified. Second, the judgment by professionals of other professionals must be made at a distance. In other words, the "local" activities of a professional—such as teaching or service to a community—cannot be invoked as criteria for professional evaluation. Such "local" concerns therefore remain functionally outside the domain of professional activity. A scholar's "research product" is, by the profession's light, the only reasonable standard of professional judgment, for it alone is public and accessible. Thus, the power of the profession remains its ability to display unity, and its unity continues to be focused in research.

Because research entitles the academic worker to the role of "expert" or "professional," academic practice becomes oriented toward achievement principally in that arena. Such focus has an isolating effect on the individual. The image of the research scholar has consequently become one of "self-denial," with "the individual forsaking discernible comforts and social graces in order to follow his calling" (Haber 284–85).

Thus, "expertise" seems to depend upon the scholar's removal (to the extent possible) from experiences of everyday life. Comforts and social graces are the least of the losses; as Wilshire suggests, "individual advancement within professions [tends] to supplant civic duty" (64). Since service, and other civil activities, hold little discernible place in contributing to or judging an individual's professional expertise, they become less important than research and are segregated more and more from it. Even teaching is typically regarded as in opposition to the pursuit of expertise. As Jacoby puts it, "professionalization leads to privatization or depoliticization, a withdrawal of intellectual energy from a larger domain to a narrower discipline" (147). Drawn away from the civic life in favor of the professional identity, one is increasingly enjoined, in Wilshire's phrase, "to clap oneself in the nutshell of one's theory, to line it with mirrors, and to count oneself king of infinite space" (72).

Under such pressures, addressing a community beyond one's own discipline quickly becomes suspect, as Russell Jacoby notes in his observation that academics are not considered "serious" professionals if they write for general audiences (153). Moreover, and more specifically in the humanities and social sciences, even those research emphases that might hold direct relevance for a nonacademic community find little or no application or inspiration in that community. The judgments rendered by scholars on the moral world at large, writes Wilshire, thus "tend to be construed in ever more technical senses, imperiling the sense of their broadly human significance, and of how they might be *true* of human life" (49). As a result, while unified professional groups demand and receive the loyalty and adherence of the academic worker, professionalism disengages the worker from public experience and involvement, thus augmenting the isolation already imposed by disciplinarity.

## Scientism

The image of knowledge and power that has emerged from the modern culture of professionalism, and that in turn supports that culture, is overwhelmingly a technological one. "Knowledge" has come to refer to the methods and instrumentations by which professionals study things as much as to the results of those studies. Those possible objects of study not amenable to a discipline's theories, as operationalized in its methods and instrumentations, might as well not exist (Wilshire 72).[17] The sum total of this reduction of knowledge to technology we call "scientism." A more complete description of scientism is provided by Tom Sorrell:

> Scientism is the belief that science, especially natural science, is much the most valuable part of human learning—much the most valuable part because it is much the most authoritative, or serious, or beneficial. Other beliefs related to this one may also be regarded as scientistic, e.g., the belief that science is the

*only* valuable part of human learning, or the view that it is always good for subjects that do not belong to science to be placed on a scientific footing. (1)

The ideology of professionalism hallows the discovery of knowledge and thus encourages scientism. It particularly encourages attempts by the social sciences and humanities to gain scientific status—and thereby strengthen their disciplinary status—by appropriating or emulating the practices of the so-called "hard" sciences. Scientism shows itself as a set of practices guided by a worldview. This worldview is not always complete, explicit, or entirely coherent, but it does display several recurring and identifiable features.

According to this adopted worldview, the modern natural sciences enjoy a consensus regarding the fundamental matters of method, stance, and theory. The social sciences and humanities can and should emulate this consensus in their own domains. The fundamental questions guiding scientific research should be ideologically neutral, detached from historical and pragmatic considerations, and directed toward the eventual construction of unified theory. Four general themes animate this worldview: the cult of objectivity, the goal of theory building, the elevation of method as the means of theory testing and construction, and faith in consistent scientific progress.

The primary element in this set of assumptions is well known: the proper stance for the researcher is one of objectivity—practical, ethical, and intellectual distance from the object of study. Objectivity is taken to be necessary for theory building and guaranteed by method. "Objectivity" here is an umbrella term for a collection of philosophical principles, a hodgepodge held together more by tradition than by any logical or philosophical coherence it might possess. The objectivist cant features the presumption that the questions worth asking, and the answers worth having, are generally empirical in nature and positivist in temperament.[18] As Wilshire correctly observes:

> To say, as many do, that positivism no longer exercises strong influence in the university is a self-deceiving fiction. Positivism was—and is to a great extent—"in the air," not just confined to philosophy departments, and practically no department in the university goes uninfluenced. In some cases it is gross and inescapable to any attentive eye. The constricted attention to "testable facts," and the cognitive as opposed to the emotive, cripples the imagination and unnecessarily restricts the scope of study. This occurs in many departments of history and economics, for example—also in "the better" departments of art history and music history, or musicology. (207)

To be sure, professionalism has produced some of its greatest cultural effects (although not without a price) in those disciplines whose "knowledge base" has been most directly tied to empirical methods and empirical outcomes: medicine, engineering, and so on. Small wonder that other emerging disciplines found that route tempting.[19]

But it has been more than just a temptation. As Stanley Aronowitz suggests, "modern science demarcates itself, not by reconstituting the object, but by defining rationality in a specific way" (8). To the extent that its definition took hold and was generalized beyond natural science, other areas of inquiry had to pursue scientific goals and practices or risk being labeled "irrational," that is, unfit to produce knowledge and therefore not deserving of professional status. That the equation of science and rationality *has been* widely accepted seems clear, both within academic institutions and society at large.[20] Thus, the onus on disciplines is obvious. Aronowitz expresses it clearly: "All inquiry is obliged to direct itself to science, or, by inference, to distinguish itself from science" (viii).

Perhaps no practical consequence of this pressure is more ironic than the modernist scholarly horror of the rhetorical. Professional scholarship generally strives to prevent as much as possible the open recognition of the rhetorical character of its own writing. In history, for example, as Hayden White points out, disciplinary and professional status could not go forward until it was settled that the coherence of history was derived from the evidence itself, not from the rhetorical inventiveness of the historian:

> As long as history was subordinated to rhetoric, the historical *field* itself (i.e., the past or the historical process) had to be viewed as a *chaos* that made no sense at all or one that could be made to bear as many senses as wit and rhetorical talent could impose upon it. Accordingly, the disciplining of historical thinking that had to be undertaken, if history considered as a kind of *knowledge* was to be established as arbitrator of the realism of contending political programs, each attended by its own philosophy of history, had to consist first of all in its de-rhetoricization. (128)

Hence producing methodically rigorous, but impersonal, reports substitutes for engaging an audience and their world, ethically and intellectually, as a persuader. The claim of such reports to our assent is based on the rigor and objectivity of their methods, rather than the ability of writers to adduce *good reasons* for an interpretation—with emphasis on both the moral and rational implications of that term "good reasons" (Toulmin 110–15; Said 15).

Second, traditional science set for itself the task of theory generation. Sorrell explains the view of scientific empiricism:

> Science is a conjunction of well-confirmed scientific theories, and scientific theories, however disparate their subject matter, may be viewed as partially interpreted logical calculi. The calculi contain axioms and postulates from which observational truths are supposed to be derived. Taken together, the calculi of the different sciences add up to the body of truths of science. (4–5)

On this view, scientific theories are unified. Such theories serve one or both of two functions: prediction and explanation. Prediction is the identification of causal mechanisms for the purpose of making inferences about future events; explanation is the invocation of causal principles to account for an already-given state of affairs. Both explanation and prediction are to be distinguished, in modern science, from the rendering of a judgment (Kerlinger 9–10; 459–62). Scientific theories are at their best when their explanatory and predictive functions are most generalizable (Feigl 10–11; Kerlinger 11). The best theory thus accounts for or predicts the broadest range of phenomena in the simplest formulation (Holton 205–6).

The reliance upon scientific method for confirmation or falsification, the third characteristic of scientism, vouchsafes objectivity. "Testability" in principle is considered one of the most basic requirements of theory.[21] The methods required for testing are held to be observer-neutral, available to anyone properly trained to verify or falsify the results of another's test (Feigl 11). Michael McGee and John Lyne summarize this "story of scientism":

> Science is universal in the sense that the logic of its inquiry is the same in any domain where knowledge is possible. The universal objective of inquiry is explanation and prediction. An event is explained by showing that it occurred as the result of laws, rules, or principles of nature and society; and knowledge of laws, rules, conditions, and so on makes prediction possible. . . . No claim will be acknowledged as fact until it has been verified by observation, and no proposition will be treated seriously even in theory unless it is possible to envision the conditions of its verification. (383)

Scientific methods allow for empirical generalization, the "raw material" of theory generation and testing.

Finally, the attitude of scientism is an optimistic one; the theme of scientific "progress" animates and supports it. Gerald Feinberg expresses this attitude as well as anyone: "As time goes on, we can expect to see each link in the chain between simple and complex phenomena grow gradually stronger. This will reinforce the view held by most physicists and many other scientists that we are dealing with a single subject matter and that a single set of fundamental laws ultimately governs all natural phenomena" (181). Scientism exaggerates this position to suggest that "the advance of science will ultimately provide definitive solutions for the problems of society" (Davis 193). Even when the optimism is not so far-reaching, science is set up within the culture of professionalism as the means of knowledge production, claiming "exclusive access to truth" (Wilshire 153).

One problem with this characterization of the process and practice of science is that, since the early part of the twentieth century, natural scientists themselves have largely abandoned it. "It is a pity, then," writes Stephen Toulmin with understated irony, "for scholars working in the humanities to continue shaping their critical attitudes and theories by relying on a contrast with modern science that—among scientists themselves—no longer even *seems* to exist" (101). Of course, the image of science as formulating its questions for research based on "the facts," rather than on the prior interests of the scientist, was never very accurate (Toulmin 101; Pirsig 97–100). Instead, this naive image of the project of science has been far more important to the social sciences and humanities in their quest for institutional clout. Page Smith points out the irony implicit in this state of affairs: "Whereas the would-be scientists talk about detachment, objectivity, neutrality, the dispassionate treatment of data, the 'hard' scientists and their biographers talk of passion and obsession, of hunches and of inspiration, of insight, excitement, and profound emotion" (282). In the age of post-Heisenberg science, when the "uncertainty principle" has become a cornerstone of research in that most fundamental of sciences, researchers in physics and the rest of the natural sciences have abandoned the objectivist view to the social scientists and humanists—if they will have it.[22]

The other problem, of course, is that the canons of traditional science, even if they *were* accepted in the physical sciences today, would not *therefore* be appropriate or useful to other areas of inquiry. It does not follow from success in one arena that the same means will produce an important or useful outcome in another. But such is the *non sequitur* on which scientism has proceeded.

## Professionalism and Research in Speech Communication

The effects of professionalization have been felt in every field, but perhaps most profoundly in those that deal in interpretive or critical research. Eagleton, Said, and Graff all discuss professionalism's effect on literary studies, for example. White does likewise for history, Wilshire for philosophy, and Jacoby for political science. Our focus is upon rhetorical and media criticism, typically resident in departments of speech communication. The thorough professionalization of this particular research community, of course, has implications of internal consequence for its practitioners and students.

But the ramifications of a professionalized rhetorical and media criticism may reverberate more broadly, for two reasons. First, critics of media and rhetoric typically study events of *public* culture, with clear pragmatic consequences, practical contexts, and frequently even pragmatic intent. Critics of rhetoric and media justify their researches in large measure on the grounds that the texts they study—from classic orations, government pamphlets, feature and documentary films, and television comedies to televangelism, medical reports, and public memorials—have obvious and consequential socio-cultural effects. Thus, we could argue that criticism's separation from public voice and public idiom and its scientistic impulse to evacuate scholarship of political or ethical considerations are even more troubling in media and rhetorical criticism than in other areas of research. Second, other fields of scholarship recently have demonstrated an intensified interest in rhetoric as a possible means to alleviate the effects of more traditional and rigid conceptions of their discourses of inquiry. The fact that a largely professionalized rhetorical criticism is even possible should sound a warning to those who would turn to rhetoric as a clear way out of the morass of professionalization that threatens to choke off their own research pursuits.

Speech, the early twentieth-century forerunner of the speech communication discipline, was formed largely as a result of interests in practical pedagogy rather than research. Departments of speech and the National Association of Academic Teachers of Public Speaking (NAATPS), now the Speech Communication Association, had as their central concern the teaching of "oral English" (Wichelns 3). But very early in the new discipline's history, the pressure to professionalize made its entrance explicitly and with rather more candor than might be considered decorous. For example, one of the NAATPS's founding members, James A. Winans, wrote in 1915 that "by the scholarship which is the product of research the standing of our work in the academic world will be improved. It will make us orthodox. Research is the standard way into the sheepfold" ("Need" 17). Winans continued, suggesting that teaching as well as reputations would be enhanced "when we have the better understanding of fundamentals and training in the methods which test and determine truth. . . . And in the process of investigation many new truths, before unsuspected, will be discovered. . . . We talk of standardization of our work; but there can be no standardization until we have standardized truth" ("Need" 18–19). He suggested that the "difficulty" would be "getting into a sufficiently scientific frame of mind" ("Need" 22). Later that year he predicted confidently, if inaccurately: "The very practical nature of our work will save us from the excesses of research" ("Should We Worry?" 199).

Although a strong tradition of liberal rhetorical research in the emerging speech field maintained itself throughout the early twentieth century in a rather uneasy relationship with a tradition of social scientific research in the discipline (Pearce 260–64), the will to professionalize continued unabated if largely unrealized. Lester Thonssen and A. Craig Baird's resistant statement in 1948 suggests the strength of that will to professionalize:

> Rhetoric, as the intermediary between the will to action and the achievement of the result, must accordingly be conceived as both a political and ethical instrument. This is another way of saying, perhaps, that there must be a *moral principle* supporting and guiding the liberal tradition. While there has been some disposition to resist the inclusion of such a principle in the scheme of learning—a circumstance resulting from our virtual deification of the so-called scientific

spirit and method—its return as an active force in the field of knowledge is necessary. A sustained faith in democracy itself depends upon it. (467)

However, as mass communication and communication research emerged in their own right in the decades following World War II, such resistance to professionalization finally all but collapsed. "Mass communication" eventually became the research venue of researchers once based in sociology, psychology, and political science, but by the late 1950s most of these pioneers were returning to studies more closely allied with their respective former disciplines. Mass communication research was largely relinquished to members of departments of speech, journalism, or radio-TV, who found in this new field the theoretical and methodological rationale by which broadcasting and journalism programs would justify their academic positions.

Both journalism and speech were once specialized areas of English department curricula—journalism being a specialized form of written English analogous to speech's focus on oral English. In addition to their common origins, departments of speech and journalism also shared the common problem of seeking academic legitimation while being viewed as skills programs (Carey 283). And, as Raymond Carroll notes, departments of radio-TV also "evolved largely from Speech departments, when a few schools established curricula during the early 1930s" (3). The courses such as "radio speaking" were natural additions to speech departments' curricula in times when most speech departments were still geared toward the practical training of teachers, clergy, and others who could use the arts of practical speaking.

Just as speech, following Winan's urging, "began getting a sufficiently scientific frame of mind," journalism attempted to further its own professionalization by staking out areas of knowledge and research. As James Carey describes it, "practical training in journalism was given the intellectual gloss by joining it to studies in ethics, history, and later in law" (284). Journalism, like speech, felt pressure to establish for itself what Carey called "a new scientific legitimacy" (286). The boom in the study of mass communication process and effects during the 1940s, primarily by sociologists and psychologists, offered journalism departments a chance to acquire "scientific legitimacy" by appropriating a field of professional knowledge and research: mass communication.

Most of the major scientific studies of mass communication, including the work of Paul Lazarsfeld, Carl I. Hovland, and others, much of which had been done immediately before or during World War II, were codified in the volumes edited by Wilbur Schramm, most notably *The Process and Effects of Mass Communication*. Schramm's books became primers on both theory and methodology in journalism departments, speech departments, and the newly emerging communication departments.

The 1949 publication of *The Mathematics of Communication* by Claude Shannon and Warren Weaver also contributed to the increasingly professional, scientific character of mass communication research, as well as contributing to its shortened name—communication (or communications) research. The mathematical model of information and communication, developed by Shannon and extrapolated by Weaver, seemed strongly to suggest that a general theory of communication was indeed possible. As Carey summarized the situation, "cybernetics and information theory had a legitimating and shaping effect for they suggested that the study of mass communications might be established on a fully scientific basis, that they contributed a core imagery and vocabulary to the field in the form of [Shannon's and Weaver's] graphic model" (285). Even more tantalizing, the general theory of communication might be reducible to mathematical form.

Everett Rogers noted the disciplinary implications of this new field of knowledge, mass communication: "We see that 1959 was really a time of transition, as communication research moved from departments of sociology, psychology, political science, and specialized institutes like Lazarsfeld's and into departments of its own" (21). These departments of communication were usually constructed from faculty, or even whole departments, originally called journalism, radio-TV, and speech.

Communication research brought with it new "options to studying journalism or the newspaper or the magazine—one could study mass communications. There were now options to studying speech, or rhetoric, or drama—one could study communications" (Carey 285). It further embraced scholarship in areas later to be termed interpersonal communication, organizational communication, and so on, areas also drawing heavily from research traditions begun in sociology and psychology.[23] The introduction of the study of communication to traditional rhetorical studies within the domain of the speech field promoted a heavy influx of scholars principally interested in methods borrowed from the behavioral sciences, and whose theorizing was often oriented primarily toward electronic and print communication rather than oral communication. Thus, speech departments found themselves driven, by the ideological demand for "unity" within a discipline, to accommodate both rhetorical studies and the scientific study of communication, although frequently neither faction felt much of a common bond with its counterpart (Brown 201).[24] The challenge has been described by both Jesse Delia and W. Barnett Pearce,[25] and was nowhere better summarized than in John Bowers's memorable epithet: "The critic thinks he knows; the scientist knows he knows" (171).

The social scientists' determination to unify the discipline around a theoretical core was loudly voiced and frequently repeated—usually by the communication researchers themselves but sometimes also by convinced rhetoricians.[26] Henry McGuckin, for example, urged communication researchers and rhetoricians to "heed with real conviction one another's contribution to what is ultimately a single purpose" (172). Carroll Arnold elaborated, suggesting that "the tendency to say that rhetorical scholars and communication scholars live in separate worlds is the consequence of simply paying too much attention to methodologies and too little attention to how we are conceptualizing the ultimate stuff being studied and how we are building toward ultimate theories about that stuff we partly share" ("Rhetorical and Communication Studies" 80). Karlyn Kohrs Campbell clearly concurred: "What all of us in this discipline seek to discover—whatever our special interests and competencies—are the processes that characterize human communication" ("Criticism" 12).[27]

By 1975, Gerald Miller—himself a dominant voice among communication researchers—had concluded confidently that "there seems to be no serious problem in achieving rapprochement between the humanistic and scientific approaches to speech communication" (239). Miller was correct, as far as his statement goes, but the rapprochement that he and others of his persuasion sought would be at a high cost to rhetorical criticism, as we shall argue in the next section. Mainstream rhetorical criticism finally capitulated to the ideology of professionalism, a victim of the disciplinary call to unity, scientizing itself and compromising or discarding altogether its earlier defense of a pragmatic, pedagogical, public orientation.

# ▓ The Professionalizing of Rhetorical and Media Criticism

It is relatively easy to document that critical inquiry in speech communication has been, to a considerable degree, professionalized. The difficulties lie in choosing, from among the seemingly endless possibilities, the evidence that most clearly marks the professionalized culture and in documenting the consequences of the disciplinization, disengagement, and scientizing of criticism. For the sake of practicality and relative brevity, we shall document the pervasive influence of professionalization by referencing "metacritical" literature—scholarly and textbook materials describing, prescribing, and justifying the particular character of critical practices within rhetorical criticism.[28]

Our intention is to construct from these various materials a text that represents a culture or discourse community—the community of professional rhetorical and media critics. No individual critic has rendered this whole text as an idealized, coherent view of criticism; what we present is a composite of voices. Although it is a textual construction, we are confident that it will have at least some resonance, some intuitive familiarity, as a legitimate way of reading what still appears to be the mainstream of contemporary criticism, what Michael Leff refers to as "modernist rhetoric."[29] Individuals whose voices we have appropriated may occasionally object that our rendering of their arguments has not captured their motives or intentions with perfect fidelity—but this objection would be beside the point. We are attempting to locate the ideological structure that serves as the primary discourse of the critical community in speech communication. It is precisely our point that we and our colleagues, as professionals, are *all* implicated at this level in norms and practices we might be unaware of or even struggling against in our own teaching and writing. Indeed, as the next section of this book shows with sometimes painful clarity, even we, the authors of this chapter denouncing the influences of professionalism, are complicitous in the very practices we are resisting here, whether we like it or not.

We shall focus primarily on the scientizing of criticism, for here is where this discourse of professionalism emerges most clearly. Scientism reproduces and sustains disengagement and disciplinization, just as it is sustained by them. We shall discuss those mutual supports and some of their consequences following our discussion of the scientization of criticism. The implications of this professionalized criticism are legion; many of them will go unremarked here, in the interest of focusing attention especially on the consequences for inventional practices in criticism.

## The Scientizing of Criticism

A review of the literature of rhetorical criticism localizes the themes of scientism we identified earlier in this chapter: preoccupation with theory building, the cult of objectivity, reliance upon method for confirmation and falsification of claims, and even the ideal of progress—although this last shows itself in some unexpected ways in critical discourse, as we shall see below.

It seems no accident that the critical community would assume the mantle of scientism in response to the calls for unification and theory building on the parts of their scientifically inclined colleagues in communication. The most obvious evidence of this tendency among those writing about criticism has been to describe science either as a model or as a different form of inquiry. Edwin Black's comparison-contrast of the scientist and the critic in 1965 certainly is the most prominent case of both of these tendencies. While acknowledging that critics and scientists pursue different ends, he concluded that science had provided "achievements to be emulated by the critic" (*Rhetorical Criticism* 9). He suggested that the influence of science on criticism had been "wholesome," in making critics "conscious of their methods," and in encouraging them "to become systematic, to objectify their modes of inquiry, and to restrict themselves to demonstrable, or at least arguable, generalizations" (2). The Committee on the Advancement and Refinement of Rhetorical Criticism, of the 1970 National Developmental Project, took a more exaggerated stance, contrasting the "critic-scientist" and the "critic-artist":

> At one extreme, we envision the critic acting much like the scientist: deriving hypotheses from systematized constructs, controlling extraneous variables, minimizing error variance, operationalizing terms, arriving at low-order inferences about classes of events with a minimum of experimenter bias. At the other extreme, we envision the critic functioning artistically: immersing himself in the particulars of his object of study, searching for the distinctive, illumining with metaphor the rhetorical transaction. (Sloan, et al. 223)

The critic-artist did not fare very well in the Committee's efforts to advance and refine rhetorical criticism.[30] In addition to the above description of the critic-artist as merely "functioning," in contrast to the critic-scientist "acting," the critic-artist consistently appeared as a role in need of defense but difficult to defend. For example, the critic-artist's "reports are hardly as unsupportable as is frequently maintained. . . . Admittedly we are hard pressed to indicate how the arguments are made convincing" (Sloan, et al. 223).[31]

That the Committee was "hard pressed" illustrates the problem of describing or justifying critical research in relation to science or in an environment wherein professional knowledge is the *desideratum* and science is respected as the only, or at least the superior, route to knowledge. Even when criticism is simply contrasted with science, the virtually inevitable result is that criticism will be viewed as inferior or, at the very least, less "advanced" in its development. Bernard Brock, Robert Scott, and James Chesebro, for example, suggest that current critical work in rhetoric is "pre-paradigmatic" (20). By this designation, they treat criticism as if it might or even should move toward a paradigmatic state as science ostensibly does in Thomas Kuhn's description of succession in scientific knowledge. The implication, of course, is that criticism remains in a primitive state by contrast to the more advanced position of science. Such comparisons and contrasts are by no means unusual.[32] But as critics continue to model their goals, stance, language, and writing practices on this image of science, only the *comparisons* between criticism and science retain much enthusiasm; the *contrasts* drawn between criticism and science have begun to seem a bit disingenuous.

Critics have embraced the goals of science perhaps from political necessity, given the prestige science has enjoyed and its installation as the premier, if not the sole, epistemology of modernity. "Theory" has become virtually the singular objective of criticism; even "judgment," which might seem a definitional end of anything called "criticism," has become a secondary and often quite expendable goal. For example, the Committee on the Advancement and Refinement of Rhetorical Criticism took criticism's principal function virtually for granted: "Whether rhetorical criticism *ought* to contribute to theory seems to us to be beyond question" (Sloan, et al. 222). Foss suggests variously that "any essay of rhetorical criticism cannot not contribute to theory" ("Criteria" 287), that "rhetorical criticism must begin with the asking of a research question so that the critic is able to contribute to rhetorical theory as a result of the study" (*Rhetorical Criticism* xi), and that "the purpose of rhetorical criticism is to explain how some aspect of rhetoric operates and thus to make a contribution to rhetorical theory" ("Constituted by Agency" 34–35). Richard Gregg counsels that "our best criticism ought to be both particular and summative. That is, it ought to illuminate particular situations and at the same time suggest hypotheses regarding human rhetorical behavior that, when added to the insights of other critics, provide generalizable understandings of the human rhetorical condition" (60). And Andrews claims that "development and refinement of rhetorical theory" is a function of criticism that, "in a sense, subsumes all others" (12).[33]

On this view, criticism is treated as scientific or "pre-scientific" in character. Bowers forwarded the notion of a "pre-scientific" criticism in 1968, arguing that the end of such criticism should be

> to contribute to an economical set of scientifically verifiable statements accounting for the origins and effects of *all* rhetorical discourses in *all* contexts. This point of view requires that rhetorical criticism be viewed as an early part of a process eventuating in scientific theory. Hence, the adjective "pre-scientific" is appropriate. The term implies that, in this frame of reference, the rhetorical critic's principal task is to produce testable hypotheses which, when verified, will have the status of scientific laws. (163–64)

Bowers's arguments were frequently so condescending toward criticism that it is a bit surprising to find critics who would agree with him. Bowers spelled out what critics "must learn" and what they "must" do in order to accomplish what science would "require" of them (166). After suggesting that criticism might have the most to contribute to the scientific enterprise by operationally defining terms, he labeled the task of operational definition "a relatively trivial matter" (167). Nonetheless, some critics have accepted this subordinate role for criticism. Roderick Hart does so explicitly: "It is in their roles as pre-scientists that rhetorical critics can add substantially to the development and refinement of synthetic, inclusive, and predictive theoretical statements about human persuasion" ("Theory-Building" 70). Others have accepted Bowers's prescription without the label of "pre-science." Horace M. Newcomb likewise argues that television criticism can open new areas for empirical research while also providing a test for criticism's conclusions (226). Brock, Scott, and Chesebro suggest that one of the ways in which criticism serves theory is to "give rise to insights that can then be phrased as principles for further use or hypotheses for further testing" (17). James Andrews agrees, suggesting that a critic "may generate hypotheses upon which new theories can ultimately be built" (13).[34]

Critics' treatment of rhetorical criticism as itself a scientific process is more common but typically less than explicit. Ernest Bormann is technically correct in pointing out that few rhetoricians would call rhetorical theory "scientific" (53). That is, no one seems to want to be caught uttering an explicit statement to that effect. However, if criticism's principal purpose is to contribute to rhetorical theory, and if rhetorical theory is treated as a functional equivalent to scientific theory, then it certainly would follow that rhetorical criticism is treated as fundamentally equivalent to a scientific activity. Contributing to theory *is* regarded as the fundamental goal of criticism by a number of critics, as we noted earlier. And the theory to which criticism contributes *is* described in ways suggesting similitude, if not identity, with scientific theory. Barry Brummett makes the case clearly:

> Rhetoricians often seem to regard their theories as close parallels to more conservative, hypothetical-deductive social science theories. Gronbeck sounds like a social scientist when he claims that Burkean scholars try to generate "a systematic set of covering propositions." Black argues that rhetorical theory, apart from the more insignificant theories derived from logical necessity, is grounded in "regularities" of psyche or discourse. McGee explicitly claims that "if it is to achieve the status of 'theory,' any prose must reliably describe, explain, and predict." Zarefsky agrees that rhetorical theory should be both testable and predictive. Swanson demands that a rhetorical study pass "objective tests of its accuracy." ("Rhetorical Theory" 97)[35]

Brummett's catalog is not exhaustive, but it is in every sense exemplary. Yet, even given the stature and accomplishment of those critics he names, it is possible to augment his case. Hart can be counted among those who treat rhetorical theory as scientific in character. He suggests that "theory is richest when it accounts comprehensively for multiple events rather than individual instances, for the comparatively unmonitored rather than the widely observed activity, for the regularized rather than the idiosyncratic" ("Contemporary Scholarship" 294). Andrews concurs as well: "By theory, we mean a body of plausible generalizations or principles that explain a complex set of facts or phenomena" (12).

Andrews's mention of "explanation" represents a further level of the infiltration of rhetorical criticism and theory by scientism. While one might expect criticism's principal operations to be interpretative and/or evaluative, contemporary critics align themselves with scientists in describing their work as primarily explanatory in nature. In summarizing the "specific analytical tasks" that the Wingspread conferees formulated for the profession, Arnold lists six; he introduces them as follows: "1. We need clearer explanations. . . . 2. We need clearer explanations. . . . 3. We need more precise explanations. . . . 4. We need fuller explanations. . . . 5. We need explanations. . . . 6. We need more precise explanations" ("Reflections" 195–96). Brock, Scott, and Chesebro describe "the critical impulse" as an awareness "of circumstances that seem to cry out for explanations" (10). Hart defines rhetorical criticism as "the business of identifying the complications of rhetoric and explaining them in a comprehensive and efficient manner" (*Modern Rhetorical Criticism* 32). Leah Vande Berg and Lawrence Wenner cite explanation as one of the "primary purposes of criticism" (10). Sonja Foss equates explanation and theory contribution in discussing the goal of rhetorical criticism ("Constituted by Agency" 34–35). Brockriede values only explanatory and some forms of evaluative criticism as "significant argument" ("Rhetorical Criticism"). If these critics' references to explanation are reflective ones—that is, if they understand explanation to be an account of causality—their views of criticism's goals align with the objectives espoused in traditional conceptions of science.[36] William Brown, in his discussion of critical research in mass media, certainly seems to be aware of the implications of his suggestion that one of the proper roles for criticism is to reach for the ultimate goal of behavioral science—prediction and control. He writes, "depending upon the individual critic's specific version of 'usable explication,' the yield from criticism may be knowledge . . . theoretically capable of leading to prediction or perhaps even control of mediated-communication outcomes, with a concomitant view of reality working like a machine" (207).

Explanation does not always appear in these accounts to *replace* understanding or judgment as proper goals of criticism. As in Wayne Brockriede's case, explanation and judgment are both recognized as legitimate goals. However, normative judgments of all varieties—ethical, political, and moral—are frequently devalued. Mark Klyn, for example, argued in 1968 that criticism "does not imply . . . any categorical structure of judgment, or even any judgmental necessity" (147). Bowers, elaborating his vision of the pre-scientific critic, explained that his view "ignores, though it does not prohibit, the critic's evaluative activities" (164). Hart seems little bothered by the recognition that "theorist-critics may be in positions to do little for the cause of justice-in-our-times" ("Theory-Building" 76).

Campbell goes further, distinguishing between "ephemeral" social criticism and "enduring" academic criticism:

> The social critic enters the arena of public controversy and appraises contemporary acts before all their consequences are clear and all the relevant facts are known. Such a critic is committed to participating in the free discussion of issues relevant to a particular time and place. The academic critic explores and analyzes whatever acts will aid in explicating the essential processes of human symbolization. Both functions are vital, and both forms of criticism need to be

affirmed, but the distinctive purposes of each need to be recognized. ("Criticism" 13–14)

Despite Campbell's acknowledgment of the importance of the appraisal accomplished by social critics, she argues that professional journals are not the proper outlets nor professional colleagues the proper audience for such work ("Criticism" 10). Campbell thus forecloses, albeit indirectly, the possibility of judgment as a legitimate function of academic criticism by privileging "explication" as the province of the professional critic.[37]

Brock, Scott, and Chesebro seem rather nonplussed by the apparent inevitability of the conclusion they draw: "Try as we may, the evaluative component appears to remain an enduring feature of any critical impulse" (13). Their ambivalence about judgment is explained by their recognition that "evaluation of others can often be awkward, upsetting, and difficult for both the critic and those being judged" (12). They never seem to emerge from this difficulty; their discussion is confused and confusing. At one point, they "hold criticism to be an art of evaluating with knowledge and propriety" (13). At another, they suggest that "the critic may choose to deemphasize the evaluative function of criticism" (16).[38]

These shifts toward explanation and the corresponding devaluations of judgment are funded by the currency of objectivity. We could not hope to make the case more succinctly or accurately than James Klumpp and Thomas Hollihan have:

> The dominant interpretation of the rhetorical critic's purpose over the last three decades has formed from the relationship of critical method to social science. Indeed, the perspective of the critic as morally neutral has sprung primarily from the linkage with the objective methods promoted by American social science during that period. The celebration of critical objectivity, rooted in a trend common to many disciplines in this century, reached its full flower in the 1960s among those attempting to find comfort in academic departments experiencing the growth fueled by increased interest in social science and social engineering. The oft-longed-for unity of such departments was often achieved around the central symbols of the common task of "building and testing theory." After agreement on goals, the social scientists' tolerance in method made room for the rhetorical critic. The result was a self-image for critics that valued "objectivity" defined as moral noninvolvement. (92)

Although Black, in his 1965 monograph, still admitted judgment as a function of criticism, his commitment to objectivity was explicit and unswerving.[39] He argued that, like scientists, critics have "two vitally important activities, which are to see a thing clearly and to record what they have seen precisely." The critic "tries to become, for a time, a pure perceiver, an undistorting slate on which an object or an event external to him can leave a faithful impression of itself, omitting nothing" (*Rhetorical Criticism*, 1965, 4).

Today, most critics, including Black, would be unlikely actually to lay explicit claim to objectivity, as Black himself did in 1965. However, critics remain mesmerized by the objectivist cant to whatever degree that they pretend toward moral neutrality or distance, that they insist upon method to ensure against the intrusion of interest or idiosyncracy, or even that they exalt subjectivity as a corrective to the excesses of objectivity, as Black did in the preface to the 1978 reissue of *Rhetorical Criticism*. More frequently, the issue of stance is passed over completely or treated with ambivalence. Most current commentators take their lead from the Committee on the Advancement and Refinement of Rhetorical Criticism, which suggested that criticism is best when "the critic immerses himself in particulars and at the same time stands, psychologically, at a distance from them. . . . Theory is made richer by the critic's involvement in the events he studies; theory is made clearer by his transcendence of those events" (Sloan, et al. 224). Likewise, Malcolm Sillars implies that all criticism is always already evaluative, no matter what its stance (3–4), but he classifies three critical approaches as "objectivist," and is able to distinguish value analysis from ideological critique on the grounds that the former is more "objective" (148). Karyn Rybacki and Donald Rybacki claim that "the problems posed by subjectivity" can be "overcome" (13). Hart suggests that the critic's "special discernment" is the capacity "to stand simultaneously in the midst of and apart from the events experienced," and to "point out features that the too-involved" individual would miss because of "the immediacy and excitement of the event itself" (*Modern Rhetorical Criticism* 33). Foss goes so far as to emphasize the subjectivity of the critic:

> Subjectivity is acknowledged . . . when the critic admits interest in and involvement with the artifact and explains the nature of the interest and involvement: "I became intrigued with this film because of how I responded to it" or "I worked on the campaign to elect Jesse Jackson," for example. The critic also acknowledges subjectivity by revealing to the reader experiences and values that affect the critic's perceptions and judgments—"I am a Democrat," "I am a feminist," "I grew up in the late Sixties," "I like abstract art," "I do not own a television." (*Rhetorical Criticism* 25)

One difficulty with Foss's account is that it is counterfactual; it is extremely rare for critics to reveal their own interests, personal characteristics, or habits in their professional writings.[40] The other is that to call involvement and personal characteristics "subjective" is simply to reproduce the subject-object dualism grounding traditional empiricist science, while favoring the other half of the pair. Such attempts to purge criticism of objectivism are doomed to the extent that they are partial attempts. So long as *part* of the collection of objectivist tenets is retained as grounds for rejecting *other*, perhaps more obviously objectionable parts, the overall philosophical position remains secure—incoherent, but secure.

Moreover, the critical community remains resistant to impulses that clearly culminate in judgment or action. The energetic—not to say hysterical—reaction from some to Philip Wander's 1983 essay, "The Ideological Turn in Modern Criticism," was one notorious case of such resistance.[41] Similarly, while critical approaches found under the general rubrics of feminism and poststructuralism (including deconstruction) may share little in common with one another beyond the impulse to question authority and dislodge traditional ways of thinking, those who write criticism from such stances have met with their share of resistance and antipathy as well. Foss observes that "Feminist criticism . . . is often met with hostility, defensiveness, or amusement. It strikes many students, associate editors, and editors as inappropriately political or ideological" ("Constituted by Agency" 47). And, while Hart apparently tries to give deconstruction a hearing in his textbook, his account fails to live up to any standard of fairness save equal time. It is difficult to be impressed with the evenhandedness of statements like: "Deconstructionists win few popularity contests" (386); or "Deconstructionists are often accused of being anarchists, who treat communication as an impossibility and who are, as a result, nothing more than radical debunkers" (386–87). It is significant that Hart classifies deconstruction as a form of ideological criticism, since most deconstructionists distance themselves from ideological critique.[42] But critical to our point is that Hart's scheme of classification allows him to set different so-called "ideological critics" off against each other:

> Marxists charge that postmodernists—or deconstructionists, as they are often called when operating as critics—play wasteful semantic games and that feminists are politically naive. Feminists resent the paternalism of Marxists but agree with them that deconstructionists play wasteful semantic games. For their part, deconstructionists feel that Marxists are tedious moralizers, that feminists take rhetoric too seriously, and that they, the deconstructionists, play wasteful semantic games but that that is the only game in town. (*Modern Rhetorical Criticism* 383)

Setting aside what some would view as inaccuracies in this account, note that these different groups of "ideological critics" have consumed each other before the chapter about them is three pages old.[43] Certainly, there may be other defensible reasons to resist ideological, feminist, and poststructuralist critiques. But it seems no accident that these forms of critique, all thematizing power, frequently culminating in judgment, and typically articulating the need for fundamental change, have encountered the resistance they have.

Critics' emphasis on method also signals a residual impulse toward the objectivity sustained by scientism. Even the choice of the terms, "method" and "methodology," suggests a scientistic influence. Critics' elaborations of "method" make the case even more clearly. Hart, for example, suggests a need for "methodologies for treating the message as a dependent variable" ("Theory-Building" 76). Lawrence Rosenfield proposes as a "methodological" concern the critic's need to decide "what sorts of measurements or readings" to take on the text (104); he suggests that the critic's reasons are "the product of 'measurement' " (103); and he elaborates various "permutations" of four "variables" (source, message, environment, critic) that articulate the stance of the critic (104–5). Method has been and continues to be of prime concern to most critics. Brock, Scott, and Chesebro claim that "methodological statements" function as a kind of "shorthand" for the choices a critic makes (510). Foss takes the point further, arguing that "what we know in the area of rhetorical criticism has come largely from a featuring of agency or method; our knowledge about criticism and the beliefs we hold about it are methodologically derived" ("Constituted by Agency" 35).

Even though critics do not now frequently claim, at least not explicitly, that their methods are their guarantors of objectivity, the continued significance of method suggests that some will toward objectivity remains, despite the relative scarcity of claims to it. That impulse does manifest itself, for instance, in the reassurance of "reliability" or the "replicability" of studies. Brockriede, for example, suggested that the critic attempts a "degree of intersubjective reliability" by risking argumentative confrontation ("Rhetorical Criticism" 167). He continued:

> when a critic advances a significant argument about a concrete rhetorical experience or about a general concept of rhetoric, a reader can confront it usefully. If he tries to disconfirm the critic's argument and fails to do so, the intersubjective reliability of that argument is increased. If he can disconfirm or cast doubt about the critic's argument, that argument must be abandoned or revised. (174)

Although Brockriede understood reliability to rest upon the potential for argument, and not upon method, the *desire* for reliability nevertheless signals a will toward objectivity.[44] Hart clearly places his confidence in the capacity of critical methods to enable replication: "Because theory necessarily builds upon some convergence or replication of insight, it would behoove some of us to refine our analytical tools so that others in the field can share in the 'how' as well as in the 'what' of our researches" ("Theory-Building" 73). Thomas Farrell seems to agree, advancing several standards for judging "non-scientific" approaches to communication, one of which is methodological rigor. Farrell poses the criterion as a question: "Could others employing the method find approximately the same things?" ("Beyond Science" 124).

The honest answer to Farrell's question, if it were posed of virtually any approach to rhetorical criticism, probably would be in the negative. Most of these approaches do not really qualify as "methods," in any meaningful sense, to begin with. They are more properly conceptual heuristics or vocabularies; they may invite a critic to interesting ways of reading a text, but they do not have the procedural rigor or systematicity that typically characterizes a method. In fact, it is arguable that they are at their best, critically, when they are least rigorous "methodologically." Still, many critics treat them as if they were equivalent to the analytic methods and instruments of science, and as if they provided a direct and universal-access bridge for the critic between "data" and theoretical generalizations.

Just as in the sciences, methods are taken by critics to be the tools with which one must be equipped in order to test hypotheses and build theory. Theory testing and building are thus two sides of the same coin for some critics. Brummett describes theory testing as understood by rhetorical critics:

> Many rhetoricians view rhetorical criticism as the means to test the regularities asserted by rhetorical theory; criticism is to rhetorical theory what experiment and other methods are to social science theory. . . . Although Clevenger sees criticism as primarily descriptive, he explicitly argues that it can and should *test* a rhetorical theory. Farrell's theoretical 'models' are informed and tested by criticism. ("Rhetorical Theory" 97–98)[45]

Foss completes the picture with her description of theory building:

> The findings of the analysis may be shown to confirm some tenet of rhetorical theory. . . . The critic also may discover that some principles or constructs in rhetorical theory need to be modified or qualified to make them more accurate or to provide more useful explanations of a rhetorical process. . . . Another way in which the critic may contribute to rhetorical theory is by formulating a new model or theory. The critic may discover that the theoretical model used for the comparison simply does not accommodate the discoveries made in the analysis and that a new theoretical explanation is needed for how a rhetorical process works. (23–24)

Foss's description demonstrates how theory "testing" leads to theory "building," on this view. And her language ("findings," "confirm," "discover," "constructs," "accurate," "explanation") seems to confirm the analogy Brummett draws between criticism and scientific method.

However, hypothesis testing is a questionable analog for rhetorical criticism. Black claims that "there is not a single case in the literature of our field in which a rhetorical theory has been abandoned as a result of having failed an application of criticism" ("A Note" 333). And Brummett argues that "rhetorical theory is *never* tested in the sense that social science theories are" ("Rhetorical Theory" 98). He explains: "A critic who finds that he or she cannot apply fantasy theme analysis to a piece of discourse will simply turn to Burke, Aristotle, or some other theory, and the 'failure' of the rejected theory never sees the light of published day" ("Rhetorical Theory" 99). Yet despite the apparent accuracy of Black's and Brummett's assessments, critics continue to claim for criticism the capacity to test rhetorical theories.

In all of this scientistic labyrinth, what of the text, the rhetoric, that a rhetorical critic engages? It does make an appearance in these accounts, all too often described as "data," "evidence," "case studies," or "samples."[46] The rhetoric that critics take up in their work is thus typically reduced methodologically to fodder with which to fill the theoretical silo. Campbell's position is perhaps the most blunt, claiming, "what must be specified are the factors that constitute critical excellence and critical outcomes or objectives that contribute to rhetorical *theory*. At this level, criticism and theory are indistinguishable" ("Criticism" 11). Campbell adds, "what we learn about the specific rhetorical acts is secondary; they become illustrations or means through which the reader apprehends the nature of symbolic processes themselves" ("Criticism" 12). Foss agrees: "Criticism no longer serves a useful purpose if it has been devoted exclusively to an understanding of a particular artifact" (*Rhetorical Criticism* 6). Hart goes so far as to suggest—twice—that "the rhetoric of plumbers' conventions, the proselytizing which occurs at meetings of the Catholic War Veterans, [and] the dialectic at the local city council meeting" would be more useful objects of the critic's attention than a presidential campaign. They are more typical, more ubiquitous, and therefore pay more "theoretical dividends" ("Theory-Building" 72; "Contemporary Scholarship" 293). The basic point appears to be that it does not matter much *what* text one chooses for criticism, because "all texts are filled with data" (Hart, *Modern Rhetorical Criticism* 45).

What remains evident, however, is the move to reduce the critical essay to a commodity or product. The Committee on the Advancement and Refinement of Rhetorical Criticism referred to this product as "findings" (Sloan, et al. 226, 227). Andrews suggests that a critic "must be able to communicate to others the results of his or her critical observation and inquiry" (5). Foss picks up the terminology of both: "The report of the findings of the analysis constitutes the bulk of the essay. . . . The critic tells what has been discovered from an application of the method to the artifact and provides support for the discoveries from the data of the artifact" (*Rhetorical Criticism* 21). Of course, the terms "findings" and "results" are not themselves problematic. The difficulty is that they are deadly accurate in describing the scope of a critical essay—it has become a product, not a representation or exploration of the critical practices behind the product.

However even if, for purposes of argument, we accepted the scientistic suggestion that it is appropriate for a critical essay to be merely a product, a report of findings, we would quickly encounter an even thornier problem: assessing the quality of this product. We may then ask, what has criticism provided us? What are its results, its findings? What theory has it built or modified—rather than merely borrowing for its purposes? Perhaps the focal

irony of the scientization of criticism, and the point at which we will culminate our discussion of it, is crystalized in Gregg's astute, if offhand, observation that "whether, if at all, the explorations of rhetorical critics have contributed to our theoretical understanding of human rhetorical behavior" is
a "question that has not received much attention" (42).

We regard the studied silence of media and rhetorical criticism on this
point, compared to the optimism of modern science, as extremely telling.
The question is a potentially embarrassing one, in two senses. On its face,
it raises the possibility that criticism is not making proper progress toward
what should be the goal of any professional discipline: contributing significantly to an encompassing "theoretical understanding" of its subject area.
But if in fact it means—as we suspect it does—that critics should be questioning the very legitimacy of this goal, this is only slightly less uncomfortable, since it forces us to question norms that have at least served to organize
our sense of ourselves as critics and professionals, and to set out instead into
what must surely seem uncharted waters. The silence of criticism on its own
ultimate theoretical productivity thus emphasizes the poor fit between a
scientized model of professionalism and contemporary critical practice.

## Disengagement of Critical Experience

As we suggested earlier, in the drive to unify a discipline, a guild is produced
that comes to sanction only research activity as truly professional work. The
will to knowledge that pervades this professional guild diminishes the importance of other realms of activity, such as teaching and participation in
political or social groups. And it segregates such larger community involvement from the experience of professional culture. The broad professional
demand for knowledge production certainly has contributed to the scientization of criticism. In addition, though, criticism's scientistic posture produces and is reproduced by the balkanization of the critic's domains of
experience and knowledge.

It probably is true that whatever public or civic voice rhetorical criticism
originally had came from critics who, in the early years of the discipline, took
their civic duty to be teaching—preparing young men and women to be
active, vocal participants in their culture. Critical pedagogy took a conservative form of which many of us might now disapprove; it frequently held up
"masterpieces" of oratory or the careers of great orators as models to be
studied and emulated.[47] But the connection of criticism to pragmatic, civil
affairs was clear and proximate (Thonssen and Baird 22), and the classroom
was the link between the two. Also clear was the recognition that the texts
produced in the larger community had material effects on individuals in real
situations, and that rhetorical critics, therefore, had the "responsibility of
considering the ethical implications of public statements" (Thonssen and
Baird 471).[48]

As the goal of knowledge production grew in importance to become the primary task of the academic professional, however, the links between the scholarly, pedagogical, and public realms were altered. By all appearances, it is the students who have fared the worst in the change. The students' role as an audience to professional criticism is frequently one of apprentice to master. Those who do become academic professionals themselves, therefore, are equipped to provide continuity to the knowledge-production industry. But those who do not—and this is the great majority of students—may well leave the university culture knowing more about how to be citizens of the academic community than they do about ways of being, thinking, and acting in a larger, public culture.

Often crucial to this academic citizenship is at least a *Jeopardy*-level familiarity with the frequently opaque language of the professionalized critic. As a test, we conducted a haphazard tour through three rhetorical criticism textbooks—not scholarly journals, but *textbooks*—and in about twenty minutes generated a partial listing of the professional critical argot academic critics inflict upon their students, an incomplete lexicon in English, Greek, Latin, and *faux*-French already numbering in the neighborhood of one hundred terms. (Germanisms had, by the time of our test, apparently come into vogue and passed back out again.)[49] Yet even if modern academic criticism were more intelligible to students, it still would only rarely speak to the hearts of such readers, "who must often wonder where the joy and appreciation is to be found in such a tedious and officious activity" (Nothstine and Copeland 22). So while students do, technically, count as an audience or market for professional criticism, they are for the most part a captive audience, whom academic critics treat with the disrespect of being frequently inaccessible and almost always disconnected from *their* interests and concerns.

The larger, general public, as a potential "audience" for professional criticism, seems to have even less of an obvious stake in listening to professional critics. Members of that group are unlikely to be much interested in the "results" of the critic's "findings," except in those cases where these readers' concrete concerns might be addressed. But to the extent that professional critics seem to value the concrete, situated event only as "data" for theoretical generalizations, as springboards for their feats of scholarly virtuosity, not as interested, consequential discourse, communities outside the academy are unlikely to find their concrete concerns noticed, much less addressed and engaged. Brock, Scott, and Chesebro observe that "if [critics] are interested in influencing society, they will almost certainly be required to convey an evaluative judgment" (506). But the scientization of criticism has rendered judgment, or any other form of engaged reaction,[50] as incidental at best to the critical work. Thus, professional critics' construal of their own professionalism alienates them from the potential public audience. But this alienation, in turn, reinforces the tendency toward scientism; if the public at large is not an audience, then the obvious audience consists of other professionals, who do value theoretical virtuosity.

It is occasionally fashionable (and the last decade has been one of those occasions) to lament the extraordinary and unwholesome influence that academics have on American society. We have listened as a former vice president of the United States, for example, attacked the "cultural elite" of the academy, media, and performing arts. At about the same time, a former secretary of education bemoaned the pernicious agenda apparently underlying the movement toward "diversity" and "multiculturalism" on American campuses. However, with apologies to Dan Quayle, William Bennett, and the rest of academia's detractors, it seems clear that the delicate fabric of society is in no danger from radicals (or anyone else) who are members of the academic critical culture.

The lines of possible contact with society, from either the left or the right on campuses, are all but severed for rhetorical and media critics as with their colleagues in other disciplines. Jacoby explains: "This conservative nightmare lifts with any daytime inspection of universities. What happened to the swarms of academic leftists? The answer is surprising: Nothing surprising. The ordinary realities of bureaucratization and employment took over" (134). As Said writes of leftist literary critics, "Eagleton, [Frederic] Jameson, and [Frank] Lentricchia are literary Marxists who write for literary Marxists, who are in cloistral seclusion from the inhospitable world of real politics" (22). Samuel Becker notes the same trend toward political disengagement in media studies, particularly in the United States. Rhetorical critics too are engaged, with rare exceptions, only with and by others of their professional kind. Scholarly critics and their criticism today scarcely participate in a public culture; to accuse them of *undue* influence is therefore to charge them with an offense of which they are altogether innocent.

The public is thus quite safe from academic criticism. In exchange, academic critics themselves are guaranteed a large measure of safety of a very different sort. The professional culture rewards critics in several ways for remaining in the professional role of *non*participant observer. One of the rewards is the designation of "expertise," which we address in the next section. Another is material reward in the forms of hierarchical and monetary advancement in the university culture.

But the cloistering of critics and the sanctioning of the professional critical role it generates seems to guarantee critics even more. Campbell suggests that "social criticism . . . will not be enduring; its importance and its functions are immediate and ephemeral." But by contrast, " 'academic' or 'professional' criticism can make an enduring contribution to the discipline" ("Criticism" 11). Thus, the durability of professional work is what recommends it; the desire to immortalize ourselves in that work seems to be the animating force. Hart makes the reward even more explicit in his suggestion that we forsake *"anecdotal fixation,* an over-extended concern for the details of time and place," for the *"conceptual record,"* the "only record that will outlive us" ("Contemporary Scholarship" 284, 285).

This "immortality" from "enduring contribution to the discipline," however, must be weighed against the contributions critics might otherwise have made to any public culture. By that measure, "immortality" shows itself to be a Faustian bargain indeed. As Richard Cherwitz and John Theobald-Osborne observe,

> After reading highly specialized rhetorical accounts of messages, one is often left with the question: Of what value is such criticism to those in society who transmit and receive communication? Or more specifically, To what extent can the insights gleaned by scholarly criticism be used constructively to promote better politics? These questions are more than trivial; for at core, the rhetorical art is a practical one, an art that we intuitively know makes a difference for the vast majority of people not ensconced in academe. It is for this reason that critics cannot sidestep or ignore such questions. (73)

One of the reasons rhetorical and media critics cannot avoid these questions is the nature of the texts they study: "The underlying pedagogical and scholarly assumption of our discipline is that communication has the power: to arouse emotions; influence the direction, intensity, and salience of beliefs; transform and nurture the development of ideas; and instigate action" (Cherwitz and Theobald-Osborne 52). Another is the question of what some critics might actually wish to do. Philip Wander and Steven Jenkins's poignant questions are worth our serious reflection:

> Let us suppose that a critic honestly became emotionally involved with his subject—that he found it important down to the very ground of his being. Are we to tell him to write about it as though he were not so interested; are we to suggest that he write about something less involving? Are we, in other words, to request the critic, for professional purposes, either to lie about or to ignore what to him is vitally important? (446)

Unfortunately, because of the ideological forces we have been examining, the professional critic must answer, "Yes." Professional critics are not in the business of involvement and advocacy; the nature of their work, as it is currently construed, demands neutrality and seeks theoretical explanation. As a result, the possibility for critics and their criticism to serve as a genuine source of knowledge, power, or ethics in a public culture is diminished almost to zero.

## Disciplining Critics and Criticism

The rise of modern departments of speech in universities took place shortly after the ideology of professionalism in American higher education began to take shape. The effects of disciplinization are not always easy to demonstrate, because disciplines are in all respects artificial abstractions, with years of accreted right and privilege, and because the very idea of a "discipline" is so familiar that it is almost invisible.[51] However, it occasionally does appear explicitly as a justification or excuse for some practice or habit, as in Hart's metaphorical warning: "Many of us in public address feel greater kinship with our colleagues in departments of history than with our cousins in speech communication studying compliance-gaining. I believe that that is a dangerous condition because it frustrates the development of holistic and analytically precise theories of human communication" ("Contemporary Scholarship" 285). Hart reminds his readers of the professional necessity of border guarding and the dangers associated with consorting with those of another disciplinary clan—our theory construction efforts will be victimized.

A more common, and telling, metaphor for the discipline is that of an economic community, within which Hart's disciplinary "kinship systems" barter goods and products. Herman Cohen, for example, observes that "the trade balance with related fields is negative. We import much more than we export. We frequently cite the work of other fields but our work is seldom cited" (287). Charles Berger virtually echoes Cohen: "The field of communication has been suffering and continues to suffer from an intellectual trade deficit with respect to related disciplines; the field imports much more than it exports" (102).

These metaphors both display and reinforce the ideology giving rise to our understanding of critical (and other) scholarship as commodity or product. They also expose disciplinarity as the restrictive and even xenophobic mechanism that it is, screening out contact with members (and ideas) of other disciplines and keeping the product "homegrown," as Berger quaintly puts it (104). For members of the profession, the product's quality often seems to be of less concern than the "Made in Speech Communication" label sewn into the lining.[52]

Supporting the research edifice and the entire professional structure, for better or worse, is the reward and punishment system explicit in disciplinarity. "Discipline," after all, is a verb as well as a noun. It is worth considering how these collective entities we call disciplines go about the work of "disciplining" individuals, rewarding decorum and good judgment, and penalizing or "correcting" inappropriate or "bad" behavior.

The grant of the title, "expert," must be counted among the principal rewards the disciplinary system can offer. In fact, it follows as a necessary entailment of the system. Because disciplines are specialized and rigidly bounded by educational and productivity requirements, they are peopled by specialists—"experts." The experts maintain their expertise to the extent that they do what the system demands, that is, contribute to "knowledge production." If scientism has created rigid and narrow criteria for what counts as knowledge, disciplinarity tends and maintains those requirements. It grants status only to those whose work meets those rigid criteria. The reward system is, as we commented earlier, inherently conservative, but it also is potentially disabling to criticism.

Critics, perhaps critics of rhetoric and media especially, are vulnerable in such a system of reward, since they study texts generated in public and popular cultures, texts that anyone who inhabits these cultures presumably already finds intelligible to some degree. Thus, when Eagleton describes the "contradiction on which criticism finally runs aground—one between an inchoate amateurism and a socially marginal professionalism" (*Function* 69), there must be some resonance for rhetorical and media critics, perhaps even more than for the literary critics with whom Eagleton is concerned. Professional critics' students and fellow citizens probably believe that they have a fair grasp of what they hear and see going on about them. Their colleagues in other academic departments probably dare to presume that they do, as well. So, how—without the professionally sanctioned title of "expert"—can an academic critic claim any more authority on such matters than any other reasonably observant, thoughtful individual?

This tension emerges rather clearly in criticism textbooks. Andrews distinguishes between critics as "serious" students of rhetoric and others who will seek to make intelligent responses to public discourse (4), and between "trained professionals" and "casual observers" (14). Similarly, Foss suggests that "we engage in the process of rhetorical criticism constantly and often unconsciously," but that adeptness and discrimination are acquired by "formal training" (*Rhetorical Criticism* 3). Hart follows suit: "Everyone is capable of doing rhetorical criticism without ever reading *Modern Rhetorical Criticism.* By having lived and talked for several decades or more, all of us have done the homework necessary to do criticism" (*Modern Rhetorical Criticism* 36). But, as he later suggests, "it is possible to become more perceptive as critics if we (1) adopt a useful set of critical attitudes and (2) ask the right sorts of questions when inspecting rhetoric" (*Modern Rhetorical Criticism* 40). Andrews also makes very clear what he considers necessary to the expert: "Becoming a critic involves the careful practice of a craft. The rhetorical critic 'practices' in the sense that any professional does, through the continuous application of specialized knowledge to situations for which he or she is trained" (61). Walter Fisher concurs, suggesting that "everyone engages in critical acts; few elevate them into an art form. The principal difference between the ordinary criticizer and the critic is knowledge" (76). He continues:

> The critic possesses special, comprehensive knowledge of the nature and functions of the objects and acts that he examines. He has at his command a wide range of models to choose from, a fine sense of the appropriateness of given models in the evaluation of particular objects of criticism, a capacity to make his

models explicit, if necessary, and he can cite attractive, convincing reasons to justify his judgments. (76)

While the tension between amateurism and expertise shows itself here, so does its approved means of resolution—professional knowledge. Small wonder that critics are highly motivated to contribute to theory and to construct elaborate technical apparatuses that enable the scientistic project. It is precisely such work, not their practical insights into public culture, that separates them from amateurs. The reward system effectively reinforces both the scientistic impulse and the civic and experiential detachment attendant upon the professional ideology. Thus, the "decorum" and "good judgment" that are rewarded by disciplinarity with the badge of "expertise" are precisely those actions that support and contribute to the ideology of professionalism.

As we suggested earlier, a discipline may also be prepared to encourage a judicious silence on the value of criticism's theoretical output. The peculiar abstractness of disciplinarity may help to explain how critics collectively have managed to avoid Gregg's important question: Have the explorations of rhetorical critics contributed to our theoretical understanding of human rhetorical behavior? Although it is the discipline that provides outlets for publications, advocacy on behalf of its members, conferences, and career placement services, it does not produce scholarship; individuals do. Individuals are rewarded (or sanctioned) for their research "production." If a research product is "good," judged by whatever measures, the discipline is enhanced, along with the individual researcher. For example, Hart notes with approval "the *field's* growing ability to produce scholarly books" ("Rhetorical Research" 2. Emphasis added). However, the same does not seem to be true in reverse. If a research product is "not good," judged by whatever measures, it is the fault of the individual. For example, Berger speculates that "it is possible that persons seeking advanced degrees in communication are, for some unknown reasons, risk averse, and therefore not particularly motivated to develop theory" (108).

Thus, it may be that we as a discipline have managed to avoid answering Gregg's question by virtue of the disciplinary truth that scholarship is not done by disciplines but by individuals.[53] That is, while the discipline is portrayed as the site of opportunity—the economy, to extend the earlier metaphor—individuals are understood as those who do or do not avail themselves of opportunities to produce. Thus, the question of what "the discipline" or a subfield has "produced" can be dismissed, for the discipline is not the producer but only the site of production. Of course, this is a naive view of material conditions and of individual autonomy, but it is a convenient naiveté. By clinging to it, disciplinarity is able to prop up an enterprise that has done little to assess the "products" of its own labor. It does so by allowing critics the luxury of never having to pose the question of what their own work, taken collectively, has produced. Unburdened by the appearance of any evidence to the contrary, the members of a discipline are thus free to assume that they are making collective progress, in the best scientistic tradition, toward the grand professional goal of increasing "our theoretical understanding of human rhetorical behavior."

Disciplinarity also contains negative mechanisms to reinforce adherence to the professional ideology. The most obvious of these are also the most materially consequential. In academia, individuals are disciplined, kept in line as it were, by the repressiveness of the tenure and promotion system. An individual is very unlikely to succeed in that system without the explicit approval of disciplinary colleagues—journal editors and referees, writers of recommendations and endorsements, and so forth. Another such repressive mechanism is the "analysis of research productivity." These are heavily quantified lists tracking, for example, the appearance of a scholar's work in the citations of fellow scholars' publications, or ranking the "most prolific scholars" in the discipline, based upon the numbers of articles published in particular journals. The justification typically offered for the compiling and publication of these bibliometric exercises is their asserted ability to provide "a yardstick by which to measure the research productivity of a faculty member" (Hickson, Stacks, and Amsbury, "An Analysis" 231). But one can certainly be forgiven for wondering whether such a "yardstick" is to be used as a measure or as a cudgel. Because of these mechanisms, the individual *must,* at least to a large degree, speak the community's discourse—and had better speak it a lot, too. To do otherwise is to risk deferrals of one's own advancement, or even unemployment. And even this serves the discipline's larger interests: after all, the fewer "experts" there are, the more precious their expertise must seem.

But other, less obvious, instruments of discipline make nonconformity "merely" uncomfortable rather than dangerous. In speaking outside the culturally cloistered, scientistic, disciplinary discourse, the academic critic runs the risk of being thought an oddball or worse. No one had to wander far at Speech Communication Association conventions in 1982 and 1989, for example, to overhear multiple, whispered conversations about Thomas Benson's "Another Shooting in Cowtown," and Michael Pacanowsky's "Slouching Toward Chicago." The reaction to such nontraditional scholarship runs the full spectrum, from *sotto voce* remarks about iconoclasm to publicly expressed complaints about those who rely upon or emulate the work of "limp-wristed, incomprehensible, beret-wearing leftists"—a characterization actually uttered publicly at a professional convention, we are both surprised and dismayed to report. This chapter, in fact, runs similar risks, for it not only speaks from at least partly outside the professional community's discourse, but also seeks explicitly to displace that way of speaking. And, of course, we are also implicating ourselves herein to the extent that our own voices have participated in the discipline's standard discourse. The three of us, along with the contributors to this volume, are consequently flirting with charges of high treason, lunacy, or both. The scientization and consequent depoliticization of criticism thus serve yet another purpose: They guard against the possibility that the critic will expose the professional system to scrutiny.

## ▨ Recovering Critical Invention from the Void

At the outset of this essay, we specifically exempted ourselves from having to provide answers to the problems we were going to raise. But we were careful to make no such ingenious promises about expressing hope, because in fact we do have some hope for professional critics, beginning critics, and their criticism.

If criticism were *absolutely* professionalized, following the dictates of the disciplinary voice we have reconstructed and explored in this chapter, the critic's inventional procedures would be all too clear. The critic would choose a text to study purely because of its representativeness or its uniqueness (Sillars 19). The "representative" text would help the critic in building a theory (Hart, "Theory-Building" 72); the "unique" text would aid in "testing its limits" (Rybacki and Rybacki 11). Once finished with this bloodless task of choosing a text, the critic would select the appropriate method for isolating and analyzing its "data." The method would discipline the critic's gaze toward only those features of the text that were relevant to the theoretical objective. The critic would render a theoretical conclusion and go on to locate another text to exploit in the same manner, while another critic might conduct a reliability check, by replicating the first "critical" venture.

If anyone actually believed that this was a fair and accurate rendition of what critics do, who would ever decide to be a critic? And if there were any critics still to be found, who would read their relentlessly dreary work? We believe that the answer to both questions is obvious: *no one would.* And this is what gives us cause for hope, even in the shadow of the professional edifice. As much as we believe that critical work in speech communication might sometimes be more interesting than it is—and we do think that from time to time—*none* of it, even on its worst days, is so utterly stupefying as the professional ideology would suggest that it should be. In fact, the critics whose words we have appropriated here to reconstruct the traces of the professional ideology—Andrews, Black, Brock, Scott, Chesebro, Campbell, Fisher, Foss, Gregg, Hart, and the rest—do not *ever* write colorless criticism; their work is engaging and provocative, sometimes delightfully maddening.

Thus, while we have no compelling or demonstrative proof, we must confess to several hunches about critics and their inventional practices. We think most critics probably choose to study particular texts because those texts interest them, whether or not they have any intrinsic or immediately obvious potential for theory contribution. We believe critics take up their practice in part because the experience itself of criticism—that vital energy and sense of moral and intellectual engagement—draws them forward. Most critics, we believe, *become* critics for reasons other than to build explanatory theories and generate "results," desiring to understand in some way how they and their readers can and should react to events in the world. And finally, we suspect that critics are at least as interested in affecting the public cultures of which they are a part as they are in being entombed in a desiccated "most prolific scholars" list.[54]

If our speculations are correct, it does these writers and teachers a grave injustice to call their observations about these texts either "objective" in the sense of being neutral, or "reliable" in the sense of being replicable (Nothstine 161–63). And if we are correct, we have located the starting point for our search to retrieve the question of critical invention in the gap between the dictates of professional ideology and the practices and experiences of critics.

But even believing, as we do, that critics and their work are not *absolutely* scientized, disengaged, and disciplined, professionalism remains the dominant discourse that the critical community speaks. As such, professionalism disciplines its adherents at least to *appear* to conform. One of the clearest ways in which critics keep up this appearance is by concealing or at least leaving unarticulated their inventional practices. They do so because they are too messy, involved, uncertain, and unscientific—in short, too "unprofessional," in the most pleasing sense of that word—to conform to the ideals of disciplinary discourse.

But critics' silence about their inventional practices has consequences. First, it catches critics up in the uncomfortable stance of arguing that inquiry in the sciences and human sciences is fundamentally rhetorical while not acknowledging the rhetorical character of their own inquiry.[55] Second, critics' silence helps to maintain and reproduce the professional ideology. It allows critics to mime and even parody science (Eagleton 92), actually believing somehow that the goals and practices of critical inquiry resemble those of the sciences; or it allows critics to continue with practices that they do not examine and to which they do not admit because they *pretend* subscription to the professional, scientistic creed. But perhaps the most serious consequences of this silence are in the criticism classroom.

## Critical Invention in the Classroom

Faced with the first assignment in the criticism class, the first response of the student—the beginning critic—might reasonably be, "Where do I *start*? How do I know what's worth *doing*?" Fair questions—indeed, crucial questions—but as long as the norms of professional criticism are reproduced without examination in criticism courses, no consistent and practical answer is likely to be forthcoming, for these are precisely the points where professional criticism remains silent. Criticism textbooks are illustrative of this problem, but they are *not* themselves the problem; they reflect the difficulties anyone encounters in teaching criticism that is still in the thrall of the professional ideology. Andrews is certainly right to observe: "One of the rhetorical critic's first problems is deciding where to begin. If one is going to undertake to explicate and interpret the rhetorical dimensions of a particular message, be it a speech, a pamphlet, an editorial, or a proclamation, it makes obvious and good sense to begin with the message itself" (16). But *what* message? And why that message? And having begun with that message, what now?

Hart offers a position on how *not* to choose: "No message is inherently worthy of study. Just because a given text fascinates the critic does not mean that study of it will be worthwhile" (*Modern Rhetorical Criticism* 46). Foss and Sillars, as well as Brock, Scott, and Chesebro, all might soften this position to some extent, maintaining that critics may legitimately choose for criticism those texts they are interested in (Brock, Scott, and Chesebro 10; Foss, *Rhetorical Criticism* 5–6; and Sillars 18–19). But Foss cautions that, while the text might be "of interest to the critic," it should also be "capable of generating insight about rhetorical processes" (*Rhetorical Criticism* 11). Brock, Scott, and Chesebro sound a similar warning:

> Any criticism will automatically have a starting point, even though critics do not consciously make such decisions. However, if these decisions are consciously made (which in some cases will mean that critics seek to uncover their perspectives), they can be more certain that the decisions are consistent with their materials, their purposes, and the sorts of judgments they intend to make. (505)

They make their point more concisely, if more obliquely, when they advise critics to "pick products that will be fruitful to criticize" (14).

Yet this is a circular answer to the problem—for one could hardly expect to know whether criticizing "the product" will be fruitful, or capable of generating insight, after all, until one has already begun to engage it as a critic. Despite Scott, Brock, and Chesebro's good intentions, neither beginning critics nor experienced critics are very likely to *know* "the sorts of judgments they intend to make" before they begin the groping, circular process of critical invention.

Even if the problems of selecting a text for critical investigation are temporarily set aside, however, the difficulties continue, for decisions must be made regarding how to approach the text, what to ask of it or say about it. That road, too, is lined with danger signs. Andrews, for example, warns that "many questions will be irrelevant or of minor significance in certain cases" (62). Both he and Hart hold out the promise that the critic's sophistication and ability to know what kinds of questions to pose will increase with "maturity" (Andrews 62; Hart, *Modern Rhetorical Criticism* 45), which may be the case, but is unlikely to offer much help or comfort in the here-and-now to the critic who is not yet "matured."

Another way that textbook authors often handle the problem of critical invention is a logical response to this dilemma: provide beginning critics with questions to pose of texts (Andrews; Foss; and Hart). Providing the questions leads to other issues, however. For example, why these questions and not others? At least this question is easier to answer: The questions provided are ones that the discourse of the professional critical community recognizes as appropriate or important. But what if a critic wishes to pose a question that is not "approved" by that community? Surely that question should not therefore be dismissed as illegitimate. This issue may be the most troublesome, because it contains the insidious potential for automatically dismissing an individual critic's own interest in favor of the concerns of the professional community.[56]

The same effect, privileging the concerns of the professional community, results from providing beginning critics with professional critics' published essays to study, since once again it asks readers to guess at the hidden *process* by studying the completed *product.* Andrews's comments on the critical essays anthologized in his textbook are typical of this pedagogical strategy: "The samples demonstrate the results of combining imagination and scholarship to reach critical conclusions. These studies are, of course, the work of mature critics, and beginning students are unlikely to emulate them. But the studies do provide points of departure for discussion and may serve as stimulants to students' own critical work" (xii). The problems here are evident: The critical essays demonstrate the *results* of imagination and scholarship but contain not a hint about the process by which imagination and scholarship bring about the result, for the reasons we have devoted this chapter to exposing.

Brock, Scott, and Chesebro's discussion reveals the same lapse between description of the critical impulse and the final product, even as they recognize that a critic "must form his or her own discourse":

> This is not intended to be a handbook on the mechanics of writing critical essays. . . . We hope this text goes behind the mechanics of writing criticism to the theory and method involved. We have sought to identify perspectives and approaches that are likely to be of value to the rhetorical critic. We hope to raise some important questions about junctures at which the critic must make decisions that will shape specific pieces of criticism. We believe that the essays included within this volume are apt to remain important to the substance of rhetorical criticism into the foreseeable future. At the same time, we have included essays that should stand as illustrations not only of each method but of critical writing. (22)

Later, they remind the reader that "we have included applications of each method because we wanted to maintain a link with the actual writing of rhetorical criticism" (502–4). But the essays, of course, can reveal nothing of the *link* to writing; that link is invention, and its presence and operation have been concealed to the greatest extent possible by the ideological mechanisms we have been tracing throughout this chapter. So again, the beginning critic is left with no choice but to *attempt* to emulate the goals and norms of these professional writings as they indirectly show themselves in published essays, and hope for the best.

Foss takes a different approach, although she also includes illustrative critical essays. She addresses the "process of producing an essay of criticism," and "provides guidelines for the critic concerning . . . (1) discovery of the rhetorical artifact and research question; (2) formulation of the critical method; (3) critical analysis of the artifact; and (4) writing the critical essay" (*Rhetorical Criticism* 11). Foss's attempt to deal with this process is a crucial effort; each of the four moments she describes constitutes at least a locus for the choices that the critic must make. However, the process of choice as she describes it soon becomes ossified as a set of regulatory, mechanistic apparatuses. In treating the eight "methods" of criticism included in the text, for example, Foss reduces each of them to a series of prescribed, businesslike techniques. Neo-Aristotelian criticism is thus routinized into the procedures of "reconstruction of context," "analysis of the rhetorical artifact," and "assessment of effects" (*Rhetorical Criticism* 75–80). Feminist criticism, likewise, becomes these procedures: "analysis of gender in the artifact," "discovery of effects on the audience," "discussion of use of artifact to improve women's lives," and "explanation of artifact's impact on rhetorical theory" (*Rhetorical Criticism* 155–60). So, while beginning critics offered these guidelines for criticism are less likely to feel completely abandoned in the inventional process, they are also less likely to find that the process recognizes or serves the interests they themselves might have in writing criticism, unless coincidentally they have the interests presupposed by the procedures themselves—not always a very likely circumstance.

Foss's text and her drift toward the mechanization of critical invention are particularly important when read together with her work assaying the limitations of criticism driven by method ("Constituted by Agency"). There she recognizes most of the limitations and difficulties we have discussed in this chapter.[57] For example:

> Our focus on method confines our criticism to a particular setting or context— in this case, an intellectual, academic one. Technical jargon, the making of minuscule distinctions among categories, and—if it shows off a method— analysis of sometimes trivial topics are made to seem relevant and appropriate by a focus on method. As a result, our criticism is likely to be of interest only to our colleagues in speech communication departments and, even then, only to those who work in our area of specialization. ("Constituted by Agency" 38)

And:

> The subjectivity of the critic is downplayed in the discourse about rhetorical criticism because we do not feature the agent or critic in that discourse. We may not do so because we are uncomfortable with subjectivity, for how can criticism be rigorous or legitimate or scientific or any number of good things if it is rooted in individual experience and bias? ("Constituted by Agency" 42)

But Foss's textbook reproduces those problems. That is neither unique to Foss nor an indictment of her work. Her work mirrors the inexorable problem faced by any critic who also teaches rhetorical criticism. Most academic critics no doubt recognize that many or most of their goals as critics are not shared by most of their students and that their inventional processes probably do not match the scientistic guise with which they cover them. Yet it is not at all clear for many critics how criticism might be taught if not on the "professionalized model." The result is that professional critics' procedures and goals become presented in mechanized and denatured form, misrepresented in the belief that doing so will make them somehow "teachable."

## Revitalizing Criticism

But despite its ambivalence toward the beginning critic and its tendency to fixate on often-arcane theory, media and rhetorical criticism nevertheless espouse sincerely the goal of "opening up" rhetorical works and their constituent media to the understanding of a wider audience, literate but nonspecialist. We believe that Foss is in earnest when she writes, "One purpose of rhetorical criticism . . . is to understand a rhetorical artifact better and, consequently, to use that understanding to help others appreciate it or to change some aspect of the society that generated the rhetorical artifact" (*Rhetorical Criticism* 6). Likewise, Hart's sincerity could not be mistaken when, in the next chapter of this anthology, he explains his identity as a critic: "I am a critic because I often do not like the language my contemporaries speak nor the policy options they endorse. I am a critic because I feel that rhetoric should move a society forward rather than backward, that it should open and not close the public sphere, that it should make people generous and not craven. I am a critic, ultimately, because I am a citizen." Implicit in both of these statements, and the many more like them one can find among the published declarations of our colleagues, is the conviction that criticism can and should make provocative and worthwhile contributions to public discussion.

Because this conviction is genuinely held, if not yet perfectly realized, media and rhetorical criticism ought to do whatever it can to escape the fate of some other branches of criticism in this century. As Said (10–12) and Jacoby (112–39) note, such movements in literary criticism as the Anglo-

American New Criticism and the French *nouvelle critique,* and much of Marxist criticism in several disciplines, once determined to be accessible and influential to the widest audience, are now all-too-seldom heard by any outside their narrowly drawn academic audiences (Said 10–12; Jacoby 112–39).

It would be naively optimistic about the institutional and cultural forces we challenge to imagine that the future of criticism will be transformed simply by our revival in this book of the question of critical invention. Yet the return to the question of critical questions is clearly a necessary precondition if criticism is to emerge from its present cloistered state in which critics are isolated from public culture, from their students, and from one another. This first step is but one of several that must be contemplated. Another step will be taken as critics experiment with different forms of writing and expression *as* critics, and with breaching the boundaries currently separating disciplines. Another step will be taken as editors tolerate departures from the standard models of professional critical scholarship, rethinking which critical practices they really want to use their institutional power to encourage. Another important step will be taken when administrators demythify the significance of disciplinary turf barriers as well as the relationships among scholarly writing, professional journals, and knowledge production. A terribly important step will be taken when teachers of criticism have access to an alternative teaching model designed to promote the values and practices of media and rhetorical criticism to a new generation of critics, enabling these beginning critics to write to and from various communities, rather than exclusively the community of professional critics. When and if this moment arrives, critics will have the opportunity to write criticism that draws strength and vitality from their initial commitments to community, to ethics, and to ideology, as well as to theory and profession, rather than struggling to conceal them.

# ▓ Notes

[1]As later sections of this chapter will demonstrate, we intend "media and rhetorical" to refer primarily to critics and criticism connected with the disciplinary history of the speech communication field. Our purpose is thus to designate a disciplinary category, rather than a purely theoretical, methodological, or substantive one. The speech communication discipline's experience with the issues of professionalization has in many ways been similar to the experience of other fields, such as history, literature, film, journalism, or sociology, and its history can be instructive to those readers more familiar with these neighboring disciplines. But speech communication, owing to aspects of its particular disciplinary history, has also faced tensions that have not generally been experienced even by substantively similar fields. Readers from other disciplines may thus find speech communication's *atypicality* instructive as well.

[2]We assume as our general stance one defended by Foucault, who argued that we are not disqualified from raising questions or problems if we do not immediately "solve" them. To impose such a stricture would be to foreclose any acknowledgment or discussion of a problem unless or until one can solve it. Instead, he suggested that it may be of at least interim value

for critics "to bring it about that they 'no longer know what to do', so that acts, gestures, discourses which up until then had seemed to go without saying become problematic, difficult, dangerous. The effect is intentional." Rather than having an "anaesthetizing" or "sterilizing" effect, his critique was intended to mobilize "a long work of comings and goings, of exchanges, reflections, trials, different analyses" ("Questions of Method" 84). Also see "Critical Theory/ Intellectual History." We hope, instead of dictating our own "solutions," to initiate discussions and experiments aimed at solving the problem we attempt to characterize in this book.

³Here our goal is in line with, and is meant to extend, the work begun by Wander and Jenkins, and supplemented by Wander. Wander suggests that "in an academic context, for example, an ideological critique would bore in, at some point, on the connection between what scholars in a given field call 'knowledge,' even 'scientific' knowledge, and professional interest. It would confront ideals professed with what they obscure in either theory or practice in light of the possibilities for real or 'emancipatory' change" ("Ideological Turn" 2).

⁴We mean by "text," in part, what we believe others reference by terms like "artifact" or "object." That is, we mean the rhetorical or media event the critic has chosen to address through critical writing. We deliberately avoid these other terms because of our discomfort with their implications. We have chosen "text" to designate that which the critic addresses for two reasons. First, it is broad enough to encompass a variety of events; it is at least as unconfined in scope as "artifact" or "object," so as to allow for the inclusion of extra-verbal acts (music, painting, sculpture) or extra-verbal aspects of verbal forms (material action and scene in a dramatic performance). Second, "text" has come to designate a critical operation rather than a fixed material object. It or "discourse," as used in most critical circles, refers to a construction or construal by the critic of the event(s) to be analyzed. See Barthes; Bové; Brummett, "How to Propose"; Foucault, *Archaeology;* and McGee, "Text."

⁵Wander and Jenkins concur: "The play of values takes place at three points in the critical act: selection, response, and communication. One discovers that a particular object holds interest over against any number of other potential objects; one tries to understand both the object and one's interest in it; and one decides what to say about it." But, as they also observe, "These questions [of value] lie at the heart of criticism as we conceive of it, but the practice of academic criticism tends to divert us from this kind of questioning" (441). They suggest what we intend here, a consideration of "the institutional context of scholarship and how it encourages and discourages certain modes of thought, research, and expression" (449).

⁶There are exceptions, but they are extremely rare. See, for example: Birdsell; and Leff, "Textual Criticism."

⁷As Robert Hariman suggests, "the writer is not the sole author of the work, which also is the product of inventional patterns provided by (and sustaining) the writer's dominant social organization. Academic discourse is made by the academic institution, and discovering the relationship between the rhetorical and epistemological dimensions of such discourse should include a critique of its institutional invention" (213).

⁸As Hariman notes, "professionalism has been a productive movement." Among other functions it has "[advanced] democratic access to learning within and without the academy" (223). And as Bruce Robbins notes, the professionalism decried by those like Jacoby overlooks the professional university's achievements in including and advancing the work of women. "Even in the worst instance," Robbins concludes, "professionalization is always partly achievement from below as well as co-optation from above" (xviii).

⁹See Wilshire; Jacoby; Smith; and Bledstein.

¹⁰See Wilshire; and Hariman. As Graff points out, this was only one of the possible forms professionalization might have assumed. We heed his warning that professionalization itself is not necessarily dangerous, but the form it takes may be (*Professing Literature,* 5).

¹¹Levine defines "discipline" as a "discrete body of knowledge with a characteristic regimen for investigation and analysis . . ." (522). Katrín Fridjónsdóttir suggests the mutual dependence of professionalism and disciplinarity (120).

[12]See Foucault, "Discourse." There he argues that disciplines negotiate what counts as true [*dans le vrai*]. He suggests that, "disciplines constitute a system of control in the production of discourse, fixing its limits through the action of an identity taking the form of a permanent reactivation of the rules" (224).

[13]Wilshire uses philosophy as an example: "It is symptomatic of the university's malaise, its distance from the common concerns of humans to build lives for themselves, that philosophers tend to be isolated in highly technical, verbalistic communication with professional fellows. The complexity and expertness of their language is the problem" (xxii).

[14]In the late nineteenth-century movement to professionalize the university, "learned societies blossomed in great profusion" (Rudolph, *Curriculum*, 156). Wilshire notes that "in the 1870s and '80s two hundred learned societies were formed in addition to teacher's groups" (64). Significant in Wilshire's description is not only the linkage of professionalism to the growth of learned societies, but also his distinction between these professional organizations and "teacher's groups." Such segregation of the professional and the pedagogical is another sign of the estrangement of civic and experiential domains from the professional.

[15]See Wilshire 49. As Cornelis Disco suggests, "the organization of professions across the specific peripheral institutions in which their members work provides professionals with a source of identity competitive with their identities as employees" (72).

[16]Certainly it is not the case that outside reviewers have completely usurped the university's evaluation function. But the outside professionals' opinions and decisions can go far in justifying a university's tenure, promotion, and merit decisions regarding individual faculty members.

[17]Also see: Hariman 218; Sorrell 9; and McGee and Lyne 383.

[18]Treatments of the question of objectivity have degenerated into something virtually useless; almost invariably, they come down to epistemological criteria, most commonly some form of empiricism (Said 14–15). The result often treads a narrow line between intellectual earnestness and farce: scholars buttressing their arguments by pointing to the impossibility of walking through walls and the like (Hikins and Zagacki 203; See also Carey 287).

[19]The field of history provides a well-known example of the temptations to objectivism that professionalism can create; see Novick. Hayden White points to historians' embrace of empirical method, as opposed to metaphysical reflection, as the basis for "permitting the kind of 'historical knowledge' produced by professional historians to serve as the standard of 'realism' in political thought and action in general" (123–24).

[20]See Aronowitz ix; and Sorrell 2.

[21]Hempel, "Logic" 185. Also see his *Philosophy*, particularly Chapter 5. "Testability" in general embraces such more specific issues as replicability, quantification, operationalization, etc.

[22]Toulmin uses the term "postmodern science" to describe post-Heisenberg views. He observes:

> In quantum mechanics as much as in psychiatry, in ecology as much as in anthropology, the scientific observer is now—willy-nilly—also a *participant*. The scientists of the mid-twentieth century, then, have entered the period of postmodern science. For natural scientists today, the classical posture of pure spectator is no longer available even on the level of pure theory; and the objectivity of scientific knowledge can no longer rely on the passivity of the scientists' objects of knowledge alone. In the physical sciences, objectivity can now be achieved only in the way it is in the human sciences: the scientist must acknowledge and discount his own reactions to and influence on that which he seeks to understand. (103)

[23]This move toward a Catholic interpretation of the discipline had its Protestant countermovements, functioning at the same time: Delia notes that the proliferation of professional guilds—specifically the development of individual national organizations in theatre, speech

pathology, and broadcasting—contributed to the break-up of departments of speech, which once typically housed all these subareas under one administrative roof, into their own individual administrative units (78). To the extent that scholars in these various areas once shared much in common, substantively or professionally, this centrifugal force discouraged the continuation of these ties.

[24]And the rhetorical scholars did not always provide a gracious welcome. For example, David Berg described in 1972 the problems of publishing rhetorical criticism of the media stemming from "a very literal and limited conception within the discipline of what constitutes 'speech' " (255). He describes his attempt in the late 1960s to get an article accepted in *Quarterly Journal of Speech*—an article that was later published in *Journalism Quarterly*. Berg was told by the editor of the *Quarterly Journal of Speech* that an article on the persuasive functions of newspapers was inappropriate for the journal. Stretching the definition of speech to cover newspapers would, according to that editor, lead ultimately to the loss of the "unique quality" of *Quarterly Journal of Speech* (255).

[25]Also see Cohen; and Benson, "History."

[26]Berlo, in 1955, lamented the absence of a "hypothetical-deductive (to use the Hullian term) theory of rhetoric," but insisted that "it is the responsibility of any experimenter to attempt to provide a theoretical rationale for any piece of research not exploratory in nature" (4). He concluded that "only through training competent experimentalists and securing the presence of a skilled methodologician on the editorial review boards of our journals will research in Speech secure the academic respect of our colleagues in the social sciences, and aid in the development of a realistic theory of rhetoric" (8). That this determination still is a dominant concern is clear in Berger's attempt to account for the "high level of fragmentation" he takes to be a difficulty of communication research and the so-called problem of "relatively little commerce among the various sub-areas of the field" (101). This despite Arthur Bochner and Eric Eisenberg's sensible, if obvious, objection:

> Not only is coherence an unrealistic objective but, even worse, the search for coherence militates against cohesion. Consider what happens when a discipline looks for a single framework, perspective, or paradigm capable of making the field as a whole seem coherent. Promoters of particularized points of view are given license to make outrageous claims about the range of issues to which their largely unspecified perspective apply . . . to universalize a perspective is to ask that "reality-under-a-certain-description" be viewed as accommodating all possible descriptions of reality. . . . No field of knowledge has ever been able to settle on a final set of terms under which all its inquiry could be subsumed." (314–15)

[27]Also see Arnold, "Rhetorical and Communication Studies"; Brockriede, "Toward a Contemporary Aristotelian Theory"; Brockriede, "Trends"; Clevenger; and Thompson.

[28]This approach will therefore tend to favor the voice of rhetorical critics over that of media critics, but to the extent that they share overlapping disciplinary histories, the difference is not as crucial as might be supposed. Our choice was driven by the fact that there are presently comparatively few textbooks on media criticism associated with speech communication—as opposed, for example to film criticism, for which numerous texts are available but which has shared little disciplinary history with speech communication. To attempt to reconstruct a disciplinary voice from such a small body of work strikes us as unfair. Where reference to those available works in media criticism, for example, Vande Berg and Wenner, is appropriate to highlight either important differences or significant convergences between media criticism and rhetorical criticism, we have attempted to do so.

[29]Leff describes "modernist rhetoric" as "an approach based in conventional social scientific notions of theory," and "probably best articulated by Roderick Hart" ("Things" 230n). Whether or not that is an accurate label, we think Leff is correct in suggesting that practitioners of both "textual criticism" and "critical rhetoric" can agree in their resistance to this main-

stream criticism. The two groups pursue different, competitive routes in their desires to supplant it, however. "Textual criticism" represents a particular position within what has been called a "renaissance" in public address scholarship. "Critical rhetoric" is but one specific stance among an array of similar but nonidentical positions that thematize discourse as power and that view criticism as a vehicle of change, sometimes radical change. Representatives of the former group include: Iltis and Browne; Leff, "Textual Criticism"; Lucas; Mohrmann; and Zarefsky. Representatives of the latter include: Biesecker; Blair, "Contested Histories"; Blair, " 'Meta-Ideology' "; Charland; Condit; McGee, "Text"; McKerrow; and Ono and Sloop.

[30]Our observations that the critic-artist does not seem to fare as well as the critic-scientist in the Committee's descriptions should not be taken as a statement of support for the critic-artist as an appropriate model. We agree with Klumpp and Hollihan's observation, that "both of these self-images alienate." They explain:

> The social scientist must alienate him/herself from his/her own involvement in the act and the artistic critic must alienate him/herself from the obvious social context and impact of the rhetorical and critical act. The result has been a criticism that seems sterile. One reads Martin Medhurst's criticism of the anti–gay rights campaign and his defense of the criticism and feels an estrangement from the morality of consequences that alienates all but the professional critic sharing the social science orientation. One reads Robert L. Scott and Wayne Brockriede's study of Harry S. Truman's elegant use of counterpoint musical form and feels the dominance of a rarified technical theory of art estranged from the impact of a rhetor who fundamentally changed our world. (92)

Also see Medhurst; and Scott and Brockriede 10–43.

[31]This despite the "Conclusion" of the National Developmental Project:

> The issue becomes: shall there be concerted action to "rhetoricize" rather than to "scientize" social and humanistic study and action? Our conferences have suggested that intolerance of differences, exacerbation of disagreement, and distrust of the content of modern education are at least in part the consequences of educational and other public policies which imply that objective, depersonalized conclusions or "truths" are or should be possible, though indeed no such possibilities do or can exist. In the tons of print and hours of sound expended upon "the cause of the present malaise," one finds almost no attention given to the fact that decision-making in a vast array of problem areas has been culturally misrepresented (as scientific) to several generations. (Bitzer and Black, eds. 244)

[32]See also Brockriede, "Trends"; Farrell, "Beyond Science"; Fisher, "Rhetorical Criticism"; and Wallace.

[33]Also see: Campbell, "Criticism" 11; Hart, "Contemporary Scholarship"; and Hart, "Theory-Building." In this context, Vande Berg and Wenner stake out a moderate position, citing Foss with approval on the goal of theory building in criticism, but listing "theory builder" as only one of several roles the critic may play, the others including interpreter, teacher, and judge (6–8).

[34]The attempt to ascribe "pre-scientific" status to critical research has its counterpart in media research as well, beginning with Paul Lazarsfeld's attempt to introduce European critical theory into American media research by bringing Theodor Adorno into collaboration with his research team in 1938. Lazarsfeld had hoped that Adorno's critical theory could generate ideas that would be empirically testable by the methods of Lazarsfeld's team. As Slack and Allor report, "attempts at convergence failed essentially because it proved impossible to translate Adorno's critical analysis into the methods and goals of other members of the radio project" (210).

[35]Brummett's references are to: Gronbeck 328; Black, "A Note" 333–34; McGee, " 'Social Movement' " 233; Zarefsky 245; and Swanson 210.

[36]See Chaffee and Berger 104–5. They list seven criteria for evaluating theory, the first of which is explanatory power: "Here we are concerned with the theory's ability to provide plausible explanations for the phenomena it was constructed to explain. Also considered here is the range of phenomena that the theory explains; the greater the range, the more powerful the theory" (104).

[37]We will take up the issue of criticism's audience and "proper" outlet further on. However, Wander and Jenkins's observation, that "the critic is but one human being trying to communicate with other human beings," is suggestive of the problem in Campbell's analysis. The division of academic criticism, which addresses professionals, from social criticism, which addresses people at large, forgets the fact that critics are also people at large and not *just* professionals.

[38]The confusion is exacerbated by one of Brock, Scott, and Chesebro's predictions: "We anticipate that the ideological nature increasingly attributed to rhetorical criticism may be perceived as a denial of the social ends and functions traditionally attributed to rhetorical criticism" (512). That criticism, which has devalued judgment as a principal operation for almost thirty years, does not now appear to *have* much of a social function is one source of confusion. But to suggest that it would be the ideological turn that might divert criticism away from a social end that it currently does not have is even more puzzling. As Wander suggests, "criticism takes an ideological turn when it recognizes the existence of powerful vested interests benefiting from and consistently urging policies and technology that threaten life on this planet, when it realizes that we search for alternatives" (18).

[39]Black would later soften his position. In the preface of the 1978 reissue of his book, he claims that, "these reflections on the subjectivity of criticism are recorded here as a corrective to this book's excessive deference . . . to an ideal of objectivity" (xiv). Two observations are in order regarding Black's modification. First, it almost certainly came too late to change the scientistic course that had been set. That is *not* to suggest that Black was singly responsible for that course, nor that he should have modified his position earlier. Black's, like other critics', statements are ones of a discourse community as much as of any individual. Had Black not made the 1965 statements or had he modified them sooner, it is quite unlikely that the course taken in criticism would have been materially different. Second, apparently trapped within the Cartesianism that so pervades modernist thought, Black simply chose the other half of the dualism in his revision. His 1978 account discusses *subjectivity* as a corrective to the overemphasis on objectivity, thus remaining within the same dualist vision with a change of emphasis. We believe that there are other options available, if only we are able to think outside of Descartes' moment. It is worth noting also, however, that Black is not alone in his occupation of the Cartesian system. See, for example, Rybacki and Rybacki 13.

[40]The only examples we can think of are: Benson, "Another Shooting"; Hill, "Reply"; and Pacanowsky. The Benson and Pacanowsky essays are clear departures in this respect and others from the norm. Hill's claims to being a McGovern supporter and a liberal were in a "Forum" essay, where presumably the norms governing such self-reference are more lax than in the typical critical article.

[41]See: Megill; Rosenfield, "Ideological Miasma"; Hill; Campbell, "Response"; McGee, "Another Philippic"; Franceasconi; and Corcoran. Not all of the respondents disagree with Wander. However, the apparent need or desire to defend his position itself points to the recalcitrance of the view attacked by Wander. Wander responded to these critics in "The Third Persona."

[42]Classifications seem a potent weapon for those who would resist some forms of criticism. Sillars divides critical approaches into two general categories—"the objectivist and the deconstructive" (10). "Deconstruction" in Sillars's text consists of virtually all types of criticism done in the last thirty years, *except* that kind which most of us would recognize as deconstruction. On Sillars's classification, Kenneth Burke, Walter R. Fisher, and Sillars himself would be decon-

structionists; those most typically associated with deconstruction—Jacques Derrida and Paul de Man—never appear in Sillars's account. Such classification *is* a way of making deconstruction seem safe, if not a means of actually carrying out the spirit of the pluralist project Sillars advocates (10).

[43]Hart's description here is not by any means the worst representation in the discipline. There are moments of understanding and sympathy with these projects to be found in his chapter. Donald Ellis's essay is an even more resistant rendition and it is founded upon a serious misreading and reduction of poststructuralist projects.

[44]To so construe reliability, however, is a reach, and a potentially dangerous one. It suggests that a critic is "right" if the reader cannot disconfirm the critic's argument, and that a critic is "wrong" if the reader disagrees or casts doubt on the argument.

[45]See Clevenger 175; and Farrell, "Critical Models."

[46]See, for example: Andrews 12; Brock, Scott, and Chesebro 17; Brockriede, "Rhetorical Criticism" 169; Foss, *Rhetorical Criticism* 11; Hart, *Modern Rhetorical Criticism* 34–35; Rybacki and Rybacki 23; Sillars 22; and Sloan, et al. 226, 227.

[47]See Thonssen and Baird v, 4. Also see Brigance, ed; and Hochmuth, ed.

[48]For a broader justification of the political-ethical obligations of the critic, see Thonssen and Baird 467–71. It is worth noting that, by 1948, when *Speech Criticism* was published, the signs of professional, scientized criticism were evident. For example, Thonssen and Baird advocated a "dispassionate, objective attitude toward the object of investigation" (20). Nonetheless, the older connection of the academic to the culture was still much in evidence.

[49]It is a sad irony: Modern criticism's life is completely intertwined with the college and university, yet modern critics are producing criticism often described as "inaccessible" to their own students—"inaccessible" being an apparent euphemism for "incomprehensible," but carrying with it as well an unintended slur against the competence of the students. Indeed, a reservation voiced by more than one reviewer of the proposal for *this* anthology was that the critical essays to be reprinted herein, drawn from academic journals, would be inaccessible to their undergraduate students.

[50]For example, Rosenfield characterizes the moment of appreciative encounter between critic and text in terms bordering on the erotic; it is tempting to describe the energetic efforts to conceal this moment of pleasure (or pain) from the public gaze as a kind of intellectual puritanism. See Rosenfield, "Experience."

[51]Indeed, we find that a significant part of the problem is that the question of critical invention, and its relation to critical practice, to theory, and to the politics and pedagogy of criticism, is a disciplinary pariah: As the modern university has divided up boundaries, our question is not *in* any discipline, by definition. The reflection on the disciplinary structures of knowledge and their implications for practice in any critical field is no one's responsibility (with the arguable exception—heaven help us—of university administrators). This is even true of "interdisciplinary studies," which may fashion curricula or research programs crossing the boundaries of several disciplines but which in almost every case assume the reality and propriety of those boundaries (Wilshire 113–14; Said 21; Graff, "Pseudo-Politics" 70).

[52]Factional rivalry exists even within the communication borders, for example between those whose loyalties are to the Speech Communication Association and those who give allegiance to the International Communication Association. Notwithstanding their nominal association with communication and the fact that they frequently work in the same departments, these two groups—and other groups affiliated with broadcasting, journalism, etc.— often have little professional communication. Reeves and Borgman's 1983 network analysis of citations of nine journals nominally related to communication found that the three Speech Communication Association-related journals (*Quarterly Journal of Speech, Central States Communication Journal,* and *Communication Monographs*) were strongly linked to one another, citing

one another's research frequently, but found no such links to any of the other tested journals, except to *Human Communication Research* (130). The other journals in their sample were *Journalism Quarterly, Communication Research, Public Opinion Quarterly, Journal of Communication,* and *Journal of Broadcasting.*

[53]The number of times that Berger refers to "one's theory," "one's own theory," and "ego," in the span of two pages, may be enlightening on this point.

[54]Burton Bledstein expresses the consequences of this tension well: "Historically speaking, the culture of professionalism in America has been enormously satisfying to the human ego, while it has taken an inestimable toll on the integrity of individuals" (xi).

[55]See: Nelson, Megill, and McCloskey, eds.; Simons, ed. *Rhetoric;* and Simons, ed. *The Rhetorical Turn.* Also see Blair, "Contested Histories."

[56]Graff recounts an example of precisely this problem. In a literature course, he assigned his students a short story whose ending apparently contradicted the well-established motivations of the main character. He then asked the students to write about this ending.

> The students had grasped the contradictions of the tale, but when they came to write their papers they had no terms for talking about contradictions except as things to be resolved. Their interpretations had been predetermined by an assumption drilled into them since high-school English, namely, that when you encounter an apparent anomaly in a literary work—especially if it's a canonized one—it's not a real anomaly. The students who read the ending as ironic did so because that is the only plausible way to make it cohere with the rest of the story. That there are occasions when the elements of a literary work *don't* cohere was a possibility they either hadn't been led to consider or had no terms to express, at least not in formal writing. Not surprisingly, it was the *better* students in the class who were least able to treat the story's contradictions *as* contradictions. This makes depressing sense: it's the students who have best mastered a particular interpretive strategy who figure to be most its captive. ("University" 76)

Graff's encounter with the professionalization of criticism among his students is doubtless far more typical than either teacher or student would care to admit. The same is probably true of his observation that it is often the "better" students who most quickly discipline themselves to keep a safe distance from critical inventiveness.

[57]Foss does identify a different reason for these difficulties than we would. Analyzing the possibilities open to critics with Burke's pentad, she suggests that the difficulties are a result of focusing too much upon method. We believe the problem goes much deeper than that, into the heart of the institutions in which we practice and into our own motivations to maintain them. Overemphasis on method, in that larger context, is as much a symptom of the problem as a cause.

# ▮ Works Cited

Almond, Gabriel A., Marvin Chodorow, and Roy Harvey Pearce, eds. *Progress and Its Discontents.* Berkeley: University of California Press, 1982.

Andrews, James R. *The Practice of Rhetorical Criticism.* 2d ed. New York: Longman, 1990.

Arnold, Carroll C. "Reflections on the Wingspread Conference." Bitzer and Black, eds. 194–99.

———."Rhetorical and Communication Studies: Two Worlds or One?" *Western Speech* 36 (1972): 75–81.

Aronowitz, Stanley. *Science as Power: Discourse and Ideology in Modern Society.* Minneapolis: University of Minnesota Press, 1988.

Barthes, Roland. "From Work to Text." *Image-Music-Text.* Trans. Stephen Heath. New York: Hill and Wang, 1977. 155–64.

Becker, Samuel L. "Marxist Approaches to Media Studies: The British Experience." *Critical Studies in Mass Communication* 1 (1984): 66–80.

Benson, Thomas W. "Another Shooting in Cowtown." *Quarterly Journal of Speech* 67 (1981): 347–406.

———. "History, Criticism, and Theory in the Study of American Rhetoric." *American Rhetoric: Context and Criticism.* Ed. Thomas W. Benson. Carbondale: Southern Illinois University Press, 1989. 1–17.

———, ed. *Speech Communication in the 20th Century.* Carbondale: Southern Illinois University Press, 1985.

Berg, David M. "Rhetoric, Reality, and Mass Media." *Quarterly Journal of Speech* 58 (1972): 255–63.

Berger, Charles R. "Communication Theories and Other Curios." *Communication Monographs* 58 (1991): 101–13.

Berger, Charles R., and Steven H. Chaffee, eds. *Handbook of Communication Science.* Newbury Park, CA: Sage, 1987.

Berlo, David K. "Problems in Communication Research." *Central States Speech Journal* 7 (1955): 3–8.

Biesecker, Barbara A. "Towards a Transactional View of Rhetorical and Feminist Theory: Rereading Hélène Cixous's *The Laugh of the Medusa.*" *Southern Communication Journal* 57 (1992): 86–96.

Birdsell, David S. "Ronald Reagan on Lebanon and Grenada: Flexibility and Interpretation in the Application of Kenneth Burke's Pentad." *Quarterly Journal of Speech* 73 (1987): 267–79.

Bitzer, Lloyd F., and Edwin Black, eds. *The Prospect of Rhetoric.* Report of the National Developmental Project Sponsored by the Speech Communication Association. Englewood Cliffs, NJ: Prentice-Hall, 1971.

Black, Edwin. "A Note on Theory and Practice in Rhetorical Criticism." *Western Journal of Speech Communication* 44 (1980): 331–36.

———. *Rhetorical Criticism: A Study in Method.* New York: Macmillan, 1965.

———. *Rhetorical Criticism: A Study in Method* [reissued]. Madison: University of Wisconsin Press, 1978.

Blair, Carole. "Contested Histories of Rhetoric: The Politics of Preservation, Progress, and Change." *Quarterly Journal of Speech* 78 (1992): 403–28.

———. " 'Meta-Ideology,' Rhetoric and Social Theory: Reenactment of the Wisdom-Eloquence Tension After the Linguistic Turn." *Rhetoric and Ideology: Compositions and Criticisms of Power.* Ed. Charles W. Kneupper. Arlington, TX: Rhetoric Society of America, 1989. 21–29.

Bledstein, Burton J. *The Culture of Professionalism: The Middle Class and the Development of Higher Education in America.* New York: Norton, 1976.

Bochner, Arthur P., and Eric M. Eisenberg. "Legitimizing Speech Communication: An Examination of Coherence and Cohesion in the Development of the Discipline." Benson, ed. *Speech Communication* 299–321.

Bormann, Ernest G. "Generalizing About Significant Form: Science and Humanism Compared and Contrasted." *Form and Genre: Shaping Rhetorical Action.* Ed. Karlyn Kohrs Campbell and Kathleen Hall Jamieson. Falls Church, VA: Speech Communication Association, 1977. 51–69.

Bové, Paul A. "Discourse." *Critical Terms for Literary Study.* Ed. Frank Lentricchia and Thomas McLaughlin. Chicago: University of Chicago Press, 1990. 50–65.

Bowers, John Waite. "The Pre-Scientific Function of Rhetorical Criticism." *Essays on Rhetorical Criticism.* Ed. Thomas R. Nilson. New York: Random House, 1968. 126–45. Rpt. in Ehninger, ed. 163–73.

Brigance, William Norwood, ed. *A History and Criticism of American Public Address.* 2 vols. New York: McGraw-Hill, 1943.

Brock, Bernard L., Robert L. Scott, and James W. Chesebro, eds. *Methods of Rhetorical Criticism: A Twentieth-Century Perspective.* 3d ed. Detroit: Wayne State University Press, 1989.

Brockriede, Wayne. "Rhetorical Criticism as Argument." *Quarterly Journal of Speech* 60 (1974): 165–74.

———. "Toward a Contemporary Aristotelian Theory of Rhetoric." *Quarterly Journal of Speech* 52 (1966): 33–40. Rpt. in Johannesen, ed. 39–49.

———. "Trends in the Study of Rhetoric: Toward a Blending of Criticism and Science." Bitzer and Black, eds. 123–39.

Brown, William R. "Mass Media and Society: The Development of Critical Perspectives." Benson ed. *Speech Communication* 196–220.

Brummett, Barry. "How to Propose a Discourse—A Reply to Rowland." *Communication Studies* 41 (1990): 128–35.

———. "Rhetorical Theory as Heuristic and Moral: A Pedagogical Justification." *Communication Education* 33 (1984): 97–107.

Campbell, Karlyn Kohrs. "Criticism: Ephemeral and Enduring." *Speech Teacher* 23 (1974): 9–14.

———. "Response to Forbes Hill." *Central States Speech Journal* 34 (1983): 126–27.

Carey, James W. "Graduate Education in Mass Communication," *Communication Education* 28 (1979): 282–93.

Carroll, Raymond L. "Context in the Study of Mass Communication: The Cases of 'Telecommunications' and 'Journalism,' " *Feedback* 27 (1985): 3–8.

Chaffee, Steven H., and Charles R. Berger. "What Communication Scientists Do." Berger and Chaffee, eds. 99–122.

Cherwitz, Richard A., and John Theobald-Osborne. "Contemporary Developments in Rhetorical Criticism: A Consideration of the Effects of Rhetoric." Phillips and Wood, ed. 52–80.

Clevenger, Theodore, Jr. "The Interaction of Descriptive and Experimental Research in the Development of Rhetorical Theory." *Central States Speech Journal* 16 (1965): 7–12. Rpt. in Ehninger, ed. 174–78.

Cohen, Herman. "The Development of Research in Speech Communication: A Historical Perspective." Benson, ed. *Speech Communication* 282–98.

Condit, Celeste. "Rhetorical Criticism and Audiences: The Extremes of McGee and Leff." *Western Journal of Communication* 54 (1990): 330–45.

Corcoran, Farrel. "The Widening Gyre: Another Look at Ideology in Wander and His Critics." *Central States Speech Journal* 35 (1984): 54–56.

Davis, Bernard D. "Fear of Progress in Biology." Almond, Chodorow, and Pearce, eds. 182–201.

Delia, Jesse G. "Communication Research: A History." Berger and Chaffee, eds. 20–98.

Disco, Cornelis. "Intellectuals in Advanced Capitalism: Capital, Closure, and the New-Class Thesis." Eyerman, Svensson, and Söerqvist, eds. 50–77.

Eagleton, Terry. *The Function of Criticism: From* The Spectator *to Post-Structuralism.* London: Verso, 1984.

Ehninger, Douglas, ed. *Contemporary Rhetoric: A Reader's Coursebook.* Glenview, IL: Scott, Foresman, 1972.

Ellis, Donald G. "Post-Structuralism and Language: Non-Sense." *Communication Monographs* 58 (1991): 213–24.

Eyerman, Ron, Lennart G. Svensson, and Thomas Söerqvist, eds. *Intellectuals, Universities and the State in Western Modern Societies.* Berkeley: University of California Press, 1987.

Farrell, Thomas B. "Beyond Science: Humanities Contributions to Communication Theory." Berger and Chaffee, eds. 123–39.

———. "Critical Models in the Analysis of Discourse." *Western Journal of Speech Communication* 44 (1980): 300–14.

Feigl, Herbert. "The Scientific Outlook: Naturalism and Humanism." *Readings in the Philosophy of Science.* Ed. Herbert Feigl and May Brodbeck. New York: Appleton-Century-Crofts, 1953. 8–18.

Feinberg, Gerald. "Progress in Physics: The Game of Intellectual Leapfrog." Almond, Chodorow, and Pearce, eds. 161–81.

Fisher, Walter R. "Rhetorical Criticism as Criticism." *Western Speech* 38 (1974): 75–80.

Foss, Sonja K. "Constituted by Agency: The Discourse and Practice of Rhetorical Criticism." Phillips and Wood, eds. 33–51.

———. "Criteria for Adequacy in Rhetorical Criticism." *Southern Speech Communication Journal* 48 (1983): 283–95.

———. *Rhetorical Criticism: Exploration and Practice.* Prospect Heights, IL: Waveland, 1989.

Foucault, Michel. *The Archaeology of Knowledge.* Trans. A. M. Sheridan Smith. New York: Pantheon, 1972.

———. "Critical Theory/Intellectual History." Trans. Jeremy Harding. *Michel Foucault: Politics, Philosophy, Culture—Interviews and Other Writings, 1977–1984.* Ed. Lawrence D. Kritzman. New York: Routledge, 1988. 17–46.

———. "The Discourse on Language." Lecture at the Collège de France. December 2, 1970. Trans. Rupert Swyer. Appendix to *The Archaeology of Knowledge.* 215–37.

———. "Questions of Method." *The Foucault Effect: Studies in Governmentality.* Ed. Graham Burchell, Colin Gordon, and Peter Miller. Chicago: University of Chicago Press, 1991. 73–86.

———. "Two Lectures." *Power/Knowledge: Selected Interviews and Other Writings, 1972–1977.* Ed. Colin Gordon. Trans. Colin Gordon, Leo Marshall, John Mepham, and Kate Soper. New York: Pantheon, 1980. 78–108.

Francesconi, Robert. "Heidegger and Ideology: Reflections of an Innocent Bystander." *Central States Speech Journal* 35 (1984): 51–53.

Fridjónsdóttir, Katrín. "The Modern Intellectual: In Power or Disarmed? Reflections on the Sociology of Intellectuals and Intellectual Work." Eyerman, Svensson, and Söderqvist, eds. 110–26.

Gibbons, Reginald. "Academic Criticism and Contemporary Literature." Graff and Gibbons, eds. 15–35.

Graff, Gerald. *Professing Literature: An Institutional History.* Chicago: University of Chicago Press, 1987.

———. "The Pseudo-Politics of Interpretation." Mitchell, ed. 145–58.

———. "The University and the Prevention of Culture." Graff and Gibbons, eds. 62–82.

Graff, Gerald, and Reginald Gibbons, eds. *Criticism in the University.* Evanston, IL: Northwestern University Press, 1985.

Gregg, Richard B. "The Criticism of Symbolic Inducement: A Critical-Theoretical Connection." Benson, ed. 41–62.

Gronbeck, Bruce E. "Dramaturgical Theory and Criticism: The State of the Art (or Science?)." *Western Journal of Speech Communication* 44 (1980): 315–30.

Haber, Samuel. *The Quest for Authority and Honor in the American Professions, 1750–1900.* Chicago: University of Chicago Press, 1991.

Hariman, Robert. "The Rhetoric of Inquiry and the Professional Scholar." Simons, ed. *Rhetoric.* 211–32.

Hart, Roderick P. "Contemporary Scholarship in Public Address: A Research Editorial." *Western Journal of Speech Communication* 50 (1986): 283–95.

———. *Modern Rhetorical Criticism.* Glenview, IL: Scott, Foresman/Little, Brown, 1990.

———. "Rhetorical Research: The Most Traditional Tradition." *Spectra,* 20, February 1989: 2–3.

———. "Theory-Building and Rhetorical Criticism: An Informal Statement of Opinion." *Central States Speech Journal* 27 (1976): 70–77.

Head, Sydney W. "The Telecommunication Curriculum: A Personal View." *Feedback* 27 (1985): 9–12.

Hempel, Carl G. "The Logic of Functional Analysis." *Readings in the Philosophy of Science.* Ed. May Brodbeck. New York: Macmillan, 1963.

———. *Philosophy of Natural Science.* Englewood Cliffs, NJ: Prentice-Hall, 1966.

Hickson, Mark, III, Don W. Stacks, and Jonathan H. Amsbury. "An Analysis of Prolific Scholarship in Speech Communication, 1915–1985: Toward a Yardstick for Measuring Research Productivity." *Communication Education* 38 (1989): 230–36.

Hikins, James W., and Kenneth S. Zagacki. "Rhetoric, Philosophy, and Objectivism: An Attenuation of the Claims of the Rhetoric of Inquiry." *Quarterly Journal of Speech* 74 (1988): 201–28.

Hill, Forbes. "Reply to Professor Campbell." *Quarterly Journal of Speech* 58 (1972): 454–60.

———. "A Turn Against Ideology: Reply to Professor Wander." *Central States Speech Journal* 34 (1983): 121–26.

Hochmuth, Marie, ed. *A History and Criticism of American Public Address.* Vol. 3. New York: Russell & Russell, 1955.

Holton, Gerald. "Toward a Theory of Scientific Progress." Almond, Chodorow, and Pearce, eds. 202–25.

Iltis, Robert S., and Stephen H. Browne. "Tradition and Resurgence in Public Address Studies." Phillips and Wood, eds. 81–93.

Jacoby, Russell. *The Last Intellectuals: American Culture in the Age of Academe.* New York: Basic Books, 1987.

Johannesen, Richard L., ed. *Contemporary Theories of Rhetoric: Selected Readings.* New York: Harper & Row, 1971.

Johnstone, Henry W., Jr. *The Problem of the Self.* University Park: Pennsylvania State University Press, 1970.

Kerlinger, Fred N. *Foundations of Behavioral Research.* New York: Holt, Rinehart, and Winston, 1946.

Klumpp, James F., and Thomas A. Hollihan. "Rhetorical Criticism as Moral Action." *Quarterly Journal of Speech* 75 (1989): 84–97.

Klyn, Mark S. "Toward a Pluralistic Rhetorical Criticism." *Essays on Rhetorical Criticism.* Ed. Thomas R. Nilsen. New York: Random House, 1968. 146–57.

Krupnick, Mark. "The Two Worlds of Cultural Criticism." Graff and Gibbons, eds. 159–69.

Kuhn, Thomas S. *The Structure of Scientific Revolutions.* 2d ed. University of Chicago Press, 1970.

LeFevre, Karen Burke. *Invention as a Social Act.* Carbondale: Southern Illinois University Press, 1987.

Leff, Michael C. "Interpretation and the Art of the Rhetorical Critic." *Western Journal of Speech Communication* 44 (1980): 337–49.

———. "Textual Criticism: The Legacy of G. P. Mohrmann." *Quarterly Journal of Speech* 72 (1986): 377–89.

———. "Things Made By Words: Reflections on Textual Criticism." *Quarterly Journal of Speech* 78 (1992): 223–31.

Levine, Arthur. *Handbook on Undergraduate Curriculum.* San Francisco: Jossey-Bass, 1978.

Lucas, Stephen E. "The Renaissance of American Public Address: Text and Context in Rhetorical Criticism." *Quarterly Journal of Speech* 74 (1988): 241–60.

McGee, Michael Calvin. "Another Philippic: Notes on the Ideological Turn in Criticism." *Central States Speech Journal* 35 (1984): 43–50.

———. " 'Social Movement': Phenomenon or Meaning?" *Central States Speech Journal* 31 (1980): 233–44.

———. "Text, Context, and the Fragmentation of Contemporary Culture." *Western Journal of Speech Communication* 54 (1990): 274–89.

McGee, Michael Calvin, and John R. Lyne. "What Are Nice Folks Like You Doing in a Place Like This? Some Entailments of Treating Knowledge Claims Rhetorically." Nelson, Megill, and McCloskey, eds. 381–406.

McGuckin, Henry E., Jr. "The Experimentalist as Critic." *Western Speech* 32 (1968): 167–72.

McKerrow, Raymie E. "Critical Rhetoric: Theory and Praxis." *Communication Monographs* 56 (1989): 91–111.

Medhurst, Martin J. "The First Amendment vs. Human Rights: A Case Study in Community Sentiment and Argument from Definition." *Western Journal of Speech Communication* 46 (1982): 1–19.

Megill, Allan. "Heidegger, Wander, and Ideology." *Central States Speech Journal* 34 (1983): 114–19.

Miller, Gerald R. "Humanistic and Scientific Approaches to Speech Communication Inquiry: Rivalry, Redundancy, or Rapprochement." *Western Speech Communication* 39 (1975): 230–39.

Mitchell, W. J. T., ed. *The Politics of Interpretation.* Chicago: University of Chicago Press, 1983.

Mohrmann, G. P. "Elegy in a Critical Grave-Yard." *Western Journal of Speech Communication* 44 (1980): 265–74.

Nelson, John S., Allan Megill, and Donald N. McCloskey, eds. *The Rhetoric of the Human Sciences: Language and Argument in Scholarship and Public Affairs.* Madison: University of Wisconsin Press, 1987.

Newcomb, Horace M. "American Television Criticism, 1970–1985." *Critical Studies in Mass Communication* 3 (1986): 217–28.

Nilsen, Thomas R. *Essays on Rhetorical Criticism.* New York: Random House, 1968.

Nothstine, William L. " 'Topics' as Ontological Metaphor in Contemporary Rhetorical Theory and Criticism." *Quarterly Journal of Speech* 74 (1988): 151–63.

Nothstine, William L., and Gary A. Copeland. "Against the Bureaucratization of Criticism." *Pennsylvania Speech Communication Annual* 45 (1989): 19–28.

Novick, Peter. *That Noble Dream: The "Objectivity Question" and the American Historical Profession.* Cambridge: Cambridge University Press, 1988.

Ono, Kent A., and John M. Sloop. "Commitment to *Telos*—A Sustained Critical Rhetoric." *Communication Monographs* 59 (1992): 48–60.

Pacanowsky, Michael E. "Slouching Towards Chicago." *Quarterly Journal of Speech* 74 (1988): 453–67.

Pearce, W. Barnett. "Scientific Research Methods in Communication Studies and Their Implications for Theory and Research." Benson, ed. *Speech Communication* 255–81.

Phillips, Gerald M., and Julia T. Wood, eds. *Speech Communication: Essays to Commemorate the 75th Anniversary of the Speech Communication Association.* Carbondale: Southern Illinois University Press, 1990.

Pirsig, Robert M. *Zen and the Art of Motorcycle Maintenance: An Inquiry into Values.* New York: Bantam New Age Edition, 1981.

Reeves, Byron, and Christine L. Borgman, "A Bibliometric Evaluation of Core Journals in Communication Research." *Human Communication Research* 10 (1983): 119–36.

Robbins, Bruce. "Introduction: The Grounding of Intellectuals." *Intellectuals: Aesthetics, Politics, Academics.* Ed. Bruce Robbins. Minneapolis: University of Minnesota Press, 1990. ix–xxvii.

Rogers, Everett M., and Steven H. Chaffee, "Communication as an Academic Discipline: A Dialogue." *Journal of Communication* 33 (1983): 18–30.

Rosenfield, Lawrence W. "The Anatomy of Critical Discourse." *Speech Monographs* 25 (1968): 50–69. Rpt. in Brock, Scott, and Chesebro, eds. 96–116.

————. "The Experience of Criticism." *Quarterly Journal of Speech* 60 (1974): 489–96.

————. "Ideological Miasma." *Central States Speech Journal* 34 (1983): 119–21.

Rudolph, Frederick. *Curriculum: A History of the American Undergraduate Course of Study Since 1636.* San Francisco: Jossey-Bass, 1977.

Rybacki, Karyn, and Donald Rybacki. *Communication Criticism: Approaches and Genres.* Belmont, CA: Wadsworth, 1991.

Said, Edward W. "Opponents, Audiences, Constituencies, and Communities." Mitchell, ed. 7–32.

Scott, Robert L., and Wayne Brockriede. *Moments in the Rhetoric of the Cold War.* New York: Harper & Row, 1970.

Sillars, Malcolm O. *Messages, Meanings, and Culture: Approaches to Communication Criticism.* New York: HarperCollins, 1991.

Simons, Herbert W., ed. *Rhetoric in the Human Sciences.* Newbury Park, CA: Sage, 1989.

————. ed. *The Rhetorical Turn: Invention and Persuasion in the Conduct of Inquiry.* Chicago: University of Chicago Press, 1990.

Slack, Jennifer Daryl, and Martin Allor. "The Political and Epistemological Constituents of Critical Communication Research." *Journal of Communication* 33 (1983): 208–18.

Sloan, Thomas O., Richard B. Gregg, Thomas R. Nilsen, Irving J. Rein, Herbert W. Simons, Herman G. Stelzner, and Donald W. Zacharias. "Report of the Committee on the Advancement and Refinement of Rhetorical Criticism." Bitzer and Black, eds. 220–27.

Smith, Page. *Killing the Spirit: Higher Education in America.* New York: Penguin, 1990.

Sorrell, Tom. *Scientism: Philosophy and the Infatuation with Science.* London: Routledge, 1991.

Swanson, David L. "A Reflective View of the Epistemology of Critical Inquiry." *Communication Monographs* 44 (1977): 207–19.

Thompson, Wayne N. "A Conservative View of a Progressive Rhetoric." *Quarterly Journal of Speech* 49 (1963): 1–7. Rpt. in Johannesen, ed. 9–17.

Thonssen, Lester, and A. Craig Baird. *Speech Criticism: The Development of Standards for Rhetorical Appraisal.* New York: Ronald Press, 1948.

Toulmin, Stephen. "The Construal of Reality: Criticism in Modern and Postmodern Science." Mitchell, ed. 99–117.

Vande Berg, Leah R. and Lawrence A. Wenner, *Television Criticism.* New York: Longman, 1991.

Wallace, Karl R. "The Fundamentals of Rhetoric." Bitzer and Black, eds. 3–20.

Wander, Philip. "The Ideological Turn in Modern Criticism." *Central States Speech Journal* 34 (1983): 1–18.

———. "The Third Persona: An Ideological Turn in Rhetorical Theory." *Central States Speech Journal* 35 (1984): 197–216.

Wander, Philip, and Steven Jenkins. "Rhetoric, Society, and the Critical Response." *Quarterly Journal of Speech* 58 (1972): 441–50.

Weber, Samuel. *Institution and Interpretation.* Minneapolis: University of Minnesota Press, 1987.

White, Hayden. "The Politics of Historical Interpretation: Discipline and De-Sublimation." Mitchell, ed. 119–43.

Wichelns, Herbert A. *A History of the Speech Association of the Eastern States* (Speech Association of the Eastern States, 1959).

Wilshire, Bruce. *The Moral Collapse of the University: Professionalism, Purity, and Alienation.* Albany: State University of New York Press, 1990.

Winans, J. A. "The Need for Research." *Quarterly Journal of Public Speaking* 1 (1915): 17–23.

———. "Should We Worry?" *Quarterly Journal of Public Speaking* 1 (1915): 197–201.

Zarefsky, David. "A Skeptical View of Movement Studies." *Central States Speech Journal* 31 (1980): 245–54.

———. "The State of the Art in Public Address Scholarship." *Texts in Context: Critical Dialogues on Significant Episodes in American Political Rhetoric.* Ed. Michael C. Leff and Fred J. Kauffeld. Davis, CA: Hermagoras Press, 1989. 13–27.

# CHAPTER 3

# WANDERING WITH RHETORICAL CRITICISM

Roderick P. Hart

*In this essay, Roderick P. Hart describes assumptions that have guided his work as a critic for the past two decades. Hart locates his interest in rhetoric, understood as "how people use language to narrow the policy options of others," and traces three sets of assumptions that characterize his criticism: political (liberal/capitalist), epistemological (investigating "the American audience through texts prepared for their consumption"), and procedural (from "fishing expeditions" to perfecting the "incomplete arguments" of scholars in other fields).*

Nobody knows where ideas come from. Certainly nobody I know, at least. To suggest the contrary is folly of the highest order. I most certainly do not know where my ideas come from. I am just grateful that they come along often enough to keep my family fed. (At the moment, I would not mind if a Really Big Idea arrived in time for me to pay a certain young woman's tuition bill.) And so I am uncomfortable even speculating about the source of critical invention. I fear that to think too much about invention will cause it to suddenly drift off on the winds, never again to waft in my direction. Like some obedient native of a pre-technological culture, I fear that raising my eyes to scrutinize the godhead of ideas will result in my being blinded for my hubris. What to do?

I have chosen to press on here, not because I know where ideas come from but because the questions the editors of this text pose are intriguing: What sorts of people do rhetorical criticism? Why do they do it? What do they do when doing it? Because all criticism is autobiographical, as George Bernard Shaw has said, I have no choice but to respond personally when trying to answer such hard questions. This, too, is a kind of hubris, but perhaps one less deserving of permanent sensory deprivation. To lose one's eyes for poetry is conceivable; for God or love, perhaps even noble. To lose one's eyes for rhetoric is daft.

Rhetoric can, however, steal one's heart. It has mine. Studying how people use language to narrow the policy options of others[1] became my occupation twenty years ago and it has preoccupied me ever since. Criticism is not something I do; it is something I am. I am a critic because I often do not like the language my contemporaries speak nor the policy options they endorse. I am a critic because I feel that rhetoric should move a society forward rather than backward, that it should open and not close the public sphere, that it should make people generous and not craven. I am a critic, ultimately, because I am a citizen.

In this essay, I shall attempt to point up three different sets of assumptions that have guided my work as a critic. As a collection of assumptions, they may not make much sense. They are the sorts of rag-tag beliefs that a person picks up without noticing, beliefs that lie safely out of range until that person is forced to confront them as I have been asked to do here. These assumptions spring from my personal upbringing, from the thinkers who influenced me along the way, and from a bevy of personality quirks that I do not fully understand but which I cannot reasonably deny. Sensible or not, these assumptions have made my criticisms. Sensible or not, they have made me as well.

## ▧ Political Assumptions

For me, all critical work is political work. The critical essay is part of an intertextual world of statement-and-response and the critic is part of a political cadre: advancing this agenda or that agenda, criticizing this use of power or that use of power, offering a new take on the world or reminding us of an older one. Over time, the critic's brow becomes almost permanently furrowed as he or she scrutinizes what people say and how they say it. And yet the best critics refuse to descend into cynicism, that hell-hole reserved for skeptics without imaginations. Instead, the best critics remember that rhetoric—the language of policy—is infinitely self-corrective and self-generative, an art of the possible. To reword the world is to remake the world, at least in part. People respond to words and to things-like-words—symbols—because they have no choice. They can, however, choose from *among* the symbols they see and hear. The critic's job is to help them do the choosing.

To be a political worker is not necessarily to be a partisan worker. Alas, not everyone agrees with this statement. Some would argue that the critic is either part of the patriarchy or opposed to it, collusive with the forces of hegemony or committed to undermining them. Such thinkers feel that a culture's rhetoric can trap a critic even before the critic traps a text. They urge a kind of radical self-awareness in criticism, a constant examination of the critic's own social, economic, and epistemological assumptions. Conducting political inventories of this sort is said to keep the forces of repression from being unwittingly reproduced in the critic's oeuvre. Guided by such inventories, words like "struggle," "marginality," "commodification," and "resistance" interpenetrate much of the work produced by contemporary critics.

And then there is postmodernism. The postmodern critic is a wag who comments breezily on the surfaces that pass for realities in modern social life. For the postmodernist, "meaning" is a problematic animal, one not worth stalking since meaning is so often deferred in day-to-day life. As a result, postmodernists explain how a text "embarrasses" itself with its inconsistent premises and linguistic absurdities. Such critics do not actually deconstruct texts as much as they oversee the inevitable self-deconstructions that texts produce. Postmodern politics, if there is such a thing, embraces radical individuality and multiperspectivism and fiercely interrogates a society's overarching myths and narratives.

I have always admired the clarity of purpose and sense of mission found in Marxian, feminist, and postmodern researches. My own criticism, alas, has been far more muddled. In part this is because of my own politics: liberal/capitalist. Because I subscribe to that agenda, I have also subscribed to much of the modernist project—that economic achievement is theoretically possible for all; that excellence, not tradition, should be society's sole measuring rod for advancement; that enduring institutions can be beneficent; that technologies, wisely used, make people's lives better.

Because modernism so powerfully determines what happens in the United States, I have studied statist discourse almost exclusively during my career. In a series of books and essays I have explored the rhetoric of the American presidency simply because executive politics matters so much in the real world. But I have also felt, perhaps because of my coming-of-age in the tumultuous sixties, that institutional politicians do not always tend the modernist hearth as I would have them tend it. This assumption has compelled me to look over the presidents' shoulders when they talk.

One of the assumptions I have made as a citizen-critic is that the most important discourses in U.S. society are deliberative in nature. If a given text is not policy-impinging, I do not study it. For many, this is an overly constraining assumption since it rules out so much cultural politics: images of women in second-grade textbooks; emancipatory themes in MTV videos; protectionist themes in commercial advertising; the xenophobic rhetoric of the cable televangelist; the crypto-Freudian overtones of modern cinema. Surely these everyday messages also affect people's political visions. Surely they open up a world of subtle insinuations that are persuasive precisely because people feel so superior to them. Surely the prosaic, but portentous, rhetoric of *Donahue* does more to mold the American mindset each day than the president of the United States does each year.

So it seems to the critic of popular culture. I do not wish to gainsay these assumptions entirely since I have learned much from cultural critics. But I make a different set of assumptions: (1) that deliberative, not cultural, discourse most powerfully affects the policy options available to the average citizen; (2) that discourse about the disbursement of public monies, and about the statutory regulation of private monies, ultimately constrains all other discourse in a modernist society; (3) that it takes a certain kind of expertise to track policy-impinging rhetoric.

Subsumed beneath these assumptions are still more assumptions: that people's cultural perceptions are constraining but that law constrains them even more tightly; that it is good to have symbolic capital (for example, Madonna) but that it is better to have capitalist capital (for example, Ross Perot); that the off-site rhetoric of *Murphy Brown* empowers women but that the on-site rhetoric of the Thomas-Hill Senate hearings empowers men even better; that African-American rap lyrics help that community deal with its frustrations, but that a new urban policy in the United States would do so far more expeditiously; that having a rainbow coalition of newscasters at 6:00 P.M. is good but that being an actor in the news is better; that the rhetoric of campus multiculturalism is stimulating but that the rhetoric of congressional redistricting is determinative.

All of this is to say that the move in the 1970s and 1980s to expand rhetorical criticism into the cultural domain carried with it a hidden danger: that the economic and regulatory clout of deliberative politics would become occluded in the academic community. With that as my worry, what do I do as a critic? Answer: I find a policy-relevant reason to launch any rhetorical investigation. Thus, the rhetoric of *Larry King Live* became important to me when it served to launch a presidential campaign in 1992. *Murphy Brown* became relevant when the star's purported offspring bedeviled the reigning vice president as well as the anti-abortion lobbies in Washington. MTV became important when it was used more advantageously by a progressive political candidate than by a conservative.

In other words, my political assumptions make me distinguish between the *policy sphere* and the *public sphere*. The latter is more encompassing than the former and therefore has a certain natural attraction to critics, especially since the pyrotechnics of popular culture are included within it. But the former is where law is made and law, it seems clear, determines *precisely and irrevocably* what people can and cannot do in their everyday lives.

My choice as a critic, therefore, has been to remember this sobering dictum when choosing which texts to study. Happily, I have not found this to be a noxious constraint since it has kept my eye trained on the modernist substratum—materialist advancement. Like other critics, I am often fascinated by the policy-distant rhetorics of popular culture but I generally steel myself against them. I do so because they distract me from the nation's bottom line—who gets what. They distract me, also, from the groups in society who have profited most from that bottom line. Historically, my Irish Catholic ancestors in Massachusetts were not among the profiteers. The scars of those denials still reside within me and they affect what I do as a critic.

## Epistemological Assumptions

What one studies inevitably affects how one studies it. Because politics is a functional art, I study quotidian texts. Because politics is a situated art, I specialize in Americanist texts. Because politics is a populist art, I typically avoid the ersatz text. Unlike many of the critics who preceded me in the field, that is, I have been comparatively uninterested in the signal oration. Politics is an art of central tendency, I have reasoned, not an art of dispersion from the mean. Democratic politics lives or dies by its ability to corral 51 percent of the vote. And so the most common text—the 51-percent text— has always had special appeal for me.

Thus, while I, like all rhetorical critics, appreciate Marie Hochmuth Nichols's magisterial analysis of Lincoln's first inaugural,[2] I have never mounted such an Olympian platform myself. Instead, I became intrigued by Ronald Reagan's first inaugural precisely because it was so undistinguished—a hodgepodge of rhetorical forms and functions that captured the hodgepodge of the Reagan presidency itself: angry rhetoric cum expedient politics.[3] Similarly, I was one of the few critics interested in Jimmy Carter's much reviled "Malaise speech" of 1979.[4] The electorate's critical reactions to Carter's address, I have argued, exposed their disapproval of theoretical politics and exposed, also, certain faultlines between Eastern and Western values. Examining an allegedly banal text like Carter's can sometimes produce uncommon insight. Or so I have felt.

Any text—exalted or ordinary—tells only what the critic asks it to tell. That is, although I have spent a great deal of time studying American presidents, I have never been terribly interested in the forty-odd chief executives themselves. Their personality tics are intriguing, to be sure, but psychobiography seems at best an arcane science. A far more productive operation is to read the American audience through the texts prepared for their consumption.

That is, the presidential tableaux can legitimately be viewed as a record of the nation's wishes and dreams and nothing more. Because presidents virtually never stray from their political leashes, it is curious that the chief executive is so often accused of "being political." Translated, that means that the president has responded with supreme delicacy to the pressure groups he has been asked to superintend. His too-careful rhetoric betrays that delicacy and it betrays, also, the public's impatience with the serial compromises required in a complex polity. In short, the real news trapped in the presidential text may well be sociological, not psychological. If read insightfully, that text can tell us who we are and who we wish to be. The president himself, in such a scheme, becomes little more than a spectacular afterthought.

When doing criticism, then, I have always tried to "read large" rather than "read small." No doubt, I have read too large for some tastes. But a given piece of rhetoric has only intrigued me if it seems to have a broader story to tell. And so I simultaneously studied the rhetoric of the American Communist Party and the John Birch Society because they had so much in common rhetorically (doctrinal constraints, for example) even though they are political antipodes.[5] In addition, I have patiently tracked the linguistic choices made by Richard Nixon, not because he alone warranted such patience but because his collected discourse revealed a fissure in American politics between absolutism and compromise.[6] In another study, I examined the pragmatic and sentimentalist motifs displayed in sharply different forms of American ritual and discovered that a nation imbeds both its conclusions and its indeterminacies in its most sacred texts.[7]

Because I see rhetorical criticism as cultural work, I have consistently oversampled rhetoric, basing most of my scholarly arguments on patterns discerned *across* texts and across a *large number* of texts at that. Such a procedure is not unique to me. Indeed, it is a hallmark of the social-scientific method. But it is a rather rare procedure for a critic to use and, in some people's eyes, it is reason enough to drum me out of the corps. Traditional critics feel that such procedures violate the integrity of the historical moment. "A discourse exists in a special time and place and then is gone forever," they claim. "The critic must show full allegiance to the phenomenology of that moment," they argue further, "and abandon forthwith any feckless grab for universal truth."

Maybe. But is it not also the case that people—audiences—live in many moments of time and that, through human memory, they are able to live again in the past (emotionally) even though the past is no longer present (literally)? In other words, is it not plausible that rhetorical effects *aggregate* within us over time and that the wise critic accounts for their cumulative influence?[8] By examining forty years worth of *Time* magazine's political coverage, for example, I and my colleagues were able to show how the institutional superstructure of the presidency—the collective unconscious, if you will—impinges upon whoever happens to be sitting in the Oval Office.[9] Similarly, by documenting the verbal and nonverbal features of television news across three presidencies in another study, we detailed how executive politics is *remade* for the American people each night and how sharply different priorities within the first and fourth estates are continually reinscribed by the nation's media.[10]

Perhaps my greatest heresy as a critic can also be laid at the social scientist's door. I have counted things. Many things. For example, I have noted the frequency with which speakers use certain kinds of words. Again using the logic of additivity, I have speculated about how unconscious rhetorical habits might affect public opinion. So, for example, I found that sitting presidents use much more optimistic and cautious language than do political campaigners.[11] This suggests two principles: (1) a president must be happy even when the electorate is angry, and (2) it is easy to pontificate when the buck stops on someone else's desk. The regularity of such patterns across very different presidencies was surprising, suggesting that institutional constraints are much more powerful than previously thought. The subtlety of these patterns is also noteworthy, suggesting that rhetoric may affect us in a variety of unconscious ways. Numbers did not reveal these things. Critical interpretation did.

The importance of a critic's epistemological assumptions was driven home for me by a team-teaching experience I had several years ago in a graduate seminar on "Persuasion and the Presidency." My colleague and I often set ourselves the task of separately analyzing the same presidential message and then presenting our results in class. Although my team-teacher and I shared much in common, we almost never agreed on what was most important about the sample text. She emphasized speaker and I audience; she featured argument and I language; she the visual and I the verbal; she the administrative and I the cultural. Because our thoughts began in such different places, we almost always arrived at different destinations. Happily, for the most part.

Such is the nature of criticism. And such is the nature of rhetorical experience. *How* we come to know greatly affects *what* we come to learn. Because rhetoric is such a vast repository of truths and visions, it takes many hands to understand it. When analyzing discourse, not everyone should feature the political over the aesthetic, the normative over the idiosyncratic, or the quantitative over the qualitative as have I. But all critics, it seems clear, should know where they started and why they started there.

## ▪ Procedural Assumptions

The doing of criticism is an individual thing. No two critics represented in this volume are exactly alike and none of them operates in the same way. Moreover, a given critic may be interested in one sort of text on Monday and a different sort on Wednesday. Likewise, critics change their modes of operation from project to project since sterility means the death of criticism. The best critic chooses the right way to examine the right text. What could be simpler?

Criticism is hardly ever this simple. Each project I have taken on over the years has surprised me (usually by taking longer than anticipated). The experienced critic becomes experienced only because he or she has traveled down so many blind textual alleys and been proved wrong on so many occasions. The critic has a hunch. He or she checks it out. The hunch proves wrong. The critic becomes intrigued by something else.

When retracing my own steps as a critic, I seem to have stumbled down four different paths. Each has proved fruitful, but only hindsight has shown me that. When I was actually doing the criticism I wandered around a great deal. My wanderings began in these places:

1. *The Fishing Expedition.* Confession is said to be good for the soul. Here is my confession: I began a book-length project without knowing exactly why. Here is what I did know: (a) that it was possible to find each of the 10,000 texts spoke by American presidents between 1945 and 1985; (b) that no critic had ever bothered to record the date, place, occasion, genre, etc. of these remarks; (c) that a computer database could be built that would let me discover the rhetorical patterns of the modern presidency; (d) I had tenure, so time was on my side.

Five years later I wrote a book, *The Sound of Leadership.*[12] When one looks at that book now, it seems as if I knew what I was doing from the beginning. Clearly a lie. I did, of course, have my hunches. I knew that a voracious mass media industry had developed in the United States and that it was pressuring the chief executive. Both, it was clear, were now locked in a battle for opinion leadership in the country. I reasoned that while presidents were being victimized by the whims of fate, by a recalcitrant Congress, and by a pesky press, presidents had the scheduling of rhetoric on their side. My book details how the presidents used that advantage and how they changed the face of American politics as a result. The book also shows that patience is the critic's greatest ally.

2. *The Curious Text.* Many critical projects begin because the critic is baffled. I, for example, became baffled when collecting the rhetoric of American atheists.[13] Atheists, I was to learn, have always been part of the American landscape even though 95 percent of the American people profess belief in God. Atheists in the United States must be a hardy lot, I imagined, but until I read what they wrote I had no inkling of how hardy they really were.

To put the matter simply, atheists use discourse like a blunt instrument. Everything I had been taught about rhetoric—that it ingratiates itself with its audience, that it adapts to audience members' needs so as not to offend them—proved untrue of the atheists. They excoriated the Church, which was to be expected, but they also excoriated teachers, scientists, legislators, novelists, painters, patriotic organizations, and others. Theirs was a scorched-earth policy. To understand why, I had to learn that rhetoric is both a social and an auto-reflexive activity and that expression often feels better than communication. I would not have appreciated these principles unless I had first noticed how silly the atheists seemed.

3. *The Bold Assertion.* A particularly good reason to do criticism is to find out if some elegant conceptual vessel really holds water. This sort of "empirical" instinct motivates the work of many critics as they treat popular texts as "proof" of some hypothesized trend or phenomenon. As I have argued elsewhere, the extra dividend of this approach is that it enriches a given body of theory even as it opens doors for yet more inquiry.[14] When the work of the wide-ranging theorist is joined with that of the careful critic, everyone profits.

One of the most compelling books ever written on American politics is James David Barber's *The Presidential Character.*[15] In that book, Barber examined the lives of modern American presidents and constructed a compelling model of presidential character. He then proceeded to categorize each chief executive on the basis of their active or passive natures and their negative or positive predispositions. Barber's work intrigued me, but I felt that he had not been systematic or comprehensive enough, nor as precise as he needed to be. Seven-hundred textual analyses later, I published *Verbal Style and the Presidency*[16] which in part operationalized Barber's notions and in part dealt with other matters. As in so many studies of this sort, I found much in the presidents' discourse that intrigued me far more than Barber's notions, but I would not have strayed into this particular thicket if Professor Barber had not blazed the trail some years earlier.

4. *The Incomplete Argument.* I remember the exact moment when one of my critical projects began. It was after reading Robert Bellah's groundbreaking essay "Civil Religion in America."[17] In that essay, Bellah argues that the American people, because of their enormous diversity, have had a special need to work out their church-state relations amicably. He traces the religious antagonisms that had flourished in the Old World and then shows how the American establishment found ways of building a "civil religion" that would bind them together as a people and provide a usable social structure for their new nation.

In 1968 Robert Bellah was an esteemed sociologist and I was a lowly graduate student. But even in that profound state of humility I knew there was more to Bellah's tale than he had told and that it was a quintessentially rhetorical tale as well. It took me nine years to get around to telling it, but I eventually did so in *The Political Pulpit.*[18] There, I argued that Bellah's civil religion was a *rhetorical* phenomenon, not an historical or sociological phenomenon, and that that was its genius. I argued further that church and state in America have decided to talk in certain ways about one another, that there are clear and definitive rules about how that conversation should go, that there are penalties associated with any significant deviation from those rules, and, most important, that these accommodations provide the sense of community a mottled nation like the United States needs in order to survive. Even today, I like to think that only a rhetorical critic could have extended Bellah's story in precisely the way it needed to be extended.

## ◼ Conclusion

Compared to most of the authors in this volume, my take on criticism is probably the most linear. I normally begin an assignment because I am vaguely troubled by some unanswered theoretical question or because a given body of texts stubbornly resists conventional modes of interpretation. My world is probably more orderly than it needs to be but I have tried to turn that weakness into a strength by reading the work of less orderly critics. Within their imaginative flights and noisy expostulations, I have often found food for thought as well as a researchable hypothesis or two. Often, my reductions of their work probably get me into a special kind of trouble. But all critics get into trouble. Getting out of trouble is what inspires their work. Mine included.

The clearest way of staying out of trouble, of course, is to read wisely and well. Therein lies the importance of a critical community. When many persons toil in the same vineyard, good wine gets made. The wanderings I have described above are unique to me and surely constitute no iron law of critical inquiry. It is not necessary for all rhetorical critics to study the policy sphere as intently as I have studied it. There are other spheres of human activity and they have their uses. My own opinion, to be sure, is that all roads lead to Rome and, more particularly, to the Roman *polis.* That is why I have positioned myself on the *Via Maximus* and why I refuse to be distracted from how laws are made, who makes them, and for whom they are made. Unquestionably, there are other kinds of critical projects to be done. And there are other kinds of critics to do them.

There are also as many ways of doing criticism as there are critics. Because of my interests and training, I choose to think of all critics as unwitting mathematicians, as persons who study a particular population of items and who learn the most when an element within that population behaves oddly. In such a scheme, the perceptive critic becomes one who (1) notices a rhetorical pattern that nobody had noticed previously, or (2) who finds a textual variation, a break in pattern, that surprises. It is at these two moments—at moments of odd continuity or sudden deviation—that the two most powerful critical questions emerge: Why this? Why now?

Rhetoric exists because people differ from one another and because rhetoric can be used to bridge the chasms between them. Not all rhetoric builds bridges, of course. Some of it creates chasms. The critic's job is to distinguish the bridges from the chasms, but that is not always easy. Did the rhetoric of the Equal Rights Amendment help or hurt the women's movement among blue-collar workers? Did Ronald Reagan's saber-rattling promote or end the Cold War? Did the Catholic church's pronouncements create the pro-life movement, the pro-choice movement, or both? None of these questions is easy to answer. Only the critic is trained by temperament and education to call a bridge a bridge and a chasm a chasm. No society can call itself humane, however, unless someone performs that function. That is what gives the critic a reason to be.

## ▨ Notes

¹This is an abbreviated form of my definition of rhetoric. For an expansion of this definition see R. P. Hart, *Modern Rhetorical Criticism* (New York: Harper, 1990), 4.

²M. H. Nichols, "Lincoln's First Inaugural," in R. Scott and B. Brock (eds.), *Methods of Rhetorical Criticism: A Twentieth Century Perspective* (New York: Harper, 1972), 60–101.

³See R. P. Hart, "Of Genre, Computers, and the Reagan Inaugural," in H. Simons and A. Aghazarian (eds.), *Form, Genre, and the Study of Political Discourse* (Columbia: University of South Carolina Press, 1986), 278–98.

⁴R. P. Hart, "Culture, Rhetoric, and the Tragedy of Jimmy Carter," in J. Andrews and J. Lucaites (eds.), *Rhetorical Practices: Theory and Criticism* (in press).

⁵R. P. Hart, "The Rhetoric of the True Believer," *Communication Monographs*, 38 (1971), 249–61.

⁶R. P. Hart, "Absolutism and Situation: Prolegomena to a Rhetorical Biography of Richard M. Nixon," *Communication Monographs*, 43 (1976), 204–28.

⁷R. P. Hart, "The Functions of Human Communication in the Maintenance of Public Values," in C. Arnold and J. Bowers (eds.), *Handbook of Rhetorical and Communication Theory* (Boston: Allyn and Bacon, 1984), 749–91.

⁸I have defended this notion more fully in R. P. Hart, "Systematic Analysis of Political Discourse: The Development of DICTION," in K. Sanders, et al. (eds.), *Political Communication Yearbook: 1984* (Carbondale, IL: Southern Illinois University Press, 1985), 97–134.

⁹R. P. Hart, D. Smith-Howell and J. Llewellyn, "The Mindscape of the Presidency: *Time* Magazine, 1945–1985," *Journal of Communication*, 41 (1991), 6–25.

¹⁰R. P. Hart, P. Jerome and K. McComb, "Rhetorical Features of Newscasts about the President," *Critical Studies in Mass Communication*, 1 (1984), 260–86.

¹¹See R. P. Hart, "The Language of the Modern Presidency," *Presidential Studies Quarterly*, 14 (1984), 249–64.

¹²R. P. Hart, *The Sound of Leadership: Presidential Communication in the Modern Age* (Chicago: University of Chicago Press, 1987).

¹³R. P. Hart, "An Unquiet Desperation: Rhetorical Aspects of Popular Atheism in the United States," *Quarterly Journal of Speech*, 64 (1978), 33–46.

¹⁴See, for example, R. P. Hart, "Theory-Building and Rhetorical Criticism," *Communication Studies*, 27 (1976), 70–77; and "Contemporary Scholarship in Public Address: A Research Editorial," *Western Journal of Communication*, 50 (1986), 283–95.

¹⁵J. D. Barber, *The Presidential Character: Predicting Performance in the White House* (Englewood Cliffs, NJ: Prentice-Hall, 1972).

¹⁶R. P. Hart, *Verbal Style and the Presidency: A Computer-Based Analysis* (New York: Academic Press, 1984).

¹⁷R. Bellah, "Civil Religion in America," *Daedalus* (Winter, 1967), 1–21.

¹⁸R. P. Hart, *The Political Pulpit* (W. Lafayette, IN: Purdue University Press, 1977).

# CHAPTER 4 [                                        ]

# THE INVENTION OF
# RHETORICAL CRITICISM
# IN MY WORK

**Michael M. Osborn**

> *In this essay, Michael M. Osborn reflects on his own critical scholarship as
> an entry-point into three central issues: What is the nature of rhetorical
> criticism? What stance should the critic assume? What questions should the
> critic ask? Osborn's answer characterizes an approach to criticism that is
> concerned with "the recovery of the rhetorical moment," the fullest
> appreciation of the products of the art of rhetoric. Osborn describes the
> influence of his background in literary studies as making him "more at
> home with the texture of vital images in discourse than with skeins of
> practical reasoning."*

**T**his chapter promises consideration of three central and related issues: (1)
what is the proper nature of the object of rhetorical criticism? (2) what
critical stance should the critic assume in response to this object? and (3)
what questions should the critic ask? In this essay I will reflect on these
questions, especially as they pertain to my own scholarship.

## I

The question of "proper object" for rhetorical criticism goes to the genesis
of my life as a scholar. After I had graduated with a master's degree in
literary studies, I had to choose between continuing in that field or going
into what was then called "Speech." I decided on Speech, and one of the
factors in that decision, I now realize, was the nature of the texts studied in
the two disciplines. Literary texts, at least in that time, were regarded as art
objects. They were to be contemplated as self-contained and self-sufficient

verbal masterworks, complete in themselves, standing out of time. Heming-way presented the point of view well in *Death in the Afternoon,* as he com-mented that the value of a "major art" can only be assessed after its timeli-ness has faded and "the unimportant physical rottenness of whoever made it is well buried," revealing finally its gleaming virtues.[1] Obviously this view has an honorable antiquity, reaching back to Longinus, who suggested that only the tests of time and diverse audiences could decide the excellence of artistic works. Hemingway and Longinus, it is clear, would reject *timeliness* and *intensity of appeal* for specific audiences as significant criteria for decid-ing on discursive excellence. Indeed, it is the secondary, inferior nature of intense but ephemeral appeal that requires Hemingway to consign reluc-tantly his beloved bullfighting to a minor place within the pantheon of the arts. Yet typically, it is these very criteria that loom large in the assessments of rhetorical critics.

As art objects, literary works do command attention in and of them-selves, and finely wrought, enduring novels often can be more intrinsically engaging than discourse that is primarily rhetorical, that exists to confront life around it and to play a role in the fate of change. But if the literary art object is often more intrinsically interesting, the same cannot be said for the nature and significance of the critical questions one poses in response to literary and rhetorical creations. At least it was true for me that the literary criticism practiced during my neophyte scholarly days too often seemed to trivialize the objects of its interests. What books was Byron reading while writing *Childe Harold's Pilgrimage,* and what is the evidence of their influ-ence, are questions that fascinate a fairly restricted audience at a relatively specialized level of interest. Rhetorical criticism, on the other hand, seemed to open a new field of inquiry, one that might contribute substantially to knowledge about human behavior. Of course the objects of rhetorical criti-cism were different kinds of objects—they were actually not objects but agents, engines of influence. They courted listeners, seeking not esthetic distance but strategic closeness. Whereas literary art objects had a certain density, themselves being the termini of attention, rhetorical productions were translucent. Through them one might see dimly configurations of power, prejudice, and piety, all witnessing and manipulating the courtship ritual. Rhetorical productions themselves had an enthymematic quality, in that they rested on foundations of faith and taste that were outside them-selves, presumably in the audiences they addressed. They had, to use a term happily offered just recently by Michael C. McGee, a *fragmentary* quality. To reconstruct a sense of that wholeness in which they once participated is a major task of rhetorical critics, just as paleoanthropologists often must seek to reconstruct an entire lost species from a few fragments of bone. Except that the work of the rhetorical critic is as much a matter of art as it is of science. Indeed, one of the special joys of rhetorical criticism is its essential creative function. Recently, as I labored to recapture the wholeness of that rhetorical energy-field to which Martin Luther King's last speech in Memphis made dynamic contribution, I commented on the artful nature of rhetorical criticism in this way:

> Criticism itself must participate in the final fate of the rhetorical event. Rhetorical artistry is not preserved entire in a monument of words; any surviving text must be fragmentary, dependent for its appreciation on the critical gloss. The critic becomes an archaeologist of the meaning surrounding the rhetorical moment. Therefore, rhetorical criticism is essential to the symbolic after-life of the artistry it contemplates. Such criticism freezes an evanescent moment for lasting contemplation: on the rhetorical critic's urn, forever shall they speak and listeners be moved.[2]

While the critic's own art work seems integral to the recovery of the rhetorical moment, it is also true that the critic's obligation as scholar is not diminished. The practice of rhetorical criticism must be marked by integrity as well as imagination; it must be a *faithful rendering of events*. The critic does not become the primary artist in the rhetorical production; rather the critic functions as the medium through which that production is preserved. If the critic wishes to argue, and to use rhetorical performance itself as evidence for a case, then in that moment the criticism itself transforms into a rhetorical performance that invites its own critical appreciation.

Obviously, this view will not be acceptable to those who argue that the criticism *ought to* or even *must* function as advocacy. Clearly, criticism can motivate advocacy, and can itself become evidence in the case we create, but some distinction may yet be desirable between the critical and rhetorical enterprises. Despite the subjectivity of all experience, the critic *qua critic* strives as much as possible to see rhetorical events through eyes unimpeded by political or personal interest. Objectivity may be an unreachable star, but nevertheless it can still guide the critical quest.

If I was drawn initially to rhetorical criticism by some intimation of its urgency in recapturing and preserving vital discursive events, I was also schooled initially to think of these events primarily in terms of speeches. I am still comfortable in giving much of my critical attention to speeches, perhaps because I remain fascinated by the power, sense of public ritual and ordeal, complexity of challenge, and risk this form of expression seems to entail. Moreover, I was much influenced early in my career by the following reflections from Hegel's *Reason in History:*

> Speeches are actions among men and, indeed, most effective ones. . . . Speeches from peoples to peoples or to peoples and princes are integral parts of history. Even granted, therefore, that orations like those of Pericles—that most profoundly accomplished, most genuine, and most noble of statesmen—had been elaborated by Thucydides, they were yet not foreign to Pericles' character. In these orations these men expressed the maxims of their people, of their own

personality, the consciousness of their political situation, and the principles of their moral and spiritual nature, their aims and actions.[3]

When we realize that the advancing species-consciousness that so fascinated Hegel often glimmers first in the minds of great orators and leaders, then the importance of significant speeches seems all the more underscored. Finally, I accepted the centrality of speeches as objects of critical concern for the simple reason that no other departments of academic study seemed inclined or equipped to deal with them as serious and unique forms of expression. If they were to be appreciated and preserved *as rhetorical events,* then rhetorical scholars must assume that moral as well as academic duty.

Having established the piety of my concern with significant speeches, I now confess that my first exercise as a fledgling rhetorician came as I studied Swift's passionate *Drapier Letters.* I never believed in making speeches the *exclusive* objects of rhetorical criticism; such misplaced sense of loyalty as one used to encounter in our discipline succeeded only in distorting the study of rhetoric by featuring a form at the expense of the function. That function, which is to form, reinforce, and dissolve the bonds of social consanguinity, can work through forms as disparate as blatant letters to the editor or television situation-comedies masquerading as entertainments as they subvert orientations and model proper actions. A considerable irony for me was to return recently to certain prominent novels, and to discover that literary critics had too often botched the job of reading their significance, because that significance was inscribed in the language of rhetoric.[4]

## II

These thoughts on the "proper object" of rhetorical criticism also suggest appropriate stances for the critic. By "stance" I mean how the critic positions her- or himself vis-à-vis the critical object in order to perform the task of criticism. This task is to appreciate as fully as possible the nature of some rhetorical interaction, taking into account the constraints of *in vivo* rhetorical performance. This appreciation enables the critic to realize the magnificence or meanness of rhetorical behavior, its summons to greatness or its outright exploitation of those whom it addresses. And the critic can then perform the creative and re-creative duties described in the previous section.

The critical object we have described can only be characterized as unstable and ephemeral, losing its original coloration as the moment of its production fades, assuming new colorations as it passes into new situations and performs new functions for new audiences. If the object is unstable, then the critic's work is correspondingly precarious. Always, rhetorical critics risk deceiving themselves and others. For these reasons, we ought to especially admire critical performance when it is well executed.

As I reflect upon my own critical stance with respect to objects of rhetorical criticism, I detect two opposing extremes of position. My first strategy was to assume that if specific rhetorical efforts resist responsible critical reading, then one ought to survey large numbers of such efforts to detect patterns of repetition or similarity as preserved in the fragmentary texts. This strategy is clearly akin to a scientific orientation, for it assumes the unreliability of single instances while it also privileges the importance of "constants" that emerge across a field of critical inspection. My point of entry into rhetorical scholarship was the *metaphor,* which at that time had only begun to impinge significantly upon the world of rhetorical scholarship.[5] To that point, literary critics had dominated the study of figuration, regarding it usually as a phenomenon within the art objects they contemplated. Therefore, they studied metaphorical meaning more as an intrinsic contextual phenomenon.[6] The realization that metaphor might also tap into deep communal and archetypal susceptibilities, that it might move mass audiences to action as well as invite individual esthetic response, had not yet dawned in the world of rhetorical scholarship. Sensing the fragility and instability of the rhetorical object, I sought to read widely among speech texts, especially as I sought to describe patterns of archetypal behavior. Thus I sought to describe certain prominent forms of metaphor in speeches across time, or I sought to identify patterns of metaphorical usage across the corpus of a rhetorician's work.[7] Perhaps I sensed that the enduring stability of archetypal meaning might somehow compensate for the instability of a given instance of rhetorical practice. For this reason, much of my early rhetorical scholarship might better be described as metacritical, on the border between theory and criticism, as it sought to identify reliable features in such fleeting phenomena.

At the other extreme from a stance so distant from specific instances and events is my recent effort to criticize King's "Mountaintop" speech. I assumed the risk—and to some extent the presumptuousness—of such criticism because I had been part of the scene of that speech. I thought I might be unusually qualified to transcend the fragmentary text to capture the largeness of the interactive process to which that speech contributed. Here I was performing what I had earlier called *close criticism,* "which engages specific rhetorical actions," in contrast with *perspective criticism,* "which places specific actions within some overall frame of rhetorical process."[8] I had gone on to describe the aims of close criticism as follows: "Close criticism aspires to an enlightened understanding of *challenges* confronted by rhetors in the moment, the *options* available in confronting these challenges, an assessment of the rhetor's *performance,* a description of the rhetoric as *consummated* in that moment when rhetor, audience, and message converge, and the various *consequences* of the interaction." Note that the close critic of rhetorical events should be singularly qualified by circumstance and preparation to perform justly and with circumspection. Ideally, close critics will have breathed the air of that rhetoric; their nerve ends will have resonated with its tensions. Such critics always run the danger of a kind of shallow impudence that offers facile judgments without a real understanding of the terrible, sometimes contradictory forces that can drive the behaviors of rhetors locked within some desperate moment. The urn for such criticism, which we described earlier, must be quite large, its colors rich and subtle, its brushwork informed by the wholeness of the events depicted.

I am aware as I write that these reflections on critical stance may raise serious questions about the efficacy of much that has passed for rhetorical criticism in our field. Of course, nothing better answers such ruminations than examples of excellent critical work, and fortunately there seem to be more and more of these as rhetorical scholarship continues to mature.

## III

What forces have shaped the critical questions I have asked and continue to ask? This difficult question requires a degree of self-understanding I am not certain I possess. The questions we ask spring from inventional processes that run deep in our natures. Moreover, each vital day in the production of scholarship brings countless small frustrations and illuminations that make up the inventional history of any scholarly production. Re-creating that kind of history in connection with any one of my published essays would be impossible at this point. Nevertheless, as I reflect upon the general trajectory of my work as rhetorical scholar, I can recall important factors and moments that might help explain the questions I have asked.

One such factor was the background of training and orientation I brought to my graduate work in rhetoric. In my literary studies I had concentrated on the make-believe world of fiction and drama and on the world of feeling and insight expressed in poetry. From the very beginning I would be more at home with the texture of vital images in discourse than with skeins of practical reasoning. A second factor was the environment I encountered during my training at the University of Florida. I was fortunate to find there a compatible group who were eager to examine new conceptions of rhetorical scholarship. Among them was Gerry Mohrmann, who shared my interest in the intersection of literary and rhetorical studies and became a lifelong friend. Douglas Ehninger, my first mentor, encouraged innovative scholarly work, and made me believe that I might make a contribution to knowledge. As my research program began to develop, Charles Morris, a philosopher who pioneered in the field of semiotics research, shared my excitement over my discoveries, convinced me that they had value, and took over the direction of my dissertation when Ehninger moved to Iowa. All in all, it was a heady environment for a fledgling scholar.

Much of what we were reacting against at that time was unimaginative

criticism, since critiqued very nicely by Edwin Black,[9] that imposed an obligatory formula on scholars assessing the speaking careers of individual rhetors. I found most such work deadly dull, and thought it offered little to what
Bacon had called "the advancement of learning." Moreover, I decided early
that I did not want to focus my study on a "man." Such studies seemed to
make the mistake of treating speeches as art objects rather than as translucent expression. In the world of art objects, speeches would always be
doomed to inferior status. Even worse, their discursive nature and values
would be distorted. But as *means* of study rather than *objects* of study,
speeches in their unique translucence might reveal configurations of behavior and culture not otherwise visible. So I decided that I would isolate an
interesting rhetorical phenomenon and study its manifestations across
speeches. Ehninger encouraged this inclination and suggested I might want
to consider the seemingly rich but lightly explored subject of rhetorical
symbolism. While excited by that possibility, I was at the same time bothered
by its complexity and vagueness. I sensed that it might open onto a vast field
of study, that there might in fact be many forms of powerful rhetorical
symbolism that would require serious and disciplined investigation. So my
inclination was to concentrate on one such form to see where this might lead
me. I was convinced that metaphor might be such a form, and that the
metaphor in rhetoric and the rhetoric in metaphor had been generally
neglected. So I set out on a long, personal odyssey in quest of rhetorical
metaphor.

From the very beginning I rejected the study of metaphor as a surface
textual phenomenon. The metaphor I wanted to study, I wrote in 1961 in
my first convention paper, functioned not as "ornament" but as "argument."[10] If we were to understand the thought patterns that flowed visibly
in the speech, we would have to find or reconstruct the fundamental, often
implicit metaphors that generated thought, both in speakers and in the
cultures they represented. Indeed, argumentation might be studied often as
the clash of basic metaphors. Such metaphors must be studied as inventional phenomena. The paper was controversial, and I was advised, probably
wisely, to let my thoughts ripen more before I ventured into print. I continued reading and thinking, and I do remember the evening when it
occurred to me that one might form a visual model of the process of
metaphor I. A. Richards had described.[11] Before I could even begin to sketch
the model on paper, I could see it vividly as though it were printed on the
wall of my study. It was an electric moment. I presented my discovery in a
research paper before Morris's seminar in the philosophy of language, and
his reaction was one of the great moments of my life: "Paul Henle [another
philosopher] once commented that there is nothing new to be said on the
subject of metaphor," he told the group. "I no longer believe that statement." Susie and I were living on my fellowship at the time, but we had steak
that evening!

Once the model was in place, my thinking began to develop very rapidly. Soon I had progressed from a static to a process model, because as a rhetorician I was sensitive to the role of audience in creating metaphorical meaning.[12] Indeed, I relocated metaphor as an "adventure in meaning" within the minds of listeners, and began thinking, beyond Richards, about the forces that might constrain the interaction of tenor and vehicle. This led me to form a theory of *qualifiers,* forms of influence that might shape this interaction. In my dissertation, I emphasized the following kinds of qualifiers: *contextual, situational, communal, archetypal,* and *personal.*[13] One of these forms, the archetypal, struck me as especially interesting. I had learned that rhetoric was indeed timely, powerful but ephemeral, and it was clear that the study of rhetoric belonged more to specific situations and audience interactions. It was the fate of rhetoric most often to become quickly dated. How then might one reconcile the presence within many rhetorical documents of metaphorical forms that appeared timeless, that appealed across many audiences and situations? My curiosity over this question turned my research in a decisive direction, leading to essays on metaphors of light and darkness, space, and the sea. Eventually I saw that metaphors that depend more on communal qualification, meanings that belong to a specific culture of usage, form a nice contrast with archetypes. I began to describe these figures as *culturetypes.*[14]

To this point it was clear that the direction of my research was towards a finer, increasingly narrow focus. It was while completing a writing assignment with the SRA company that this direction began to turn. The challenge seemed simple enough: I had merely to summarize and simplify the traditional principles of rhetorical style in a small book for an anticipated readership of advanced undergraduates. What I quickly rediscovered was the truth of nineteenth-century philosopher Herbert Spencer's observation: *no one had ever identified such principles within a comprehensive theory.*[15] There were a few scattered observations about the rhetorical functions of language, most of them admonitions to be simple, clear, etc., accompanied by a catalog of figures of speech. Inclusion within this catalog seemed more by tradition than by principle. What I had to do then was to pick up the challenge where Spencer had left it—I had to discover and construct these principles, and the meta-principles that in turn tied them together into a coherent theory. I must say that I *felt* this challenge more than I was able to articulate it for myself; that is, until I was finally able to solve the problem.

What I did was to study the more prominent figures of speech in various contexts until I was able to see underlying categories of functions that they performed and to which they variously belonged. Moreover, it was clear that these functions were related, in the sense that one such function would seem to be preparatory to the next in a sequential, circular pattern that one might read across an entire campaign of related discourses. The arc of the circle began with strategic depiction, as rhetors sought to influence the way that auditors perceived the subjects of discourse. Most vital metaphors, it seemed to me, did much of their work within this basic function. But this function led to another, the control of feeling, as rhetors sought to fan audience response to what they perceived. The next task was to transform these feelings into a shared sense of group membership as rhetors sought to mobilize audiences into action groups. To achieve this group identity, it would be necessary to develop a kind of folk theater that would be accepted as truth, and that would include images of heroism, villainy, martyrdom, and ideal identity. The rhetor also must cultivate a specific vocabulary of vital symbols that expressed the values of group membership. Linking with the group function was the rhetoric of action, both implementing and sustaining concerted behaviors toward desired ends. The final point on the arc was ritual behavior that celebrated and affirmed group values and accomplishments, and that reinforced vital forms of perception. Thus the linkage back to strategic depiction would be effected.

When I was able to frame, identify, and describe this interlocking structure of functions, then for the first time I was able to state the significance of metaphor within a more comprehensive theory of style. As this theory has developed in subsequent writings, the focus of my thought has continued to broaden. From stating the function of metaphor within a theory of style, I have gone to stating the theory of symbolic action within a larger theory of rhetorical process,[16] and that theory I am now contemplating within an even larger frame of social organization. Thus the trajectory of my scholarly life has tracked into specialization and out again into generalization, and as I have traced that curve the kinds of critical questions I have asked of discourse have varied accordingly.

## ■ IV

While many of the critical questions I have asked have been suggested by my own scholarly interests, I have been constantly influenced by the work of other rhetorical scholars. Recent theoretical discoveries have created a profusion of ways to assess rhetorical practice, enriching and expanding the inventional processes of rhetorical criticism. In this final section I wish to sketch a way to access these expanded options through four propositions which center on the nature and work of rhetoric itself.

1. *Rhetoric fashions an integrated system of evidence, proofs, and arguments.* This view of rhetoric's identity suggests that the critic view rhetoric more as a rational system created in quest of assent and consent. It presumes that people are often susceptible to an overall arrangement of evidence, combined into proofs, combined again into arguments, which seeks to convince listeners of the fundamental rightness and soundness of a position in con-

flict. This proposition derives from the integrated systems approach outlined in Aristotle's *Rhetoric*. In addition to considering specific forms of evidence, proofs, arguments, and the relations among them, the critic responding to this perspective may also examine patterns of arrangement that structure a single discourse or the many discourses within a rhetorical campaign. The critic may well be alert to the presence of enthymemes, formed often by the interplay of premises both developed in discourse and embedded within the culture of the audience. As joint creations, enthymemes can connect rhetor, discourse, and audience in a sense of shared meaning.

2. *Rhetoric structures experience in terms of plotlines.* The conception of human existence as an aimless, drifting iteration of births and deaths, beginnings and endings, without destination or meaning beyond its own immediate needs and satisfactions, is intolerable in public rhetoric. The tendency of such rhetoric is to cast public life in terms of a melodrama, heavily moralistic, replete with two-dimensional heroes and villains (simply observe the rhetorical displays in a typical political campaign). I first encountered this perspective on rhetoric in an intriguing observation in George Campbell's *The Philosophy of Rhetoric,* in which he described metaphor as "an allegory in miniature." Campbell's observation suggests to me that the language of public discourse is deeply embued with moral colorations, and that it is replete with potential stories, either waiting to be told in discourse or to be played out implicitly in the minds of an audience. This perspective has been popular among contemporary critics, especially as developed in the ideas of Kenneth Burke, Ernest Bormann, and Walter Fisher.

For Burke, rhetoric is a *drama* of competing identifications in which speakers strive to overcome division and separation and to draw near their listeners by sharing visions, experiences, images, values, pieties, hierarchies, emotions, dialects. The critical vocabulary that has developed around this hub of dramatistic conception invites critics to consider rhetorical performance in terms of actors, scenes, agents, agencies, and purpose—the famous Burkean "pentad."[17] Competing rhetors try in turn to drive wedges into the identification rituals, to discredit them, to distance their opponents from listeners and to replace them in such positions of esteemed closeness.

Bormann emphasizes the fantasy-play of experience.[18] Humans constantly spin out fantasies to surround themselves—their cocoons become their reality. The prevailing fantasies of public life supply exciting visions of purpose and destination and offer models of disciplined, pious living. To understand a people we must resurrect these organic fantasies and examine the extent to which actual life-conditions developed in response to their plotlines—in short, determine the extent to which reality conformed to the folk art of their fantasies.

Fisher has pursued what he calls the *narrative paradigm,* suggesting that the fundamental nature of humans is that of story-telling.[19] He insists that the rational perspective (our first propositional perspective) is at best only partial, and that it robs us of a sense of the wholeness of experience. The requirements for good story-telling in fiction—there must be engaging beginnings, exciting conflicts, and satisfying conclusions or denouements, in which the characters in the story get what they deserve—spill over into life narratives as well, Fisher insists. Even our most intellectual activities, as when we engage in debate and pursue dialectical inquiries, should be viewed as episodes within the wider context of the stories we are living.

3. *Rhetoric activates arrays of powerful symbols.* This perspective offers a view of language-in-use as a universe of communication resources in which certain powerful systems of symbols develop and move. The effectiveness of rhetoric often depends on how artfully a rhetor engages these systems. Here obviously belongs my notion of archetypal metaphor, for it postulates a system of powerful metaphors defined by their attachment to fundamental forms of experience. An examination of the most potent metaphors within fifty-six world-historical speeches suggested that this system might include metaphors of light and darkness, the sea, spatial contrasts, mountains, war, the human body, sexuality, disease and cure, and the family.

As I noted earlier, there may be also a contrasting category of powerful symbols that one might call *culturetypes.* The essence of this contrast is that culturetypes are timely and culture specific. They evolve and change along with the drift in culture. One such group of symbols was described by Richard Weaver as *ultimate terms* or *god-and-devil terms,* defined by the way they express deeper value tendencies of a culture. Writing for his own time, the decade of the 1950s, Weaver pointed to such words as "progress," "scientific," "modern," and "efficiency," in contrast with such devil-terms as "communism" and "un-American." Such words, he suggested, had an unusual power to move audiences when invoked successfully in discourse.

Another, more recent discovery within the culturetypal category of powerful symbols has been made by Michael Calvin McGee. McGee has isolated what he calls *ideographs,* certain abstract words and expressions that function as compressed ideology. They offer concentrated expressions of the underlying ideology or political beliefs of a people. Rhetors may use them as ultimate sanctions for courses of action. Thus words like "freedom," "liberty," "rugged individualism," and "We the People" may be especially rich with potential to move audiences. McGee's discovery has proved most useful when applied in rhetorical criticism. When I use the concept, I often combine it with the study of *icons,* defined as pictorial or concrete embodiments of ideographs. Such images may seem to possess a secular-sacred quality, precisely because they are so laden with political values. The Statue of Liberty and the frontiersman as an icon for individualism are good examples. My suggestion is that the *combination* of ideograph and icon may be especially potent in popular discourse, because it offers the virtues of both abstract and concrete rhetorical expression.

4. *Rhetoric is an instrument of power.* The rhetorical critic who responds to this perspective has an inherent distrust of popular discourse. The assumption may be that power itself is usually malevolent, in service to its own selfish interests, and that popular discourse simply places a pleasant mask on ugly motivations. The function of the critic is to strip away the mask of the implicit structure of interests and assumptions we have come to accept without question that in effect constrains us. The aim of such criticism is emancipation.

To illustrate the assumptions undergirding this critical perspective, we need only cite one of its more influential proponents, Michel Foucault: "Truth isn't outside power, or lacking in power . . . truth isn't the reward of free spirits, the child of protracted solitude, nor the privilege of those who have succeeded in liberating themselves. Truth is a thing of this world. . . . And it induces regular effects of power. Each society has its regime of truth, its 'general politics' of truth. . . ."[20]

One remarkable feature of this perspective is that it places the critic in a heroic, even Promethean position. The critic brings the fire of her or his superior knowledge of rhetoric and its stratagems to the unmasking of discourse, to the end that readers might be saved from possible victimage. To engage in such criticism is by necessity to assume an activist posture and to renounce the traditional role of the scholar who is a mere observer upon life. (It is these critics who would insist on the "mere"; their position is that the old scholarly robe was itself designed by power sources so that the pursuit of knowledge—always dangerous to established power—might be relegated, enfeebled, and controlled.)

Within the activist posture required by this critical perspective, the old academic values of detachment and objectivity are scorned. One such critic asks feelingly "why ignoring the murder of men, women, and children following from actions justified in public address should count as a triumph of scholarly restraint."[21] Why, indeed. One of the major contributions of the "rhetoric is power" perspective may well be the restoration of passion and personal engagement in the critical act. And that is no small gift.

As I reflect upon this plenitude of perspectives on the nature of rhetoric, and how they enrich the inventional processes of criticism, I become aware of the spiritual distance we have traversed in the thirty years since I began work in this discipline. There is a marvelous human story here, to which so many have contributed so substantially. As a collective human enterprise, scholarship is surely a noble venture.

## ▓ Notes

[1] Ernest Hemingway, *Death in the Afternoon* (New York: Scribner's, 1960) 99.

[2] "The Last Mountaintop of Martin Luther King, Jr.," *Martin Luther King, Jr., and the Sermonic Power of Public Discourse*, eds. Carolyn Calloway-Thomas and John Louis Lucaites (Tuscaloosa, AL: University of Alabama Press, in press).

[3] Georg Wilhelm Friedrich Hegel, *Reason in History: A General Introduction to the Philosophy of History*, trans. Robert W. Hartman (New York: Liberal Arts Press, 1953) 4–5.

[4] "Rhetorical Depiction," *Form, Genre, and the Study of Political Discourse*, ed. Herbert W. Simons and Aram A. Aghazarian (Columbia: University of South Carolina Press, 1986) 79–107.

[5] Kenneth Burke, that trailblazer in rhetorical and literary studies, had laid the foundations for an appreciation of the rhetorical significance of metaphor in *Permanence and Change: An Anatomy of Purpose* (New York: New Republic, 1935).

[6] We first characterized contextual, communal, and archetypal forms of meaning in Michael Osborn and Douglas Ehninger, "The Metaphor in Public Address," *Speech Monographs* 29 (1962): 223–34.

[7] Examples of longitudinal studies were "Archetypal Metaphor in Rhetoric: the Light-Dark Family," *Quarterly Journal of Speech* 53 (1967): 115–26, and "The Evolution of the Archetypal Sea in Rhetoric and Poetic," *Quarterly Journal of Speech* 63 (1977): 347–63. An example of focus upon the overall production of a speaker was "Vertical Symbolism in the Speeches of Edmund Burke," *Studies in Burke and His Time* 10 (1969): 1232–38.

[8] "A Philosophy of Criticism," remarks at the Eastern Communication Association Convention, 1988.

[9] *Rhetorical Criticism: A Study in Method* (New York: Macmillan, 1965).

[10] "The Use of the Image in Great Debate," paper presented to the Southern Speech Association Convention, April 1961.

[11] *The Philosophy of Rhetoric* (New York, 1936) 89–114.

[12] Both forms of model appear in the Osborn and Ehninger essay.

[13] "The Functions and Significance of Metaphor in Rhetorical Discourse," unpubl. Ph.D. diss., University of Florida, 1963.

[14] This term first appears in my *Orientations to Rhetorical Style* (Chicago: SRA, 1976).

[15] *Philosophy of Style: An Essay* (New York: Appleton, 1892).

[16] See my "Rhetorical Depiction" essay.

[17] See his discussions in *A Grammar of Motives* (New York: Prentice-Hall, 1945) and *A Rhetoric of Motives* (New York: Prentice-Hall, 1950).

[18] Ernest G. Bormann, *The Force of Fantasy: Restoring the American Dream* (Carbondale: Southern Illinois University Press, 1985).

[19] Walter R. Fisher, *Human Communication as Narration: Toward a Philosophy of Reason, Value, and Action* (Columbia: University of South Carolina Press, 1987).

[20] Michel Foucault, "Truth and Power," in *The Foucault Reader*, ed. Paul Rabinow (New York: Pantheon, 1984) 72–73.

[21] Philip Wander, "The Ideological Turn in Modern Criticism," *Central States Speech Journal* 34 (1983): 8.

# PART II

## CRITICAL INVENTION: MAXIMS, COMMENTARIES, AND CASES

# MAXIM 1

## *CRITICISM REQUIRES UNDERSTANDING AND PURSUING ONE'S OWN INTERESTS*

# CHAPTER 5

# FEMINIST CRITICISM AND
# *THE MARY TYLER MOORE SHOW*

**Bonnie J. Dow**

*In this commentary, Bonnie J. Dow locates the beginnings of her critical study of* The Mary Tyler Moore Show *in the recurring presence of the show in her life: as a program she watched with her family on Saturday nights as a child, as an afternoon ritual when the show was in syndication, and even as a comfortable and comforting anchor when she moved to a new city. Her enjoyment of the program eventually merged with her growing interest in feminism and discourse.*

## COMMENTARY

By 1988, when I began to write the essay that would become "Hegemony, Feminist Criticism, and *The Mary Tyler Moore Show*," I felt like I had been watching *The Mary Tyler Moore Show (TMTMS)* all my life. I almost had. It debuted on prime-time television when I was in elementary school, and watching it was a Saturday night event for my family. When it moved to syndication in the late 1970s, I watched the reruns almost daily after school. When I moved to Minneapolis in 1987, watching *TMTMS* every night comforted me during a time when I was lonely, living in a large city where I knew few people. Watching television is and always has been an immensely comfortable experience for me, one that I do not hesitate to admit that I enjoy (unlike many television critics, who hold the strange attitude that they really have no use or respect for the medium that they study—except for PBS, of course).

When I began to experiment with rhetorical criticism of fictional television in graduate school, I decided to write about *TMTMS* not only because it was an ideal artifact for exploring contemporary feminism, a prior interest of mine, but also because I knew it well enough that I was comfortable making generalizations about the entire series (which spanned seven years and almost two hundred episodes). In my experience with criticism of television series, the most useful insights apply to the series as a whole and are supported by numerous episodes. This is particularly true for an intensely generic form like situation comedy that draws persuasive power from the ability to hammer home the same message again and again.

The decision to approach *TMTMS* from a feminist perspective is a fairly obvious one, given the program's place in television history. All of the reading that I did about *TMTMS,* both in initial reviews of the show in the popular press and in more formal works on television history, commented on the program's status as the first sitcom influenced by feminism. Given the resistance to feminism in the 1970s (and since), the fact that *TMTMS* was so successful begged for a rhetorical explanation. However, few of the critical treatments of the program that I read attempted any kind of considered feminist evaluation and those that did seemed to leave out what I saw as distinctive about a *rhetorical* approach: a concern with how discourse functions for an audience. So my general question became: How was *TMTMS,* a program about a single, seemingly independent, working woman able to appeal successfully to a television audience accustomed to domestic sitcoms in which leading female characters were usually wives or mothers with little real power or independence?

As I began to watch *TMTMS* with a "critical" eye I found that my more specific inquiries about its feminist content were guided by my appreciation of the generic features of sitcoms. For example, I found myself asking: What is significant about the female characters in this show (particularly Mary Richards, of course), and what is the relationship of these characters to each other and to the male characters? How are those roles and relationships different from female roles and relationships in past sitcoms (and television in general)? Such questions reflected not just feminist concerns, but issues related to generic appeal. Given the power of genre to guide understanding, viewers are likely to understand a sitcom as much in relation to other sitcoms as in relation to their lives external to television. That is, Mary Richards's perceived atypicality would come from her difference from other female television characters more than from her difference from women in the life experience of viewers.

Moreover, the questions that began as questions about genre were also useful for investigating the feminist implications of the show. For example, a standard generic question I asked was: If all sitcoms are driven by a problem/solution narrative, then what kinds of problems occur in this show and how do they get solved? This led to: What is the role of Mary Richards, the main character, in that process? When you read the final essay, it's easy to see that these two questions, basic as they are, turned out to be the most fruitful in terms of leading me to significant patterns in *TMTMS.*

All of these questions reflect my particular bias of viewing television with an eye for comparison. For example, I've done further work on other, more recent sitcoms with feminist implications and I always find myself asking how they compare with *TMTMS*. Yet this habit has led me to understand that criticism relies on some kind of implicit or explicit comparison at every level. In the case of *TMTMS*, I specifically was concerned with generic and historical comparisons, but in most cases critics seem to ask questions that follow two general lines: "How is this discourse *like* something else (whatever that thing may be) and why is that illuminating or important?" and/or "How is this discourse *different from* something else and why is that illuminating or important?" (For more explanation of this perspective, see Adena Rosmarin, *The Power of Genre*, University of Minnesota Press, 1985.) The emphasis on comparison underscores my earlier conviction about the importance of extensive experience with the discourse—the better you know your subject matter, the more informed your comparisons will be.

To begin the process of answering the questions I had developed, I took detailed notes each time I watched an episode of *TMTMS*. I did not own a VCR at the time, so such written detail was necessary as well as helpful. Later, when I studied my collected notes on forty or fifty episodes, I found that they acted as a filter that allowed me to see patterns that I had not heretofore noticed. For instance, from repeated comments in my notes such as "Mary comforts," "Mary agrees to help," and "Mary gives advice," I began to notice the prominence of Mary Richards's problem-solving and emotional support functions across all kinds of plotlines. While I had begun this process assuming that the several episodes in the series' history that specifically addressed some kind of "feminist" issue (such as equal pay, equal opportunity, or sexual freedom) would be important to my analysis, I found that *TMTMS*'s recurring message about the role of women was as apparent in episodes that had no such feminist angle as in those that did. In fact, only one such explicitly "feminist" episode, the one in which Mary Richards hires a female sportscaster, was included in the final essay.

When I began to see these patterns across episodes, the essay began to take shape for me. The evidence that I had gathered indicated that, despite alteration in some superficial characteristics, the character of Mary Richards functioned much like female characters from past domestic sitcoms in terms of her relationships with other, specifically male, characters. Although my vital comparisons were taking shape, I had not yet found a way to discuss their importance on a more abstract level. Answering the second half of the compound question underlying criticism ("why is that illuminating or important?") gave me some trouble.

The result of this difficulty was that the version of the essay that I submitted for publication was extremely descriptive but lacked the all-important attention to "theoretical significance." The first reviews of the essay all said that I was not clear about the importance of what I was claiming. I had made an attempt to introduce the essay with a discussion of the assumptions of feminist criticism, but all of my experience with feminist criticism came from literary study and I learned, via some pointed observations from reviewers, that dealing with television was quite different from dealing with literature.

This was my first attempt at television criticism, and I was dealing with a problem of having no basis for comparison in the area of theoretical significance. My experience with the literature on women and popular culture and television and hegemony was limited, thus I was handicapped in arguing how my essay fit within this tradition. My reviewers kindly directed me to some reading, and the revised version of the essay was framed quite differently. The final version, in fact, has a paragraph devoted to the problems of transferring assumptions from feminist literary study to television.

Although it appeared at the time that the changes required were enormous, with hindsight I see that the majority of the analysis remained essentially the same as in the original version; what changed was the framing and interpretation of that analysis. In the conclusion section of the original version, I alluded to hegemony when making the claim for the limited progressiveness of *TMTMS*, but the entire mention of hegemony in that draft occupied about two sentences. The reviewers and the editor concurred that the use of hegemony should be expanded to provide an overall frame for the essay, a move that clarified the intent and the importance of the analysis enormously. *TMTMS* was, in fact, an ideal case study for making an argument about feminism and hegemony, and the reviewers directed me toward a terminology that became very useful.

Interestingly, my first revision of the manuscript, which made a strong argument for *TMTMS* as an example of hegemonic strategies working to contain feminism, opened a new area for disagreement. At least one reviewer claimed that the new version left too little room for the possibility that the show might contain *mixed* messages about feminism. I had landed myself in the middle of a current debate within media studies about how "open" texts were, how "active" audiences were, and how possible it was for viewers to "resist" the hegemonic message of a text. In the next revision, I qualified my claims a bit, arguing that *TMTMS* was interesting precisely because it had the potential to be interpreted in more than one way. However, I believed (and still do) that textual analysis of hegemonic strategies is equally as valuable as audience research, particularly for feminist critics, and I was able to add a brief section to the conclusion in which I made that argument.

In general, the essay was changed in some significant ways by the review process; though most of these changes were clearly beneficial, a few still trouble me. During most of the review process I was still a graduate student, however, and I felt that I was in no position to argue with many of the demands made by the editor and the reviewers. On the other hand, I realize now that the essay was fairly raw when I first sent it to be reviewed, so I am grateful that enough initial promise was seen in it to warrant requests for revision.

In total, I did four revisions of "Hegemony, Feminist Criticism, and *The Mary Tyler Moore Show*" in the eighteen months between when I submitted it and it appeared in print. The last of those revisions was required to shorten the piece because of space limitations in the issue for which it was intended. I regret parts of that final edit because I think it weakened the coherence of the essay and eliminated some important supporting material.

Contrary to my experience since, I struggled more with this essay *after* I submitted it for publication than I did before submitting it. That is, I did not find *TMTMS* a complex text to work with in terms of finding a focus for my analysis or discerning significant rhetorical strategies. However, the work of the revision process was a valuable learning experience through which I discovered that the negotiation that occurs between an author and her reviewers/editors is, in some cases, as important to the creative process as the critic's solitary struggle with the text.

Although they challenged my patience (and my ego) at points, the inquiries and suggestions offered by the readers of "Hegemony, Feminist Criticism, and *The Mary Tyler Moore Show*" did the project much more good than harm. I was blessed with readers who were sympathetic to the purpose and potential of the analysis and who genuinely wanted to make it better. Because of this early, positive experience, I now perceive the review process as an opportunity to augment and refine my ideas rather than as a threat to their survival. While this sanguine view requires perseverance and a willingness to compromise, its reward is often a stronger and more informed piece of criticism.

# Hegemony, Feminist Criticism, and *The Mary Tyler Moore Show*

Bonnie J. Dow

Recent scholarly essays call for greater attention to feminist issues in media studies (Dervin, 1987; Treichler & Wartella, 1986). The feminist agenda in communication is a broad one, encompassing a myriad of issues, contexts, methodological approaches, and goals. This situation reflects the fact that feminist analysis of communication is a dynamic and growing concern. This essay contributes to this dialogue through a critical study of *The Mary Tyler Moore Show*, illustrating the hegemonic processes at work in television discourse about women.

Initially, this essay offers a brief review of feminist perspectives on popular culture and discusses the place of this analysis within a feminist critique of television. Moreover, the essay details the basis for a critical approach to television that focuses on its hegemonic effects, particularly in the negotiation of oppositional ideology. The usefulness of these concepts will be illustrated through an analysis of *The Mary Tyler Moore Show (TMTMS)* as an example of television programming that was, in many ways, an early response to social changes brought about by the feminist movement of the late 1960s. *TMTMS* will be used to illustrate conclusions about the working of hegemonic devices that contradict feminist ideology on television. Finally, this analysis will be used as the basis for discussing the further implications of an awareness of hegemony for a feminist critique of television.

## FEMINIST PERSPECTIVES ON POPULAR CULTURE

"Feminist perspective" may be an ambiguous phrase to some. The recent interest in popular culture criticism with a feminist focus has produced a variety of works from differing perspectives. Some critics appear to view popular culture as a sphere that is largely opposed to valorization of the female in any form; much feminist psychoanalytic work on film contains this discouraging message (De Lauretis, 1984; Kuhn, 1982; Mulvey, 1989). Other perspectives argue for a resistant reading through which discourse of the seemingly dominant ideology can be interpreted as empowering for women (Byars, 1987) or through which we can begin to discover a "feminine aesthetics" (Modleski, 1982, p. 105). In addition, Radway (1984) has highlighted the usefulness of reader-response methods in understanding how women read romance novels and through her critique of the politics of mass culture analysis (1986). More recently, a collection of essays edited by Baehr and Dyer (1987) has extended the feminist critique of television to examine women's situations as writers, actors, producers, and audiences.

All of these perspectives contribute to the ongoing dialectic about the role of women within popular culture, as producers, products, and spectators. The present analysis is intended to add to the body of work on feminism and popular culture by illustrating the possibilities for contradiction of feminist premises through hegemonic processes. One of the projects of an ongoing feminist critique (Press, 1989) must be to examine how women are devalued in the process of cultural reproduction. The critical perspective chosen here explores the subtle manifestations of hegemony in television by focusing on narrative structure and character interaction.

While literary study is the birthplace of feminist criticism, television and literature cannot be easily transposed. For example, while feminist critics of literature can focus on literature produced by women as a way to explore a feminine poetics or to ameliorate the historical white male bias of literary studies and the literary canon, feminist critics of television always deal with the discourse of the dominant ideology. Despite recent labor gains by women, it is no stretch to acknowledge that the institutions that sponsor and produce popular television are largely controlled by men and are permeated with patriarchal ideology that is revealed in television programming. However, in the years since the resurgence of the feminist movement, the television industry has attempted to respond to the changing social climate. Thus, we now have more women in television production, as well as increased numbers of women in more powerful roles on the screen, in both news and entertainment programming (Baehr & Dyer, 1987). Despite these numerical increases, however, the hegemonic process limits possibilities for substantive change: the effects of that process are the focus of this analysis.

## ■ HEGEMONIC PROCESSES IN TELEVISION

Gitlin's (1982) work on television and hegemony provides a compelling and persuasive account of television's incorporation of social change and oppositional ideology. Drawing on Gramsci, Gitlin (p. 429) offers what he calls "a lexicon for discussing the forms of hegemony in the concrete." Generally, hegemony or hegemonic processes refer to the various means through which those who support the dominant ideology in a culture are able continually to reproduce that ideology in cultural institutions and products while gaining the tacit approval of those whom the ideology oppresses. In Gitlin's view, television furthers hegemony through incorporation of radical ideology, or what Barthes (1973, p. 150) has called "inoculation." In this process, one protects the dominant ideology from radical change by incorporating small amounts of oppositional ideology.

Thus, television adjusts to social change by "absorbing it into forms compatible with the core ideological structure" (Gitlin, 1982, p. 450). So, for instance, the demands made for increased minority and female representation result in higher visibility for these groups on television, although the situations and characters through which they are depicted may implicitly work to "contain" the more radical aspects of the changes such representation implies. Some limited changes in content result, but the general hegemonic values remain intact (Gitlin, 1982). Thus, those who champion the oppositional ideology may be satisfied that their demands are having an impact on television, while those who create the programming actually have made only cosmetic changes in representation of the disputed group.

However, the hegemonic system is not a perfect monolith; it does not produce inescapable ideology. When subversive ideology is incorporated, some of it sticks, albeit in a less stringent form. To retain its dominance, the hegemonic system must change, and these changes produce "leaks" or contradictions (Gitlin, 1982, p. 449). The point of a hegemonic perspective is not that television never changes—it clearly does—but that it is less progressive than we think. The medium adjusts to social change in a manner that simultaneously contradicts or undercuts a progressive premise.

## TMTMS, FEMINISM, AND HEGEMONY

The enormous popularity of *TMTMS* in its first run (1970–77) makes the program a particularly appropriate subject for an analysis of how television responds to social change. After a slow start, the show was consistently in the top twenty rated programs for six of the seven years it was broadcast (Brooks & Marsh, 1985). *TMTMS* was popular with critics as well as viewers. Hough (1981, p. 221) described it as "one of the most believable, lucid, and lovable portrayals of the single woman in American society of the seventies" and noted that, "while there are a thousand sitcoms in television history, 'The Mary Tyler Moore Show' will probably still be among the top ten in terms of historical and social significance."

Moreover, the point in social and television history at which the show appeared makes it noteworthy as a feminist text. Arriving as it did on the crest of the developing women's liberation movement, *TMTMS* was informed by and commented on the changing role of women in American society. One of the show's creators, James Brooks, observed that although the show did not explicitly address the issues of the women's movement, "we sought to show someone from Mary Richards' background being in a world where women's rights were being talked about and it was having an impact" (quoted in Bathrick, 1984, pp. 103–104).

Indeed, the character of Mary Richards as an independent career woman on *TMTMS* challenged a television tradition that had stereotyped women as "goodwives," "bitches," "victims," and "courtesans" (Meehan,

1983). Although the "single woman" premise had been successful in *That Girl* (1966–1971), its Ann Marie character had been watched over and protected by her father and her fiancé. Her adventures in the big city seemed like little more than a premarital fling, and by the end of the series she was headed for domestic bliss. In contrast, Mary Richards was in her thirties, mature, and ambitious. When the show ended, she was thirty-seven and remained romantically unattached.

*TMTMS* was undoubtedly influenced by the developing women's liberation movement. If the show had appeared even five years earlier, its chances for success would have been lessened (Gitlin, 1983). Both James Brooks's comment and the premise of the show itself demonstrate that *TMTMS* was intended to be a departure from the tradition of sexist portrayals of women on television. Consequently, the show's popularity is surprising, both because of the audience's exposure to decades of traditional depictions of women on television and because of general resistance to many aspects of the feminist movement. Thus, analysis of *TMTMS* reveals ways in which television adapts to social resistance as well as social change.

A number of hegemonic devices work to contradict the progressive feminist premise of *TMTMS*. This section concentrates on three: family roles, intra-gender relationships, and the generic constraints of situation comedy. In the following sections I argue that, despite its workplace setting, *TMTMS* offers a traditional picture of the female within the family through Mary Richards's implicit roles as wife, mother, and daughter. The relationship of Mary Richards to the larger female community reinforces the public/private dichotomy that devalues women's relationships as well as positioning Mary as an idealized token version of the successful, single woman. The conventions of the situation comedy as a genre constrained the development of positive and progressive female characterizations on *TMTMS*. Arguments are supported by examples of specific episodes that exemplify dramatic patterns in the program's history.

## THE *TMTMS* "FAMILY"

The presentation of a family structure is common to many of the most successful comedies in television history, from *I Love Lucy* to *All in the Family* to *The Cosby Show*. Because a sitcom is short in length and typically limited in setting, the situation and the characters tend to change little from episode to episode. Consequently, the characters have strong connections to each other and to the situation.

The "domestic" situation comedy inherently limits role possibilities for women. In the sitcoms preceding *TMTMS*, leading female characters were primarily wives and/or mothers who had no identity beyond the home and little real power within it, at least in comparison to the husbands/fathers.

Programs such as *Father Knows Best, The Donna Reed Show, The Dick Van Dyke Show,* and *The Brady Bunch* are examples. The patriarchal structure of the traditional, white, middle-class family was reinforced in years of sitcom programming in the 1950s and 1960s.

Although *TMTMS* was not the first comedy to feature a woman in the workplace, the program is often noted as the precursor of a number of successful comedies in the 1970s that used a workplace setting. The regular cast of the show, which was set in a Minneapolis television newsroom (WJM-TV), included Lou Grant, producer of the news; Mary Richards, associate producer and later, producer; Murray Slaughter, news writer; and Ted Baxter, anchor. For the first four years of the show, Mary Richards's neighbor and best friend, Rhoda Morgenstern, and their landlady, Phyllis Lindstrom, were also regulars. Although scenes were occasionally set in Mary's home, the majority of the action took place in the newsroom, the focus of the show. In the last four years of the show, the character of Sue Ann Nivens, the hostess of the *Happy Homemaker* show at WJM, was added, and the role of Georgette Franklin Baxter, Ted Baxter's girlfriend and later his wife, was expanded.

It can be argued that these characters behaved in many ways as an extended family. Although "all sitcom is 'domestic' or family-oriented if we expand the definition to non-blood-related groups that function as families" (Mintz, 1985, p. 116), programs differ in the extent to which the groups they feature function as *traditional* families. Indeed, it could further be argued that, while programming had previously concentrated on blood or legal relations, *TMTMS* ushered in an era of nontraditionally structured television families that included such programs as *Laverne and Shirley, Kate & Allie,* and *Who's the Boss.* All cases involve a group of people who care about each other, are committed to their relationships, and form bonds because they live and/or work together. Allowing this broader "family" circumscription, then, the concept of "patriarchy" may refer to "any kind of group organization in which males hold dominant power and determine what part females shall and shall not play, and in which capabilities assigned to women are relegated generally to the mystical and aesthetic and excluded from the practical and political realms" (Rich, 1979, p. 78).

In considering *TMTMS* as representing nontraditional family relations, we can analyze Mary Richards in terms of her three major roles: daughter, wife, and mother. While these roles are not always kept distinct, each plays out repeatedly.

### Mary as Daughter

*TMTMS* may be characterized in terms of Lou Grant's paternalism toward Mary Richards and, in turn, her submission to his professional and personal authority. Mary consistently seeks Lou's approval and advice; he guides and protects her. For example, in one episode, Sue Ann Nivens's boyfriend makes a pass at Mary. Mary becomes upset and takes her problem to Lou, who with fatherly indignation, offers to "kill him" and then, more seriously, advises Mary to tell Sue Ann. Ultimately, Mary listens to Lou and comforts Sue Ann, and the situation is happily resolved. This illustration echoes the pattern of the classic father-and-child problem-solving plot familiar from *Father Knows Best* or *Leave It to Beaver:* The child has a problem and goes to the father, who tells the child to do "the right thing," which the child intuitively knows she should do anyway. With the advice and pressure of the parent, the child overcomes her reluctance and does what is required; the situation is happily resolved, demonstrating the father's wisdom.

An episode in which Mary asks for a raise also demonstrates the parent/child nature of Mary and Lou's relationship. Lou tells her that they must confront the station manager together, arguing that the station could afford to lose one of them but not both. When they are refused and threaten to quit, the station manager does not object. Mary is thoroughly demoralized by unemployment, but Lou is confident that the station manager will eventually give in. At the end of the episode, she and Lou go back to see the station manager, who offers them a $5000 raise for them to split—double what Mary had expected. Once again, despite Mary's reluctance, Lou's recommendation proves successful.

Lou's patriarchal superiority is underscored by the negative consequences that result when Mary refuses his advice. After being promoted to producer, Mary meets a female swimmer and is convinced she would make a good sportscaster for WJM. Lou ridicules the idea, and Mary accuses him of sexism. However, Lou grants Mary the ultimate authority as producer and Mary hires the woman. In her first broadcast, the new sportscaster reports nothing but swimming news because, we find out, she does not believe in contact sports. Mary is forced to fire her. At the conclusion, Mary tells Lou that she was wrong about the sportscaster and bemoans her failure to strike a blow for women. Lou assures her that she has indeed proven something: "that a woman has the chance to be just as lousy in a job as a man." Like a good parent, Lou allows Mary to make and learn from her own mistakes, (and it is doubly interesting that this object-lesson involves female "incompetence").

*TMTMS* was replete with similar episodes in which Mary, the daughter figure, solicits advice from the older and wiser Lou, the father figure.[1] Under Lou's tutelage, Mary copes with her problems. The daughter role can be viewed as a hegemonic device that works to contain Mary's independence. *TMTMS* tells us that Mary cannot really "make it on her own" either personally or professionally without fatherly guidance. In this fashion, Mary's independence is domesticated.

### Mary as Wife and Mother

At the same time that Mary is Lou's dutiful daughter, she also acts as a nurturing wife/mother to Lou and to other characters. It is her general responsibility to maintain interpersonal relations, and she does this through personal advice, support, and mediation of conflict.

Mary is constantly accessible; her friends, who drop by at any time, are received warmly. When Ted Baxter cannot have a child, he comes to Mary, who reconciles him to the idea of adoption. When Ted has sexual problems, his wife Georgette comes to Mary for advice. When Sue Ann feels threatened by her sister, she seeks comfort from Mary. Later in this same episode, Sue Ann becomes so demoralized that she takes to her bed, convinced that she is no longer wanted or needed. Although Sue Ann has consistently treated Mary unkindly, Mary assumes nurturing responsibility.

Mary's role as nurturer is established in the series' first episode, when Lou shows up drunk at Mary's apartment the night after he hires her. His wife is out of town and he decides to write her a letter on Mary's typewriter. Despite the fact that he interrupts a visit from Mary's former boyfriend, she accommodates him, viewing his behavior as "kind of sweet" rather than intrusive. Later in the series, Lou decides to redecorate the living room as a surprise for his wife. He seeks Mary's advice, and she enlists Rhoda, her neighbor, for the job. Following Lou's divorce, he consistently turns up at Mary's apartment for dinner, seeking the wifely/motherly functions that he misses. Whenever a "woman's touch" is needed, Mary is there.

Mary is the ideal mother-surrogate in these situations. Like other typical sitcom mothers such as Harriet Nelson or June Cleaver, she is other-centered, sublimating her own feelings or needs to those of her "family." The idea that only Mary can adequately fulfill these "womanly" functions is reinforced in the rare instances in which she flatly refuses to perform. Even when she attempts to assert herself, she returns to her accommodating patterns by the end of the episode. For example, when a former WJM staff member returns for a visit, Lou decides that a party at Mary's home would be appropriate (most social interaction outside the office takes place in Mary's apartment). Mary refuses this imposition, suggesting Lou's house for the party. On the given night, she arrives early at Lou's to assist with preparations, only to find Lou in a state of total and carefree unreadiness. It is clear that Lou has counted on Mary's last-minute assistance, and when, recognizing the manipulation, she refuses to comply, Lou redirects his manipulation. The guests, he claims, knowing Mary, will *assume* that she helped him, and so she will be blamed for the mess. Mary frantically begins to clean.

Two aspects of this situation are significant. First, Mary is obviously concerned about how others assess her traditional "womanly" qualities and would not want to be viewed as an inadequate homemaker or hostess. Second, this example emphasizes Mary's role as social facilitator for the group. Lou's confidence that Mary will take over the preparations demonstrates his (and the guests') realization of her role, and Mary's acceptance of it is clear when she in fact gives in. The nurturing aspect of Mary's character is not just an extension of the fact that she is a "nice" person. Her friend and colleague Murray Slaughter is a nice person too, but he does not perform the nurturing and interpersonal facilitation that Mary does.

Mary's sensitivity, relationship skills, and willingness to spend her time and energy on the problems of others are symptomatic of her status as mother to the group. Like the traditional mothers of domestic sitcoms, she derives her value as a person from what she can do for others. Interestingly enough, the lyrics of the theme song from *TMTMS* echo this assumption: "Who can turn the world on with her smile? / Who can take a nothing day and suddenly make it all seem worthwhile?" In *TMTMS* Mary is a woman in a man's world, and her primary function is to enhance the lives of others in ways men supposedly cannot: "The patriarchy looks to women to embody and impersonate the qualities lacking in its institutions . . . such qualities as intuition, sympathy, and access to feeling" (Rich, 1979, p. 80).

This analysis illustrates the contradictions that exist within *TMTMS*. Although it took the sitcom from the home to the workplace, it did not significantly alter the traditional male/female roles of the genre. Superficially, *TMTMS* seems progressive, but the interaction of its characters demonstrates the hegemonic patterns that undercut Mary's status as a liberated woman.

## THE FEMALE COMMUNITY ON *TMTMS*

The above section demonstrates how Mary Richards's situation as a familial adjunct to other characters can be seen as a hegemonic device defusing the threatening aspects of the "independent" woman. In their traditional forms, as they are used on *TMTMS*, the daughter/wife/mother personae are demeaning to women, suggesting that their judgments and concerns are less important than those of others, particularly males.

This section examines Mary's relationships with other women. Assessing the portrayal of female relationships on television can provide insight into the nature of women's valuation as a group. Two major issues arise from the portrayal of interaction within the female community on *TMTMS*: the division between Mary's public and private lives, and the extent to which Mary is depicted as a token successful female.

It can be argued that television, by focusing on women's relationships with men and thereby assuming their ultimate importance in women's lives, undermines the importance of female community (see Tuchman, 1978). *TMTMS* conforms to this pattern. Mary's relationships with women are consistently depicted as secondary to her relationships with men. In the primary dramatic arena, the newsroom, Mary is the only woman. While this may suggest that Mary is a woman who can make it in a man's world, it also suggests that women's public success depends on them cooperating with male-defined structures of power. Sue Ann Nivens enters the show not as a "newsman" but as the host of the *Happy Homemaker* show; her character is sketched so as to prevent female bonding. Sue Ann's job and her interests fall in traditionally female areas. She is man-hungry and constantly in pursuit of Lou, which makes her relationship with Mary competitive rather than cooperative.

In the first four seasons of the show, Mary has close relationships with Rhoda Morgenstern, her neighbor, and Phyllis Lindstrom, her married landlady. Because Rhoda and Mary are closer in age and both single, their bond is closer. In many ways, the relationship between the two women is positive; they are supportive, caring, and cooperative with each other, and neither views their relationship as a substitute for satisfying relationships with men (see Bathrick, 1984). However, Mary's successful interpersonal relationships with Rhoda and Phyllis at home further extend the division between the public and the private in *TMTMS.*

### Public and Private Realms

Traditional thought prescribes that women are suited for the private, personal realm, and men for the public, professional one. The stereotypical characteristics assigned to men and women reflect this division; men are aggressive, competitive breadwinners, and women are passive, nurturing homebodies (see Welter, 1966). *TMTMS* does not deny this perspective. Mary's interaction with close female friends is home-centered and largely involves personal rather than professional issues. At work, Mary is surrounded by men, and her one female relationship (with Sue Ann Nivens) is neither close nor supportive.

Another aspect of the private/public division is that its boundaries are more fluid for men than for women. Men are able to work and compete successfully in the public sphere and still return home to fulfill private roles as husbands and fathers. This is evident in *TMTMS* as well. While Rhoda and Phyllis rarely appear in work contexts, Mary's male colleagues are frequently seen outside of the newsroom.

### Female Tokenism

On the surface at least, Mary is a positive character. She is bright, attractive, well liked, has a good job that she performs well, and is generally happy. The other female characters on *TMTMS* do not fare as well. Sue Ann is constantly seeking fulfillment through men; Georgette is an addle-brained blonde who is devoted to the egocentric and insensitive Ted; Rhoda has a

less than satisfying job, is overweight, and is unsuccessful in romantic relationships; and Phyllis is an eccentric, narcissistic wife and mother who often
is frustrated by her circumscribed role. Moreover, Rhoda and Phyllis cannot
get along with each other despite their common friendship with Mary, again
reinforcing the idea that only Mary can be successful in all contexts, and
perhaps, that non-extraordinary women cannot get along with each other.

Mary's isolation as the sole woman in the newsroom and her portrayal
as the only reasonably successful and fulfilled woman in *TMTMS* demonstrate her tokenism. Mary succeeds in the public realm only by succumbing
to male expectations that she fulfill traditional female roles. She is successful, likeable, and admirable in the eyes of the other women and men on
*TMTMS because* she is submissive and unassertively nurturing and, thus, has
successfully adapted herself to the male culture. Moreover, Mary's isolation
as the only thoroughly positive female character in the private realm promotes perception of her as an ideal woman who is different from most. The
token woman is "separate[d] . . . from the wider female condition; and she
is perceived by 'ordinary' women as separate also, perhaps even stronger
than themselves" (Rich, 1986, p. 6). As the sole well-adjusted female character, Mary is figuratively isolated from and literally outnumbered by the
unfulfilled female characters of Rhoda, Phyllis, and Sue Ann.

In the end, Mary is no one's equal. She is inferior to other, specifically
male, characters in the public realm, where her success depends more on
interpersonal than professional skill, and she is superior to other female
characters in the private realm. This imbalance posits Mary Richards as a
token stab at a positive portrayal of female independence. In contrast to
Mary, *TMTMS* tells us, most women, like Rhoda, Sue Ann, Georgette, and
even Phyllis (who constantly looks for ways to improve her marriage), are
dissatisfied and continue to seek fulfillment through men. Mary's superiority
comes from a particular kind of power that she has gained through compliance with male expectations. She has learned to adapt better than other
female characters. In their own ways, Rhoda, Phyllis, and Sue Ann still resist
or simply cannot meet the demands of patriarchy, while Mary has met those
demands and is rewarded for her efforts. The hegemonic message derived
from a comparison of Mary with other female characters is that compliance
produces more happiness than resistance.

■ **GENRE CONSIDERATIONS**

The hegemonic devices at work in *TMTMS* cannot be separated from generic considerations. The familial roles within which Mary Richards operates
are a product of the conservatism of situation comedy as a genre and the
replicative nature of television. In his discussion of the medium's "recombinant" nature, Gitlin (1983, p. 63) notes that "executives like to say they are

constantly looking for something new, but their intuition tells them to hunt up prepackaged trends and then recognize the new as a variant of the old." *TMTMS* presents us with a "new" premise and old characters. A sitcom about a single, ambitious woman is daring until you surround her with a recognizable husband/father figure and a group of children to nurture. At that point, she becomes Donna Reed repackaged as a working woman.

The tendency of television programming to rehash traditional themes and roles is intensified by the conservatism of the sitcom, which is "committed to the prevention of change and the protection of the present" (Grote, 1983, p. 72). At the end of the episode, no radical change has occurred, and "everything goes back as it was at the beginning of the episode" (Grote, 1983, p. 68). Once the character's personalities, relationships, and interaction patterns have been established, program makers are unlikely to change them without risking damage to the success of the show.[2] Although one or all of these factors are challenged in some way within each episode, the problem ultimately is resolved in a fashion that requires no fundamental adjustment of the situation (Grote, 1983).

The first few episodes of a sitcom are designed to establish the situation firmly. The elements that make *TMTMS* problematic from a feminist perspective can be seen in the first episode of the series, in which Mary arrives in Minneapolis and gets her job at WJM. In the first scene we see an argument between Phyllis and Rhoda over Mary's apartment. Instantly, Mary is the mediator, trying to satisfy both women. Rhoda, who has been outside washing the windows, is swathed in bulky clothes and looks particularly unattractive next to the perky, pretty Mary. Phyllis reveals to Rhoda Mary's reason for moving to Minneapolis: the man she had dated for two years was unwilling to marry her. Thus, it is established that Mary did not come to the city seeking her independence for its own sake, but as a reaction to being refused the traditional role she desired.[3]

The next scene shows Lou Grant interviewing Mary for a job at WJM. Mary clearly has no qualifications for the job, yet Lou comments on her "spunk" and decides to give her a chance. Thus, we have the first example of Lou's paternalism toward Mary. Lou tells her, "If I don't like you, I'll fire you. If you don't like me, I'll fire you." It is interesting that Lou's standards for Mary are based on personal factors rather than professional ones, indicating that Mary's success in the newsroom will depend upon her likability rather than her professional merit. At this point, we have already seen several indicators of patterns that will recur in the series: Mary's superiority to Rhoda, Lou's paternalism, and the importance of Mary's interpersonal qualities.

Indeed, the first episode displays most of Mary's eventual roles; by the end of it, she is nurturing a drunken Lou in her apartment. In this scene, Mary is saying a final good-bye to her boyfriend, who has followed her to Minneapolis. On the surface, Mary's refusal to continue a relationship with him seems to testify to her conviction to be independent. However, the fact that Lou is there as well suggests an opposite conclusion: that Mary is able to reject her possibilities for traditional bliss with the boyfriend because she has found new possibilities in her developing daughter/mother relationship with Lou.

Having established its basic premises in the first episode, in typical sitcom fashion *TMTMS* does not tamper with them. Mary grows older and more mature, but her patterns do not change significantly. Many episodes center on threats to these patterns, as Mary variously tries to reject Lou's authority, assert herself, and reject the nurturing role. However, the show always travels its circular path and returns Mary to docility by the conclusion. Indeed, in the last episode, the patriarchal patterns remain. As the WJM "family" prepares to split up after the station has been sold, Lou, in his paternal role, arranges to bring Rhoda and Phyllis, who have left Minneapolis, back to console Mary. Even on this occasion, Phyllis and Rhoda bicker over Mary's attention, reinforcing Mary's superiority and bringing her mediating skills to the fore. Significantly, Mary acknowledges the relationships she has formed, saying, "Thank you for being my family."

The problems of *TMTMS* and its portrayal of women are neither minor nor obvious. To depict Mary as a truly self-sufficient and self-determined woman would have required a complete reworking of the very basics of the series' situation. The hegemonic devices are there from the beginning, and they are reinforced throughout. Mary Richards is a successful single woman, but only at the expense of conforming to traditional expectations in the roles she plays for others. In addition, although Mary's friendships with women enhance her private life, the contrast between her success and their lack of it implies that the route to happiness is found in compliance with patriarchal norms; the resistance that Rhoda, Phyllis, and Sue Ann represent leads to dissatisfaction.

## ON READING MARY RICHARDS

Two issues growing out of this analysis deserve attention. The first, the value of recognizing strategies of hegemony in television discourse about women, is integrally related to the second, which concerns the validity of critical readings of television.

### Women, Hegemony, and Television

Feminist critics need to attend to the tension that exists between the poles of feminism and patriarchy in narratives such as *TMTMS,* as well as to how audiences might negotiate that tension. As a product of the dominant ideology, television may never be all that feminists desire, but its problems require continual redefinition. Viewing a program such as *TMTMS* with the benefit of hindsight permits such redefinition and offers possibilities for future investigation.

Such investigation likely would show that variations on the family paradigm have been used in other instances to devalue women within television programming. For example, although *Kate & Allie* has been touted as a positive portrayal of women (Alley, 1985), the fairly clear allocation of traditionally male/husband/father and female/wife/mother characteristics between its two female leads indicate elements of a patriarchal family paradigm.

Other distinct methods perform hegemonic functions similar to those explored here (for an example, see D'Acci, 1987). A recent situation comedy that has been compared to *TMTMS* is a strong candidate for this type of analysis. *Murphy Brown,* which focuses on the life of a woman who is a successful television journalist and avowed feminist, depicts the title character as embodying traditionally male characteristics; she is aggressive, competitive, and often insensitive. Moreover, her public success is counterbalanced by difficult family and romantic relationships and, in general, loneliness. It could be argued that these factors work hegemonically to contain positive evaluations of a feminist character by exploiting myths about the masculinity of feminists and their sacrifice of personal happiness.

These examples underscore the idea that television is recombinant and that strategies proven successful at defusing feminist content in one situation are likely to be used in another. In developing a feminist critique that includes the development of feminist theory for television (Press, 1989), critics must make note of such patterns.

### Criticism and Audiences

On another level, however, this reading of *TMTMS* may very well not be viewed as definitive. (See Grossberg & Treichler, 1987; Radway, 1986; and Rakow, 1986 for rejection of "preferred" reading claims.) While this essay has argued that the hegemonic patterns in *TMTMS* are both evident and troublesome, some may read *TMTMS* differently. Byars (1987, p. 294), for example, notes that a previous negative reading of *TMTMS* was countered during its presentation by an audience member who claimed that "Mary had meant a great deal to her, and to other women; she had represented for them 'independence' " and "had inspired them."

This contrast in opinions should not be surprising. It is precisely such divergent readings that ensure the success of television (Fiske, 1986). In the end, Mary is threatening to no one. She is passive, deferent, and womanly enough within her surrogate family to quiet the fears of those uneasy with women's liberation. For champions of feminism, Mary is a symbol of the possibilities for women—she is independent and still happy. This is the process through which hegemony is maintained. Enough difference is introduced to give the appearance of change, yet enough remains the same to avoid upsetting the balance within the dominant ideology. Thus, the claim is not that television *"manufactures"* ideology, but that it *"relays* and *reproduces* and *processes* and *packages* and *focuses* ideology." (Gitlin, 1982, p. 430, italics in original). However, in this processing, some "ideological seams" (Radway, 1986, p. 110) are exposed, allowing for contrasting evaluations as audiences assign "different values to different portions of the text and hence to the text itself" (Condit, 1989, p. 108). Not all viewers saw Mary Richards as a "contained" feminist symbol, but the text of *TMTMS* offers mixed messages that limit claims for the program's progressiveness.

Although different evaluations of a program's message are possible, the hegemonic patterns isolated here are not my own creation. They exist within the *TMTMS* narrative and are available for conscious or unconscious articulation by viewers. In the 1970s, it was not necessary to watch *TMTMS* to know that the program was about a single, "liberated" woman. Nonetheless, audience research has recently promoted a methodological vision that threatens to obscure the legitimate functions performed by the type of criticism offered here. As critics we assume that we are able to see and explain what others cannot because we are trained to do so. Scholarly readings should be expected to be different from audience readings; the former must be considered and attuned to the subtleties that audience members may experience but not articulate.

Although audience research can enhance our conclusions and perhaps offer some sociological comprehension, it does not replace critical insight. To act as though it can is to erode our own credibility. Feminist critics are in a particularly precarious position with regard to this issue. Those critics with the knowledge and training to recognize and interpret patriarchal ideology in television discourse should not be silenced simply because audiences caught in cultural hegemonic patterns may not acknowledge what is happening. In that context, critics need to go beyond what audiences might tell them.

Each type of criticism offers a different type of insight. They are complementary, and each can add to a feminist critique (Rakow, 1989). The commitment to the need for real change that is part of the feminist agenda makes it imperative that we explore every reasonable path that enriches the diversity and usefulness of a feminist critique of television.

## ▦ Notes

[1]Interestingly, the proscription against incest that typifies a true father-daughter relationship is implicitly revealed in an episode late in the series in which Mary asks Lou for a date. Lou comes over to Mary's house for dinner, and both are extremely nervous and uncomfortable.

They decide to end the suspense and they kiss, during which both begin to giggle. Agreeing that a dating relationship will never work, they settle down to talk about the office. Clearly, the patterns created in their father-daughter relationship prohibit romance.

[2]There are a few exceptions to this general rule, and Grote (1983) cites *M\*A\*S\*H* as an example.

[3]The creators of *TMTMS* had originally conceived of Mary Richards as a divorced woman, but CBS executives vetoed the idea, explaining that viewers would not accept such a character because of Mary Tyler Moore's previous popular role as the dutiful and happy wife on *The Dick Van Dyke Show*. But "the network feared that the mass audience wouldn't accept the proposition that an attractive and competent woman on the far side of thirty had never been married" (Gitlin, 1983, p. 214). These incidents show hegemonic considerations at work from the outset of the show's creation.

# ▥ References

Alley, R. (1985). Values on view: A moral myopia? *Critical Studies in Mass Communication, 2*, 395–406.

Baehr, H., & Dyer, G. (Eds.). (1987). *Boxed in: Women and television.* New York: Pandora.

Barthes, R. (1973). *Mythologies.* London: Paladin.

Bathrick, S. (1984). The Mary Tyler Moore Show: Women at home and at work. In J. Feuer, P. Kerr, & T. Vahimagi (Eds.), *MTM: "Quality Television"* (pp. 99–131). London: British Film Institute.

Brooks, T., & Marsh, E. (1985). *The complete directory to prime time network tv shows, 1946–present* (3d ed.). New York: Ballantine.

Byars, J. (1987). Reading feminine discourse: Prime-time television in the U.S. *Communication, 9*, 289–303.

Condit, C. (1989). The rhetorical limits of polysemy. *Critical Studies in Mass Communication, 6*, 103–122.

D'Acci, J. (1987). The case of Cagney and Lacey. In H. Baehr & G. Dyer (Eds.), *Boxed in: Women and television* (pp. 203–226). New York: Pandora.

De Lauretis, T. (1984). *Alice doesn't: Feminism, semiotics, cinema.* Bloomington: Indiana University Press.

Dervin, B. (1987). The potential contribution of feminist scholarship to the field of communication. *Journal of Communication, 37(4)*, 107–120.

Fiske, J. (1986). Television: Polysemy and popularity. *Critical Studies in Mass Communication, 3*, 391–408.

Gitlin, T. (1982). Prime time ideology: The hegemonic process in television entertainment. In H. Newcomb (Ed.), *Television: The critical view* (3d ed.) (pp. 426–454). New York: Oxford University Press.

Gitlin, T. (1983). *Inside prime time.* New York: Pantheon Books.

Grossberg, L., & Treichler, P. (1987). Intersections of power: Criticism, television, gender. *Communication, 9*, 273–287.

Grote, D. (1983). *The end of comedy: The sit-com and the comedic tradition.* Hamden, CT: Archon Books.

Hough, A. (1981). Trials and tribulations—Thirty years of sitcom. In R. Adler (Ed.), *Understanding television: Essays on television as a social and cultural force* (pp. 201–224). New York: Praeger.

Kuhn, A. (1982). *Women's pictures: Feminism and cinema.* New York: Routledge & Kegan Paul.

Meehan, D. (1983). *Ladies of the evening: Women characters of prime-time television.* Metuchen, NJ: Scarecrow Press.

Mintz, L. (1985). Situation comedy. In B. Rose (Ed.), *TV genres: A handbook and reference guide* (pp. 107–129). Westport, CT: Greenwood Press.

Modleski, T. (1982). *Loving with a vengeance: Mass-produced fantasies for women.* London: Methuen.

Mulvey, L. (1989). *Visual and other pleasures.* Bloomington: Indiana University Press.

Press, A. (1989). The ongoing feminist revolution. *Critical Studies in Mass Communication, 6,* 196–202.

Radway, J. (1984). *Reading the romance: Women, patriarchy, and popular literature.* Chapel Hill, University of North Carolina Press.

Radway, J. (1986). Identifying ideological seams: Mass culture, analytical method, and political practice. *Communication, 9,* 93–123.

Rakow, L. (1986). Feminist approaches to popular culture: Giving patriarchy its due. *Communication, 9,* 19–24.

Rakow, L. (1989). Feminist studies: The next stage. *Critical Studies in Mass Communication, 6,* 209–215.

Rich, A. (1979). *On lies, secrets, and silence: Selected prose, 1966–1978.* New York: W. W. Norton.

Rich, A. (1986). *Blood, bread, and poetry: Selected prose, 1979–1985.* New York: W. W. Norton.

Treichler, P., & Wartella, E. (1986). Interventions: Feminist theories and communication studies. *Communication, 9,* 1–18.

Tuchman, G. (1978). The symbolic annihilation of women by the mass media. In G. Tuchman, A. K. Daniels, & J. Benét (Eds.), *Hearth and home: Images of women in the mass media* (pp. 4–38). New York: Oxford University Press.

Welter, B. (1966). The cult of true womanhood, 1820–1860. *American Quarterly, 18,* 151–174.

# CHAPTER 6 ⬜

# THE CAMPAIGN
# FOR CIVIL DEFENSE

Elizabeth Walker Mechling
and Jay Mechling

*In this commentary, Elizabeth Walker Mechling and Jay Mechling describe how a chance to write on "Cold War campaigns" triggered questions, images, and personal memories from their childhoods in the 1950s. Writing criticism became the chance for them to answer some of these questions, make sense of the images, and reconcile the memories.*

## COMMENTARY

The idea to write an essay on the civil defense campaign of the 1950s–60s and on social movements resisting the campaign came to us through the sort of serendipity many scholars relish. One of the things scholars do at their scholarly conventions is sit in hotel bars and in airport waiting lounges talking about ideas and plotting together the next collaboration on a convention panel or book project. These small groups make up the larger "invisible colleges" of colleagues who depend upon each other for thoughtful criticism, ideas, and encouragement. In this case, three critics were working on Cold War texts and wanted to put together a panel on "The Rhetoric of Cold War Campaigns" for the 1988 meeting of the Western Speech Communication Association. As the conversation developed, one of the group turned to us and asked, simply, "What would you two want to do?" We looked at each other and began to free-associate ideas about what Cold War campaigns might interest us. Most of the images evoked during that stream-of-consciousness (however distracted we were by the "help" we were getting from our friends around the table) included the bomb and its emblematic mushroom cloud. Those images, in turn, evoked personal memories.

**118**

*Snapshot: Frank Walker is worried about his family. Living in south Florida, there are constant reminders of the threat of nuclear attack. To the north is Cape Canaveral and the fledgling space program. To the west lies Miami International Airport, a natural target. To the south sits a Strategic Air Command base at Homestead. To the east, of course, is the Atlantic Ocean. Nowhere to run. Frank cannot afford to build a bomb shelter and Florida houses do not have basements. So he designates a closet in the house as the most protected shelter in case of nuclear attack, and he fills a footlocker with bottled water, canned goods, first aid supplies, books, games, and seeds. Ruth and the five children know what to do in the case of attack. The seven Walkers will huddle in that closet, a mattress against the door, for as long as it takes to hear the all-clear signal.*

*Snapshot: June Mechling puts in long hours through the 1956–57 school year planning with other mothers an evacuation exercise for the children at Treasure Island Elementary School in Miami Beach, Florida. The PTA decided that they needed a plan for getting children from the school to their homes in the case of imminent nuclear attack. The mothers work for months assembling the plan, creating a telephone tree, lining up drivers, and so on. On the day of the drill, everything goes smoothly. As a safety patrol officer, sixth-grader Jay leads a group of children out of the school on a march down a street, across a bridge (the traffic halted by the local police), and to a parking lot full of cars waiting to carry the children to their homes. The mothers gather in the Mechling home to have drinks and celebrate a smooth drill, the point of which (though none would say this) is that the children can die at home rather than at school.*

This is the madness we sought to understand. How could our parents, perfectly reasonable people, act in this way? How could we, cynical preadolescents then, also take this world as "natural"? How were we so easily socialized into Lifton's "nuclear culture"? How did some people in the 1950s resist the socialization, even to the point of creating social movements engaging in civil disobedience meant to thwart civil defense planning? The questions were real and troubling. This was no mere scholarly exercise of choosing an "interesting" topic. The stakes of self-understanding were high, both in retrospect for understanding our nuclear socialization, and in prospect for understanding what possibly pathological worldviews have become normal, "naturalized," for us in the 1990s. These questions led us to settle upon the civil defense campaigns and resistances as the texts we would analyze for the panel.

Most of our ideas for essays come in just this way. Some cultural experience strikes us as odd or puzzling. After talking about it for a while and getting more excited about the puzzle the more we talk about it, we usually resolve to write about the puzzle, using writing as our way of figuring it out. Our first joint work on theme parks began with such a puzzlement, as have our subsequent essays on sugar, on animal rights campaigns, and on the ABC Persian Gulf War special for kids. Indeed, our major individual projects—Elizabeth's work on free clinics and Jay's on the Boy Scouts of America—arose out of genuine cultural questions rooted in personal experiences.

So the puzzling texts present themselves first. We do not begin with a theory or method or hypotheses and then search for a case study to demonstrate or illuminate the theory. Rather, we bring to the text a repertoire of tools and ideas and fashion an approach we think appropriate to the text. Our educations have been thoroughly interdisciplinary, Elizabeth's in English and speech communication and Jay's in the conjunction of literary criticism, art criticism, history, anthropology, sociology, psychology, geography, and more that makes up an American studies training. Our training suits our cognitive styles, which is to say we consider the interdisciplinary imagination playful, eclectic, and inventive, seeing connections everywhere. The search for workable ideas and approaches should not end at the borders of the discipline. The borders, after all, are the most exciting place to be, both in cultures and in intellectual disciplines. The interdisciplinary imagination has a good enough map of the disciplines and a good enough compass (or sense of the goal) to draw upon whatever works best to solve the puzzles of the meanings of the text. As in Wallace Stevens's poem, "Thirteen Ways of Looking at a Blackbird," there are many ways to reinscribe the "meanings" of a text, and (still in Stevens's spirit) those meanings or truths we discover will always be partial and emergent. From the pragmatic perspective, our critical practice must be in concert with our moral and political goals; the practice must take us where we want to go. And "to work best" is a comparative judgment made by and within an interpretive community. The rhetorical critic must persuade readers that a given interpretation of texts finds some "truth" about the texts and their cultural contexts.

This is not to say we do not have some familiar starting points for every inquiry. For example, it always profits us to ask what Kenneth Burke would say about the text, so it seems clear that his dramatism and his attention to symbolic narratives on the mythological level appeal to our sense of the goals of culture criticism. Similarly, we always become smarter about a text when we ask what Peter Berger, Gregory Bateson, and the symbolic anthropologists (Mary Douglas, Victor Turner, Clifford Geertz) would have to say in an imagined group discussion about the text. And, of course, we always learn something new by asking what difference gender, race, ethnicity, social class, age, sexual orientation, or other human particularities make in creating and receiving the meanings of texts.

This way of operating has become more and more naturalized in our critical writing over the years, as we realized when the first round of reviewers' reports from the *Western Journal of Speech Communication* (now the *Western Journal of Communication*) asked for, as the editor put it, "a stronger theoretical basis." The first manuscript version of our essay did not address theory. We sat down to reconstruct our theoretical perspective from our critical practices, that is, from the manuscript in front of us. We wrote a new section, "Criticism in the Pragmatic Attitude," explaining our theoretical approach, though neither pragmatism nor the neopragmatism of Rorty, Bernstein, West, and others is best described as a "theory." We had to condense a lot of our thinking in a few pages, and we wished we had a whole essay to lay out a model of rhetorical criticism in the pragmatic attitude. Perhaps we shall. But we satisfied ourselves that we had articulated something of our approach, and the reviewers seemed pleased on the second round of reading.

The new section notwithstanding, the development of theory was not our primary aim at the outset of our study. The "text" was central, but at the beginning the "text" was some generalized memory of the civil defense campaign. Rhetorical critics need texts, so our first step was to search for the rhetorical artifacts we would study. The debate was a public one, so we looked mainly at the magazine articles (and some books) that constituted the debate. The discourse of the resistance is a bit harder to come by. As Elizabeth discovered in her work on the free clinic movement, most social movements generate ephemeral printed texts unlikely to be preserved in the usual library and institutional collections. Elizabeth's study of the free clinic movement was possible largely because one of the physicians active in the movement saved every scrap of paper that came his way. Fortunately for us, the Swarthmore College Peace Collection had files of social movement materials documenting some of the resistance to the civil defense campaigns.

Culture criticism now looks at a greatly expanded range of what we would call "texts," so we knew from the outset that we should think broadly about the debate over civil defense, even if we did not include every text in our analysis. We paid attention to the maps and photographs accompanying articles in magazines, and we were struck especially by the similarities between the drawings in fallout shelter pamphlets and the drawings common in magazine advertising in the 1950s. As teenagers we had both read Pat Frank's *Alas, Babylon*, a nuclear war novel set in Florida, and we knew that Philip Wylie (author of the apocalyptic novel *Tomorrow!*) was an early proponent of civil defense measures, so we returned to the fiction of the 1950s to understand how those texts may have contributed to nuclear culture. Our assumption that film and television provided the most important grand, mythic narratives led us to survey those media. We focused our critical attention on *On the Beach* and the *Twilight Zone* episode "The Shelter," because those texts played such a large role in the public discourse, but we easily could have extended our analysis to the science fiction films of the 1950s, to nuclear apocalyptic comic books, perhaps to *Mad Magazine*, and beyond. We knew intertextual relations were some of the most interesting aspects of the debate. Believing it more important to interpret a few, key texts in depth rather than create an uncritical inventory of texts and a map of their connections, we relegated these other texts to footnotes and, sometimes, to our file drawers.

Notice that we keep saying "we" in this discussion of how the essay came to be written. We began writing together when we began living apart in the late 1970s. Teaching at universities eighty miles distant (and a hard, congested commute), we lived apart four days a week and were together for long weekends. We reckoned that it would be good to have something beyond exhaustion and institutional complaints to bring us together on weekends, and we saw writing together as a positive force in our married life.

Writing together is far more difficult than solitary authorship. Many university merit review processes diminish the importance of joint authorship, sometimes only "counting" a joint article as "one-half a publication." While such skepticism may be warranted in the natural sciences, where people are added to a list of authors for minimal contribution, joint authorship in the humanities is quite another matter. In humanistic culture criticism the writing is no mere, flat report on the research. The humanist discovers what she knows and means through the writing, and when the writing is that important, more hands do not make light work. We joke that Elizabeth writes the verbs and adjectives and that Jay writes the nouns and adverbs, and those who know us well see the inside joke. A sense of humor helps. We both read all the texts and supporting materials and then engage in lengthy discussions about how to interpret the texts and about how to organize the essay. From a very sketchy and tentative outline, we usually take responsibility for writing the first draft of different sections, though sometimes only one of us will attempt the first draft. Then the real joint writing begins, as we meld the drafts, cut, paste, fill holes, and so on until we have an essay that satisfies us both.

Even so, the first version of the civil defense essay was long, and adding the section on "Criticism in the Pragmatic Attitude" meant that we had to cut even more in subsequent drafts. Sacrificed was a description and analysis of a speech by Edward Teller, answering the Gerald Piel speech (which we did describe and analyze). We were drawn to the details of that debate and could write a whole essay comparing those two speeches; perhaps we will, someday. In earlier drafts we addressed more explicitly the racial and social class nuances of the dispersal strategy, but at readers' urgings we demoted Dean MacCannell's provocative analysis to a footnote. Similarly, our original notes toward the essay explored in greater depth the gender politics encoded in the civil defense materials, but we abbreviated this dimension, in large part because Elaine Tyler May's fine book about the American family in the Cold War had just appeared. Finally, we resisted the temptation to create a conversation between this essay and the "Hot Pacifism and Cold War" essay we were working on simultaneously (and which appeared in the *QJS* in 1992). It was tempting to take advantage of the New Class thesis emerging in the pacifism essay and fold it back into the final revision of the civil defense essay, but the final revision is no time to introduce a new argument. Still, it is relevant for understanding the civil defense essay that we were immersed at the same time in the rhetoric of 1950s pacifism.

The opportunity to revise and shorten the essay also meant that we had to reconsider matters of organization and structure. One of the things we disagreed upon early was how much of our conclusion to give away in the early pages of the essay. Jay prefers the approach Stephen Jay Gould uses in his monthly essays for *Natural History*, wherein Gould usually poses a puzzle of some sort and begins working through it, recording all the dead-ends, complications, and such before arriving finally at the solution, much as a detective arrives at the solution in the last pages of a novel. Humanists seem most comfortable with this sort of narrative, and one will find in history and literary criticism journals many essays constructed this way. Another element of the humanist's rhetoric is to write an essay without subheadings, assuming that a well-written essay makes clear its organization and coherence without artificial signposts along the way.

Elizabeth warned against this approach. In her experience the editors, reviewers, and readers of essays in rhetorical criticism like to have the full thesis up front, with clear organization and subheadings. Perhaps this is the result of too many debaters in the profession. In any case, Elizabeth knew the conventions of the genre and thought the essay should follow those conventions. Jay prevailed, against Elizabeth's better judgment, and the reviewers' comments vindicated her view. One reviewer wrote, "The whole paper is, frankly, bass-ackwards. . . . The emphasis should be on the claim, not the examples. In fact, your best statement of a thesis is in your conclusion." We revised the essay accordingly, laying out our thesis at the outset and creating subheadings meant to clarify the organization of the essay. The reviewers liked the changes. Showing uncharacteristic restraint, Elizabeth did not say "I told you so."

Now, it is true that we should not make too much of this instance. We do not write as well as Gould and what we thought was artful might have been vague and clumsy. But putting aside for the moment the question of how well we executed our intentions in the first manuscript version of our essay, our experience suggests that the discipline of rhetorical criticism might not be served well by the present rhetorical conventions for the writing of rhetorical criticism. At a time when other disciplines are posing interesting questions about the ideological implications of their rhetorical conventions and are experimenting with new forms of discourse, the practice of rhetorical criticism seems to us inordinately conservative and conventional. One reviewer thought we "intruded" into the essay "much more than is needed," but the intrusion of the critic into the scene under study is precisely what is happening in, say, the new ethnography advocated by James Clifford and others. It is hard to tell if the conservative nature of the rhetoric of rhetorical criticism is due to the gatekeepers (the editors and reviewers) or, more probably, to the self-censoring of authors. Certainly it would be healthy for some journal or volume editor to invite explicitly unconventional, experimental approaches to writing rhetorical criticism.

The purpose of sociological thinking, wrote C. Wright Mills in *The Sociological Imagination*, is "to connect private troubles with public issues," a notion later endorsed by the women's movement in its insistence that, politically, the private is public. There is no better motto for American culture criticism. The act of reflexive culture criticism—that is, the unpacking of one's own cultural assumptions, the discovery of cultural contingency in the beliefs one most takes for granted—is a political act to the extent that it links the public and private. Only when we understand the ways in which our social locations and interests work to influence our views of the world can we sort the "is" from the "ought." Approached with the right attitude, the radical relativizing, the debunking, the deconstruction of the critic's own world should leave the critic not an immobilized victim in a web of cultural determinism but a social actor who understands both the limits of his or her knowledge and the necessity of making choices about his or her own lives and about the lives we influence. We live in a William Jamesian world of "forced options," so we had best arm ourselves both with the self-knowledge of contemporary culture criticism and with clarity about the intended (and unintended) consequences of our work.

# The Campaign for Civil Defense
# and the Struggle to Naturalize the Bomb

**Elizabeth Walker Mechling**
**and Jay Mechling**

**R**evisiting the texts of the public debate in Fifties America over civil defense induces in the critic reared in that era an eerie vertigo. Our current perspective feels privileged not just because we now know so much more about the destructiveness of nuclear weapons than did that first generation living in the atomic era, though certainly their (our) naivete is shocking. There was a desperate madness in those first years when Americans were attempting to understand the Bomb. Is one to laugh or cry at Chicago's plan "to tattoo its citizens with their blood types—underneath the armpits because arms might be blown off—in case radiation sickness called for quick transfusions,"[1] or at New York City's plan to train pigeons to respond to supersonic whistles as part of the post-attack communications network?[2] The times invited black humor, as when Toledo's Mayor Michael DiSalle joked with reporters covering a gathering of civil defense directors and mayors that Toledo's plan against attack was to "erect large neon signs on its buildings pointing the way to Cleveland and Detroit."[3] And the makers of the 1985 film, *The Atomic Cafe*, created a powerfully political black comedy simply by making a montage of 1950s government civil defense films, theatrical films featuring atomic war, and television commercials in which an animated Bert the Turtle sang a jingle aimed at teaching children to "duck and cover."[4]

Revisiting the civil defense debate of the Fifties also induces in the critic a vertigo of blurred genres. Nonfiction public discourse and science fiction mixed so thoroughly during the era that the critic comes to realize how important were the relationships between those two sorts of narratives and a third sort of text, everyday social reality. Descriptions of the creation of vigilante leagues in Las Vegas and Bakersfield, leagues meant to provide armed resistance against the refugees from Los Angeles in case of an evacuation or a nuclear attack, come not from a grade-B film script, but from the newspapers of 1961.[5] The man who equipped his fallout shelter with four rifles and a .357 Magnum for use against neighbors who might try to follow him and his family into the shelter was not a character from the September 29, 1961, *Twilight Zone* episode entitled, "The Shelter"; rather, he was an Austin, Texas, hardware dealer who explained to reporters what he would do if his neighbors got into his shelter before he did. "I've got a .38 tear-gas gun," he warned, "and if I fire six or seven tear-gas bullets into the shelter, they'll either come out or the gas will get them."[6] For Americans devouring a diet of western films and immensely popular television series like *Gunsmoke, Wagon Train,* and *Bonanza,* firearms had become as indispensable a fallout shelter provision as were food and water.

We argue that the Fifties debate over civil defense, and especially over fallout shelters, was a proxy debate over the larger salient issue of the tension between individualism and community in Fifties America. This issue, of course, is unique neither to the 1950s nor to American culture. Every group must define for its members the meaning of the "self" and its relationship to others. What complicates the American case, however, are particular traditions and languages of individualism practiced by Americans in their everyday lives. Earlier traditions, such as those Robert Bellah and his colleagues call "biblical" and "civic," gave weight to the community as a check on the practice of a vigorous American individualism.[7] But it is the latest tradition of individualism, the "expressive," that poses the greatest threat to the social fabric. And although the tradition of expressive individualism has roots in the nineteenth century, the tradition developed fully in the twentieth. More to the point, the popularization of psychological theories and vocabularies as "folk theories" of the self, a development crucial to the ideology of expressive individualism, reached full force in the 1950s and 1960s. It is this conflation of expressive individualism and the civil defense campaign that created a particular, historical tension between the rhetoric of civil defense and the practices of everyday life.

We offer a socio-rhetorical analysis of the American public debate over civil defense, from the late 1940s through the early 1960s.[8] During those first fifteen years of American experience with nuclear discourse, the federal government attempted to induce in American citizens the political, social, and psychological acceptance of the atomic bomb as a new reality and atomic power as a new possibility.[9] This campaign to induce in Americans what Robert Jay Lifton has called "nuclearism," an "embrace of the bomb as a new 'fundamental,' as a source of 'salvation' and a way of restoring our lost sense of immortality," had many faces.[10] It is the debate over civil defense, and in particular the debate over fallout shelters, that concerns us here, as we examine the language and strategies of that debate in order to understand how government and other rhetors attempted to "naturalize" the bomb (as Roland Barthes might say) and how other parties attempted to resist the totalizing language of the civil defense campaign with a language of their own.[11]

We shall describe at the outset the theoretical perspective that guides our inquiry. To practice rhetorical criticism in "the pragmatic attitude," as we shall show, requires that the critic ground the public discourse in the practices of everyday life. Next, we shall examine, both chronologically and thematically, the public policy debate itself, striving to understand the rhetorical choices and outcomes of that debate in terms of the practices of everyday life in the United States of the 1950s. Finally, we shall comment on what seem to us to be the advantages of rhetorical criticism in "the pragmatic attitude," as demonstrated by this case study.

## ▨ CRITICISM IN THE PRAGMATIC ATTITUDE

The rhetorical critic serves the larger project of cultural criticism to the extent that socio-rhetorical criticism increases our understanding of the dialectical relationship between communication and social relations. Formalist approaches to language and to nonverbal communication are insufficient until the critic shows how the discourse is grounded in actual social practices. The critic discovers in the social practices (*praxis*) of everyday life the customs and narratives people share in the ongoing interpretation of their shared circumstances. Those customs and narratives may have patterns in their form and content, and the critic seeks to understand through these patterns the "structures of everyday life" of a people. The lives have structure and the symbolic discourse has structure, and the two structures have some relationship the critic seeks to understand.

There are several so-called "paradigms" or, more modestly, theoretical models of rhetorical criticism that address the dialectic between social practices and relations, on the one hand, and symbolic discourse, on the other. We draw our own approach from American pragmatism, a philosophical orientation that has all the strengths of British and Continental critical theory since "the linguistic turn," with the added fillip of drawing our attention to the actual practices of everyday life.[12] The anti-theoretical stance of pragmatism suggests that it would be improper to speak of a "pragmatic paradigm" for rhetorical criticism, though we note with approval recent commentaries on the implications of neopragmatism for the study of rhetoric.[13] It might be better to describe, instead, the broad outlines of how one undertakes criticism "in the pragmatic attitude."[14]

The pragmatic approach requires that the close reading of a particular rhetorical text be accompanied by the critic's study of the *structures and practices of everyday life* in the society that is home for the text. In some cases the critic may need to do this work independently, but in most cases the critic may draw upon a growing body of interdisciplinary scholarship in which historians, sociologists, anthropologists, folklorists, sociolinguists, psychologists, cultural geographers, and others collaborate to map the structures of everyday life. These structures, or social practices and relations, constitute the interpretive field for the multiple meanings of a text.

Put differently, the rhetorical critic must understand the "commonsense, taken-for-granted" reality that a people use to interpret messages aimed at them.[15] Everyday life is filled with verbal and nonverbal narratives, and within these narratives we find the cultural *commonplaces,* dense symbols that become the vocabulary for highly connotative communication.[16] Moreover, in the twentieth century we find these commonplaces most often in the folk and mass-mediated cultural systems.[17] Commonplaces draw their power not from some putative "universal" meaning (as some formalist analysis suggests) but from their grounding in particular experience.

Those undertaking the "ethnography of communication" provide a piece of what must come together for rhetorical criticism in the pragmatic attitude. Carbaugh, for example, examines the discourse of Americans on Phil Donahue's television talk show in order to discover both the native genres of speaking and the categories of "personhood" used by Americans within those genres of everyday talk.[18] Carbaugh is especially interested in cultural discourse *about* speaking, and (drawing upon previous work by Katril and Philipsen) he shows how discourse on the "Donahue" show reveals native understandings of speech, self, social roles, and the tangled relationships between these native categories.[19] What Carbaugh has done is to move the ethnography of speaking from the face-to-face scene to a more general, public, cultural scene of discourse.[20]

Similarly, metaphorical analysis needs to be grounded in experience. Too often the critic takes a formalist, rather than a pragmatic, approach to metaphors. That is to say, too often the critic finds clusters of terms within a text and concludes that the audience must understand those metaphors in the ways the formalist analysis suggests. But metaphors are not just the stuff of political oratory and other public discourse. People speak metaphorically all the time, even about speech itself, as Carbaugh and Reddy show in their analysis of folk metaphors about speaking.[21] Lakoff and other sociolinguists have shown us the large repertoire of American metaphorical speaking and what those metaphors tell us about American thought.[22] People learn and practice metaphors and other cultural resources (or commonplaces) in their everyday folk cultures, so no metaphoric analysis is complete without the analysis of folklore.[23]

The rhetorical critic should look to the ethnography of everyday life in order to understand how metaphors in a text might replicate, elaborate, or contradict the lived experiences of the audience. The critic will find in the structures of everyday life that cultural commonplaces appear in formulaic, verbal, and nonverbal narrative structures that may have a grammar and an aesthetic all their own. Part of the critical task is to discover those formulae, those "folk" grammars and aesthetics. Too often the critic brings to texts ethnocentric assumptions about the normative structures and aesthetics of persuasive texts. In particular, we see a critical bias toward a Western, Eurocentric, elite aesthetic, what anthropologist Robert Plant Armstrong calls the "synthetic" aesthetic, when there are good reasons for believing that many of the structures of everyday life are organized by what Armstrong calls a "syndetic" aesthetic. "The synthetic work [of art]," writes Armstrong, "owns inherent principles of *development.* It proceeds through the execution and resolution of opposites. Its successive units are different from one another; and insofar as successive phases grow out of prior ones, the synthetic work is linear." In contrast, he observes out of his expertise in Yoruba sculpture, narrative, song, and dance, the "syndetic work . . . grows in accordance with extrinsic principles; its *growth* is through repetition of the same or of a small inventory of similar units. It does not develop; there is no entailment of the subsequent to be found in the prior."[24] When critics approach a syndetic text (like Russell Conwell's famous address, "Acres of Diamonds") with critical assumptions appropriate to synthetic texts, the critics come away stymied or puzzled that such a poorly constructed text was so successful with the audience.[25] Critics working in the pragmatic attitude realize that there are *folk aesthetics* that members of an audience bring to their understanding of texts.

The pragmatic approach to rhetorical criticism, then, requires that textual analysis be undertaken in a dialectic with the study of the structures of everyday life in the home society of the text. Society, in this view, is a vast network of structures of signification, of verbal and nonverbal narratives. People perceive and remember these narratives not in isolation but as part of a system, a gestalt. Accordingly, an important aspect of the critic's task is to explore the *intertextuality* of this whole system.[26] Texts refer to each other, the ability to understand some texts depends upon experience with others, vocabularies from one text bleed into others, and so on.

The analysis of a public policy campaign, therefore, might look to the intertextuality between the campaign's narratives and the narratives of everyday life. Our choice of the civil defense campaign offers special opportunities and insights as a case study of this approach, for the civil defense campaign was the first major public policy campaign undertaken in a public field increasingly dominated by television and other mass media.[27] Moreover, we have a wealth of scholarship on the practice of everyday life in America of the 1950s, so the campaign for civil defense works well for demonstrating what we have in mind for criticism in the "pragmatic attitude."

## THE EVOLUTION OF CIVIL DEFENSE STRATEGIES

The public debate over civil defense began in the late 1940s with the loss of the American atomic weapon monopoly.[28] In 1949 President Truman ordered a study of civilian defense, and on January 12, 1951, he signed the bill creating a federal Civil Defense Administration. Truman and others understood what the American public did not, that is, that notions about bombs and civilian defense forged in World War II were a deceptive, grossly inadequate base upon which to build civilian defense against atomic bombs. The architects of a campaign for civil defense immediately saw the rhetorical dilemma they faced. "Keeping civilians in a constant state of fear," explained *Time* in its cover story of October 2, 1950, "would produce impossible local demands on governments and provoke the panic in an emergency which would compound catastrophe. Kept in a state of induced calm—even if that were possible—people would get apathetic."[29] So the rhetors responsible for selling civil defense to the American audience would have to frame their campaign carefully; too much emphasis upon danger would either panic citizens or drive them to fatalism, while too little would fail to stir the apathetic.

In the politics of nuclear culture, governments and people take action in order to avoid the use of nuclear weapons. The arms build-up was, of course, the fundamental strategy in the ritual drama of "deterrence." But government planners also saw that civil defense plans were an equally important element in an overall strategy meant to discourage the use of nuclear weapons. Only two basic civil defense approaches seemed feasible to strategic planners: dispersal and evacuation of the population from cities, or fallout shelters.

**Dispersal and Evacuation**

While there always was recognition that shelters would have to play a part in a comprehensive civil defense package, early campaigns favored dispersal and evacuation. It seems clear from the public literature that one motive for preferring these strategies was revulsion against the thought of hiding underground. *U.S. News and World Report* previewed a new book, *Must We Hide?*, introducing to the American public the strategy of dispersal, of decentralizing America's cities, spreading both industrial, residential, and strategic zones out into satellites or huge concentric circles, or along major highways.[30] Thus, explained the magazine, New York City makes a good target with its 21,000 persons per square mile, but Los Angeles makes a poor one with only 3,000 persons per square mile.[31] Even the *Bulletin of Atomic Scientists* supported dispersal, devoting the entirety of its September, 1951, issue to the idea.[32] Dispersal seemed to even the most pacifistic atomic scientist a workable deterrent. But centrally planned dispersal would be an extremely expensive project. Moreover, dispersal was going on in any case, as the Fifties witnessed the suburbanization of American residential patterns.[33]

The role of evacuation in the early civil defense plans and campaign suffered a fate similar to that of dispersal. Even when the technology of delivering nuclear weapons led planners to believe that they would have hours after the first alert, the logistics of evacuating large cities seemed insurmountable to many. Gene Marine, *The Nation*'s West Coast correspondent and resident of San Francisco, used the occasion of finding a civil defense pamphlet, *It's Your Life* (San Francisco Disaster Council and

Corps), in his mailbox to show how ridiculous the evacuation plans for San Francisco would be in the case of an atomic attack.[34] The confirmation of the existence of Soviet ICBMs and their fifteen-minute warning time eventually made evacuation hopeless.

Besides, evacuation seemed provocative in a way dispersal did not. The debate over evacuation began to focus less on logistics and more upon the fundamental paradox of civil defense—namely, that evacuating a city during international crises might seem to the enemy a prelude to a first strike and, therefore, actually increase the risk of nuclear war by inviting the enemy to strike in response to evacuation. Thus, by the late Fifties the most widely discussed civil defense strategy was the shelter.

## The Fallout Shelter

The earliest stage of the campaign for civil defense built upon the recent experiences of Americans during World War II. Newsreel images of the London blitz led the general American public to think of immediate postwar shelters as "bomb shelters" against the blast and fire, but as news of the firestorms of Tokyo became general knowledge, few held the view that atomic age shelters would do much near ground zero. Indeed, while mass circulation magazines spoke of "air raid shelters" through most of the 1950s, the increasingly preferred terms were "atomic bomb shelter" and "fallout shelter."

Most of the public and private discourse by Americans during World War II pictured a cooperative community working together toward a just goal. Newsreel commentaries, theatrical films, and other narratives told stories of cooperative group efforts on the battlefield and on the home front. These stories included tales of self-sacrifice for others on both fronts. The first attempts at legitimating the notion of civil defense relied upon the war experiences of Americans, but with the added complication of the atom bomb.

Civil defense advocates assumed that their first task was to clear away the vast ignorance and accompanying inflated fear Americans had about atomic weapons. The usual approach in the mass circulation magazines was to paint an imaginary scenario of what would happen if the bombs started dropping on, say, New York City. The *Time* cover story of October 2, 1950, posed this "Horrendous Hypothesis," positing a single 50-megaton bomb detonated half a mile over Union Square. But after describing the destruction the initial blast would create, the *Time* writers imagined a scenario in which a coordinated civil defense system would respond from the undamaged periphery of the blast. Firefighters, physicians, construction crews, Boy Scouts, and dozens of other categories of helpers would mobilize to provide for the survivors. The New York City Welfare Department had plans "to organize such big chain restaurants as the Horn and Hardart automats to prepare food . . . ; clothing would be requisitioned from the big department stores."[35]

Still, *Time* made it clear that the logistics, especially the medical, were frightening. The 600,000 pints of blood that would be needed to care for the estimated 100,000 casualties would fill 17 freight cars, and the city's 17,000 doctors (or however many survived the blast) would be unable to give adequate care to the injured. *Time* then sounded a theme that would persist throughout the next twelve years of the debate:

> People would have to be taught to look out for themselves. . . . But the necessity went beyond that.
>
> Said one state medical officer: "These booklets are all right. But people have to be trained. . . . Everyone must become his brother's keeper."
>
> As a matter of fact, if every department enrolled all the volunteers they said they needed, one out of every ten people in the city would have a specific job in the army of civilian defense. Many more would have to help out at a moment's notice. The biblical injunction to love thy neighbor was being forced on men by man's own unneighborliness. Communism and the atom had posed a problem of total war in which civilians were totally involved.[36]

This passage raises several themes that came to dominate civil defense advocacy. Central was the relatively new idea of total war in which *every citizen is a "soldier"* in an "army of civil defense." By this vision, Americans had a duty to be prepared to be self-reliant in an emergency. But this was not the self-reliance of an isolated individual. Rather, there emerged here an understanding of self-reliance as a quality that serves the collectivity. "Preparation of the private mind and will to meet [war] anywhere, any time, in any form," wrote Philip Wylie in a 1951 article for *The Atlantic Monthly*, "is *the* fundamental requirement not just for the defense of cities but for victory." "What the circumstance amounts to, for the urban dweller," Wylie reasoned,

> is this: from the day of the declaration of another war, or the season of imminent war, he will be a front-line soldier. His conduct, as much as that of troops, will determine the outcome.
>
> In preparing himself to stand by his city he will find the courage which does not and cannot exist in defense or evacuation schemes. Furthermore, in readying his city to aid other stricken cities, and in knowing that they have the training to help his city, he will have a second bolster to his determination. These are active, offensive, humanly positive, and characteristically American attitudes and ways of behavior.[37]

Wylie's exhortation shared with the writers on the staff of *Time* and *U.S. News and World Report* a vision that Americans surviving an atomic attack will rally and cooperate. Individual preparedness, therefore, was an expression of commitment to the group, an extension (under new circumstances, to be sure) of the wartime sense of cooperative community.

The *every-citizen-a-soldier theme*, therefore, necessitated a second theme that arose in the earliest stage of the campaign for civil defense, namely, the *knowledge-is-power theme*. This theme wedded an American faith in rationality with a faith in technology to argue that civil defense is possible in the nuclear age. "It is in our nature to find the better way of doing a thing—of finding a solution to any problem," asserted the authors of a 1960 pamphlet designed as a text for a civil defense course:

> Through intelligent action we lay bare the mysteries of a threat—and then act to overcome it. The threat of modern weapons is no exception: we are learning ways to blunt their effects.
>
> Some excellent measures already exist. Through research, education, and training, other protective means will be developed. As in the past, the dangers cannot be wished away. Intelligent planning and hard work will be necessary. Indifference is a luxury we cannot afford.[38]

Those planning the civil defense campaign in the 1950s had a new term, "fallout," that was the source of a great deal of public confusion and anxiety. The *demystification of fallout* became, therefore, a fundamental rhetorical strategy throughout the Fifties and into the Sixties.[39] The 1949 *U.S. News and World Report* article on Dr. Lapp's book lamented the fact that atomic secrecy "has bred rumors, fantastic stories, many distortions."[40] John W. M. Bunker, Dean of the Graduate School at MIT, reassured our public jitters in 1951 by arguing that if "fear is accompanied by understanding, if we know what to expect, then in spite of fear we by and large act credibly and usefully when the test comes."[41] After acknowledging the initial dangers of blast and heat in an atomic bombing, Bunker proceeded patiently to demystify "radiation" and "fallout." "Invisible, like X rays," wrote Bunker, nuclear radiation "has great penetration without causing any sensation in the person receiving it. Like X rays, a small amount does no harm, more will make one ill, and too much can cause death." But Bunker assured his readers that the "great danger from this source is the first ten seconds," and that taking cover will protect the individual. Most people in an atomic attack would receive radiation doses from which they would recover. "The body cells have a power of recovery from radiation damage which has not been measured for man, but it is certainly substantial." "Decontamination," he explained, "is a long word which means removal of dirt from surfaces where the dirt has become radioactive or consists in part of radioactive fragments caused by an A-bomb explosion."[42]

The demystification of fallout continued to follow these twin strategies—assure people that radiation is a natural background to the universe, and assure them that they can easily cleanse themselves of the more dangerous kind of dirt. In explaining to its readers that food would not be radioactive, *Popular Mechanics* noted that

> an astonishing number of people have a grossly mistaken idea about fallout. There's nothing spooky about it. It is a substance like dust or dirt. It falls to Earth

like dust. It can be washed away or swept up and removed, like dust. Unlike ordinary dust, it gives off X rays that can damage living tissue, which is why people must hide from it behind dense material that stops the rays. But fallout radiation decays fast. In two days it is less than one percent of what it was at one hour.[43]

The paradigmatic moment in the rhetorical demystification of fallout occurred with the government's publication and distribution of several million copies of the 1958 brochure, "Facts About Fallout Protection." After explaining what fallout is and how ill prolonged exposure to radiation can make a person, the pamphlet informs the audience that the key is placing "dense material" such as earth, sand, even books and magazines, between oneself and the fallout. "If you think you have been in a fallout area," explains the pamphlet, featuring a reassuring drawing of an individual taking a shower, "wash yourself and your clothes thoroughly. If you can't wash your clothes and dispose of the water, leave your clothes outside." In summary, concluded the pamphlet, fallout is dangerous, but the average citizen can protect himself or herself against the danger.[44] "Be prepared," intoned the civil defense publications, invoking the motto of the Boy Scouts, a familiar institution in suburban America. Part of being prepared was gaining knowledge about fallout and decontamination.

Strangely, all the talk about fallout and decontamination would have had a special appeal to Americans of the 1950s. Anthropologists have shown how powerful a cultural symbol is dirt, especially in its threat to contaminate the human body.[45] The body stands, moreover, as a symbol of the social order, so threats to the body become, *mutatis mutandis,* threats to the social order. Dirt disturbs order. Thus, the metaphoric cluster CLEAN/DIRTY taps a fundamental human symbolism. But we need to add that cleanliness was an especially potent symbol for Americans in their everyday lives in the 1950s. The critic marvels at the way "clean" and metaphors of cleanliness pervaded 1950s talk. Perhaps in the American mind the Depression of the 1930s and the war years seemed "dark," "dirty," and "disorderly," something to be put behind them as they emerged in the sunlight and prosperity of the 1950s. Millions of Americans moved from the "dirty" city to the new and clean suburbs. The everyday aesthetics of suburban Americans favored "clean lines" in everything from kitchen appliances to patio furniture to automobiles.[46] Advertisements on television were dominated by cleaning products, linking prosperity, happiness, and cleanliness. Civil defense explanations of fallout as just another kind of "dirt" and the importance of "decontamination" would have appealed to most citizens. The strategy was to *domesticate* fallout, both in the sense of taming it and in the more important sense of linking it to routine chores in the home.

As all the talk about fallout and decontamination made clear, survival would depend upon citizens' taking shelter. Although public shelters had their advocates throughout the debate, the emphasis in the 1950s and 1960s discourse was upon home shelters. The effort to "domesticate" fallout was part of the larger effort to "domesticate" the entire issue of survival. Americans had a duty to survive, but the unit of survival (as the unit of living) was to be the suburban family. Americans would come to understand the fallout shelter issue in terms of the family and of the family home. Government rhetors attempted to exploit this "intertextuality" between images of the home and images of the fallout shelter.

The campaign for Americans to build fallout shelters responded directly to developments in foreign affairs. Whenever the Cold War heated up, fallout shelters became an issue again. CIA Director Allen Dulles brought to the August, 1959, U.S. Governors' Conference in San Juan, Puerto Rico, classified documents to bolster Governor Nelson Rockefeller's proposal for the governors to get their citizens to build private shelters. Rockefeller had made headlines in July by sponsoring a New York plan that would make home shelters compulsory. Convinced that an adequate family-sized basement shelter could be built by "do-it-yourself" homeowners for $150 and by a contractor for $500, Rockefeller's Special Task Force on Protection from Radioactive Fallout had recommended a state law requiring fallout shelters in all new buildings, including private homes.[47] Despite the considerable public resistance against the idea, the *Time* writer covering the story accepted the argument made by Rockefeller and his task force. "But these criticisms missed the essential point," said *Time*, "that deterrent power will deter only to the extent that the enemy is convinced of the U.S.'s willingness to use it—and the willingness would be a lot plainer if the nation's citizens had the protection of fallout shelters." This was the message that Dulles carried to the other governors at the San Juan conference, namely, that a nationwide system of private fallout shelters "would blunt the effectiveness of nuclear blackmail."[48] Despite Dulles's plea for the plan as an important adjunct to American foreign policy, the U.S. governors were not persuaded.

Over the next year, Rockefeller became the important point man for the private shelter campaign. On March 4, 1960, he delivered an extemporaneous speech on the "Importance of Shelters in Nuclear Age" [*sic*] at a luncheon of the Men's Civil Defense Seminar of the New York State Civil Defense Commission, and the speech appeared within a month in *Vital Speeches*.[49] At the same time, the April issue of *Foreign Affairs* featured an article by Rockefeller on "Purpose and Policy," in which he laid out the foreign policy alternatives facing the United States in five important areas.[50] The Rockefeller speech established themes that were to persist at the center of the shelter controversy for the next few years. Shelters play an important role "in strengthening the hand of our government in its pursuit of peace with justice, in its efforts to deter attack, and to deter the use of nuclear blackmail as a means of destroying this country's will to resist."[51] Shelters, therefore, are a form of insurance policy that costs one hundred dollars per person sheltered, and who in the audience wouldn't pay one hundred dollars to save his child's life? It is a citizen's duty to save lives, including his own, argued Rockefeller. Finally, the governor played the most valuable trump card of Cold War discourse: "The Soviets are doing it," he warned; "they have compulsory shelters in new construction. . . ."[52]

Rockefeller's comparison between a family fallout shelter and a family insurance policy was aimed, no doubt, at reinforcing the domesticity theme. But despite its obvious appeal, the theme did not seem to work. The Rockefeller initiative in the fallout shelter campaign came to an abrupt end with the state legislature's rejection of the plan and with Rockefeller's increasing preoccupation with presidential election year doings. The campaign had never really gained momentum. By mid-1961, Americans had built only nine thousand private shelters and the issue seemed resolved.[53] Then, in July of that year, the Soviet Union found a way to revive the issue.

President Kennedy came before a nationwide television audience on the evening of July 25, 1961, to explain what he intended to do about Soviet actions in and around Berlin. After reminding his audience of the strategic and symbolic importance of Berlin, Kennedy outlined the response he was making to Soviet provocations. First, he was going to supplement the defense build-ups begun earlier in the year. Second, he was reorganizing the nation's civil defense planning, with an emphasis upon identifying and stocking existing private and public fallout shelters:

> In the event of attack, the lives of families which are not hit in a nuclear blast and fire can still be saved, if they can be warned to take shelter, and if that shelter is available.
> We owe that kind of insurance to our families and to our country. . . .
> In the coming months I hope to let every citizen know what steps he can take without delay to protect his family in case of attack. I know that you will want to do no less.[54]

Kennedy was using Rockefeller's "insurance" and "family protection" metaphors, tropes aimed at reinforcing the view that building a family shelter was simply a domestic duty. But Kennedy was appropriating the family insurance metaphor in the service of a very different shelter program. Judging the earlier campaign for home shelters to have failed, the president attempted to shift public policy in the direction of public shelters. The $207 million bomb shelter program Kennedy sent to Congress shortly after his Berlin Crisis speech included $93 million for "surveying basements, subways, abandoned mines, and other underground caverns which could be used as radiation shelter space,"[55] $10 million for radiation measuring devices to be used by civil defense and rescue workers, and $7.5 million to build shelters in all new federal buildings.[56] The aim, finally, was to find shelter space for 45–50 million Americans.

Despite Kennedy's desire to create public, community shelters, his Berlin Crisis speech immediately renewed interest in private fallout shelters. *Time* reported on the boom, from Dallas' Acme Bomb & Fallout Shelters Co. to Sacramento's Atlas Bomb Shelter. "For two years I've starved in this business," one Orlando, Florida, shelter builder explained to *Time*. "But since Kennedy's defense talk, I've averaged two sales a day at $2,195 each."[57] Business was greatest in California, reported *Time:* "Fox Hole Shelter, Inc., offshoot of a swimming-pool firm that got into shelters two years ago by turning its original product upside down, has already sold 236 Fox Holes from San Luis Obispo to San Diego."[58] Charlatans of all sorts entered the market.

The cover story for the September 15, 1961, issue of *Life* magazine promised to tell readers "How You Can Survive Fallout," claiming that "97 out of 100 people can be saved." The special section began with a letter from President Kennedy outlining the government's actions to identify and stock public shelters and urging citizens "to read and consider seriously the contents of this issue of LIFE. . . . The ability to survive coupled with the will to do so therefore are essential to our country."[59] The accompanying feature article showed readers drawings and construction plans for three different kinds of shelters that could be built for modest expense. The drawings are remarkable for the orderliness and high spirits they portray in the sheltered family.

Critics of fallout shelters complained about the claims in *Life* and in a November syndicated series of newspaper articles about both the number of lives to be saved and the comforts of living in shelters. An editorial in *The Nation* mocked the newspaper articles for showing an illustration of "a beautiful blonde in shorts taking goodies out of a well-filled freezer next to her bed. The power company has been unaffected by the bombs and she and her family (not shown) will eat their fill of unspoiled delicacies while the radiation dies down."[60]

This rush to buy fallout shelters in the wake of Kennedy's Berlin speech was short-lived, and by May of 1962 *Time* was attributing the demise of the private shelter business to the combined effects of a "lull in the cold war plus the Kennedy Administration's decision to stress large-scale, community shelters over backyard bunkers."[61] Yet, the scare did produce a substantial public debate about fallout shelters and civil defense in general, and it is in the details of that debate that we find the richest discourse for discovering how the shelter debate was over a good deal more than holes in the ground.

First, the critic is struck by the pervasiveness of the *rebuilding civilization theme* driving much of the discourse in favor of shelters. There is in American Protestant eschatology a strong strain of Manichaeanism, of the early Christian heresy that painted the world as caught in a struggle between the Kingdom of Darkness and the Kingdom of Light. Apocalyptic visions are central to this eschatology, and the stunning scale of destruction possible with nuclear weapons made it difficult for many Americans to resist seeing in the atom bomb the Apocalyptic fire prophesied in the Book of Revelation.

But there were secular as well as religious interpretations of the bomb and the Apocalypse. "Typically," writes an historian of the decade, "the science fiction imagination of the fifties foretold not an ending but a beginning; the world crashes in ruins, but the survivors in those ruins pick themselves up and go on from there, as survivors always have."[62] The advantage the survivors have is of starting over, bereft of the complexities and dead-ends of the civilization that was lost when the bombs fell. The drama becomes one of what shall be selected from the past to pass on to the future.

Like this fiction of a post-nuclear war, much of the rhetoric in the campaign for shelters took the view that the chance to rebuild civilization might not be such a bad thing. "In Malibu," reported a *Time* article on the resurging interest in home shelters,

> Missile Scientist and Electronics Manufacturer Bernard Benson, his wife, and seven children had a $15,000 shelter built to withstand any bomb damage but a direct hit. Along with food and water, Benson had stocked his hideout with beer and a 1925 edition of the *Encyclopedia Britannica.* A nuclear attack, says he, will set civilization back at least one generation; with the 1925 *Britannica* to tell him how, he will start life over again at the national norm.[63]

A *Time* cover story the week of October 20, 1960, described an upbeat scenario. Most Americans would emerge from their shelters finding not a scorched earth but pretty much the green land they left. "With information gleaned from radio reports and radiation-detection devices, with trousers tucked into sock tops and sleeves tied around wrists, with hats, mufflers, gloves, and boots," explained *Time,* "the shelter dweller could venture forth to start ensuring his today and building for his tomorrow."[64] Within two weeks, things will have returned to normal. "This must necessarily be the most critical phase of the thermonuclear war," explained *Time,* picking up the official position on civil defense preparedness as a civic duty, "for the nation that can arise most quickly and strongly will be the nation that best survives."[65]

Usually accompanying the theme of rebuilding civilization was a related theme, that of a *heroically cooperative community* emerging from the shelters to help one another. While most Americans would have to be on their own for a few weeks after emerging from their shelters, admitted a *U.S. News & World Report* article, people would work together until the government could help out. Based upon people's working together in the face of natural disasters, civil defense planners were counting on that same spirit. "People would band together to protect themselves against looters," predicted *U.S. News,* "pool their supplies and set up group kitchens to conserve food and fuel. Foraging parties would set out to find more food and fuel. Makeshift hospitals and nurseries would be set up to care for the sick and the children. All these things Americans have done in the past—and would do again if the bombs drop."[66]

In all, these narratives of the sheltered life seemed to be saying, a nuclear war might not be so unpleasant. Well-informed and well-prepared citizens would simply move underground for two weeks, at most, and emerge to help one another rebuild their communities. Americans would survive, and their survival would amount to a rebirth (perhaps a resurrection, if Lifton is correct about the mythic power of nuclearism). Our way of life would continue, even would prevail, if enough Americans could be persuaded to prepare to shelter themselves.

## The Resistance

Not all the public rhetoric in the late 1950s and early 1960s came from the proponents of shelters. As a counterpoint to the science fiction that took an optimistic view toward a post-apocalyptic world, one science fiction text, Nevil Shute's *On the Beach* (1957), became a remarkable presence running through the debate. As a novel and then as a 1959 theatrical film directed by Stanley Kramer and starring Gregory Peck, Ava Gardner, Anthony Perkins, and Fred Astaire, *On the Beach* became a benchmark text for people on both sides of the civil defense debate.[67] Rockefeller singled out the film for criticism in his March 4 speech. A basic objective of any military operation, explained the governor, is "to break the people's will to resist. I don't know how many of you have seen the movie 'On the Beach'," he continued. "I know some of my kids saw it, and I want to tell you, that is a great way to destroy peoples' will to resist, because they come out of that movie saying, 'There is nothing we can do.' "[68] In describing and analyzing the Rockefeller civil defense program for the readers of *The Bulletin of Atomic Scientists*, Ralph E. Lapp also fell into using *On the Beach* as symptomatic of a fatalism that was interfering with people's dispassionate consideration of civil defense plans.[69]

Civil defense officials recognized the problem they faced. In a *Commonweal* article covering favorably the hearings of the Special Subcommittee on Radiation of the U.S. Congress Joint Committee on Atomic Energy, one author blamed the film for the public's general impression "that any nuclear attack would be a total one. And, most unfortunately, this belief has been reinforced by such improbable pictures of nuclear war as that which was presented in Neville [*sic*] Shute's story. . . . Other experts who appeared before the subcommittee were equally concerned about the impressions and attitudes created by *On the Beach.*"[70] On the other side, student protesters borrowed the motto, "There Is Still Time, Brother," from the film when they demonstrated against Operation Alert on May 3rd of 1960.[71] Rarely in rhetorical campaigns has a popular culture text so dominated the public discourse as did *On the Beach.*

Nor was the 1960 protest the first of its kind. Pacifist social movement organizations perceived early in the Cold War that civil defense programs amounted to a form of militarism in a world where new weapons and new military tactics made obsolete the distinction between combatants and non-combatants.[72] Pacifists took seriously the civil defense campaigns' argument that every citizen would be a "front-line" soldier in World War III, and they concluded, logically, that their conscientious objection to war should include conscientious objection to civil defense operations. As early as 1951–52 the War Resisters League distributed a leaflet outlining three courses of action open to the ordinary citizen in case of nuclear attack:

(1) Clear out of the country now, while the going is good.
(2) Carry a Geiger counter to detect radiation, stay away from windows, keep water in your bathtub, wear a dogtag around your neck to show your bloodtype, practise [sic] crawling under the bed, and hope for the best.
(3) (If 1 and 2 do not appeal to you) See that war does NOT break out. Because "There is no defense against atomic bombs, and none is to be expected. Preparedness against atomic warfare is futile and, if attempted, will ruin the structure of the social order." (Emergency Committee of Atomic Scientists, Albert Einstein, Chairman.)[73]

In this and other texts of resistance, the rhetors adopted the strategy of relanguaging the civil defense discourse, saying directly (and sometimes brutally) what the language of the civil defense rhetors tried to "domesticate" and naturalize. Apparently the social movement rhetors recognized early that the federal bureaucracy emerging in postwar America was one that had learned well the power of language to define reality, and that opposition to civil defense would have to unmask the government's double-speak. "We would do well," wrote two pacifists in a related context, "to follow Camus' prescription for clarity and refuse to let vague abstraction mask the harsh reality; refuse to say of the man condemned to death: 'He's going to pay his debt to society,' but rather 'They're going to cut his head off.' "[74] This relanguaging of violence became a key rhetorical strategy in the campaign against civil defense and stood in marked contrast to the clean and safe imagery of the government discourse.

"Operation Alert," a national Civil Defense "mock thermonuclear attack" drill scheduled for June 15, 1955, offered pacifists the first opportunity for nonviolent resistance against what they took to be the involuntary conscription of all citizens into a military exercise.[75] The Fellowship of Reconciliation prepared for the drill by publishing and distributing "A Sane Man's Guide to Civil Defense: Being a Glossary of Terms Useful for the Citizen Hoping to Remain Unvaporized after the Bombs Drop."[76] The pamphlet relanguages the new civil defense vocabulary, such as

DOG-TAGS—Small metal identification tags being circulated through milk and other commercial companies. If tag is not vaporized, will be used to identify unvaporized remains, if any, by survivors, if any and if interested. . . .
SHELTER—A now-obsolete hole in the ground in which citizens of target city were supposed to crouch for protection against air-raids. Earth-shaking force of

H-bomb explosions would crush underground shelters for miles around; flames from fireball would suck oxygen out of any that remained uncrushed, thus simultaneously suffocating and roasting inhabitants.

When the 1955 drill began, a group calling itself the Provisional Defense Committee and working out of the offices of the War Resisters League in New York City committed civil disobedience in a park near City Hall by refusing to take shelter when the sirens sounded. Police quickly arrested 28 protestors, including Provisional Defense Committee leaders Dorothy Day, A. J. Muste, Ralph DiGia, Kent Larrabee, and Bayard Rustin. During their trial and in publications by the group, the protestors explained their view that "civil defense, especially in our nuclear age, is an intrinsic part of the military machine, the preparation for war, to which they conscientiously object."[77] The judge found the defendants guilty (some had pled guilty as an act of conscience) and issued suspended sentences. The same group of pacifists protested the July 20, 1956, civil defense drill, making the same arguments as the year before. Nineteen were arrested protesting that day's drill in New York, and Dorothy Day led another 12 pacifists who were arrested for failing to take cover during the July 12, 1957, drill.[78]

A professionally printed handbill announcing "Civil Defense Protest Day" on May 3, 1960, during that year's "Operational Alert," reiterated the point that "Civil defense is no defense." After describing the destruction and chaos that a single hydrogen bomb would wreak on New York City, the authors of the handbill invited citizens to join the protest: "Your life, the lives of your families and children, depends on the prevention of war and not in playing wasteful civil defense games." The handbill then recommended to the citizen a range of possible acts, from writing letters to the governor and mayor to inviting arrest through civil disobedience. "Those who refuse to take shelter," explained the authors, "will do so not out of any light impulse to break the law, but on grounds of conscience. They have not reached their decision without careful thought." Finally, the authors connected theirs with other well-known causes and traditions of political resistance: "Those who know of the recent sit-downs in the South, who remember the struggles of women to get the vote and of Labor to organize will recognize the American tradition in these methods of non-violent resistance."[79]

By the 1961 drill date, the Civil Defense Protest Committee had grown considerably. A news release announcing plans to protest the April 28 nationwide Civil Defense drill claimed that over 500 protestors committed civil disobedience in the 1960 drill; clearly, the organizers expected as many in 1961.[80] The printed handbill for the 1961 protest, entitled "Brave Men Do Not Hide," again made the "no defense" argument and mustered quotations from Eleanor Roosevelt, New Jersey Governor Meyner, and Ohio Senator Young in order to support the authors' view that the only defense is peace. The 1961 handbill drew stark contrast between cowardice/bravery and between childishness/maturity in confronting the Bomb:

> It is easy, when the sirens whine, to run down into a basement or cower in a doorway. But that will not protect your child. It will not save your family. Brave men do not hide from danger. They face the danger openly and fight against it. The greatest danger now is war. The real defense against hydrogen bombs is peace.
>
> The men who plan Civil Defense are good men but they threaten the safety of America because they are trying to convince us we can survive another war. *We cannot survive another war.* We will find our safety in disarmament, not in basements. We appeal to the Civil Defense Officials to stop playing children's games. We appeal to them to act like grown men and to speak the truth to the citizens of New York.[81]

So the authors of these texts drew carefully upon reliable appeals to family safety and to conscience in making their case for a pacifist response to civil defense. Most powerfully, though, these authors and others in the anti-nuclear, peace movement of the 1950s and 1960s repeatedly returned to the contrasting set SANE/INSANE in order to capture rationality on the side of those opposing civil defense.[82] In a decade that placed high value on rational expertise in general and upon psychological and other social science expertise in particular, the critics of civil defense had found a key metaphor for discrediting the government's own "expert" plans and planners.[83]

The opposition to civil defense measures, especially private shelters, also generated a public debate over *lifeboat ethics* in 1950s America. In response to newspaper and magazine reports that many shelter owners were equipping their shelters with guns to repel intruders, the Rev. L. C. McHugh wrote in the Jesuit magazine, *America,* a brief essay on "Ethics at the Shelter Doorway." McHugh shocked even some of his fellow editors at *America* by arguing that it was morally justifiable for a shelter owner to protect his family and shelter by whatever means possible, including armed violence.[84] This view, which has some legitimation in the history of the Church's moral theology, caused an immediate controversy. Washington's Episcopal Bishop Angus Dun fired back at McHugh. "I do not see how any Christian conscience can condone a policy which puts supreme emphasis on saving your own skin without regard for the plight of your brother," said Bishop Dun. "Justice, mercy, and brotherly love do not cease to operate, even in the final apocalypse."[85] Dun also raised the social class question, noting that some families cannot afford individual family shelters.[86] Besides, said the Bishop, appealing finally to a Social Darwinian sensibility related to the vision of a heroic collectivity, "the kind of man who will be most desperately needed in a post-attack world is least likely to dig himself a private mole-hole that has no room for his neighbor."[87]

A moralist of a different sort addressed the lifeboat ethics of the fallout shelter that same fall. The September 29, 1961, episode of *Twilight Zone* (just entering its third season on CBS) was a half-hour videoplay, "The Shelter," written by series creator Rod Serling. In that story, it is a UFO scare that sends a family to its fallout shelter and triggers the transformation of a close community of neighbors into a bigoted, violent mob trying to batter down the shelter door. The alert is suddenly cancelled as the UFOs are identified as harmless satellites, but the shelter family and their neighbors know that their relations will never be the same again.[88]

There were other voices that shared Serling's view that, rather than rise as a heroic collectivity from the rubble of a nuclear attack, Americans were more likely to revert to an ugly struggle for survival. For some analysts, this outcome was foreshadowed by public reponse to Kennedy's July 25 Berlin Crisis speech. "The public panic, the theological disputes on the limits of Christian charity, and the activities of fast-buck shelter entrepreneurs," wrote Ronald Steel in a *Commonweal* essay, "have unleashed an element of savage social irresponsibility that lurks beneath American individualism."[89]

To arguments about the illusion of civil defense and the troubling ethical questions raised by shelters, some critics added an argument that tapped into the same fears the civil defense rhetors had counted on— namely, the argument that civil defense increased the likelihood of nuclear holocaust. In a November 10, 1961, speech delivered in San Francisco before The Commonwealth Club of California, *Scientific American* publisher Gerard Piel argued carefully his thesis that shelter building actually made a Third World War more likely, and that "civil defense is an illusion."[90] Piel raised, once more, the theme that critics of civil defense had raised since the early Fifties, namely, the "paradox" of civil defense: "In all humanity, we must encourage measures that can save the lives of individuals. In the national interest, one must seek to minimize the number of casualties. But if such measures enhance the feasibility of thermonuclear war, then they may also raise the probability of war" (p. 240). Piel explained to his audience in great detail the likely effects of nuclear attack and the nature of the real threat. Erroneous military theory, argued Piel, led the government to suppose that fallout is the greatest danger, whereas far more serious are the incendiary effects of an attack, against which fallout shelters are useless. "We are assured," said Piel, getting finally to his Apocalyptic vision, "that the empty world of 'On the Beach' is pure fiction. But the firestorms of a thermonuclear war could work an irreversible disruption of the social and moral fabric of Western Civilization. The kind of society that would emerge from the shelters may be guessed from the kind of society that is preparing to go into the shelters now" (p. 243).

Piel's examples of the sorts of people preparing to enter shelters were not pretty. The new consciousness "erupts in an ugly way, at the middle level, in the vigilante league of Las Vegas and Bakersfield against the prospective flood of refugees from Los Angeles. It shames our people," he continued, "before the world in the climax of American privatism that prescribes a sawed-off shotgun as equipment for the family fallout shelter" (p. 244). "The social cost of going underground," concluded Piel, "would not fall short of the total transformation of our way of life, the suspension of our civil institutions, the habituation of our people to violence and the ultimate militarization of our society" (p. 244). Piel urged disarmament as the only way out of the deadly paradoxes of the thermonuclear age.

By the Spring of 1962, Americans were over their brief panic and the issue of fallout shelters again became moot. *U.S. News and World Report* took a sampling of American opinions in the Fall of 1961 and quoted liberally from the interviews to document the degree to which the "prevailing attitude is one of fatalism."[91] The fatalism had a fair dose of cynicism. There was some feeling that the campaign for civil defense was "misleading and dishonest," "hypocritical and absurd on its face."[92] On October 14, 1961, *The Nation* editorialized against the shelter campaign with strong charges. "The shelter as a symbol of safety may make people feel better before the holocaust," wrote the editors, "but it will not protect the vast majority if the holocaust comes. The shelter campaign is the dirtiest deception ever perpetrated on a nation of sheep."[93] Roger Hagan escalated the attack on the shelter campaign a few weeks later in a long article in *The Nation*. The civil defense officials, charged Hagan, are guilty of bad faith. They know that America will never have an adequate shelter system, so "they have found a cheap alternative, and it is the public-relations man's way out: to convince the people that they are sheltered even when they are not. That is the great ugliness of the moment."[94]

Whatever the combination of fatalism and cynicism, neither the American public nor Congress was succumbing to the heavily financed campaign for civil defense and fallout shelters. In searching for that active response lying somewhere between fatalism and apathy, the rhetors failed dramatically and had squandered in the process a good deal of the government's credibility in the matter of Cold War strategy.

In October of 1962, the Cuban Missile Crisis once again heated up the Cold War, but a public opinion survey conducted early in 1963 showed that when Americans were asked to choose from a list of seven issues the one most important to the United States, they ranked fallout shelters seventh.[95] Whereas in a 1960 sample 21% of Americans admitted having considered building a fallout shelter and in late 1961, 48% had considered the possibility, only 25% had considered such in the post-Cuba lull. A majority of Americans "favored" shelters abstractly, but few built them.[96]

While it is difficult to pinpoint the reasons why Americans never really embraced civil defense programs—ironically the one aspect of nuclearism that had an action component for the average citizen—our examination of the multiple texts resisting civil defense suggests that the rhetoric of the resistors may have been closer to the practices of everyday life than was the civil defense rhetoric. Certainly the novels, television dramas, and films about nuclear war reinforced the language and imagery of groups like the Provisional Defense Committee. The texts of resistance built their narratives around the fundamental paradox of civil defense—namely, that civil defense might make war more likely. That argument alone may have been forceful enough to induce fatalism in some, active resistance in others. But the rhetoric of resistance also tapped a fundamental tension in American life, and it is to that tension we finally turn.

### The Tension between Home and Community

The Second World War created in most Americans a sense of global challenge to which Americans arose collectively. Both in the armed services and on the home front, public discourse stressed cooperation, collectivity, and community. The force fields of public rhetoric during the war were centripetal, pulling things toward the center. The war accelerated the concentration of power in large organizations begun in the Depression, as college trained technocrats came to assume their mantle of planning power. The managed economy of the 1930s led naturally to the managed war of the 1940s.

All of this was backdrop for a new set of forces converging in the 1950s. Demographic forces were now centrifugal, spinning populations out from the cities into new suburbs. Americans were engaged in their own version of a policy of dispersal, and the single-family, ranch-style home became the desired norm. Suburbanized Americans were faced with the need to redefine "community" in an institutional setting that was neither rural nor urban.

Moreover, the emerging domestic ideal of the 1950s elevated the nuclear family and its home as the institution that would bring order and security to American life. As historian Elaine Tyler May notes, the rhetoric legitimating the new domesticity attempted to make stable private life a public duty and virtue. But in the debate over private and public shelters, for example, the home shelter tapped into a more powerful, private domestic image. Advocates of home shelters saw their alternative use as a "cool family room," and the iconography of the home shelter campaign featured two striking images—one of the full larder to be stored in the shelter, a reassuring sign of American abundance, and the other of a nuclear family going about its domestic business in a living space aesthetically similar to the design world of the 1950s.[97] But in these design similarities lurked an obvious contradiction. Whereas the new ranch-style American home was open, rambling, and spacious, the fallout shelter was closed, small, and dark. Americans wanted homes with picture windows and other design features dissolving the sharp boundaries between inside and outside; they wanted simultaneously the security of a family home and the feeling that they could connect with their neighborhood.[98]

Public worry about these matters began to surface in the 1930s, first in the musing of culture critics as they reflected upon the meaning of the Great Depression as a laboratory for understanding American civilization. Commentators since Tocqueville had remarked on the peculiar American tensions between competitive individualism and social community, but it was not until the twentieth century that critics began to sense some of the cultural contradictions of capitalism as it was practiced in its bourgeois American version.[99] Sociologist Robert S. Lynd, who conducted the famed Middletown studies (1925, 1937) with Helen Lynd and their team of researchers,[100] warned readers in 1939 that "The pattern of the culture *stresses individual competitive aggressiveness against one's fellows as the basis for personal and collective security.*"[101] Lynd recognized that competitive individualism is a piece of a larger American political theory, one born in the eighteenth century and rooted importantly in capitalism's theories of the market and of the rational, self-interested economic actor.

Clearly, this political theory had become problematic in 1930s America, as market capitalism proved itself lacking and as government moved to manage the economy in search of a way out of the Depression. There emerged shortly after World War II a planned corporate capitalism subsequently taken for granted in the Fifties and Sixties. So Americans in the Fifties were experiencing full-blown the contradiction between a persistent cultural mythology of markets, individualism, and freedom on the one hand and a managed economy where the individual mattered less than the common good, on the other.

The ambiguities and contradictions between bourgeois values of freedom and equality and capitalism's actual structuring of social relations were sometimes encoded in popular culture narratives of the Fifties. This is Wright's reading of the shifting formula of the western film from the "classical plot" prevalent from 1930 through the mid-Fifties to the "professional plot" prevalent in the late Fifties and Sixties.[102] The western film provides a mythic narrative that "addresses this conflict and provides a resolution. . . . The myth asks . . . how do we, as autonomous, self-reliant individuals, relate to the society of others, a society of morality and love?" Since neither extreme answer to a cultural contradiction is possible, the most powerful cultural myths satisfy the audience by providing a narrative affirming both poles and the "naturalness" of the ambiguity.

It is against this backdrop of the contradictions between treasured cultural mythologies and transformed political economies that the fallout shelter issue came to be a useful "text" for public debate over the nature of American individualism and community. The several themes of the debate—from "every-citizen-a-soldier" through "informed self-reliance" through the vision of a heroically cooperative community emerging from the shelters—all addressed in one way or another troubling questions suggested by experience with competitive individualism without the check of collective social responsibility. Fallout shelters, as Piel put it, represented "the climax of American privatism." Would Americans cooperate in a nuclear crisis, or would savage individualism take over? Is the cultural myth of the redemptive grace of Apocalyptic violence viable in a world of nuclear weapons? Are American science and technology really sufficient to meet the challenge of defense in the nuclear age? And are federal government bureaucrats capable of realistic planning?

The rhetoric of the campaign for civil defense answered each of these questions by affirming the value of expertise and a vision of redemptive community, but the audience was never persuaded. It is possible that the average American's failure to follow the civil defense advice was a form of psychological avoidance, an unwillingness to face harsh realities and make some sacrifices during a decade that drew so much of its meaning from the fact that it was so different from the unpleasant realities and sacrifices of the 1930s and 1940s. But it is more likely, in our view, that Americans understood clearly the ways in which the debate over civil defense in general and over fallout shelters in particular was an exploration of the troubling trajectory of American competitive individualism. In rejecting the civil defense campaign, Americans were rejecting that ugly future and opting instead for any collective alternative vision that would make war less likely while it affirmed American community. Experience with and resistance to the civil defense campaign of the 1950s and early 1960s made the American public a more skeptical audience for future government rhetoric, as the apologists for the building war in Vietnam were about to discover.


■  CONCLUSION

Even as this article goes to press, journalists and governments are declaring the "end of the Cold War" and the beginning of a remarkably new relationship between the superpowers. Yet, to see the developments of 1989 and 1990 as remarkably new is to understand how fundamental has been "Cold War culture" in the lives of Americans for the past forty years. And a crucial psychological and social element of Cold War culture has been "nuclearism," the acceptance of nuclear weapons as part of our ordinary, everyday, taken-for-granted lives.

If Lifton is correct, "nuclearism" draws its energy from complex psychological motives surrounding death and survival, but nuclearism did not just arise from those motives. Nuclearism is just as much a product of persuasive campaigns aimed at naturalizing through language the Bomb, fallout, shelters, and the practice of our everyday lives as a form of deterrence. Our goal in this essay has been to offer a critique of the language and narrative strategies used by those charged with persuading Americans to participate in a credible civil defense program.

But persuasive campaigns appear in historical contexts, and accounting for the civil defense rhetors' choices of tropes and themes is only one way to historicize the campaign. For a persuasive campaign, really, is the site of several discourses. Some of the discourses, as in the case of the social movement rhetoric resisting civil defense programs, are full-fledged participants in the contest. Many more discourses, however, may speak less directly to the issue at hand but be important resources for people's understanding the campaigns. Thus, the persuasive campaign for civil defense was the site of a contest of narratives and was the site of an intertextual conversation, of sorts, where texts as disparate as home architecture, television dramas, feature films, and everyday conversation about family safety collided to create the interpretive field for Americans' attitudes toward government pleas to participate in civil defense plans and training. In the end, the narratives resisting civil defense must have seemed closer to the actual practices of everyday life, for Americans never included large-scale participation in civil defense programs as part of the "nuclearism" of the era.

To fully historicize this debate over civil defense, then, requires that the critic historicize not just the most obvious texts in the debate but as many of the other verbal and nonverbal texts as possible, making the intertextuality of the debate a central point of the criticism. To this task we brought the tools of what we call "criticism in the pragmatic attitude," attempting to demonstrate (within the constraints of space and purpose) how one public campaign can be understood best by historicizing several of its most important intersecting texts.

Our call for historicizing the texts in the "intertextual conversation" of a public persuasive campaign should not panic critics into thinking that they must become historians. That worry has sent too many critics scampering back to the safety of formalist analyses of texts. Rather, we simply wish to point critics in the direction of work already being done by historians, folklorists, art critics, sociologists, anthropologists, psychologists, and others working on the reconstruction of the forms and conditions of the practice of everyday life. Socio-rhetorical criticism should be a collaborator in this interdisciplinary project to determine how symbolic communication induces social practices.

## ▊ Notes

The authors wish to thank Wendy Chmieleuski, Curator of the Swarthmore College Peace Collection, for her kind assistance in this research. A travel grant from the University of California Institute on Global Conflict and Cooperation, based at UC San Diego, made possible part of the research for this essay.

[1]"Waiting for September," *Time*, 56, 14 August, 1950: 8.

[2]"The City Under the Bomb," *Time*, 56, 2 October, 1950: 14.

[3]"Barely Time to Duck," *Time*, 56, 16 October, 1950: 22.

[4]Historian JoAnne Brown describes this and other civil defense educational programs aimed at children in her essay, " 'A Is for *Atom*, B is for *Bomb*': Civil Defense in American Public Education, 1948–1963," *Journal of American History*, 75 (1988): 68–90.

[5]Roger Hagan discusses these stories from the *Los Angeles Times* and from the *San Francisco Chronicle* in "When the Holocaust Comes," *The Nation*, 193, 4 November 1961: 341–347.

[6]"Gun Thy Neighbor?" *Time*, 78, 18 August 1961: 58.

[7]See Robert N. Bellah, Richard Madsen, William M. Sullivan, Ann Swidler, and Steven M. Tipton, *Habits of the Heart: Individualism and Commitment in American Life* (Berkeley: University of California Press, 1985). See, also, the essays gathered in Charles H. Reynolds and Ralph V. Norman, eds., *Community in America: The Challenge of Habits of the Heart* (Berkeley: University of California Press, 1988). We should note, as have some of the critics of *Habits,* that the exclusively white, middle-class character of the authors' informants limits our generalizations to that population.

[8]This debate provides more "moments" of the sort first analyzed by Wayne Brockriede and Robert L. Scott in *Moments in the Rhetoric of the Cold War* (New York: Random House, 1970). For further contributions to the study of Cold War rhetoric, see the essays gathered in Martin J. Medhurst, Robert L. Ivie, Philip Wander, and Robert L. Scott, eds., *Cold War Rhetoric: Strategy, Metaphor, and Ideology* (Westport, CT: Greenwood Press, 1990).

[9]Martin J. Medhurst, "Eisenhower's 'Atoms for Peace' Speech: A Case Study in the Strategic Use of Language," *Communication Monographs*, 54 (1987): 204–220.

[10]Robert Jay Lifton and Richard Falk, *Indefensible Weapons: The Political and Psychological Case Against Nuclearism* (New York: Basic Books, 1982), 87.

[11]Our reference to Barthes (e.g., *Mythologies* [New York: Hill and Wang, 1972]) here is simply a way of signalling that nuclear discourse invites semiological and semiotic inquiry. See, for example, Jack Solomon Fisher, *Discourse and Reference in the Nuclear Age* (Norman: University of Oklahoma Press, 1988) and the entire issue of essays devoted to "Nuclear Criticism" in *Diacritics* (Summer 1984).

[12]Jay Mechling, "William James and the Philosophical Foundations for the Study of Everyday Life," *Western Folklore*, 44 (Oct. 1985): 301–310.

[13]Janet Horne, "Rhetoric After Rorty," *Western Journal of Speech Communication*, 53 (Summer 1989): 247–259, and John Lyne, "The Culture of Inquiry," *Quarterly Journal of Speech*, 76 (1990): 192–224. In reviewing Richard Rorty's new book, *Contingency, Irony, and Solidarity* (New York: Cambridge University Press, 1989), Lyne finds fault with Rorty's "lack of a *rhetoric* of universality" (p. 195). A disappointed "fan" of Rorty ("disappointed" because Rorty has not turned to a fully rhetorical approach to language and reality), Lyne finds more promise in the "prophetic pragmatism" built by Cornel West in his *The American Evasion of Philosophy: A Genealogy of Pragmatism* (Madison: University of Wisconsin Press, 1989). For West, who seems alert to social class and race in ways that escape Rorty, the *"goal of a sophisticated neopragmatism is to think genealogically about specific practices in light of the best available social theories, cultural critiques, and historiographical insights and to act politically to achieve certain moral consequences in light of effective strategies and tactics"* (p. 209).

[14]Eugene Rochberg-Halton, *Meaning and Modernity: Social Theory in the Pragmatic Attitude* (Chicago: University of Chicago Press, 1986).

[15]Basic to this approach is the view that "common sense" is a cultural belief system every bit as legitimate (perhaps even more so) as more formal systems, such as science. Alfred Schutz's crucial attention to common sense rests upon William James's privileging of that system. See, for example, Alfred Schutz, "Common-Sense and Scientific Interpretation of

Human Action," in *Collected Papers: I, The Problem of Social Reality,* ed. Maurice Natanson (The Hague: Martinus Nijoff, 1973), 3–47, and Clifford Geertz, "Common Sense as a Cultural System," *Antioch Review,* 33 (1975): 5–26.

[16]We like using "commonplaces," following Walter J. Ong, *Orality and Literacy: The Technologizing of the Word* (London: Routledge, 1982), 110, though there are other suitable terms. Marchand, for example, identifies several patterned, repeated, culturally resonant "visual cliches" in his analysis of American advertising. See Roland Marchand, *Advertising the American Dream: Making Way for Modernity, 1920–1940* (Berkeley: University of California Press, 1985), 235–284.

[17]Jay Mechling, "An American Culture Grid, With Texts," *American Studies International* 27 (1989): 2–12.

[18]Donal Carbaugh, *Talking American: Cultural Discourses on DONAHUE* (Norwood, NJ: Ablex Publishing Corp., 1988).

[19]Ibid., 122–125. Here Carbaugh builds upon the work represented by Tamar Katriel and Gerald Philipsen, " 'What We Need is Communication': 'Communication' as a Cultural Category in Some American Speech," *Communication Monographs,* 48 (1981): 301–317.

[20]A related move is that made by Gusfield and others in bringing together interactionist, social-constructionist, dramaturgical sociology, on the one hand, and rhetorical criticism on the other in the study of "the culture of public problems." See, for example, Joseph R. Gusfield, *The Culture of Public Problems: Drinking-Driving and the Symbolic Order* (Chicago: University of Chicago Press, 1981), Joel Best, "Rhetoric in Claims-Making: Constructing the Missing Children Problem," *Social Problems,* 34 (1987): 101–119, and Kathryn A. Woolard, "Sentences in the Language Prison: The Rhetorical Structuring of an American Language Policy Debate," *American Ethnologist,* 16 (1989): 268–278.

[21]Carbaugh, 122–124, and M. Reddy, "The Conduit Metaphor," in *Metaphor and Thought,* ed. A. Ortony (Cambridge: Cambridge University Press, 1979).

[22]George Lakoff and Mark Johnson, *Metaphors We Live By* (Chicago: University of Chicago Press, 1980), and George Lakoff, *Women, Fire, and Dangerous Things: What Categories Reveal about the Mind* (Chicago: University of Chicago Press, 1987).

[23]See, for example, Alan Dundes' analysis of a single American proverb, "Seeing is Believing," in *Interpreting Folklore* (Bloomington: Indiana University Press, 1980), 86–92, and his analysis of "the literalization of metaphor" in "Projection in Folklore: A Plea for Psychoanalytic Semiotics," *MLN,* 91 (1976): 1500–1533.

[24]Robert Plant Armstrong, *The Powers of Presence: Consciousness, Myth, and Affecting Presence* (Philadelphia: University of Pennsylvania Press, 1981), 13.

[25]Elizabeth Walker Mechling and Jay Mechling, "Retilling *Acres of Diamonds,*" unpublished paper delivered at the meeting of the Speech Communication Association, November 3–6, 1988, in New Orleans. A. Cheree Carlson's "Narrative as the Philosopher's Stone: How Russell H. Conwell Changed Lead into Diamonds," *Western Journal of Speech Communication,* 53 (Fall 1989): 342–355, offers an interesting Burkean reading of the speech but still fails to recognize the non-Western aesthetic by which Conwell constructed the text. Closer to our point is Michael Leff and Andrew Sachs, "Words the Most Like Things: Iconicity and the Rhetorical Text," *Western Journal of Speech Communication,* 54 (Summer 1990): 252–273.

[26]Especially illuminating on this matter is Susan Stewart's *Nonsense: Aspects of Intertextuality in Folklore and Literature* (Baltimore, MD: Johns Hopkins University Press, 1979).

[27]It is worth noting, in this regard, that Jameson considers "intertextuality" as a distinctive aesthetic feature of the postmodern code. See Fredric Jameson, "Postmodernism, or The Cultural Logic of Late Capitalism," *New Left Review* 146 (1984): 67.

[28]Paul Boyer tells the story of the earliest years (1945–1950) of America's accommodation to the atomic age. See his *By the Bomb's Early Light: American Thought and Culture at the Dawn*

*of the Atomic Age* (New York: Pantheon Books, 1985). See, especially, chapter 26, "The Reassuring Message of Civil Defense," 319–333.

[29]"The City Under the Bomb," *Time*, 56, 2 October, 1950: 12.

[30]Ralph E. Lapp, *Must We Hide?* (Cambridge, MA: Addison-Wesley, 1949).

[31]"The Truth About Atomic Bombs and Defense Against Them," *U.S. News & World Report*, 26, 29 April, 1949: 11–13.

[32]The prestigious *Bulletin of the Atomic Scientists*, 7 (1951) explored the dispersal strategy with an editorial ("The Only Defense"), ten essays, and "Dispersal—A Selected Reading List."

[33]Elaine Tyler May, *Homeward Bound: American Families in the Cold War Era* (New York: Basic Books, Inc., 1988) 169; Thomas Hine, *Populuxe* (New York: Knopf, 1986), 42. Dean MacCannell has made an interesting argument about the conscious and unconscious cultural politics of the suburbanization of America as part of the 1950s doctrine of deterrence, noting (among other things) the fact that the strategy leaves poor, black, urban dwellers to absorb the hit at ground zero. If MacCannell is correct, then the transition from early, explicit discussion of dispersal to the seemingly benign discourse over structural changes like suburban high schools and shopping malls represents less a change of taste than an elaborate encoding of hidden motives. See Dean MacCannell, "Baltimore in the Morning . . . After: On the Forms of Post-Nuclear Leadership," *Diacritics* (1984): 33–46.

[34]Gene Marine, "Our Stupid Civil Defense: Playing Politics with National Survival," *The Nation*, 184, 9 February, 1957: 111–115.

[35]"The City," 14.

[36]"The City," 14.

[37]Philip Wylie, "A Better Way to Beat the Bomb," *Atlantic Monthly*, 187, February 1951: 42. Within ten years, Wylie had changed his mind about civil defense and testified in Congress against shelters. See the account in the editorial, "The Great Illusion," *The Nation*, 192, 11 March, 1961: 197–198.

[38]Office of Civil and Defense Mobilization, "Personal Preparedness in the Nuclear Age" (Washington, DC: U.S. Government Printing Office, December, 1960) 6.

[39]This is part of what Robert J. Lifton refers to as the "domestication of the Bomb" in postwar America. See Robert J. Lifton, *The Broken Connection: On Death and the Continuity of Life* (New York: Touchstone Books, 1979).

[40]"The Truth," 11.

[41]John W. M. Bunker, "After an A-Bomb Falls," *Atlantic Monthly*, 188, September, 1951: 56.

[42]Bunker, 58–59.

[43]Richard F. Dempewolff, "Don't Let the Cries of Doomsday Panic You . . . ," *Popular Mechanics*, 117, April 1962: 114.

[44]Federal Civil Defense Administration, "Facts About Fallout Protection" (Washington, DC: U.S. Government Printing Office, April 1958).

[45]See Mary Douglas, *Natural Symbols: Explorations in Cosmology* (New York: Vintage/Random House, 1973), and Barbara Babcock-Abrahams, "Why Frogs Are Good to Think and Dirt Is Good to Reflect On," *Soundings*, 58 (Summer 1975): 167–181.

[46]Hine, 59–81.

[47]"Against the Silent Killer," *Time*, 74, 20 July, 1959: 19.

[48]" 'Right to Die'," *Time*, 74, 17 August, 1959: 22.

[49]Nelson A. Rockefeller, "Importance of Shelters in Nuclear Age: Protection from Nuclear Blackmail and War," *Vital Speeches*, 26 (April 15, 1960): 411–413.

[50]Nelson A. Rockefeller, "Purpose and Policy," *Foreign Affairs*, 38 (1960): 370–390.

[51]Rockefeller, "Importance," 412.

[52]Rockefeller, "Importance," 413.

[53]Editorial, "The Shelter Racket," *The Nation*, 193, 23 September, 1961: 169–170.

[54]John F. Kennedy, "The Berlin Crisis," *Vital Speeches*, 28 (August 15, 1961): 644.

[55]Ronald Steel, "The Cost of Survival," *Commonweal*, 75 (October 13, 1961): 63.

[56]"—And for Civil Defense, Kennedy Asks Fresh Start," *U.S. News & World Report*, 51, 7 August, 1961: 36.

[57]"Shelter Skelter," *Time*, 78, 1 September, 1961: 59.

[58]"Shelter," 59.

[59]*Life*, 51, 15 September, 1961: 95.

[60]Editorial, "Reader, Be of Good Cheer," *The Nation*, 193, 25 November, 1961: 413–414.

[61]"Boom or Bust," *Time*, 79, 18 May 1962: 20.

[62]Paul A. Carter, *Another Part of the Fifties* (New York: Columbia University Press, 1983), 248. Perhaps the best example of this genre is Walter M. Miller, Jr., *A Canticle for Leibowitz* (New York: Bantam, 1959).

[63]"All Out Against Fallout," *Time*, 78, 4 August 1961: 11.

[64]"The Sheltered Life," *Time*, 78, 20 October 1961: 25.

[65]"The Sheltered Life," 25.

[66]"If Bombs Do Fall on U.S.—What People Look For," *U.S. News & World Report*, 52, 25 September, 1961: 54.

[67]Americans probably reacted more to the American film than to the British novel, though the latter was available in paperback. Pat Frank's novel, *Alas, Babylon* (New York: Bantam, 1959) was also popular reading in this period, but it never moved into the public discourse as did *On the Beach*.

[68]Rockefeller, "Importance," 412.

[69]Ralph E. Lapp, "Rockefeller's Civil Defense Program," *Bulletin of Atomic Scientists*, 16 (April 1960): 135.

[70]Vincent Wilson, Jr., "Surviving the Bomb," *Commonweal*, 74 (May 26, 1961): 224.

[71]Stanley Meisler, "Charade on Civil Defense," *The Nation*, 190, 11 June 1960, 508.

[72]Lawrence S. Wittner, *Rebels Against War: The American Peace Movement, 1941–1960* (New York: Columbia University Press, 1969), 264–265.

[73]War Resisters League, "Civil Defense: A Message to Every Citizen" (New York: War Resisters League, n.d.), Document Group No. 311, "Civil Defense Protest Committee (formerly Provisional Defense Committee)," Swarthmore College Peace Collection, Swarthmore, PA.

[74]Stephen Cary and Robert Pickus, "Reply to Critics," *The Progressive* (October, 1955): 18. This was the conclusion to a forum on the 1955 pamphlet, *Speak Truth to Power*, in which a working party of the American Friends Service Committee offered a way to connect pacifist thought with international affairs.

[75]Reporters described and, one might say, ridiculed "Operation Alert" without mentioning the protests, in "Best Defense? Prayer," *Time*, 65, 27 June, 1955: 17–18.

[76]Fellowship of Reconciliation (New York, n.d.). In Document Group No. 133, Swarthmore College Peace Collection.

[77]Arthur Brown, "What Happened on June 15?" (New York: Provisional Defense Committee, n.d.), n.p. This is a 12-page, professionally printed pamphlet describing the protest and trial and presenting the moral and legal issues as seen by the defense (in the Swarthmore College Peace Collection, Document Group No. 311). An editorial, "The Rights of Non-Conformity," in *Commonweal*, 62, 15 July, 1955: 363–364, agreed that prosecution of the

protestors constituted a serious threat to acts of conscience, especially when the protestors were disobeying an order for a *"mock* emergency" (their emphasis).

[78]See the following documents in Document Group No. 311 in the Swarthmore College Peace Collection: letter from protestors Dorothy Day, Ralph DiGia, Robert Gilmore, and Kent Larrabee to Gov. Averill Harriman, July 17, 1956; War Resisters League leaflet, "The Only Real Defense"; and a mimeographed handbill, "Today—July 20." See, also, the editorial, "Pacifists Arrested," *Commonweal*, 44, 3 August, 1956: 432–434, and the editorial, "Aspirations and Realities," *Commonweal*, 46, 16 August, 1957: 483–484. Each year, the editors at *Commonweal* explained that, although the editors themselves supported nuclear tests and participated in air raid drills, they were worried about the courts' view that civil rights could be suspended in the absence of a "clear and present danger."

[79]Civil Defense Protest Committee, "Civil Defense Protest Day." See, also, the documents, "Civil Defense Protest, A Call to Sanity, Tuesday, May 3, 1960," and "The Truth About Civil Defense," both by the Civil Defense Protest Committee. Document Group No. 311, Swarthmore College Peace Collection.

[80]Between 1,200 and 1,500 protestors participated in the 1961 rally. See Carl Dreher, "Hazards of Civil Defense," *The Nation*, 192, 10 June, 1961: 495.

[81]Civil Defense Protest Committee, "Brave Men Do Not Hide," in Document Group No. 311, Swarthmore College Peace Collection. Also in that file are the April 20, 1961, news release, the leaflet "Civil Defense Protest—A Call to Sanity, Friday, April 28, 1961," and a mimeographed information sheet handed out to the protestors. By 1961 the Civil Defense Protest Committee could boast among its "sponsors" such public figures as Living Theatre directors Julian Beck and Judith Molina, Norman Mailer, Paul Goodman, Kenneth Clark, Nat Hentoff, Dwight MacDonald, Lewis Mumford, and David Riesman.

[82]Compare this with the SICK and MADNESS clusters of vehicles discovered in the rhetoric of Cold War "idealists" Henry Wallace, William Fulbright, and Helen Caldicott by critic Robert L. Ivie, "Metaphor and the Rhetorical Invention of Cold War 'Idealists,' " *Communication Monographs*, 54 (1987): 165–182.

[83]On valuing expertise and rationality in the 1950s, see John Patrick Diggins, *The Proud Decades: America in War and Peace, 1941–1960* (New York: W. W. Norton & Company, 1988), 247–263.

[84]L. C. McHugh, "Ethics at the Shelter Door," *America*, 105 (September 30, 1961): 824–826.

[85]Quoted in "The Sheltered Life," *Time*, 78, 20 October, 1961: 23.

[86]"Shelter Morality," *Commonweal*, 55, 27 October, 1961: 109.

[87]"Shelter Morality," 109.

[88]Marc Scott Zicree, *The Twilight Companion* (New York: Bantam Books, 1982), 226–227.

[89]Ronald Steel, "The Paradox of Civil Defense," *Commonweal*, 75, 16 March, 1962: 638.

[90]Gerard Piel, "The Illusion of Civil Defense," *Vital Speeches*, 28, 1 February 1962: 239.

[91]"If the Bombs Do Fall," 52.

[92]"The Realities of Civil Defense," *Commonweal*, 74, 26 May, 1961: 220.

[93]Editorial, "What the Citizen is Not Being Told," *The Nation*, 193, 14 October, 1961: 237.

[94]Hagan, 342.

[95]Gene N. Levine and John Modell, "American Public Opinion and the Fallout-Shelter Issue," *Public Opinion Quarterly*, 29 (1965): 271.

[96]Levine and Modell, 277–278.

[97]May, 103–108, discusses the mother's role in civil defense preparedness and in making the shelter a well-stocked version of home. See the drawings of shelter life in such articles as

"Atomic Hideouts," *Popular Mechanics*, 109, March 1958: 146–148; "Before the Siren Sounds," *Popular Mechanics*, 114, October 1960: 196–199; and "You *Can* Build a Low-Cost Shelter Quickly," *Popular Mechanics*, 116, December 1961: 85–89. On the 1950s aesthetic of American homes and fallout shelters, see Hine, 48–58, 135–138.

[98]On the design of suburban American homes and neighborhoods, see Clifford Edward Clark, Jr., *The American Home, 1800–1960* (Chapel Hill: University of North Carolina Press, 1986), 193–236.

[99]Karen Horney, *The Neurotic Personality of Our Time* (New York: Norton, 1937).

[100]Robert S. Lynd and Helen Merrell Lynd, *Middletown: A Study in Contemporary American Culture* (New York: Harcourt and Brace, 1929) and *Middletown in Transition: A Study in Cultural Conflicts* (New York: Harcourt and Brace, 1937).

[101]Robert S. Lynd, *Knowledge for What? The Place of Social Science in American Culture* (New York: Grove Press, Inc., 1939), 71.

[102]Will Wright, *Sixguns and Society: A Structural Study of the Western* (Berkeley: University of California Press, 1975).

# CHAPTER 7

# THE FRANKENSTEIN MYTH
# IN CONTEMPORARY CINEMA

Thomas S. Frentz
and Janice Hocker Rushing

*In this commentary, Thomas S. Frentz and Janice Hocker Rushing describe how their study of the "Frankenstein myth" stemmed in part from their own uneasiness about technology in their lives. The project began, they report, because various events had prompted them to reflect on their ambivalence about the role of technology in their personal and academic lives. Rushing and Frentz share the conviction that finished criticism has more integrity if these triggering experiences are not discarded once the writing is begun, but are instead preserved as a reference point to provide bearings for the critic in the refining and explaining that is to come.*

## COMMENTARY

"The Frankenstein Myth in Contemporary Cinema" began when we saw *The Terminator* on television. Like many who viewed this film (having been conditioned, perhaps, by *Conan the Barbarian*), we expected little more than an evening of pumped-up posing, gratuitous violence, and monosyllabic mumbling. We were not, of course, disappointed. But we were also more than a little blown away by the relentlessness of the film's twenty-first-century cyborg and the bleakness of its postapocalyptic vision. For us, criticism typically starts as this kind of gut-level, unexamined intuitive feeling about a text(s). If we don't feel intensely about it one way or another—it can be hate, love, disgust, surprise, fear, awe, perplexity—we don't write.

Although criticism must eventually develop beyond this initial reaction that Robert Pirsig refers to in *Zen and the Art of Motorcycle Maintenance* as "preintellectual awareness," we try to honor it throughout the process. For us, this intuitive feeling is the purest "moment" in which the opposition between the critic-as-subject and the text-as-object is broken down, and it

**155**

generally provides the "seed crystal" for the unfolding of the more reasoned aspects of the critique. We have discovered that the finished product has more integrity if we re-member its genesis in feeling even as we inevitably dis-member it intellectually to refine, revise, and explain. In our work, criticism typically unfolds as a series of analogies between the text and us as potential critics. That is, something in the text links up with something in us to form an insight or a problem that insists upon our attention. Such analogies usually multiply and they never occur in an orderly fashion. We often talk to other people about these analogies in seeking to solve the problem, develop an idea, or test some idiosyncracy. If the analogies are numerous and/or intriguing enough we are almost compelled to work them out in writing. Many of these efforts lose steam, are soon forgotten, and/or end up in the circular file. A few are as tenacious as the Terminator, and evolve into full-blown analyses.

In the case of *The Terminator*, all sorts of analogical connections began to occur. Janice thought of Langdon Winner's *Autonomous Technology* and Jacques Ellul's *The Technological Society,* both of which worried that technological perfection would render humans obsolete. She also remembered she had been dreaming for some time of technologically constructed men, some with neck bolts and others with missing limbs, and despite Tom's suggestion that these nocturnal events were simply residue fears that his recently repaired neck discs and "scoped" knee were but signs of things to come, she had learned over time not to dismiss such synchronistic occurrences out of hand. We also realized that just about every major appliance in and around our house had gone berserk or quit in the last few months. Not only was this irritating in and of itself, but it prompted some abashed semiphilosophical musings concerning our own dependence on our technological trappings. Furthermore, we had just purchased, only about a decade after everybody else, a personal computer. Tom was touchy about giving up his legal pad. "It has no right," he used to complain, "to ask me whether I am *sure* I want it to do something. If I wasn't sure, I wouldn't have asked!" The *coup-de-grace* came when our Imagewriter II refused to print the draft of an idea we had on technology developing a mind of its own. Consciously and unconsciously, our ambivalence about technology—the seed crystal of this paper—had infiltrated itself into our personal and academic lives.

Although we were intrigued by the above analogies, they lay fallow for awhile until Tom and his son saw *Rocky IV*. Some years earlier, we had written an essay on the original *Rocky*, and, as such, felt a curious moral compulsion to at least *see* the seeming infinity of sequels. But having endured *Rocky III*, Janice simply could not be induced into the next ring of movie Hell. And so when Tom returned from the Saturday afternoon matinee, strode into the study muttering, "Yo—Janice! Ya gotta see this one!," a condescending "Yeah—sure" was her unimpressed response. Thinking that her coauthor/spouse, who always did have a disturbing taste for the cinematically banal, was on another one of his temporary testosterone highs, Janice ignored him. Maybe he would go away. But beneath the transparently embarrassing politics of this film, Tom insisted, was an interesting subtext about the intrusion of technology into contemporary life—both Russian and American. Moreover, he noted that the similarities between the giant Russian prizefighter in *Rocky IV* and the equally inflated cyborg in *The Terminator* might index an evolutionary pattern concerning humanity's unfolding relationship to technology.

Against her better judgment, Janice saw *Rocky IV,* and although she conceded that Tom was probably right about the technological subtext and the similarities between Ivan Drago and the Terminator, the gap between this politically romanticized melodrama and its apocalyptic sci-fi counterpart seemed too great. Tom agreed, and again the project was put on hold. But we continued to be haunted by the problem of technology, and eventually two related ideas revisited us. One was the concept of "rhetorical narration," which Tom had discussed previously in his Van Zelst lecture and Janice had extended in her earlier work on the New Frontier. Rhetorical narration was the notion that cultural myths evolve slowly over time and that singular texts—be they speeches, films, or television programs—often articulate specific marker events in a larger unfolding story that tells something significant about the psyche of the culture. The second connection occurred when we recalled the character of Roy Batty, a humanly crafted replicant in the cult favorite *Blade Runner,* about which Janice had written before in another context.

We then pieced these events together with *The Terminator* and came up with the basic idea for the article. We felt that the characters of Ivan Drago, Roy Batty, and the Terminator represented important stages in humanity's evolving relationship with technology. Moreover, the three films in which these characters played central roles seemed to comprise a rhetorical narrative insofar as they charted how technology was gradually becoming independent from humanity. Should this independence ever occur, *The Terminator* at least seemed to suggest, the worst prophecy of technological determinism, whereby machines would eliminate humanity, would come to pass. We also recognized, as other critics have noted, that this general story was itself merely a recent extension of a much more widespread myth—one that began for Western civilization with the Prometheus story, which showed the consequences of stealing fire from the gods, and continued through industrial times in Mary Shelley's classic *Frankenstein.*

Given the kernel idea, writing the first draft became a matter of solving two problems. We had to integrate some fairly diverse theoretical materials—the technological determinism literature of Winner and Ellul and the rhetorical narration idea along with its rhetorical and mythic entailments—into a coherent critical framework. We then needed to allow that critical frame to illuminate meanings from the films while those meanings reverberated back and guided us to rethink the perspective at the same time. In the process, we followed our general rule to watch the films we were writing about again and again until we would begin spontaneously to speak to each other in a restricted code consisting totally of lines from the characters. A hazard of this occupation is that it does evoke odd stares when we do this in public.

On June 16, 1987, we submitted the manuscript to *Critical Studies in Mass Communication,* presumably, given its title, an ideal forum. Although most submissions undergo significant changes and the reviewing process is lengthy, this particular process was unusually protracted: Twenty-two months passed from submission to acceptance. During that time, the essay engaged the attention of seven people—the two of us, four reviewers (two original and two added later), and the journal editor—and underwent two full revisions and a third significant editing (four drafts in all). Throughout the review process, the readers and editor liked our writing and much of our analysis of the films, but questioned the rationale for addressing the technology problem and the theoretical bases of our critical framework.

On September 25, 1987, we received reactions to our initial paper from two reviewers and a letter from the editor, suggesting that while we could revise and resubmit the manuscript in accordance with the suggestions of the reviewers, we might not want to take our work in those directions. After immediately concluding (as we typically do) that the readers were massively brain-damaged for not buying every phoneme we wrote, we began to see (as we typically do) that all had read the manuscript carefully and had made excellent suggestions. One reviewer, obviously a feminist, alerted us to the literature that linked technology with gender and to implications concerning gender within these films. The second reviewer and the editor—in quite different ways—were concerned that our critical framework seemed "dated" and that its "universalist" cast was out of keeping with the literature readers of this journal would be likely to know. We interpreted these remarks to imply that our piece was not in keeping with the emerging postmodernist (in the broadest sense) orientation of *CSMC.* The challenge to us was legitimate: If we expected to publish our piece in this journal, we would have to either revise our critical framework in light of more avant garde theoretical perspectives, or show how our own perspective was superior to them.

Our second draft, resubmitted May 26, 1988, tried to meet these challenges. As we always do, we included a detailed letter in which we cited each significant objection and how we attempted to address it. This draft reflected three important modifications. First, we developed a mythic perspective that synthesized some of the work of depth psychologist C. G. Jung, moral philosopher Alasdair MacIntyre, rhetorical scholar Kenneth Burke, novelist Mary Shelley, and a wide variety of contemporary writers on gender. Second, we used this mythic frame to reconcile competing perspectives on technology—the viewpoint of neo-Marxists (likely to be familiar to readers of

*CSMC*), who saw technological determinism as a stance that limited action and choice, and of technological determinists like Winner and Ellul (from our first draft), who countered that technology was rapidly obliterating choice and determining action. Our argument here was that our mythic perspective "historicized" these two seemingly antithetical views of technology as different phases in an ongoing, evolutionary process—that is, technology is on its way toward autonomy, but it is possible to avert the apocalypse if certain choices are made soon. Finally, we fleshed out the gender entailments in the three films, now noting that the patriarchal myth seemed destined to separate humanity from technology, while its repressed feminine alternative exhibited the potential to reunite the human with the machine.

We received the response to our second draft on August 26, 1988. Because we had radically altered the theoretical materials making up our critical framework, the editor asked two new readers to join the original two in reviewing this version. The two original reviewers were satisfied with our revisions and both recommended publication. One of the new reviewers was not enthusiastic, saying that s/he saw nothing theoretically new in our work. The second new reader recommended publishing the piece in a condensed form, but suggested that our analysis be grounded, not in the ongoing theoretical controversy over technology, but rather in the literature of science fiction criticism. Given the lack of unanimity among the four reviewers and the fact that the editor's space in the journal was rapidly filling up, he was uncertain whether we could accommodate the competing suggestions and make the necessary changes in the time still available.

This was a "near death experience" for our project. But, as survivors of NDEs (as they are known in the trade) usually are, we were energized by this experience and decided to rise to the occasion. To this day, we don't think the editor expected us to reassemble this considerably bullet-ridden thing, itself beginning to resemble a "Frankenstein's monster" sewn together from diverse "theory parts" in several fits of less than divine inspiration. Perhaps the editor hadn't seen *The Terminator*—or at least hadn't seen it as many times as we had—and so he couldn't have known how thoroughly we had internalized Der Arnold's few lines as well as his miraculous capacity for resurrection. Promising on August 31, 1988, that "We'll be back," we sent him a third revision on September 28, 1988. In it, we dropped the theoretically oriented literature on technology and, taking our cue from one of the new reviewers, allowed the technology problem to grow out of the science fiction criticism literature. We then wove the new science fiction orientation more fully throughout the entire essay, although the critical framework and textual analysis were not changed significantly.

The editor accepted this revision on October 6, 1988. He still thought the essay was too long and asked that we cut an additional five pages. We did this and returned it to him on October 11, 1988. It appeared in the March 1989 issue of *CSMC*.

What do we think of this work in retrospect? We are mixed. At this writing (a little more than three years after publication), we both still like the article, which has launched us on a longer-term project in the same general area. But we do wince a little now in reading it over. We understand the space limitations all editors must work within, and that most authors have an inflated sense of the importance of their own prose. But in the spirit of self-reflection that this book invites, we will go ahead and share our own inflation: We both feel that cutting those final five pages from the last draft was unfortunate. In particular the "Critical Framework" section seems to suffer the most, appearing choppy and cryptic, with too few transitions from point to point. Because this is our theoretical contribution in this work—synthesizing several diverse approaches into a singular mythic perspective—we lament that it is not set forth as clearly as it was in earlier drafts.

The two of us do not agree on everything, however. Tom, for example, thinks that the second draft was the strongest and potentially most theoretically subversive form of the paper. That draft argued that the "dated" mythic perspective could resolve a controversy between two more current bodies of theoretical literature on technology. To the extent that that argument was sound, it would have reaffirmed the value of mythic criticism of cultural texts and, by so doing, subverted the charge that such approaches were passe. When that material was dropped and the science fiction criticism literature substituted in its place, the article, for Tom, was somewhat depotentiated because it now grew out of "aesthetic" or "poetic" materials, which, in Tom's view, are not as important theoretically as the socially and politically inspired literature they replaced.

Whereas Janice shares some of Tom's feelings on this, she—being less conspiratorial by nature—feels that the science fiction literature was relevant and provided a useful and more direct departure point for the critical framework section as well as for the analysis itself. In addition (she reminds Tom), the body of sci-fi lit-crit was fun to read and has become an important knowledge base for much of our later research. Besides, do we really have to accept the conventional wisdom that aesthetics isn't as important as politics? She may be right on this. Tom's still thinking about it.

# The Frankenstein Myth
# in Contemporary Cinema

**Janice Hocker Rushing**
**and Thomas S. Frentz**

**V**irtually from the beginning, we humans have carried on a love-hate relationship with the tools we have made. Currently we are enchanted with fully mediated "home entertainment centers," with user-friendly personal computers, and with the optimistic conviction that solutions to such social problems as disease, the greenhouse effect, and the nuclear threat will surely emerge through advances in technology. And yet, detractors from the automatic equation of moral with technological progress continue their attempts to break the spell we are under, pointing out that chronic electronic bliss grows couch potatoes, that artificial intelligence may prove to be our obsolescence, and that the side effects of the "cure" are often worse than the malady.

Although the debate over technics pervades the scholarship of social, philosophical, and rhetorical critique (Barrett, 1978; Ellul, 1964; Farrell, 1976; Farrell & Goodnight, 1981; Marcuse, 1964; McLuhan, 1965; Mumford, 1970; Slack, 1984; Williams, 1974; Winner, 1977), the most profound insights into how technology is and might be experienced by the culture as a whole often emanate from the literary and cinematic genre of science fiction. Critics of science fiction note that its attitude toward "the machine" reflects "both an invitation and a warning; it is simultaneously fascinating and threatening, both superior to and somehow inferior to the punier humans who build, operate and sometimes are subjugated by it" (Porush, 1985, p. 7). A "strange split personality" exists both in reality and in fiction, claims Patricia Warrick (1980, p. 206): "Man intellectually and emotionally rejects electric technology at the same time that he increasingly comes to rely on it."

Most science fiction critics place works dealing with the theme of humanity versus the machine into one of two broad categories: "utopian" or "dystopian." Utopian fiction employs positive images of the robot as "the visible sign of the triumph of reason, the Enlightenment dream of human progress" (Fitting, 1987, pp. 349–350), generally aestheticizes the machine (Porush, 1985, p. 9), is often set in the far distant future, is imaginatively speculative, and operates on the "open-system model" of cybernetics in which animate and inanimate are not sharply differentiated and systems can transform themselves by exchanging energy, matter, and information with the environment (Warrick, 1980, pp. 161, 130–202).[1] Dystopian fiction creates foreboding images of the robot (Fitting, p. 350), regards the machine as a malevolent threat (Porush, p. 9), extrapolates from and exaggerates present conditions in imagining the future, and operates on the "closed-system model" of cybernetics in which the whole is the sum of its parts and equilibrium in a system occurs when maximum entropy is achieved (Warrick, pp. 161, 130–202).

In this study, we are concerned with the current form of the dystopian vision, specifically as it has evolved from Mary Shelley's *Frankenstein* (1818/ 1934). Isaac Asimov (1981, pp. 160–162) labels such science fiction "the Frankenstein complex" and claims that Shelley's original novel represents a "peak of fear," not only that machinery will harm us but that it will supplant us. The story's basic and familiar outline is that a technologically created being appears as a surprise to an unsuspecting and forgetful creator. "A ghost appears in the network. Unanticipated aspects of technological structure endow the creation with an unanticipated *telos*" (Winner, 1977, p. 280). The maker is then threatened by the made, and the original roles of master and slave are in doubt. As Shelley acknowledged by subtitling her novel *A Modern Prometheus,* the Frankenstein complex recapitulates the Greek myth of creation: like Prometheus, Dr. Frankenstein enters forbidden territory to steal knowledge from the gods, participates in overthrowing the old order, becomes a master of technics, and is punished for his transgression (Warrick, 1980, pp. 2–38).

Four critical insights regarding the Frankenstein complex inform our analysis. First, many critics recognize that such dystopian stories are not only based on myth but have attained the status of myth and archetype themselves (Haasen, 1975, p. 142; Neisser, 1966; Porush, 1985, p. 2; Warrick, 1980). Second, several critics maintain that popular works of art in this vein expel fears which are at least partially repressed and unconscious (Fitting, 1987; Jameson, 1971, pp. 404–406; 1979). Third, critics generally recognize that this myth expresses a process of increasing mechanization of the human and humanization of the machine, a process moving toward an ultimate end in which the machine is god and the human is reduced either to slavery or obsolescence (Asimov, 1981; Gordon, 1982; Porush, 1985; Sanders, 1982; Warrick, 1980, pp. 38, 207; Wymer, 1982, p. 47). Finally, critics often note that the dystopian myth (as well as science fiction in general) is gendered in various ways, often echoing and occasionally exposing the general patriarchal bias of technology within our culture (Broege, 1983; Creed, 1986; Geduld, 1973; Gordon, 1982; Palumbo, 1982; Wolfe, 1979, pp. 55–85).

While these conclusions are essential to understanding how we experience the darker side of our relationship to technology, they do not fully reveal the social significance of this relationship as an intensifying problem for contemporary society. Thus, while it seems evident that the Frankenstein complex is mythic in nature, the social function of this myth remains problematic unless it is linked to the cultural psyche that it manifests. In addition, although it is correct, in our view, to regard dystopian fictions as the expression of unconscious fears, a conception of the myth as evolving rather than static suggests that the tensions unearthed in such popular art are not always dissipated. Moreover, whereas it is clear that dystopian fiction expresses an advance toward a frightening end, an understanding of the internal structure of the myth's elements is necessary in order to determine the point (if any) at which that end might be successfully averted. Finally, although we agree that the Frankenstein complex is engendered, we argue that its repressed feminine aspect is revealed, at least in some instances of the myth, to be a key to reversing its movement toward a deterministic *telos*.

In what follows, we draw from depth psychology, rhetoric, and gender studies to build a critical framework. We then critique three contemporary films that represent crucial markers in the evolution of the myth. We close by offering some implications of our critical perspective and analysis for the reinterpretation of the dystopian myth and for the conduct of other cultural studies.

## ▦ CRITICAL FRAMEWORK

Carl Jung (1966, p. 98) writes: "Every period has its bias, its particular prejudice, and its psychic malaise. An epoch is like an individual; it has its own limitations of conscious outlook, and therefore requires a compensatory adjustment." Every cultural era, in other words, like every individual, is predisposed to "see" certain things and to ignore others. That which a person dislikes and does not wish to recognize about oneself is repressed into unconsciousness (purposely forgotten), where it carries on an active life away from the strictures of the ego, erupting into consciousness in such processes as dreams and projections, which *compensate* for the one-sided attitude of the conscious ego. Jung (1971) calls this repressed part of the personality the *shadow*, for it is the dark mirror image cast by the stance of the conscious self and inextricably attached to it. The shadow, however, is not a mere counterpart to consciousness in a homeostatic psyche. Rather, it is "a moral problem that challenges the whole ego-personality," and its recognition is "the essential condition for any kind of self-knowledge" (Jung, 1971, p. 145). The shadow is a threat to consciousness as long as it remains unrecognized; if assimilated, productive change becomes possible.

Since ". . . the psyche of a people is only a somewhat more complex structure than the psyche of an individual" (Jung, 1971, p. 470), it is appropriate to speak of a "cultural shadow," born in response to the limitations of the conscious perspective of an era and often appearing in the guise of archetypal symbols (see Davies, Farrell, & Matthews, 1982). If the shadow of a cultural epoch is always the repressed negation of what the collectivity consciously affirms, then the unconscious compensation for progress is the fear of being systematically replaced by technology. Whereas, in an individual, the *shadow erupts in dreams, in a culture, it does so through the "visions of artists and seers" (Jung, 1966, p. 104). Jung (1971, p. 478) regarded the cinema as one of the prime outlets for such visions, for it "enables us to experience without danger to ourselves all the excitements, passions, and fantasies which have to be repressed in a humanistic age."

As important as any singular shadow dream may be to the individual dreamer, the fuller significance of one's shadow is only realized in the context of a *series* of dreams, for the shadow is a symbolic narrative that evolves over time. Unlike Freud's *id*, which consists of ahistorical, preverbal, sexual, and aggressive drives, the shadow "is the way an individual refuses to own and author his life's text, his own self." It is "linguistic and hermeneutical, and consists of meaningful but dissociated narrative units" (Wilber, 1983, pp. 276–277). The shadow becomes comprehensible to the dreamer to the extent that she or he can understand some underlying coherence among these disconnected units. Similarly, whereas public shadow visions such as films may be important as singular events, their cultural meaning is more completely realized when they are critically associated into meaningful wholes (Frentz, 1984). Traditionally, the historical text that unites singular public expressions into a narrative is called a "myth."

If a cultural shadow is best understood as a repressed but evolving myth, then a method is needed to assess internal changes in the structure of that myth as it moves toward its completion. Kenneth Burke's "dramatistic pentad" (scene, act, agent, agency, and purpose) is a critical tool for interpreting mythic motivation (1969a, p. xv).[2] In any myth, one element may be featured as "figure" and the others as "ground." Burke (1969a, p. 15) also considers possible "ratios" or "principles of determination," generated by placing any two terms together. By extension, a myth can be examined from the perspective of a highlighted ratio, which forms the figure around which the other terms cluster as ground. The dominant term or ratio in a myth can also be used to interpret its entelechial principle, which animates the narrative to evolve toward its optimal end state. "There is," Burke (1968, p. 17) writes, "a principle of perfection implicit in the nature of symbol systems; and in keeping with his nature as symbol-using animal, man is moved by this principle."

Clearly, the ratio between human *agent* and the products of technical reason as *agency* (tool) dominates the Frankenstein story. Furthermore, the evolutionary direction of the drama is from relative *identification* toward increased *division* of agency from agent, that is, from tool as simple extension of the body toward machine as agency-turned-agent with a purpose of its own. Asimov (1981, p. 154) explains:

> The further a device is removed from human control, the more authentically mechanical it seems, and the whole trend in technology has been to devise

machines that are less and less under direct human control and more and more seem to have the beginning of a will of their own. A chipped pebble is almost part of the hand it never leaves. A thrown spear declares a sort of independence the moment it is released.

If this division were to be completed, such that technology totally co-opted the human functions of rational thinking and action, and even of emotion, then humans themselves would be expendable. Burke (1969b, p. 14) notes that locating the entelechial motive in a tragedy would entail showing how that motive *ended*, that is, "the identifying of that motive with a narrative figure whose acts led to some fitting form of *death.*" The shadow myth of technology grown autonomous prophesies a "fitting form of death" for the human agent and thus is a recurring nightmare of contemporary life.

But if the cultural shadow represents not only a menace but also an opportunity, it is important to ask whether there is any way that the direction of movement expressed in the Frankenstein myth can be altered so that it does not reach its tragic perfection. Commenting on dystopian fiction, Ihab Hassan (1975, p. 131) offers a clue: "Prometheanism, I think, veers toward the demonic when it denies the female principle of creation. . . . (Significantly, Mary Shelley's Frankenstein never consummates his relation to Elizabeth, nor is his relation to any man or woman but perfunctory.) There is a dark, moon-like side to Promethean nature . . . a side shaped by Maternal forces. That side Prometheus can never afford to ignore" (see also Warrick, 1980, p. 38). Prometheanism, or the advance of technological progress, is predominantly a *masculine* myth that tends to ignore values associated with the feminine and with nature, which are often symbolically equated (Griffin, 1978; Kolodny, 1975; 1984; Merchant, 1980; Rakow, 1988). However, a feminine principle is always already enfolded within this patriarchal myth (Kristeva, 1984), and if the productive potential hidden in this ominous narrative is to be understood, the engendered dialectic operating at its core should be examined.

In the theory of depth psychology, antithetical entelechial impulses inhere in the masculine and feminine archetypal principles. Masculine consciousness moves from the center of the psyche outward in an analytical pattern of abstraction and separation (Whitmont, 1986, p. 142). We have already noted the particular form of this general pattern as a division of agency from agent in the Frankenstein myth. Conversely, feminine consciousness moves from the periphery toward the center in an analogical pattern of inclusion and identification (Whitmont, 1986, p. 142). In terms of the Frankenstein myth, agent strives to recollect agency as an interdependent part of an expanded cultural identity. If the repressed feminine aspects of the dystopian tragedy could be consciously recognized, then the entelechial pattern that motivates the feminine principle might be able to redirect the movement of the shadow myth, and in so doing alter its evolution toward a more productive societal end.

The Frankenstein myth unfolds against the backdrop of two oppositional motives: the tendencies toward division and identification. Our analysis thus proceeds in two parts. We first trace the dominant, patriarchal theme
of the myth through three contemporary films that represent phases in the
evolution of the agent/agency ratio: *Rocky IV* (1985), *Blade Runner* (1982),
and *The Terminator* (1984).[3] This theme manifests itself not so much as the
overt oppression of feminine by masculine symbols as through the advancing division of agency from agent as agency is progressively perfected. We
then examine the films again, focusing upon the secondary, more opaque
theme of facing and identifying with the shadow through the integration of
the feminine principle.

## ■ THE PERFECTION OF AGENCY

*Rocky IV.* Beneath its ideological transparencies, *Rocky IV* suggests that
people have extended themselves through and become dependent upon
their tools to act for them and that technology is thus making over the
human agent (regardless of nationality) in its own image, systematically
restructuring its scene and emptying it of moral purpose. Although the
robot in *Rocky IV* is not the main character, the film does chart the early
stages of human obsolescence through increasing mechanization. As *Rocky
IV* suggests, technology accomplishes the transformation of humans quite
differently in the United States than it does in Russia. In America, technology is primarily for "recreative" pleasure, and it already dominates the scene
in the form of televisions, fast automobiles, cordless telephones, motorized
kiddie cars, and household robots. Here, citizens experience the impact of
technology from the outside in. Paulie, for example, is everyone's Ugly
American. Soft, greedy, manipulative, and whiny, he typifies the consequences of recreational technology; unable to survive without his comics
and his television, he grows fat on junk food which his "female" robot, a sort
of Stepford wife without the flesh, retrieves for him. "She," on the other
hand, progressively takes on more human (i.e., stereotypically feminine)
qualities as Paulie grows even more sedimented than he was. She learns to
talk to him in terms of endearment, and Paulie explains to an astonished
Creed, "That's my girl. . . . She loves me." As Paulie leaves for Russia, she
nags him about taking his toothbrush. He responds with characteristic
crudeness, "When I get back, I'm gonna have her wires tied."
    Ever since Rocky won a moral victory in his Creed fight, he has walked
a thin line in the sequels between moral integrity and Paulie's decadence,
descending further into the temptations of wealth in each film, and requiring the rigors of spartan retraining for each redemption. By *Rocky IV*, his
living situation is not only blatantly ostentatious but also obviously mechanized, and he is once again losing his edge. All of his interactions with his

son emphasize a technologized scene: As Rocky arrives home early in the film, Rocky Jr. greets him through the lens of a video camera, warning him (with a bit too obvious childlike wisdom), "Don't go too fast or you'll get out of focus." As Rocky washes his Ferrari, the kid washes Paulie's robot, and their conversation is obscured by a radio turned up too loud. And when Rocky prepares to leave for Russia and tucks Junior in bed, father reminds son, "Don't forget to feed your robot." Even Adrian, previously the rock of good sense who protested the gadgetry the *nouveau riche* lifestyle brought her family, has succumbed and, by this fourth film, is patently dull and mechanical. When Rocky tells her he is going to Russia to fight Drago, she is confused. "And for that [Rocky's choice to fight Drago], you're willing to lose everything?" she asks, indicating the comforts of home.

As another victim of recreational technology, Apollo Creed is a sadder case than Paulie or Adrian, for he has genuine talent. But his talent has been diluted by a different variant of recreational technology—the televised spectacle, the pseudo-event, the electric circus—which, although good for the image, extracts its pound of flesh from the person as moral agent (Boorstin, 1962). By flattering appearance, pseudo-events break down human substance, hollow out the soul, and replace it with nothing but style. The opening act to Creed's exhibition match with Drago, with James Brown singing a telling "Living in America," is a carnival so overproduced and banal that Rocky and Adrian wince in recognition. It is a fitting scenic prelude for the tragedy to come; when empty posturing meets mechanized physical perfection, the outcome is quick, brutal, and final. Creed's death reveals the ultimate consequence for the human agent evacuated by technological recreation.

While American recreational technology erodes from the outside in, leaving purged vessels of stylized veneer, Russian technology "re-creates" the human agent from the inside out, perfecting nascent physical potential through blood doping, steroid ingestion, and Nautilus for the state. As Drago's publicist explains to the press: "It's a matter of science, evolution, isn't it, gentlemen? Drago is the most perfectly trained athlete—ever. . . . It's physically impossible for this little man [Rocky] to win. Drago is a look at the future." David Edelstein (1985, p. 67) writes of Drago: ". . . Rising up out of a pit for an exhibition match with Apollo Creed . . . he's like a socialist-realist Frankenstein's monster." Wearing a Nazi-like military uniform, backlighted, and shot from low angles through a smoky mist, Drago appears in the beginning of both fight scenes more as a futuristic *fascist* Frankenstein. Though Soviet technology leaves the agent cruel and "hard," rather than harmless and "soft," the cost of such physical consummation is the anesthetizing of the human spirit: feelings, creativity, compassion, self-awareness. Paulie may be a mushroom and Apollo Creed an image, but Drago is an automaton: dull, efficient, and relentless. His comments always resemble the vocalized print-out of a computer. "You will lose," he tells Creed before their fight. Looking down at a dying Creed, Drago remarks matter of factly, "If he dies, he dies." "I cannot be defeated. I defeat all men," he intones after Creed's destruction. "I must break you," he tells Rocky moments before their own encounter. As the two slap gloves together in the obligatory prefight handshake, a metal clink resounds from Drago's fist; he is the mechanized "dragon" of Russian re-creational technology.

The refusal of the dreaming individual, or culture, to look at its own shadow is generally represented in the Frankenstein myth by humans who will not see the consequences of what they have created (Small, 1972, p. 164). The prototype for this motif occurs in Shelley's novel when Victor Frankenstein is immediately repulsed as his handiwork opens his eyes. Frankenstein refuses to look at his creation, leaves the laboratory, and tries to forget him by going to sleep. "Technology, then, allows us to ignore our own works. It is *license to forget*" (Winner, 1977, p. 315). Until the end of *Rocky IV*, all the characters (except Rocky, on occasion) similarly fail to notice the extent to which technology has drained them. Certainly, Paulie does not reflect on his own degeneracy. With his totally impassive face, it is not apparent that Drago sees anything clearly, much less that his own technocratic make over has made him vulnerable by robbing him of "heart." And from the moment Creed first catches a glimpse of Drago (appropriately, as a televised image), he is so obsessed with planning his comeback that he pays no attention to Drago's re-created strength. When Rocky warns his aging friend, "You don't want to hear this, but maybe the show is over," Apollo protests vehemently. Prancing arrogantly in the prefight spectacle, and unaware of the irony, he says to himself, "God, I feel born again!" as he enters into his own demise.

*Blade Runner.* Within the futuristic time frame of *Blade Runner* (2019), technological agency has extended itself further toward its entelechial end.[4] In *Rocky IV*, the products of technical reason could significantly alter the human being, from without and within, but they still operated *on* the agent. In *Blade Runner*, agency as genetic engineering uses the DNA molecule to create synthetic agents (replicants) "from scratch." While it is true that these replicants share genetic substance with their human makers, their very consubstantiality makes them, paradoxically, more divided from each other. For, like an amoeba that replicates itself by splitting its cellular substance in two, the human agent has projected itself outward in space (in this film, the replicants are placed *literally* in "off-world" space) and now faces an alter ego: separate, nearly complete, and at the borderline of autonomy.

In *Blade Runner,* the question of who is in control, the humans or their agencies, has arrived at a perilous point. "Commerce is our goal here at Tyrell," the film's futuristic Dr. Frankenstein tells bounty hunter Rick Deckard, and Eldon Tyrell has certainly controlled the androids' genes to enhance their fitness as tools; the female "pleasure models" are more beautiful, the combat officers more strategically intelligent, and the assassins stronger than their human counterparts. Tyrell is aware, however, that technical efficiency only provides freedom for other activities when concern is eliminated about malfunctions. Thus, he has cannily built a safeguard into his Nexus 6 series: they are not genetically programmed for emotion (presumably, the catalyst for the development of free will), and, just in case they do begin to generate emotion spontaneously, they are preprogrammed to "die" after four years.

Nevertheless, human control is more elusive than Tyrell would like to admit; technology's vastly expanded influence is evident in the way it has restructured the scene in its own image. Technology is no longer *in* the scene; it *is* the scene. "Nature" has virtually disappeared, and the line between outside and indoors seems insignificant, as light rarely penetrates the dark, smoky haze of either. Harlan Kennedy (1982, p. 65) notes that, "As in *The Road Warrior,* we're in a world welded from the waste-materials of past epochs: Scrap-Heap Futurism." Michael Sragow (1982, p. 33) writes, "The city itself becomes a metaphor for a society that's lost organic growth. . . . The metropolis appears bloated yet constrained, like an overstuffed, glittering garbage can."

Technology has also redefined the relationship between humanity and its agencies. The real humans in *Blade Runner* make Paulie, Adrian, and Apollo Creed seem vibrant by contrast. The ever-present street people are alienated scavengers in a multilingual Tower of Babel. Although the city has the feel of stultifying overpopulation, no one seems to live near anyone else. (The wealthier by now have escaped to off-world suburbs.) Tyrell, a paranoid recluse, lives in an inaccessible penthouse high atop a grotesque, pretentious structure in downtown L.A., a fitting image for the perversion of the hierarchy of technical reason he has ascended. The police chief who forces Deckard back from retirement is a calloused bigot who refers to replicants as "skin jobs." Deckard describes himself in an early voice over as "Sushi, that's what my ex-wife called me. Cold fish." The most poignant symbol of the humans' descent is J. F. Sebastian, the genetic engineer who works for Tyrell. Occupying an entire glum apartment building by himself, he manufactures "friends" to keep him company, and perhaps also to ward off the knowledge that he is fast becoming extinct; at age 25, he has "Methuselah Syndrome" ("accelerated decrepitude") and, like the desperate replicants, not long to live.

*More human than human* is the motto at Tyrell Corporation, and, indeed, the replicants display a much richer array of human qualities than do the people. Deckard's narration is a weary rehashing of Philip Marlowe's self-reflections, but replicant leader Roy Batty speaks poetically and wonders about "his own place between animals and angels, men and machines" (Kennedy, 1982, p. 65). Two of the replicants (Leon and Rachael) carry photographs, supposedly of family members, in order "to give them the feeling (literally, the *impression*) that they have a human past. . . . For to have a past, whether your own or one you have created, is also to have a future" (Desser, 1985, p. 175). While the humans are too catatonic to suffer or to react angrily to the techno-commercial exploitation of their home, the replicants are furious at their enslavement. Whereas no human in the film cares about any other human, the replicants care passionately for each other; though murderous, they are more loyal to their own than are the human beings.

Unlike most critics (Desser, 1985; Kael, 1982), we regard Rachael as the film's most sentient sign that the characteristics of creator and created have shifted places. Manufactured without a termination date, but implanted with memory chips from Tyrell's niece, she is the only character who does not know what she is, and whose self-definition changes in the course of the narrative from "human" to "replicant." Rachael acts with mechanical indifference during the first half of the story, when she thinks she is human, as if she were imitating how the people around her seem to her. When she begins to suspect that she is a replicant, however, she drops her condescending facade and begins to act humanely. She shows initiative in escaping from Tyrell and questions Deckard intensely about her origins. After she shoots fellow replicant Leon in order to save Deckard, and Deckard tells her the shakes are "part of the business," she reflects tearfully on her ontological status: "I'm not *in* the business. I *am* the business!" Her aesthetic sense is awakened as she begins to play the piano. And she forms a relationship with Deckard. Although she can be seen as acting in a traditionally feminine manner with him (to his "Say you want me," she replies, "I want you"), this submissiveness, we believe, is more appropriately interpreted as the hesitant uncertainty that accompanies trying out each aspect of her "new" identity as nonhuman.

As was the case in *Rocky IV*, the people in *Blade Runner* do not consciously see their own shadows walking among them. None of the "average" people can tell the difference between a human and a replicant, and even the experts are sometimes fooled. Rachael wonders about this and asks Deckard if he has ever "retired" a human by mistake. He answers "no," but his expression reveals that this is an obvious risk of the business. Rachael also asks whether Deckard thinks that the work at Tyrell is a benefit to the public. He answers: "Replicants are like any other machine. They're either a benefit or a hazard. If they're a benefit, it's not my problem." It is an answer that calls to mind the questionable Western assumption "that technology is essentially neutral, a means to an end" (Winner, 1977, p. 25). But *Blade Runner*'s most near-sighted person, both literally and symbolically, is also the most "rational." Just as Victor Frankenstein failed to provide a place for his monster in society, Eldon Tyrell refuses to take moral responsibility for his creations. And just as Apollo Creed's pride veiled from him the dangers that technology posed for him, Tyrell is unable to see that what he calls his "fail-safe device" is inadequate to protect him from his prodigies' revenge.

His *reason* is impressive, but his eyesight is failing, and his *wisdom* is as artificial as the big-eyed owl that guards the entrance to his factory and home.

If the replicants are more human than humans, then it might be expected that they, in contrast to the real people, ironically might "see" the predicament of both agent and agency better than their creators. In fact, visual and verbal images of eyes accompany the replicants throughout the film as a sign of their visionary acuity. In the opening shots, two full-screen images of a replicant's eye are interspersed between scenes of the polluted city; factory fires are reflected in the iris, linking the industrial scene to its product. In their search for Tyrell, Roy and Leon visit Chew, the eye maker. Perfectly expressing the transference of identities that has taken place, Roy taunts Chew with, "If only you could see what I've seen with your eyes." As Leon lays a false eye on Chew's shoulder, Roy says of Tyrell, "Not an easy man to see, I guess."

As if to make fun of the fact that humans do not see as well as they do, the replicants act out black comic burlesque scenes employing eyes. When Leon pins Deckard against a car and prepares to kill him by poking out his eyes, he speaks with an oxymoronic mixture of matter-of-fact brutality: "Quite an experience to live in fear, isn't it? Wake up. Time to die." At the home of Sebastian, Pris paints a grotesque black mask around her eyes, which she coaxes Sebastian into proclaiming "beautiful." Roy holds up fake eyes to Sebastian and says, with a grin, "We're so happy you found us." (Of course, it was the superior-seeing replicants who found *him*.)

Most significantly, Roy kills Tyrell by completing Leon's aborted act; he places his thumbs underneath Tyrell's trifocals and gouges out his eyes as a prelude to crushing his skull. Roy's killing of Tyrell, a Biblical "eye for an eye," is revenge for Tyrell's myopia: his failure to see the consequences of his creative deeds. The poignancy in this hideous scene is that Roy understands the consequences of his own deed clearly. Like Dave Bowman's act in *2001*, this is a murder/suicide (except this time the machine kills the human), for Roy is dependent on Tyrell for any hope of further life. Finally, after Roy has almost killed Deckard but then inexplicably decides to let him live, he delivers his own eulogy, a lament on the ephemerality of his race's sight:

> Quite an experience to live in fear, isn't it? That's what it is to be a slave. . . . I've *seen* things you people wouldn't believe. Attack ships on fire off the shoulder of Orion. I've watched seabeams glitter in the dark near the Tannhauser gate. All those moments will be lost in time—like—tears—in rain. Time to die.

Roy's eyes close and, like Apollo Creed, he meets an "untimely" death. Unlike Creed, however, Roy has entered his own demise with his inner eye wide open.

*The Terminator.*[5] The time traveler in this film, Kyle Reese, explains to

Sarah Connor that the life he came from is "one possible future" for humanity. Indeed, *The Terminator* represents most clearly the tragic consequences for humanity, should this shadow story ever be played out to its completion. In contrast to both *Rocky IV* and *Blade Runner,* in which technology is divided from but still dependent upon human agents, technology in *The Terminator* is fully autonomous.

In this post-nuclear context of 2029, technology has virtually completed its task of reconstructing the environment in its own image. Gargantuan tanks roll relentlessly through the "scenery," which, like that of *Blade Runner,* is another scrap heap of waste materials from the past. Unlike the scenery of *Blade Runner,* however, this landscape of discarded metal and human bones is all there is: no commercials lure the rich to off-world colonies, and no wooded mountains await the heroes' escape. Because their plight is so desperate, these future humans are no longer passive, as they were in *Rocky,* or dull and alienated, as they were in *Blade Runner;* they have awakened from their somnambulism and are fully aware that their shadows are alive, well, and threatening their pitiful existence. Unfortunately, it is almost too late for this newly found consciousness to do them any good. For their hunted condition has reduced them to the status of cornered animals. The brands they wear on their arms are signs that they have lost that most human of characteristics: the capacity to choose; as an endangered species, their only mode of intervention is to battle the machines.

At the outset, the people of *The Terminator*'s present are much like the average, contemporary Americans in *Rocky IV:* tuned into recreational technology and blissfully tuned out of the eventual consequences of their comfortable and convenient lifestyle. Sarah and her roommate Ginger use the requisite modern inventions: hair dryer, telephone answering machine, and scooter. Ginger's perpetual life-support system is a Sony Walkman, which she keeps connected even when making love. A revved-up dance bar is named the "Tech Noir." When the Terminator visits the present, however, the people who cross his path are instantly restricted to the choices of the people of the future: kill or be killed (and, for all but Sarah, the first "choice" is purely academic). Sarah becomes as hunted as the future's guerrillas, her every *act* an automatic *reaction* to the Terminator's.

As separate beings who develop wills of their own, *Blade Runner*'s replicants were close to controlling their own destinies; they did not, however, possess the capacity to extend their immortality by reproducing their own kind. The computer network in *The Terminator,* only 10 years later, has found this key. This reproductive capacity breaks the umbilical cord that keeps technology dependent on its human parent and creates a seemingly unbridgeable generation gap. It also co-opts the most basic feminine form of creation: that of giving birth. In addition, since *Blade Runner*'s replicants were created in the image of a *human* maker, they were synthetic reproductions of the near-whole human agent, and, as the humans grew progressively more obsolete, the replicants grew more human than human. But the Terminator's roots are electric circuitry, itself generated by machines. He is created in the image of a *technological* maker and, as such, is a reproduction of a human part: that of technical reason. Whereas both Drago's and Roy's material substance was organic, the Terminator's is inorganic; he looks human on the outside, but is the most recent triumph in a series of sophisticated robots from the future. "He's not a man. A machine. A terminator. Cyberdigm Systems Model 101," Reese tells a disbelieving Sarah. "The 600 series had rubber skin; we spotted them easy. But these are new. They look human. Sweat, bad breath, everything—very hard to spot." He is, then, a more advanced incarnation than either Drago or the replicants of the entelechial end of this myth, which is the perfection of rational/technological *agency,* not of the whole human being.

We have already noted how technological agency progressively redefines the scene and the human agent with each advance in the myth. *The Terminator* represents the most perfected form yet of agency-determined *purpose.* Drago's purpose was the improvement of human efficiency; technology had not yet developed a separate intention. The replicants in *Blade Runner* did develop a purpose of their own (delaying their own mortality), but they were still dependent on their human makers to fulfill it. But *The Terminator*'s future computers have generated a purpose that they may act upon without human help. As Kyle "reminisces" to Sarah: "It was the machines—Defense Network Computers. New—powerful—hooked into everything. They say it got smart. A new order of intelligence. Then it saw all people as a threat, not just the ones on the other side. Decided our fate in a microsecond—extermination." Presumably, the Defense Network Computers had been created as elaborate safeguards against nuclear holocaust. Their "decision" to eliminate the human race by starting a war echoes Jung's prophecy in 1922 that "fire-arms go off of themselves if only enough of them are together" (1971, p. 465), as well as Winner's warning that "the foundations of technological society are less reliable than some had hoped" (1977, pp. 295–296). If humans have finally awakened to realize that the computers are now the master and humanity the slave, the humans must be exterminated lest they try to reclaim from technology the capacities they so blindly gave away. The Terminator's name captures well both his purpose and the fact that technology and humanity have exchanged places as agent and agency. "Termination" is a term ordinarily not applied to human homicide but reserved for the cessation of mechanical functions, which have no purpose other than to serve as agencies for human intention. Since humans now serve no function for the machines, they might as well be liquidated.

When agency determines purpose rather than vice versa, however, purpose loses its customary association with morality, which is a "flaw" in the perfection of agency. The Terminator is *rational,* for example, but not *reasonable.* "You can't reason with him," Kyle says, although he is the pure embodiment of technical reason. Furthermore, he has no need for community. Whereas Frankenstein's monster pleaded with his creator to make a place for him in human society, and *Blade Runner*'s replicants at least found society with each other, the Terminator has no such limitation and is unhampered by angst over any of his killings. "He was just being systematic," Kyle tells the police to explain why the Terminator killed all women with the name "Sarah Connor" who preceded *the* Sarah Connor in the Los Angeles telephone directory. The metal skeleton that emerges from the ashes in the climactic battle scene with Sarah, free from all human bodily or communal constraints, seems a macabre caricature of the humanists' moral conception of a "core self."

As has been the case with other humans in this myth, the people of the present are so dependent on their technological devices that they do not see the Terminator for what he is. The film has a great deal of "fun," not only with the Terminator's masterful use of the humans' technology against them but with people dying while relying upon the latest mechanical gadgets. The Terminator's first act upon entering 1984 is to rip the heart out of a punker who refuses to give up his technology-inspired metallic clothes. His next victim is a local gun shop clerk, whose inventory would warm the heart of any *Soldier of Fortune* devotee. Ginger does not hear the Terminator enter her apartment (not that it would have saved her) because she is hooked up to her Walkman. Sarah gives away her whereabouts by leaving a message on her answering machine, which the Terminator is by now monitoring. In addition, it takes Sarah several near misses to see that the Terminator is somewhat unusual. And, even after the Terminator's inhuman survival of multiple shootings, the police try to convince Sarah he is just wearing a bulletproof vest. They tell her to "get some sleep" (recalling Dr. Frankenstein's attempt to forget) as the Terminator crashes through the police department's doors in a muscle car.

Predictably, the nonhuman Terminator sees the situation quite clearly, not with the existential understanding of Frankenstein's monster or of Roy Batty but with the "tunnel vision" necessary to fulfill his mission. And, since his "human" body is merely a disguise, he does not need his imitation eyes to see what to do. After one of them has been damaged, he inserts an Exacto knife into his orb with clinical detachment, plucking the synthetic organ from its socket and leaving a demon-red glow in its place. His optic mutilation is not, like Roy's, an act of revenge (the most perfected machines have no emotions) but of *efficiency*. As the Terminator's outer shell continues to decompose, turning his face into a nesting ground for flies, he sits on a bed in a seedy hotel room plotting his next move. An almost equally squalid janitor hollers through the door, "Hey Buddy, ya gotta dead cat in there?" The Terminator prepares a measured, computerized response: "Fuck you, asshole!" The entire scene seems a particularly rich materialization of Burke's wry observation that the human race is "rotten with perfection."

## ■ FACING THE SHADOW

Although most humans in these films are oblivious to their condition in relation to technology, a few people appear cognizant that the patriarchal path is leading toward extinction. In the first two films, this heightened vision is correlated with some contact with the *feminine*, either symbolized as nature or actualized in individual women. Those who recognize the shadow side of technological progress seem to do so because they identify their own escalating enslavement by technology with the prolonged historical subjugation of women and feminine values to patriarchal social structures and their technological extensions. To the extent that a predominantly male social order reintegrates into its consciousness a feminine perspective that it has itself long repressed, the resulting expanded consciousness may be whole enough to reclaim technology as a part of itself. As might be expected, however, facing the shadow is a formidable task, and those who attempt it in the three films meet with variable success.

*Rocky IV.* Unlike Paulie, Apollo Creed, and Drago, Rocky does eventually see that his glossy lifestyle is robbing him of spirit. Despite his macho persona, Rocky's instinct in all the previous films has been to humanize himself through contact with Adrian. Since Adrian is now too corrupted by the overtechnologized comforts of home to provide a psychological anchor, this time he regains his equilibrium through contact with the unspoiled *land* as a symbol of the feminine. Rocky's attraction to the frozen, yet energizing fecundity of the earth suggests an attempt to escape the ravages of all technology on the human purposive agent. In the obligatory fight-training montage, the camera juxtaposes Rocky outside *working*—chopping wood, piling stones for fences, towing loaded carts—with Drago inside *working out*—running on treadmills, hitting impact machines, lifting metal weights. The contrast is one between the human who *acts* through intrinsic purpose and the humanoid who *moves* through the manipulation of someone or something else (Burke, 1968, p. 53). Cut off from nature, Drago's training-as-movement deadens the spirit as it perfects the body. Reunited with nature through unencumbered work, Rocky's training-as-action conjoins body and spirit into the consummate warrior.

The disturbing thing about Rocky's "vision" is that it distorts his psyche into "an individualism bordering on the psychotic" that J. Hoberman (1986, p. 44) thinks is characteristic of several films like *Rocky IV*. Following Susan Sontag (1974/1980), Hoberman notes that *Rocky IV* relies on typically fascist themes, such as emphasis on the physical and instinctual over the intellectual, rebirth of the body and community through worship of an irresistible leader, the challenge and ordeal of the elemental, extravagant effort and endurance of pain, and the vertigo before power, symbolized by the majesty of mountains (p. 45). The spiritual fervor of Rocky's training, a recurrent theme in all four films, is now depicted in the archetypal terms of a descent into hell. "Now you're gonna go through hell—worse than any nightmare you ever dreamed," proclaims Rocky's trainer and guru, "but in the end, you're gonna be the one standing." Certainly, the ending scene of the film, in which Rocky awakens the slumbering individualism of Drago (significantly, by opening a gash under his *eye*), and converts the Russian people, including a Gorbachev look-alike, into a hysterically pro-Rocky mob, deserves the critical ridicule it has received.

Rocky does awaken to the shadow cast by technological progress over his culture and his self, and it is partially his encounter with the symbolically feminine land that not only prepares him to see but to convert his enemies to seeing. Why, then, does his experience turn him into a dangerously zealous fanatic rather than a person who has regained his balance? Rocky's *hubris* is exacerbated because his attitude toward nature remains patriarchal: he uses rather than identifies. This is represented most vividly in the triumphant climax of his training sequence, when he ascends, on foot, not the steps of a municipal building in Philadelphia (as in the first two films) but a rugged mountain peak, absorbing its power for his own individualistic purposes. Rocky succumbs to what Jung (1971, p. 119) calls "psychic inflation": through a meeting with a life-renewing symbol of the collective repressed feminine, he feels a godlike power, for he is now "the fortunate possessor of *the* great truth which was only waiting to be discovered, of the eschatological knowledge which spells the healing of the nations." Psychically inflated individuals, Jung (p. 120) states, "are seized by a sort of pathos, everything seems pregnant with meaning, and all effective self-criticism is checked." Because Rocky does not become one with the land but uses it to enhance his power as a single combat warrior, he unwittingly follows a course that led humans to lose control of technology in the first place: that is, the attempt to control it through force (to defeat Drago) only hastens humans' divorce from machines and machines' dominance over humans (Winner, 1977, pp. 238–251, 311).

*Blade Runner.* Like Rocky, *Blade Runner*'s Deckard eventually comes to see the threat of technology against his humanity. Also like Rocky, his awakening is linked to the feminine; by this time, however, technology has so thoroughly dominated his immediate environment that very little "nature" is left (symbolized further by the absence of any major "real" women characters in the film). His association with the feminine is thus limited to the technologically created female replicants. Each confrontation with one of these women leaves him, in contrast with Rocky, more self-critical and less militant. Like a lucid dreamer, he starts to realize he is dreaming while not yet completely awake and begins a dialogue with his own unconscious (Garfield, 1974, pp. 143–178).

When Rachael prompts Deckard to tell her the truth about her origins and she sadly leaves his apartment, he expresses in narration confusion over his psychic state: "Replicants weren't supposed to have feelings. Neither were blade runners. What the hell was happening to me?" Later, after first deceiving and then shooting the replicant Zhora as she tries to escape, his feelings become stronger, and he muses: "The report would be routine retirement of a replicant, which didn't make me feel any better about shooting a woman in the back. There it was again—feeling in myself—for her, for Rachael." And when he kills Pris in a violently bloody scene, his facial expression indicates he is more repulsed by his act than relieved by his momentary respite from danger.

In killing the two women replicants, Deckard attempts a radical form of the usual patriarchal tactic for handling errant technology (i.e., apply further control [Rushing, 1989]). But, through his care for Rachael, he has already begun to assimilate values usually associated with the feminine, such as concern for life, sensitivity, empathy, emotionality, and cooperation (Rakow, 1988, p. 62; Rothschild, 1981). These qualities interfere with a detective's necessary detachment, and he realizes that the women he kills are indeed "more human than human." Like real women and, increasingly, like himself, they are enslaved by the technological extensions of patriarchal reason. Thus, his increasing consubstantiality with his victims forces him to see his acts as cold-blooded murder, not just "retirement." More generally, once the feminine entelechial process is reactivated in Deckard through his identification with the female replicants, he can re-collect other aberrant aspects of technological agency into his own consciousness (even Roy, who is bent on destroying him). His oneness with the replicants is underscored when Roy "toys" with Deckard near the end, letting him dangle precariously from the rooftop and then reminding him that it is a fearful experience to be a slave. Sitting alone in stunned silence, Deckard registers in his narration recognition of what he shares with those who have "died":

> I don't know why he saved my life. Maybe in those last moments he loved life more than he ever had before—not just *his* life—anybody's life—my life. All he wanted were the same answers the rest of us want. "Where do I come from? Where am I going? How long have I got?" All I could do is sit there and watch him die.

Deckard is awakened, then, through his identification with the feminine, the experience of thralldom, and the recognition of the brutality of his own acts. He seems also to have realized that, whatever the solution to the problem of technology, it will not be achieved by divorcing himself from it, by attempting further *mastery* of it, or by co-opting feminine power in order to inflate his own patriarchal ego. Rather, it requires an act of reconciliation, of, quite literally, "getting ourselves together." Rachael is both technology *and* woman, and he reunites himself with both by loving her. As Deckard returns to his apartment after his final encounter with Roy, he retrieves Rachael and finds an origami unicorn, symbol of resurrection, left by detective Gaff. Deckard and Rachael escape their polluted scene, which is probably beyond the possibility of rehumanization. As they fly over what look like the Rocky Mountains, Deckard's final narration reveals his attitude: "Gaff had been there and let her live. Four years, he figured. He was wrong. Tyrell had told me Rachael was special—no termination date. I didn't know how long we'd have together. Who does?" Unlike Rocky, he enters the mountains humbly to make a new and tentative beginning.[6]

*The Terminator.* Whereas Deckard became conscious of his shadow slowly and painfully, *The Terminator's* people of the future are, as we pointed out earlier, fully alert from the beginning. Likewise, Sarah also wakes up totally when she finally realizes that Kyle is not crazy and that the Terminator is really what Kyle says he is. But these people are awake because they must kill or be killed, not because throwing off sleep will allow them to regain their humanity. Once the shadow is an entirely separate and autonomous entity, it is not any longer, as it still was in *Blade Runner,* consubstantial with humanity. It can be faced and fought, but not reassimilated into consciousness. Furthermore, since all humans, both feminine and masculine, are now enslaved by technology, each sex is reduced to its most primitive functions in order to ensure survival. Men are valuable as warriors, and women for their ability to give birth to warriors (or, as is also the case with Sarah, to become warriors themselves). Although Kyle does fall in love with Sarah, his encounter with her is only important insofar as it produces the child who will become leader, not because he needs to empathize with her enslavement or integrate her characteristics into his own consciousness. When a pregnant Sarah rides out into the desert at the end of the film, the fertility implied in the biological/natural link is mitigated by the dark clouds gathering forebodingly in the distance. If things ever come to this, *The Terminator* seems to say, sexual politics will be irrelevant, "nature" will be obliterated, and humankind's only chance will be to rid itself of *all* technology and start over again at a tribal level.

## ▥ IMPLICATIONS

At the beginning of this essay, we noted the widely accepted practice of classifying science fiction as either "utopian" (open system) or "dystopian" (closed system). In contrast, our analysis suggests that the dystopian impulse is dialectical, creating a tension between apocalyptic and slightly more sanguine visions.[7] If this interpretation extends to other works, the Frankenstein myth advocates that the machine is currently a largely unseen malignancy which will indeed result in the degeneration or death of humanity in the future, but only if the prescription for remedy implanted within the myth itself is not heeded. Specifically, the myth suggests that the medicine for cultural psychic health lies within, as a form of *inner seeing* rather than *outer control.* Thus, although we share Warrick's enthusiasm for open-system fiction that provides metaphors for the imaginative transcendence of the present, we cannot endorse her clear preference for such fiction over dystopian stories as social criticism. Open-system narratives provide a "speculative leap" (Warrick, 1980, p. 198), a "radical and discontinuous jump into a future time" (p. 161). Of dystopian, closed-system fiction, she writes,

> The story dates; the events pictured in the fiction, except for the destruction of the computer, have actually occurred, and society generally continues on unperturbed, except for a distraught humanist here and there wringing his hands despairingly. It just may be that an image of something better in the future has a greater corrective effect on society than the image of something worse. (p. 165)

But our perspective implies that "something better" can follow "something worse" only if that "something worse" is first assimilated into consciousness. If it is not, the "something better" that Warrick hopes for will remain, we fear, in the fantasy realm of the fictive imagination and not in the sociocultural sphere of life as lived.

In order to reach these conclusions, we have presumed interpretive possibilities for myth, a communicative form long vilified in mass media criticism (e.g., Fitting, 1987; Jameson, 1979; McGee, 1980). Specifically, we envision some myths (what we are calling "shadow myths") as revelatory insofar as they visualize the repressed as a precursor to social change. Seen in this way, such myths are rhetorical, not in that they advance the interests of a particular social group but in that they narratively advocate a view that simultaneously subverts the dominant cultural ideology and affirms a new image (Fisher, 1970). It is not in the nature of myths, of course, to argue logically for a point of view or to spell out a specific course of action. It is in the nature of a shadow myth, as a cultural analogue to an individual's shadow dreams, to present the hibernating culture with an accurate, though frightening, disclosure about what it has been repressing. An individual who gives such a series of dreams their due would try out various paths for dealing with them: for integrating them into consciousness and taking action in waking life. The person thus establishes an ongoing dialogue with the dreams, in which the dreams "comment" on their author's conscious acts, and the person makes decisions about what to do. Similarly, mythic art has long carried on such a dialogue with the culture; one of the tasks of the critic, as we see it, is to offer interpretations of this "conversation." In saying this, we acknowledge that many narrative structures are vehicles of domination and repression, but we do emphasize that restricting the concept of "myth" to those particular functions places unnecessary limitations on critical analysis. It would be unfortunate if the assumption that myths are always mystifying were to take on a cast that reproduces such mystifying myths themselves: that is, that serves to perpetuate an increasingly dominant critical world view and thus unintentionally forecloses opposing readings.

## Notes

¹At one point, Warrick (p. 198) claims that open-system fiction is not truly utopian because it does not solve the problems defined in dystopian literature; however, she also states that there is a high correlation between closed system and negative views, and open system and positive views (p. 100). Warrick also discusses a third category, the "isolated model," consisting mostly of short stories of the 1930s and 40s that were instrumental in creating a positive image of robots, but pertaining to a hypothetical system which is isolated from its surroundings (pp. 102–129).

²For an application of the pentad to analysis of mythic change in a series of films, see Rushing (1986).

³Because science fiction is preeminently concerned with contexts that are removed in time and/or place from the present, stories that comment on the present stage of the human/technology relationship often occur outside that genre. *Rocky IV* is included here for this reason.

⁴*Blade Runner* is based on Philip K. Dick's novel, *Do Androids Dream of Electric Sheep?* (1969). However, as Peter Fitting (1987) has pointed out, the novel and the film suggest significantly different conclusions concerning the humanity/technology relationship; our comments are thus confined to the film.

⁵*The Terminator* takes place within two time frames, the future (2029) and the present (1984). Since the robot is constructed in the future and sent to the present, our comments concerning the state of technology are relevant to both time frames.

⁶David Desser (1985, p. 178) makes a similar point concerning the ending scene when he writes, "Deckard must put aside his distrust of women, must transcend his emotional aloofness, must finally make the ultimate commitment to give of himself and his humanity. . . . Man merges with his creation." For an opposing reading of this ending, see Fitting (1987).

⁷Andrew Gordon (1982) has similarly questioned the purely optimistic impulses of *utopian* science fiction.

## References

Arendt, H. (1958). *The human condition.* Chicago: University of Chicago Press.

Asimov, I. (1981). The myth of the machine. In *Asimov on science fiction* (pp. 153–163). Garden City, NY: Doubleday.

Barrett, W. (1978). *The illusion of technique: A search for meaning in a technological civilization.* New York: Anchor.

Boorstin, D. J. (1962). *The image or what happened to the American dream.* New York: Atheneum.

Broege, V. (1983). Electric Eve: Images of female computers in science fiction. In R. D. Erlich & T. P. Dunn (Eds.), *Clockwork worlds: Mechanized environments in SF* (pp. 183–194). Westport, CT: Greenwood Press.

Burke, K. (1968). *Language as symbolic action.* Berkeley: University of California Press.

Burke, K. (1969a). *A grammar of motives.* Berkeley: University of California Press.

Burke, K. (1969b). *A rhetoric of motives.* Berkeley: University of California Press.

Creed, B. (1986). Horrors and the monstrous-feminine: An imaginary abjection. *Screen, 27,* 44–70.

Davies, R. A., Farrell, J. M., & Matthews, S. S. (1982). The dream world of film: A Jungian perspective on cinematic communication. *Western Journal of Speech Communication, 46,* 326–343.

Desser, D. (1985). *Blade Runner:* Science fiction & transcendence. *Literature Film Quarterly, 13,* 172–179.

Dick, P. K. (1969). *Do androids dream of electric sheep?* New York: Signet.

Edelstein, D. (1985, December 10). Going for the biff-bam-bang. *Voice,* p. 67.

Ellul, J. (1964). *The technological society* (J. Wilkinson, Trans.). New York: Alfred A. Knopf.

Farrell, T. B. (1976). Knowledge, consensus, and rhetorical theory. *Quarterly Journal of Speech, 62,* 1–14.

Farrell, T. B., & Goodnight, G. T. (1981). Accidental rhetoric: The root metaphors of Three Mile Island. *Communication Monographs, 48,* 271–300.

Fisher, W. R. (1970). A motive view of communication. *Quarterly Journal of Speech, 56,* 131–139.

Fitting, P. (1987). Futurecop: The neutralization of revolt in *Blade Runner. Science-Fiction Studies, 14,* 340–354.

Frentz, T. S. (1984, May). *Mass media as rhetorical narration.* Paper presented at the Van Zelst Lecture in Communication, Northwestern University, Evanston, IL.

Garfield, P. L. (1974). *Creative dreaming.* New York: Simon and Schuster.

Geduld, C. (1973). *Filmguide to 2001: A Space Odyssey.* Bloomington: Indiana University Press.

Gordon, A. (1982). Human, more or less: Man-machine communion in Samuel R. Delaney's *Nova* and other science fiction stories. In T. P. Dunn & R. D. Erlich (Eds.), *The mechanical god: Machines in science fiction* (pp. 193–202). Westport, CT: Greenwood Press.

Griffin, S. (1978). *Women and nature: The roaring inside her.* New York: Harper and Row.

Hassan, I. (1975). *Paracriticisms: Seven speculations of the times.* Urbana: University of Illinois Press.

Hoberman, J. (1986, March). The fascist guns in the west. *American Film,* pp. 42–48.

Jameson, F. (1971). *Marxism and form.* Princeton: Princeton University Press.

Jameson, F. (1979). Reification and utopia in mass culture. *Social Text, 1,* 130–148.

Jung, C. G. (1966). Psychology and literature. In *The spirit in man, art, and literature* (pp. 84–105, R. F. C. Hull, Trans.). New York: Bollingen Foundation.

Jung, C. G. (1971). *The portable Jung* (J. Campbell, Ed., R. F. C. Hull, Trans.). New York: Viking.

Kael, P. (1982, July 12). Baby, the rain must fall. *The New Yorker,* pp. 82–85.

Kennedy, H. (1982, July–August). 21st century nervous breakdown. *Film Comment,* pp. 66–68.

Kolodny, A. (1975). *The lay of the land.* Chapel Hill: University of North Carolina Press.

Kolodny, A. (1984). *The land before her: Fantasy and experience of the American frontier, 1630–1860.* Chapel Hill: University of North Carolina Press.

Kristeva, J. (1984). *Revolution in poetic language* (M. Waller, Trans.) New York: Columbia University Press.

Marcuse, H. (1964). *One-dimensional man: Studies in the ideology of advanced industrial society.* Boston: Beacon Press.

McGee, M. C. (1980). The ideograph: A link between rhetoric and ideology. *Quarterly Journal of Speech, 66,* 1–16.

McLuhan, M. (1965). *Understanding media: The extensions of man.* New York: McGraw-Hill.

Merchant, C. (1980). *The death of nature: Women, ecology, and the scientific revolution.* San Francisco: Harper and Row.

Mumford, L. (1970). *The pentagon of power: The myth of the machine* (Vol. 2). New York: Harcourt, Brace, Jovanovich.

Neisser, U. (1966). Computers as tools and as metaphors. In C. R. Dechert (Ed.), *The social impact of cybernetics* (pp. 71–93). New York: Simon and Schuster.

Palumbo, D. (1982). Loving that machine; or, the mechanical egg: Sexual mechanisms and metaphors in science fiction films. In T. P. Dunn & R. D. Erlich (Eds.), *The mechanical god: Machines in science fiction* (pp. 117–128). Westport, CT: Greenwood Press.

Porush, D. (1985). *The soft machine: Cybernetic fiction.* New York: Methuen.

Rakow, L. (1988). Gendered technology, gendered practice. *Critical Studies in Mass Communication, 5,* 57–70.

Rothschild, J. (1981). A feminist perspective on technology and the future. *Women's Studies International Quarterly, 4,* 65–74.

Rushing, J. (1986). Mythic evolution of "The new frontier" in mass mediated rhetoric. *Critical Studies in Mass Communication, 3,* 265–296.

Rushing, J. (1989). Evolution of "The new frontier" in *Alien* and *Aliens:* Patriarchal co-optation of the feminine archetype. *Quarterly Journal of Speech, 75.*

Sanders, J. (1982). Tools/mirrors: The humanization of machines. In T. P. Dunn & R. D. Erlich (Eds.), *The mechanical god: Machines in science fiction* (pp. 167–176). Westport, CT: Greenwood Press.

Slack, J. D. (1984). *Communication technologies and society: Conceptions of causality and the politics of technological intervention.* Norwood, NJ: Ablex.

Small, C. (1972). *Mary Shelley's Frankenstein.* Pittsburgh: University of Pittsburgh Press.

Shelley, M. (1934). *Frankenstein.* New York: Harrison Smith and Robert Haas. (Original work published 1818)

Sontag, S. (1980). Fascinating fascism. In *Under the sign of Saturn* (pp. 73–105). New York: Farrar, Straus, Giroux.

Sragow, M. (1982, August 5). "Blade Runner": Stalking the alienated android. *Rolling Stone,* pp. 33–34.

Warrick, P. (1980). *The cybernetic imagination in science fiction.* Cambridge: Massachusetts Institute of Technology Press.

Whitmont, E. C. (1978). *The symbolic quest: Basic concepts of analytical psychology.* Princeton, NJ: Princeton University Press.

Wilber, K. (1983). *Up from Eden: A transpersonal view of human evolution.* Boulder, CO: Shambhala Press.

Williams, R. (1974). *Television: Technology and cultural form.* New York: Schocken Books.

Winner, L. (1977). *Autonomous technology: Technics-out-of-control as a theme in political thought.* Cambridge: Massachusetts Institute of Technology Press.

Wolfe, G. K. (1979). *The known and the unknown: The iconography of science fiction.* Kent, OH: Kent State University Press.

Wymer, T. L. (1982). Machines and the meaning of human in the novels of Kurt Vonnegut, Jr. In T. P. Dunn & R. D. Erlich (Eds.), *The mechanical god: Machines in science fiction* (pp. 41–52). Westport, CT: Greenwood Press.

# MAXIM 2

# *CRITICISM IS WRITTEN TO AND FOR AN AUDIENCE*

# CHAPTER 8 [                    ]

# RHETORICAL STRUCTURE
# AND *PRIMATE*

**Thomas W. Benson**

*In this commentary, Thomas W. Benson explains his own sense of
identification with his audience as a professional, a teacher, and
writer-scholar, for whom critical writing discharges obligations to both
students and colleagues. Benson's attraction to the documentary films of
Fred Wiseman led him to search for ways to share his understanding and
appreciation of Wiseman's* Primate *with this community, and his
commentary recounts the tensions and choices involved in revising his work
for the* Quarterly Journal of Speech.

## COMMENTARY

I have been interested in the documentary films of Fred Wiseman since
seeing his first two films—*Titicut Follies,* at the State University of New York
at Buffalo (in, I think, about 1968, in an exhibition sponsored by one of the
film's backers, Warren Bennis, who was then a provost at SUNY Buffalo),
and *High School,* which I saw for the first time at the 1969 San Francisco Film
Festival, when I was a visiting assistant professor at the University of California, Berkeley.

I had been teaching at SUNY Buffalo since 1963, where I had introduced courses in the history and criticism of narrative and documentary film
in addition to courses in rhetorical criticism and the history of public address.

I admired the intelligence and aesthetic achievements of Wiseman's
work. In the late sixties, at a time of social upheaval, of distrust and protest
against the Vietnam War and institutions of oppression, Wiseman's films
spoke strongly to my own sense of alienation from authority. Wiseman's
films also seemed to offer a rich way to tap into understandings of how

**184**

people communicated in situated, face-to-face interaction and how complex discourses (his films) communicated with audiences who were treated as active and intelligent (and flattered for being active and intelligent).

Why write rather than seek some other form of expression? I define myself professionally as a teacher and writer-scholar. Bringing a piece of scholarship to written form is part of what I feel I owe my students and colleagues. It is setting aside time to do part of society's homework, in aid of shared social knowledge—monitoring our institutions and practices, and encouraging critical reflection. And scholarly writing, despite its difficulties and disappointments, I experience as deeply rewarding for its own sake in enlarging understanding, exercising mind and spirit, and satisfying the yearning for serious communication. Scholarly writing is a way to participate in the world and to attempt to make a contribution. I was raised in a family where it was a male virtue to not talk very much. Becoming a teacher and scholar has been a personally liberating experience for me, but it always carries with it, in addition to my sometimes deep stage fright, a conscientious sense of inhibition, a repugnance about talking too much and advertising myself.

The original version of this essay was written in the summer of 1981, in preparation for a presentation at the annual convention of the Speech Communication Association in Anaheim in November of that year. I had already been doing preliminary work on *Primate* when a former doctoral student and coauthor on various projects invited me to participate in a panel he was organizing for the Anaheim convention. I worked on the film over a period of weeks, constructing notes based on a detailed, scene-by-scene analysis; the analysis was accompanied by slides shot from frames of the film. The critic-respondent was an old friend, Walt Fisher, whom I had first met at the SCA-NEH Pheasant Run conference in the spring of 1970.

At Anaheim, Herman Stelzner asked me if I would submit the *Primate* paper to *The Quarterly Journal of Speech,* of which he was then editor; I said I had written the essay in the hope that it might be suitable for *QJS,* and that I would probably send it to him. But I already had another essay in press at *QJS,* which was scheduled to appear shortly after the 1981 convention. That essay, "Another Shooting in Cowtown," was by far the longest ever published in the journal and was somewhat unconventional in form. Although the essay was generally well received, I heard of some complaints that it was not fair for one author to be given so much space in the journal, thus depriving other authors of access to a resource crucial to tenure and promotion. And so I refrained from sending the *Primate* essay to Herm Stelzner during the remainder of his editorial term. I did not want to place him in the position of being doubly criticized for giving me still more space in the journal during his term. Over the period 1981–85 I presented various versions of the *Primate* paper in lectures at the University of Texas, the Eastern Communication Association, the Society for Cinema Studies, Auburn University, and the University of Maryland, as well as in classes at Penn State University. Professors and students at these occasions always provided strong encouragement and asked questions that helped in the ongoing process of rethinking and revision.

When Walter Fisher took over as the new editor of *QJS*, I figured that the clock had been reset and that it was now appropriate for me to submit the work to the gatekeeping process. I spent most of the Christmas break in 1983, and then January and February 1984, working on the essay, revising and extending it for review. I sent it to *QJS* on February 23, 1984. The reviews praised the essay as criticism but asked for clearer statements of the theory that drove the criticism and explained its general significance. There were several useful stylistic and structural suggestions. At the end of spring semester 1984 I again turned to the paper, and sent a revision to Walt Fisher at the end of June. On October 9, 1984, Walt wrote to say that the two associate editors (whose comments he included) advised publication, but that he himself was not ready to accept it without further revision. He requested that I omit or sharply condense the paper's discussions of the work of Anthony Trollope, James Agee, and Nadine Gordimer, and introduce a more compelling theoretical grounding, such as Stanley Fish's notion of "self-consuming artifacts."

I would prefer not to tell this next part, but I've started the story, at the request of the editors of this volume, so I'll finish. I did not want to take Walt's advice, which I saw as driving me away from a paper that was groping for a complex critical understanding and toward a paper that followed a text-illustrates-theory format, a format that seemed to me likely to offer a false clarity at the expense of understanding. It is hard for me, just a few years later, to sort out the merits of the situation, to tell how much was an author's appropriate defense of his vision and how much was just my own ego and stubborn self-indulgence. In any case, Walt's letter graciously invited a response: He ended his letter by writing, "If I have been unclear or wrong-headed, call and let us discuss things. Cordially, Walt." I made some changes in the manuscript, based on this latest round of reviews, where I was convinced the reviewers' suggestions improved things, then wrote Walt explaining my views. We then talked on the phone. I recall arguing pretty strongly, though in friendly terms, both in that letter and in our phone call. On December 6, 1984, I sent Walt my final, revised version, which he accepted for publication in the May 1985 issue of the journal.

In the end, Walt and his editorial readers prompted me to revise in ways that improved the essay. Some of the revisions were made simply by accepting direct suggestions by the reviewers. More often—and I think this is typical—I found myself unable or unwilling to accept a direct suggestion, but able to use the suggestion as indicating some problem with the reader's understanding that I might be able to repair in a different way. I frequently tell my students who are starting out in journal publishing to read all editorial suggestions not as absolute directives to be mechanically accepted but as symptoms of some failure of the author to be clear in substance or style, and to try and rewrite accordingly.

As I look at the essay now I cannot really say I am "satisfied" with it. There are many thousands of scholarly journals, but this essay was written specifically for *QJS*, and for no other. I worked hard over a period of years to understand how to write the essay, and in the end even lobbied a bit to have it appear in the form in which it appeared. Yet I recoil at gaps in the logic of the paper, and at its sometimes inflated and pontifical tone. I wish that there were more close textual analysis of the film, but the paper was already rather long for a journal article. I am not entirely pleased with the theoretical frame of the paper, in which, for example, the film is considered from the perspectives of deliberative, forensic, and epideictic rhetoric; these passages, though they seem to me true, also seem of less theoretical interest than some of what emerges as part of the close reading, in which I attempted to suggest Wiseman's implicit theories of how texts may induce complex and active responses in collaboration with audiences. In many ways, I am never satisfied that I have written anything as I had originally envisioned it; on the other hand, the writing and revision process always introduces happy surprises that go beyond what was originally envisioned.

I did get one more chance with the paper, when Carolyn Anderson and I decided to use it as the basis for a chapter in a book on Fred Wiseman's films, *Reality Fictions*. The chapter on *Primate* as it appears in the book adds some additional detail about the film from the perspective of its human subjects—research workers at the Yerkes Regional Primate Research Center of Emory University, where the film was made, who accused Wiseman of inaccuracy and betrayal. Carolyn became the coauthor of the paper as it was prepared for the book, and, at least from my point of view, the paper takes on a different and more meaningful shape when it appears in the context of a more extended analysis of Wiseman's films that involves both close readings and close historical attention to matters of production and reception, thus extending the purely "textual" (and intertextual) approach taken in the *QJS* version of the paper.

Well, maybe all of this amounts to no more than professional gossip and, yet again, an exercise in self-promotion. But a large and growing body of literature in the rhetoric of inquiry and the political economy of scholarly publishing argues that our shared, published knowledge is importantly shaped by institutional forces and the influence of disciplinary traditions and fashions.

The story told in these reflections may show merely that in the end an old friendship prevailed over good editorial judgment, and that despite a carefully planned system of blind reviewing, an essay that was recommended for publication by the editorial referees might in the end have been rejected, or at least radically revised, had it been submitted by a doctoral student, but instead was published as the author could be persuaded to revise it. I hope the story is more edifying than that, perhaps showing something of the complexity of the writing and reviewing process, of the urge to remain silent and the urge to speak, and of the tensions between "criticism" and "theory" in rhetorical studies as they presently express themselves in the writing and gatekeeping process.

# The Rhetorical Structure of
# Frederick Wiseman's *Primate*

Thomas W. Benson

The mission of rhetorical critics is to pay close attention to the communicative potentials of symbolic forms, to understand not only the forms themselves but also what listeners, readers, and watchers are likely to make of those forms. Rhetorical critics inquire into meaning, not simply in an artifact but also in the pragmatics of that artifact: that is, in how a human being can, or did, or should use that artifact. Rhetorical critics are interested not only in *what* meaning emerges from a text or artifact, but also in *how* it emerges. This is a complicated matter, but it seems apparent, at least, that a critical account must do more than propose a reduction of its text to a theme or an effect: the game of critical truth or consequences. In rhetorical situations, the connections among referent, author, text, and reader are always mutual.

Even if focused pragmatically on the "effect" of a text, a rhetorical critic is usually going to do best if he or she is attentive to the details of the text; to the contexts, both internal and external, that give that text meaning; and to the forms and processes that connect to create meanings. For modern rhetorical criticism, a meaning-centered approach brings to the text a curiosity not simply about the structure of the text, nor about the clues to the author revealed by the text, nor about the extent to which the text mirrors "reality," but also about the ways in which the text invites an audience to make meanings. The text implies its audience and the interpretive actions of its audience.

I propose to examine the rhetoric of Frederick Wiseman's documentary film *Primate*.[1] Wiseman helps us to understand how meanings are made by audiences, and how audiences turn "facts" into symbols with which to comprehend their world.

## FACTS, AUTHORS, AND READERS

To understand how Wiseman's *Primate* works, and its significance to studies in rhetoric and film, we need to see it as part of a developing tradition, a continually evolving dialogue in the arts and social sciences of the past century. To place Wiseman fully into the context of Western cultural developments is clearly beyond the scope of this essay, and so I propose instead

**189**

to begin with a brief discussion of two authors who are clearly precursors of Wiseman. Anthony Trollope, a nineteenth century master of political realism and personal romance, and James Agee, a twentieth century documentarist who turned facts into imaginative activities, help us to trace the development of the issues of audience action and the transformation of facts.

Anthony Trollope understood that fictions are made by authors in collaboration with their audiences. In the first of his Palliser novels, *Can You Forgive Her?*—its title itself is addressed to readers—Trollope addresses his reader directly. He has been describing how his heroine, Alice Vavasour, jilted the virtuous John Grey because she felt she might have fallen in love with her own cousin, the scoundrel George Vavasour. She even promises to marry her cousin, thinking she can help him. But she soon discovers her mistake, and understands that she can never love George—and of course, that she cannot permit herself to return to John Grey. In the midst of Alice's muddle occurs this passage:

> She had done very wrong. She knew that she had done wrong. . . . She understood it now, and knew that she could not forgive herself.
>
> But can you forgive her, delicate reader? Or am I asking the question too early in my story? [We are on page 384 of an 800 page novel]. For myself, I have forgiven her. . . . And you also must forgive her before we close the book, or else my story will have been told amiss.[2]

Trollope here asserts what every author of fiction knows: that the novel is not simply the invention of the actions of its characters, but the invention of the actions of its readers, in collaboration with those readers.[3] The *meaning* of Trollope's novel is not simply in the story of Alice's redemption, it is in the pleasure we take in wishing for and welcoming that redemption.

Another short passage from Trollope bears on our second methodological point, that a critic needs to attend both to details and to contexts in constructing a balanced account of meaning. Alice is in the Alps with her cousins. The idle George Vavasour is described as lounging on a "bench, looking at the mountains, with a cigar in his mouth." George expresses his contempt for hikers who climb the mountains for exercise, or for study. "They rob the mountains of their poetry," says George, "which is or should be their greatest charm." He goes on:

> "The poetry and mystery of the mountains are lost to those who make themselves familiar with their details, not the less because such familiarity may have useful results. In this world things are beautiful only because they are not quite seen, or not perfectly understood. Poetry is precious chiefly because it suggests more than it declares. Look in there, through that valley, where you just see the distant little peak at the end. Are you not dreaming of the unknown beautiful world that exists up there;—beautiful, as heaven is beautiful, because you know nothing of the reality? If you make your way up there and back to-morrow, and

find out all about it, do you mean to say that it will be as beautiful to you when
you come back?"

"Yes—I think it would," said Alice.[4]

By this point in the novel, we have come to recognize Alice's virtue and
George's sinfulness, and so Alice's simple "yes" carries considerable force.
It is clear from the discussion that Alice, and Trollope, invite the reader to
take pleasure and wisdom from the details of everyday reality, and from the
relations of those details, and even from the effort that it takes us to trudge
up the mountain for a clearer view of them. Trollope's invitation to detail
has nothing in common with that other sort of nineteenth century amateur
scientism that reduced the world to a statistic.

Charles Dickens, especially in *Hard Times,* shows us the terrible consequences of the misplaced love of facts, and John Fowles uses another facet
of this mentality in two of his best novels, *The Collector* and *The French
Lieutenant's Woman,* both of which are in large part variations on his theme
of the horror of the impulse to factualize, possess, name, count, and fragment the world of nature, to reduce it to our order and our use.[5] For
Trollope, the alternative to George Vavasour's vague and lazy romanticism
is not science, but a common sense feeling, a willingness to face the details
of the world, and to see their relations and their consequences.

Americans have had an especially interesting time trying to cope with
"the facts." Our literature, journalism, and popular arts have been dominated in this century by various forms of flight to and from facts. From
Upton Sinclair to Norman Mailer, from Robert Flaherty to *60 Minutes,* from
the newsreels to *Real People,* we have searched after the facts, and have found
that facts are not enough, even if we could agree on what "the" facts are.
Artists have told us over and over again that art may be too disconnected,
and science too reductive, to bring us into a proper relation with our world.

The issue is posed with special poignancy by James Agee, in a passage
from his documentary essay on Depression sharecroppers in Alabama, *Let
Us Now Praise Famous Men:*

> If I could do it, I'd do no writing at all here. It would be photographs; the rest
> would be fragments of cloth, bits of cotton, lumps of earth, records of speech,
> pieces of wood and iron, phials of odors, plates of food and of excrement.
> Booksellers would consider it quite a novelty; critics would murmur, yes, but is
> it art; and I could trust a majority of you to use it as you would a parlor game.[6]

And yet Agee is writing a book, and not simply trading in objects, as his
writing shows very well. In a later passage, Agee describes the dresses of one
of the tenant farm women:

> Mrs. Gudger: I have spoken already of her dresses. I think she has at most five.
> . . . Three are one-piece dresses; two are in two pieces. By cut they are almost

identical; by pattern of print they differ, but are similar in having been carefully chosen, all small and sober, quiet patterns, to be in good taste and to relieve one another's monotony. I think it may be well to repeat their general appearance, since it is of her individual designing, and is so thoroughly a part of the logic of her body, bearing, face and temper. They have about them some shadow of nineteenth-century influence, tall skirt, short waist, and a little, too, of imitation of Butterick patterns for housewives' housework-dresses; this chiefly in the efforts at bright or 'cheery,' post-honeymoon-atmosphere trimming: narrow red or blue tape sewn at the cuffs or throat. But by other reasons again they have her own character and function: the lines are tall and narrow, as she is, and little relieved, and seem to run straight from the shoulders to the hem low on the shins, and there is no collar, but a long and low V at the throat, shut narrowly together, so that the whole dress like her body has the long vertical of a Chartres statue.[7]

The passage is remarkable not simply for its factuality, its close attention to detail, but also for the way it relates those details, gives them a meaning in the life of the person whose dresses are being described, and calls on us to bring to the description a cultural sophistication that is almost certainly unfamiliar to Mrs. Gudger. The final reference to the statues of Chartres Cathedral is only the most explicit indication that the entire passage is addressed to educated and prosperous readers, and not to the tenant farmers with whom Agee in so many ways identifies himself imaginatively.

The issues raised by Anthony Trollope in the 1860s, and by James Agee in the 1930s are still with us, though transformed. Certainly in the past decade and a half one of the most profound inquirers into American facts has been the documentary filmmaker Frederick Wiseman, who has produced, beginning with *Titicut Follies,* in 1967, some fifteen major documentary films. Wiseman's films have much to teach us about the uses to which we can put "the facts" about everyday reality, and about the rhetorical actions that film makers and their audiences perform.

## ▓ THE RHETORIC OF *PRIMATE*

*Primate,* shown on public television for the first time in 1974, was shot at the Yerkes Primate Research Center in Atlanta. Immediate and later reaction to *Primate* was sharply divided between those who charged that Wiseman had unfairly attacked the Yerkes scientists and those who applauded the film as a profound attack against vivisection. That is to say, the majority of commentators for and against the film seemed to recognize it as a rhetorical act in the narrowest sense—as persuasive discourse in the forensic and deliberative modes, accusing a group of particular scientists of cruelty to animals, and attacking the policy of public support for animal research.

A rhetorical critic could sensibly and conveniently proceed through the film on these narrow grounds. We would extract from the film its implicit accusations and propositions, examine the proofs Wiseman offers to support them, and attempt to assess both the extent to which the film might be persuasive and the extent to which we, as critics, could support the proofs as "good reasons" to accept the propositions and accusations. Nothing could be more straightforward.

But such a critique, though it would have its uses, would be seriously incomplete, because it would fail to account for the way the audience is likely to understand the film. Rhetorical critics in the last two decades have discovered that non-oratorical persuasive actions can be analyzed with the rigorous tools of traditional rhetorical criticism. But they have also followed Kenneth Burke in understanding that all symbolic actions, and not just those most narrowly didactic, can be encompassed by a rhetorical criticism that is interested in the whole enterprise of sharing meanings in human communication.[8] It is this latter, larger sense of rhetorical criticism to which we must turn, I think, to understand how Fred Wiseman's *Primate* invites us to share its meanings.

What does Wiseman's *Primate* mean? *Primate* invites us to experience a horrified, comic rage at the arrogance, hypocrisy, banality, and destructiveness of our fellow humans and ourselves. Like most of Wiseman's films, *Primate* is not simply accusatory, it is paradoxical, and this of course contributes to the frustration of Wiseman's opponents—both in the film community and in the various institutions that he has explored in his documentaries.

*Primate,* like Wiseman's other documentaries, is in black and white, with synchronous sound, but with no direct verbal commentary by Wiseman. The film is 105 minutes long—feature length—and contains, according to an analysis by Liz Ellsworth, 569 shots.[9] That works out to an average of 11 seconds per shot for *Primate,* approximately half of the average shot length of 22 seconds in Wiseman's *High School.*[10]

The unusually large number of shots in *Primate* is not simply a fact, but a clue, both to the rhythm of the film and to its method of building meanings. We would expect that with briefer shots the meanings would emerge to a great extent from the structural relations among shots—from editing or montage—and that the shots themselves would be very likely to be highly condensed in their imagery and iconography. This pattern of condensation and montage does much to account for Wiseman's method.

*Primate* is addressed not to particular crimes, nor even to social policy, but to our attitudes about human action. The film is not merely forensic or deliberative, it is existential.

I have said that the film follows a pattern of condensation and montage. I propose to get closer to the film's method by examining how certain major structural features of the film invite us to construct meanings. I will discuss three major structures: Comparison, Sequence and Continuity, and Sound/

Image relations. Rather than treat these structural features separately and sequentially, I will layer them in the discussion that follows, because they work together to achieve Wiseman's effects.

*Primate*'s effect depends very heavily upon the family of rhetorical structures that may be collected under the heading of comparison: analogy, contrast, metaphor, identification, irony, and comparison itself. Our response to the film depends upon our willingness to compare men to apes, and to judge their relations in terms of the increasingly complex comparisons we are invited to draw. The film opens with a long series of shots in which we may first notice the ambiguity of the film's title, which applies equally well to men and apes. We see a large composite photograph, with portraits of eminent scientists, hanging, presumably, on a wall at the Yerkes Center. Wiseman cuts from the composite portrait to a series of eight individual portraits, in series, then to a sign, an exterior shot of the Center, and then a series of four shots of apes in their cages. The comparison is obvious, though not particularly forceful, and it depends for its meaning both upon the structure Wiseman has chosen to use—at least he does not intercut the apes and the portraits—and upon our own predictable surprise at noticing how human the apes look.

Slightly later in the film, still very near the beginning, occur a pair of sequences that are crucial to how we will experience the rest of the film. Researchers are watching and recording the birth of an orangutan. The descriptive language is objective, but not altogether free of anthropomorphism: for example, it is hard not to refer to the female giving birth as the "mother."

Immediately following the birth sequence, we watch women in nursing gowns mothering infant apes: the apparatus of American babyhood is evident—plastic toys, baby bottles, diapers, baby scales, and a rocking chair. To reinforce the comparison, we hear the women speaking to the infant apes:

> "Here. Here. Take it. Take it. Come on." [says the first woman, offering a toy to an infant ape].

Then another woman enters the nursery, also dressed in gown and mask.

> "Good morning, darlings. Good morning. Mama's babies? You gonna be good boys and girls for Mommy?"

A moment later she continues:

> "Mama take your temperature. Come on, we'll take your temperature. It's all right. It's all right. It's all right. It's all right."

Then a man enters and hands cups to the infants. He says:

> "Come on. Come on. Here's yours."

The rhetorical effect of this sequence is to reinforce our sentimental identification with the apes. And this scene, by comparison, makes even more frightening a sequence that follows close upon it, in which a small monkey is taken from its cage, screaming, as a man with protective gloves pins its arms behind its back and clamps his other hand around its neck.

After these sequences, every image in the film invites us to continue enacting comparisons, as part of the process by which we actively make meanings out of the images. Those who object to Wiseman's methods argue that his comparison of apes and people is a cheap shot, an obviously sentimental ploy to make monkeys out of primatologists. Although there is something to be said for this view, since it is quite clear that Wiseman is showing us comparisons whose meanings are predictable, the problem is complicated. Wiseman's comparisons do not stay at the simple level of the infant scene, but grow increasingly complex throughout the film. The infant scene not only predisposes us sentimentally, it also rehearses us in the exercise of comparative thinking. The researchers themselves invite the comparison. Their use of the dramatic apparatus of American baby care is not something Wiseman forced upon them, though admittedly he takes advantage of it. And at a deeper level, those scientists who object to a sentimental willingness to object to vivisection are placed in the paradoxical situation that the primary justification for their research is that, biologically, apes are such close relatives of people. The defenders of such research must seek funding for their research on the grounds that apes are biologically analogous to humans; but they must also seek to justify their practices upon those apes by arguing that, ethically, apes are not analogous to humans. *Primate* makes it very difficult for viewers to buy that argument, by inviting them to identify with the apes at an aesthetic, subjective level. This is why comparison is so central to Wiseman's film: comparison both justifies and condemns the research, and Wiseman exploits that comparison not simply to attack vivisection, or scientific research in general, but also to engage us in actively considering the paradoxes of our institutions and ourselves.

And this is why those scientists and reviewers who attacked *Primate* had such a frustrating time of it. Wiseman invites his audience not simply to condemn particular scientists for foolishness or cruelty to animals, and not just to reason about the policy of animal research. Instead, Wiseman reframes the whole question, inviting us to look with our common sense at the whole context of human action at Yerkes, to employ our own abilities to identify with the apes, to feel horror and shame at the actions of our fellow humans.

Wiseman's peculiar rhetorical talent is to help his audiences identify with oppressors and oppressed: we feel pity, fear, and rage on behalf of the victims, with whom we identify; and we feel the shock of horrified recognition in realizing that the oppressors are acting in our name, as members of this society: teaching our children, butchering our meat, administering our institutions, and toying with the generation and termination of life in a primate research center.

Comparison works in another way in the film. Wiseman establishes a dialectic between acts of kindness to the apes, and acts that we are likely to perceive as cruelty. Do the acts of kindness balance the acts of cruelty—is there a journalistic attempt at fairness here? Not really. We understand that in this institution the apes are subject to human domination, mutilation, and termination. In such a situation the acts of kindness do not balance the acts of heartless research. Rather, kindness is reduced to hypocrisy, a lie told to ease the consciences of the scientists and to keep the apes under control. Far from balancing the harshness of the research scenes, the scenes of kindness turn the research into a cruelty and a betrayal.

We can perhaps forgive Wiseman his unsympathetic methods, because we realize that the shame and rage we direct at the primate researchers is directed at them as representatives of ourselves. It is not that we cannot forgive them—we cannot forgive ourselves.

And what makes Wiseman's films so devastating is that there is no easy liberal solution. Wiseman's films are not about corruption, they are about something that is much more nearly indivisible from our daily lives, and about institutions that—even when they have some modifiable policies—are never going to be able to resolve the paradoxes they were set up to deal with. Problem films are almost always optimistic, in that every problem implies a solution. Wiseman's films do not imply any solution to the enterprise of being human.

And here we have another reason why *Primate* is so frustrating to the scientists who have attacked it. They realize that they must defend themselves on the deliberative issue of the justification for their research. But *Primate* goes beyond deliberation—one cannot expunge the effect of *Primate* on a susceptible viewer with an argument addressed to policy. And yet—and here's the rub—Wiseman's film is relevant to that deliberative issue, even as it goes beyond it. The rhetoric of non-oratorical forms frequently presents us with this paradox: that it implies a stance toward deliberative matters that its opponents cannot refute adequately with a deliberative reply.

Let us examine briefly another sequence in *Primate*. It is the climactic sequence of the film, a little over twenty minutes, and 100 shots, long. In it, researchers remove a gibbon from its cage, anesthetize it, drill a hole in its skull, insert a needle, then open its chest cavity, decapitate it, crack open its skull, and slice the brain for microscopic slides. It is a harrowing sequence. From a structural standpoint, Wiseman uses the techniques we have noticed earlier. The images are often highly condensed, with big closeups of needles, drills, scalpels, the tiny beating heart, the gibbon's terrified face, scissors, jars, vises, dials, and so on.

We are invited to engage in our continued work of making comparisons and metaphors: the gibbon is easy to identify with, in its terror of these silent and terminal medical procedures. We are the gibbon, and we are the surgeons. At another level, we see the gibbons' cages as a sort of death row, and call upon our memories of prison movies when we see the helpless fellow gibbons crying out from their cages as the victim is placed back into its cage for a twenty-five-minute pause in the vivisection.

Wiseman has carefully controlled sequence and continuity in this section of the film, first by placing the scene very near the end of the film, so that it becomes the climax of the preceding comedy, and then by controlling its internal structure for maximum effect. The sequence is governed by the rules of both fiction and documentary. As in *cinema verite* documentary, we do not know until almost the very last second that the gibbon is certainly going to die. Earlier in the film we have seen monkeys with electrodes planted in their brains, so we are able to hope that the gibbon will survive. We keep hoping that he will live, but as the operation becomes more and more destructive of the animal, we must doubt our hopes. And then, with terrible suddenness, and with only a few seconds warning, the surgeon cuts off the gibbon's head. We feel a terrible despair that it has come to this. But the sequence continues through the meticulous, mechanical process of preparing slides of the brain. Finally we see the researchers sitting at the microscope to examine the slides for which the gibbon's life has been sacrificed—and for us, as viewers, the discovery ought to be important if it is to redeem this death. The two researchers talk:

> "Oh, here's a whole cluster of them. Here, look at this."
> "Yeah. My gosh, that is beautiful."
> "By golly, and see how localized. No fuzzing out. . . ."
> "For sure it does not look like dirt, or . . ."
> "No, no, it's much too regular."
> "I think we are on our way."
> "Yeah. That's sort of interesting."

The whole operation, which viewers must experience as pitiable and frightening, seems to have been indulged in for the merest idle curiosity, and, if they cannot distinguish brains from dirt, at the lowest possible level of competence.

Our suspicions are confirmed a few minutes later when a group of researchers seated at a meeting reassure each other that pure research is always justified, even if it seems to be the pursuit of useless knowledge.

We have already mentioned the sound/image relationships in this sequence in discussing the structural uses of comparison and continuity. But let me point to some special issues that relate to Wiseman's use of sound. At many places in the film, people talk to apes, creating a dramatic fiction that the apes can understand and respond to human speech. But in the vivisection sequence, no word is spoken to the victim. This silence is almost as disturbing as the operation itself, because a bond of identification offered earlier is now denied. Its denial, in this context, becomes part of an action that we see as sadistic. It is interesting that Wiseman's critics in the scientific community object that he has made a misleading use of sound. Their argument is that one cannot understand scientific research just by watching it take place, and that the audience needs to be told what it is seeing and why it is justified in scier 'ific terms. The absence of a narrator forces us to see the film as an existential drama, and to believe in the reality of the gibbon's death as important in and of itself. But that is the point. This is not a debate between Wiseman and the primatologists on the costs versus the benefits of vivisection. Presumably there are good reasons to be offered by both sides of that debate. Wiseman works at a different level, inviting us to question whether any verbal justification is relevant to what we have seen. Wiseman uses his "reality fictions"—the term is his—to address our subjective con- sciousness, and his films do not depend for their effect upon objective accuracy (whatever that is), or immediate political utility.

Although Wiseman has frequently referred to himself as a documentary film maker, he has never professed to provide an objective description of reality. In fact, he seems to have coined the term "reality fiction" as a partly tongue-in-cheek way of declining to be described as part of the *cinema verite* tradition, with its implied claims of transparency and unmanipulated reality. Wiseman has frequently described his editing method as a process of fic- tion-making in which bits and pieces of photographed actuality are re- assembled to see what can be found in the material.

And yet a very large percentage of the praise and detraction of Wise- man's films centers on the issue of accuracy. Those who praise the films often seem to accept them as literally true, and discuss not the films but the people in them. And those who object to the films often do so on the basis of their alleged inaccuracy or lack of objectivity. Wiseman usually brushes aside both the praise and the blame, though he has often been quite open about his methods. He allows his admirers the meanings they find in the films, and he typically responds, as he did to an objection made by Geoffrey H. Bourne, Director of the Yerkes Center, that Bourne did not object to the film when he saw it for himself, but only after he began to see how he looked to others.[11]

One of the more interesting objections to Wiseman's accuracy is made by Karl Heider. Heider, an anthropologist and ethnographic film maker, argues that one of the primary attributes of a successful ethnographic film is that it "show the structure of a whole act."[12] One of Heider's key examples of a film that fails to depict whole acts is Wiseman's *Primate*.

A major weakness of Frederick Wiseman's 1974 television film, "Primate," was that, although he spent one month shooting and two hours of screen time on bits of scientific experimentation at the Yerkes Primate Research Center in Atlanta, the film never followed a single experiment as a whole act. The approach had interestingly different effects on different viewers. Laymen (including television critics) were simply horrified by the picture of senseless butchery in the guise of science; one friend of mine who is familiar with that sort of research could fill in the gaps for himself and was fascinated by the film; more thoughtful viewers reacted strongly against the film itself on the grounds that it made no attempt to communicate an understanding of primate research by presenting whole acts, but only used scenes of gore to play on the audience's emotions and turn them away from such research.[13]

I have quoted Heider at some length to try to do justice to the shape of his argument.[14]

Heider's objections deserve careful scrutiny, and there are five important considerations that deserve to be mentioned. First, it is curious that in a passage in which he is describing the importance of "wholeness" Heider does not provide a full description of *Primate*, thus denying to Wiseman the structural completeness he proposes as his standard of accuracy.

Second, and obviously, Wiseman does not present his films as ethnographic documents, and so it is not clear why the standards Heider proposes for ethnography should be applied to *Primate*.

Third, Wiseman does provide, in at least one case, a dramatic account, with beginning, middle, and end, of one experiment. The vivisection of the gibbon takes approximately twenty minutes of screen time: it begins when the gibbon is taken from its cage, it provides some background on the stated desire of the scientists to check some previous research, it proceeds through the surgery to the examination of slides and the agreement that the procedure has been a success. Of course, Wiseman's account is anything but neutral, but it does have the three-act structure that Heider accuses the film of lacking.

Fourth, it is interesting to note that in developing his case against *Primate,* Heider devotes very little space to the film itself, and concentrates instead on audience reactions to the film. Implicitly, Heider seems to be struggling with the difficulty that philosophy, science, and rhetoric have recently begun to re-examine in a new light. Is Heider implying that the standard of a film's accuracy is to be found not in its correspondence to an "objective" reality, but in what an audience makes of it? Apparently not, because Heider prejudges the matter in favor of the primatologists—the lay audience's reactions to the film are dismissed as "emotional." Heider seems to imply that if the audience had the whole story, they would understand and support primate research.

A major difficulty of ethnographic—or any other—film is that accuracy cannot be measured simply in terms of the correspondence of the film to the actuality it describes. Every theorist of ethnographic film, including Heider, recognizes that completeness is impossible. Every film that explains one culture to another must confront the dilemma of point of view: if the film is made purely from the point of view of the subject culture, it will be unclear to the audience; if the film is translated into the point of view of the audience, it will necessarily introduce elements that are unfamiliar to, and therefore untrue for, the subject culture. Hence the question of accuracy often reduces itself to the struggle over point of view. Clearly it would have been possible for a film maker to make a film sympathetic to the point of view of the primatologists: but that was not the point.

But, fifth, by far the most interesting and challenging of Heider's arguments is his standard of "whole acts." The chief danger of Heider's "whole act" standard is that it can easily reduce a sensible principle to a naive and inappropriate technical reductionism. In principle, Heider is convincing when he argues that it is a mistake to focus on what he calls the "peak" of a cultural event, "that part of the act which involves the most energy and activity and draws the most attention."[15] Even if the peak activity is the focus of one's interest, that peak cannot be properly understood without some context, and in ethnographic reporting, the cultural context would include some placement of the activity in its natural setting in time and space, including the relevant events that led up to and succeeded the event. And a full understanding of the whole act might require not simply extended observation but verbal commentary about the invisible and implicit cultural substructures that give meaning to the act. Clearly, from the point of view of the scientists, Wiseman withholds from his audience the contextual information that might either distract us from the horrors or justify the horrors in the name of scientific knowledge or human use.

But why should Heider assume that the "act" being described by *Primate* is scientific-research-as-understood-by-scientists? Heider's argument rests on the unsupportable assumptions that the ethnographer is explaining "them" to "us"; and that any social action is, firmly, finally, and naturally what it is. Wiseman correctly violates both assumptions, in my view. *Primate* is not about a "them"—it is about us. The scientists are not a foreign culture but our agents, acting like us, and on our behalf. And what a social action "is" is a matter of definition, duration, and point of view. A behavior may possibly be what it is, but an action is a socially constructed human product, subject to understandings (and misunderstandings) from a variety of perspectives, more than one of which can be accurate.

A human action, as rhetoricians from Aristotle to Kenneth Burke have told us, is a behavior waiting for a name. If a man kills another, it is for others to judge whether the act is an accident, manslaughter, or murder. From the point of view of the victim, the act is the end of life. From the point of view of the perpetrator, the act may be the culmination of a quest (revenge) or the beginning of an ordeal. From the point of view of the community, the act is a legal fact, to be dealt with as a matter of justice. Any one of their points of view is capable of being understood as a "whole act," and yet they are obviously different renderings of a single set of events, variously understood (and not by any means necessarily misunderstood).

Similarly, in the narrative arts, the form of the whole work guides the reader in defining the action that is represented. In a recent novel, *July's People,* Nadine Gordimer describes the experiences of a White South African family hiding in the bush with their former servant, July, during a revolution. It is not at all clear that the family will survive the ordeal. The novel ends when the wife runs off, alone, to seek rescue from a helicopter. From one point of view, the novel is disastrously incomplete, since we do not learn whether she is actually rescued or, if she is, what happens to her husband and child. The novel seems to end too soon, before its action has been completed. But that is just the point. It is only when the novel has ended that we realize that the action of the novel is not, as we had thought it might be, about the escape, successful or not, of this family. Rather, we see, when it ends in the woman's headlong flight through the bush, the action of the novel is the woman's transformation from a housewife to "a solitary animal at the season when animals neither seek a mate nor take care of young, existing only for their lone survival, the enemy of all that would make claims of responsibility."[16] The strong feeling that Gordimer's novel is incomplete forces us, as readers, to reevaluate what we take the novel to be about, at the same time recognizing our own predispositions toward melodrama.

Let me cite one other example, to show how the process may work in a different way. American student viewers almost always feel that Sergei Eisenstein's *Potemkin* is too long. The fourth "act" of the film climaxes with the famous massacre on the Odessa steps, which is capped, briefly, by the answering guns of the Potemkin coming to the aid of the victims. Then comes a fifth "act," in which the Potemkin cruises off from Odessa and goes to meet the fleet. It is not clear to the mutineers on the Potemkin whether the fleet will open fire on them. At the last moment, the sailors of the fleet refuse to fire. Why does the film seem too long to American students, and why would Eisenstein have mishandled his dramatic forms? It is a question of what *Potemkin* is *about.* American students are inclined to see *Potemkin* as melodrama, in which a mutiny leads to the massacre on the Odessa steps and the vengeance of the Potemkin's reply. At that point, the story, if it is to be taken as a conventional melodrama of victimage and revenge, is over for them. The meeting with the fleet is an anticlimax, an emotional letdown, and a narrative flaw. Did Eisenstein include the last act because historical facts constrained him to do so? Probably not, since he took many liberties with history in fashioning the film. Again, it is a question of what the film is about. For Eisenstein, the film is about the achievement of revolutionary solidarity. Seen from this point of view, the meeting with the fleet becomes a dramatic and ideological extension that follows logically and meaningfully from the scene on the Odessa steps. A film that appears, if regarded as a bourgeois melodrama, to be too long, appears to fit the structure of a "whole act" if it is redefined as a drama of revolutionary solidarity.

*Primate* is a film with a point of view, and it is certainly not sympathetic to scientific research. But Heider's "whole act" standard is both misleading and misapplied. Wiseman records, constructs, and communicates a whole act that transcends vivisection as a political issue to examine the experience of being human. The whole act that Wiseman records, and in which he invites his audience to participate, is an act of identification with both the scientists and their victims. And Wiseman constructs his film in such a way that viewers become actively involved in constructing its meanings.

The act of identification that we perform as viewers of Wiseman is not undifferentiated, not simply a sympathetic embrace of all that is. We identify with the apes and the scientists, but in different ways. In identifying with the apes, we are able to feel the horror and helplessness of their position; in identifying with the scientists, we are able to feel responsible. There is, of course, another identification possible, and one which may complicate the matter further. Do we not also identify with "Fred Wiseman," the implied author of *Primate?*[17] The implied author of *Primate* is not simply saddened or outraged at the apes' victimage, nor does he seek redemption in political reform.

Wiseman's elusive narrative point of view, depending upon strategies of action and identification, places a strain upon critical language. Throughout this essay, I have employed the first-person plural pronoun in discussing audience response. I have said that "we" read the film in this way or that. I have done so partly as a way of identifying with the reader whose actions I am proposing to describe, and as a way of pointing to the way in which Wiseman's method hinges upon identification and division among his audience, himself, and his subjects. The use of the first-person pronoun has the disadvantage, in academic and critical argument, of seeming both overly familiar and presumptuous, and may even seem to beg the question of effect, presuming that "we" the viewers will see the film as "I" the critic describe it. But a third-person usage does not avoid the problem of critical question-begging, and may distort not only the critical perspective but the critical interpretation by suggesting an objective assessment by the critic about how "they" will read the film. The meaning of a film, that is, the meaning "in" or "intended by" a film, even when understood by its audience, is not irresistible.

*Primate* achieves its peculiar effects with a curious combination of generic styles that include both comedy and horror. The comedy of the early birth and baby sequences is magnified and pushed in a less sentimental direction by the many scenes in which the scientists observe, discuss, and manipulate the sex lives of the apes. The distortion of sexual behavior, in the name of understanding sexual behavior, sometimes reduces sexuality to mechanics, as in the many scenes where apes are stimulated to erection and ejaculation by means of electrodes implanted in their brains, or the scene in which a technician masturbates an ape with a plastic tube in one hand while distracting the ape with a bottle of grape juice in the other. At other times, the scientists seem gossipy, as they sit and whisper about sex outside a row of cages. The effect of the sex scenes is comic, and undermines the dignity of the presumably scientific enterprise we are watching.

But along with the comedy, there is an undercurrent of horror, at times straightforward, at times almost surrealistic. Sometimes the horror occurs in small moments: a technician tries to remove a small monkey from its wire cage. He reaches inside the door of the cage, and grasps the monkey, which tries to evade capture by clinging to the front of the cage next to the door, an angle that makes it difficult for the technician to maneuver it out of the door. The technician reaches up with his other hand and releases another catch, revealing that the whole front of the cage is hinged. The front of the cage swings open, and the technician grasps the clinging monkey from behind, as our momentary pleasure at the comedy of the impasse gives way to a small despair: there is no escape.

At other times, the scientists are framed to seem sinister, as when the surgeon who vivisects the gibbon is shot in closeup, from a low angle, a large surgical light shining over his shoulder. And because of the structure of the film, in which a strictly observational point of view is maintained, we are never quite sure what will happen next. It quickly becomes clear to us that the scientists, for all their expressed good will, are capable of anything, and so we approach even the mildest procedures with dread, not knowing what horror they are likely to reveal. We can identify with the scientists as our representatives—even, perhaps, as analogies for Wiseman, who is, after all, observing the observers—but we do not trust them.

And for all of his unobtrusiveness as a narrator, Wiseman puts a considerable distance between himself and his subjects. From very early in the film, Wiseman adopts a convention of sound-image relationships that makes for an ironic distance. In an early scene, we observe a resident scientist talking with another man about gorilla sexuality. As we continue to listen to their conversation, Wiseman's camera begins to gaze about on its own. We *hear* the official line, but we begin to *see* other things. That wandering camera begins to stand for Wiseman's—and our—free curiosity, refusing to be locked into the conventions of place and point of view. A profound relation is thus established, in which filmic consciousness, and our consciousness, is willing to be interested in its own questions, rather than just those suggested by the speakers. Wiseman's use of sound-image relations here is something far more sophisticated than the heavy-handed *cinema verite* rhetoric that zooms in on the nervous hands of a speaker we are thus invited to doubt. Wiseman does not obviously use cutaways as a method of bridging gaps in continuity or as a way of underlining possibly deliberate misrepresentations. Nor does he obviously cut, within a scene, to images that cannot be accounted for as literally part of the immediate context. Rather, he makes us active participants in the process of building meanings by wandering beyond the speaker's concern to the context in which it occurs, or, conversely, by gazing uninterruptedly at the actuality of everyday institutional reality rather than brushing actuality aside in favor of its rationale or product.

Wiseman looks at the "facts" of social reality, and reveals the structures that underlie them. He implicates his viewers in the social world that is described, and in the process of making meanings out of his film.

There is a danger for Wiseman here. He is skating very close to the thin ice of despair, and of that currently fashionable despair which adopts an anti-political cynicism as a substitute for responsibility to social particulars.[18]

## CONCLUSION

I said at the outset that Wiseman could not be accurately pigeon-holed as the filmic equivalent of a forensic or deliberative orator, suggesting that he has gone beyond indicting his subjects or offering a policy. Part of Wiseman's usefulness to us as viewers is the way he resists the sterility of fixed genres. But it may be that we can understand Wiseman as offering us something akin to Lawrence Rosenfield's notion of epideictic.[19] Rosenfield writes of epideictic rhetoric as a celebration of the radiance of being, and he wisely notes that even condemnatory rhetoric can function as an affirmation of Being's excellence and availability. When Wiseman works for us, we are perhaps experiencing, through the comedy and the cruelty, a larger sense that comedy and cruelty are recognizable to us as alternatives to the human excellence that they imply by denying. If, as Karl Wallace wrote, the substance of rhetoric is good reasons,[20] Wiseman's *Primate* offers us good reasons to look more honestly at ourselves.

## Notes

[1] *Primate* is the eighth film in Frederick Wiseman's continuing series of documentaries on American institutions, which include *Titicut Follies* (1967); *High School* (1968); *Law and Order* (1969); *Hospital* (1970); *Basic Training* (1971); *Essene* (1972); *Juvenile Court* (1973); *Primate* (1974); *Welfare* (1975); *Meat* (1975); *Canal Zone* (1977); *Sinai Field Mission* (1978); *Manoeuvre* (1979); *Model* (1980); *The Store* (1983).

[2] Anthony Trollope, *Can You Forgive Her?* (Oxford: Oxford University Press, 1973), I, pp. 383–84.

[3] This is the sort of relationship that Kenneth Burke refers to as "a communicative relationship between writer and audience, with both parties actively participating." Kenneth Burke, "Antony in Behalf of the Play," *The Philosophy of Literary Form* (Berkeley: University of California Press, 1973), p. 329.

[4] Trollope, pp. 44–45.

[5] Fowles states the same theme autobiographically and polemically in his text for *The Tree;* John Fowles and Frank Horvat, *The Tree* (Boston: Little, Brown, 1979), unpaginated.

⁶James Agee and Walker Evans, *Let Us Now Praise Famous Men* (1941; rpt. New York: Ballantine Books, 1966), p. 12.

⁷Agee and Evans, p. 250.

⁸See, for example, Martin J. Medhurst and Thomas W. Benson, ed., *Rhetorical Dimensions in Media: A Critical Casebook* (Dubuque, IA: Kendall/Hunt, 1984).

⁹Liz Ellsworth, *Frederick Wiseman: A Guide to References and Sources* (Boston: G. K. Hall, 1979), pp. 102–58.

¹⁰Ellsworth, pp. 34–57. For an analysis of *High School* cf. Thomas W. Benson, "The Rhetorical Structure of Frederick Wiseman's *High School*," *Communication Monographs*, 47 (1980), 233–61. See also Thomas W. Benson and Carolyn Anderson, "The Rhetorical Structure of Frederick Wiseman's *Model*," *Journal of Film and Video*, 36 (1984), 30–40.

¹¹Frederick Wiseman, *New York Times*, 22 December 1974, p. 33.

¹²Karl Heider, *Ethnographic Film* (Austin: University of Texas Press, 1976), p. 82.

¹³Heider, p. 84.

¹⁴Heider refers to *Primate* at two other points in his book: once in a table on p. 108 that restates the charge of fragmentation; and once on p. 121, where, in a discussion of consent, he notes the exchange of charges between Wiseman and Geoffrey Bourne in the *New York Times*.

¹⁵Heider, p. 85.

¹⁶Nadine Gordimer, *July's People* (New York: The Viking Press, 1981), p. 160.

¹⁷The concept of implied author refers not to the actual author of a text but to the consciousness that is implied as controlling the point of view of the work. See Wayne C. Booth, *The Rhetoric of Fiction* (Chicago: University of Chicago Press, 1983), pp. 71–76.

¹⁸Cf. William Stott's discussion of social documentaries versus human documents: "Human documents show man undergoing the perennial and unpreventable in experience, what happens to all men everywhere: death, work, chance, rapture, hurricane, and maddened dogs; as John Grierson said, the theme of such documents is 'la condition humaine.' Social documentary, on the other hand, shows man at grips with conditions neither permanent nor necessary, conditions of a certain time and place: racial discrimination, police brutality, unemployment, the Depression, the planned environment of the TVA, pollution, terrorism." William Stott, *Documentary Expression and Thirties America* (New York: Oxford University Press, 1976), p. 20.

¹⁹Lawrence W. Rosenfield, "The Practical Celebration of Epideictic," in *Rhetoric in Transition: Studies in the Nature and Uses of Rhetoric*, ed. Eugene E. White (University Park: The Pennsylvania State University Press, 1980), pp. 131–55.

²⁰Karl Wallace, "The Substance of Rhetoric: Good Reasons," *The Quarterly Journal of Speech*, 49 (1963), 239–49.

# CHAPTER 9 ⬚

## CONSTITUTIVE RHETORIC AND THE *PEUPLE QUÉBÉCOIS*

**Maurice Charland**

*Maurice Charland's commentary traces a project superficially similar to Thomas Benson's in the previous commentary: writing and revising an essay for a scholarly journal. However, in Charland's case, he was a comparative newcomer to the audience and community he addressed: a Canadian writing about Quebec nationalism for the largely American audience of the* Quarterly Journal of Speech *in the "language" of the American study of rhetoric, which has no counterpart in the Canadian communication curriculum in which he began his education. Charland's commentary, compared to Benson's, is thus much more the story of initiation, as a critic, into a new community and language.*

## COMMENTARY

I did not initially set out to write an essay for the *Quarterly Journal of Speech.* That came much later. I was, like many a doctoral student, struggling to develop a dissertation topic. Something to do with public culture, but what? Two things happened. The first was the rising tide of nationalism in Quebec, my home. The second was the hiring by Iowa (where I was studying for my Ph.D. in communication) of Michael McGee, a rising star in speech communication's version of rhetoric. I had never studied rhetoric, which had no presence in Canadian communication studies. But as I came to know McGee and his work and thought about the news from home, it seemed that I might be able to explain something, at least to myself, and be able to take a stand on the theoretical terrain of cultural theory that I was discovering. My intuitions were rough and unformed, but I sensed that the usual premises of rhetorical studies did not render the Quebec case well. What struck me was that, while for my American friends and fellow students, national identity was unproblematic and politics was concerned with deliberation and reasonableness, from my perspective national identity was extremely problematic and politics seemed far more linked to "being" than reason. As I read McGee's "In Search of 'The People'," I realized that much of it could be applied to Quebec.

The story of writing the thesis is one that I will not go into here, save to say that it was at times a pleasure, at times a drama, and at most times an ordeal. But I should underline that at its genesis, the project was less intended than emergent, and that once it was set in motion I often felt that the best I could do was not to let it overwhelm me as I tried to guide it to completion. I was so absorbed with that task that I never gave any thought to what might follow from it. And when it was finally defended and deposited, I had no desire to return to it, at least for a good long while.

I had pretty much ruled out turning my thesis into a book until I received an unsolicited request for a manuscript from a university press. I enthusiastically sent off my dissertation and awaited the press' review. I then started fiddling with the text until, six months later, I received the reviewer's comments. The review was perceptive and ambivalent. I would have a book, if I rewrote the text basically from scratch! After another six months of studying how it could be revised, I decided not to pursue the project. While dissertations are often laborious, the genre also permits a certain economy of detail and research. What is crucial in the doctoral thesis is the development of a specific theoretical argument within narrow disciplinary frames. The rest is incidental. Not so with a book: It must be comprehensible to general readers who bring their own agenda to it. The broad strokes in which I had drawn Quebec history from 1760 to 1980 would have been inadequate to those whose main interest was Quebec affairs, while my rhetorical concerns might have appeared arcane. Retelling the story of Quebec nationalism in the terms a Quebec historian could appreciate and a rhetorical theorist could value was not worth the effort. I wanted to keep up to date with the field, and not be dragged back into rewriting my thesis for the equivalent of another committee. So there I was, with a manuscript whose scope was too narrow for a book—but not too narrow for a journal article.

While I still did not fully consider myself a rhetorician, I decided to submit a manuscript to the *Quarterly Journal of Speech*, in part, because I thought the arguments I wished to make would be of interest to its readership, in part because it is a national journal (ego and tenure review demand the most prestigious journal possible) and in part because the journal was highly regarded by former professors and classmates to whom I could prove my academic coming of age. Also, since graduate school my interlocutors had been primarily rhetoricians, even though my arguments were usually against rhetoric's conventional principles. Better to write to them than to those who would not care about the point I was trying to make. Ultimately, in retrospect, the article was a performance, to prove something to myself, my colleagues, my professors, and my friends. To "get published." As a friend paraphrased Dr. Hook: There ain't no thrill like when you get your picture on the cover of the *QJS*.

My task began in earnest once I had decided to submit an article to *QJS*. To go from dissertation to journal is not just a matter of lifting a chapter, adding a beginning and concluding paragraph, and buying a stamp. Dissertations are extended works; articles offer short, self-contained arguments that address specific debates within a field. In addition, *QJS* is a disciplinary and association journal. It addresses a particular community that shares a particular literature and intellectual heritage. I needed to speak in terms that would be understood, that would establish my membership in their community. And so I reread Kenneth Burke. Also, I returned to other sources within rhetorical studies: McGee of course, for I was truly indebted to his thought, but also Edwin Black and Walter Fisher, who seemed to be addressing questions similar to my own.

I would be writing to rhetoricians, but my intent was to issue a kind of challenge. Thus, my project also required that I establish my difference. And so I framed my essay in terms of both Burke and Louis Althusser (the French Marxist philosopher). Both can be found in my dissertation's bibliography, but their explicit presence was minor. Roland Barthes and Frederic Jameson were similarly enlisted. None of these authors was absolutely necessary. I had no interest in developing a commentary or exegesis of some great thinker. My intellectual habits and writing strategy are more those of a *bricoleur,* a hobbyist-tinkerer, who crafts his works from available materials even if they are decontextualized in the process.

When I began to work on the article, I had been teaching Althusser, and realized that the concepts "subject" and "interpellation" underlay what I had been trying to say all along. Indeed, they likely influenced the dissertation itself, for I had read Althusser in graduate school. As for Burke, "identification" would provide a familiar reference point for what I had to say. But what was that exactly? I reread my dissertation and an earlier article presented at the second Alta conference on argumentation, and thought again about the initial inspiration for the thesis. My intuition was that claims were often warranted by an audience's identity, but that identities themselves are ultimately rhetorical constructs. Furthermore, it appeared to me that these were elicited through an effect of narrative. This then was what the article would be about, and I would have to develop and systematize it.

At one level, I was involved in a major "cut-and-paste" operation, but more fundamentally this was a new article, sharing only some primary texts and a few key ideas with its antecedents. My dissertation features the term "constitutive discourse," which inspired the crisper and more theoretical sounding "constitutive rhetoric" of my title. My dissertation chapters formed the basis for my description of Quebec affairs and the "White

Paper," my primary text. On a notepad and later on an outline processor, I brainstormed, I dissected my ideas, and I tried to order them. There would be a descriptive component; there would be an epistemological claim; there would be a discussion of narrative form; there would be some claim linking discourse to political action. I found myself confronting (but not of course resolving) the big questions: individual vs. collective action; materialism vs. idealism; text vs. performance. I was developing a sense of what I would need to write around. I saved paragraphs and sections in separate files; I kept alternate versions; I dated them. Slowly, a structure for the work emerged.

The essay was not written quickly. At least six months went by between beginning this revision piece and submitting it. I wanted the work to be accessible to the reader ignorant of Quebec and unfamiliar with what, at the time, I called a "structuralist" orientation, but I did not want to sacrifice theoretical substance. More than that, I did not want to face a rejection letter and so spent a great deal of time crafting sentences. I tried to keep them short. I used paraphrase and repetition for the sake of clarity. And most importantly, I sought to maintain a dialectic between my theory and my case.

I wanted the piece to be regarded theoretically, and not be considered primarily descriptive of an episode in Quebec political life. And so was born my hook and lead: I began by raising a theoretical distinction and I invoked Kenneth Burke's authority to secure its significance. Having made a few sweeping generalizations, it was necessary to elaborate specifics of the case and their relevance to my argument. My chapters would provide some of that, but again major revision was necessary. I wanted to emphasize the problem of national identity and so highlighted differences and discord.

A draft assembled, I read it over and over and over again. I checked the spelling, the flow, the clarity. Finally, I mailed it off and waited. Six months or so later, I received a response. One reviewer loved it, another felt it unfit for publication, and a third recommended publication but perceptively pointed out its weaknesses. Most notably, in the initial draft Kenneth Burke pretty much disappeared after the opening paragraph. Where had he gone? The editor assured me the essay would be published, but encouraged me to consider the reviewers' comments. Back to Burke's books. I scanned the index of each one for "rhetoric" and "ideology." I found suitable quotations that would illustrate or better state what I was attempting to say. In the process, I learned a great deal about Burke and the essay became somewhat "Burkean." Also, a reviewer asked how one could account for the emergence and success of new constitutive appeals. I had not wanted to grapple with "persuasiveness" in this essay. Indeed, the essay adopted "identification" as a counterpoint to "persuasion" as rhetoric's key term. But the reviewer's point was well taken, and so I struggled to respond. Another four months had passed. Enough was enough. I returned the corrected essay.

Six years after the Alta conference paper, more than three years after my dissertation defense, and two years after the beginning of my revisions, the essay was in print. The pleasure was great. More astounding, however, was that the essay was then read by people I did not know. I had never given any thought to what is so self-evident: Publication is ultimately a form of communication.

# Constitutive Rhetoric:
# The Case of the *Peuple Québécois*

**Maurice Charland**

In the *Rhetoric of Motives,* Kenneth Burke proposes "identification" as an alternative to "persuasion" as the key term of the rhetorical process. Burke's project is a rewriting of rhetorical theory that considers rhetoric and motives in formal terms, as consequences of the nature of language and its enactment. Burke's stress on identification permits a rethinking of judgment and the working of the rhetorical effect, for he does not posit a transcendent subject as audience member, who would exist prior to and apart from the speech to be judged, but considers audience members to participate in the very discourse by which they would be "persuaded." Audiences would embody a discourse. A consequence of this theoretical move is that it permits an understanding within rhetorical theory of ideological discourse, of the discourse that presents itself as always only pointing to the given, the natural, the already agreed upon.[1] In particular, it permits us to examine how rhetoric effects what Louis Althusser identifies as the key process in the production of ideology: the constitution of the subject, where the subject is precisely he or she who simultaneously speaks and initiates action in discourse (a subject to a verb) and in the world (a speaker and social agent).[2]

As Burke recognizes, "persuasion," as rhetoric's key term, implies the existence of an agent who is free to be persuaded.[3] However, rhetorical theory's privileging of an audience's freedom to judge is problematic, for it assumes that audiences, with their prejudices, interests, and motives, are *given* and so extra-rhetorical. Rhetorical criticism, as Grossberg points out, posits the existence of transcendental subjects whom discourse would mediate.[4] In other words, rhetorical theory usually refuses to consider the possibility that the very existence of social subjects (who would become audience members) is already a rhetorical effect. Nevertheless, much of what we as rhetorical critics consider to be a product or consequence of discourse, including social identity, religious faith, sexuality, and ideology is beyond the realm of rational or even free choice, beyond the realm of persuasion. As Burke notes, the identifications of social identity can occur "spontaneously, intuitively, even unconsciously."[5] Such identifications are rhetorical, for they are discursive effects that induce human cooperation. They are also, however, logically prior to persuasion. Indeed, humans are constituted in these characteristics; they are essential to the "nature" of a subject and form the basis for persuasive appeals. Consequently, attempts to elucidate ideo-

**211**

logical or identity-forming discourses as persuasive are trapped in a contradiction: persuasive discourse requires a subject-as-audience who is already constituted with an identity and within an ideology.

Ultimately then, theories of rhetoric as persuasion cannot account for the audiences that rhetoric addresses. However, such an account is critical to the development of a theoretical understanding of the power of discourse. If it is easier to praise Athens before Athenians than before Laecedemonians, we should ask how those in Athens come to experience themselves as Athenians. Indeed, a rhetoric to Athenians in praise of Athens would be relatively insignificant compared to a rhetoric that constitutes Athenians as such. What I propose to develop in this essay is a theory of constitutive rhetoric that would account for this process. I will elaborate this theory of constitutive rhetoric through an examination of a case where the identity of the audience is clearly problematic: the independence movement in Quebec, Canada's French-speaking province. There, supporters of Quebec's political sovereignty addressed and so attempted to call into being a *peuple québécois* that would legitimate the constitution of a sovereign Quebec state.

Central to my analysis of the constitutive rhetoric of Quebec sovereignty will be Althusser's category of the subject. Examining what Michael McGee would term Quebec's rhetoric of a "people," I will show how claims for Quebec sovereignty base themselves upon the asserted existence of a particular type of subject, the "Québécois." That subject and the collectivized "peuple québécois" are, in Althusser's language, "interpellated" as political subjects through a process of identification in rhetorical narratives that "always already" presume the constitution of subjects. From this perspective, a subject is not "persuaded" to support sovereignty. Support for sovereignty is inherent to the subject position addressed by *souverainiste* (pro-sovereignty) rhetoric because of what we will see to be a series of narrative *ideological effects*.

## ▨ THE QUEST FOR QUEBEC SOVEREIGNTY

In 1967, the year of Canada's centennial, a new political association was formed in Quebec. This organization, the *Mouvement Souveraineté-Association (MSA)*, dedicated itself to Quebec's political sovereignty as it proclaimed the existence of an essence uniting social actors in the province. In French, Quebec's majority language, the *MSA* declared: "Nous sommes des Québécois" ("We are *Québécois*") and called for Quebec's independence from Canada.[6] This declaration marked the entry of the term "Québécois" into the mainstream of Quebec political discourse. Until that time, members of the French-speaking society of Quebec were usually termed "Canadiens français" ("French-Canadians"). With the *MSA*, a national identity for a new type of political subject was born, a subject whose existence would be presented as justification for the constitution of a new state. Thus, the *MSA*'s declaration is an instance of constitutive rhetoric, for it calls its audience into being. Furthermore, as an instance of constitutive rhetoric, it was particularly effective, for within a decade of the creation of that *mouvement*, the term "Québécois" had gained currency even among certain supporters of the Canadian federal system, and Quebec voters had brought the *MSA*'s successor, the *Parti Québécois (PQ)*, to power.

Quebec voters gave the *Parti Québécois* control of the Quebec government on November 15, 1976. The party obtained 41.4% of the popular vote and won 71 of 110 seats in the *Assemblé nationale*, Quebec's legislature.[7] This election marked a major transformation in Canada's political life, for the *PQ* asserted that those in Quebec constituted a distinct *peuple* with the right and duty to political sovereignty, and was committed to leading Quebec, Canada's largest and second most populous province, out of Canada.

The *PQ*'s major campaign promise was to hold a referendum on Quebec's political sovereignty during its first term of office. In preparation of this plebiscite, the Quebec government issued, on November 1, 1979, a formal policy statement, a "white paper," that outlined a proposed new political order in which Quebec would be a sovereign state associated economically with Canada.[8] While the Quebec-Canada economic association would include free trade, a customs union, a shared currency and central bank as negotiated, and the free movement of persons across the Quebec-Canada border, each government would have the full sovereignty of a nation-state.[9] The White Paper asserted that those in Quebec constituted a *peuple* and called upon them to support this project by voting OUI in a forthcoming referendum. Such a positive vote by the Quebec electorate would mandate their provincial government to negotiate for the envisioned new constitutional status with the federal government in Ottawa.[10]

The White Paper, as it articulated the reasons for Quebec's political independence, was a rhetorical document. It offered a variety of arguments demonstrating that *Québécois* were an oppressed *peuple* within the confines of Canada's constitution who would be better off with their own country. These arguments were presented in the context of the constitutive rhetoric of the "peuple québécois." This constitutive rhetoric took the form of a narrative account of Quebec history in which *Québécois* were identified with their forebears who explored New France, who suffered under the British conquest, and who struggled to erect the Quebec provincial state apparatus.

The Referendum on sovereignty-association was held May 20, 1980. Although a majority of the populace voted against the measure, over 45% of the French-speaking population assented to their provincial government's interpretation of Quebec society.[11] Those voting OUI granted the legitimacy of the constitutional claims the White Paper asserted. Clearly, even if a majority of *Québécois* were not ready to seek sovereignty, a *malaise* powerful enough to dominate political debate and government priorities existed in the province. There was a strong sense in which "Québécois" was a term antithetical to "Canadien."

The election of the *Parti Québécois* and the strength of its *souverainiste* option in the Referendum reveals the significance of the constitutive rhetoric of a "peuple québécois." While some might consider the White Paper to be a rhetorical failure because less than half of Quebec's French-speaking population opted for independence, the outcome of the Referendum reveals that its constitutive rhetoric was particularly powerful. This rhetoric, which presents those in Quebec as *Québécois* requiring and deserving their own state, constituted at least close to half of Quebec voters such that they, as an audience, were not *really* Canadians.

What the debate in Quebec reveals is that the very character of a collective identity, and the nature of its boundary, of who is a member of the collectivity, were problematic. In other words, in Quebec there existed a struggle over the constitution of political subjects. In Quebec, the possibility of an alternative *peuple* and history was entertained. Thus, the movement for sovereignty permits us to see how peoples are rhetorically constituted.

### ☐ "PEUPLE" AS LEGITIMATING PRINCIPLE

As Michael McGee has noted, the term "people" can rhetorically legitimate constitutions.[12] Not surprisingly then, the independence debate in Quebec, as it developed since the formation of the *MSA*, centered upon whether a *peuple québécois* exists, and more importantly, on whether that *peuple* is the kind of "people" that legitimates a sovereign state. In Quebec, competing claims were made as to the nature of the *peuple*. Consider, for example, Claude Morin's polemical history of Quebec-Ottawa constitutional disputes from 1960 to 1972, where he distinguishes the emergent Quebec collectivity from its predecessor, French-Canada, as he identifies the perspective of the Quebec government: "Like many other peoples, Quebeckers have experienced an awakening of self-consciousness. They want to assert themselves, not as French-speaking Canadians, but as Québécois, citizens who, for the moment, suffer the want of a country that is their own."[13] In Morin's view, not only are those in Quebec *Québécois,* but they constitute the kind of *peuple* that warrants a sovereign state. Morin's observation confirms that populations can at different historical moments gain different identities that warrant different forms of collective life. Furthermore, if we consider that Morin's observation is contentious and partisan,[14] and that many in Quebec would contest his assessment of their collective identity, we find confirmation of McGee's further assertion that the identity of a "people," as a rhetorical construct, is not even agreed upon by those who would address it.[15] Rather, supporters and opponents of Quebec sovereignty both seek to justify their position on the basis of what they assert is a will intrinsic to their version of the *peuple's* very being. Their rhetoric is grounded in the constitution of *Québécois* as political subjects.

The debate over sovereignty in Quebec clearly reveals the degree to which peoples are constituted in discourse. Those in Quebec could be "Québécois"; they could also be "Canadiens français." The distinction is crucial, for only the former type of "peuple" can claim the right to a sovereign state. Indeed, the debate in Quebec permits us to see the radical implication of McGee's argument, for not only is the character or identity of the "peuple" open to rhetorical revision, but the very *boundary* of whom the term "peuple" includes and excludes is rhetorically constructed: as the "peuple" is variously characterized, the persons who make up the "peuple" can change. Thus, consider the rather extreme counter-argument to Morin's claim that a *peuple québécois* exists and is gaining self-awareness, as articulated by William Shaw and Lionel Albert, two Quebec opponents of sovereignty, who conversely assert that no Quebec *peuple* exists, that the term "Québécois" properly only applies to residents of the City of Quebec, and that the term as used by Quebec nationalists constitutes a "semantic fraud":

> Separatists measure the degree of their penetration of the public con-sciousness by the extent to which the people are willing to call themselves *Québécois.* The more they can persuade the French Canadians in Quebec to call themselves *Québécois,* the easier the task of insinuating the idea that those French Canadians who happen to live in eastern or northern Ontario or in northern New Brunswick are somehow "different" from those living in Quebec. Once that idea has been established, then the idea that Quebec's borders, which are criss-crossed daily by tens of thousands of French Canadians, could some-how be thought of, not as casual signposts along the highway, but as a full-fledged international boundary, can also be established.[16]

Shaw and Albert display a keen sensitivity to the workings of the *péquiste* rhetoric of collective identity, even if as advocates, these opponents of Quebec independence assert that a French-Canadian *peuple* "really" exists out-side of rhetorical construction. What Shaw and Albert ignore, of course, is that the French-speaking *peuple* or nation that they assert exists also be-comes real only through rhetoric. Indeed, the possibility of political action requires that political actors be within a "fictive" discourse. More precisely, as Althusser asserts: "there is no practice except by and in an ideology."[17] Political identity must be an ideological fiction, even though, as McGee correctly notes, this fiction becomes historically material and of conse-quence as persons live it.

## ■ THE RHETORIC OF INTERPELLATION

As we have seen, rhetorical claims for a sovereign Quebec are predicated upon the existence of an ideological subject, the "Québécois," so constituted that sovereignty is a natural and necessary way of life. Furthermore, and hardly surprisingly, the ultimate justification for these claims is the subject's character, nature, or essence. This is so because this identity defines inherent motives and interests that a rhetoric can appeal to. The ideological "trick" of such a rhetoric is that it presents that which is most rhetorical, the existence of a *peuple*, or of a subject, as extrarhetorical. These members of the *peuple* whose supposed essence demands action do not exist in nature, but only within a discursively constituted history. Thus, this rhetoric paradoxically must constitute the identity "Québécois" as it simultaneously presumes it to be pregiven and natural, existing outside of rhetoric and forming the basis for a rhetorical address.

We find a treatment of this constitutive phenomenon in Edwin Black's discussion of the "second persona."[18] As Michael McGuire observes, Black's process of transforming an audience occurs through *identification*, in Burke's sense.[19] However, to simply accept such an account of this process would be inadequate. It would not fully explain the significance of becoming one with a persona, of entering into and embodying it. In particular, to simply state that audiences identify with a persona explains neither (1) the ontological status of those in the audience before their identification, nor (2) the ontological status of the persona, and the nature of identifying with it. In order to clarify these ontological issues, we must consider carefully the radical edge of Burke's identificatory principle. Burke asserts that, as "symbol using" animals, our being is significantly constituted in our symbolicity. As Burke puts it, "so much of the 'we' that is separated from the nonverbal by the verbal would not even exist were it not for the verbal (or for our symbolicity in general[)]."[20] In this, Burke moves towards collapsing the distinction between the realm of the symbolic and that of human conceptual consciousness. From such a perspective, we cannot accept the 'givenness' of "audience," "person," or "subject," but must consider their very textuality, their very constitution in rhetoric as a structured articulation of signs. We must, in other words, consider the textual nature of social being.

The symbolically based critique of humanist ontology implicit in Burke has been developed in a tradition sharing much with him, that of structuralism.[21] Structuralist semiotics and narrative theory have deconstructed the concept of the unitary and transcendent subject. And, with rhetorical theory, they share an appreciation of the power of discourse, of its effects. Thus, in order to develop the radical implications of Burke's lead, it is to this tradition that I will turn.

Althusser describes the process of inscribing subjects into ideology as "interpellation":[22]

> I shall then suggest that ideology "acts" or "functions" in such a way that it "recruits" subjects among the individuals (it recruits them all), or "transforms" the individuals into subjects (it transforms them all) by that very precise

operation which I have called *interpellation* or hailing, and which can be imagined along the lines of the most commonplace everyday police (or other) hailing: "Hey, you there!"[23]

Interpellation occurs at the very moment one enters into a rhetorical situation, that is, as soon as an individual recognizes and acknowledges being addressed. An interpellated subject participates in the discourse that addresses him. Thus, to be interpellated is to become one of Black's personae and be a position in a discourse. In consequence, interpellation has a significance to rhetoric, for the acknowledgment of an address entails an acceptance of an imputed self-understanding which can form the basis for an appeal. Furthermore, interpellation occurs rhetorically, through the effect of the addressed discourse. Note, however, that interpellation does not occur through persuasion in the usual sense, for the very act of *addressing* is rhetorical. It is logically prior to the rhetorical *narratio*. In addition, this rhetoric of identification is ongoing, not restricted to one hailing, but usually part of a rhetoric of socialization. Thus, one must already be an interpellated subject and exist as a discursive position in order to be part of the audience of a rhetorical situation in which persuasion could occur.

## ▓ THE "PEUPLE" AS NARRATIVE IDEOLOGICAL EFFECT

Events in Quebec demonstrate that the "peuple" is a persona, existing in rhetoric, and not in some neutral history devoid of human interpretation. But note, personae are not persons; they remain in the realm of words. As McGee observes, a "people" is a fiction which comes to be when individuals accept living within a political myth.[24] This myth would be ontological, constitutive of those "seduced" by it. In Quebec, what McGee terms the myth of the "people" is articulated in the Quebec government's White Paper. This document, speaking in the name of the independence movement, as institutionalized in a party and a government, offers a narrative of Quebec history that renders demands for sovereignty intelligible and reasonable.

The White Paper's narrative of the *peuple* since the founding of New France, through the British Conquest, the development of Canada into a federated state, and the setting up of the Referendum on Quebec sovereignty is, in McGee's sense, a myth. It paradoxically both reveals the *peuple* and makes it real. This making real is part of the ontological function of narratives. Indeed, as Jameson points out, "history . . . is inaccessible to us except in textual form, and . . . our approach to it and the Real itself necessarily passes through its prior textualization, its narrativization in the political unconscious."[25] Because the *peuple* exists as a subject in history, it is only intelligible within a narrative representation of history. In other words, this *peuple*, and the individual subject, the *Québécois*, exist as positions in a text.

Narratives "make real" coherent subjects. They constitute subjects as they present a particular textual position, such as the noun-term "peuple québécois" as the locus for action and experience. Roland Barthes well expresses this ultimate textuality of narratives when he asserts that: "Narrative does not show, does not imitate; the passion which may excite us . . . is not that of a 'vision' (in actual fact, we do not 'see' anything)."[26] In other words, narratives work through a representational *effect.* Texts are but surfaces; characters are, in a sense, but "paper beings," to use Barthes' phrase. These paper beings *seem* real through textual operations. The distinct acts and events in a narrative become linked through identification arising from the narrative form. Narratives lead us to construct and fill in coherent unified subjects out of temporally and spatially separate events. This renders the site of action and experience stable. The locus of yesterday's acts becomes that of today's. Consequently, narratives offer a world in which human agency is possible and acts can be meaningful.

All narratives, as they create the illusion of merely revealing a unified and unproblematic subjectivity, are ideological, because they occult the importance of discourse, culture, and history in giving rise to subjectivity, and because, as G. H. Mead and Freud have made clear, subjectivity is always social, constituted in language, and exists in a delicate balance of contradictory drives and impulses. Narratives suppress the fact that, in a very real sense, no person is the same as he or she was a decade ago, or last year, or indeed yesterday. In raising the ultimate "falsity" of narratives, my intention is not, however, to decry them and hold out for some unmediated consciousness. Nor am I here concerned with a philosophical critique of the subject in Western civilization. My intention is to show the degree to which collective identities forming the basis of rhetorical appeals themselves depend upon rhetoric; the "peuple québécois," and "peoples" in general, exist only through an ideological discourse that constitutes them. Furthermore, if the subject in all narratives is ideological, a "peuple" is triply so, for it does not even have a unitary body corresponding to its imputed unitary agency and consciousness. The persona or subject "peuple québécois" exists only as a series of narrative ideological effects.

In the rhetoric of Quebec sovereignty, the "Québécois" is a collective subject. It offers, in Burke's language, an "ultimate" identification permitting an overcoming or going beyond of divisive individual or class interests and concerns.[27] This identity transcends the limitations of the individual body and will. This process of constituting a collective subject is the *first ideological effect* of constitutive rhetoric. If a *peuple* exists, it is only in ideology, as McGee makes clear. That ideology arises in the very nature of narrative history. To tell the story of the *Québécois* is implicitly to assert the existence of a collective subject, the protagonist of the historical drama, who experiences, suffers, and acts. Such a narrative renders the world of events understandable with respect to a transcendental collective interest that negates individual interest. Consider the following passage from the White Paper's account of early French North America:

> Our ancestors put down their roots in American soil at the beginning of the 17th century, at the time the first English settlers were landing on the East coast of the United States. As they were clearing the land of the St. Lawrence valley, they explored the vast continent in all directions, from the Atlantic to the Rocky Mountains, and from Hudson Bay to the Gulf of Mexico. Through discovering, claiming, and occupying the land, *Québécois* came to consider themselves North-Americans.
>
> In 1760, our community was already an established society along the St. Lawrence. North American by geography, French by language, culture, and politics, this society had a soul, a way of life, traditions, that were its very own. Its struggles, its successes, and its ordeals had given it an awareness of its collective destiny, and it was with some impatience that it tolerated the colonial tie.[28]

In a radically empiricist mood, I could assert that a society *qua* society has no soul, no struggles, no successes. Clearly, history proceeds by the acts of individuals. But, of course, individuals can act in concert or as a mass, they can respond to apersonal historical forces, and we can interpret the sum total of their individual actions with respect to a collective agent. Historical narratives offer such interpretations. In the telling of the story of a *peuple*, a *peuple* comes to be. It is within the formal structure of a narrative history that it is possible to conceive of a set of individuals as if they were but one. Thus, the "struggles" and "ordeals" of settlers, as a set of individual acts and experiences, become identified with "community," a term that here masks or negates tensions and differences between members of any society. The community of *Québécois* is the master agent of a narratized history.

In the above passage, note also how the past is presented as an extension of the present through the use of the pronoun "our" and the term "Québécois" as signifiers of both eighteenth century settlers who termed themselves "Canadiens" and those living in Quebec today. The White Paper, and histories of peoples in general, offer a "consubstantiality," to use Burke's expression, between the dead and the living. This positing of a transhistorical subject is the *second ideological effect* of constitutive rhetoric. Here, ancestry is offered as the concrete link between the French settlers of North America, those in Quebec today, and a collectivity. Time is collapsed as narrative identification occurs: today's Quebec residents constitute a *peuple* and have a right to their own state because members of their community have discovered, claimed, and occupied the land. This interpretive stance is perfectly reasonable. It is also perfectly tautological, for it is a making sense that depends upon the a priori acceptance of that which it attempts to prove the existence of, a collective agent, the *peuple québécois*, that transcends the limitations of individuality at any historical moment and transcends the death of individuals across history.

Form renders the "Québécois" a real subject within the historical narrative. The "Québécois" does not, however, become a free subject. Subjects within narratives are not free, they are *positioned* and so constrained. All narratives have power over the subjects they present. The endings of narratives are fixed before the telling. The freedom of the character in a narrative is an illusion, for narratives move inexorably toward their *telos*. The characters in a story are obviously not free. Only in Woody Allen's *The Purple Rose of Cairo* can characters abandon their script and walk off the screen. What Allen's film and Barthes' analysis of narratives so clearly illustrate is that narratives are but texts that offer the illusion of agency. The subject is constituted at the nodes of a narrative's surface. What Walter Fisher terms "narrative probability" is a formal and ideological constraint upon the subject's possibilities of being.[29] To be constituted as a subject in a narrative is to be constituted with a history, motives, and a *telos*. Thus, in the rhetoric of Quebec sovereignty, "Québécois" is not merely a descriptive term, but identifies and positions the Quebec voter with respect to his or her future.

The White Paper presents *Québécois* as agents, capable of acting freely in the world. However, the narrative's existence as a text is predicated upon *Québécois* asserting their existence as a collective subject through a politics of independence. In the White Paper on sovereignty, *Québécois* are constituted in the choice of national solidarity. As Burke observes is the case in ideological narratives, the White Paper effects an identification of the temporal sequence of its plot with the logical development of an ultimate principle.[30] In the resultant hierarchy, *Québécois* are free to choose only one course of action:

> The Will to Survive
> Sooner or later, this society would have shaken off the colonial yoke and acquired its independence, as was the case, in 1776, for the United States of America. But in 1763 the hazards of war placed it under British control. . . . Faced with this defeat, francophones spontaneously chose to be faithful. There could be no question of passing over to the winner's camp to reap the benefits that awaited them. They would adapt to the new situation, come to terms with the new masters, but above all preserve the essential of that which characterized our *peuple:* its language, its customs, its religion. At all costs, they would survive.[31]

The freedom of the protagonist of this narrative is but an illusion. This illusion of freedom is the *third ideological effect* of constitutive rhetoric. Freedom is illusory because the narrative is already spoken or written. Furthermore, because the narrative is a structure of understanding that produces totalizing interpretations,[32] the subject is constrained to *follow through,* to act so as to maintain the narrative's consistency. A narrative, once written, offers a logic of meaningful totality. *Québécois*, precisely because they are the subjects within a text, within a narrative rhetoric, must follow the logic of the narrative. They must be true to the motives through which the narrative constitutes them, and thus which presents characters as freely acting towards a predetermined and fixed ending.

## ▨ THE EFFECTIVE POWER OF CONSTITUTIVE RHETORIC

The ideological effects of constitutive rhetoric that I have outlined are not merely formal effects inscribed within the bracketed experience of interpreting a text. In other words, these do not only permit a disinterested understanding of a fictive world. What is significant in constitutive rhetoric is that it positions the reader towards political, social, and economic action in the material world and it is in this positioning that its ideological character becomes significant. For the purpose of analysis, this positioning of subjects as historical actors can be understood as a two-step process. First, audience members must be successfully interpellated; not all constitutive rhetorics succeed. Second, the tautological logic of constitutive rhetoric must necessitate action in the material world; constitutive rhetoric must require that its embodied subjects act freely in the social world to affirm their subject position.

Audiences are, to use Althusser's famous phrase, "always already" subjects. This is to say that if we disregard the point at which a child enters language, but restrict ourselves to "competent" speakers within a culture, we can observe that one cannot exist but as a subject within a narrative. The necessity is ontological: one must already be a subject in order to be addressed or to speak. We therefore cannot say that one is persuaded to be a subject; one is "always already" a subject. This does not imply, however, that one's subject position is fixed at the moment one enters language. Indeed, the development of new subject positions, of new constitutive rhetorics, is possible at particular historical moments. The subject is a position within a text. To be an embodied subject is to experience and act in a textualized world. However, this world is not seamless and a subject position's world view can be laced with contradictions. We can, as Burke puts it, encounter "recalcitrance."[33] In addition, as Stuart Hall observes, various contradictory subject positions can simultaneously exist within a culture:[34] we can live within many texts. These contradictions place a strain upon identification with a given subject position and render possible a subject's rearticulation. Successful new constitutive rhetorics offer new subject positions that resolve, or at least contain, experienced contradictions. They serve to overcome or define away the recalcitrance the world presents by providing the subject with new perspectives and motives.

Thus, for example, the subject position "Québécois" arises from a rearticulation of two positions, that of "Canadien français," and that of the Quebec resident and voter with a collective will ostensibly represented by the Quebec government. Because some French-Canadians live outside of Quebec and not all those in Quebec are French-speaking, the identity "Canadien français" cannot permit the articulation of a French-speaking nation-state in North America. As the White Paper never fails to remind its audience, to be "Canadien français" is to be a member of an impotent minority without a proper homeland. The White Paper, penned by the Quebec government, invokes the contradiction of being a member of a French-speaking collectivity, or *nation*, that does not have a sovereign state apparatus, for the Quebec government remains subject to Canada's Federal government in Ottawa, and French-Canadians are subjects of the Federal state, a state that can be represented as ultimately foreign.

French-Canadians in Quebec had to live the contradiction of not being exclusively subjects of the state they collectively controlled. "Québécois" resolves this contradiction at the discursive level, by identifying the populace with a territory and a francophone state, rather than with an ethnic group. Constitutive rhetorics of new subject positions can be understood, therefore, as working upon previous discourses, upon previous constitutive rhetorics. They capture alienated subjects by rearticulating existing subject positions so as to contain or resolve experienced dialectical contradictions between the world and its discourses. The process by which an audience member enters into a new subject position is therefore not one of persuasion. It is akin more to one of conversion that ultimately results in an act of recognition of the 'rightness' of a discourse and of one's identity with its reconfigured subject position.

The White Paper's constitutive rhetoric, as it articulates the meaning of being "Québécois," is not a mere fiction. It inscribes real social actors within its textualized structure of motives, and then inserts them into the world of practice. The White Paper offers a collectivized subject position that constitutes those in Quebec as members of a *peuple* which is transcendent of the limits of their biological individuality. This position thus opens the possibility for them to participate in a collective political project. The White Paper's narrative is characterized by a set of formal ideological effects that permit it to be intelligible as one accepts and enters into the collective consciousness it articulates. The White Paper offers, therefore, a particular instance of narrative rhetoric that, in Fisher's language, "give[s] order to human experience and . . . induce[s] others to *dwell in* [*it*] to establish ways of living in common, in communion in which there is sanction for the story that constitutes one's life" (italics added).[35] This dwelling place is, of course, prerequisite to the power of the rhetoric of Quebec sovereignty. To be *Québécois* as configured by the White Paper is to embody in the world the narrative and the motives it ascribes to members of the *peuple*.

To enter into the White Paper's rhetorical narrative is to identify with Black's second persona. It is the process of recognizing oneself as the subject in a text. It is to exist at the nodal point of a series of identifications and to be captured in its structure and in its production of meaning. It is to be a subject which exists beyond one's body and life span. It is to have and experience the dangerous memories of British conquest and rule. It is to live towards national independence. Then, the power of the text is the power of an embodied ideology. The form of an ideological rhetoric is effective because it is within the bodies of those it constitutes as subjects. These subjects owe their existence to the discourse that articulates them. As Burke puts it: "An 'ideology' is like a god coming down to earth, where it will inhabit a place pervaded by its presence. An 'ideology' is like a spirit taking up its abode in a body: it makes that body hop around in certain ways; and that same body would have hopped around in different ways had a different ideology happened to inhabit it."[36] Thus, from the subjectivity or point of view of the embodied *souverainiste* discourse, not only would there exist "good reasons" for supporting sovereignty, but good *motives* as well, motives arising from the very essence of the *Québécois'* being. Within the White Paper's account is embedded a "logic," a way of understanding the world, that offers those in Quebec a position from which to understand and act.

## ◼ IDENTIFICATION WITH A CONSTITUTIVE RHETORIC

If the White Paper and historical narratives were but dead history, mere stories, their significance to ideology could easily be dismissed. However, constitutive rhetorics, as they identify, have power because they are oriented towards action. As Althusser and McGee both stress, ideology is material, existing not in the realm of ideas, but in that of *material practices*. Ideology is material because subjects enact their ideology and reconstitute their material world in its image.[37] Constitutive rhetorics are ideological not merely because they provide individuals with narratives to inhabit as subjects and motives to experience, but because they insert "narratized" subjects-as-agents into the world.

The insertion of subjects into the world is a product of both the identificatory and referential functions of the White Paper's historical narrative and its ideological effects. In particular, it is the third ideological effect, the constitution in action of a motivated subject, that orients those addressed towards particular future acts. Since narratives offer totalizing interpretations that ascribe transcendent meanings to individual acts, the maintenance of narrative consistency demands that a certain set of acts be chosen. This is amplified in the White Paper because it offers a narrative without closure. The White Paper offers an unfinished history: the *peuple québécois* has yet to obtain its independence. Thus, the *Québécois* addressed by the

White Paper must bring to a close the saga begun by the subjects of the White Paper's history. In other words, while classical narratives have an ending, constitutive rhetorics leave the task of narrative closure to their constituted subjects. It is up to the *Québécois* of 1980 to conclude the story to which they are identified. The story the White Paper offers is of a besieged *peuple* that has always continued to struggle in order to survive and to assert its right to self-determination. Nevertheless, in this account, each advance is blocked by the colonial power. The story proceeds through the recounting of a series of episodes, each exhibiting the same pattern.

As we have already seen, the White Paper asserts that the new *peuple's* aspirations were blocked by British conquest. This act of conquest recurs in other guises at other moments in the *peuple's* saga. Thus, in the rhetoric of Quebec sovereignty, for example, the victims of the conquest of 1760 become the protagonists in the parliamentary wrangles of 1837. Individual subjects, the *Québécois*, and their collective subject, the *peuple*, are somehow the same, even though the actual personages, institutions, material conditions, and struggles have changed. *Québécois* as explorers become political subjects. Thus, the White Paper asserts:

> The Parliament of Lower Canada, where the language was French, proposed laws and a budget that were submitted for approval to the Governor, who exercised executive power on behalf of London. The *peuple's* will was often blocked by the veto of the Governor, particularly sensitive to the interests of the English minority of Lower Canada and those of the imperial power. The consequent tension was leading, by 1830, to exasperation. The representatives drew up a set of resolutions in which they expressed their demands: control by the Assembly of taxes and spending, and the adoption of urgent social and economic measures. The Governor refused and dissolved the House. In the elections that followed, the *Patriotes*, headed by Papineau, won 77 out of 88 seats with 90% of the vote. To the same demands, the Governor responded by dissolving the House once again.[38]

The rhetorical significance of this passage is twofold. First, it typifies the text's constitution of a subject subjugated by Britain. Note how it confronts victory with power. In doing so, it highlights what can be presented as an inherent contradiction of "French-Canadian" as a subject position that interpellates French-Canadians both as French ethnic subjects and Canadian political subjects. Second, this passage, again typically, rearticulates this subject position: it articulates "Québécois" as a *political* subject battling on the terrain of parliament. In doing so, it dissolves any possible contradiction between loyalty to an (ethnic) nation and the federal state and it articulates both a site for and an object of struggle: the Quebec state apparatus and its legitimate institutions.

The White Paper offers a narrative characterized by a teleological movement towards emancipation. If the root cause of the struggle of the *peuple* is the natural impossibility of the *peuple* to exist without self-determination, control of the state machinery becomes the point of resolution of a drama that began while *Québécois* were still under the rule of the French king. The narrative offers sovereignty as the ultimate point that must be reached in order to attain narrative closure and liberate its subjects. The White Paper offers no alternative but for *Québécois* to struggle against annihilation. To offer but one example among many, the recounting of the 1837 uprising by a nationalist party known as the *Patriotes* and their speedy defeat makes clear that *Québécois* are constituted in a struggle for life itself, a struggle, furthermore, that cannot be won militarily:

> After their lone victory at Saint-Denis, the *Patriotes* were crushed at Saint-Charles and Saint-Eustache. The repression was cruel: hundreds of *Patriotes* were imprisoned and twelve were hanged; here and there, farms were ablaze.[39]

Within the context of contemporary attempts to secure Quebec's independence, the White Paper offers a condensed historical narrative of the *peuple québécois* as teleologically moving towards emancipation. The historical account of the White Paper is decidedly presentist and rhetorical, for a society of the seventeenth century is identified with a society today: the seventeenth century colonists who termed themselves "Canadiens" are termed "Québécois"; past struggles are presented as warranting action in the present. The particular issues over which nineteenth century parliamentarians battled are rendered in ideological terms that are then applied to current battles between Quebec and Canada's Federal government. Each episode in the history moves the *peuple* as subject towards the Quebec Referendum on sovereignty-association. The narrative form provides a continuity across time in which the practices of the past are increasingly identified with the present day order. Thus, the British Conquest, parliamentary wrangles, and the rebellions of 1837, find their counterpart in the "imposition" of a Canadian constitution:

> At the constitutional conferences of 1864 and 1866, the Quebec delegates and those of the other provinces were pursuing very different goals. Upper Canada in particular wanted a supraprovincial parliament, endowed with as many and as important powers as possible, that would have presided over the fates of the new country; Quebec, on the other hand, wanted to grant itself a responsible government, enjoying a large degree of autonomy, that would guarantee once and for all the existence and progress of the Quebec *peuple*—and that would have been its *real* government. The opposition between a centralized federalism and a decentralized confederation was already making itself felt. The first idea finally won out. Granted, *Québécois* acquired an autonomous responsible government, but with its autonomy limited to jurisdictions seen then as being primarily of local interest.[40]

The *peuple québécois* is presented as preceding the Canadian state. Confederation, like the Conquest, the defeat of the *Patriotes*, and the unification in 1849 of the predominantly English-speaking colony of Upper

Canada with the predominantly French-speaking colony of Lower Canada disrupted the movement of the *peuple* towards the "natural" ideal of its own constitution, responsible government, and a state. The implicit presumption that political structures should provide a means for the articulation and execution of a *peuple's* aspirations, as connoted by the term "peuple" itself, is set in opposition to this account of Canada's formation. The government in Ottawa is not a *real* government. Ottawa's power is represented as illegitimate. The Quebec *peuple* is frustrated, denied progress and its very existence. This narrative's movement towards closure is frustrated by the English presence. The emancipation of the *peuple* is blocked by the pattern of conquest and resistance *(narratio interrupta)*. The conquerors stand against narrative teleology as well as history's grand laws.

In the rhetoric of Quebec sovereignty then, the Government of Canada does not arise from the Quebec *peuple* and hence disrupts the teleological flow of history that the narrative form provides. Canada is an antagonist in this life-drama of a *peuple*. As such, Canada must be overcome so that the tensions in the mythic narrative and in history can be resolved. The "natural" principle that *peuples* attain control of their future is denied because Ottawa will preside over destiny. Within the context of the repression of the *Patriotes,* this new order does not arise from the *peuple québécois* but from external constraints. Confederation is but another manifestation of the Conquest to which, in this account, the *peuple* never assented: *Québécois* never acquiesce, but always struggle within the constraints of the possible. The change heralded by Confederation was but a small gain within the British system. Confederation is not the end of the struggle, only a new battleground. On this terrain, the *peuple* is threatened by a political reality that denies its very being.

The White Paper, having constituted *Québécois* in a struggle for survival, moves them and the narrative into the present. The current constitution that the independence movement opposes is represented as forming the basis for the continued subjugation of the *peuple:*

> The institution of the Canadian federal regime thus sanctioned, and favored as well, the hegemony of a Canada become English. It is quite natural that in such a regime the interests and aspirations of *Québécois* and Francophones in other provinces should take second place. In 1885, for example, all Quebec took the side of Louis Riel, who was fighting for the survival of francophone communities in the West. On the other hand, the federal government fought him and Louis Riel died on the scaffold.[41]

Any possibility that Confederation was advantageous for Quebec is denied. The will of the *peuple,* as instantiated in historical practice, is shown to be undermined in the federal regime. The White Paper describes various defeats of the will of the *peuple* in Confederation: Louis Riel fought for "survival" and climbed the scaffold; rights to French language education outside Quebec were denied; *Québécois* were forced to participate in British wars.[42] The accounts form a tragic tale; the francophones in Canada including the *peuple québécois* are without control of their circumstances.

The narrative concludes by identifying a threat to its very existence as a narrative. Canadian Confederation would deny that Québécois exist and so would deny the very possibility of this constitutive rhetoric and so of an audience inhabiting it. As the White Paper puts it: "The very balance of the system, as the Canadian majority wants it, requires that Quebec remain a province—or perhaps a territory—among ten others, and forbids the formal and concrete recognition of a Quebec nation."[43] This version of Quebec would require a revision of the meaning of "Québécois" such that it no longer positioned its subjects as members of both a nation and state. The "Québécois" would be but the Quebec resident, who might also be a French-Canadian defined in ethnic terms. Thus, in its concluding summary exhorting *Québécois* to vote OUI in the Referendum on sovereignty-association, the White Paper characterizes a NON vote as constituting:

> Only a brutal ending to the healthiest form of progress, one that leads an entire *peuple*, as naturally as an individual, to its maturity. We would simply fall back into line, remain in the state of oblivion kindly granted us by those outsiders who have been keeping a close eye on our progress. . . .
>
> On the contrary, we believe that we are mature enough, and big enough, and strong enough, to come to terms with our destiny. Because that is what is true.[44]

To be constituted as a *Québécois* in the terms of this narrative is to be constituted such that sovereignty is not only possible, but necessary. Without sovereignty, this constitutive rhetoric would ultimately die and those it has constituted would cease to be subjects, or at least would remain, like children, partial and stunted subjects, lacking maturity, responsibility, and autonomy. In consequence, true *Québécois* could not vote NON. Only a OUI vote would be in harmony with their being and their collective destiny: "Indeed, the choice should be easy, for the heart as well as the mind. We need only give a little thought to how faithful we have been in the past and how strong we are at present; we must think also of those who will follow us, whose futures depend so utterly on that moment."[45]

In sum, the White Paper calls on those it has addressed to follow narrative consistency and the motives through which they are constituted as audience members. Its rhetorical effect derives from their interpellation as subjects and on their identification with a transhistorical and transindividual subject position. It is in this sense of textualizing audiences, therefore, that we can understand the process Black treats in his discussion of the second persona and McGee discusses in his study of the "people." From this perspective, we can see that audiences do not exist outside rhetoric, merely addressed by it, but live inside rhetoric. Indeed, from the moment they enter into the world of language, they are subjects; the very moment of recognition of an address constitutes an entry into a subject position to which inheres a set of motives that render a rhetorical discourse intelligible. These subject positions are bequeathed by the past, by yesterday's discourses. Furthermore, the contradictions between discourses as well as the dialectic between discourse and a changing concrete world open a space for new subject positions. Tensions in the realm of the symbolic render possible the rhetorical repositioning or rearticulation of subjects.

## ■ CONCLUSION

Early in this essay, I identified two problems deserving examination: the first regarding the ontological status of those addressed by discourse before their successful interpellation; the second regarding the ontological status of the persona and the process by which one is identified with it. I have treated the latter problem by introducing the concept of the subject and by showing that audiences are constituted as subjects through a process of identification with a textual position. This identification occurs through a series of ideological effects arising from the narrative structure of constitutive rhetoric. As for the first problem I posed, I have in a sense circumvented it through my analysis. Persons are subjects from the moment they acquire language and the capacity to speak and to be spoken to. As such, constitutive rhetoric is part of the discursive background of social life. It is always there, usually implicitly, and sometimes explicitly articulated. It is more than a set of commonplaces, but is the con-text, the pre-rhetoric that is necessary to any successful interpellation.

Our first subject positions are modest, linked to our name, our family, and our sex. As we enter the adult world, they become more complex, as different constitutive rhetorics reposition us with respect to such formal and informal institutions as the state, the economy, the church, and the school. Thus, though we are subjects through language, and indeed can only speak as subjects, our subjectivity and ideological commitments are not fixed at our first utterance. As Quebec public address illustrates, particular subject positions can undergo transformation: "Canadien français" can become "Québécois," an identity permitting claims for a new political order. At particular historical moments, political rhetorics can reposition or rearticulate subjects by performing ideological work upon the texts in which social actors are inscribed.

In this essay, I have suggested that Burke's privileging of the term "identification" and an understanding of rhetoric's constitutive and ontological effect, as suggested by structuralist discourse theory, have certain consequences for the theory and practice of rhetoric. A theory of constitutive rhetoric leads us to call into question the concept, usually implicit to rhetoric's humanist tradition, of an audience composed of unified and transcendent subjects. If we are left with a subject, that subject is partial and decentered. History, and indeed discourse itself, form the ground for subjectivity. Consequently, even what Fisher terms "narrative fidelity" has an ideological character, for the experiential ground to which narratives would be faithful are always already ideologically framed within the very being of the experiencing subject.[46]

Because ideology forms the ground for any rhetorical situation, a theory of ideological rhetoric must be mindful not only of arguments and ideographs, but of the very nature of the subjects that rhetoric both addresses and leads to come to be. Indeed, because the constitutive nature of rhetoric establishes the boundary of a subject's motives and experience, a truly ideological rhetoric must rework or transform subjects. A transformed ideology would require a transformed subject (not a dissolving of subjectivity). Such a transformation requires ideological and rhetorical work. This can proceed at two levels: (1) it can proceed at the level of the constitutive narrative itself, providing stories that through the identificatory principle shift and rework the subject and its motives; (2) it can also proceed at the aesthetic level of what Williams terms the "structure of feeling" and Grossberg describes as the "affective apparatus."[47] Since, as Fisher observes, the truth of a narrative resides in its "fidelity," which is an aesthetic quality, new true narratives become possible as new modes of aesthetic experience emerge and gain social meaning. Ideological rhetorical practice is not restricted to explicitly political public address, but can include a range of aesthetic practices, including music, drama, architecture, and fashion, that elicit new modes of experience and being.

The significance of the rhetorical tradition is that it has long realized that discourse has eminently political and practical effects. In recognizing the contingency of the social, it offers the possibility of social critique and the development of *praxis*. However, in order to overcome the constraints of ideology, rhetorical theory must see through the 'givenness' of what appears to be the delimitable rhetorical situation, where the ontological status of speaker, speech, audience, topic, and occasion offer themselves as unproblematic. It must recognize that ultimately, the position one embodies as a subject is a rhetorical effect.

## ▉ Notes

[1]By ideology I mean a symbolic system, the discourse of which (1) is "false" in the sense that it is based on the presuppositions of some "terministic screen," (2) denies its historicity and linguisticality—pretending to but present a naturally or self-evidently meaningful world, (3) denies or transforms contradictions, and (4) legitimates and structures power relations. As such, my usage is much like the one suggested in, Anthony Giddens, *Central Problems in Social*

*Theory: Action, Structure and Contradiction in Social Analysis* (Berkeley: University of California Press, 1979), 165–197.

[2]For a discussion of discourse-based theories of the subject, see, Kaja Silverman, *The Subject of Semiotics* (New York: Oxford University Press, 1983), 43–53, 126–131.

[3]Kenneth Burke, *A Rhetoric of Motives* (1950; rpt. Berkeley: University of California Press, 1969), 50.

[4]Lawrence Grossberg, "Marxist Dialectics and Rhetorical Criticism," *Quarterly Journal of Speech* 65 (1979): 249.

[5]Kenneth Burke, *Language as Symbolic Action: Essays on Life, Literature, and Method* (Berkeley: University of California Press, 1966), 301.

[6]Mouvement Souveraineté-Association, founding political manifesto, 1968, in *Le manuel de la parole: Manifestes québécois*, ed. Daniel Latouche and Diane Poliquin-Bourassa (Sillery, Quebec: Editions du boréal express, 1977) vol. 3, 97.

[7]André Bernard and Bernard Descrôteaux, *Québec: élections 1981* (Ville LaSalle, Québec: Editions Hurtibise HMH, Limitée, 1981), 15, 23.

[8]Quebec (Prov.), Conseil exécutif, *La nouvelle entente Québec-Canada: Proposition du Gouvernement du Québec pour une entente d'égal à égal: La souveraineté-association.* Quebec: 1979. This document, a soft cover book sold in bookstores, consists of a foreword, six chapters which explain the Quebec government's reasons for seeking sovereignty, and a concluding direct address by Quebec's premier, René Levesque, calling for a OUI vote in the forthcoming referendum. The significance of the document arises from its clear articulation of Quebec's rhetoric of sovereignty as it had developed for over a decade in Quebec public address, and from its institutional status, offering the official rhetoric of the government's pro-sovereignty position.

[9]Quebec, *La nouvelle entente*, 62–64.

[10]As adopted by the Quebec *Assemblé nationale*, 20 March 1980, the following question appeared on the ballot:

"Le Gouvernement du Québec a fait connaitre sa proposition d'en arriver, avec le reste du Canada, à une nouvelle entente fondée sur le principe de l'égalité des peuples; cette entente permettrait au Québec d'acquérir le pouvoir exclusif de faire ses lois, de percevoir ses impôts et d'établir ses relations extérieurs, ce qui est la souveraineté—et, en même temps, de maintenir avec le Canada une association économique comportant l'utilisation de la même monnaie; aucun changement de statut politique résultant de ces négociations ne sera réalisé sans l'accord de la population lors d'un autre référendum; en conséquence, accordez-vous au Gouvernement du Québec le mandat de négocier l'entente proposée entre le Québec et le Canada?

OUI        NON

The Government of Québec has made public its proposal to negotiate a new agreement with the rest of Canada, based on the equality of nations; this agreement would enable Québec to acquire the exclusive power to make its laws, levy its taxes and establish relations abroad—in other words, sovereignty—and at the same time, to maintain with Canada an economic association including a common currency; no change in political status resulting from these negotiations will be effected without approval by the people through another referendum; on these terms, do you give the Government of Québec the mandate to negotiate the proposed agreement between Quebec and Canada?

YES        NO."

Quebec (Prov.), Directeur Général des élections, *Rapport des résultats officiels du scrutin, référendum du 20 mai 1980*, 9.

¹¹In the May 1980 referendum on "sovereignty-association," 85.6% of eligible voters cast valid ballots. Of these, 40.4% voted OUI. See, *Rapport des résultats,* 19. Among francophones, the vote was slightly higher and is estimated at 46%. See, Jean-Claude Picard, "Le gouvernement et le Parti Québécois analysent l'échec référendaire de mardi," *Le Devoir,* Thursday, 22 May 1980.

¹²Michael C. McGee, "In Search of 'The People': A Rhetorical Alternative," *Quarterly Journal of Speech* 61 (October 1975): 239.

¹³Claude Morin, *Quebec versus Ottawa: The Struggle for Self-Government, 1960–1972,* trans. Richard Howard (Toronto: University of Toronto Press, 1976), 5.

¹⁴Claude Morin's text was written as a reflection on his experience of federal-provincial relations as a high-ranking civil servant. He was also an early and active proponent of sovereignty and member of the *PQ* who became a cabinet minister in the *PQ* government.

¹⁵McGee, 246.

¹⁶William F. Shaw and Lionel Albert, *Partition* (Montreal: Thornhill Publishing, 1980), 143–144.

¹⁷Louis Althusser, *Lenin and Philosophy and other Essays,* trans. Ben Brewster (New York: Monthly Review Press, 1971), 170.

¹⁸Edwin Black, "The Second Persona," *Quarterly Journal of Speech* 56 (April 1970): 109–119.

¹⁹Michael D. McGuire, "Rhetoric, Philosophy and the *Volk:* Johann Gottlieb Fichte's *Addresses to the German Nation,*" *Quarterly Journal of Speech* 62 (April 1976): 135–136.

²⁰Burke, *Symbolic Action,* 5.

²¹Burke reveals a structuralist tendency in his discussions of the formal interplay between the elements of his "pentad," which are constitutive of motives. While Burke differs with the French structuralist tradition, particularly in holding on to the concept of "act," his denial of a foundational character for any of his pentadic terms and his sensitivity to unresolvable ambiguities do lead him, just like the French structuralists, to consider the agent's constitution in symbolic structures. See Frank Lentricchia, *Criticism and Social Change* (Chicago: University of Chicago Press, 1983), 66–83.

²²"Interpeller" is a rather commonly used French verb which designates the act of calling upon someone by name and demanding an answer. It is not surprising that Althusser, in the quote that follows, uses the example of a policeman's hailing, since a person who is *interpellé* is usually under some constraint to respond. Thus, the term is used to refer to the questioning of ministers by members of parliament and to the formal address of a judge or bailiff as part of a legal act. *Petit Larousse illustré,* 1979, s. v. "interpeller," "interpellation."

²³Althusser, 174.

²⁴McGee, 244.

²⁵Fredric Jameson, *The Political Unconscious: Narrative as a Socially Symbolic Act* (Ithaca: Cornell University Press, 1981), 35.

²⁶Roland Barthes, *Image, Music, Text,* trans. by Stephen Heath (New York: Hill & Wang, 1977), 124.

²⁷Burke, *Rhetoric of Motives,* 194.

²⁸Québec, *La nouvelle entente,* 3. The primary language of Quebec public discourse is French. As such, political life proceeds through a French "terministic screen." To be true to the political consciousness of that society, this essay is based on the analysis of the French primary texts. It is for this reason that I continue to use the terms "peuple" and "Québécois" throughout this essay. Note specifically that "peuple," the French term for "people" is a singular noun; in French, one would write "the people is." Note also that there is no adequate

translation of "Québécois." The closest equivalent, "Quebecker," lacks all of the French term's nationalist connotations. While analyzed in French, cited passages are presented in English translation for the reader's convenience. My translation is in large measure based on the simultaneously published official English version of the White Paper: *Québec-Canada a New Deal: The Québec Government Proposal for a New Partnership between Equals: Sovereignty-Association* (Quebec: 1979).

[29]Walter Fisher, "Narration as a Human Communication Paradigm: The Case of Public Moral Argument," *Communication Monographs* 51 (March 1984): 8.

[30]Burke, *Rhetoric of Motives*, 197.

[31]Quebec, *La nouvelle entente*, 3–4.

[32]Paul Ricoeur, *Hermeneutics and the Human Sciences*, ed. and trans. John B. Thompson (New York: Cambridge University Press, 1981), 278–279.

[33]Kenneth Burke, *Permanence and Change: An Anatomy of Purpose*, 2nd rev. ed. (Indianapolis: The Bobbs-Merrill Company, Inc., 1954), 255.

[34]Stuart Hall, "Signification, Representation, Ideology: Althusser and the Post-Structuralist Debates," *Critical Studies in Mass Communication* 2 (June 1985): 107–113.

[35]Fisher, 6.

[36]Burke, *Symbolic Action*, 6.

[37]McGee and Althusser adopt a similar strategy in order to assert the materiality of meaning. Althusser argues that, "Ideology . . . prescrib[es] material practices governed by a material ritual, which practices exist in the material actions of a subject in all consciousness according to his belief" (Althusser, 170). Similarly, McGee, after tracing out the relationship of myth to ideology, asserts: "Though [myths] technically represent 'false consciousness,' they nonetheless function as a means of providing social unity and collective unity. Indeed, 'the people' *are* the social and political myths they accept" (McGee, 247).

[38]Quebec, *La nouvelle entente*, 5.

[39]Quebec, *La nouvelle entente*, 6.

[40]Quebec, *La nouvelle entente*, 7–8.

[41]Quebec, *La nouvelle entente*, 11.

[42]Quebec, *La nouvelle entente*, 11–12.

[43]Quebec, *La nouvelle entente*, 44–45.

[44]Quebec, *La nouvelle entente*, 109–110.

[45]Quebec, *La nouvelle entente*, 118.

[46]Fisher, 8.

[47]Raymond Williams, *Marxism and Literature* (New York: Oxford University Press, 1977), 128–135; Lawrence Grossberg, "Is There Rock after Punk," *Critical Studies in Mass Communications* 3 (March 1986): 69–70.

# CHAPTER 10

# PSEUDO-PRIVATE AND THE PTL MINISTRY SCANDAL

William L. Nothstine

*This commentary, by William L. Nothstine, recounts the transformations of an essay on the role of the media in the PTL Ministry scandal: from a short piece submitted to a magazine of political opinion, to a professional conference paper, to a manuscript submitted and revised for a scholarly journal. In each form, considerations of audience led to revisions of content, style, and organization. In Nothstine's case, the impulse to express his critical conclusions in the language of his chosen readers was in a state of tension with his original interests in the project. Eventually he concluded that the project had too little resemblance to what had originally prompted him to write about the PTL scandal, and consequently he shelved the project.*

## COMMENTARY

Unlike the other critical essays in this anthology, "Public, Private, and Pseudo-Private" was not published elsewhere, although it almost was. It began in 1987 as a short magazine submission, was transformed into a convention paper, and finally became a manuscript for journal submission in 1989. Based on the cumulative effect of these incremental changes, I decided to withdraw the manuscript from journal review and file it away.

In many ways, my original interest in the PTL Ministry scandal was unremarkable. During the height of the scandal, roughly from March to May of 1987, the images of Jim and Tammy Bakker seemed everywhere in the popular media, and like many Americans I found the sideshow atmosphere fascinating. ABC's Ted Koppel compared the whole business to "a national soap opera," but I found it to be closer to an auto accident: Although I was a little ashamed of myself, I just couldn't resist staring. I began collecting magazine and newspaper articles, and taping the major TV appearances of the main figures in the scandal. My collection was more than haphazard, but hardly exhaustive. Beyond satisfying the voyeuristic curiosity I shared with many Americans about the scandal, I thought perhaps the materials might be useful as a case for study in the classroom. In part because my writing interests were in a different area, I had no plans to write and disseminate a critical essay concerning the Bakkers, the media, or any of the other themes eventually played out in the following essay. That came later.

By chance, at about this time a colleague invited me to contribute a paper to a convention panel she was organizing on the intriguing-sounding subject of "scandal management." None of the writing projects I had under-way seemed to fit the bill, but we discussed some possibilities, including the PTL scandal. Since it had received so much media attention, and since coincidentally I had already accumulated quite a bit of background material on the topic, we tentatively decided that I should investigate the PTL scandal, although neither of us had any particular idea yet of *what* I might have to say, as a critic, about the scandal. Convention planning deadlines being what they are, we knew I had six or seven months to research and write a paper if the panel proposal was accepted (as it eventually was). Like many of my colleagues who submit abstracts of papers for conventions when the papers are as yet unwritten, I counted on the muses of criticism to visit with inspiration in a timely manner.

I wouldn't say they visited, but they did leave me a "while you were out" note. The following week, browsing through old files, I rediscovered "Pseudo-Private Lives," a short piece by Charles Krauthammer in *The New Republic,* about the blurring of "public" and "private" in the media cover-age of political figures. I had saved the article for no clear reason other than that I found it interesting and well written. I think that's important: In saving the Krauthammer article, and in collecting the materials on the PTL scandal, my choices were responses to a series of coincidences, driven by my own intellectual curiosity more than by any explicit axe to grind, whether theoretical, religious, or ideological. And had it not been for the unexpected phone call from my colleague, whatever interest I had in these issues and incidents would almost certainly never have played itself out in writing.

Rereading Krauthammer's essay, I found his observations suggested interesting conclusions about the case of the Bakkers. Since *The New Republic*'s editorial policy at that time had not yet fully turned the corner from laggard-progressive to neo-conservative, this struck me as a convenient and topical opportunity for me to write for a different (and larger) audience than the journals and conventions of my field provided. I set to work and soon turned out a 1,000-word manuscript, which I sent to *The New Republic.* Its rejection was quick and perfunctory, and (except for a handful of public presentations based on it and the few obituary remarks herein) that manu-script was consigned to oblivion and need concern no one ever again.

That original 1,000-word piece asserted that Jim and Tammy Bakker's most typical *public* appearances in the media featured the characteristic actions and implied standards of judgment associated with *private* display—hence they were, using Krauthammer's term, pseudo-private displays. The essay listed several examples of the Bakkers' behavior demonstrating this point, and concluded by observing that this shift went a long way toward explaining why the media coverage of the two focused on how tacky or tasteless they were, rather than how dishonest or impious they were. The essay was thus a simple form of criticism by analogy: The insights Krauthammer had reached regarding several political figures recently in the news could be usefully extended to the case of the Bakkers as well. The case of the Bakkers also allowed the conceptual point to be stretched from the political arena to the religious, since the Bakkers were evangelists, but the main purpose was to demonstrate a noteworthy feature of the Bakkers' media coverage, nothing more.

However, it gradually became much more. The convention paper that followed a few months later was over twice the size of the original piece. The convention version had by no means become the essay that follows in this volume, since convention papers are normally not accountable to the same professional and rhetorical demands that journal articles are. This was most noticeable in the style and tone of the language, which still showed my enjoyment of irony and word play. In fact, one sentence I wrote for the convention paper delighted me so much that I called a colleague up, long-distance, and dictated it into her answering machine for her amusement. (By contrast, I can't imagine reading a single sentence written for the version in this book into anyone's answering machine, even if it was a local call.)

Nevertheless, the differences between the convention version and the original version are striking. The *New Republic* version was organized inductively, building to its thesis in what I fancied to be a crescendo; the convention paper was organized deductively, with the thesis first and the proof deployed afterward. Elliptical arguments, some of them little more than familiar allusions, were replaced for the convention by more complete syllogisms. The most important difference, however, was in the substance and justification of its main argument. What began as an assertion about the seemingly bullet-proof media personae of the Bakkers gradually but undeniably became a study of the changes worked by the modern media upon our culturally shared sense of the true and the good. The Bakkers' case, once in the spotlight by itself, now shared the stage with this evolving theoretical argument. As the form and content were recast from social criticism to scholarly criticism, the paper's voice changed, too: Where once it spoke in a simple and vigorous public idiom, intended for the audience of *The New Republic*, it now spoke in an intricate and brittle professional dialect intended for a scholarly audience. A bristling layer of citations formed over the top, protecting the delicate inner argument and deflecting blows outward onto such targets as Aristotle and Hannah Arendt, both of whom made their first appearance in this version of the manuscript.

After the convention, I sent a slightly revised version to a journal in my field for editorial consideration. It went through two rounds of revisions and began a third, a process dragging on for eighteen months. The reviewers were always encouraging, but their strong suggestions for revisions moved the essay in directions I found less and less interesting, and in some cases philosophically offensive. One change, not specified by my reviewers but driven by the same process, was the gradual transformation of the tone from cynical to moral. The last few paragraphs of the version included in this book would have been incongruous in the original *New Republic* piece, but they were consistent with the tone of the final version. And as I revised, I gained appreciation for the complementary rhetorical functions that Jim and Tammy Bakker served in their public appearances, and—yes—even a kind of grudging respect, or at least sympathy, for Tammy Bakker.

But the most noticeable change was that the case of the PTL Ministry scandal no longer shared center-stage with the theoretical argument about public media; the Bakkers were being escorted quickly but firmly off to the side. In part this is because scholarly journals in my field prefer academic criticism to ephemeral social criticism. The fact that a year and a half had passed since I first submitted the manuscript to the journal became a disadvantage, because during that time the Bakkers had mostly faded from the public eye. As the editor wrote to me in October 1989, "Partly, I believe, because of the most recent news about the theatrics of Jim Bakker's trial, I am not convinced that these people really *matter* very much." Rather, the editor suggested, the Bakkers were "a soon-to-be-forgotten minor blip on the radar trace of the late 1980s." Theoretical issues are less fleeting than public notoriety (and, one suspects, more in keeping with the dignity of a scholarly journal). The choice was clear: If I wanted to pursue the publication of the paper, Jim and Tammy could be no more than a convenient example of a theoretical point.

Following this shift, the strictures of formalized method—rather than whether I had said anything useful to know about the PTL Ministry scandal—became central in justifying my critical conclusions. Little by little, the responsibility for my critical claims was taken out of my hands and turned over to "method" and "system." The editor wrote to me, "One part of the argument for significance, given that you have chosen a scholarly arena in which to make it, has to be a more careful statement about your research methods." The easiest way to make such a statement, of course, is if one has followed the dictates of a critical method—recognized, identified, elaborated, and formalized. But this I had not done. Instead, my claims were based to an embarrassing extent on my own observation, intuition, and judgment. I had attempted to clarify the premises and principles of my reasoning, and I worked to clarify them further, but recasting that explanation as a section entitled "Research Methods" would have been absurd and not entirely honest.

Another comment by the editors illustrates the problem from another direction: "Neither the reviewers nor I expect social-scientific defense of your 'sample size,' but we are looking for a little more evidence that you went about your 'data-gathering' (i.e., your selection of communication events on which to focus) *systematically.*" A process that had not been "methodical" or "systematic," *as the editor meant those terms here,* had now to be described after the fact as if it fit that mold. (And, of course, since the manuscript had by now swollen to 10,000 words, this *post hoc* discussion of "methodology" should not increase the length of the manuscript. . . .)

At about this time I found myself taking on unwelcome and time-consuming administrative duties, and I put the PTL scandal on the back burner with few regrets. Perhaps one more round of revisions would have gotten it into a journal, perhaps not—hardly an inconsequential consideration for an untenured professor—but it now bore little resemblance to the piece I had originally been interested in writing. I believe both the original essay and the final version made defensible arguments, albeit very different ones. But the manuscript was moving farther and farther from my own research and writing interests in the philosophy of criticism. This meant additionally that the PTL essay, if published, would not appreciably advance my "research program." There were few benefits to be derived from continuing to revise a manuscript I felt so little connection with, and I gladly diverted my energy toward more interesting and rewarding projects. The version in this anthology is the last full revision before I withdrew the essay from editorial consideration.

# Public, Private, and Pseudo-Private: Ethics and Images in the Collapse of the PTL Ministry

William L. Nothstine

At the zenith of its power in the mid-1980s, the PTL ("Praise The Lord") Ministry represented the focus of an enormous media empire.[1] The Ministry's founders, Pentecostal evangelists Jim and Tammy Bakker, recognized earlier than most the incredible power the electronic media offered to evangelists. Perhaps it is fitting, then, that the slow collapse of the PTL Ministry—beginning in the spring of 1987 and featuring widely flung accusations of deceit, adultery, homosexuality, blackmail, embezzlement, fraud, and hostile corporate takeovers—was played out in all of its garish detail before the cameras and microphones of the media. So natural was the fit between the Bakkers and the media that, a year later, when a similar sex scandal engulfed rival televangelist Jimmy Swaggart in the spring of 1988, it was inevitable that the media would seek some reaction from the already beleaguered Bakkers, after the round-robin of denunciation and accusation between the two sides during the PTL scandal. Even amid the flurry of indictments handed down in the spring of 1989, leveling criminal charges of mail and wire fraud against Jim Bakker in connection with Ministry activities, the Bakkers themselves—stripped of their network, their ministry, and their expensive lifestyle—still seemed to have ready, if not always friendly, access to the media.[2]

The Bakkers' durability stems from their status as forerunners of what political commentator Charles Krauthammer has called pseudo-private display.[3] ABC interviewer Ted Koppel pronounced the daily stream of revelations and charges around the Bakkers "a national soap opera."[4] Yet the intrusive presence of the media can actually work to the advantage of those who suffer it. Many celebrities before the Bakkers have capitalized on the diminishing privacy they enjoy by manufacturing pseudo-private lives—thoroughly public media images packaged and presented as glimpses into private lives. But, though they did not invent it themselves, the Bakkers took this effect to lengths without recent equal.

Krauthammer's suggestive observations are worth clarifying and extending in their own right. The same is true of understanding the ignominious collapse of the once-powerful PTL Ministry. But the full implications of the phenomenon of pseudo-privacy go markedly beyond Krauthammer's initial sketch, and reach past the downfall of one television ministry. A fuller elaboration will show the importance of this phenomenon in understanding the evolution of public communication within the rhetorical tradition. This elaboration will require clarifying the transformation worked by the electronic media upon the traditional categories of public and private discourse. This transformation makes possible the emergence (and dominance) of a third mode of display and experience, the pseudo-private. A discussion of the characteristics of pseudo-private display will show how this transformation may be exploited to alter our perceptions of both the candor and the morality of the persons and events we come to know this way. This last is of importance beyond the fate of the Bakkers. The dislocation of public and private has implications for our perceptions of all celebrities and political or religious figures. The PTL scandal, in this sense, is merely a theoretically egregious instance of a larger issue that I intend to explore: the consequences of the media-induced transformation of "public" and "private" from descriptions of *physical* places to descriptions of *metaphorical* places.

## PUBLIC, PRIVATE, AND PSEUDO-PRIVATE

Pseudo-privacy represents a third kind of communicative experience, separate from the public and the private. Though we do not widely recognize or appreciate its significance and character, it is pervasive in our media society, the inevitable consequence perhaps of the fifteen minutes of celebrity Andy Warhol assured us we would each someday be guaranteed. Pseudo-private display has recognizable features, and can alter, subtly or radically, our perceptions and judgments of those whom we experience in this way.

In our culture we respect as a matter of custom the difference between public and private. Political philosopher Hannah Arendt notes that this distinction "corresponds to the household and the political realms, which have existed as distinct, separate entities at least since the rise of the ancient city-state."[5] Moreover, Arendt reminds us that from the Greek tradition we have come to regard public and private not as realms that differ merely in degree, but as different orders of experience, and as practical contraries. "The 'good life,' " observes Arendt in her discussion of Aristotle's commentary on civic life, ". . . was not merely better, more carefree or nobler than ordinary life, but of an altogether different quality."[6] The dimensions of this qualitative difference include the communicator's role, the audience's expectations, and the standards of rationality and morality thought applicable to the communicator's role.

Yet the precise nature of the correspondence that Arendt notes—between public and political, and between private and household—has been transformed in a most fundamental way since Aristotle drew upon his observations of ancient Athens. In Aristotle's world, the correspondence was metonymic: physical location determined one's communicative persona or role. There were physical sites (the legislature, the courtroom, the public gathering) where one went to enact one's public role, and one could not sensibly be called a *public* figure anywhere else. When one retreated to the household, one gave up one's public persona and became a private figure— "private" because deprived of the physical and communicative arena for being most-fully human, to the classical way of thinking.[7] Joshua Meyrowitz argues that this difference resulted directly from the limits that physical space placed upon the flow of information. That is, one had to position oneself in certain places to see and hear certain things.[8]

At approximately the same time as Arendt's reflections on the public tradition, sociologist Erving Goffman first demonstrated the extent to which our role behaviors change as a result of the various ways in which space may be bounded by barriers to perception.[9] As examples, Goffman's analysis suggests the following: Theatrical performers who drop their role when backstage; medical personnel who adopt their professional demeanor upon entering the examination room with the patient and abandon that role as soon as the patient is gone; garage mechanics whose deference to the customer ends when they leave the front office and return to the working area; or political candidates whose on-stage or on-camera behavior is carefully modulated and "presidential," yet who maintain informal rapport with staff members and reporters aboard the campaign jet between stops.[10] Goffman links role performance directly to the influence of physical space upon perception, as when he notes, "Very commonly the back region of a performance is located at one end of the place where the performance is presented, being cut off from it by a partition and guarded passageway."[11] In all of these cases, perceptual barriers—even something as seemingly transparent as a partly drawn curtain or a half-closed door—mark the location for a change from public to private role.

Goffman discusses not "public" and "private," but rather "front region" (that is, "the place where a performance is given")[12] and "back region" (that is, "a place, relative to a given performance, where the impression fostered by the performance is knowingly contradicted as a matter of course").[13] However, the parallels between the elements of Goffman's analysis and our traditional understanding of "public" and "private" are clear. In this regard it is most significant that Goffman relates front region and back region as practical contraries—not merely *different* orders of performance, as Arendt describes them, but *opposite and antithetical* ones. The image created through social performance in one region is "knowingly contradicted" in the other. This nuance of Goffman's analysis is essential to our traditional, largely unexamined view of "public" and "private."

However, in contemporary Western life—and perhaps nowhere more so than in the United States—electronic (and, in a different way, print) media have transformed the relationship between physical location and communicative persona. Because our physical location no longer has the same power to limit our access to information, the physical location of the person no longer predicts the persona or role that individual will assume. As a consequence, "public" and "private" have lost their metonymic connection to physical location, and have instead become spatial metaphors. We continue to speak of them as "realms," as if they were concrete places, but they have become "modes," ways of performing and experiencing essentially independent of physical location.

As metaphor, "public" and "private" carry with them systems of associated commonplaces.[14] With "public," we typically associate elements from one or both of two clusters of commonplaces. The first cluster stresses the artistic dimension of things public, such as *strategic, formal, contrived, inauthentic, or onstage.* The second cluster features the moral dimension of public life, including such associations as *noble, exemplary, representative, or popular.* With "private" we typically associate the opposites of these commonplaces, such as *spontaneous* rather than strategic, *informal* rather than formal, *natural* rather than contrived, or *backstage* rather than onstage. Similarly, the moral ideals implied by our typical sense of "private" are *graciousness* rather than nobility, *charm* rather than greatness, being *typical* rather than being exemplary. However, because these terms are no longer anchored in physically distinguishable settings, interaction among these systems of commonplaces is changing the meaning of our communicative practice even as we maintain our earlier habits of thinking and speaking about "public" and "private." We thereby live up to Marshall McLuhan's characterization of the limits on modern self-understanding in an electronic society: We live mythically and integrally, but continue to think in language that has not kept pace with change.[15]

As a consequence of this dislocation, although we continue to pay lip service to the public/private distinction, this observance is frequently blurred almost beyond recognition in contemporary practice. Many Americans feel, for example, that former presidential candidate Gary Hart's private indiscretions are of a different realm, a different order of action and experience, than are his public campaign tactics. Yet when Americans are pressed to account for the collapse of Hart's 1988 presidential campaign in the wake of the Donna Rice scandal, the typical answers almost immediately begin to confuse the two categories. For example, one sometimes hears the waning of Hart's popular support explained by reference to the maxim that a man who lies to his wife would probably also lie to the American voter—an explanation that succeeds by failing to distinguish between public and private standards of conduct. Only slightly more discriminating are those explanations beginning from the premise that a man who would actually encourage reporters to catch him in a scandalous indiscretion, as did Senator Hart, is probably unfit for the demands of high office. Our consensus that the public and the private are realms of different stature, values, and truths has become a fuzzy consensus at best.

This dislocation of public and private has also undermined a second, related, consensus that we share: the consensus that what is public can no longer be private, and vice versa. In Aristotle's Athens, this assertion would have been the nearly literal equivalent of "what takes place outdoors can no longer be indoors." However, the truth of that innocuous claim becomes a good deal less self-evident today when, by turning on my television, I can be both "in my living room" and "at a Cubs game" at the same time. Meyrowitz's argument applies once again: Physical location no longer determines the information we have access to, the experiences we can have, or the communicative roles we can play. Yet, significantly, the commonplaces embedded in our everyday language-use preserve the worldview of an age when this distinction still applied. While we talk of public and private as the practical opposites of one another, a more accurate and useful description would be that "public" and "private" are metaphors whose *associated commonplaces* are clustered in consistently antithetical patterns: strategic/spontaneous, noble/gracious, formal/informal, contrived/natural, inauthentic/authentic, intimate/distant, "onstage"/"backstage."

Out of this dislocation, based on the confusion of physical space with communicative role, emerges the hybrid realm of the pseudo-private, within which the opposite of "public" is no longer "private," but rather "genuine," "spontaneous," or "authentic," the commonplaces *associated with* private. At the heart of this third communicative realm is suspicion of technique. Krauthammer writes,

> Political imagery derives mainly from public actions. But public actions are suspect, precisely because they are undertaken in the knowledge that they will be observed. A glimpse of private life can shape a public image far more powerfully [than can a public statement], not just because the private revelation is more titillating, but because it has what public action can never have: the air of unself-consciousness, and thus the stamp of sincerity.[16]

From this practical paradox has emerged a potent weapon in the armory of the public figure: pseudo-private display, presenting the *appearance* of private action through the public media. This widespread phenomenon has recognizable features, features that bring home with ironic vengeance Arendt's characterization of public life as "better or nobler than ordinary life."

Pseudo-private disclosure is, of course, thoroughly public in at least one sense. It does not include the "high government official who has been saying one thing for weeks," notes Krauthammer, nor even the fact that the official "is reported to believe 'privately' the opposite." Rather, this disclosure enters the realm of the pseudo-private only when "this private confession . . . appears on the front page of *The New York Times.*"[17]

Pseudo-private disclosure is identified by framing cues, traces at some level asking us to overlook how the message has been shaped and timed and processed for popular consumption, and to focus instead on what appears to be spontaneous and uncontrived—hence, seemingly private. As the familiarity of Krauthammer's example shows, the delivery of these cues often need not be overburdened with subtlety; simply labeling a disclosure "private" is often enough to achieve the effect, even when this labeling is done in glaringly public circumstances. Overall, however, the effect of framing cues tends to be incremental and additive: One framing cue does not necessarily make a display pseudo-private, and one pseudo-private display does not necessarily transform a media image. Further, these framing cues may be nondiscursive as well as linguistic and discursive: scenic elements, dress, audio and video editing, all can become tokens of spontaneity, candor, or intimacy.

These framing cues, verbal or nonverbal, are the means by which the dislocation of public and private is accomplished. Just as any metaphor may be evoked by the systematic appearance of its associated commonplaces, aspects of the roles and rules appropriate to private settings can be evoked in public communication by framing cues—traces of either physical settings or role behaviors normally associated with the private sphere. If traces suggestive of a particular *physical location* or a particular *role or figure* traditionally considered as belonging to the public realm are shown packaged together with the verbal or nonverbal tokens of the private realm—whether language, behaviors, settings, or objects—our tendency is to experience them through the lens of the commonplaces of privacy. Therefore, one may identify framing cues by examining mass-mediated messages for traces of, or references to, physical situations or communicative roles strongly associated with the private sphere.

Pseudo-private display titillates its audience with the possibility of a revealing peek behind a mask, around a facade, over a transom, or beneath a skirt. And as with all such peekaboo games, what we see in pseudo-private disclosure usually matters less than our conviction that we were not meant to see it. Pseudo-private display has unique rhetorical power to the extent to which it is made to appear artless and uncontrived. The posture of the pseudo-private disclosure is antirhetorical; it implicitly claims kinship with the documentary genre, purporting to show a reality that is unaffected by strategic political considerations or technical manipulation. It seeks to be regarded as inartistic proof, as evidence that does not require artifice to be persuasive, whose truth is self-evident and whose ethical character is unproblematic. And yet pseudo-private display is thoroughly rhetorical—it is persuasion seeking to be effective by donning the guise of nonpersuasion.[18]

As such, its power represents the McLuhanesque extension of our well-established trust in the nonverbal over the verbal, especially when the two are perceived as incongruent.[19] Just as we tend to rely on nonverbal indicators of sincerity, on the conventional wisdom that they are harder to manufacture than the verbal, so we rely on pseudo-private portraits of motives or values because they are presented together with traces suggesting that they are intimate or revealing.

This is the first of two ways in which pseudo-private display can influence our judgments: by appearing more genuine or candid than "purely" public display, seeming to have "the stamp of sincerity." The case of Jim and Tammy Bakker demonstrates this function.[20] In the following two sections, framing cues typically associated with the Bakkers' discourse will be discussed, followed by an analysis of these cues' influence on the Bakkers' apparent sincerity.

## ■ RECOGNIZING FRAMING CUES: THE BAKKERS "AT HOME"

Under the temporarily ignored supervision of the media, we were allowed many glimpses at the Bakker lifestyle, before and during the PTL scandal. A PBS *Frontline* documentary on the Bakkers, broadcast in January 1988, featured an excerpt from an informal video tour of their Palm Springs home, given to the PTL faithful by the Bakkers before the scandal broke in the spring of 1987:

*Jim:* (seated on a couch in the living room) We're kind of taking you into our secret hideaway.

*Tammy:* (clutching a stuffed animal, walking into the bedroom) Not very many people get a chance to show you their bedroom, but you never know what you're going to see in PTL.

*Jim:* (on couch) Tammy's out in the kitchen now.

*Tammy:* (off-camera) Lunch is almost ready, Jim![21]

There have been many such moments, all having little homey touches that project the illusion of nontechnique. The same documentary included another clip originally shown to PTL viewers, in which Jim Bakker proudly, one might almost say gleefully, showed off his vintage Rolls Royce, one of a collection, taking the reporter and camera operator for an evidently impromptu ride through the desert near the same Palm Springs redoubt.[22] The framing cues apparent in these instances include tokens seeming to suggest spontaneity, if not sheer amateurism: The camera following Jim into his Rolls is hand-held and wobbly; for the home-tour scenes a single camera is used, panning stiffly between the two; the sound is miked poorly and often hollow and tinny. The overall effect certainly denies the supporting presence of a sophisticated worldwide, satellite-based telecommunication network. By seeming to deny the contrived and "onstage" character of the events, the framing cues contribute to the seeming rejection of public display. The wobbly camera, perched on the camera operator's shoulder, is also reminiscent of the subjective point-of-view any of us would experience, were we actually there with Bakker—thus not only denying the presence of a *sophisticated* public medium, but of *any* public medium whatsoever.

Other traces indicative of pseudo-privacy may be found in these scenes, as well. Our commonplace sense of "public" figures is that we would not normally be given a tour of their bedroom or a joyride in their favorite car; we too strongly associate distance and formality with such figures and their roles to expect such behaviors. Therefore, the seeming inclusion of the audience in informal, even intimate, activities such as these further reframes the televised presence of these persons from public to pseudo-private, by providing traces of both private locations and behaviors appropriate to private roles. These examples all serve to help identify framing cues; their cumulative effect on our perceptions of the Bakkers will be considered below.

The Palm Springs home was the setting for a variation on this theme after scandal drove the Bakkers from their residence at Tega Cay. The Bakkers invited the media into their home again, letting themselves be seen *au naturel* to demonstrate that the scandalous publicity was not disrupting their household. Tammy chatted and giggled, and Jim wielded a hammer in some light repair work around the house, while the cameras whirred and clicked. The reader has only to imagine the national networks descending on his or her own home, with vans, lights, cables, microphones, and the rest, to imagine how intimate and spontaneous such a moment could possibly have been.

Production techniques alone are not the only means by which framing cues may be delivered; another tactic for pseudo-private display focuses our attention more directly on the communicative personae of the persons involved. A feature of the examples noted above, one that could easily be multiplied by examining televised images of the Bakkers before, during, and after the PTL scandal, is a certain naiveté, and (despite the polish of some aspects of technical presentation), aesthetic amateurism.

## ▨ PSEUDO-PRIVACY AS SIGN OF CANDOR: BELIEVING THE BAKKERS

Nowhere is this aesthetic amateurism better seen in the present case than in Tammy Bakker's media persona, a persona that has let the Bakkers push pseudo-private display toward limits that were, before now, only theoretical.

Certainly Tammy Faye Bakker is an inviting target for the cynic. But this misses the source of much of her appeal: Tammy's on-air demeanor is tailor-made for pseudo-private display. On *Nightline*, in May 1988, while Jim Bakker's responses to interviewer Ted Koppel usually advanced a case, Tammy veered away from the abstract and complex, toward the simple and concrete. For example, compare the responses by Jim and Tammy, when Koppel asked about their plans for the future:

*Jim:* . . . Ted, you know, I hope that people will let us move on into God and not spend the rest of our life in, as you said, a soap opera that the whole world has looked on. I feel so sad that I've been a part of something to bring this much, you know, pain and sorrow to the body of Christ.

*Tammy:* Well, you know, Jim, well, the thing I can't believe is that we are the— probably the most normal people there ever was [sic], and I just look—I wake every morning, and I say, "I can't believe this has happened. I'm the oldest of eight kids. We had an outdoor bathroom all the time I was growing up. I mean, me, just the normal of normal that this happened to. Or that anybody would be that interested in us. It's just hard to believe."[23]

Granted, a determined reader could impose quasi-syllogistic order on Tammy's answer, but her utterance clearly seems to lack the argumentative directness of Jim's reply—especially when we remember that Koppel's question was about their future plans. Tammy Bakker's habits of explanation borrow from cinema verite, if not the home movie: They favor detail and uninterpreted image, presented one after the other, rather than abstraction; they prefer verbal montage rather than argument.[24] Here it was not within production values that the framing cues were embedded, even Tammy's references to what Goffman would certainly call "back region" elements are not decisive in reframing the event; rather the framing is accomplished by the role Tammy plays, or the persona she assumes.

Tammy's persona is one far more readily associated with the private sphere than with the public, and therefore functions as a framing cue just as surely as manipulation of recording technique in previous examples. Although her public reputation is, in part, derived from her fame as the author of books on how to keep sexual excitement alive in marriage, and as what *Newsweek* has called "the flashy-trashy *femme fatale* in a leopard-skin pantsuit and four-inch stiletto heels," Tammy Faye Bakker's pseudo-private image is naive and childlike.[25] Like a child, Tammy under fire on camera is apparently without guile, especially compared to Jim's more straightfor- wardly rhetorical posture. On *Nightline,* while Jim rebutted charges and built a case in support of their actions, Tammy often interrupted, contrib- uted *non sequiturs,* or added chatty ornament to remarks by others. She frequently broke into nervous giggles at inappropriate moments, suggesting a desperate eagerness to please. Her remark above captures the absence of guile: The persona we see in such moments of contrived candor probably *cannot* believe that the public would be so interested in anyone as normal as she. Whether Tammy actually sees herself that way is beside the point; what seems clear is that her pseudo-private persona *does.*

And that is the key: Tammy's on-air naiveté, like that of any child, promises us that her displays in the public media are nevertheless candid and authentic—hence, it frames her presence as not "really" public at all. A revealing example comes from the Koppel interview, in response to Kop- pel's first question: Why had the Bakkers ended their seclusion from the media? Jim Bakker's two-minute reply began with a reading of verses 12–16 of Psalms 38, then concluded with a list of reasons, both for their seclusion and their decision to end it:

> We wanted to protect our children. We wanted to really just cling to each other and see God. But it won't stop, and we're getting, really, thousands of letters. And people say, "We want to hear from you, Jim and Tammy. We want to know what went on. We want to know where you are or how you feel." And we chose to come out today, and we actually chose your program. We even had—I guess we had invitations just to about every program to come on, but I felt that you're not only tough, but I felt you would be fair and give us a chance to share with people all over the country.[26]

Koppel's irritation with Bakker's answer was obvious. As soon as Bakker finished answering, Koppel quickly attempted to corner the two, mistakenly expecting Tammy Bakker to be an easier target than her husband. Koppel retorted, "All right, well, I hope I live up to both of your expectations. Let's start with the tough. You may consider this to be a tough question, Mrs. Bakker: Is it going to be possible to get through an interview with both of you without you wrapping yourselves in the Bible? . . ."[27]

Tammy Bakker's answer picked up Koppel's mixed metaphor and ran with it, in a triumph of stream-of-consciousness over the syllogism. "Well the Bible is a protection. It's a very real protection. It's a comfort. That's, I think, the biggest reason we wrap ourselves in the Bible—it's so comforting. Jesus said, 'When I go away I'll send a comforter to you,' and he has, that's been our comfort during this."[28]

Koppel's remark to Tammy was two-leveled. At a semantic level, it could be paraphrased roughly as a *question:* "How likely are you to bring up the Bible throughout the rest of this interview?" Yet even without the advantage of hearing and watching Koppel deliver this line, it is evident here from the transcript alone—for example, his mock-polite remark, "You may consider this to be a tough question, Mrs. Bakker"—that Koppel was being sarcastic. His intended meaning was much closer to an *injunction:* "Answer my questions directly and without quoting the Bible during this interview." Conversational context, conventional idiom, and nonverbal cues all pointed very strongly to this second interpretation; it seems fair even to say that only someone with a childlike lack of conversational skills would have missed the second interpretation. By answering as she did, Tammy left Koppel with two choices: Either he could assume that she recognized his sarcastic intent and chose to respond by begging the question (that is, by invoking scripture yet again); or he could assume that she failed to recognize his sarcasm for what it was and had tried to answer the literal meaning of the question as best she could. Although he was demonstrably suspicious to the point of hostility when Jim Bakker had invoked scripture not a minute before, Koppel now chose to ignore the same from Tammy and quickly shift tactics, drifting on to the feud between the Bakkers and the Reverend Jerry Falwell. Koppel's rout demonstrates that what appears *strategic* coming from Jim Bakker—invoking scripture as a response to a hard question from an interviewer—is shrugged off as *naive* coming from Tammy Bakker.

The general principle underlying the discussion of pseudo-privacy so far may be formulated as follows: The presence of framing cues, transforming our experience of individuals' public or private actions into the pseudo-private, tends to make those individuals' claims and actions more plausible, their motives less suspect; if their utterances are not strictly *believed*, at least they are not as likely to be challenged.

But Koppel's rhetorical predicament was not simply that Tammy Bakker's presence on *Nightline* was reframed as pseudo-private display; he was doubly hamstrung by the fact that his own presence there was *not* pseudo-private, but rather more traditionally public. Koppel was clearly bound by the rules of public decorum (bear in mind the explicit spatial connotations of this word), and was thereby unable to respond to Tammy's answer in the manner he (or anyone) might do privately. *Informally,* or *backstage,* or *off-the-record,* Koppel might have challenged Tammy Bakker's pseudo-private performance: Are you serious? Do you expect me to believe this from you? But such informal, private rejoinders would only be available in public to Koppel if he had the availability of framing cues to discount *his own* publicness. He did not; and, as an interviewer whose role was a public (not pseudo-private and definitely not private) one, he could only respond within the communicative limits of his own role. Therefore he had little practical choice except to pass over Tammy's obtuse answers, regardless of his private opinion as to her motives.[29]

An equally glaring example of this principle was provided a month later, on 18 June 1987. The preceding days had seen media coverage awash in claims of betrayal made by Jim and Tammy Bakker, claims that rival televangelist Jerry Falwell had broken his promise to act only as "caretaker" of the troubled PTL Ministry in March of that year. When Falwell assumed full control over the ministry and its holdings (including the right to evict the Bakkers from their Tega Cay parsonage), it was a tearful Tammy who defended her family in a meeting with the press on the parsonage grounds. Jim Bakker was not present, except by implication. The following lament by Tammy was replayed frequently by the networks that afternoon and evening. "I would like to say I hope that Jerry Falwell and his family never have to suffer the way that they've made our family suffer. I wake up every morning wishing that they had killed me. And Jim does, too."[30] Such melodramatic stuff might be greeted with derision if it were to come from a public figure in a public setting. But such a remark from Tammy, a woman who has spent years as a television figure and yet apparently never mastered the codes of decorous behavior one expects of television personalities, appears plausible; at the very least, it is passed along by the media without comment.

Thus, examining the Bakkers' media images during 1987 and 1988 suggests that our experience of any figure can be removed from the public to the pseudo-private by reframing the presence of the media to discount its publicness. When this happens, a measure of rhetorical invulnerability is bestowed upon that figure's discourse: Not that the figure becomes more credible, but rather that serious challenge to his or her claims becomes much more difficult and unlikely. One obvious but effective way of accomplishing this transformation is by manipulating production values to downplay technical sophistication. More cunning tactics involve bringing the media into the home for a share in ostensibly private conversations, as one would with any friend. These techniques are most familiar to us, perhaps, as staples of political campaign spots; the Bakker's peculiar genius has less been in the technical staging of their pseudo-private display than in their ability to keep a seemingly naive and garrulous Tammy in the spotlight.

It is important to qualify my argument at this point. I do not contend that all of the examples of framing cues I have used here to illustrate my thesis are the result of deliberate calculation, although doubtless many of them are. To claim that Tammy Faye Bakker is *deliberately* as ingenuous as she appears to be would be as nonsensical as claiming that Ronald Reagan was *deliberately* more photogenic than Walter Mondale during the 1984 presidential campaign. Not all of the framing cues to which we were exposed in our experience of the Bakkers were contrived, nor is it decisive for my argument to prove that they are. My argument so far rests only on the function of these cues, when present, and on the tendency of all of us to view persons and events through these framing cues whenever we are exposed to them.

## PSEUDO-PRIVACY AND MORAL STANDARDS: JUDGING THE BAKKERS

Pseudo-private display influences our judgments of the figures involved, in ways both obvious and subtle. The first of these functions, as Krauthammer has indicated, is that information presented in this way is granted a claim to plausibility and sincerity that is not available to explicitly public messages. Yet pseudo-privacy is more than a collection of techniques for manipulating perceived truth-value, or defending against attack upon utterances whose truth-value is dubious. It is also a mode of action and experience, within which we may come to "know" such figures as the Bakkers. The function of this mode of action and experience is the suspension of customary (that is, public) grounds for moral and ethical judgment of the persons we witness this way.

Koppel's irritation with the Bakkers was clear from the tone of his question, above; equally clear from his tone there and throughout the interview was that he rejected the Bakkers' piety as hypocritical, if not downright dishonest. But Koppel's censure misses the point. In the pseudo-private, the categories of judgment that count are not simply honesty and piety, as we might consider appropriate for public figures, but also (and, sometimes, little other than) grace and taste. Pseudo-private display has the tactical advantage of inviting judgment primarily on aesthetic standards, rather than exclusively on moral or ethical ones. While the public realm is the realm where, as Hannah Arendt wrote, individual greatness and nobility matter most, greatness is an unsuitable standard for the private realm, and—by extension—for the pseudo-private.[31] In the pseudo-private sphere, where these two worlds collide, we frequently judge not how great or noble a person is (as would be appropriate to public display), but rather how charming or enchanting (as would be appropriate in one's private home). True, many of the Bakkers' less-friendly observers might maintain that they failed dismally the tests of grace and taste, but what of it? The point is that time thus spent decrying the Bakkers as tasteless is time during which the issues of honesty and piety (in which the critics' judgment of the Bakkers might be far more damning) are not even being raised. Many a scandal-ridden celebrity, politician, or religious leader would count that trade as a bargain.

Here the Bakkers—especially Tammy—are in their element.[32] Because their television career has, for years, played down the difference between onstage and backstage, the transition from one category of judgment to the other is far simpler for the Bakkers than it would be for, say, Jimmy Swaggart, whose backstage (private) life is more sharply separated from his onstage (public) performance.[33]

In this regard, Jim and Tammy Bakker enjoy a peculiar rhetorical advantage in that they represent a conjunction of different styles of display: Of the two, Jim is the more comfortable with and adept at the discourse and manners of traditionally public display, while Tammy is obviously more naturally at home in pseudo-private display. Thus, Jim Bakker's argumentative exchanges with Koppel, for example, were always conducted from comparative rhetorical safety, because of Tammy's presence alongside him. In the extended exchange below, notice how Koppel must repeatedly attempt to extricate himself from discussion of "shopping" with Tammy to force Jim back into a discussion of PTL Ministry finances. The excerpt begins with Jim Bakker's reply to charges made earlier that day by Jerry Falwell, and repeated by Koppel, that the Bakkers had asked for six-figure lifetime salaries (and more) from the financially racked Ministry:

*Jim:*    Well, that was just some suggestions of where to start, and honestly, if—we'd go back to PTL and work for nothing, if God wants that.

*Koppel:* Yeah, well, maybe you would, but you didn't, and the fact of the matter is, not only did you not work for nothing, you worked for a great deal. Jerry Falwell today claims that now that the accountants are beginning to sort their way through all the paperwork, that they have found that over the past year, for example, you paid yourselves, or the board paid you, in salary and in dividends and in bonuses, a total of $1.9 million. Now, that's a far cry from working for nothing, isn't it?

*Jim:* Uh huh. Yes, and I'm not sure of those figures, but I think we've made a lot of mistakes, and I'm very sorry about it, and the—the board of directors, with me out of the room, always voted our salary. We—Tammy and I had nothing to do with our salary. And that doesn't excuse it, because we are the president, or were the president of the ministry, and we should have said, "No." And we did say, "No" many times, but our board cared about us, and they would tell us that Jim and Tammy, you earn every penny that we give you. In one week, I raised $30 million, at one time last year, and Tammy's records and our books and all have brought in literally millions of dollars, and instead of royalties, we took a salary controlled by the board of directors, and I feel that we—we should have said, "No, we'll just—we will not receive this." And the board did it out of love, they cared about us, they really did.

*Koppel:* Well, let's just talk numbers.

*Tammy:* And they told us they thought we were worth it.

*Koppel:* I'm sorry?

*Tammy:* They told us that they thought we were worth it, because I would go every time and tell them, you know, we don't deserve it, and they will all tell you I have said that to them. And they said, "Listen, you guys, you're worth it to us," you know, so—

*Koppel:* They also said you were kind of like a shopping machine. I mean, you would go out and—

*Tammy:* I do like to shop. I probably am well-known for my shopping.

*Koppel:* Yeah, it's—

*Tammy:* But I am a bargain-hunter.

*Koppel:* Extravagantly, though, I mean we're not talking about a little item here and a little item there, or a couple of dresses—how many mink coats, how many cars, you know what I mean, we're talking—

*Tammy:* I don't shop for cars, and I don't shop for mink coats. I do a lot of my shopping at places like T.J. Maxx's and the outlet stores. I shop outlet stores an awful lot, and I enjoy shopping. It's kind of a hobby to help my nerves.

*Koppel:* Jim Bakker—

*Tammy:* Better than a psychiatrist.

*Koppel:* Well, it may not be cheaper, the way you've been going at it, but let me—

*Tammy:* Maybe not.

*Koppel:* Let me—let me come back for a moment to the overall question of finances here. . . .[34]

Once Tammy has blithely repositioned the Bakkers in the pseudo-private, even a self-described "tough" questioner like Koppel must concentrate his energy to keep the implicit standards of judgment in the realm of honesty and ethics, not taste and materialism. Perhaps it is no coincidence, in connection with this principle of "safety" or "invulnerability," that while it was not uncommon for Tammy Bakker to appear in the media without her husband during the PTL scandal, for example on interview shows, rarely if ever did Jim Bakker appear without Tammy.

The Bakkers' ministry has always been associated with an upwardly mobile Pentecostalism that paralleled their own lives. Two features identify this Pentecostalism: a charismatic focus on the lives and times of the evangelists themselves, and a gospel of material pleasures as the sign of God's special blessing. Yet, despite Jim's occasional lapses into high display such as his vintage Rolls Royce, the Bakkers' materialism was mostly middle class: Sears and T.J. Maxx, not Saks and Neiman-Marcus.[35] What is of critical importance here is not *where* the Bakkers shop, but rather that—unlike with Gary Hart or Jimmy Swaggart, Ollie North, or other figures who faced scandal at about the same time—we *know* where they shop, and that this has been made somehow relevant in forming a judgment of them.

The trappings of this materialism, their household and lifestyle, have always been near the center of popular debate about the Bakkers. It is striking that during the scandal itself they were rarely asked to respond substantively to the many allegations of fraud, embezzlement, and so on— certainly Koppel did not ask them to do so; his idea of a "tough question" was handled rather easily by the Bakkers, as we saw in the exchange above. Rather, the popular treatment of their fall from grace was more often about the features of their pseudo-private lifestyle; about their charm rather than their piety; about their taste rather than their honesty. A newspaper article in March 1988, syndicated by Knight-Ridder Newspapers, commemorating the first anniversary of the PTL scandal, is typical of this pattern: The story devoted two paragraphs to the indictments against the Bakkers; the remaining seventy-three paragraphs focused on such details as the price of the ring Tammy wore at the interview, the age of Jim's unemployed parents, and the treatment of Jessica Hahn (Jim Bakker's alleged lover-turned-blackmailer) by the same cosmetic surgeon who transfigured pop superstar Michael Jackson.[36] Even wire service coverage of the impending collapse of the PTL ministry and the forced sale of all its assets in bankruptcy, in April 1988, was scarcely seen as an occasion to pass, invite, or even suggest moral judgment upon the Bakkers' actions.[37] By publicly playing up the Bakkers' private quirks and tastes, media coverage has moved our dominant image of them to the pseudo-private. Because of this shift, the harshest popular judgment ever passed against the Bakkers during the scandal seems to be that their taste failed to measure up to a level appropriate to the wealth they accumulated—that they are, in a word, tacky. Ethics, piety, and virtue dropped almost completely out of the picture.

## ■ CONCLUSION: PSEUDO-PRIVACY
## AND PUBLIC ACCOUNTABILITY

The results of pseudo-private display can be impressive. Our pseudo-private experience of Jim and Tammy Bakker gives us a sense of intimacy with them that no amount of nude photo layouts in *Playboy* will ever win for Jessica Hahn. If, indeed, it were only a question of creating a greater sense of intimacy through the electronic media, then the case of the PTL scandal might be simply one more case, albeit a slightly offbeat one, of celebrities manipulating the media to their advantage.

What deserves our concern is not simply that pseudo-private display can blunt the seriousness of charges raised by interlocutors, although this is demonstrably true: During 1987, a year of seemingly perpetual scandal, perhaps only Lt. Col. Oliver North dodged the noose of civic accountability with equal panache. Indeed, the likes of Gary Hart and Joseph Biden, who saw scandal quickly derail their 1988 presidential ambitions, must look with wonder upon the ease with which the Bakkers blunted our sense of the seriousness of the (far more grave) accusations they faced by transferring our experience of them to a wholly different realm in which what we see is less important than what we agree to ignore. Rather, we should be troubled, as citizens and as observers of public discourse, to find that public discussion, through which we expect to hold public figures to standards of public accountability, may so easily be degraded to pseudo-private display—taking with it the centrality of honesty, piety, and integrity upon which the very idea of public accountability is founded. Pseudo-private display does something worse than make figures appear more honest or pious than perhaps they are; continued exposure makes less likely even the attempt to challenge figures on these grounds.[38] Suspicion of technique, upon which pseudo-private display is founded, has not made us wiser or more critically discerning; instead it tempts us to lower our expectations for public discourse in general.[39]

We therefore risk being betrayed by our own language: Pseudo-private display is *not* simply public display with minor, updated variations in technique. True, it is commonly found in physical locations traditionally considered public, and it involves persons we would ordinarily consider public figures. But the dislocation of "public" and "private" by the electronic media—by which both terms have been transformed into metaphors—means that physical location is no longer decisive in differentiating the two. Failure to recognize that "public" and "private" are now metaphors provides the opening within which pseudo-privacy operates. While the two terms were anchored metonymically in physical sites, they could sensibly be discussed as practical contraries. But when the media allow the commonplaces of one to interact with the other, allow the traces of sites and roles appropriate to the private to become mingled with messages traditionally expected to be public, the result is not merely more artful public display, but something quite different: a mode of display in which argumentative standards change, as do the appropriate standards for judgment of conduct.

After all, what has made the term "public" so important to us in our culture is not the mere physical trappings of public spaces, but rather its association with codes our culture considers important: standards of rationality, rules of conduct, precepts of morality. Display ungoverned by these rules, even when it occurs in sites traditionally considered public, is not simply a new kind of public display; it is in fact no longer public display at all, at least as we traditionally or conventionally understand that word "public."

So long as we cannot rethink the relationship within which our expectations about "public" and "private" now stand with respect to contemporary communicative practice, adequate standards for acting and judging in our communicative world will continue to elude us.

# ▓ Notes

[1] At its peak, the PTL Ministry's worth was estimated at $203 million, including the income from the 161 stations that aired its programming. David Brand, "God and Money," *Time* 3 August 1977: 48.

[2] The examples used to illustrate my analysis, below, were drawn chiefly from three sources, beginning after the scandal reached public proportions in March 1987: television news coverage of the Bakkers (primarily on Cable News Network); talk-show interviews with the Bakkers, including the Bakkers' 27 May 1987 appearance on *Nightline* and Tammy Bakker's 12 December 1988 appearance with talk-show host Sally Jesse Raphael; and televised documentaries related to the scandal, including "Praise the Lord" (PBS, 26 January 1988), and "Thy Will Be Done" (PBS, 6 April 1988). Other sources, such as on-line information searches, were also relied upon and are identified below. It is not the purpose of this essay to produce an exhaustive accounting of all media appearances, public or pseudo-private, by the Bakkers; obviously the total of their media appearances during the height of the scandal is far too great to treat here.

[3] Charles Krauthammer, "Pseudo-Private Lives," *The New Republic* 23 May 1983: 12–14.

[4] *Nightline,* Executive Producer Richard Kaplan, ABC, 27 May 1987. Transcription of Show no.1567 (New York: Journal Graphics, Inc., 1987) 2.

[5] Hannah Arendt, *The Human Condition* (Chicago: University of Chicago Press) 28.

[6] Arendt 36–37.

[7] I have relied upon Arendt's more elaborate discussion of the relationship between "private" and "privation"; see: Arendt 58–73.

[8] Joshua Meyrowitz, *No Sense of Place: The Impact of Electronic Media on Social Behavior* (New York: Oxford University Press, 1985). See, for example, his "Introduction: Behavior in Its Place," 1–9.

[9] Erving Goffman, *The Presentation of Self in Everyday Life* (New York: Doubleday Anchor Books, 1959) 106–140.

[10]Goffman 106–10.

[11]Goffman 113.

[12]Goffman 107.

[13]Goffman 112.

[14]Max Black, *Models and Metaphors* (Ithaca: Cornell University Press, 1962) 38–47. See also: George Lakoff and Mark Johnson, *Metaphors We Live By* (Chicago: University of Chicago Press, 1980). The argument developed here, with respect not only to metaphor in general but also to spatial metaphor in particular, relies upon William L. Nothstine, " 'Topics' as Ontological Metaphor in Contemporary Rhetorical Theory and Criticism," *Quarterly Journal of Speech* (May 1988) 151–163.

[15]See: Marshall McLuhan, *Understanding Media: The Extensions of Man*, 2nd ed. (New York: Signet Books, 1964) 19.

[16]Krauthammer 12.

[17]Krauthammer 12.

[18]Two useful discussions of the denial of persuasive intent as a persuasive strategy have guided me here: Herbert W. Simons, *Persuasion: Understanding, Practice, and Analysis*, 2nd ed. (New York: Harper and Row, 1986), Chapter 15 "Analyzing Persuasion in the Guise of Objectivity," 307–328; and F. G. Bailey, *The Tactical Uses of Passion: An Essay on Power, Reason, and Reality* (Ithaca: Cornell University Press, 1983).

[19]Mark L. Knapp, *Essentials of Nonverbal Communication* (New York: Holt, Rinehart, and Winston, 1980) 12–13.

[20]We might as appropriately look at the stream of "kiss-and-tell" books that flooded the bookstores during the summer of 1988, written by former Reagan administration officials. Perhaps the most notorious of these were: Donald T. Regan and Charles McCarry, *For the Record* (New York: Harcourt, Brace, Jovanovich, 1988); and Larry Speakes and Robert Pack, *Speaking Out* (New York: Scribners, 1988). The thesis of this essay is equally applicable—indeed, perhaps even more urgently so—to political figures as to religious figures. This is sharply demonstrated by *Time* magazine's excerpting of Regan's titillating accounts of President Reagan's deference to the First Lady's obsession with astrology. The publisher's assertion that "the decision to print excerpts of *For the Record* had less to do with personality than history" faces tremendous evidence to the contrary: not only the circus atmosphere surrounding the publication of the excerpts, but also the fact that history had all but forgotten the revelations a year later. See: "A Letter from the Publisher," *Time* 16 May 1988: 4.

[21]"Praise the Lord," Producers William Cran and Stephanie Tepper, *Frontline*, Executive Producer David Sanning, PBS, 26 January 1988. Transcription by the author.

[22]"Praise the Lord," 26 January 1988. This scene, and the one described immediately above, were broadcast to the audience of the PTL network before being used in Cran and Tepper's documentary.

[23]*Nightline* 15–16.

[24]The image of the outdoor bathroom, whose connection to Koppel's question seems tenuous, is nevertheless a favorite of Tammy's, and it has occurred with some frequency during Tammy's media appearances after the PTL scandal broke. As late as December, 1988, Tammy was still resurrecting the outdoor bathroom, this time in reply to talk show host Sally Jesse Raphael:

> *Raphael:* How does somebody—how does the normal American family get caught up in all of this? Did you ever dream—If some, could somebody have come to this little girl from Minnesota . . . could somebody have said to her, "One day they're going to have you on the cover of a magazine. One day you're going to be caricatured on 'Saturday Night Live'?"

   *Tammy:* I would have said there was no possible way. We had an outdoor bathroom.
   I was the oldest of eight children. . . .

(*Sally Jesse Raphael,* 12 December 1988. Transcription by the author.) Here the relevance
of the image to the question asked is more obvious, yet not so obvious that the reader may not
find its appearance somewhat indecorous.

[25]Jean Seligmann, "The Inimitable Tammy Faye," *Newsweek* 8 June 1987: 69.

[26]*Nightline* 3.

[27]*Nightline* 3.

[28]*Nightline* 3.

[29]Koppel's predicament also highlights an ironic consequence of the dislocation of public
and private. Even though they were engaged in conversation together on the same live broadcast, the Bakkers and Koppel were not present within the same communicative mode: Tammy
Bakker's presence was pseudo-private, while Koppel's was public. Hence their displays were
accountable to different standards of conduct, to Koppel's dismay.

[30]Reported on Cable News Network, 18 June 1987. Transcription by the author.

[31]Arendt 52.

[32]More evidence of how frequently and easily the Bakkers can blur this line: both Ted
Koppel's May 1987 *Nightline* interviews with the Bakkers and Sally Jesse Raphael's December
1988 interview with Tammy Bakker took place in the Bakker's home (or, in Koppel's case, with
the Bakkers at home and Koppel in the studio). In the midst of the Raphael interview, Tammy
fretted that her house needed dusting.

[33]A comparison with the case of Jimmy Carter suggests that this preparation of the
audience, by repeated and incremental exposure to pseudo-private display, may be necessary
to prevent the effect from backfiring. Compared to his recent predecessors, Jimmy Carter's
"backstage" life frequently crossed over into his "onstage" performance as president. Yet for
Carter, pseudo-private display (including framing cues spanning the range from his appearance for a nationally televised address in a cardigan sweater to the antics of his eccentric
relatives, most prominently his brother Billy) seemed to produce a less-positive reaction, even
if that reaction was not always well-voiced. Billy Carter, in particular, was at best a diverting
sideshow to the Carter presidency; at worst he was an embarrassment and a liability. The
analysis of pseudo-privacy so far suggests two possible explanations for this: First, the office of
the presidency may be especially resistant to the transition to pseudo-privacy. Second, and more
directly relevant to the present discussion, Jim and Tammy Bakker had a much longer time over
which to accustom their audience to experiencing them in the pseudo-private mode, whereas
Carter moved in a short time from relative anonymity to the presidency, leaving comparatively
little time to accustom us to viewing him through the lens of pseudo-private display.

   [34]*Nightline* 5–6.

[35]Sources already mentioned provide numerous examples of this attention to be found
during the scandal's height. For example, "The Inimitable Tammy Faye" catalogues Tammy's
attraction to "shoes and cubic zirconiums," and describes in some detail her passion for
shopping binges. Often this attention, in matters that might otherwise seem undeserving,
approached the level of farce. Koppel's *Nightline* interview dwelled at some length on the rumor
of an "air-conditioned dog house" for the Bakker's dog, Max (16). This was later picked up by
*Newsweek* ("Heaven Can Wait," 8 June 1987: 62) and was also featured in the infamous music
video. The same *Newsweek* article featured a photo montage of a ceramic dachshund and other
statuary from the Bakker's home, cited as examples of "excess" (61). This trend reached its
apparent zenith on 22 November 1987 when the syndicated comic strip "Bloom County"
mentioned the air-conditioned dog house in a strip caricaturing the Bakkers.

[36]Elizabeth Leland, "PTL: A Year Later," *The Muncie Star,* 20 March 1988: B8.

[37]As an illustration of this point, none of the news items, retrieved on-line through the Newsgrid information service under the keyword "PTL," during the week following the April 1988 announcement that the Internal Revenue Service had revoked the tax-exempt status of the PTL Ministries, gives more than passing mention to charges of blackmail, or mail or wire fraud, then associated with the demise of the ministry. The first item, "PTL Leaders Vow to Fight the IRS Ruling Stripping . . ." (25 April 1988, item 1844), mentions only "the high salaries of the Bakkers," and that PTL officials "blamed big salaries paid to Jim and Tammy Bakker for PTL's troubles." A second item from the same search, "IRS Revokes Tax-Exempt Status of U.S. Television . . ." (22 April 1988, item 1551), mentions the Bakkers' "extravagant" lifestyle and the sex scandal involving Jessica Hahn, but lapses significantly into passive voice at the mention of "thousands of dollars from a trust fund set up to assure her silence about her celebrated sexual encounter with Bakker," passing over the question of agency and responsibility. The remaining Newsgrid item, "TV Evangelist Jim Bakker Asks to Return to . . ." (22 April 1988, item 1506), does use the word "sins" in connection with Bakker's actions, but only in reporting Bakker's characterization of his own behavior. Even these references to possible public wrongdoing by the Bakkers are uniformly brief and ambiguous, as the influence of the shift from public experience to pseudo-private would lead us to expect.

[38]Indeed, although a full investigation of the question would be beyond the scope of this essay, the apparent rhetorical invulnerability of Ronald Reagan's so-called "Teflon Presidency," in which scandals and reversals never seemed to "stick" to the Chief Executive himself or affect his credibility with Americans, may well stem from exactly the phenomenon being considered here.

[39]Syndicated columnist David Broder's description of a glaring example from the summer of 1989 is worth quoting at length:

> One of the perverse rules of behavior of the Washington press corps is our tendency to savor being told secrets while ignoring what is on the public record. Eight years ago, there was a huge furor when William Greider published the previously private views of budget director David Stockman on the perils of the fiscal policy he had helped create and move through Congress.
>
> Stockman's phrases—his observation, for example, that "the hogs were really feeding" when the special interest lobbies finished with the tax bill—created a sensation. Stockman had made the comments in what were originally off-the-record, one-on-one conversations with Greider.
>
> The man who now holds Stockman's job as director of the Office of Management and Budget, Richard G. Darman, late last month sounded an equally urgent note of alarm about the selfishness of fiscal policy. But in contrast, he scarcely caused a ripple.
>
> Darman's mistake was that he didn't leak his views to a single reporter but stood up and delivered them, of all places, at the National Press Club.

See: "Budget Troubles No Less than under Past Administration," *Chicago Tribune*, Sunday 6 August 1989; Section 5:11. Broder's point is well-taken: the on-the-record public speech, which we still imagine to be the best way to place an issue on the public agenda, pales in its rhetorical force compared to pseudo-private display.

# MAXIM 3

## CRITICISM IS BOTH SERVED AND CONFINED BY THEORY AND METHOD

**258**

# CHAPTER 11 

## THE METAPHOR OF FORCE
## IN PROWAR DISCOURSE

Robert L. Ivie

*In this commentary, Robert L. Ivie recounts how the rigor of theory and method helped him gain distance on his topic of research, American war rhetoric. He describes his study of the case of the War of 1812 as part of a larger critical project stemming from his ambivalence about his own military service during the Vietnam era. To give himself the distance he felt he needed to undertake a project so close to his own intense experiences, Ivie began his study not with the war most close to him, but to one separated in time and cultural space: the War of 1812. Ivie also sought perspective on his subject in part by embracing a theoretical approach that would allow him distance from his texts.*

## COMMENTARY

Reflecting ten years later upon the process of writing "The Metaphor of Force in Prowar Discourse: The Case of 1812" reminds me that the essay was ten years in the making, the product of a larger project on the rhetoric of war that began in graduate school upon my return from two troubling years of active duty in the United States Navy during the Vietnam era. Throughout those two years, the longest of my life, I confronted the moral dilemma of obliging a patriotic duty at the expense of contributing to a wrongful cause. Stymied by my circumstances as a military instructor stationed at a naval air training facility in Millington, Tennessee—thus protected from combat as well as prevented from protesting the war—the dilemma eventually transformed itself into a quest for understanding and, perhaps, absolution from the purgatory of inaction and indecision over questions of moral purpose, specifically those surrounding the justification of war. Thus, I renewed my graduate studies with a desire to discern how we talk ourselves into war and quickly discovered an affinity between my burning question and Kenneth Burke's probing investigation of rhetorical motives.

Realizing that I was too close to the immediate experience of the Vietnam war, that I needed distance and breadth of perspective to initiate my study of American justifications of war, I began planning a dissertation that would employ Burke's conceptual machinery in an analysis of presidential war messages from 1812 forward. Following James Andrews's lead, I set out "to discover any consistent appeals which contribute toward a pattern of pro-war oratory." Burke's ideas seemed especially amenable to providing a method of intrinsic criticism, or systematic study of rhetorical strategies as symbolic action. The War of 1812 provided an intriguing starting point because not only was it the young republic's first declared war but also it had been labeled by historian Samuel Eliot Morison as "the most unpopular war that this country has ever waged, not even excepting the Vietnam conflict."

The first result was a term paper in 1972 that investigated what C. Wright Mills called "vocabularies of motive" by drawing upon Burke's notions of hierarchy and victimage, his dramatistic pentad and ratios, and various strategies of identification to analyze James Madison's war message of June 1, 1812, and the antiwar arguments of three of Madison's most prominent Congressional critics—Daniel Sheffey, Richard Stanford, and John Randolph. In addition to yielding a method of analysis, which I employed soon thereafter in a doctoral dissertation comparing seven presidential justifications for war, this initial study of war rhetoric in 1812 suggested essential differences between the symbolic orientations of prowar and antiwar speakers—a lead I did not investigate further until several years later when Ronald Hatzenbuehler and I undertook a joint project on Congressional decision-making in the early republic.

Upon further examination, the rhetorical struggle between proponents and opponents of war in 1812 underscored the importance of understanding war as a matter of choice grounded in symbolic action. Thus, I set about writing a paper that rejected deterministic images of war and advocated instead, by way of example, a comparative analysis of opposing strategies employed by prowar and antiwar speakers to dramatize an essentially ambiguous situation. This paper, presented in 1976 at the annual meeting of the Western Speech Communication Association, metamorphosed over the next five years into a reconceptualization of war rhetoric. As the initial draft submitted to *The Quarterly Journal of Speech*, it contained the seed of an idea that developed through two revisions into its final published form.

The 1976 draft appears in retrospect more prescient than perhaps it actually was. Nevertheless, I remember shipping it off to the editor of *QJS* with the uneasy sense that it contained an important notion not yet fully grasped. I had ventured as far as I could without benefit of the kind of dialectic that comes from serious editorial review. I hoped I had produced something sufficiently substantive to prompt the kind of critique that helps perplexed writers find their bearings. Indeed, the response confirmed the unrealized potential of the piece, encouraging me to keep searching for an elusive gestalt and providing Delphic guidance toward that end.

What I had achieved by this point was a rudimentary sense of the importance of integrative images to the rhetorical process, including the rhetorical process of scholars theorizing about war and involving mechanistic metaphors that cast human nature and the causes of war into a deterministic mold; rhetoric, ironically, was employed by scholars no less than by proponents of war to occlude choice. Thus, the extended debate in 1812 provided a valuable case study in how the option of peace was transformed rhetorically over a period of months (and, as I later discovered, years) into a perception of war's necessity.

My analysis of this debate was guided by a dramatistic orientation and thus untethered by mechanistic tenets to a content-analytic listing of recurring themes, or so I thought. I adopted (mostly implicitly) an organic metaphor to capture the integrative function of rhetorical action between and among what, for the most part, were Republican advocates and Federalist opponents of war with Great Britain. What emerged most clearly was the existence of competing perspectives, two relatively integrated symbol systems diverging along party lines, each grounded on different premises, with one more capable of enveloping the other in its legitimizing rhetoric. I had discovered that a different image guided each side's definition of the situation and that various reinforcing rhetorical strategies of argument, arrangement, and style had been concocted on their behalf. The outcome of the debate was a result of one image outmaneuvering the other.

Nevertheless, a tension between mechanistic and organic accounts of rhetoric's justificatory form and function continued to confound my search for an explanatory gestalt. The mechanistic inclination guided me toward a systemization of three sets of themes (intrinsicality of harms, intentionality of hostilities, and feasibility of redress), each with its subthemes (for example, intrinsicality of harms was characterized as itself a function of three additional "operations": one to specify the adversary's noxious behaviors and establish a concretization of damages, another to identify a universality of effects, and a third to substantiate the lawlessness of the adversary's conduct). This systemizing of themes, abstracted from the constituting language of the debate, served as a convenient template for comparing Republican and Federalist cases as they "evolved" in stages from prewar through transitional to prowar rhetoric. I set out to find the intrinsic coherence of belligerence, a coherence that had been constructed within an inherently ambiguous situation, by charting the evolution of recurring themes and presentational tactics in a justificatory structure that functioned as a "catalyst" for war. Presentational tactics were conceptualized as language devices for communicating the substance and salience of themes (themes that served as decision criteria) when evidence available to rhetors remained otherwise inconclusive.

This peculiar mixture of organic and mechanical thinking led to a linear search for an integrative structure, yielding among other things the observation that Republican rhetors had woven the image of the enemy's hostile intentions into the very fabric of their prowar discourse. One presentational tactic Republicans employed, I noted among a list of others, was to characterize the British enemy through decivilizing metaphors that were consistent with an ascribed motive of recolonizing the United States and inconsistent with England's professed goal of defending itself against the French. As something of an afterthought, I noted that the significance of such a tactic transcended its role as a catalyst for war in 1812 because it illustrated a way of engaging an underlying image of savagery that aroused the nation's fear and provoked its anger. In this way, I began tentatively to merge previously independent lines of critical inquiry, one of which had just culminated in a forthcoming essay on images of savagery while the other was still being revised to resubmit for editorial review. Again, my *QJS* readers displayed remarkable patience, advising me to drop the catalyst and feature the metaphor. But just how to feature the metaphor continued to baffle me until I began thinking of it less as a presentational mechanism and more as the seed of a motivating idea, the source of a guiding image.

Understanding metaphor as the linguistic source of rhetorical invention was the insight that finally brought the project to fruition, its gestalt derived from the metaphor of force. Force could now be understood as the principal war-legitimizing figure manifested, extended, and literalized through decivilizing vehicles, structures of argument, and various other rhetorical forms. This was the insight that guided both my analysis and my evaluation of Republican prowar rhetoric and its motivating perspective. It was the insight that transformed a structuralist analysis of savagery's three dimensions into a holistic understanding of its unity as an image.

Metaphor became the unifying principle and rhetorical dynamic that has animated my investigation of war-justifying discourse for a decade since. It has led me to explore the typology of decivilizing vehicles revealed in Ronald Reagan's rhetorical construction of the Soviet threat; to examine Harry Truman's strategic appropriation of the plain style as a literalizing medium of the image of Soviet savagery; to investigate the metaphorical construction of freedom's feminine fragility as the threatening reciprocal of savagery's masculine force; to devise a procedure for locating metaphorical concepts constraining the rhetorical invention of Cold War critics; and to examine the self-neutralizing cluster of motivating metaphors in the Johnson administration's Vietnam war rhetoric. Thus, a rhetorical theory of war has begun to emerge within a unified line of investigation, the key characteristics of which first became synthesized within a framework of critical inquiry into Cold War motives.

The rhetorical perfection of the metaphor of force into an attitude of belligerence raises the related question of what self-defining metaphor could inspire the construction of such a threatening image of the enemy. Accordingly, the critical quest that a decade ago yielded the gestalt of force turns now down the dark path of fear into the metaphorical depths of a nation's rhetorically constituted sense of insecurity.

# The Metaphor of Force
# in Prowar Discourse:
# The Case of 1812

Robert L. Ivie

One of the radical differences between classical and contemporary theories of rhetoric is the role each accords to metaphor. Within its classical context, metaphor is a trope of resemblance which, along with other figures of speech, adorns the essential features of discourse. As I. A. Richards observes, it is viewed as a "happy extra trick with words" which contributes only a "grace or ornament or *added* power of language, not its constitutive form."[1] Conversely, many contemporary theorists subscribe to the dictum that metaphor is "the omnipresent principle of language."[2] Thought itself is metaphoric. Paul Ricoeur considers metaphor "the rhetorical process by which discourse unleashes the power that certain fictions have to redescribe reality."[3] Perelman and Olbrechts-Tyteca contend that it influences "the life of notions."[4] Kenneth Burke argues that "every perspective requires a metaphor, implicit or explicit, for its organizational base." Entire schools of scientific research "are hardly more than the patient repetition, in all its ramifications, of a fertile metaphor" which provides "the cue for an unending line of data and generalizations."[5] No mere rhetorical ornament, metaphor is instead the linguistic origin of our most compelling arguments.

Burke recognizes, as a principle of symbolic action, the necessity of extending the figurative to the literal world. Nevertheless, he warns that the value of seeing one thing in terms of another is easily lost if the two are treated identically. Persons, objects, and events "possess *degrees of being* in proportion to the variety of perspectives from which they can with justice be perceived."[6] Phenomena should be considered tentatively from various points of view in order to counter natural tendencies toward the reduction of whole to part. Analogical extensions, that is, need to be multiple and flexible, not singular and rigid. Yet there is the ever-present temptation of literalizing one metaphor to the exclusion of others.

Nowhere is the temptation to literalize a fertile metaphor any stronger or more consequential than in deliberations about war and peace. Prowar rhetors perform the ritual of victimage as they cultivate images of a savage enemy. Through analogical extensions, they articulate a theme of diabolism that, taken literally, goads nations into defending themselves against barbarians bent upon subjugating innocent peoples. Voices of belligerence, disguised in the overtones of pacific ideals, promise salvation to those who would vanquish satan's surrogate.[7]

It is difficult to imagine a more powerful call to arms than one based on the image of savagery. Accordingly, the transformation of its primary metaphor from a mere trope of resemblance into a thoroughgoing definition of reality is a matter deserving close analysis. Whenever "a *similarity* is taken as evidence of an *identity*,"[8] it behooves us to understand how the inference is effected. This paper examines the process of literalization as it was enacted by those who advocated America's second war with Great Britain. Attention is focused on their choice of decivilizing vehicles, their affirmation of threatening expectations, their suggestion of rational demonstrations, and their subversion of competing perspectives. These four operations are indicative of resources generally available to prowar rhetors who draw upon the master trope of force to accuse an adversary of hostile motives. Together they represent a basic mode of discourse in which arguments are produced from metaphors through the principle of terministic perfection.[9] Each is examined within the context of the War of 1812 in order to draw a clear illustration of how literalization occurs and why it is important.

## ■ DECIVILIZING VEHICLES

America's declaration of war against Great Britain on June 18, 1812, was the culmination of a decade of tensions accompanied by an abundance of vituperative rhetoric. The issues, as characterized by majority-party Republicans, led to a justification for war that depended largely on images of savagery. Like the claims so often made against enemies, Republican charges of British barbarity were persistent, thematic, and pervasive to the point of portending the ruination of American independence. The young republic's rights, honor, and sovereignty had been trampled upon by an international bully who would stop at nothing short of recolonizing a commercial rival. The nation could be rescued only by an application of force equivalent to that of the advancing enemy. War, therefore, was the sole option for a people determined to remain free; or so the situation appeared after a metaphor was stretched to its limits.

This stretching of the metaphor by prowar Republicans exploited a variety of decivilizing vehicles in order to decipher and censure the motives behind England's conduct. Favoring the language of power and physical abuse, spokesmen recounted a series of "depredations" in which America had been "trampled," "trodden," "bullied," "kicked," and "pounded" by Great Britain. The perpetrator of these violent actions was portrayed variously as a beast of prey, common criminal, ruthless murderer, haughty pirate, and crazed tyrant whose appetite for commercial monopoly was insatiable. Each of these vehicles contributed in turn to an overall vision of malevolence which, in Roger Brown's judgment, put "the worst possible construction on British policies and motives without mentioning settlements, the shifting course of negotiation, and possible alternative interpretations of British intentions."[10]

As Brown notes, the actual sequence of events did not necessitate the particular interpretation given it by Republican partisans. America's problems had developed within a context of international strife much wider than the immediate conflict with Britain. The United States had suffered a number of infringements upon its maritime rights, especially since 1803, largely because commercial restrictions in the form of blockades and counterblockades had become a principal instrument of warfare between two great empires. Beleaguered Britain was determined to dominate the seas, both to counter Napoleon's supremacy on the land and to force a reopening of trade with the Continent. Sailors from American merchantmen frequently were impressed to man the ships of the Royal Navy while Continental markets for American grain, cotton, and tobacco were blockaded by England's executive Orders in Council. France also issued Decrees which forbade American trade with Great Britain and authorized the confiscation of violators' property. The United States refused to yield its right as a neutral nation to trade with either belligerent. When tensions led in 1807 to an attack on the American frigate *Chesapeake* by H.M.S. *Leopard,* Congress responded with an experiment in economic coercion designed to protect the country's maritime rights. During the next four years, the nation tried embargo, non-importation and non-intercourse, none of which achieved its declared objective. Finally, Britain was identified as the intransigent enemy of American sovereignty, and war was declared to save the new republic from the threat of an early demise.[11]

Ironically, as Bradford Perkins notes, there was actually less cause for war in 1812 than in previous years, especially since England finally had repealed the hated Orders in Council. Even though slow transatlantic communications prevented Americans from learning of their victory over "the chief symbol of discord" in time to prevent a final commitment to hostilities, there were earlier "omens of concession" that could have induced a longer wait for news had not hardened attitudes led Congress to act otherwise.[12] Britain's insensitivity to American complaints and preoccupation with the struggle against Napoleon had frustrated a bad situation even further, ultimately allowing sufficient time for a rhetorically-charged metaphor to evolve into a Republic theory of British diabolism.

This evolvement of the metaphor occurred steadily as Republicans turned repeatedly to decivilizing vehicles of violence and physical confrontation. Tropes, initially drawn upon to assail Britain's conduct, were suggestive as well of Britain's diabolical motives. The *possibility* of an adversary's goals being similar in quality to its coercive behavior eventually became the *conclusion* that British conduct and British intentions were identical. The enemy meant to subdue an upstart nation of freemen, for nothing was more instinctive than to satisfy a raging appetite for commercial dominion by brutally attacking a vulnerable rival. Means, that is, could be expected to conform to the ends they served, and the vicious assaults on American commerce seemed to be no exception to the rule. As abuses continued, they merely confirmed what Republicans were conditioned to expect by the terms of their primary metaphor.

The steady movement through decivilizing vehicles toward the final image of Britain's savage motives was readily apparent in the speeches and letters of Republicans between 1807 and 1812. Following the *Chesapeake* incident of 1807, rhetors availed themselves of decivilizing language primarily to characterize and condemn British depredations and incidentally to suggest a possibility of evil intentions. George Washington Campbell, for instance, compared attacks on his country to a previous assault on Denmark. Depicting the common aggressor as both criminal and beast of prey, the Congressman from Tennessee reminded his colleagues that the "so much famed British lion, stretched forth his merciless paw, fastened its fangs upon her capital, murdered her people, and robbed her of her navy."[13] Richard M. Johnson also drew upon images of force when he complained in a circular letter to his constituents that American seamen were being "torn from their families, their friends, their country"—that "all the kindred ties of the human heart [were being] broken asunder by a British press gang."[14] Joseph Desha warned his constituents that "the gigantic strength of [Britain's] navy has enabled her to trample the rights of neutrals under her feet."[15] Vermont's James Fish interpreted the British to be saying quite simply, "I have abused you; humble yourself, succumb to me, and I will make such satisfaction as I think fit."[16] Like other Republicans in the House, John Eppes responded in kind by proclaiming his country would forever refuse "to bend to lawless power."[17] Almost imperceptibly, the verbs depicting Britain's conduct as strictly coercive began to reappear through similar verbs attributing only hostile motives to the enemy. Those haughty freebooters—who had variously murdered, plundered, robbed, torn, broken, trampled, and abused their unfortunate victims—likewise were intent upon wresting inherent rights from the hands of Americans.[18] The refusal "to bend" amounted in turn to a circumscribing of America's motives by the same kind of verbal reflex.

Many in the majority party initiated the policy of economic coercion in 1807 either hoping or believing that a momentarily deranged England would soon return to its senses after losing the coveted trade with America. The embargo was something of a test of England's determination. As Burwell Basset, a Republican Congressman from Virginia, privately wrote early in 1808: the British "must be made to feel the pressure of a restrained commerce before they will open their eyes to what justice to us and their own good requires. Such is the demonial influence of jealousy that it injures itself and the object it most wishes to cherish. Their merchants are ardent to monopolise. To this use the British whould [sic] subvert the seas and are blind to the fatal blow they are giving to commerce itself. . . . It cannot be doubted that a judicious use of this power [i.e., embargo] will bring England to her senses."[19] Uninhibited commercial jealousy had gotten the better of Britain's rational faculties.

Even when America's resolve proved too feeble to put Britain's true motives to the test—that is, when domestic political pressures forced Congress to retreat from embargo and adopt much weaker forms of economic coercion—Republicans never abandoned metaphors which prompted images of "demonial influence." By the end of 1808, Madison's brother-in-law James G. Jackson was telling Congress that "the shark of the ocean" was "scouring every sea and driving everything from its surface." The law of nations, he added at another point, had been "trampled under foot." Britain was determined that "our pride shall be humbled."[20] In 1809, Desha complained of Britain's "fangs of despotism" and "the voracious jaws of the monster of the deep" as he warned that the enemy "has outstripped the piracy and perfidy of barbarism. Grasping at universal monopoly, she abandons moral and religious principles, tramples on sacred faith, sports with national law, and arrogantly demands tributary exactions calculated to bring us into a state of bankruptcy, and render us abject vassals instead of a sovereign and free people."[21] Again in 1810 he referred to Britain as "our inveterate, rapacious, and relentless enemy" whose aggressions were without parallel "even in times of barbarism" and whose government "in all cases substitutes power in place of right." Our "most important and inherent rights are about to be wrested from our hands" by an adversary who had "never pardoned our independence."[22]

Finally Madison called Congress into session late in 1811 to put "the United States into an armor and an attitude demanded by the crisis." England was "trampling on rights which no independent nation can relinquish."[23] According to Peter B. Porter, Chairman of the House Committee on Foreign Relations, the British had "advanced with bolder and continually increasing strides" to the point of "trampling on our persons."[24] Henry Clay wrote that the enemy was "every where pounding us."[25] Porter warned that if the nation "tamely submitted to one cool, deliberate, intentional indignity," it "might safely calculate to be kicked and cuffed for the whole of the remainder of [its] life."[26] Throughout the war session, Republicans extended this image of British brutality to its ultimate conclusion which, according to Jonathan Roberts, "would be absolute recolonization."[27] The United States, John C. Calhoun resolved, must resist "the colonial state to which again that Power is endeavoring to reduce us."[28] Nothing seemed more necessary by 1812 than to declare war on a nation which had plotted, in Thomas Gholson's words, "the dismemberment of the U. States."[29]

No language could have provided a better vehicle for prowar rhetoric.

Figures of British power, when turned into threatening images of evil intentions, made self-defense the prime motive for an "appeal to the God of
Battles."[30] Further, the image was practically self-confirming. Constructed
from the stuff of metaphor, it directed attention to British behavior which
appeared most consistent with diabolical motives, filtered from view experiences that tended to disconfirm evil intentions, and recalled to mind deep-
rooted prejudices against an erstwhile foe.[31] Given the basic perspective
(supplied essentially by metaphor) that Great Britain was driven by savage
impulses, Republicans experienced relatively few difficulties in crafting a
logic which verified their worst expectations.

## ▨ AFFIRMATION OF THREATENING EXPECTATIONS

Literalizing the metaphor required some means of verifying its power to
predict the future course of Britain's conduct toward America. Otherwise,
the image of barbaric intentions remained a mere analogy vulnerable to the
criticism that England's conduct and motives were most accurately defined
by qualities other than savagery. Lacking a record of firm resistance to
British encroachments, Republicans could only speculate, not establish, that
the enemy's hostility was unbounded. As late as 1810, in fact, even Republican congressmen continued to suggest that an act of firmness, "a manly
stand," would cause Britain to recede.[32] Yet active resistance was politically
infeasible without prior verification of the enemy's diabolical motives.
Therefore, solving the problem of verification depended upon developing a
passive test of Britain's persistence, and the passage of Macon's Bill No. 2 in
May of 1810 accomplished just that. The new law offered to defend the
nation's rights against either belligerent if one of them repealed its Orders
or Decrees and the other refused to follow suit within three months thereafter.[33] A British, not American, initiative was now required to disprove hostile
intentions.

The rationale for the test embodied in Macon's law was effected through
a quasi-logical argument which simulated pure disjunctive and hypothetical
deductions.[34] Given the thesis (suggested by decivilizing vehicles) that Britain harbored evil intentions, Republicans quite simply fixed their attention
on two possibilities: *either* the British were determined to force their will on
the United States at any cost, *or* they would respect American rights when
provided a sufficient opportunity to do so. Further, *if* they truly respected
America's sovereign rights, *then* they would respond rationally to Macon's
law by suspending the Orders in Council; but *if* they were bent upon subjugating the former colonies, *then* they would hold fast to their Orders. The
syllogistic form of this argument was itself appealing, even if the legitimacy
of the argument's basic assumptions was questionable. Certainly the mix of
possible motives behind England's conduct was more complex than the two

alternatives set upon by Republican legislators, and the definition of "sufficient opportunity" was subject to honest differences of opinion, especially when determining whether Macon's law provided a reasonable opportunity to repeal the Orders without jeopardizing England's position vis-à-vis Napoleon. Nonetheless, the appearance of sheer rationality compensated for lingering doubts over any such ambiguities. What began as a fluid, suggestive trope of resemblance had emerged as a rigid, probative line of reasoning which presumed to test independently the very metaphor from which its own premises were drawn.

When the opportunistic Napoleon obligingly, even if ambiguously, offered to revoke his Decrees, Madison proclaimed on November 2, 1810, that one of the two belligerents had met the requirements of Macon's law.[35] On December 5, Madison added that the British government showed no intention of relinquishing its Orders. Republicans seized upon this turn of events to denounce England as America's true enemy. Ezekiel Bacon, writing to Joseph Story after hearing of Napoleon's offer, concluded that a *"resort to arms* must as you suggest be the ultimate result of a perseverance by G. Britain in her orders in Council."[36] In the words of congressman John Rhea, the United States had made a "conciliatory" gesture; France "preferred a friendly and amicable intercourse"; England continued to violate "the neutral rights of the United States"; and, therefore, "Great Britain has itself only to blame for the state of things that will be."[37]

This same line of reasoning was carried into the war session. Madison's message to the new Congress stressed that Great Britain not only refused to revoke its Orders but actually increased its demands on the United States despite "successive confirmations of the extinction of the French decrees."[38] France had passed the test of Macon's law, according to presidential decree, by expressing its willingness to respect American rights. Britain, though, persisted in its mercantile cupidity even at the expense of American sovereignty. Within the framework of a narrow hypothetical-disjunctive logic, Republicans had affirmed their worst expectations. The enemy, indeed, was bent upon America's destruction, for as Samuel McKee told his congressional colleagues:

> The law of May, 1810, was enacted with a hope that the terms thereby offered to the belligerents, respectively, would induce the one or the other to accept them, and withdraw their orders or decrees. And an expectation was also entertained, that if one of the parties could be induced to relinquish their orders or decrees, the other party would follow the example; and, if this just expectation should be met by a perseverance of either of the parties in their orders or decrees, after their adversary had accepted the invitation thus given, it would test the sincerity of the various and repeated declarations made by them, respectively, that their orders and decrees, affecting our commerce, were reluctantly issued in their own just defence.

McKee concluded, as did most Republicans, that the "fixed and determined hostility of one of the parties toward the United States would be (as it certainly now is) most clearly proved."[39]

Other arguments were presented throughout the session either to reinforce the syllogistic progression toward McKee's final conclusion or to establish further grounds for declaring war. Various observers, Winn and Reeves among them, have reported the most significant of these arguments elsewhere.[40] The point to make here, however, is that the language and logic of prowar rhetoric were essentially interdependent. The validity of a master trope had been "proved" but in the manner of logic embellishing metaphor, not the other way around. Indeed, the aura of rational demonstration was so important to literalizing the metaphor that explicit, quasi-logical proof was only one of the means found to adorn the image of British savagery. Also embedded in prowar discourse were implicit, stylistic suggestions of the case against Great Britain.

## ▮ SUGGESTIONS OF RATIONAL DEMONSTRATION

As the syllogistic argument confirming Britain's evil intentions took shape, the structure of militant discourse became assertive and its tone magisterial, especially at points where evidence regarding British and French actions was insufficient to substantiate key premises. Leading Republicans affected a declarative stance, complete with diction that purported "factuality," to compensate for a lack of corroborating facts or the existence of conflicting data. Henry Clay, for instance, announced that there was "complete proof that [Great Britain] will do every thing to destroy us."[41] The evidence was never so complete, but the full weight of his authority and credibility as Speaker of the House was committed to an unqualified, presumptive affirmation of knowledge which left doubters assuming the burden of proof.

Madison's presidential declaration of the "successive confirmations of the extinction of the French decrees" likewise insinuated, in the manner of an unqualified and authoritative assertion of truth, that the matter at hand was beyond dispute.[42] In so doing, he reinforced a premise which Republicans needed to accept if they intended to uphold the deductive line of reasoning central to their case against Britain. Without some backing of the kind afforded by Madison's statement, the premise was easily undermined by persistent reports of continuing French actions against American commerce.[43] If France's Decrees remained in force, Macon's bill provided no mechanism for condemning England. The bill, though, had authorized the president, when he determined the evidence sufficient, to certify which belligerent was no longer in violation of America's commercial rights. His magisterial authority reinforced by the decorum of a legal proclamation,

Madison institutionalized a doubtful interpretation of the situation with language that left no room for argument nor any hint of uncertainty.

Another expedient for suggesting good reasons was adopted by the House Committee on Foreign Relations. In this case, literalization was more the result of arrangement or narrative structure than of diction and declarative syntax. Calhoun, speaking for the committee, suggested the image of a determined and advancing foe by the very way he reviewed the events of the decade. To support the committee's recommendation for war, Calhoun arranged the complaints against Great Britain into a spatio-temporal sequence of increasingly direct attacks on American sovereignty. Strict chronology was ignored when, first, he complained of blockades in Europe, next of impressments at sea, then of Britain supporting Indian uprisings on the American frontier, and finally of the Henry affair involving a British "secret agent" sent to agitate against the body politic itself: In short, encroachments were arranged climactically through space and (by implication) time, progressing from the Continent to the high seas, to America's borders, to within its borders. Inferences of hostile intentions were stated more strongly with each recounting of another transgression, ending on "there is no bound to the hostility of the British Government towards the United States; no act, however unjustifiable, which it would not commit to accomplish their ruin."[44] By arrangement itself, that is, Calhoun had managed to convey spatial and chrono*logical* "evidence" of an advancing enemy and thereby to support further the image he had expressed months earlier in the metaphor of a "swelling evil." As he had warned then, the "evil still grows, and in each succeeding year swells in extent and pretension beyond the preceding."[45] From dehumanizing diction to decivilizing *dispositio,* the effect was to reinforce the claim that Britain's motives were manifestly savage.

The metaphor of force found the signs of its verification in diction, syntax, and arrangement, as well as logic. Each constituent of the rhetorical act expressed the validity of the trope, and together they transformed it into a perspective on reality. All that was required to round out the process of literalization was for prowar rhetors to establish British savagery as the only viable image of reality.

### ■ SUBVERSION OF COMPETING PERSPECTIVES

Federalists, together with a few Republican dissidents, presented a more materialistic and impersonal view of the situation than had been advocated by the majority party. The United States had a great deal to lose and very little to gain from a war with Great Britain, they reasoned, because war would not "remedy the evil which we experience."[46] The real evil was something other than British motives, something besides human volition. "The present state of the European world," Daniel Sheffey insisted, "is the primary cause from which those principles that have so seriously affected our commerce have received their origin. And to me it appears vain to expect that our neutral rights will be respected, until the causes which have subverted every venerable principle . . . shall no longer exist."[47] Circumstances, not men with evil designs, had caused Britain to impinge upon America's rights. Current circumstances had undermined the old European balance of power which previously protected the rights of weaker neutrals. Americans, Federalists argued, must adapt to new realities that were beyond their power to influence rather than delude themselves into exercising "any right to the full extent of its abstract nature." The United States must avoid "pretensions, right in theory [but] urged without due consideration of our relative power."[48] Even considering the Orders in Council, opportunities for commerce were still rich and extensive.[49] The nation must learn, Sheffey added, to acknowledge and "participate in the evils (in some shape) which have fallen on the community of civilized man."[50] In short, from the perspective of those who opposed war, the nation should adapt to the world of conditions rather than flail at illusionary evildoers supposedly out to enslave freemen. Peace was "the policy which most comported with the character, condition, and interest of the United States."[51]

Prowar Republicans attacked this opposing view of the situation in several ways, including various efforts to contradict its promise of material advantages, to neutralize its account of impersonal causality, and to predict its ruinous consequences if endorsed. Porter, for instance, argued that peace could not promise commercial prosperity, even as compensation for national submission. The effect of the Orders had been "to cut up . . . about three-fourths of our best and most profitable commerce."[52] Clay, among others, maintained that if "pecuniary considerations alone are to govern, there is sufficient motive for the war."[53] In short, Republicans claimed that the opponents of war were making false promises of peace with prosperity.

Further, Republicans argued that these same antiwar views offered a naive account of the enemy's real motives: England was driven by hostility toward the United States, not by objective circumstances beyond the control of all nations. To neutralize the view of Federalists and dissident Republicans, Calhoun turned their own argument against them. Noting that John Randolph had asked how we can "hate the country of Locke, of Newton, Hampden, and Chatham; a country having the same language and customs with ourselves, and descending from a common ancestry," Calhoun answered that "powerful indeed must be the cause which has overpowered it."[54] Americans had not jumped quickly and easily to a favored conclusion, he seemed to say, but instead had resisted the truth about satanic England until all hope for more impersonal accounts had proved false.

Not only were promises of material advantages and theories of circumstantial causes invalid, according to Republicans, but the antiwar perspective was also faulty because of the terrible consequences it could perpetrate on an unsuspecting nation if adopted. Even if, from a strictly pecuniary point of view, defense should happen to "cost more than the profit," Calhoun emphasized, a timid and "calculating avarice" must never "disgrace the seat of sovereignty" and blind the nation to "the laws of self-preservation."[55] Commercial ties were dangerous "means for estranging the affections of many from our republican institutions," Johnson added, especially while Britain harbored "her present hostile disposition."[56] And as Clay put the matter, "We are invited, conjured to drink the potion of British poison actually presented to our lips," "to submit to debasement, dishonor, and disgrace—to bow the neck to royal insolence," and to risk the nation's "freedom and independence" on the slim hope that Great Britain might abstain from "self-aggrandizement."[57] The view of antiwar spokesmen was branded as unrealistic because it required too great a risk of those who were asked to adopt it. These criticisms, combined with the Federalists' decision to minimize their participation in the debate, left the Republican vision of savagery as the dominant, most "realistic" perspective on the crisis with Great Britain.[58]

## ■ FORCE: MASTER TROPE OF PROWAR DISCOURSE

Attending to the metaphor of force and its literalization provides a key to understanding not only the justification for war in 1812 but also the development of prowar rhetoric generally. Images of savagery, which are themselves fundamental to victimage rituals, require a language which communicates the enemy's coerciveness, irrationality, and aggressiveness.[59] As is now apparent, Republicans found in the language of force just such a vehicle. Casting Great Britain into the role of a monstrous beast preying upon its innocent victim, they were able to convey a sense of urgency and inevitability about the fate awaiting America. Britain's coercive means and aggressive ends were identical; appeals to reason were futile; the drive to destroy had blinded the beast even to its own best interests. Force defined the enemy's conduct, the enemy's methods, the enemy's motives, and the victim's recourse—all to the exclusion of other possibilities. Logical forms and suggestions of rationality verified the definition and contributed to its reification as the sole view of reality. Reason was on the side of the victim, not the aggressor. The organizational base of the image of the enemy had been reduced to the metaphor of force, and war therefore seemed thoroughly just, absolutely necessary. Force was the master trope of Republican prowar discourse, the figure rhetors sought most to literalize.

To appreciate the significance of the metaphor of force and its literalization in prowar discourse more generally, it is useful to compare the language of Madison's Republicans to that of rhetors who have addressed other crisis situations. Between 1798 and 1800, for instance, the United

States faced a crisis with France over issues very similar to those which led to war with England in 1812. The conflict with France, however, did not result in a formal declaration of hostilities. It only "smoldered and sputtered," never bursting into "full flame."[60] Throughout the crisis, representatives of the Federalist majority insisted that France would "relinquish her aggressions" if the United States called the Directory's bluff.[61] America needed only to remain alert and militarily prepared while keeping open the channels of diplomacy, for the threat was one of subversion, subterfuge, and seduction, not direct physical confrontation. While acknowledging the power of the French armies, Federalists insisted the Directory lacked the will to attack directly any but the demoralized and disarmed nations of the world. As Robert G. Harper explained to his constituents, the French would not attempt to invade the United States "provided we keep up our preparations and continue to display a firm countenance. Should we be induced, by any deceitful appearance held forth by them, to relax and sink into careless security, they will think us an easy prey and, no doubt, attempt to devour us." In his view, "Our wisdom . . . consists in a state of watchful and vigorous preparation."[62]

France as the tenor of Federalist metaphors affected the image of an adversary who was far less coercive, irrational, and aggressive than Great Britain had appeared in 1812. On its periphery, the image allowed for a dimension of force, but at its center was the metaphor of seduction. Federalists did speak of the United States being "plundered" by "a nation of robbers," and did warn that "the Tyger always crouches before he leaps on his prey."[63] More fundamentally, though, these decivilizing vehicles were integrated into the nucleus of the adversary's image by repeated use of terms such as "syrens," "wiles," "sweet songs," "veils," "opiates," "hood-winked," "blinded," "enticed," "duped," "dazzled," "lull," "coax," "snare," "trick," "artifice," "schemes," and "deceit." The threat of French seduction could be met effectively by "sounding an alarm" that "opened the eyes" of those who had been "hood-winked" and "lulled to sleep" by the "opiates" of a deceitful foe. Congress was called upon "to draw aside the veil" which was "spread before the eyes of the people" in an attempt to "blind" them of the necessity for a strong defense.[64] The opposition Republicans were performing as French "syrens" by singing their "sweet, enchanting song," and French "intrigues" had been pushed even into some of the first offices of our Government.[65] There was no greater danger than from this "secret corruption," for it was "owing to this cause that all the Republics in Europe had been laid prostrate in the dust; it is this system which has enabled the French to overleap all natural and artificial obstructions; to subjugate Holland and Italy, to destroy the Helvetic Confederacy, and force a passage through rocks and mountains, which have been for ages sacred to the defence of liberty." Subverted by the seductions of "foreign agents and domestic traitors," those unfortunate republics had "crumbled into fragments" upon receiving the "slightest shock."[66] So long as the United States resisted the allure of a deadly temptress, however, and left no weak points unguarded, there was every reason to expect the danger to subside.

The French were portrayed as essentially rational adversaries who depended upon deception more than force to attain their objectives. Their advance was neither inevitable nor immune to the influence of continued diplomacy. The metaphor of force, in other words, did not dominate the image of the adversary in 1798–1800 as it did in 1812. It was instead modified by a second metaphor, thus making the call to arms that much harder to justify.

On the other hand, nearly a century and a half later Franklin Roosevelt took full advantage of decivilizing language to alert the nation to Hitler's unrelenting advance against civilization.[67] He cultivated images of storms, disease, and brutality in his "Quarantine" address at Chicago in 1937, warning that the "storm will rage till every flower of culture is trampled and all human beings are leveled in a vast chaos." The "epidemic of world lawlessness" was spreading.[68] "Storms from abroad," he added in 1939, were warnings of an enemy's "strident ambition and brute force."[69] The president compared the enemy to predaceous animals and violent criminals when, in the fireside chat of December 28, 1940, he maintained that "no man can tame a tiger into a kitten by stroking it." No nation could hope to appease the Nazis, nor would Roosevelt "pay tribute" to a "gang of outlaws" any sooner than he would condone invaders who had "attacked, overrun and thrown into the modern form of slavery" citizens of Europe.[70] The Germans were characterized in September of 1941 as "international outlaws," "raiders," and "pirates," who were "hammering" at America's rights while holding other nations "by the throat." They were the "rattlesnakes of the Atlantic," and "when you see a rattlesnake poised to strike, you do not wait until he has struck before you crush him."[71] Drawing upon still another decivilizing vehicle of force, Roosevelt condemned the "mechanized might" of the Axis nations.[72] Hitler had created a following of "puppet states," and the "forward march" of his "hordes," his "regimented masses," was designed to "mow down" the principles of common humanity.[73] Hitler's methods and Hitler's goals were one and the same. The president, in his campaign to prepare a nation for battle, had turned to the timeless archetype of force as if it were, in Michael Osborn's words, the "bedrock of symbolism," one of those "basic, unchanging patterns of experience" to which people are "unusually susceptible" during "moments of great crisis."[74]

The role of force as the master trope of prowar discourse is apparent as well in Ronald Reid's study of New England rhetoric during the French War of 1754–1760. Reid observes that British Americans portrayed France as lusting for power and as fighting in barbaric and uncivilized ways while trying to conquer North America. His hypothesis is that nations "display an amazing willingness to fight" when they "are persuaded that (1) their territory, especially the center of their territory, is endangered, (2) the enemy is a barbarian who threatens their basic values and (3) the prospects for victory are good."[75] The image of the barbarian's unrelenting advance toward the center of a nation's territory, that is, imposes upon its citizens a choice between war and submission. Literalizing the metaphor of force is the principal means of developing such a threatening image of the enemy's advance; and when the metaphor evolves into an image of savagery—thus symbolizing the antithesis of civilized values—submission requires a greater risk than most nations are willing to take, regardless of their prospects for victory. The prospects of war, compared to enslavement, seem good when attributions of evil intentions have been transformed into "facts" which no "sane" or "rational" person any longer questions.

Above all else, the function of prowar rhetoric is to establish a "realistic" image of the enemy's savagery in order to eliminate peace as a viable alternative to war. The metaphor of force is the constitutive form of that image, and the rest of prowar discourse serves largely to embellish the trope until its literalization has been completed. Decivilizing vehicles—including references to acts of nature, mechanized processes, predaceous animals, barbarous actions, and violent crimes—supply a varied set of terms that call attention to an adversary's mindless dependence upon naked power. Quasi-logical arguments, such as the hypothetical-disjunctive ratiocinations of Republicans in 1812, lend added authority to the metaphor by "verifying" its most threatening implications. Stylistic suggestions of rationality pervade the discourse of war rhetors and serve to reinforce quasi-logical arguments. And neutralizing attacks on alternative metaphors leave the master trope of force with lessened competition for its claim on reality. Operations such as these determine most directly whether the power of a single fiction will be unleashed to redescribe a whole reality, whether one metaphor will be reified to the exclusion of all others. They are the means whereby rhetors may choose to create "subjective illusions" that give immediate cause for war regardless of any other perspective from which the world of international conditions might justly be perceived.[76] No trope is inherently more understandable nor seemingly more realistic during times of crisis than that of force. When embellished by the art of rhetoric into a full-blown image of savagery, it transcends all definitions of reality and elevates every issue to a desperate struggle for survival. The act of literalizing the metaphor, that is, represents something far more substantial than a happy extra trick with words. It is the defining of reality itself.

# ▓ Notes

[1] I. A. Richards, *The Philosophy of Rhetoric* (New York: Oxford University Press, 1965), p. 90.

[2] Richards, pp. 92–93.

[3]Paul Ricoeur, *The Rule of Metaphor*, trans. Robert Czerny (Toronto: University of Toronto Press, 1977), p. 7.

[4]Ch. Perelman and L. Olbrechts-Tyteca, *The New Rhetoric: A Treatise on Argumentation*, trans. John Wilkinson and Purcell Weaver (Notre Dame: University of Notre Dame Press, 1969), p. 404.

[5]Kenneth Burke, *The Philosophy of Literary Form: Studies in Symbolic Action*, 3rd ed. (Berkeley: University of California Press, 1973), p. 152; and Kenneth Burke, *Permanence and Change: An Anatomy of Purpose*, 2nd ed. (Indianapolis: Bobbs-Merrill Company, Inc., 1965), p. 95.

[6]Kenneth Burke, *A Grammar of Motives* (1945; rpt. Berkeley: University of California Press, 1969), pp. 503–504.

[7]Robert L. Ivie, "Images of Savagery in American Justifications for War," *Communication Monographs*, 47 (1980), 279–294.

[8]Burke, *Permanence and Change*, p. 97.

[9]Dan F. Hahn, "Metaphors, Myths, and American Politics," *Et cetera*, 35 (1978), 257, 262.

[10]Roger H. Brown, *The Republic in Peril: 1812* (1964; rpt. New York: W. W. Norton and Company, Inc., 1971), p. 38.

[11]Bradford Perkins, *Prologue to War: England and the United States, 1805–1812* (Berkeley: University of California Press, 1961); and Ronald L. Hatzenbuehler and Robert L. Ivie, "Justifying the War of 1812: Toward a Model of Congressional Behavior in Early War Crises," *Social Science History*, 4 (1980), 453–477.

[12]Perkins, pp. 3, 300, 418. See also Reginald Horsman, *The Causes of the War of 1812* (Philadelphia: University of Pennsylvania Press, 1962), p. 14. In Horsman's judgment, "Actually what is really surprising is not that America declared war on England in 1812, but that she had not done so several years earlier. In many ways it is easier to show why America should have gone to war in 1807 or 1809 rather than in 1812."

[13][*Annals of Congress*] *Debates and Proceedings in the Congress of the United States, 1789–1824* (Washington, D.C.: Gales and Seaton, 1824–1856). 10th Congress, 1st Session, col. 2016. Hereafter referred to as *Annals*.

[14]Noble E. Cunningham, Jr., ed., *Circular Letters of Congressmen to Their Constituents, 1789–1829* (Chapel Hill: University of North Carolina Press, 1978), II, 10 April 1808, 552. Hereafter referred to as *Circular Letters*.

[15]*Circular Letters*, II, 29 March 1808, p. 541.

[16]*Annals*, 10th Congress, 1st Session, col. 2117.

[17]*Annals*, 10th Congress, 1st Session, col. 2045.

[18]*Annals*, 12th Congress, 1st Session, Joseph Desha, col. 487.

[19]Burwell Bassett, Letter to Joseph Prentis, 25 February 1808, Webb-Prentis Collection, University of Virginia. I am indebted to Professor Ronald Hatzenbuehler of Idaho State University for the excerpts from letters by Bassett, Gholson, and Bacon as cited here and in footnotes 29 and 36.

[20]*Annals*, 10th Congress, 2nd Session, see his remarks cols. 655, 635, 640, 637.

[21]*Circular Letters*, II, 25 February 1809, 625, 627.

[22]*Annals*, 11th Congress, 2nd Session, cols. 1301–1302, 1304–1305, 1309, 1311–1312.

[23]*Annals*, 12th Congress, 1st Session, col. 13.

[24]*Annals*, 12th Congress, 1st Session, cols. 375, 414.

[25]"To ———," 18 June 1812, *The Papers of Henry Clay*, ed. James F. Hopkins (Lexington: University of Kentucky Press, 1959), I, 674. See also "To Jesse Bledsoe," 18 June 1812, p. 675.

[26]*Annals*, 12th Congress, 1st Session, col. 415.

[27]*Annals*, 12th Congress, 1st Session, col. 503.

[28]*Annals,* 12th Congress, 1st Session, col. 482.

[29]Thomas Gholson, Letter to ———, 1812 (fragment), Brunswick Co., Va., University of Virginia.

[30]*Annals,* 12th Congress, 1st Session, John A. Harper, col. 656.

[31]Examples of American prejudices against the British are numerous. See, for instance, the discussion by Kurt W. Ritter and James R. Andrews, *The American Ideology: Reflections of the Revolution in American Rhetoric* (Falls Church, Virginia. Speech Communication Association, 1978), pp. 6–12. They argue that the strategy of American revolutionaries was to degrade the British by representing them as "literally and figuratively raping America." This was to be taken as a symptom of the moral decline of England and was designed to "wean colonists from old affections" and "to construct an image of America totally independent from (and superior to) Great Britain."

[32]*Annals,* 11th Congress, 2nd Session, Joseph Desha, col. 1312.

[33]Brown, pp. 22–25.

[34]Perelman and Olbrechts-Tyteca, pp. 193–194, discuss the concept of quasi-logical arguments.

[35]Brown, pp. 23–25; and Perkins, pp. 245–252.

[36]Ezekiel Bacon, Letter to Joseph Story, 22 October 1810, Joseph Story Collection, Library of Congress.

[37]*Annals,* 11th Congress, 3rd Session, cols. 893–894.

[38]*Annals,* 12th Congress, 1st Session, col. 11.

[39]*Annals,* 12th Congress, 1st Session, cols. 507–508.

[40]Larry James Winn, "The War Hawks' Call to Arms: Appeals for a Second War with Great Britain." *Southern Speech Communication Journal,* 37 (1972), 402–412; Clyde E. Reeves, "The Debates on the War of 1812: Parliament and Congress Compared." Diss. University of Illinois 1958.

[41]"Speech Urging Passage of the Embargo Bill," I. 1 April 1812, in *Papers of Henry Clay,* 642.

[42]*Annals,* 12th Congress, 1st Session, col. 11.

[43]Perkins, pp. 253–257.

[44]*Annals,* 12th Congress, 1st Session, col. 1552.

[45]*Annals,* 12th Congress, 1st Session, cols. 476–477.

[46]*Annals,* 12th Congress, 1st Session, Daniel Sheffey, col. 621.

[47]*Annals,* 12th Congress, 1st Session, col. 626.

[48]*Annals,* 12th Congress, 1st Session, "Address of the Minority to their Constituents," cols. 2200, 2202.

[49]*Annals,* 12th Congress, 1st Session, "Address of the Minority," col. 2207.

[50]*Annals,* 12th Congress, 1st Session, Sheffey, col. 626.

[51]*Annals,* 12th Congress, 1st Session, "Address of the Minority," col. 2198.

[52]*Annals,* 12th Congress, 1st Session, col. 415.

[53]*Annals,* 12th Congress, 1st Session, col. 599.

[54]*Annals,* 12th Congress, 1st Session, cols. 482–483.

[55]*Annals,* 12th Congress, 1st Session, col. 479.

[56]*Annals,* 12th Congress, 1st Session, col. 460.

[57]*Annals,* 12th Congress, 1st Session, col. 600.

[58]Perkins, pp. 351–353 discusses the Federalists' strategy of minimizing their participation

in the war debate in order to give Republicans ample opportunity to destroy their credibility with voters.

[59]Ivie, "Images of Savagery," pp. 284, 292.

[60]Alexander DeConde, *The Quasi-War: The Politics and Diplomacy of the Undeclared War with France, 1797–1801* (New York: Charles Scribner's Sons, 1966), p. 326.

[61]*Annals,* 5th Congress, 2nd Session, cols. 1344–1345.

[62]*Circular Letters,* I, 10 February 1799, 151; and 20 March 1799, 172.

[63]*Annals,* 5th Congress, 2nd Session, John Allen, cols. 1478, 1480; and *Circular Letters,* I, Robert G. Harper, 20 March 1799, 172.

[64]*Annals,* 5th Congress, 2nd Session, Harper, cols. 1748–1749.

[65]*Annals,* 5th Congress, 2nd Session, John Allen, col. 1482.

[66]*Annals,* 5th Congress, 2nd Session, Harrison G. Otis, cols. 2017, 1961–62.

[67]See also William E. Rickert, "Winston Churchill's Archetypal Metaphors: A Mythopoetic Translation of World War II," *Central States Speech Journal,* 28 (1977), 108–109.

[68]Samuel I. Rosenman, ed., *The Public Papers and Addresses of Franklin D. Roosevelt* (New York: Harper and Brothers, 1950), VI, 407, 408, 410.

[69]Rosenman, VIII, 1–2.

[70]Rosenman, IX, 636, 638, 639.

[71]Rosenman, X, 385, 387, 389, 390.

[72]Rosenman, X, 526.

[73]Rosenman, X, 439, 441, 443, 444.

[74]Michael Osborn, "Archetypal Metaphor in Rhetoric: The Light-Dark Family," *Quarterly Journal of Speech,* 53 (1967), 115, 119–120, 125.

[75]Ronald F. Reid, "New England Rhetoric and the French War, 1754–1760: A Case Study in the Rhetoric of War," *Communication Monographs,* 43 (1976), 269–270, 284.

[76]Quincy Wright, *A Study of War,* 2nd ed. (Chicago: University of Chicago Press, 1965), p. 1503. For his analysis of the war-justifying role of symbols in general and the theme of diabolism in particular, see pp. 1083–1103.

# CHAPTER 12 ⬜

## PREMILLENNIAL APOCALYPTIC

**Barry Brummett**

*In this commentary, Barry Brummett stresses the importance of theory in his own criticism. Yet Brummett is by no means a slave to method. His commentary uses words like "faith" and "hunch" to describe the attitude with which he approaches texts and begins the tentative process of selecting a theoretical approach to his text. Brummett's study of premillennialist rhetoric exemplifies his faith in action—the theoretical approach settled on in that study is reached only after some experimentation with ways of reading the text suggested by other theories.*

## COMMENTARY

My interest in apocalyptic rhetoric spans a number of published articles and convention papers. The essay in this book was my first article on the subject. My latest effort is a book. In negotiating with various publishers over bringing that book out, I was asked by one editor why I became interested in apocalyptic discourse in the first place. It was a loaded question, because the *subject matter* of apocalyptic, especially *contemporary* apocalyptic rhetoric, is not what one might call "respectable" in the academic tradition. People who truly believe that the world is about to end are considered on the cultural and intellectual fringe by many people, *especially* by mainstream academics. Indeed, when I first submitted the essay in this book to an academic journal, one reviewer sent back a downright abusive tirade questioning why anyone would want to study the discourse of (in his or her words) crazy people.

Because the editor's query was a loaded question, it put me on the spot. And perhaps for the same reason, I had not given much conscious thought to the question before. I was being asked why I became interested in the subject matter, but because of the sensitive nature of that subject matter, I was being asked to explain *myself*. In that moment, the relationship between the critic as a professional analyst and the critic as a person was brought to the foreground. That is the relationship that I think is or should be central to the critical process, and a relationship that I would like to feature in these remarks.

For me, criticism has always been the product of personal involvement and theoretical inspiration. Good criticism, I believe, requires both. The criticisms I have published have always concerned subject matters that I cared about strongly: political rhetors or groups or movements that I admired or despised; rhetorical situations that I found fascinating or intriguing; forms of literature, movies, or television that I personally enjoy. The same was true of apocalyptic discourse. Because of my religious upbringing and beliefs, I have always been aware of apocalyptic themes, although not as a *primary* concern. I understood that these ideas were the preoccupations of certain subgroups, if not my own, within the larger Church. I have always been fascinated by people who express their personal fears and obsessions by cloaking them in terms and symbols belonging to another order of discourse. I believe that this is what opponents of gay rights do in appropriating religious discourse to express their aesthetic preferences, for instance, and of course I argue that apocalyptic discourse does the same. Not being a very risky person myself, I am both awed and appalled by those who risk their rhetorical "all," as so many apocalyptics do in committing themselves to specific dates for the end of the world.

But there have been many subject matters that I have not addressed in criticism even though I found them personally fascinating. In the early 1980s, several African American children in Atlanta were killed by an unknown assailant. The circumstances resembled the earlier "Zebra" killings in San Francisco, a subject that I *had* studied, and so several people suggested to me that I write about Atlanta. I found the *subject* horribly fascinating, but I was and I remain *theoretically* uninspired. That is to say, I could think of no systematic explanation or way of thinking about the Atlanta murders that would generate insights about that experience. I could find no methodical way (or method, if you like) of saying something beyond the obvious about those murders. And so I left them alone.

By *theory* here I mean a system for understanding experience, usually involved in a set of questions or issues to consider that a person can apply to some subject matter so as to gain a better understanding of the subject matter. There are theories for everything: I have a theory for how to start my old blue clunker of a car and for why it does *not* start sometimes; I have a theory about what is eating the bean plants in my garden and for how to stop it; and there are many theories of how discourse works in life. Those last theories are what I use to say something about my experience of communication.

I do criticism when I experience the conjunction of both a real personal involvement in a subject matter *and* a realization that some theoretical explanation fits that subject matter and can be used (by me) to say something interesting and insightful about it. Typically, the beginning of the critical process involves a dialectic between those two prerequisites. I am unable to say which of the two comes first. Usually, I will read some interesting news item, and I will think about what it means, what the implications are, what is going on in the deeper levels of discourse about the item. And then it will come to me that a theory that I have read recently, or about which I have *also* been thinking, has some relevance to that news item. It seems to me that I could fit the two together and, in the process, say something new and interesting about the subject. But was it my ongoing thinking about the theory that directed my attention to that news item in the first place? I don't know.

I don't know the answer to that question because I think that a lot of criticism is saved by *faith* alone, in advance of works. In the early stages of many studies, I have simply had a hunch that I would be able to say something non-obvious or interesting about what was going on in some kinds of discourse. I had faith that the theory I was using would help me to notice things that others had not. I had faith that the subject matter was sufficiently deep and complex to allow new insights to be brought out of it. But I have never been able to see my way clearly to the end of any study when I was just beginning it, and the apocalyptic essay is no exception.

In the present essay, I began with a fascination for several apocalyptic texts that were currently popular, such as *The Late Great Planet Earth* or several pamphleteers who were setting specific dates for the apocalypse. I wanted to understand that discourse better, but I was unaware of a theoretical framework that would help me to do so. So I turned to other scholars of apocalyptic, and read widely in their commentaries. It seemed to me as if writers such as McGinn, Tuveson, and Barkun were discussing issues directly related to rhetoric without making that link clear. At the same time, I had been thinking about Karlyn Kohrs Campbell and Kathleen Jamieson's theory of rhetorical genres. Gradually, it became clear that Campbell and Jamieson could be used to make nonrhetorical theory serve rhetorical ends, to make the apocalyptic scholars I had been reading "talk" about apocalyptic as a rhetorical genre. With that realization came Campbell and Jamieson's *structure* of situational, substantive, and stylistic hallmarks of a genre. And that structure then provided an organized way to look at apocalyptic. I could then return to the subject matter and reconfigure/reconceptualize it following the structure provided by the categories of the theory.

The structure that theory provides constitutes the set of questions that the critic asks about the subject matter so as to generate insights about it. Useful criticism is, for me, not simply a wallow in a text. It is guided by an order inherent in a theory. The resulting act of criticism, whether it emerges in a paper or simply in an insight held by the critic, is a rewriting and reordering of the subject matter so as to see it more clearly. The naive observer experiences life, but the critic lays the template of a theory over life and says, "If you see it *this* way, additional levels of meaning and significance emerge."

The essays you read in this book are by academics, all of us professional rhetorical critics. We publish the results of our studies in scholarly journals and books, which are largely read by other academics. What's the point? The question is crucial to how criticism is done. Many of us begin our careers being motivated to publish criticism so as to get tenure, to be blunt about it. But that motivation cannot sustain the critical enterprise, personally or even institutionally. I think that considering what value lies within the whole enterprise of rhetorical criticism helps us to understand how the process itself works.

The value in rhetorical criticism lies in returning to that conjunction of the personal and professional with which I began these remarks. Rhetorical criticism should help people to understand their experience more richly, to see levels of meaning and significance that they would not have seen before, and to instill in people habits or techniques of "reading" discourse. Several implications follow from that claim.

Criticism must be *generalizable*. The reader must be enabled to use the criticism so as to understand other experiences better. For that to happen, the way or pattern of understanding that is embodied in the theory must be generalizable. If the reader is enabled only to understand the particular apocalyptic texts studied in my essay, then I think it has failed. If the reader can better understand a new set of texts she encounters next week, so much the better. And if the reader acquires an expanded repertoire of ways to understand all sorts of texts, apocalyptic or not, that would be best of all. Generalizability comes from theory, not subject matter.

Criticism is not necessarily concerned with *accuracy*. I have made several assertions about what is going on in apocalyptic discourse. This will sound strange, but whether those things are "really" going on is beside the point, it seems to me. The reason is that, as noted in the paragraph just above, I don't really care whether you understand Tim LaHaye's book better now. What I want my essay to do is to give you "practice" using a conceptual structure (the theory) to help you to see meanings in experience more richly. As long as that structure helps you to see meanings in experience *generally*, I don't care whether it is entirely accurate about the meanings in the focal experience that the criticism is "about."

Criticism must be *disseminated*. I am personally unhappy with the prospect of the critical essays I have written moldering away in journals, because to the extent that they do, then my criticism cannot help people to experience life more fully and richly. Academics ought not to be content with mere academic publication. Criticism should be passed on to as many people as possible. The best route that academics have for reaching the public is, obviously, students. I have used the apocalyptic essay, and every other criticism I have ever published, in my classes: I have taught my students using the criticisms of others. I have used techniques and insights of criticism to write opinion pieces for local papers, thus passing on ways of understanding experience through that avenue.

The personal and the professional can be paired, respectively, with subject matter and theory, or with real life involvement and the ability to say interesting things about that involvement. So I will end on the theme with which I began. Good criticism talks to you about what you have experienced, but it tells you that there is more to see than you have suspected. It shows you something more, and sends you out to live with ears and eyes that are more widely opened.

# Premillennial Apocalyptic
# as a Rhetorical Genre

**Barry Brummett**

This essay describes as a rhetorical genre *apocalyptic,* that branch of eschatological discourse which holds that the world will end with a bang.[1] Apocalyptic discourse bemoans the distressing state of the world, predicts a radical end to this epoch by way of cosmic, total, cataclysmic change (the arrival of the Messiah, return of Christ, etc.) and foresees a *millennium*—the establishment of a radically new order in which good and righteousness are triumphant.[2] Familiar ancient examples are the *Book of Daniel* and *The Revelation to St. John.*

Although some writers ignore the distinction,[3] most scholars divide apocalyptic into two camps, premillennialism (millenarianism) and postmillennialism (utopianism). Premillennialists believe that the Change, the apocalypse, will come very soon and must happen *before* the millennium can occur. Postmillennialists expect the apocalypse, whether the return of Christ, the ultimate perfection of human nature, or some other culmination to come *after* the millennium.[4] The rhetoric of postmillennialists is tame, even noncommittal, concerning the apocalypse itself, since it may not occur for many centuries. Postmillennial apocalyptic also tends to merge into other genres. Thus, this essay will focus on the rhetoric of the more explicit and distinct premillennials or millenarians, whose discourse trembles with the thrill of impending doom. I shall use "apocalyptic" to mean the premillennial sort, unless otherwise noted.

First, I shall briefly explain what I mean by a genre, show how apocalyptic is distinct from its generic neighbor the jeremiad, and indicate why apocalyptic may need to be treated as an umbrella term for sub-genres in future research. Second, the bulk of the essay explains why apocalyptic's situational and substantive characteristics qualify it as a genre.[5] This essay should enable critics to identify apocalyptic rhetoric and to understand better how discourses of the genre appeal to their audiences.

## I

The idea of genre recently has excited much interest among rhetorical critics.[6] In claiming that apocalyptic is a genre, I shall defend a view of genre which sees it not merely as a convenience of classification but as an aid to understanding and explanation. Campbell and Jamieson argue that "the rhetorical forms that establish genres are stylistic and substantive responses to perceived situational demands."[7] Following Campbell and Jamieson, I shall argue that apocalyptic is a genre of discourses which address one *type* of perceived situational exigency with consistent forms of rhetorical style and substantive argument. I shall treat style and substance as a single complex category because of their close interrelation.

Apocalyptic is a genre that is distinct from its nearest generic neighbor, the jeremiad. Ronald Carpenter, in "The Historical Jeremiad as Rhetorical Genre," defines his subject as "a secular treatise which accomplishes its goals rhetorically by a process leading readers to view themselves as a chosen people confronted with a timely if not urgent warning that unless a certain course of atoning action is followed, dire consequences will ensue."[8] Apocalyptic is different from the jeremiad on several counts: (1) Apocalyptic sees dire consequences as inevitable; there is no question of atoning, although there is the possibility of preparing. Apocalyptists await The End, not the fulfillment of a mission in this world. (2) Apocalyptic always includes an expectation of the millennium; thus, the dire consequences are welcomed. (3) Carpenter argues that the jeremiad "achieves its objectives indirectly, through the reader's imaginative interpretation of the treatise." Kurt W. Ritter's review of the jeremiad makes the same argument.[9] But apocalyptic is indirect, it is quite explicit, and recent apocalyptic is even more explicit than traditional.[10]

Sacvan Bercovitch defines the jeremiad as the "political sermon."[11] Bercovitch seems to be using the term "jeremiad" sometimes to refer to postmillennial apocalyptic, with its emphasis on repentance, atonement, progress, and the gradual transformation of this era into the millennium,[12] whereas this essay examines the premillennialists.

Finally, although I shall show that premillennial apocalyptic always addresses the same sort of audience experiencing the same sort of exigency, with similar rhetorical strategies, future research may reveal that apocalyptic is actually an umbrella term for several sub-genres. That is because the specific purposes to which apocalyptic rhetoric is put vary widely; each separate rhetorical intention might define a sub-genre. For instance, some scholars argue that apocalyptic provokes social action, and they point to the millenarianism of Roger Williams.[13] Others argue that apocalyptic encourages passive withdrawal from society, while still others argue that it has caused both reactions.[14] Some scholars argue that apocalyptic is subversive, and point to its role in fomenting the American Revolution as well as to its customary stance as a heresy against established religions.[15] Others argue that apocalyptic has often been used by established governments, or has been apolitical, or has been both subversive and conservative.[16] This essay, however, considers the rhetorical force of the larger genre of premillennial apocalyptic. For whatever social or political purpose it furthers, apocalyptic is used "to spur the reader" rhetorically in the direction one would spur him or her,[17] and this essay shows why and how.

In the next section, I shall examine scholarly reviews of original texts in the Judeo-Christian tradition, up to about 1900. Although few of these scholars give as much as a nod to apocalyptic as rhetorical, I shall recast their findings into a rhetorical perspective.[18] To demonstrate that apocalyptic is neither outmoded nor purely religious, I shall also examine some selected examples of recent religious[19] and civil[20] apocalyptic.

## II

### Situational Characteristics

Scholars of apocalyptic have consistently identified a common exigency which apocalyptic addresses. Apocalyptic is always a response to meaninglessness, failure of points of reference, and bewilderment about how to understand the present. That exigency also defines the audience for apocalyptic. The audience is the isolated individuals, subgroups, or even whole cultures who suffer from acute anomie. Scholars of apocalyptic agree almost universally that it arises in response to "the collapse of a well-ordered world view which defines values and orders the universe for a people, thrusting them in the unchartered chaos of anomie and meaninglessness."[21] One experiences the present time as one of "broken continuities,"[22] in which important values, groups, and patterns of life are subject to unpredictable change.[23]

A brief look at periods of flourishing apocalyptic shows them to be times of social and physical change, in which old systems of meaning could no longer explain the world. Jewish apocalyptic flourished during the troubling times of the Captivity[24] and again "between the testaments" in response to the twin challenges of Rome and Christ.[25] The Reformation forced re-examination of religion, and so caused apocalyptic discourse.[26] The French Revolution provoked political uncertainty, an exigency that prompted apocalyptic.[27] The period around the American Civil War brought forth profuse apocalyptic, for "people at every level of society felt the passing of the old order and sought in various ways to restore for themselves some kind of power, order, security, and personal meaning under fast-changing conditions."[28]

Barkun argues that "disasters" are the source of apocalyptic, for these "movements almost always occur in times of upheaval, in the wake of cultural contact, economic dislocation, revolution, war, and natural catastrophe."[29] What makes an event or circumstance a "disaster" is not the gravity of the times in any absolute sense but rather the *perception* that things have gotten out of human *control*.[30] It is the human reaction of "anxiety and insecurity" that calls forth apocalyptic—not crisis itself but a failure of received ways of coping with crisis.[31] Thus, although 18th-century England experienced less change than did other eras which saw much apocalyptic, the lack of a cultural ability to assimilate and chart change called forth the doomsday rhetoric.[32]

Recent religious apocalyptic is also explicitly addressed to those with a sense of anomie and doom. Its proponents see the world "on a collision course,"[33] and feel that "man's problems have grown too great for him to solve."[34] This sense of hopelessness and loss of control is felt as the harbinger of "the greatest devastation that man has ever brought upon himself. Mankind will be at the brink of self-annihilation when Christ suddenly returns to put an end to the war of wars called Armageddon."[35] Despair has reached a crisis, for "objectively considered, it seems that we have indeed come to that day."[36] Civil apocalyptic's audience is explicitly identified as suffering the exigency of anomie and meaningless: "You are reading this book because you are perceptive enough to sense that something is terribly wrong out there,"[37] or perhaps "you have a vague, general feeling that things aren't exactly right."[38]

### Stylistic-Substantive Characteristics

Apocalyptic counteracts the exigency of meaninglessness and anomie in very much the same way each time. At the most basic level, premillennial apocalyptic always includes the three main themes of bemoaning the present, expecting the imminent apocalypse, and foreseeing a golden millennium. To develop those themes, the twin strategies of creating a system of meaning and building a sense of community are employed.

*A system of meaning.* Apocalyptic typically offers its audience a system of meaning to replace that being lost. Substantive arguments designed to explain the apocalyptic meaning system are geared to *purpose* and *control.*

Apocalyptic argues that the universe is guided by a purpose or destiny and that the events of this life manifest the unfolding of that purpose: "To the apocalyptist history is presented as a continuity which can be viewed as a whole, is complete, and is moving toward a goal."[39] History has a meaning because no event lies outside a predetermined pattern of development, guided by a cosmic purpose. Typically, apocalyptic identifies that purpose explicitly; in both old and new religious apocalyptic the purpose is the will of God.[40] Some scholars have traced all teleological thinking in the West to ancient apocalyptic's view of history as purposive.[41]

When one lives and where that era falls in the development of history are all-important. Burke argues that a hallmark of mystic or purpose-oriented discourse is the identification of the individual with the unfolding pattern of history.[42] Apocalyptic addresses what is happening to the audience *now*, it describes their particular situation as the warm-up act to the

Main Event, presaging the culmination of historical purpose. Apocalyptic thus imbues its audience with a sense of urgency about present events.[43] This sense of the present as special can be seen in the ancient Hebrews, who saw their own history as fitting into the overall pattern and who expected the Messiah momentarily.[44] So also did the apocalyptic Puritans in England and America see their own time as history's culmination.[45]

Civil apocalyptic also defines a purposive force driving history toward the end predicted: "The trends are irreversibly beyond the point of no return."[46] They are "the natural laws of cause-and-effect"[47] or "the law of consequences" appointed by God Himself.[48] Since the forces of history invoked are "immutable law," civil apocalyptic is highly deterministic.[49] For Ruff, the purpose that is driving events is the cycle of inflation which must complete itself.[50] Abert sees cycles in history as well,[51] but his purpose is a cycle of overconsumption and overproduction. Smith offers an historical review designed to show the effects of debasing the currency, hyperinflation, which is the source of present woes.[52] Hackett blames the impending war on the "inexorable advance of Marxism-Leninism" and on "Russian imperialist expansionism."[53]

A second form of argument promises control over meaninglessness. Recall that apocalyptic addresses a psychological exigency, not mere disaster but disaster for which people have no symbolic remedy. Thus, the control over events that apocalyptic restores is symbolic rather than practical. By naming the present time and its overwhelming problems as special in the Great Plan, apocalyptic helps people to gain symbolic control over their difficulties and to celebrate them, in three ways. Apocalyptic restores control, first, by giving people a better understanding of their present difficulties which had seemed so enormous and beyond comprehension. Apocalyptic "beliefs provide both an explanation of the present state of things and an indication of how it will be resolved."[54] One's present difficulties and confusions are given "validation by incorporation into a transcendental scheme of meaning."[55] As a "form of explanation," apocalyptic tells "us why we are in the dreadful circumstances of the present."[56] Apocalyptic gives one a familiar and predictable set of coordinates by which to chart the unfamiliar and capricious present. And by forecasting an imminent and radical change of circumstances, followed by a golden period of vindication for the righteous, apocalyptic reconciles one to present troubles not only as temporary but as tickets to future rewards.[57]

Specific causes of anomie are explicitly mentioned by apocalyptic so that they can be encompassed within a system of meaning. Referring to the Israeli occupation of Jerusalem as a prediction of the Bible, Lindsey explicitly argues for the meaning-giving function of apocalyptic: "It is like the key piece of a jigsaw puzzle being found and then having the many adjacent pieces rapidly fall into place."[58]

Civil apocalyptic always includes "a grisly list of unpleasant events"[59] in the near future, "the likes of which the world has never seen."[60] These woes are explained by and proof of the orderly force of purpose in history. "The nation is about to undergo its greatest test since the Civil War,"[61] a test that will include civil collapse and martial law, "labor strikes, commercial turmoil, international trade wars, urban strife, food riots and, sometimes, shooting wars."[62] Repressive government countermeasures and international chaos are ahead.[63] "It is too late for us to avoid the economic crisis that looms just ahead,"[64] a crisis that promises "total destruction."[65] Hackett foresees the world entering a third world war which will include the collapse of nations and the nuclear destruction of some cities.[66] Yet these woes are explained and given meaning by being incorporated into the apocalyptic meaning system.

A second sense in which apocalyptic provides audiences with a sense of control and meaning is in its reading of the signs of impending doom. Apocalyptic allows its audience a measure of control over their problems by demonstrating techniques of reading them *as signs*.[67] To corroborate the evidence of one's personal woes, apocalyptic points to signs "in which the laws of nature appeared to have been set aside, any abnormal or inexplicable happening."[68]

The signs of the apocalypse are always understood as ambiguous and figurative.[69] They require interpretation. Apocalyptic employs a dogmatic style which insists that its interpretation of the end signs must be true.[70] The reading of the signs is often not done by rational demonstration but by vivid dramatization. Apocalyptic relies on story and drama to present the interpretations to an audience: "Such beliefs are incapable of rational demonstration; they can only be revealed, that is, presented or manifested in symbolic and dramatic forms."[71]

Bipolar dramatization is highly rhetorical insofar as it serves political ends in *this* world. Luther's enemies were the Church of Rome and the Turks, and so he identified those parties with the monsters of *The Revelation to St. John*.[72] Seventeenth-century England saw itself as a latter day Israel fulfilling the Jews' original contract with God and its enemies in a correspondingly Satanic role.[73] The ancient Jews identified their persecutors among the Gentiles as the prophesied signs and agents of the end.[74] Apocalyptic served political purposes for both North and South during the American Reconstruction and was used by the early settlers of America to justify inhabiting the new world and suppressing its natives.[75]

The dogmatic reading of the signs is important to recent discourse. Lindsey argues that "the Bible contains clear and unmistakable prophetic signs,"[76] and McBirnie similarly notes that "Jesus said there would be many clear, visible signs of his Return."[77] In identifying contemporary events as those predicted by esoteric Biblical prophecy, this discourse describes the difficulties experienced by its audience as signs of the end: religious apostasy, war, national revolutions, earthquakes, famines, etc.

Religious apocalyptic is used today rhetorically to motivate actions and attitudes in pursuit of secular ends. Lindsey interprets Biblical prophecy as identifying the Soviet Union, China, Arabs, Libya, etc., as agents of Satan.[78] McBirnie identifies as demonic portents the World Council of Churches, drug abuse, and the European Economic Community.[79]

Reading the signs for the public is a central argument of civil apocalyptic. Ruff reviews the "signs that controls are coming" from the government.[80] Abert offers long lists of signs, not only economic problems but every other sort of distress from depletion of the ozone to astrological wonders, bad weather, and contemporary religious practice. He provides a list of specific signs of the end, any three of which will mean the apocalypse is upon us.[81] Smith's fifth chapter is a heavily documented catalogue of signs that the collapse is near, and he insulates these signs from counterargument by claiming that "informed, intelligent observers should not be deceived by interludes of moderation in money and price inflation rates into believing that the long-run acceleration toward hyper-inflation has been halted or reversed."[82] Hackett indulges in long lists of bureaucratic acronyms to rival the most mysterious signs of *Revelation*, and also claims that "the warning was as clear as any given by Hitler before the Second World War."[83]

Civil apocalyptic addresses political and social issues through interpretation of signs. Ruff, perhaps influenced by his Mormon background, sprinkles his book with arguments in support of families and against women's liberation and extra-marital sex. He even translates the Latter Day Saints' doctrine of storing enough food for one year into purely practical advice for weathering the apocalypse.[84] Abert extends his apocalyptic warnings into social advice, counseling his audience on "How to Have a Healthful Kitchen" and advising them to lose weight, eat brewers' yeast, etc. He stresses the need not only to grow one's own food but to do so organically.[85] Smith grinds his axe against government regulations and calls for their complete dismantling.[86] Hackett, a British general, uses his apocalyptic in a self-serving way to trumpet "the United Kingdom, a country of critical importance to the Alliance," and he sees the climax of the coming war as the nuclear destruction, not of Chicago or New York, but of Birmingham, England.[87]

A third sense in which apocalyptic provides audiences with control is in its promise of a new order that will not fail or turn incomprehensible. The present age will be removed "totally, favorably, and summarily,"[88] through a "sudden and spectacular change."[89] "A more perfect order" will follow the change, radically different from the present.[90] Because the new age is ushered in by sanction of Ultimate Meaning, it can be counted on; its stability and imperviousness to decay make it grounds for a new order that will not fail. The new order vouchsafed for the community of the elect in religious apocalyptic truly is millennial, for "wrong will ultimately fall"[91] and "God's kingdom will be characterized by peace and equity, and by universal spirituality and knowledge of the Lord."[92]

Civil apocalyptic follows the genre closely in its depiction of the millennium, the good times, which follow the apocalypse. Hackett foresees the disintegration of the Soviet Union, which will end the war and usher in a time of peace, prosperity, and international cooperation.[93] For economically troubled citizens, Abert claims that "once you have taken the steps outlined in this book, I can assure you that you will observe the darkening clouds of economic and social disorder with a kind of serene confidence that conveys to everyone that you are managing your own tomorrow."[94] Other economic writers claim that "if enough of us do the right thing, we may come out of this stronger than we went into it," because "this can be a time of great opportunity right now, and more times of opportunity will come when things bottom out."[95] Others contend that "it is quite likely that a few simple preparations and adjustments by those who anticipate the future will result not only in survival, but prosperity in the brave new world that follows."[96] Life after the apocalypse will be idyllic in ways that go beyond economic issues: "People will eventually find themselves returning to an 'old time' morality, with the pace being slower, simpler, virtues being emphasized, greater respect for nature," etc. In short, civil apocalyptic comforts an audience disaffected with the present order by promising that "a new order of life will be established."[97]

*A builder of communities.* Apocalyptic pictures the world in bipolar terms as a dramatic conflict between good and evil, God and Satan, Jews and Gentiles. Dramatization constructs in-groups and out-groups because it turns around antagonist and protagonist: "Apocalyptic presentation is highly dramatic in form. In its desire to present a picture of the conflict between good and evil, the apocalyptic text deliberately creates . . . a set of easily visualized scenes and strongly drawn characters that because of their imaginative power remain fixed in the reader's mind."[98]

Bipolar dramatization, by giving them no middle ground, enlists the audience on the side of good. Since the apocalypse will settle the struggle favorably for the good and disastrously for the evil, it is by way of group membership that people's fates will be determined. The apocalypse and its signs are only revealed to a special group and they ultimately reward only that group.[99] This attitude of the elect as special is exemplified by the collective self-consciousness and self-examination of the Puritans.[100] Thus, a frequent feature of apocalyptic rhetoric is the belief that the elect will be taken out of the world, "raptured," to spare them the tribulation befalling the damned.[101] Apocalyptic movements usually have been in the minority throughout history, a status often explicitly encouraged because it reinforces the uniqueness of the elect.[102]

Contemporary religious apocalyptic also uses the traditional community-building strategy. McBirnie urges his audience to see themselves as "God's spiritual 'remnant.' These spiritually alive people bear all the responsibility for God's work in the world at this time."[103] Only these few, the "Bible-believing Christians," will escape the trauma of the end.[104] The rest of humanity will not be saved, and thus this discourse relies heavily on the bipolar dramatizations of traditional discourse.[105]

Civil apocalyptic also functions as a builder of communities, although I shall argue at the end of this paper that in this respect it sometimes differs from traditional form. Abert urges the formation of teams of survivalists, and he gives several plans for the construction of whole communities set apart from the world, a civil equivalent of the "rapture."[106] Other apocalyptists make entry into the community of the elect easy, for one need not "be terribly smart if you can identify the basic trends and make some very simple decisions."[107] Civil apocalyptic uses the traditional appeal of being a minority, warning that "you too may be laughed at if you begin now to make preparations,"[108] but that this community is of special importance, for "it is always a minority that changes the course of a civilization" and "there is little hope in sight for the brainwashed adult majority."[109] For those who may be drawn to this discourse by dissatisfaction with identities that are based on old systems of meaning, some civil apocalyptic offers "A New You" if you will join the elect.[110]

The building of civil communities is stylistically enhanced with bipolar dramatizations. An Enemy is always named. Hackett, of course, pits NATO against the Warsaw Pact. Ruff blames political leaders who are "acting in their own economic or political self-interest, are fools, or are just plain wrong."[111] Smith also blames government officials as "inflationists,"[112] and refers to them as "the Washington gang."[113]

Apocalyptic movements often cluster around a prophet who guides the interpreting of the signs and serves as the magnet around which the community of the elect will draw.[114] Traditional religious apocalyptic built communities around someone who had a claim to a prophet's or priest's stature. Recent religious apocalyptic also stresses the reverend qualifications of its authors.

Holding an exclusive key to the mystery of historical purpose validates the claims of civil rhetors and sets them above the usual run of pundits as prophets around which a community of the elect could rally. So it is quite common to find civil apocalyptists claiming that with the exception of them and their followers, "few of us understand the process,"[115] that "most financial advisers don't understand money" and "most [investors], novices and professional alike, lack knowledge of either monetary history or economic science. Thus, they do not understand what's happening, where it will lead, or what to do about it."[116] Hackett makes the same charge about military and political leaders regarding the upcoming Armageddon.[117]

### ■ III

Traditionally, those premillennialists who reject progress have been a minority in an otherwise optimistic society. However, in the past few years social observers have noted a more general disillusionment with progress in our society. This rejection of progress may be exacerbated by the fact that television can make us all vicarious victims of disaster. If apocalyptic arises from the ashes of progress, but if more and more people have lost faith in progress, then is the majority of our society becoming predisposed to premillennial apocalyptic appeals?

A number of observers also have noted that most of the disasters which befell humankind in the past were natural disasters: flood, fire, earthquake, famine.[118] Although traditional apocalyptic was certainly aware of the role of people in bringing about disaster such as war, it emphasized natural misfortunes. But in our time we have tamed nature and found it to be more or less predictable. Recent apocalyptic seems to place more of an emphasis on human-made disasters. Many of the economic woes of civil apocalyptic are brought on by inept or malicious government officials. Wilder and Hanson note that ancient apocalyptic was objective and communal: salvation happened to people as a group and came to them from a source outside themselves.[119] Modern apocalyptic, these authors claim, is subjective: people are saved individually, by themselves, and often as a result of their own efforts. While my review of modern apocalyptic shows Wilder and Hanson to be too extreme in drawing such a rigid distinction between ancient and modern, it does seem that some recent apocalyptic includes more elements which are personal or subjective. We often hear these days of Christ referred to as a "personal savior," Ruff and others advocate that each family or person should privately store food and gold for the coming collapse, etc. This emerging feature of subjectivity, put together with the feature of a human source of disaster, leads to this question: Is modern apocalyptic coming to define communities of people as the problem rather than the solution, as the cause of the end rather than as a locus of salvation? Have the Soviet Union and government bureaucrats replaced the plague as preeminent signs of the end?

If these questions are answered in the affirmative, modern apocalyptic may become self-fulfilling. No amount of ancient lamentation about an earthquake or an illness that would end the world would bring on the misfortune. But modern apocalyptic may breed in people the sort of mistrust and hatred of others that will bring on precisely the end foretold. If we expect the Soviet Union to be the Beast, we are likely to take measures which will ensure that it becomes exactly that. More studies are needed to examine the effects of apocalyptic, studies that can warn us if the rhetoric becomes self-fulfilling. Future research into apocalyptic must answer the question, Can our world still afford this venerable symbolic remedy for humanity's misfortune?

# ▓ Notes

¹Literally, apocalypse means revelation or lifting of the veil. John C. Heald, "Apocalyptic Rhetoric: Agents of Anti-Christ from the French to the British," *Today's Speech,* 23 (1975), 33; Bernard McGinn, *Visions of the End* (New York: Columbia University Press, 1979), p. 2.

²J. F. C. Harrison, *The Second Coming* (New Brunswick, N.J.: Rutgers University Press, 1979), p. 8; McGinn, p. 6. Postmillennialists alter the order of that sequence; see below.

³Michael Barkun, *Disaster and the Millennium* (New Haven: Yale University Press, 1974), p. 2.

⁴See Harrison, p. 7, and Ernest Lee Tuveson, *Millennium and Utopia* (Berkeley: University of California Press, 1949), pp. vii, 7–14. Norman Cohn describes Nazism and Marxism as postmillennial ideologies in *The Pursuit of the Millennium* (New York: Oxford University, 1970).

⁵This essay's goals also need to be distinguished from two other works on apocalyptic rhetoric in the field of communication. Heald's article, *op cit.,* is an interesting review of some historical, secular uses made of apocalyptic; it does not attempt to describe apocalyptic generally as a genre, or to apply such analysis to contemporary discourse. William L. Burke, in "Notes on a Rhetoric of Lamentation," *Central States Speech Journal,* 30 (1979), 109–121, does review some recent apocalyptic rhetoric. He does not, however, systematically outline clear rhetorical characteristics of the genre, nor does he link present apocalyptic to the historical tradition which helps to explain it. In consequence, although he promises to reveal its "symbolic dynamics," he offers mainly a descriptive review of apocalyptic without giving in-depth reasons why it should be expected to arouse commitment.

⁶Karlyn Kohrs Campbell and Kathleen Jamieson, *Form and Genre* (Falls Church, Va.: SCA, 1978); Walter R. Fisher, "Genre: Concepts and Applications in Rhetorical Criticism," *Western Journal of Speech Communication,* 44 (1980), 288–299; Thomas M. Conley, "Ancient Rhetoric and Modern Genre Criticism," *Communication Quarterly,* 27 (1979), 47–53.

⁷Campbell and Jamieson, p. 19. Conley argues persuasively that rhetorical genres must include formal elements that go beyond messages alone, and suggests that audience expectations define genres (p. 47). Bruce Gronbeck, in "Celluloid Rhetoric: On Genres of Documentary," in Campbell and Jamieson, p. 155, argues that genres are made of message characteristics plus extra-textual considerations which he calls "sociocultural rules." Conley's expectations and Gronbeck's rules seem very similar, and I would like to consider them both under the heading of what Campbell and Jamieson called "perceived situational demands." This essay follows the position that the rhetorical situation is defined by the perceptions of the parties to a rhetorical transaction.

⁸In Campbell and Jamieson, p. 104.

⁹Kurt W. Ritter, "American Political Rhetoric and the Jeremiad Tradition: Presidential Nomination Acceptance Addresses, 1960–1976," *Central States Speech Journal,* 31 (1980), 153–171. Carpenter, p. 104.

¹⁰These three distinctions may be illustrated in Jonathan Schell's "Reflections (Nuclear Arms—Part I)": "Extinction by nuclear arms would not be the Day of Judgment, in which God destroys the world but raises the dead and then metes out perfect justice to everyone who has ever lived; it would be the utterly meaningless and completely unjust destruction of mankind by men." Schell's mournful article is a jeremiad; the argument he describes and attacks is apocalyptic. In *The New Yorker,* 8 February 1982, p. 69. Reprinted in Jonathan Schell, *The Fate of the Earth* (New York: Knopf, 1982).

¹¹Sacvan Bercovitch, *The American Jeremiad* (Madison, Wisc.: University of Wisconsin Press, 1978), p. 4.

¹²Ibid., p. 12.

¹³W. Clark Gilpin, *The Millenarian Piety of Roger Williams* (University of Chicago, 1979), p. 63; James H. Moorhead, *American Apocalypse* (New Haven: Yale University Press, 1978), p. 7; Barkun, p. 11; Walter Schmithals, *The Apocalyptic Movement*, trans. John G. Steeley (Nashville: Abingdon Press, 1975), pp. 38–9.

¹⁴McGinn, pp. 32–3; Paul D. Hanson, *The Dawn of Apocalyptic* (Philadelphia: Fortress Press, 1975), hereafter *Dawn* p. 406; Schmithals, p. 24; Timothy P. Weber, *Living in the Shadow of the Second Coming* (New York: Oxford, 1979), pp. 45–6 and 82–3; Moorhead, p. 9.

¹⁵Barkun, p. 1; Moorhead, p. 5; Ronald F. Reid, "Prophecy in New England Victory Sermons, ca. 1760: A Study in American Concepts of Historical Mission," Baylor University Wilcox Lecture, 1979, pp. 13–18; Schmithals, p. 215.

¹⁶McGinn, pp. 30–2; Katherine R. Firth, *The Apocalyptic Tradition in Reformation Britain, 1530–1645* (Oxford: Oxford University, 1979), p. 5.

¹⁷Schmithals, pp. 216, 255; Moorhead, p. 8; Barkun, p. 44.

¹⁸Amos N. Wilder, "The Rhetoric of Ancient and Modern Apocalyptic," *Interpretation*, 25 (1971), 550, comes closest to treating apocalyptic as rhetorical. He tends to restrict his focus to language use, however, and he is also not explicitly concerned with its generic characteristics as argued here. I have not reviewed these ancient original texts myself because to do so would require a knowledge of several languages such as Hebrew, Greek, Latin, Italian, which I do not possess; instead, the essay builds on past scholarly efforts.

¹⁹The books examined are Hal Lindsey, *The Late Great Planet Earth* (N.Y.: Bantam Books, 1970) and William Steuart McBirnie, *Anti-Christ* (Dallas: Acclaimed Books, 1978). Lindsey's book has sold nearly ten million copies, while McBirnie's volume is based on his consulting work for the successful motion picture "Damien."

²⁰These works see social collapse due to war or economic depression. Howard J. Ruff, *How to Prosper During the Coming Bad Years* (N.Y.: Warner Books, 1979, 1981); Geoffrey F. Abert, *After the Crash* (N.Y.: Signet, 1980); Jerome F. Smith, *The Coming Currency Collapse* (N.Y.: Bantam, 1981); General Sir John Hackett, *The Third World War* (N.Y.: Berkeley Book, 1979); Other forms of civil collapse such as racial strife and class wars are alluded to in the sources reviewed here. In the social realm, this apocalyptic predicts as radical a change as does any religious apocalyptic.

²¹Amos N. Wilder, p. 550; Paul D. Hanson, "Old Testament Apocalyptic Reexamined," *Interpretation*, 25 (1971), 455, hereafter "Old"; Paul D. Hanson, *Dawn*, p. 2.

²²Wilder, p. 447.

²³Schmithals, p. 35.

²⁴Frederick Van Der Meer, *Apocalypse* (London: Thames and Hudson, 1978), p. 29.

²⁵D. S. Russell, *Between the Testaments* (Philadelphia: Muhlenberg Press, 1960), p. 93.

²⁶Firth, p. 9.

²⁷Harrison, pp. 5, 207.

²⁸Weber, pp. 83–4, 41.

²⁹Barkun, p. 45.

³⁰Ibid., p. 58.

³¹Russell, p. 95; Schmithals, p. 20; Harrison, pp. 218, 222; McGinn, p. 31.

³²Harrison, pp. xv–xvi. This feature of apocalyptic is distinctly *pre*millennial and opposed to the postmillennial or utopian ideal of progress, for if one believes that the future will improve, then the world is once more within some measure of control. Rather, apocalyptic in the premillennial sense of an *imminent* doom often arises from the loss of faith for some people in progress, from a feeling that tomorrow cannot get better. See Barkun, p. 27; Tuveson, pp. 1, 16, and 203; Schmithals, pp. 231–2; Schmithals describes Marx as such a utopian,

p. 237, and Barkun also sees Marxism and Nazism as traceable to postmillennial apocalyptic, p. 31. See also Hanson, *Dawn*, p. 1, and Eric Hoffer, *The True Believer* (1951; rpt. New York: Harper and Row, Perennial Library, 1966), pp. 23–4. Although Hoffer does not focus explicitly on apocalyptic, many of his descriptions of the true believer seem to encompass the interest of this essay.

[33]Lindsey, p. 7.

[34]McBirnie, p. 1.

[35]Lindsey, p. 34 and p. 31.

[36]McBirnie, p. 8; Lindsey, pp. 164–5.

[37]Ruff, p. 16.

[38]Abert, p. 4.

[39]Schmithals, p. 17.

[40]McGinn, pp. 7–8; Hanson, *Dawn*, p. 406; Russell, p. 97.

[41]Schmithals, p. 218.

[42]Burke, p. 288; Wilder, p. 442.

[43]Schmithals, p. 18, and p. 36; Harrison, p. 288; Weber, p. 52.

[44]Tuveson, p. 4.

[45]Gilpin, pp. 2–3.

[46]Ruff, pp. 35–6.

[47]Smith, p. 124.

[48]Abert, p. 52.

[49]Ruff, pp. 39 and 363.

[50]Ruff, pp. 39 and 363.

[51]Abert, p. 29.

[52]Smith, pp. 3–19.

[53]Hackett, pp. 45–46.

[54]Harrison, p. 220.

[55]McGinn, p. 31.

[56]Barkun, p. 56.

[57]Ibid., p. 52; Harrison, pp. 8–9; Russell, p. 94.

[58]Lindsey, p. 47.

[59]Ruff, p. 27.

[60]Smith, p. 82.

[61]Ruff, pp. 16–17.

[62]Smith, p. 57.

[63]Ruff, pp. 144–152, 325.

[64]Abert, p. 3.

[65]Smith, p. 129.

[66]Hackett, pp. 401–3; Chaps. 25 and 26.

[67]Schmithals, pp. 215, 25.

[68]Harrison, p. 42.

[69]Firth, p. 6.

[70]Weber, pp. 182, 36.

[71]McGinn, p. 36; Schmithals, p. 14.

[72]Firth, Chap. 1.

[73]Gilpin, p. 11.

[74]Russell, p. 109.

[75]Moorhead, pp. 14, x.

[76]Lindsey, p. 7.

[77]McBirnie, p. 6.

[78]Lindsey, Chaps. 5–7.

[79]McBirnie, pp. 26, 92–3, 94–5, 102–7.

[80]Ruff, p. 81.

[81]Abert, Chap. 1; pp. 42–52, 259.

[82]Smith, pp. 55–69, 123.

[83]Hackett, pp. xi–xiv, 45.

[84]Ruff, pp. 36–7, 161–2, 166–7, 247.

[85]Abert, pp. 150–7, 210–30.

[86]Smith, p. 152.

[87]Hackett, p. 46, Chap. 25.

[88]Barkun, p. 56.

[89]Hoffer, p. 13.

[90]Hanson, *Dawn*, p. 408.

[91]McBirnie, p. 132.

[92]Lindsey, p. 165.

[93]Hackett, pp. 394–400; Chapt. 28.

[94]Abert, pp. 271–2.

[95]Ruff, p. 17, 33.

[96]Abert, p. 29.

[97]Ibid., pp. 84, 262.

[98]McGinn, p. 6. see also Schmithals, p. 22; Firth, p. 246; Wilder, 44 and 446.

[99]Russell, pp. 95–6; Harrison, pp. 6, 8.

[100]Gilpin, p. 5.

[101]Weber, p. 70.

[102]Hanson, *Dawn*, p. 2.

[103]McBirnie, p. 2.

[104]Ibid., pp. 130–1, 139; Lindsey, p. 99.

[105]McBirnie, p. 4; he argues that history is "dualistic."

[106]Abert, pp. 231–49.

[107]Ruff, p. 27.

[108]Abert, p. 29.

[109]Smith, p. 151.

[110]Abert, p. 150.

[111]Ruff, pp. 16–17.

[112]Smith, p. 55.

[113]Ibid., p. 127.

[114]Harrison, p. 11.
[115]Ruff, p. 46.
[116]Smith, p. xiv.
[117]Hackett, pp. 87–90.
[118]Barkun, pp. 201–2.
[119]Wilder, p. 452; Hanson, "Old," pp. 455–6.

# CHAPTER 13 [                    ]

# THE RHETORIC OF DEHUMANIZATION

Martha Solomon

*In this commentary, Martha Solomon characterizes her own approach to criticism somewhat differently from the accounts of Brummett and Ivie, earlier in this section, by downplaying the role of theory in her early critical choices. Solomon gravitated toward the study of the infamous Tuskegee syphilis medical reports because of more general interests, but as her background reading increased her understanding of the consequences of those reports, she discovered a fit between certain theoretical writings and her emerging interpretations of the texts. Yet Solomon also notes that a critic's theoretical point-of-view may well change over time, suggesting very different ways she might approach the text were she to return to it today.*

## COMMENTARY

I have always relied on the kindness of strangers.
—Blanche DuBois, *A Streetcar Named Desire*

For me, inspiration for critical projects has often come, if not from strangers, at least from strange places. When I wrote "The Rhetoric of Dehumanization: An Analysis of Medical Reports of the Tuskegee Syphilis Project," I was at Auburn University, some twenty miles from Tuskegee, Alabama. James H. Jones, the author of *Bad Blood: The Tuskegee Syphilis Experiment*, which exposed the racism in the study, had recently spoken at Auburn University. But neither of those facts directly influenced my interest in this project. Indeed, I did not hear Jones's lecture nor know of the Tuskegee syphilis project until a colleague, who found little to like in living in a small Southern college town, expressed unusual enthusiasm (for her) for the lecture. It was in reporting her untypical enthusiasm for the lecture that I mentioned the topic to my husband. After a few minutes of animated discussion, he speculated: "There's an important article for you in that study."

The idea intrigued me enough that I began to explore the possibilities. Reading Jones's book, I found to my disappointment that his analysis that racism facilitated the study's continuance was convincing. He had, in a sense, preempted one avenue I as a rhetorical critic might pursue. However, I had a strong intuition that my husband's prediction of an article lurking here was accurate. My contribution was to be the rhetorical critic's inherent interest in how texts work. Then, I began to consider looking at the medical reports of the Tuskegee project themselves, since those were the texts that initially made the information about the study public. At first, I was stymied because Auburn had no medical school with an attendant library that would have the necessary journals; and getting materials xeroxed through interlibrary loan can be a tiresome, time-consuming, and sometimes frustrating task. But one of the unfailingly helpful librarians at Auburn's Ralph Brown Draughon Library suggested that our veterinary medicine school had an excellent collection of medical journals and might prove helpful. In fact, I was able to obtain copies of almost all the medical reports in one visit there. Thus, with little effort on my own part, I had a full set of texts discussing what had become a highly criticized study that had prompted the development of federal standards for the use of human subjects.

Although the details of how these reports came to my attention make this case different from other critical projects I have undertaken, my experience in this instance resembles almost all of the studies I have done in two respects. First, I am always primarily interested in *how* and *why* texts work for particular audiences. Believing that audiences construct meanings on and around works, I am fascinated by what in a work excites or irritates an audience member. Thus, rather than trying to determine what a rhetor "means" in a text or attempting to reconstruct the rhetorical situation surrounding the text, my focus is always on that complex, subtle, and elusive connection between a work and the audience it influences.

Second, I prefer to study texts that I know have worked or failed to work for a particular audience. Popularity is one signal of a text's influence. For example, I was drawn to *The Total Woman* because it was a best-seller, to *Chariots of Fire* because it was a popular and Academy Award–winning movie, and to Robert Schuller because he has survived and prospered as a televangelist. Political success, as in the case of the STOP ERA movement, is another indicator of a text's "working" for some audience. I am particularly intrigued by texts that work for an audience of which I do not consider myself to be a member. Thus, the medical reports of the Tuskegee syphilis study were precisely the kinds of texts I find myself drawn to explore because they had obviously been very successful in obscuring the ethical issues inherent in the project for the medical community.

Thus, unlike many critics I do not engage texts with a theoretical question or project in mind. Until recently, I have not had theoretical issues that direct my critical efforts. Nor did I, as some critics do, choose these texts because they were a type of discourse—scientific writing—that I have decided to explore. In short, this essay grew out of a concatenation of a general question that concerns most critics and the happy chance of locating a set of texts that played an important role in what became a national scandal.

As the project unfolded, what attracted my attention as a rhetorical critic was a small point in Jones's book. He reported that until the study was brought to public attention in the early 1970s by a Public Health Service official only one letter from the medical community had objected to the project although it had been reported in thirteen progress reports published in medical journals over almost forty years. The seemingly inexplicable silence of the medical community was in striking contrast to the widespread public outrage it produced in 1972. Why in forty years had only a single physician objected to what public opinion regarded as an atrocity? Racism was too simple an answer. Certainly, the United States had had and retains elements of a racist ideology. But it was not credible to me that all but one of the estimated 100,000 physicians who read those reports were blinded by their racism to the human consequences of the disease. Moreover, many physicians who read the studies were themselves African Americans. From my rhetorician's perspective, it seemed that the answer must lie in the nature of the discourse itself and how it functioned to produce their shared insensitivity.

The studies themselves were dry reading. Perusing them, I was impressed anew with the clinical sterility of scientific reporting. That reading experience led me to my first glimmer of insight: These were doctors and health officials writing to and for other doctors and health officials. They used all the techniques of scientific writing to wipe clean any "subjective" human elements from their reports in order to present their findings "objectively." Thus, I envisioned this project in part as a study of how the generic parameters of scientific reporting influence perceptions and systematically obscure some crucial elements of the reality they are recording.

Specifically, I wondered what particular factors in the reports had obscured the ethical issues that so upset persons outside the medical profession when they learned of the nature of the study from the media. I soon realized that those outside the medical profession, regardless of their ethnic background, identified, in the Burkean sense, with the men in the study, while the physicians who wrote and read the reports did not. This suggested the appropriateness of Kenneth Burke's idea of consubstantiality; this connection, in turn, prompted me to consider the depictions within the reports and suggested the pentad as a method that might be generative.

Although the details of this project differ from other work I have done, I frequently begin with Burke and his notion of identification. Starting there, of course, reflects my primary interest in why and how texts work for particular audiences; or to put it in Burkean terms, why audiences identify with the rhetor and his/her perspective. But I must also admit that although I begin with Burke, I almost never end up with him. While I gain insights and understanding from asking questions drawn from the pentad, the resultant analysis has a cookie-cutter predictability that does not satisfy me. This problem, I believe, inheres in most pentadic analyses. Burke's pentad is difficult to use effectively with subtlety, and Burkean analyses seldom tell me things I did not see for myself.

For this essay, however, I never got beyond Burke or pursued other approaches. At that time, Burke seemed the natural avenue for answering the questions I wanted to explore. If I were doing the essay today, I might draw on what I have learned about Foucault's ideas on the rules governing discourse, or pursue notions from cultural studies about hegemony, or consider the spheres of argument concept that Thomas Goodnight has proposed. But even a decade later, I remain convinced that in light of my interests, the texts, and the overtly political content, Burke offered a compelling heuristic. I should note that I find doing more than one "pass" with Burke's pentad and considering alternate depictions to be a very fruitful exercise regardless of whether I pursue that method in an essay. Indeed, I enjoy "playing" with the pentad as a means of exploring how texts can be parsed and how different construals suggest disparate interpretations.

One problem in working with Burke's pentad is that I see layers or series of depictions and often have difficulty sorting out what elements belong in which depiction. That was certainly true in this case. Initially, I tried to make all the pieces fit into a single pentadic analysis; despite my efforts, that approach did not work. Finally, two interpenetrated strands seemed to emerge from the medical reports. First, the bulk of the material in the reports was clinical observation of the impact of the disease. What loomed large in those details was the subjects of the study as the place where the disease was taking its toll. This realization led me to my first successful pentadic pass through the material: the patient as scene with syphilis as the actor. This depiction dehumanized the men being studied and accounted for why concern for them was eclipsed. Then, I revisited my observation that these were medical professionals writing for doctors. What, I wondered, made that bond so strong? The answer seemed to lie in the role or persona that the authors assumed in the texts. I began to tease out a second depiction: the depiction of the study. In that case, the men being studied became the agency through and by which the medical community was studying a phenomenon and contributing to human knowledge.

Two things united these depictions. In each case, a group of humans was moved from their usual status as agents to fulfill other roles in the depictions, scene in one case and agency in the other. Both depictions obscured their humanity. Additionally, on another level, viewing subjects (whether human or animal) as scene and agency seemed characteristic of scientific writing generally. These two observations became the core of my critical argument.

Discussing how these two features worked for the audience and drawing the implications of my analysis provided the final part of the essay. In the discussions of function and implications, I moved from describing the texts to evaluating and assessing them. For me, these sections are the easiest and most enjoyable part of writing essays because here I can attempt to answer the central question of how texts work and speculate about why audiences connect with some texts so forcefully.

This essay was an unusually easy one to write. From the beginning the materials themselves seemed to suggest the approaches to take. However, the process was not without its problems. On the one hand, teasing out the two depictions took some time because the strands were so interrelated and subtle. On the other hand, I found myself leaving out so much of the texts as I developed my pentads that I felt uncomfortable. Frequently, when writing criticism, I am troubled by how much of the material remains untouched and undiscussed in the analysis. Whenever I finish a project, I am keenly aware that I have, to borrow the terminology of Roland Barthes, created my own texts on and around the work I am studying. In this case, however, by far the largest portion of the medical reports consisted of clinical details and statistical data that did not seem to play a direct rhetorical role, except in establishing the tone of the reports as "objective" and "scientific."

As I wrote, I also felt myself constrained by Jones's analysis. His conclusions about the implicit racism in the Tuskegee study are compelling. My problem was, in a sense, to move beyond that important dimension of the study and explore a different, and in a sense, broader rhetorical problem. This need to negotiate a space for my ideas is common in doing criticism. Because I like to work on popular cultural texts, I am often writing analyses after other authors have commented on the works. Thus, I am always in danger of simply reiterating their observations or offering a fuller account than they have to support similar conclusions.

Finally, I should note that writing is for me a slow creative process. I labor over the language in some sections, particularly the justification and rationale for the study. It is not unusual for me to struggle with one or two paragraphs for several hours, while other portions flow rather quickly. Because I try to be precise, I find myself consulting a dictionary frequently. Moreover, I change directions and revise my arguments as I work with the texts themselves, trying to articulate my thoughts carefully and coherently. In this case, as in virtually every essay I have done, the introductory paragraphs, particularly those previewing the argument, are the last I write. I find myself sharpening and altering my focus in the process of writing as I realize what I want to say.

Finishing a project is both gratifying and frustrating. While I like the sense of developing and articulating an argument and I feel good about having "proved" my case, I am always a bit disappointed at the finished product. This sense of the inadequacy of an essay to one's initial conceptualization of it is, to my mind, inherent in the process of developing a critical argument. Requirements of length and focus make full articulation of one's ideas impossible.

The reviewers' comments on this essay suggested few substantive revisions, but they did press me to organize the argument more clearly and to focus it more sharply. Usually I have been fortunate, as in this case, in getting practical, constructive guidance from reviewers.

I followed the reviewers' suggestions about the essay rather closely. Although I am familiar with authors' horror stories about how reviewers want to control the essay, few editors or reviewers have tried to write an essay for me. In this case, they simply helped me argue what I wanted to say more effectively. The only comment I resisted was one reviewer's suggestion that I be more "outraged" about the studies. Because I tend to write on texts of which most persons in our profession (myself among them) disapprove, I am frequently urged to be more disparaging or condemnatory in my analysis. My goal has always been to explain rhetorical processes, not make social judgments. I recognize that all criticism is inevitably political and ideological to some extent, but I make an earnest effort to show how texts work rather than judge whether it is just that they should have worked at all.

Rereading this essay seven years after its publication was pleasurable. I like what I wrote, and I remain convinced that my assessment is accurate and fair. I would do it differently—not necessarily better—if I were doing it today. This essay has always been one of which I am fond; it was easy to write and I said something I wanted to say about the lures and dangers of scientific allegiance to "objectivity." I hope the essay is accessible enough for students and lay persons to make them alert to the terrible and wonder-working power lurking in language.

# The Rhetoric of Dehumanization:
# An Analysis of Medical Reports
# of the Tuskegee Syphilis Project

**Martha Solomon**

**A**n "Inhuman Experiment," "Official Inhumanity," and "An Immoral Study" were epithets the press used to describe the Tuskegee syphilis study when Jean Heller reported the details of it in July 1972.[1] The Tuskegee project was a forty-year longitudinal study conducted by The United States Public Health Service (PHS) to trace the "natural history" of untreated syphilis in the adult male Negro. PHS officials periodically conducted blood tests, physical examinations, X rays, and, finally, autopsies on 399 men with syphilis and 201 members of a control group who were free of the disease. Not only was no treatment administered to the men with syphilis, but they were discouraged and even prevented from seeking treatment outside the program (Jones 178). Since the disastrous consequences of untreated syphilis were well-known before the study began in 1932 and since satisfactory treatment was available even then, the ethical and moral ramifications of the study were profound. Public reaction to Heller's report forced a national investigation. An *ad hoc* committee appointed by the federal government to investigate the study concluded that such a longitudinal study was "ethically unjustified in 1932" and urged stronger restrictions on the use of human subjects. Senator Ted Kennedy's hearings on the study confirmed this view and resulted in the revamping of HEW guidelines for human experimentation (Jones 211, 214).

In his detailed study of the case, *Bad Blood: The Tuskegee Syphilis Experiment,* James H. Jones traces its history and examines the rationale provided by PHS officials and the individuals involved. Jones's thorough analysis indicates clearly the role of racial prejudice, confused medical thinking, and bureaucratic dynamics in instigating and continuing a passive observation of the devastating effects of syphilis on human subjects. His book highlights the "moral astigmatism" of the persons responsible (*Atlanta Constitution* 4A, quoted in Jones 14). However, despite the thoroughness of his analysis, Jones does not explore one very significant facet of the Tuskegee project: why the thirteen "progress reports" of it which appeared in major medical journals from 1936 to 1973 did not outrage the medical community. Although these reports clearly delineated the nature of the study and its devastating consequences on the men involved, their publication generated virtually no criticism (Jones 257–58). In light of the vehement public reaction to Heller's 1972 report, the thirty-seven-year silence from the medical community is particularly striking.

My purpose is to examine the published reports of the Tuskegee study to determine the ways in which they obscured ethical issues. I contend that the published reports, reflecting the constraints of scientific writing, emphasized what Burke calls "the principle of discontinuity" (Burke 50). In Burke's terms, the reports encouraged readers to dissociate themselves from the subjects by highlighting the differences between the two groups and by dehumanizing the men involved. Rhetorically, the generic conventions of scientific writing not only encouraged neglect of ethical questions but also played an important role in the study's continuation. In brief, I argue that the reports of the study functioned rhetorically to diminish and obscure the moral issues involved. As a case study of scientific reporting, my analysis suggests that scientific writing employs rhetorical conventions which by their very nature tend to obscure or de-emphasize any ethical, "non-scientific" perspective.

A scholarly view of scientific reporting as rhetorical has become widespread. For example, Simons identifies specific factors such as the prestige of the journals and the "appearance of impersonal detachment and passivity" in the language of scientific articles as having a persuasive effect (*Persuasion* 33). With a similar perspective Kenneth Burke, contrasting the scientistic and dramatistic uses of language, avers that "even if any given terminology is a *reflection* of reality, by its very nature as a terminology it must be a *selection* of reality; and to this extent, it must function also as a *deflection* of reality" (45). Even "scientific" language is heavily rhetorical, for it necessarily obscures some aspects of the reality it reports. Paul Newell Campbell, probing the implications of one rhetorical feature, the author's *persona,* in scientific discourse, argues that scientists cannot escape revealing attitudes in their discourse, despite their claims for objectivity and neutrality, because the act of symbolizing entails the expression of "those attitudes, beliefs, biases, opinions" that constitute the *persona* of such discourse (404). Other scholars have explored additional dimensions of scientific rhetoric.[2]

Although the Tuskegee study provides a good case study of scientific reporting for several reasons,[3] enabling us to understand better how such writing functions rhetorically, the justification for the analysis derives ultimately from the suffering of the subjects themselves. Largely uneducated and seduced by small incentives offered by members of the medical community, the men unwittingly undermined their health and shortened their lives. Among the consequences of untreated syphilis were blindness, deep skin lesions, insanity, heart disease, and early death (Jones 1–4). Using the euphemism "Bad Blood," the medical staff handling the study apparently tried to convey to the men that they were victims of syphilis (Jones 5–6). But the message was only partially understood. As one patient's widow noted, "I thought the doctors were trying to help him. I didn't know better."[4] A survivor reported, "I thought they was doing me good" (Quoted in Jones 160). Unsuspecting patients labored under a terrible misconception while investigators periodically reported on health problems that developed because they remained untreated. As a consequence of this miscommunication and the silence of the more knowledgeable medical community, as many as 100 men may have died from syphilis-connected diseases (Jones 2).[5] Understanding the role scientific rhetoric played in this tragedy is, thus, the focus of this study.

The remainder of the essay falls into five sections: (1) a brief background of the Tuskegee study, (2) an analysis of the depiction of the disease in the research reports, (3) an examination of the description of the study itself in these same reports, (4) a discussion of the rhetorical function of (2) and (3), and (5) a consideration of rhetorical implications.

## ▨ BACKGROUND OF THE TUSKEGEE STUDY

To understand the Tuskegee study one must know something of its background. Concerned with the widespread incidence of syphilis among rural Southern Blacks, PHS officials in the late twenties began a treatment program funded by a private philanthropy. Unfortunately, the project lapsed in the early thirties when the private funding ceased. But by that time PHS officers had identified many Blacks suffering from syphilis and had established contacts in the Macon County area. Since a lack of outside support prohibited full treatment, the staff perceived an opportunity to take advantage of their groundwork in a new way—an observation of the course of untreated syphilis. As one doctor noted, "The thought came to me that the Alabama community offered an unparalleled opportunity for the study of the effect of untreated syphilis" (Jones 91).

The Tuskegee situation was ideal for several reasons. First, many of the cases had received no treatment and were, thus, in the terminology of the study, "pristine." Second, the victims were Black. Earlier controversy had developed over whether syphilis affected Blacks differently than Whites. Tuskegee provided an opportunity to explore that question. Third, Tuskegee offered the possibility of a prospective study, which could follow the course of the disease rather than simply catalog its effects after the fact. This was particularly significant since the only major study of the effects of untreated syphilis, by Bruusgaard in Oslo, catalogued the conditions of White patients at various stages of the disease who came to his clinic but were not treated (Jones 91–93). Bruusgaard did not trace the disease's course by following particular patients. Tuskegee could provide an effective contrast to his methodology.

From their perspective, PHS officials, constrained by funding from providing treatment, made a virtue of necessity. They instituted a non-therapeutic, longitudinal, prospective study of syphilis in adult male Blacks. Such studies, which withhold treatment beneficial to the individual patient, are usually justified on the grounds that they provide information which will enlarge medical knowledge. As Charles Fried explains in his essay on "Human Experimentation: Philosophical Aspects," "In therapeutic experimentation a course of action . . . is undertaken in respect to the subject for the purpose of how best to procure a medical benefit to that subject. In nontherapeutic experimentation, by contrast, the sole end in view is the acquisition of new information" (699). Such studies, in yielding valuable information, can be condoned morally because they benefit the larger group although not the individual (Fried 701).

Officials who conducted and reported the Tuskegee project thus perceived their work as a legitimate and, indeed, beneficial undertaking. Unable to offer complete treatment, they tried to learn what they could about the ravages of syphilis. Kept from performing their job of treating disease, they assumed a new role: medical experimenters.

Even after Heller's exposé in the *New York Times*, there were those who defended the study. To vindicate the procedures used, they pointed to changed medical standards and the nature of the Tuskegee undertaking as a "study project" rather than a "treatment clinic."[6] Moreover, they supported the decision not to offer the highly effective penicillin when it became available because the major damage already had occurred in the subjects and the impact of the drug itself might have been harmful (Kampmeier 1251). Defenders also contended that the study's goal of tracing the results of untreated syphilis was appropriate and, from a broad view, even beneficial since the increased medical knowledge of the disease might have improved prevention and treatment (Kampmeier 1251; Jones 81–112; Vonderlehr et al. 260). Robert M. Veatch outlines the philosophical grounding for this approach in "Codes of Medical Ethics: Ethical Analysis" when he notes that medical practitioners may condone studies which are not beneficial to the individual patient if the information gained will "render service to humanity" (173). Clearly, from the first, some complex ethical issues surrounded the nature of the study, although the apparently unintentional misleading of the patients about the nature of their disease and its treatment was unacceptable (Wooten 18).

If we grant that the study did present difficult ethical issues, we must wonder why these were not even raised until it had been underway almost forty years. No attempt was made to conceal the study or to disguise its nature. Between 1936 and 1973 at least thirteen "progress reports" appeared in major medical journals with an estimated readership of 100,000.[7] One article, for example, spelled out the reduced life expectancy and increased disability of the untreated subjects (Pesare, Bauer, and Gleeson 201, 213). But, according to Jones, only one member of the medical profession or public objected to the study prior to the strenuous response of Peter Buxton, a PHS officer, which resulted in wide press coverage. That single letter dated June 1963, twenty-seven years after the first widely published report of the study, was filed at the Center for Disease Control in Atlanta with the notation, "This is the first letter of this type we have received." Moreover, Buxton contends that his objections met strong opposition and provoked heated defenses of the study but produced little immediate action (Jones 190). Apparently, the directors of the study did not perceive its ethical ramifications and depicted it in published reports so that its moral implications were not salient to most readers.

An examination of the reports suggests that the depiction of the patients in two contexts (in relation to the disease itself and as elements in the study) dehumanized them and helped the readers and authors dissociate themselves from the afflicted men. In describing the ravages of the disease, the reports highlighted the disease as a dynamic agent acting on and within the patients as scene. Explaining the study and its purposes, the journal accounts featured the doctors as noble agents pursuing knowledge and the afflicted patients as their agency for gaining information. The reports, then, offered a double-layered depiction: the study as a quest for scientific knowledge by impartial observers who note the activity of the disease on patients. Both depictions dehumanized the patients and highlighted the role of the experimenters as impartial observers and knowledge seekers. In so doing, the rhetoric obscured key ethical issues. Using Burke's pentad to explore these two depictions of the patients in greater detail can elucidate the rhetorical processes at work.

## ▮ DEPICTION OF THE DISEASE: THE PATIENT AS SCENE

The journal accounts of the study depict the disease as a dynamic agent bent on destroying its "host" through the cardiovascular and central nervous systems. The patient is the scene in and on which the disease operates. The emphasis is on the actions of syphilis and its results, particularly its contributions to early death and disability.

The initial report of the Tuskegee project, read at the 1936 AMA convention before appearing in the journal *Venereal Disease Information*, reveals a depiction of the disease which persists throughout the study. The agent is syphilis whose effect is "the production of morbid processes involving the various systems of the body" and "disability in the early years of adult life" (Vonderlehr et al. 26). The study would, therefore, focus on the disease's particular effects: "Subsequently in more detailed analysis of the material attempts will be made to describe and evaluate specific changes brought about by the disease in the infected individual with particular reference to the cardiovascular system" (Heller and Bruyere 34). This act of disabling the victim is accomplished through impairment of the cardiovascular and central nervous systems: "Study of the untreated syphilitic and presumably non-syphilitic individuals under the age of forty indicates" that syphilis "tends greatly to increase the manifestations of cardiovascular disease. . . . Cardiovascular and central nervous system involvements were from two to three times as common in the untreated syphilis group as in a comparable group receiving even an inadequate treatment" (Vonderlehr et al. 261–65). Since the disease results in death, reports of increased morbidity among the untreated are not surprising. As the second report concludes, "The life expectancy of a Negro man with syphilis between the ages of 25 and 35 who is infected with syphilis and receives no treatment for his infection is on the average reduced by about 20 percent" (Heller and Bruyere 38). The reports catalog the ravages of syphilis in detail, furnishing frequent comparison to nonsyphilitic subjects. As the study progresses, details drawn from autopsies confirm the impact of the disease by describing its pathological signs (Peters et al. 127–48).

The scene of the disease's activities is, of course, the victim, but reports avoid such emotionally connotative language. The second article "deals particularly with the effect of the disease on the life span of the human host" (Heller and Bruyere 34). The first report of the study also contains the metaphor of victim as host or donor: "Such individuals seemed to offer an unusual opportunity to study the untreated syphilitic patient from the beginning of the disease to the death of the infected person" (Vonderlehr et al. 260). The more common designations of the victim as scene are "Male Negro" (which appears in the title of nine of the thirteen articles), "patients," "syphilitics," and "individuals." The third report of the study, published in 1946, clearly illustrates the depiction of the patient as scene. "Briefly, the study is a continuing attempt to follow the natural history of syphilis, uninfluenced by treatment, in adult male Negroes, with special attention to its effect on the cardiovascular system" (Deibert and Bruyere 301). As scene, the patient displays "manifestations," "presents evidence of," and "exhibits appreciably more morbidity" (Vonderlehr et al. 263; Deibert and Bruyere 313).

The reports, then, depict the disease as dynamic agent whose impairment of the central nervous system takes place in the "scene" of the patient. This emphasis on act is one with philosophical realism wherein "material objects exist externally to us and independently of our sense experience" (Hirst 77). One of the hallmarks of realism is that it minimizes the role and significance of the observer. Events, happening in an "out there," are recorded by a neutral, detached "observer" who sees them as they exist. A "realistic" attitude thus emphasizes the objectivity and detachment of the observer, while removing attention from his/her role or possible intervention in the events being reported.

■ **DEPICTION OF THE STUDY:
THE PATIENT AS AGENCY**

The journal articles also characterize the study itself. The agents or actors are the PHS doctors whose credentials, affiliations with the Public Health Service, and usually prestigious titles are listed as author information in each article. Not only are their credentials explicitly listed, but they are depicted implicitly as members of a dedicated, self-sacrificing "team" (Rivers et al. 395). This view of the actors reveals itself in a 1955 report: "The contribution of time, thoughts, and energy of many individuals with the full knowledge that the fruits of their efforts would not mature until years later, and in other hands, has been vital. As in all such lifetime studies the devotion of these scientists and public health workers to the search for knowledge for the sake of knowledge and with selflessness must here be acknowledged" (Peters et al. 128).

The primary activity of these agents is observing, a passive act rather than a dynamic one. Articles are sometimes subtitled "observations" of various facets of the disease. They also "follow" and "survey the patients" (Deibert and Bruyere 301; Rivers et al. 391). The only dynamic acts of the doctors involve conducting tests or autopsies as part of the observational process. A 1950 report reveals the passivity and detachment of the directors in their recording of observations: "When the effect of differences in age distributions between the untreated syphilitics and the non-syphilitic controls was removed by a standardization procedure, significant differences in the combined mortality and morbidity could be demonstrated between the two groups" (Pesare et al. 213). One report praised the excellent, thorough care the doctors extended to the patients, noting its pragmatic impact. "The excellent care given these patients was important in creating in the family a favorable attitude which eventually would lead to permission to perform an autopsy" (Rivers et al. 394). The irony is striking: the "excellent" medical care, consisting in part of denying treatment, encouraged participation in a procedure to document syphilis's devastating effects.

The purpose guiding the doctors is clear—the pursuit of knowledge which may benefit mankind. As one early study notes, the primary problem in controlling syphilis is learning how treatment can prevent its transmission. But a secondary goal is understanding "the effect which treatment has in preventing late and crippling manifestations." Tuskegee provided a unique opportunity "to compare the syphilitic process *uninfluenced* by modern treatment, with the results obtained when treatment has been given" (Vonderlehr et al. 260, italics mine). A report eighteen years later in 1954 pinpoints the values and purposes of the study. It notes that in 1930 "no accurate data relative to the effect of syphilis in shortening of life" and "no accurate history of the disease leading up to these complications" were available. "This *information* was necessary in order to *evaluate* the effectiveness of programs of public health control with a *reasonable* degree of *understanding* of the natural history of the disease." The italics, which are mine, highlight the directors' focus on acquiring knowledge. The report documents shortcomings and gaps in the Bruusgaard study. Later, the authors assert that "such a study was needed to assist in the planning and execution of the national venereal disease control program which was then being planned for a later time" (Shafer et al. 685–87). A later report refers to the clear difference between the populations involved in the Tuskegee and Bruusgaard studies (race being primary), reaffirming implicitly the value of the project in filling out scientific knowledge. A "tabular listing" highlights the superiority of the Tuskegee project (Schuman et al. 544). Of special significance is the study's prospective, long-term nature. Unlike earlier work, the Tuskegee study's particular contribution is to trace the course of the disease across time. Clearly, the investigators feel the study is justified because it adds to scientific knowledge.

While no precise description of the scene within which the investigators work appears in reports of the study, the depictions of agents and purposes clearly imply its nature. Tuskegee is the geographical setting, but the larger medical and scientific communities are the scenes which provide the real context of the study. The doctors, observing the disease and examining the patients in Macon County, frame their activities as medical investigations. Thus, findings are reported in medical journals rather than popular periodicals, and a 1954 report presents a lengthy rationale that details the study's significance not only among other investigations of syphilis but also to public health programs (Shafer et al. 684–85). Another explicit reference to the scene as the medical community appears in the report entitled "Twenty Years of Followup Experience in a Long-Range Medical Study" (Rivers et al. 391–95). Even in a discussion of the "non-medical" aspects of the study, this essay claims that "the experiences recounted may be of value to those planning continuing studies in other fields." It concludes that "several points . . . may benefit anyone now engaged in planning or executing a long-range medical research study," finally observing that "the gains to medical knowledge derived from the horizontal, long-term study of illness and health are only just beginning to be realized" (Rivers et al. 391, 394–95). The report thus rhetorically sets the study's scene within a medical community which is just recognizing the significance of such projects.

The final pentadic element, agency, is clear: the patients suffering from syphilis are the instruments or means through which the doctors achieve their purpose. The initial report of the study notes, "The material included in this study consists of 399 syphilitic Negro males who had never received treatment, 201 presumably non-syphilitic Negro males; and approximately 275 male Negroes who had been given treatment during the first two years of the syphilitic process" (Vonderlehr et al. 260). While this perspective of patients-as-agency is inherent in the nature of such a medical project, regarding human subjects as agencies tends also to dehumanize them in a most literal sense: "The shortening of life expectancy observed in man" has "a counterpart in the white mouse, in which animal it has been shown by Rosahn that a syphilitic group has a significantly lessened life expectancy" (Olansky et al., "Untreated Syphilis" 177). Although the attitude toward the patients as agencies is usually detached, occasionally a hint of condescension appears. A 1954 report, for instance, examining the possibility that environmental factors might be a confounding factor in the observed impact of syphilis, comments on the "nonchalant attitude of the patients toward calendars and time-reckonings." The description of their diet concludes "these men like relatively few dishes. As a rule they were interested only in meat (pork or chicken, never beef) and bread, and would select vegetables only upon the suggestion they do so" (Olansky et al., "Environmental Factors" 697). In a similar vein, the report in 1953 dealing with non-medical aspects of the study suggests the naïvete and limited perspectives of the patients: "Incentives for maximum cooperation of the patients must be kept in mind. What appears to be a real incentive to an outsider's way of thinking may have little appeal for the patient. In our case, free hot meals meant more to the men than $50 worth of free medical examination." Significantly, the researchers also note that "because of the low educational status of the majority of the patients, it was impossible to appeal to them from a purely scientific approach" (Rivers et al. 394, 393).

The central focus of these studies concerns purpose. While the results and analyses of the disease's course comprise the bulk of the articles, the discussions function solely to fulfill the objective of increasing "scientific" knowledge. This emphasis on purpose corresponds, as Burke notes, to philosophical mysticism, which is "the consciousness that everything we experience is an element and only an element in fact, i.e., that in being what it is, it is symbolic of something else" (50–51). This perspective deflects attention from actual human suffering to the function of the study in advancing medical knowledge. Implicit is a valuation of knowledge regardless of the human costs. By stressing the loftiness of the study's purpose, the depiction eclipses the agency used to achieve the goal. The study is more important than the individuals involved because it is a part or symbol of a larger and more significant scheme.

## ▉ RHETORICAL FUNCTION

These depictions of the disease and the study, reducing the Tuskegee patients to scene and agency, are common to reports of non-therapeutic projects, for the essence of such endeavors is the observation of a disease to catalog its effects and course. Moreover, they reflect the constraints of the genre of scientific writing, which prizes detachment and objectivity in the assessment and reporting of results. From the Tuskegee studies, we can identify four features of scientific investigation that impinge on the genre of scientific reporting: (1) the scientific method encourages the perception of distinctions and the investigation of their significance; (2) objectivity and detachment are desiderata; (3) science assumes knowledge as a primary value; and (4) the scientific approach is consistent across subject matter areas. In a culture which values the scientific method these elements are accepted almost without question. They become strategies enabling us to rise above our biases and predispositions when making observations.

However, while they may de-personalize our activities in many ways, these elements structure, constrain, and focus our perceptions. They can hamper our thinking if they distort our vision and obscure what should be salient features of reality. Within the reports of the Tuskegee project, these features of the scientific approach, acting as generic constraints, produce a malevolent, if unintended, distortion of reality. The generic constraints, working in concert with the perhaps unconscious racism of the experimenters, produce a powerful but unintentionally unethical rhetoric.

The realization of the generic features outlined above function to dehumanize the patients, to develop a powerful basis for communication within the medical community, and to play enthymematically on the reader's esteem for knowledge. In so doing, the rhetoric encourages myopia and insensitivity in both writers and readers in three broad ways.

First, the depictions deflect attention from the patients by casting them as scene and agency. The consequence is dehumanization and a process of division (as opposed to identification) between patients and the scientific community. A depiction focusing on the acts of the disease necessarily highlights the disease as a dynamic force, controlling and even crippling the "scene" it inhabits. While this view may be accurate, it associates a sense of inevitability with the disease's progress which detracts from the patient's role and self-determination.

Also, stemming from an approach which prizes discriminatory powers and encourages categorization of phenomena on the basis of small distinctions, the reports highlight a relatively minor difference (skin color) between groups of subjects as it obscures their more numerous and significant resemblances. The scientific approach itself encourages investigators to assume the importance of the factor distinguishing one group of subjects from another and to rationalize the project on that basis. Not only are the subjects dehumanized by their status in the study, but also race (the primary factor distinguishing them from the subjects in Bruusgaard's earlier study and from most of the investigators) becomes a key variable in the Tuskegee project. Inherently, then, the study's avowed purpose of tracing the impact of syphilis on Blacks creates the basis for the dissociation between investigators and subjects. Instead of encouraging questions about the validity of racial stereotypes, the study implicitly justifies their significance. Science encourages the acquisition of knowledge to the point of becoming inadvertently a mechanism for encouraging racism.

Reporting the demographic background of the subjects further highlights the differences between them and the medical community. The use of "Male Negro" to designate the patients is significant. Without belaboring the racial elements in the study, one can still assume that this "Male Negro" title does little to establish common ground between the patients and the almost exclusively white readers of medical journals. Other terms used to refer to the victims are equally distancing. "Syphilitic," for instance, reduces the person involved to a simple manifestation of disease, or a "host" like the white rats mentioned earlier. Far from being led to identify and thus empathize with the subjects, readers of the journal articles are implicitly encouraged to distinguish themselves from the men studied.

Moreover, the use of these "scientific" terms for men suffering from syphilis plays into the scientific assumption that detachment is methodologically appropriate regardless of subject matter. The genre, in other words, encourages investigators to select such terms for the men and endorses their usage as appropriate for scientific reporting. Inherent in the genre, then, is a sometimes misleading and potentially destructive convention.

The terms and depictions employed in reports of the Tuskegee study, by highlighting the principle of discontinuity, obscure the moral and ethical implications of the materials being presented (Burke 50–51). Interestingly, the organization of the study itself, which involved frequent rotation of doctors and little sustained contact with the subjects, reinforced this rhetorical distancing from the participants themselves (Jones 187).

Second, in direct contrast to the distancing between "Male Negroes" and the readership of the medical journals, the project directors establish a powerful basis for identification between themselves and the medical community by emphasizing the purposes of their study. Although the doctors are withholding treatment which could alleviate the suffering of victims, they re-define their activities as the observing of the consequences of the disease "uninfluenced" by treatment. Like medical scientists in research centers, they are pushing back the frontiers of knowledge. Knowledge becomes an absolute value: to learn is important, perhaps of paramount importance. Gaining knowledge fulfills one's professional roles and responsibilities. Thus, a commitment to research and the search for knowledge, powerful sources of identification between the doctors in Tuskegee and the larger medical community, enables the reports to cement professional bonds throughout the medical community.[8]

Third, on a more general level the focus on the study's purpose has powerful rhetorical impact because it plays enthymematically on the reader's esteem for knowledge. If knowing is a positive value, then efforts to gain knowledge are desirable. The Tuskegee study, therefore, is clearly a reasonable and even admirable activity. Moreover, in Burkeian terms, the focus on knowledge as a purpose rather than agency elevates it to an absolute value. Questions about the means used to gain the knowledge or even the value of the knowledge itself are eclipsed. Scientific inquiry becomes an activity beyond and above social critique. The depiction of the study as a scientific quest for knowledge thus not only gives it a mystical justification but also elevates it above mundane considerations of costs and effects. What is learned is important, regardless of the economic or human costs.[9]

Furthermore, by accentuating the distance between researchers and subjects while emphasizing lofty purposes, the study presents the medical community as an admirable elite. The process of disseminating information about the study through scientific medical journals enhances this image. Doctors talking to other doctors who share their attitudes and understand their professional commitments creates a closed communication network that reaffirms the bonds within the medical fraternity as it isolates the researchers from outside assessment. Society's respect for medical and scientific research further insulates the study. The process of communicating the results of the study, then, tends to obscure its ethical ramifications as it appeals subtly but forcefully to the shared values and self image of the readers.

At the same time that the definition of and focus on the study's purpose helps create an almost mystical justification, its very longevity reinforces its value. Described in a 1953 report as "one of the longest continued medical surveys ever conducted," the study gains validation through its continuity (Rivers et al. 391). The periodicity of the reports and the reiterated references to earlier articles confer the presumption of value on it. The Tuskegee study as a continuing investigation becomes almost sacrosanct.

## ▉ RHETORICAL IMPLICATIONS

As a case study of the generic constraints of scientific reporting, the Tuskegee project suggests several observations. First, it reveals clearly that features inherent in the genre helped reinforce and even rationalize the latent racial prejudice of the investigators (Jones 60). The conventions of detachment and scientific discrimination accentuated the polarization between subjects and investigators. Significantly, there is no evidence that the authors manipulated the genre for their own ends. Rather, in this case, the genre itself encouraged a continuation of societal myopia and insensitivity.

Second, the study suggests that the genre of scientific reporting which deals with human subjects may be particularly prone to such problems because its very nature encourages detachment and divorces us from appropriate as well as inappropriate human reactions. In this respect, the fact that scientific rhetoric makes no distinction in its approach among inanimate objects, animals, and human beings is noteworthy. A genre which is in many ways insensitive to significant differences in content has severe limitations as a medium of communication. Clearly, a rhetor has some control over any genre, but generic conventions may be so powerful, pervasive, and esteemed by society that they severely restrict rhetorical choice. Rhetors inculcated with those generic conventions may become insensitive to alternatives and blind to the limitations and assumptions inherent in them.

Third, the study clearly indicates that the posture of much scientific reporting as objective and value-free is misleading. The scientific process itself structures and skews our perceptions. What emerges from our observations and appears in our reports is, at best, one slice of reality. If the perspective distorts our observations significantly, as it did in the Tuskegee project, the result is unethical, even if unintentionally so. Such reports are particularly malevolent because they wear the mask of objectivity and truth.

Finally, the broadest rhetorical ramification of the type of scientific reporting discussed here is the creation of a discontinuity between scientific inquiry and more concrete and specific human concerns. All the factors mentioned above contribute to the process: the creation of a discontinuity between subjects and observers, the identification of observers with a larger medical community, and the elevation of the quest for knowledge to an absolute value. In concert, these rhetorical strategies suggest and implicitly reinforce an "in-out" group attitude which isolates scientists from the larger community. Such reporting, by emphasizing the principle of discontinuity discussed by Burke, encourages readers to dissociate themselves from other human beings and to regard the subjects as "scenes" or "agencies" in their endeavors. The possible consequences of such depictions are vividly evident in the Tuskegee study.

The Tuskegee study reveals how rhetorical conventions can obscure the vision and perceptions of rhetors and their audiences. The features distinctive to scientific reporting, "objectivity" and "detachment," can encourage our neglect of crucial human concerns. Rhetorical conventions can become not mere shapers of discourse, but perceptual blinders. Such conventions, when they facilitate stereotypical thinking and distorted vision, become dangerous intellectual straitjackets.

In essence, the Tuskegee study reveals the hollowness of claims that scientific language is always neutral, objective, and value-free. Detachment from the content being discussed can be valuable in helping us exercise our reason and monitor our judgments. But such detachment or objectivity assumes that reason must always dominate human activities. It urges the preeminent value of rationality in the conduct of our lives and in our research. While all of us appreciate the importance of reason in human affairs, we also recognize the value of human emotion in tempering our behavior. Insistence on objectivity and detachment is a great asset in the pursuit of knowledge, but this stance reflects only one aspect of a broad spectrum of human concerns. These qualities embody one beneficial perspective, one set of values. As the Tuskegee study shows, this perspective and the language which conveys it can mislead even well-intentioned people. If allegiance to objectivity and detachment blinds us to other values, it produces neither humane behavior nor sound science.

## ▓ Notes

[1]"Inhuman Experiment" 16, "Official Inhumanity" II 6, "An Immoral Study" 2D, Jones 221.

[2]Wander, 226–35, Kelso 17–29, Simons 115–30, J. A. Campbell 375–90, and Mechling and Mechling 19–32.

[3]For example, the diversity of authors involved abrogate questions of individual idiosyncracies in report writing. Second, the lack of reaction in the medical community indicates clearly the impact of the reports in obscuring ethical questions. Finally, the thirteen progress reports provide a complete and manageable corpus.

[4]Carrie Foote quoted in Brown 12. Jones also reports that the men thought they were being "doctored" for a disease rather than merely observed to trace its course (5–6).

[5]Brown estimates the number at 250 (13).

[6]Seabrook 2A, "The Forty Year Death Watch" 16. Cf. Capron 692–94 for a discussion of "beneficial" versus "non-beneficial" research.

[7]Jones 257–58, estimate of Dr. Donald Printz quoted in Seabrook 2A.

[8]One may speculate that public health officers assigned to rural Alabama did not enjoy the most prestigious of assignments. Participation in a large scale study which was reported periodically in national medical journals undoubtedly made the assignment more attractive. As Jones notes, the study provided not only a relief from the tedium of clinic treatments, but also "the intellectual excitement of becoming researchers on a scientific experiment, one that their superiors regarded as very important." Moreover, for physicians with scientific ambitions, the Tuskegee study afforded opportunities "to publish and advance their careers" (Jones 186).

[9]Significantly, the discovery of penicillin's great efficacy in treating syphilis encouraged continuation of the study, although the information the study yielded had little practical value. That penicillin could obliterate the ravages of syphilis made learning about its consequences more urgent, for they would soon become part of medical history. Reports after penicillin's discovery argued that it "can never be duplicated since penicillin and other antibiotics are being so widely used in the treatment of other diseases thereby affording a definite treatment for syphilis" (Jones 179). The focus on the study's purpose thus provided a justification for its continuation regardless of its practical value.

## ▓ References

"An Immoral Study." *St. Louis Post-Dispatch* 30 July 1972: 2D.

Brown, Warren. "A Shocking New Report on Black Syphilis Victims." *JET* 9 Nov. 1972: 12–17.

Burke, Kenneth. *Language as Symbolic Action.* Berkeley: University of California Press, 1966.

Campbell, John Angus. "The Polemical Mr. Darwin." *Quarterly Journal of Speech* 61 (1975): 375–90.

Campbell, Paul Newell. "The *Personae* of Scientific Discourse." *Quarterly Journal of Speech* 61 (1975): 391–405.

Capron, Alexander Morgan. "Human Experimentation: Basic Issues." Ed. Warren T. Reich. 4 vols. *Encyclopedia of Bioethics.* New York: Free Press, 1972. 2: 692–97.

Deibert, Austin V. and Martha C. Bruyere. "Untreated Syphilis in the Male Negro: III. Evidence of Cardiovascular Abnormalities and other Forms of Morbidity." *Journal of Venereal Disease Information* 27 (1946): 301–14.

Fried, Charles. "Human Experimentation: Philosophical Aspects." *Encyclopedia of Bioethics.* Ed. Warren T. Reich. 4 vols. New York: Free Press, 1978. 2: 698–702.

Heller, J. R. and P. T. Bruyere. "Untreated Syphilis in the Male Negro: Mortality During 12 Years of Observation." *Journal of Venereal Disease Information* 27 (1946): 34–38.

Hirst, R. J. "Realism." *The Encyclopedia of Philosophy.* Ed. Paul Edwards. 8 vols. New York: Macmillan, 1967. 7: 77–83.

"Inhuman Experiment." *Oregonian* 31 July 1972: 16.

Jones, James H. *Bad Blood: The Tuskegee Syphilis Experiment.* New York: Free Press, 1981.

Kampmeier, R. H. "The Tuskegee Study of Untreated Syphilis." *Southern Medical Journal* 65 (1972): 1247–51.

Kelso, James A. "Science and the Rhetoric of Reality." *Central States Speech Journal* 31 (1980): 17–29.

Mechling, Elizabeth Walker and Jay Mechling. "Sweet Talk: The Moral Rhetoric Against Sugar," *Central States Speech Journal* 34 (1983): 19–32.

"Official Inhumanity." Editorial. *Los Angeles Times* 27 July 1972: II6.

Olansky, Sidney, Stanley Schuman, Jesse J. Peters, C. A. Smith, and Dorothy Rambo. "Untreated Syphilis in the Male Negro." *Journal of Chronic Diseases* 4 (1956): 177–85.

Olansky, Sidney, Lloyd Simpson, and Stanley H. Schuman. "Environmental Factors in the Tuskegee Study of Untreated Syphilis." *Public Health Reports* 69 (1954): 691–98.

Pesare, Pasquale J., Theodore J. Bauer, and Geraldine Gleeson. "Untreated Syphilis in the Male Negro." *American Journal of Syphilis, Gonorrhea, and Venereal Disease* 34 (1950): 201–12.

Peters, Jesse J., James H. Peters, Sidney Olansky, and Geraldine A. Gleeson. "Untreated Syphilis in the Male Negro: Pathologic Findings in Syphilitic and Nonsyphilitic Patients." *Journal of Chronic Disease* 1 (1955): 127–48.

Rivers, Eunice, Stanley H. Schuman, Lloyd Simpson, and Sidney Olansky. "Twenty Years of Followup Experience in a Long-Range Medical Study." *Public Health Reports* 68 (1953): 391–95.

Schuman, Stanley H., Sidney Olansky, Eunice Rivers, C. A. Smith, and Dorothy S. Rambo. "Untreated Syphilis in the Male Negro." *Journal of Chronic Disease* 2 (1955): 543–58.

Seabrook, Charles. "Study Genocidal—CDC Doctor." *Atlanta Journal* 27 July 1972: 2A.

Shafer, J. K., Lida J. Usilton, and Geraldine A. Gleeson. "Untreated Syphilis in the Male Negro." *Public Health Reports* 69 (1954): 684–90.

Simons, Herbert W. "Are Scientists Rhetors in Disguise? An Analysis of Disuasive Processes Within Scientific Communities." *Rhetoric in Transition: Studies in the Nature and Uses of Rhetoric.* Ed. Eugene E. White. University Park: Pennsylvania State University Press, 1980, 115–30.

———. *Persuasion: Understanding, Practice, and Analysis.* Reading, Mass.: Addison-Wesley, 1976.

Smart, Ninian. "History of Mysticism." *Encyclopedia of Philosophy.* Ed. Paul Edwards. 8 vols. New York: Macmillan, 1967. 5: 420.

"The Forty Year Death Watch." *Medical World News* 18 Aug. 1972: 15–17.

Veatch, Robert M. "Codes of Medical Ethics: Ethical Analysis." *Encyclopedia of Bioethics*. Ed. Warren T. Reich. 4 vols. New York: Free Press, 1978. 1: 172–79.

Vonderlehr, R. A., Taliaferro Clark, O. C. Wegner, and J. R. Heller, Jr. "Untreated Syphilis in the Male Negro." *Venereal Disease Information* 17 (1936): 260–65.

Wander, Philip C. "The Rhetoric of Science." *Western Journal of Speech Communication* 40 (1976): 226–35.

Wooten, John T. "Survivor of '32 Syphilis Study Recalls a Diagnosis." *New York Times* 27 July 1972: 18.

# CHAPTER 14 ☐

# CICERO'S REDEMPTIVE IDENTIFICATION

**Michael C. Leff**

*In this commentary, Michael C. Leff takes a somewhat ironic look at the writing of one of his early essays on Cicero's Catilinarian orations. Leff dryly describes the spirit of his search for a method with which to approach Cicero's texts as bordering on the opportunistic. When one theoretical approach seemed unable to draw much of interest from his text, Leff describes himself as casting about from one theory to another without asking whether it was his own assumptions that might have needed reexamination. Leff is ambivalent in retrospect about the outcome, suggesting that while the finished essay was not without its insights, his fixed attention to a narrowly drawn method ultimately restricted his ability to draw conclusions about Cicero's texts.*

## COMMENTARY

I no longer remember precisely when I wrote the first version of this essay. It was a long time ago—Lyndon Johnson was president and I was a graduate student. Somewhat later, with help from my friend Jerry Mohrmann, I revised the essay for publication in *Explorations in Rhetorical Criticism,* a book (edited by Mohrmann, Charles Stewart, and Donovan Ochs) that was designed to open new approaches to criticism. Like the book in general, the essay did not command a wide audience, and as the years passed, I more or less forgot about it. Consequently, I was surprised and a bit dismayed when the editors of this volume indicated that they wanted to reprint the essay along with some of my reflections about it. At this distance, my own essay seemed alien, and in rereading it, I had the eerie sense that it not only belonged to a different time and place but to a different person altogether.

Distance is a technical term that refers to the stance a critic takes in

**323**

relation to the object of study. The young man who wrote the essay that follows, like most of his contemporaries, believed that critical distance was a good thing; it preserved objectivity and allowed space for the application or construction of theory. More recently, fashions have changed, and critics often emphasize the value of "engagement." Objectivity is no longer assumed to be either possible or desirable, and with increasing frequency and vehemence, critics are asked to abandon the role of disinterested spectators and to recognize their function as rhetorical advocates.

My current view falls somewhere between these two positions, since I try to practice a kind of interpretative criticism that simultaneously involves distance and engagement. From this perspective, the end of criticism is not to build or test "theory" but to understand the utterance of another person. Such understanding is never "objective," since it depends upon an interaction between the discourse of the interpreter and the discourse of the other, and this interaction occurs between two positioned subjects and not in some zone of impersonal, objective neutrality. The interpreter attempts to assimilate a text that is distant or alien into his or her understanding, but the discourse the critic produces is always other than the discourse that is being studied, and the critic's understanding can never replicate another person's understanding of the world. Interpretative criticism, then, is a never-ending oscillation between distance and engagement, between identifying with the other and maintaining distance from the other.

Since self-understanding is incomplete and mutable, the critic's position is not entirely stable. Time passes, fashions change, and the accumulated weight of the interpretative discipline, which opens the critic to different rhetorical voices, gradually begins to change the critic's own view of rhetoric. Little wonder, then, that, after more than two decades, my essay seems so distant that commentary on it requires an act of critical self-reflection almost as complex as the interpretation of some other person's text.

On first reflection, the essay seemed to originate by accident. It just happened that my reading of Burke's *Rhetoric of Motives* coincided with a frustrating effort to engage the rhetoric of Cicero's Catilinarian Orations. In studying the Ciceronian texts, I had followed the then conventional method that began with an argumentative analysis. The objective was to lay bare the logical structure of the texts—to identify the key premises, show their relationship to one another, and locate the evidence supporting the premises. The more I tried to groom the text into this tidy form, however, the more clearly I realized that the endeavor was futile. Cicero's speeches just did not behave like the speeches of intercollegiate debaters. They did not march from premise to premise in an even stride, but they ambled through images, innuendoes, and emotional outbursts whose power I could sense but could not explain. At this point, Burke came to the rescue. He offered a way to encounter the symbolic dimension of rhetorical discourse, and an approach that could give a rational account for things that did not seem rational on the surface. In particular, his "theory" of redemptive identification allowed for an explanation of Cicero's apparently irrational tendency to exaggerate.

The details of this story do indeed refer to matters of coincidence, but, on further reflection, the plot line has a familiar ring. It embodies a general pattern that entered into the consciousness of rhetorical critics at the time and exerted a powerful influence on the orientation they adopted toward their work. The key element in this pattern is a fixation on theory—or more specifically on theory, conceived after the social scientific model, as a coherently organized body of principles distanced from and superior to any particular instance of practice. Operating on this basic premise, the critic is positioned to move in a vertical direction. That is, critical explanations proceed either downward from abstract, theoretical principles to specific practices or upward from practices to principles. In either case, explanation rests upon principles distant from and more abstract than anything manifest in rhetorical practice. To put this point negatively, the critic is discouraged from attending to rhetorical developments within specific cases or moving laterally across cases, except insofar as comparative study becomes grist for a theoretical mill that refines the raw material of practice into abstract regularities.

My own essay was grounded firmly, though unconsciously, in the vertical, theoretical orientation. Having found the existing "theory" inadequate for my purposes, I did not pause to consider whether the resistance of the texts suggested a flawed conception of the nature of theory and its relationship to critical practice. Instead, I hastened to find another "theory" as a replacement. This reaction was hardly accidental; it reflected the temper of the time. The essay rested comfortably within *Explorations in Rhetorical Criticism*, since the book as a whole represented an effort to multiply theoretical perspectives. The editors had instructed each contributor "to sketch a theoretical position and apply it," but in my case, the instructions were unnecessary. Already infected by the same pseudo-pluralistic virus, I had performed the required steps in the earlier version of the paper.

This bias distorted both my use of Burke and my reading of the speeches. Instead of attempting to understand and assimilate Burke's complex critical position, I tore a section of the *Rhetoric of Motives* loose from its context and rearranged it into a tidy methodological grid. Had I studied Burke more attentively, I would have discovered an alternative conception of theory per se, rather than an alternative theory in the conventional sense. By adopting a wider Burkean perspective, I might have seen the theorist as a positioned subject engaged in a kind of rhetorical practice, and I might have recognized the possibility of grounding interpretative work in cases rather than in disembodied abstractions. This same narrowing of vision also limited my approach to Cicero's texts. Unaware of other possibilities, I had assimilated the technical lore of classical rhetoric into a modern frame of reference. I did not view the standard classical system as a loose inventory of strategies grouped for convenience under a limited number of headings. I merely assumed that the system constituted a "theory" and that it ought to provide a method for critical inquiry. As a result, the conventional categories, which I, along with many others, still retained even as we appropriated new "theories," appeared as separate and distinct modules to be invoked in methodical order. The critic first read down through the text to analyze its argumentative appeals, and then invoked the same procedure to analyze its style. This fragmented approach, which runs contrary to the spirit of both Burke and Cicero, left me in a position where I could not read across a text so as to understand the interactions among argument, style, and context. Consequently, I floundered until I could borrow a "theory" that accounted for one of the prominent features in Cicero's speeches (that is, the extensive use of hyperbole), and I then fixed attention on that feature. This exercise was not without some value, but for reasons I did not then understand, it blocked a more fully realized interpretive effort. As Robert Cape has demonstrated recently (in his 1991 dissertation, "On Reading Cicero's Catilinarian Orations"), a more fluid use of the standard categories yields a much more sensitive reading of the *Catilinarians.*

Despite these misgivings, I still retain a certain fondness for the young man who wrote the following essay. He makes a noteworthy attempt to produce some sparks by striking a set of venerable texts against the thought of an important contemporary rhetorician. At times the interaction really seems to work, especially in the analysis of the metaphors of disease, parentage, death, and rebirth. In general, his problem is that he does not understand his own position as a critic. Note that when he comes to state his purposes in the last paragraph, he resorts to an almost meaningless jumble of phrases—something about living texts, historical documents, the grand possibilities of theory, and split-level realities. He does not realize that if he wants to understand other people's utterances, he must first make a serious effort to understand his own purposes. Given the blindness and confusion of this essay, I doubt that he will ever sort things out adequately, but he really seems committed to the task of opening old texts to contemporary understanding, and if he persists in this endeavor, he might improve his own self-understanding.

# Redemptive Identification:
# Cicero's Catilinarian Orations

**Michael C. Leff**

$F$ew events in ancient history are as well documented as the conspiracy of Catiline in 63 B.C.[1] Lucius Sergius Catiline was a member of a noble but impoverished Roman family. A man of talent and ambition, he sought status and wealth through political advancement. Despite his connections and ability, however, Catiline was thwarted three times in his desire to gain election to the consulship, and after his last defeat in 63 B.C., he was desperate. Deeply in debt, deserted by his most powerful ally, and deprived of any hope of recouping his losses, Catiline launched a conspiracy to overthrow the government and force a program of debt cancellation, *nova tabula*. The plot called for a rising in the city coupled with attacks on Rome from the Italian countryside. From its beginning, the plot offered little hope of success. Most Italians had recently gained Roman citizenship and were not inclined to test the strength of the Roman government without powerful support. Catiline did manage to raise a force of a few thousand ill-equipped troops, but this rag-tag army was no match for the regular troops which the government mobilized. The conspiracy collapsed as suddenly as it had emerged.

According to Cicero, the conspiracy was one of the most momentous events in human history.[2] He asserted that the incident marked the "bloodiest and cruelest war in the memory of man" (III.x.25), that the conspirators not only intended to stage a coup, but to burn down the whole city of Rome and invite savage Gauls to dance on its ashes (IV. xi.11–12), that Catiline was the author of every crime in the state, and that the conspiracy was responsible for all evil in Rome (I.vii.18,xiii.31–32,II.x.22–23). He immodestly praised himself as the sole savior of Rome (III.x.25), and he alleged that reaction against the conspiracy caused a total identification of "good" men which promised a permanent solution to the problems of the state (IV.viii.14–15). All these assertions were patently false. They grossly exaggerated the intent of the conspirators, the danger of the conspiracy, and the nature of the response to it.

For the historian, it is enough to know that Cicero overstates his case. Consequently most recent histories of the conspiracy note the problem, but do not attempt a detailed explanation of its cause. Furthermore critics of discourse have not examined this pattern of exaggeration. But Cicero's use of hyperbole is so frequent and so blatant that one must suspect that it reveals a crucial and perhaps subconscious premise that colors the orations as a whole. The purpose of this essay is to investigate this question of hyperbole, and its methodology will come from Kenneth Burke's theory of redemptive identification.

In his essay "Freud and the Analysis of Poetry," Burke begins, "The reading of Freud I find suggestive almost to the point of bewilderment."[3] The rhetorical critic could say much the same about Burke. Ranging over a seemingly limitless number of subjects from sociology to poetry, his writings are extensive, interrelated, and filled with seminal ideas. Under the circumstances, it is difficult to explicate even one of Burke's more specific concepts and contend that it is an accurate abstract of his thought. A more useful approach is to use Burke as he uses Freud, by adapting and assimilating a Burkean concept to one's own purposes, and appropriately such an adaptation can begin through an analysis of Freud's general theories of guilt and redemption.

Freud's *Civilization and Its Discontents* applies the techniques of psychoanalysis to the problems of society. Freud contends that guilt arises in civilization in much the same way as in individuals and that the existence of civilization, in and of itself, intensifies the problem of psychic adjustment. In fact, he concludes that guilt is the single most important problem faced by civilization.[4] According to Freudian theory, civilization exists in order for people to work together in harmony. This harmony of diverse interests demands an inhibited love-aim, in the sense of "love thy neighbor" as opposed to erotic love. Consequently, civilization must control the ego's desire for pleasure; it must curb certain forms of aggression. Unfortunately, this situation creates tension between the desire for aggressive pleasure seeking and the need for union within a human community.

Repression ultimately relies on some form of authority. In the early stages of human development, the child is governed by the external authority of his parents. At a later stage this authority is internalized as the "super-ego." Through the influence of his parents and of the culture as a whole, the individual creates a super-ego which confines the aggression of the ego. The function of the super-ego is especially complicated because it is internalized. External authority can control only overt behavior, but the super-ego is omniscient. While renunciation of errant behavior is often sufficient to allay external authority, it cannot mollify the super-ego. Consequently the tension between the ego and super-ego is never fully resolved, and civilized man is hopelessly caught-up in the tragic conflict between personal instinct and societal mores. The result is a sense of guilt which is sometimes, though not always, unconscious.

The sense of guilt becomes particularly keen when an individual experiences misfortune. So long as things are working to one's advantage, the super-ego's restriction is weak or easily disregarded, but when misfortune occurs, civilized man becomes disconcerted about possible violations of conscience, that is, the super-ego. In the primitive state, man blames ill-luck on a totem or a fetish, but the super-ego developed by civilization forces a conception of self-guilt; the individual is likely to view external misfortune as the result of his own improper conduct or thought. Moreover, this malaise may affect entire societies as well as individuals. In other words, a civilization may exhibit neurotic symptoms.

Naturally, societies develop means of eliminating or reducing guilt. One convenient mechanism is to distinguish sharply between one's own society and that of his neighbors. Aggression is often directed toward some alien force: "The advantage which a comparatively small cultural group offers of allowing the [aggressive] instinct an outlet in the form of hostility against intruders is not to be despised. It is always possible to bind together a considerable number of people in love, so long as there are other people left over to receive the manifestations of their aggressiveness."[5] In short, we love to find someone our whole society can hate. This concept is familiar to rhetoricians who have studied the tactics of "bloody shirt" orators, "red-scare" politicians, and anti-Semites.

Society also can find refuge in religion. In Freud's view, religion reduces guilt by manufacturing a spurious external authority, an outside force which absorbs the guilt arising from the tensions of society: "They [religions] claim to redeem mankind from this sense of guilt, which they call sin."[6] Anyone who has read more than a few sermons knows how important the notion of redemption of sin is to the preacher.

To Freud, then, guilt is an inevitable result of the conflict between natural instinct arising from the ego and inhibitory mechanisms located in the super-ego. This tension is converted into a sense of sin which blames all frustration on violation of the conscience. By analogy, societies are seen as liable to fall victim to this malady as well as individuals. The result is a powerful but often inexplicable guilt syndrome. This guilt, in turn, may be reduced or displaced through the use of external scapegoats or the invention of redemptive mythologies.

One need not extend Freud's argument very far to apply it to criticism, but some extension is needed in terminology. Fortunately Burke's theory of redemptive identification represents an adaptation and application of Freud's guilt concept to literary and rhetorical concerns.

Burke filters Freud's theory through the screen of traditional humanistic terminology. In particular, he notes the dialectical polarity which occurs in redemptive rhetoric and provides a vehicle for examining the phenomenon in the context of discourse. His basic conceptions, however, are very close to those of Freud. His view of sin and redemption, the redemption of sin through a common foe or through a symbol of the power of good, and misfortune as an impetus toward self-recrimination are all consistent with Freud.

Redemptive identification occurs through the process of shared guilt.[7]

The consubstantial bond linking the parties in this sort of rhetorical transaction is a common self-conception of sinfulness. This sin is externalized by projecting it on an alien force which acts as a scapegoat. The scapegoat serves as a receptacle, a symbolic vessel, for the "iniquities of those who would be cured by attacking it."[8] Expressed in another way, the persecutors attribute to a sacrificial victim all the sins which plague them internally and then are purged of sin by the actual or symbolic destruction of the victim.

The process, in Burke's terminology, is dialectical, for it operates through antithetical contrasts arising from division and synthesis. The ritual requires three steps: (1) the scapegoat originally merges with its persecutors in the sense that both share the same inequities; (2) the victim is then symbolically divided from its persecutors; and (3) a second merger occurs, this time the result of the "unification of those whose purified identity is defined in dialectical opposition to the sacrificial offering."[9]

The scapegoat appears in two primary forms, as the principle of good and as the principle of evil. This polarity results from the dialectical nature of the process. The victim must be separable from the rest of society along lines which can be defined in abstract, normative terms. Also it must serve as the receptacle of all sin because the externalization of sin requires that all guilt be dissociated from those seeking purgation. Finally, the victim is made a locus of power; only the powerful would have sufficient force to account for or purge so virulent a concept as that of national iniquity.

Two examples from Burke illustrate these forms of redemptive identification. The symbolism of Christ's passion represented purgation through sacrifice of the personified principle of good. The sins of mankind were poured into the Christ vessel, and when he died these sins perished with him. Through Christ's death man was redeemed. The Nazis, on the other hand, attempted unification through a common foe, utilizing the evil principle. The German defeat in the First World War caused extreme cultural dislocation. The traditional values of the society, imperial autocracy, militaristic organization, and capitalistic economic prosperity had been destroyed. The resulting sense of misfortune caused anxiety to mount and feelings of guilt developed which exercised a powerful grip on the German mind. The stage was set for Hitler's use of the Jew as sacrificial victim, and the Jew was depicted as the embodiment of all sin; his uncleanness polluted everyone and by his destruction the German nation would be purified.

Such, in brief, is Burke's theory of redemptive identification. Its affinity with Freudian theory is clear and its usefulness for rhetorical criticism is promising. It also appears to offer the most satisfactory explanation for the exaggeration that characterizes Cicero's Catilinarians.

Roman society in the age of Cicero and Augustus was unstable. This era was one of transition from republic to empire, which one historian aptly titled "The Roman Revolution." The government of the state was transformed from traditional oligarchy to imperial autocracy, the economy from agrarian simplicity to mercantile complexity, and the social mores from a belief in asceticism to open hedonism. And, at least for the educated classes, the pagan Roman religion no longer had any spiritual authority.[10]

It is always dangerous to draw analogies between one society and another, but both the Weimar Republic and late Republican and early Imperial Rome shared a sense of impending disaster. For the Romans the shock of cultural and social change was reinforced by political instability and civil war. Important leaders like the Gracchi and Saturninus were assassinated, and the disastrous conflict between Marius and Sulla set a precedent for brutality and cynicism previously unimagined in internal Roman politics. Freudian doctrine would lead us to expect symptoms of anxiety in such a society, and our suspicion is verified by the literary record. For example, in the introduction to his *Histories,* Livy recommends history as the best means of curing the sickness of his times (I.i), and the Elder Seneca speculates in his *Controversiae* that the decline of eloquence is due to moral decay (I.7.). Other examples of the same theme might be cited to support this hypothesis, but our concern is with the Catilinarian conspiracy, and there can be little doubt that it incited a feeling of guilt.

Sallust, our second contemporary source for the conspiracy, belonged to a political faction opposed to Cicero. His *Bellum Catilinae,* therefore, forms a useful comparison to check issues of fact and interpretation against the account provided by Cicero. Sallust argued that the conspiracy was a foul and guilty compact, and the topic of moral decadence emerged as the theme of his introduction. He noted the high ethical standards of the ancient Romans, and then recorded their fall from honor: "Avarice destroyed honor, integrity and every other virtue and instead taught men to be proud and cruel and neglect religion and every other virtue and to hold nothing too sacred to sell. . . . At first these vices grew slowly and sometimes met punishment, later on, when the disease spread like a plague, Rome changed; her government once so just and admirable became harsh and unendurable."[11] Catiline was both a prime example and a cause of this terrible corruption: "He [Catiline] was incited also by the corruption of a society plagued by two opposite but equally disastrous vices—love of luxury and love of money. . . . In short, all who were in disgrace or afflicted by poverty or consciousness of guilt were Catiline's intimate associates. And if anyone innocent happened to become friendly with him, the temptations to which daily intercourse with Catiline exposed him soon made him as evil a ruffian as the rest."[12] In these passages, we note an aura of guilt occasioned by misfortune and dishonor. The corruption afflicted all Roman society, but it was especially apparent in the person of Catiline. The point is underscored by the use of disease images. Catiline, infected with the disease of the times, attracted all those like him and polluted the healthy with whom he came into contact.

Although less explicit and less dramatic, a similar view of the conspiracy is conveyed by Virgil and Seneca the Elder, writers of the Augustan age. For example, in Book VIII of the *Aeneid*, Aeneas is given a shield which Vulcan decorates with scenes from later Roman history, and Catiline appears in the portrait of evil: "Elsewhere the deep Gates of hell were represented, the domicile of the damned and the torments they suffer—Catiline hangs from the edge of a terrible precipice, shrinking away from the Furies above him. But the righteous are set apart."[13] The image of the Furies, relentless agents of retribution, is particularly vivid, and the separation of the righteous from Catiline calls to mind the dialectical polarity between scapegoat and persecutors. A variation on this theme appears in Seneca's *Suasoriae* when he recalls the great deeds of Cicero's consulship, "the host of the conspirators, the discovery of the guilty pact, and the stamping out of the sin of the nobles."[14] One might argue that Virgil and Seneca view the conspiracy through the bias of Cicero and Sallust, and so their special attention to the guilt involved merely reflects their sources. Nevertheless, they were not forced to accept the hyperbole of earlier writers. Therefore, the probable conclusion is that guilt and the conspiracy are closely related in the minds of many Romans in the late Republic and early Empire. Furthermore the materials cited establish that Catiline sometimes assumes a symbolic function; that is, his conspiracy is regarded as more than a literal threat to the safety of the Roman state in one particular instance. His name is associated with guilt in much the same way Cicero's is associated with eloquence. This guilt theme is most fully developed, however, by Cicero himself.

In his attack, Cicero exaggerates the intent of the conspirators, and he exaggerates their allegedly evil character. The orations abound with examples of both. In the middle of the first speech, for instance, Cicero exaggerates intent when he hurls this invective against his opponents: "Here, here in our very midst, Conscript Fathers, in this most sacred and dignified council of the whole world, are men who plan for the destruction of all of us, who plan for the destruction of this city and even the destruction of the whole world" (I.iv.9). Throughout the orations, Cicero persists in arguing that the conspirators planned indiscriminate slaughter and the destruction of Rome through fire (III.iv.8). The extent of his passion is revealed in the introductory lines of the third speech where he boasts of saving "the state, citizens, the lives of you all, your property, your fortunes, your wives and your children" (III.i.1). The full force of his hyperbole becomes apparent in the final speech. In demanding severe penalties against the conspirators, Cicero has this vision:

> For I seem to see this city, the light of the whole world and the fortress of all nations suddenly involved in one general conflagration. In my imagination I see on the grave of the fatherland the wretched unburied heaps of corpses. Before my eyes rises the countenance of Cethegus and his madness as he revels in our death. . . . So we in the case of these men who have wished to murder us, our

wives, our children, who have tried to destroy all our homes and this common dwelling of the state, who have done this that they may set up the tribe of the Allobroges amid the ruins of this city and on the ashes of a burnt out empire, if we shall be most stern we shall be considered merciful. . . . This Lentulus summons the Gauls to overturn the foundations of the state, he instigates the slaves, he invites Catiline, he assigns us to Cethegus to be murdered, the other citizens to Gabinus to be slaughtered, all Italy to Catiline to be devastated and plundered (IV.vi.11–13).

All this is a magnificent display of rhetorical virtuosity, but it is neither true nor relevant to the point at issue in the debate. While the exaggeration in this passage is unusually extensive, the continued repetition of similar and equally false assertions is a dominant characteristic of the orations.

In the first two speeches, the critic might explain Cicero's exaggeration of conspiratorial intent on the grounds that it is an appropriate rhetorical response to a situation where concrete evidence is lacking. This sort of argument will not do, however, in the case of the third speech; Cicero had obtained all the proof he needed, and the conspirators already had been convicted by the Senate. Since this speech so well illustrates the magnitude of Cicero's hyperbole, it will be profitable to examine the oration and the circumstances surrounding it in some detail.

On the night of November 7, 63 B.C., Catiline left Rome and repaired to Etruria where his allies were recruiting an army. A number of other conspirators, led by the dissolute nobles Lentulus and Cethegus, remained in the city. The two groups intended to coordinate the attack of the Etrurian army with disturbances in Rome. These plans were known to Cicero, but he lacked sufficient evidence to arrest the conspirators who were still within the city walls. As a consequence, his dramatic invectives of early November were not followed by any decisive action. Meanwhile, the conspiracy sputtered in the hands of Lentulus, Cethegus, and their lieutenants.

By a stroke of luck, Cicero finally managed to gain the legal evidence he needed against the conspirators in early December. Ambassadors sent to Rome by the Allobrogian Gauls were rebuffed by the Senate, and the conspirators then invited them to lead their tribe into an alliance with Catiline. The Allobroges concluded that the conspiracy had no chance of success and divulged the plot to their patron Fabius Sanga, who reported it to Cicero. The Allobroges were enlisted as counterspies and instructed to express interest in the conspiracy and to demand letters pledging the support of its leaders. On the night of December second, Lentulus, Cethegus, and Statilius gave their letters to the envoys. The Gauls then departed, supposedly on their way to meet Catiline in Etruria, and another of the conspirators, Volturcius, accompanied them to deliver both written and oral messages to Catiline. The whole party was intercepted at the Mulvian bridge.

The next day, Cicero convened the Senate and summoned Statilius, Lentulus, Gabinius, and Cethegus who were still unaware of what had happened. When the evidence against them was presented, they confessed their complicity in the plot and were convicted by the Senate. After adjournment, Cicero hastened to the forum to deliver his "Third Oration Against Catiline." In his earlier speeches he sought to rouse public opinion by bold assertion; now he added a more subtle tactic—exaggeration of the intent of the conspirators by distorting the evidence. He presented four pieces of evidence to justify the arrest of the conspirators: the testimony of the Allobroges, the letters from the conspirators to the Allobroges, the letter carried by Volturcius, and his account of the oral message to Catiline.

The testimony of the Allobroges reveals the names of the leading conspirators and a general account of the services demanded of them, as well as some miscellaneous information about Lentulus' superstitiousness. Such evidence certainly proves that an illegal plot is afoot and indicates the parties involved, but it reveals nothing about the details of the conspiracy. Moreover, Cicero is vague in recounting the Allobrogian testimony, merely asserting that they affirmed that some form of "murder and arson" was contemplated (III.iv.10). This source, then, does not justify Cicero's extravagant assertions about the nihilistic aims of the conspirators.

Secondly, Cicero offers in evidence the letter carried by Volturcius: "You will know who I am from him whom I am sending to you. Be brave and consider into what a situation you have brought yourself; and see what you now need and take care to secure for yourself the aid of all, even of the lowest classes" (III.v.12). The authenticity of this letter is beyond question, for an almost identical version of it is reproduced by Sallust. Since Lentulus is identified as its sender, the letter does prove collusion between Lentulus and a public enemy, but it is hardly a model of unambiguous prose. We have no further information about the intentions of either Lentulus or Catiline except that they considered making an appeal to "the lowest classes."

Next there is the meager evidence provided by the letters of Statilius, Cethegus, and Lentulus pledging support to the Allobroges. These documents, however, say only that the conspirators would do what they promised (III.v.10). Obviously the pledge is vague. Coupled with the testimony of the Allobroges themselves, it does prove that something treasonous is imminent, but Cicero still has no basis for his strongest accusations.

Finally, and most important, there was the matter of the oral message Lentulus sent to Catiline through Volturcius. When given the promise of a full pardon, Volturcius confessed his guilt and revealed the content of the message Lentulus entrusted to him. According to Cicero, it indicated that the conspirators intended to "set fire to the city in every part, just as it had been apportioned and allotted, and kill a vast number of citizens, and that he [Catiline] should then be ready to intercept the fugitives and join his leaders in the city" (III.iv.8). If this paraphrase represented an accurate report of Volturcius' testimony, Cicero at last would have had justification for some of his stronger allegations against the conspirators. Sallust, however, presented a different version of Volturcius' story: "He [Lentulus] also sent a message by word of mouth: what, he asked, was Catiline's idea—since he had been declared a public enemy by the Senate—in refusing to enlist slaves? All was ready at Rome according to his order and there must be no delay on his part in advancing nearer."[15] Thus, Sallust did not acknowledge any specific information about the execution of the plot in his rendering of the testimony.

When the two versions of this incident are compared, there is little reason to accept Cicero's account. Catiline had already given detailed orders concerning the plan of action before departing to Etruria. There was no reason why Lentulus should have repeated these instructions concerning arson and murder to Catiline. Moreover all of the other messages were couched in the vague language we would expect of conspirators. There was no motivation for Lentulus to send a message of the sort Cicero described. On the other hand, we would expect an acknowledgment that plans already agreed to were ready for action.

On the basis of this analysis, we are forced to conclude that Cicero deliberately overstates the goals of the conspirators by tampering with the evidence. He never proves his charge of indiscriminate murder and unrestricted incendiarism, and it is quite clear that he consistently distorts the intent of the conspirators both through bold assertion and manipulation of specific evidence.

A second and even more pronounced form of exaggeration occurs when Cicero attacks the character of Catiline and his allies. He devotes much of the Catilinarians to the depravity of any and all persons associated with the conspiracy, and even by the standards of antiquity, Cicero is unusually vehement. By the time our orator leaves the podium, he has accused Catiline of every imaginable form of corruption, madness, and debauchery.

A particularly clear example of this hyperbole occurs late in the first oration. Here, Cicero lists the "personal crimes" of Catiline claiming that he has been stained by the unholy trinity of crime, corruption, and lust. He accuses Catiline of "leading youth astray," "dissipating his personal fortune," and even of murdering his wife. Finally, Cicero hints darkly about a sin so great that he hesitates to mention it for fear of bringing the wrath of the gods on the state (I.vi.13–14). The reference is to the rumor that Catiline had killed his own son. The most shocking of these charges could not have had any basis in fact. Catiline had associated with the most patrician circles in Rome for some time and had there been any real suspicion of such crimes, he could hardly have remained in this rarified society. The lack of specific legal action against him also must make us skeptical about Cicero's veracity.

Cicero is equally savage about Catiline's public life. In fact, Catiline's public misconduct is so villainous that Cicero has the personified state cry out against his sins: "She [Rome], Catiline, thus confers with you, and as it were, though silent speaks: 'No crime for some years now has come into existence except through you, no outrage without you; you alone have killed many citizens . . . you have been able not only to neglect the laws and the courts but even to thwart and destroy them' " (I.vii.18). In another speech, Cicero repeats the same argument in his own voice, charging that Catiline has been a partner in every crime committed in Rome. His hyperbole reaches a crescendo as he proclaims that "no murder, no foul lewdness" in recent memory has been accomplished without Catiline lending a hand in it (II.iv.7–8).

Cicero has vitriol enough for it to spill over to the other conspirators. Among the plotters, Cicero detects a clique composed of parricides, assassins, and sundry other criminals. Their crimes are of such a magnitude that no prison could contain them (II.x.22). In addition, there is a special coterie of softer, more personal criminals. Within this category lurk all of Rome's adulterers, all of the unclean and impure rascals of the city who whiled their hours in sensual pleasures, sprinkling poison and waving daggers (II.x.22). In general, the conspiracy is manned by a brigade of the damned. While no one can doubt that the conspirators were an unsavory crew, we may still believe that at least a few of Rome's adulterers managed to stay clear of the plot.

As one might expect, Cicero and his allies—including not only all the respectable citizens of Rome but also the immortal gods—are the precise opposites of Catiline's thugs. Cicero praises himself with an abandon equal to his denunciation of Catiline. He presents himself as a savior clad in the toga of peace protecting the innocent from lunatic criminals (III.x.23). He assumes full credit for saving both Rome and the rest of the world and immodestly delights in explaining his signal honor of having won a vote of thanksgiving while still a civilian (III.vi.15). He asserts that his actions have had a salutary effect on the politics of the nation. Good men have come to their senses and, roused by a common danger, they have joined together in order to crush evil. His conception of the unanimity of support behind him is revealed when he says, "This is the only known case since the founding of the city in which all men absolutely agree" (IV.vii.14); "After a strife with this order [the Equestrians] for many years, this day and this case have recalled them to you [the Senate]. And if we maintain this union consummated in my consulship, I assure you that hereafter no civil and domestic strife will come to any part of the state" (IV.vii.15); and "All the orders are united in purpose, heart and voice to save the state" (IV.ix.18). Like Virgil, Cicero makes a hard and fast dichotomy between Catiline and the forces of good. This contrast is most fully developed in the following antithesis: "For on this side fights modesty, on that fraud; on this righteousness, on that crime; on this steadfastness, on that madness; on this honesty, on that deceit; and finally on this side justice, temperance, fortitude, prudence, all the virtues contend with injustice, extravagance, cowardice, recklessness, all the vices; lastly abundance with poverty, good reason with bad, sanity and insanity and finally fair hope against deepest despair" (II.xi.25).

By now it is painfully obvious that much of Cicero's consular oratory is composed of extravagant hyperbole. The real task is to explain why he used such a tactic. One possible explanation is to contend that he has some specific political goal in mind and that exaggerated praise and blame further this goal. Such a theory is particularly tempting in light of Cicero's political doctrine of *concordia ordinum* which is implied in passages which extol the "good" men in the state and celebrate their union against Catiline.[16] No doubt this motive accounts for some of the hyperbole, but it is unconvincing as an explanation of the whole phenomenon. At times Cicero's overstatement constitutes a positive drawback to his political objectives. In the first oration, the exaggerations perform the useful function of diverting attention from the poverty of legal evidence. On the other hand, his total lack of restraint in the second oration renders it incredible (III.ii.4). Sallust testifies that popular opinion was not hostile to Catiline until nearly three weeks after Cicero's second oration,[17] that is, at about the time that Lentulus and his cronies were caught red-handed. Consequently if Cicero's program of distortion arises out of the rational desire to steer his countrymen toward his own political platform, it is apparent that Cicero is trapped by his own snare, a victim of what Burke calls cunning identification.

Finally, the political account of this exaggeration runs afoul of the third oration. Tactically, the hyperbole is more skillful and probably more effective, but one wonders why Cicero goes to the trouble of altering the evidence at all. More than enough proof is available to convict the conspirators and put them out of operation. The conspirators within Rome have been contained, and Cicero has consistently argued that once the plot within the city is quashed there is no cause for fear. Why then does he persist in calling the conspiracy a threat to all civilization and later demand the execution of the conspirators? As a last resort, one might argue that Cicero is a vain man, and to satisfy his vanity, he wants to appear as the savior of the Roman way of life. This is true, but it explains nothing, for it simply says that Cicero exaggerates because he feels a need to exaggerate.

The best explanation results if we move to the psychological and ritual dimensions of the situation. We see that Cicero's hyperbole functions to change Catiline from a man representing a specific external threat to the government to a symbol representing an internal threat to the integrity of society. In other words, Catiline becomes a scapegoat. The use of exaggeration is necessary because the real Catiline is neither powerful enough nor dangerous enough to serve as a victim in this sacrificial drama. Thus, the danger of the conspiracy is magnified, and vivid pictures are drawn of what would occur if the conspirators were left unchecked.

When we recall the steps in Burke's dialectic of the scapegoat, it becomes apparent how closely Cicero's rhetoric of exaggeration fits the pattern. The victim must be originally merged with the persecutors. This much is given to Cicero. Catiline's conspiracy is an act of civil violence from within the state and from within the ranks of the nobility. The scapegoat now must be *totally* isolated from the rest of society. This step requires the application of Cicero's art because he must make a desolate and desperate conspirator appear as the soul of evil and as a virulent threat. As a consequence, Cicero invokes repeated ritual incantations which associate the conspirators with all sin. Hence the insistence that all crime springs from Catiline's corruption and that the conspiracy magnetically attracts every particle of iniquity within the society ("all the adulterers, all the impure"). Hence also the distortion of evidence when it serves little practical purpose and the demand for the death of the captured conspirators. Finally, Cicero creates a dialectical polarity that separates the "good" men from the minions of the conspiracy. This is accomplished most notably in the antithetical juxtaposition of normative terms used in the extended antithesis of the second oration ("on this side fights modesty, on that fraud"). The third step, a union of those redeemed by the persecution of the victim, is represented by Cicero's argument that respectable men have ceased warring and closed ranks in opposition to the common foe ("all the orders are united"). Whatever the practical consequences of these orations, they also constitute a symbolic rite of purgation.

The hypothesis that the sense of guilt is the driving force in the rhetoric of the Catilinarians is reinforced when we examine Cicero's use of metaphor. Metaphoric clusters referring to disease, corruption, parentage, and rebirth occur regularly in the speeches, often in close proximity. Such patterns reveal the symbolic direction of the discourses and put us in touch with the level of artistic creativity that Burke terms "dream." The analysis of symbolism provides the best means of comprehending the subconscious "dancing of attitudes" in the discourses.

The use of disease images is a natural and explicit outgrowth of Cicero's tendency to concentrate on the conspirator's corruption. Both the conspiracy in general and Catiline in particular are associated with various kinds of sickness and diseases. Reference to the mental illnesses involved in the conspiracy is particularly frequent. In the third oration, for example, Cicero maintains that some of those sympathetic to the conspiracy may yet be recalled to a healthy state of mind (*mentis senari*). Catiline is repeatedly described as mad (*furor*) or insane (*amentia*), and Cicero suggests that this condition is pathologically rooted in his nature. The images involving physical disease are more relevant to our argument. In the *Pro Murena*, a speech delivered in the interval between the second and the third Catilinarian, Cicero speaks of Catiline as though he were an infection (*contagio*). Elsewhere the word *morbus* (sickness or disease) is used to describe Catiline's effect on the state. Our orator labels the conspiracy as an abundant and pestilent (*pernicosa*) bilge water (*sentina*) of the state, but the most frequently used medical term is *pestis* (pestilence, plague, or infectious disease). It recurs throughout the first two speeches in passages such as this one, "If this man alone is executed, I know that his disease in the state can be checked for a time, but it cannot be completely crushed." The same type of metaphor also appears in *Pro Murena* where Catiline is called an insatiable disease *(pestis immanis)*. Taken together these metaphors create an image of physical and mental corruption through madness, infection, and disease. In this way the evil of the conspiracy is located within the body politic and Cicero paves the way for atonement and exorcism.

Images of sickness are often coupled with some sort of purgation metaphor. In *Pro Murena* the citizens seek to cast Catiline's disease out of the state (xxxix.85); in the first oration Cicero wishes to pump the bilge water out of the state (I.v.12), and in the second speech Cicero declares the state relieved because it has "spewed" out Catiline like a pestilence (II.i.2). The most noteworthy example of this symbolic purgation is contained in the first Catilinarian, the theme providing the symbolic underpinning for the oration as a whole. Faced with the uncomfortable situation of having to argue that Catiline is a dangerous criminal, but lacking solid evidence, Cicero cannot demand a formal resolution to exile Catiline. In answer to this rhetorical dilemma Cicero develops the argument that Catiline should leave the city voluntarily and take the rest of the conspirators with him. This would draw off entirely the infection polluting the state and remove all traces of corruption. If Catiline alone is driven from Rome, "the danger will remain and it will be hidden deep in the veins and vitals of the state. Just as often men sick with a grievous disease and tossed about in a burning fever drink cold water and at first seem to be relieved, but later are much more grievously and violently afflicted, so this disease in the state though relieved by the punishment of this man will grow worse as long as the rest remain. Therefore let the wicked depart; let them separate themselves from the good; let them assemble in one place" (I.xiii.31–32). In this instance the disease metaphor is closely linked to the dialectical antithesis between the wicked and the righteous. Purgation of this internal disorder must be complete, and no traces of it can be left to reinfect the society. The correspondence between this image and the destruction of the scapegoat is too obvious to require comment.

If Catiline is the sickness which afflicts the state, then Cicero is the physician attempting to cure it. This metaphor, dramatizing the positive side of the dichotomy, develops in the course of the second and third orations. In one interesting passage Cicero announces that his function is to cure those conspirators who still are capable of being healed and to destroy those who are beyond the curative power of the state: "That which can be healed I will cure in some way or other, the members which must be cut off I will not allow to remain in the state" (II.v.11). Cicero thus appears as the ritual medicine man who not only treats symptoms but also eliminates the root cause of disease. In the third oration the same metaphor occurs, but this time the Senate plays the role of physician (III.vi.14). The disease metaphor is a symbolic complement of Cicero's use of hyperbole. The dialectical opposition between good and evil parallels an equally antithetical contrast between the physician and the disease. The concept of sickness also emphasizes the internal nature of the disorder, and the purgation theme corresponds to the purification gained through destruction of the sacrificial victim.

The symbolism of redemptive identification still requires one last step—the merger of those purified by the death of the scapegoat. The bond created by this final union is readily expressed in terms of familial relationships: "Note also that the goat, as the principle of evil, would be in effect a kind of 'bad parent.' For the alienating of iniquities from the self to the scapegoat amounts to a rebirth of the self."[18] In other words, this form of identification completes itself metaphorically in terms of parentage and rebirth. Both themes appear in Cicero's orations.

The metaphoric significance of the parent arises from his role as creative force; the parent is the cause of something. If the offspring proves evil or corrupt, the parent shares the guilt. On the other hand, the author of sin is a sort of father himself, for his pollution is transmitted to others, and we have already noted how strongly Cicero warns his audience about the generative power of corruption. Extending the argument analogically, the state, which is the common parent of all, participates in the iniquities of all its citizens and is threatened by the evil citizen. The resulting sense of sin abstractly inheres within the polity and is shared by all its members. The externalization of such guilt becomes a matter of urgent concern.

Cicero's use of personification in making the state stand *in loco parentis* to Catiline indicates the extent to which Catiline's "sins" are projections of Cicero's own society. The middle sections of the first Catilinarian exploit this issue with striking force. Attacking his opponent for criminal activity against society, Cicero reasons that "if your parents hated and feared you and you could not be reconciled to them in any way, you would, I think, withdraw somewhere from their gaze. Now your native country, the mother of us all, hates and fears you and decides that you have had no single thought for a long time save for her destruction" (I.vii.17). The combination of hate and fear represents both the repugnance resulting from causing something evil and the anxiety created by the emergence of a corrupt rival competitor.

Cicero's argument is that the state despises Catiline in the same way that a parent hates a degenerate son. A state can only hate one of its citizens if its personified value system is threatened. This set of beliefs and values is internalized as the super-ego. If Freud is correct in asserting that whole civilizations have super-egos, we may conclude that the immoral behavior of any one member of society can cause a widespread sense of guilt similar to the conflict between ego and super-ego in the individual. When the society is particularly anxious or "neurotic," the guilt is dramatically heightened. Relief from the guilt is sought by projecting it into a single receptacle and by experiencing a rebirth when that receptacle is destroyed.

In one sense, Cicero's use of images of birth and conception does little more than restate the message conveyed by the parental metaphor. Again, the point is that the pollution of the conspiracy is internal. Witness this passage from *Pro Murena:* "Plans have been conceived in this state, gentlemen, for destroying the city, slaughtering the citizens, obliterating the name of Rome. I, in the garb of a citizen, with the assistance of you and all honorable men, by my foresight will dismember and crush this hideous thing which the state has conceived and is now bringing to birth" (xxxvi.80). In another sense, the conception metaphor is used to symbolize the culmination of the identification ritual. The joy and relief Cicero expresses at the capture and arrest of the conspirators is expressed in terms of a rebirth. He says that the occasion marks a day of rejoicing and that the days are "no less pleasant and illustrious in our sight on which we are saved than those on which we are born—because the joy of being saved is certain" (III.i.1). Much the same sentiment is revealed when, in a passage from the fourth speech already quoted, Cicero speaks of the union of the orders "consummated" in his consulship. Thus the ritual is completed.

The journey from Freud and Burke to Cicero and Catiline now is completed. What we have discovered is simply that the Burke/Freud theory of guilt and redemption provides special insight into the rhetoric of Cicero's Catilinarian orations. Such an approach, of course, does not preclude more traditional and less fanciful readings of the text. Nor does it argue for universal application of this one method. It does point to a fruitful direction for the rhetorical critic. The records of argumentative discourse in a society exist as historical documents. They may be culled for information about a past era and used to clarify issues of fact. These documents, however, also tell us something about men's thoughts and attitudes; no one can make a serious argument without saying a great deal about himself.

Critics have long understood that the spirit of an age is reflected in aesthetic works, but the potential of polemic or practical discourse as a cultural index has not been effectively exploited. There is a temptation to concentrate on the text of the debate or oration or pamphlet in order to witness the practical conflict of one idea set against the other; we become so absorbed in the ideas themselves or in the process by which they are argued that it is easy to forget that these data may be applied to a wider field. Certainly the critic must undertake a careful analysis of the text, but that text once had life and once expressed its message under the pressure of the historical and psychological urgency of human needs. The critic, then, must face two realities, that of the document and that of the theory which explains the document in humane terms. The theory of redemptive identification can assist the critic in bringing these realities together.

# ▇ Notes

¹See E. G. Hardy, *The Catilinarian Conspiracy in its Context: A Re-study of the Evidence* (Oxford, 1924). In general, I have followed Hardy in reconstructing the events of the conspiracy. Among the other important studies are: Lester Hutchinson, *The Conspiracy of Catiline* (New York, 1967); R. E. Smith, *Cicero the Statesman* (Cambridge, 1966); Gaston Boissier, *La Conjuration de Catilina* (Paris, 1905); Torsten Petersson, *Cicero: A Biography* (New York, 1963): 240–286; and E. D. Eagle, "Catiline and Concordia Ordinum," *Phoenix* 3 (1949): 15–31.

²Louis E. Lord, *Cicero: The Speeches with an English Translation: In Catilinam I-IV–Pro Murena–Pro Flacco–Pro Sulla* (London, 1964): vii. Unless otherwise noted all quotations from the speeches of Cicero are taken from this translation.

³Kenneth Burke, "Freud and the Analysis of Poetry," in *The Philosophy of Literary Form: Studies in Symbolic Action* (New York, 1957): 221.

⁴Sigmund Freud, *Civilization and Its Discontents*, trans. James Strachey (New York, 1962): 81.

⁵Freud, *Civilization and Its Discontents*, p. 61.

⁶Freud, *Civilization and Its Discontents*, p. 83.

⁷On redemptive identification, see Kenneth Burke, *A Grammar of Motives and A Rhetoric of Motives* (Cleveland, 1962): 555–556. For the concept of the scapegoat which underlies the theory of redemptive identification, see *A Grammar of Motives*, pp. 406–408; *Permanence and Change: An Anatomy of Purpose* (Los Altos, Calif., 1954): 14–17; "The Rhetoric of Hitler's 'Battle,'" in *The Philosophy of Literary Form*, pp. 164–190. A summary and interpretation of Burke's concept of redemption is provided by William Rueckert, *Kenneth Burke and the Drama of Human Relations* (Minneapolis, 1963): 145–153.

⁸Burke, *A Grammar of Motives*, p. 406.

⁹*Ibid.*

¹⁰See Ronald Syme, *The Roman Revolution* (Oxford, 1939).

¹¹Sallust, *The Conspiracy of Catiline*, trans. S. A. Handford (Baltimore, 1963): Section 10.

¹²Sallust, *The Conspiracy of Catiline*, Sections 5 and 14.

¹³Virgil, *Aeneid*, trans. C. Day Lewis (New York, 1953), VIII, pp. 665–669.

¹⁴Seneca, *The Suasoriae of Seneca*, trans. W. A. Edward (Cambridge, 1928), VI, p. 26.

¹⁵Sallust, *The Conspiracy of Catiline*, p. 44.

¹⁶Cf. M. Cary, "Rome in the Absence of Pompey," in *The Cambridge Ancient History*, ed., S. A. Cook, F. A. Adcock, and M. P. Charlesworth, IX (Cambridge, 1965): 506. On the policy of *concordia ordinum* in general, see Hermann Strassburger, *Concordia Ordinum* (Leipzig, 1931).

¹⁷Sallust, *The Conspiracy of Catiline*, p. 42.

¹⁸Burke, *A Grammar of Motives*, p. 407.

# MAXIM 4

## CRITICISM RARELY TRAVELS A STRAIGHT LINE TO ITS END

# CHAPTER 15 [

# PUBLIC MEMORIALIZING
# IN POSTMODERNITY

**Carole Blair**

*In this commentary, Carole Blair describes how her study of the Vietnam Veterans Memorial, in collaboration with Marsha Jeppeson and Rick Pucci, nearly "imploded" at an early stage, when the coauthors were unable to come to agreement on what kind of response the Memorial seemed to evoke. Only after some struggle did they conclude that this problem was in fact the key to a new argument; that is, that a vital part of the Memorial's rhetorical character was its radical multivocality, its capacity to speak in many voices and evoke many responses simultaneously. Blair's essay recounts how the three critics transformed what had been a blind spot into a suggestive and original point of view on memorializing.*

## COMMENTARY

This account of the accompanying essay must begin by recognizing two potential problems. First, my account is mine, not Marsha Jeppeson's or Rick Pucci's. My coauthors' accounts of inventing this essay would be very different from this. The problem should not be dismissed; this is a very partial sketch. Second, I was concerned that I might be so contaminated by my participation in the larger project of this book that my story would fail to account for what "really happened," as Marsha, Rick, and I constructed our essay on the Vietnam Veterans Memorial. I was wrong about that; I don't think I understood what happened until contemplating the larger project. Just as this book attempts a first step toward exposing the professionalization of rhetorical criticism in general, I've moved closer to recognizing how implicated my own practices have been in that professionalization. So, while this is principally a story about how the accompanying essay came to be, it's also a story about what I didn't know or at least didn't acknowledge during the process.

**344**

I had occasion to visit the Vietnam Veterans Memorial many times; I lived in the Washington area for awhile, and during that time I visited the site frequently. I actually don't know how many times I went there, but I would guess about thirty. In my first visit, I knew I would someday write about the Memorial. I was profoundly moved by it. And I knew even then that my response was more than the sum of its parts. Yes, I knew people whose names were inscribed on the wall; finding each of them was a wrenching ordeal, but I felt compelled to do it. And yes, I was drawn to the unusual, genre-busting design of the wall. I remember thinking how appropriate it was that the Memorial honored the dead and missing but still managed to parody the body counts that were trotted out as signs of "victory" or "progress" during the Vietnam conflict. But even those components of my reaction weren't the sum of my feelings or a measure of the depth of my response. Why did I feel compelled to go back to the Memorial over and over? Why was it such a draw for me? What made it different for me than the other noteworthy sites in Washington, to which I paid a second or third visit only if friends visited and we went out to "see the sights" of Washington? How could this granite marker, and later its additive statue and flag, evoke such emotion? I knew that, if I ever found the answers to those questions, I would be able, in fact compelled, to write about the Memorial.

In the five years between my departure from the Washington area and my arrival at University of California, Davis, I would read others' commentaries on the Vietnam Veterans Memorial. There were six critical essays written in our field alone. While I learned a great deal from my occasional reading, there was little in it that helped me to understand my own response. That made it even more clear to me that I *had* to write about this thing, that I had to figure out what about the Memorial was so utterly engaging. But I still waited, because I was completely frustrated by my attempts to understand its power.

At UC, Davis, Marsha and Rick, who were then students, asked me (separately) to read and comment on an essay each had written in prior criticism courses. Both essays had to do, in varying degrees, with the similarities and differences between the Vietnam Veterans Memorial and the NAMES Project International AIDS Memorial Quilt. Though the papers were very different in orientation, both were quite insightful. Both lacked what I believed was probably necessary to turn them into publications or conference papers—a clear theoretical base and/or generalized implications for rhetorical theory or criticism.

The time had come for me; my interest was piqued again. Both Rick and Marsha were serious about pursuing their projects. Both were so sensitive to the nuances of the two memorials that I thought we might, together, figure out the power of the Vietnam Veterans Memorial. So I suggested that the three of us work together on an essay. Their compromises were to let me and each other in on their projects; mine was to deal with the AIDS Quilt, which I had not yet seen.

Marsha, Rick, and I met time and again to discuss our essay. We would discuss the similarities and differences between the two memorials, our own reactions to them, and possible theoretical bases or implications that would make our essay "fit" for publication in a scholarly journal. We had no difficulty with the first task. Our discussions about the similarities and differences were lively, productive, and nuanced. More than once, those conversations were engaging enough to attract strangers to join them. In fact, we probably owe some of our insight to those who added to our discussions.

When it came to discussing our own reactions to the memorials, it appeared that our project might implode. We simply could not agree on what responses the memorials evoked. Our temporary blunder was to not see the productive value of our seemingly irresolvable conflict. We were all trying to turn the memorials into univocal artifacts and our essay into one that provided *the right answer*. The point, of course, was that the memorials are both radically multivocal in their rhetoric. Still, it took us a while to realize that our disagreements were precisely the point of, not an impediment to, our essay.

Our realization about the multivocality of the memorials helped us toward our theoretical position. So did our observation that rhetorical critics who had written about the Vietnam Veterans Memorial had not treated the specificity of its language—that of memorial architecture. Writings about "postmodernity" should have occurred to me immediately as the key, for they would have allowed us to deal with these issues directly. But it wasn't until we began to think about the implications of something we already knew—that there was a groundswell of national-scope memorial activity in the United States—that we reached for our theoretical stance. Since the Vietnam Veterans Memorial's dedication, the AIDS Quilt, Civil Rights Memorial, Free Speech monument, Korean War Memorial, Kent State memorial, and the Astronauts Memorial had all at least been proposed; some of them had been constructed. Could our era—arguably a postmodern one—harbor a penchant for a new memorializing rhetoric? If so, what were its characteristics and conditions? What about the specific cultural language of architecture could help to account for it? Would all of these new memorials rearticulate the tensions of postmodernity? Our theoretical position resulted from all of these considerations.

But we had to be careful with our theoretical stance. We could not argue that there was a new, objectively observable "genre" of postmodern architecture. For one thing, postmodern criticism is suspicious of such claims. For another, we weren't working with enough "instances" of such memorials to make a genre claim, even had we wanted to (which we didn't). So what we had to do very carefully was to write *suggestively toward* the idea or hypothesis of an emerging memorial discourse, and to argue that new memorials might be read productively *as if* they were part of this new discourse.

We hypothesized that a new memorial architecture might reflect some, but not all, the characteristics of postmodern architecture. Furthermore, we suspected, given our research of later memorials, that the Vietnam Veterans Memorial probably was the first "voice" in this new discourse and that it set out the possibilities for further memorializing. Finally, we decided that the AIDS Quilt appropriated that same discourse and further radicalized it.

I volunteered to draft the essay, because I was more familiar with the literature of postmodernity and postmodern criticism than either Rick or Marsha. In fact, because of our different levels of understanding, we probably made a better team than if we had all been equally knowledgeable. Postmodern criticism is notoriously difficult, and those who engage in it tend to fall into using its dense, forbidding prose as a consequence of using its ideas. But since we were committed to this project as a threesome, it was vital that we all understand and agree on *all* of its contents. Because Marsha and Rick were less likely to be trapped in the linguistic thicket of postmodern critique, they were the perfect initial referees for the early drafts of the paper. If one of them didn't understand or accept the legitimacy of a sentence, it didn't make it into the final draft.

The early drafts of the essay actually were quite similar to the "finished" product; we never made it as far as the AIDS Quilt. We didn't give up on it; the three of us are working on a separate paper about it now, and Rick has written his master's thesis on it. The accompanying essay does not address the AIDS Quilt for a very simple reason: No journal editor would have dreamed of accepting an essay that threatened to be fifty pages long. We pushed the patience of *Quarterly Journal of Speech*'s then editor Martha Solomon with the length of the essay as it now stands. We had no choice but to reorient the project toward just one of the memorials and to promise each other we would write the second essay.

That made an enormous change in what we argued in the essay. Much of what we had seen and discussed in the Vietnam Veterans Memorial was the result of having considered it in relation to the AIDS Quilt, and vice versa. Some of the issues we wished to explore had to be dropped, because they wouldn't have made sense in the absence of our comparative-contrastive case. For example, we might have argued that the Vietnam Veterans Memorial wall is in some important senses multiply metaphorical—it can be seen as a book, as the outstretched arms of a human embrace, as the rise and fall of a lifecycle, as a sequential representation of the domestic experience of the war, and as a composite of the notorious body counts. By contrast, the AIDS Quilt literalizes the memorial function by incorporating into itself valued possessions of the persons who have died. Its symbolism is, as a result, arguably more direct, more concrete (no pun or irony intended), and more oppositional than that of the Vietnam Veterans Memorial. Such arguments must wait, however, for a separate essay.

Our essay also does not address the fact that its character grew out of our disagreements. It's not that we wished to hide our conflict. We simply believed that any such "personal" revelations would have been excised in the journal review process. Although our disagreements shaped the essence of our paper, they needed to be recast so as to provide the requisite sense of "distance." And so we smuggled our disagreements in under the guise of other critics' conflicting assessments and reactions. Of course, that seems ridiculous. But our own disagreements had occurred in conversations over lunches and drinks, not in the privileged arena of published writing.

Our essay does not speak to our inclination to write about the Vietnam Veterans Memorial, for much the same reason. Critical scholarship gives no apparent credence to a critic's personal reactions or to the depth of those reactions. A critical essay's merit is judged, in part, by its ability to justify the historical/political significance of the rhetorical event it criticizes or to argue that an analysis of that event helps us to understand rhetoric more generally. So, our responses to the Memorial could not have served as justification for a scholarly essay. Instead, to justify yet another essay on the Vietnam Veterans Memorial, we quoted other people's reactions, essentially conceding that the Memorial's ability to affect them was more important than its capacity to affect us.

Perhaps there is one positive aspect of not having revealed our personal reactions in the essay. I'm still not certain that I can comprehend fully the intensity of my own response to the Vietnam Veterans Memorial. It wasn't until I faced writing this essay on invention that I began to grasp one of the factors that must have made my response to the Memorial so pronounced. I had intended to suggest here that the Memorial had evoked a deeply personal response and that was why I wanted to write about it. Somehow I believed that would adequately answer the question of why I wrote about the Memorial rather than remaining content with a passing interest in it. But of course, my intended response begged the question. I, like other critics, am interested in a great many things that I have not been even tempted to write about. And I'm sure any critic would answer the question of why s/he wrote about a rhetorical event by saying that s/he had a strong personal reaction to it. The question still remained, as I realized only when concentrating on this book. I was still divesting the critical process of my own personal engagement with the Memorial.

As I thought about the question further, I realized that at least one of the answers had to do with how my personal history was tangled up in the history of the Vietnam conflict. I was four years old when the first American was killed in Vietnam and twenty when the last was killed. Every night during those years, I ate dinner while watching the "war" on TV news. I remember being sickened by the sights I saw. I remember the terror that I would actually *see* my cousin, the guy down the street, or one of my friends blown up by a mortar shell or picked off by a sniper. And every few months, I would listen to the president of the United States—Lyndon Johnson and later Richard Nixon—say why the United States had to be involved *in spite of* the views of American citizens, even in spite of a *majority* of that group.

It was not just that watching real suffering and death while I ate my peas became so "natural," a frightening enough consequence. It was also that I, and no doubt other children my age, had no hope of holding on to the innocence and idealism of youth. Nothing I saw on television squared with the principles or "truths" about American virtue that I learned about in school. The Vietnam Veterans Memorial honors those Americans who fought and died in Vietnam. For me, it marks one other thing: my childhood prematurely turned adult and sharply skeptical because of the Vietnam conflict.

# Public Memorializing
in Postmodernity:
The Vietnam Veterans
Memorial as Prototype

**Carole Blair, Marsha S. Jeppeson, and Enrico Pucci, Jr.**

Public commemorative monuments are rhetorical products of some significance. They select from history those events, individuals, places, and ideas that will be sacralized by a culture or a polity.[1] Barry Schwartz distinguishes between chronicling and commemorating, arguing that, "Commemoration lifts from an ordinary historical sequence those extraordinary events which embody our deepest and most fundamental values" (377). Though the epideictic function of public commemorative monuments may be their most obvious rhetorical feature, these monuments also display tendencies toward the political or deliberative. Conflicts over whom or what to memorialize and in what ways have occurred frequently, and these conflicts often are registers of present and future political concern.[2] Moreover, commemorative monuments "instruct" their visitors about what is to be valued in the future as well as in the past. As Griswold notes, "The word 'monument' derives from the Latin *monere,* which means not just 'to remind' but also 'to admonish,' 'warn,' 'advise,' 'instruct' " (691).[3]

The 1980s gave us a particularly striking and evocative, if unusual, commemorative monument—the Vietnam Veterans Memorial in Washington, D.C. The critical commentary it has engendered as well as its extraordinary rhetorical power have rendered the Memorial an artifact of considerable significance.[4] Lang calls the Vietnam Veterans Memorial "the most emotional ground in the nation's capital" (68). Fish describes some of the reactions: "People have cried at the wall, prayed there, screamed in anger and in pain, found friends and comforted strangers. And always they touch it" (25). Members of the design jury commented that, "There's no escape from its power," and described it as "totally eloquent" (Scruggs and Swerdlow 63). The design jury's report concluded that, "The designer has created an eloquent place where the simple meeting of earth, sky, and remembered names contain messages for all who know this place" (qtd. in Ashabranner 38).[5] Howard K. Smith remarked that the Memorial's "final result has the quality of magic" (qtd. in Scruggs and Swerdlow xiv).

The rhetorical power of the Memorial is multiplied by its reach. It has enormous drawing power, and it is "reproduced" and "replicated" in popular culture products, thus expanding the range of possible impact. The

**350**

Vietnam Veterans Memorial is the most visited memorial site in Washington, D.C., attracting between 12,000 and 15,000 visitors per day (deBlaye 263). It has been reproduced on postcards, T-shirts, buttons, brochures, posters, and books. Moreover, it was "the first national war monument introduced to the public through television" (Haines 7).

But this monument's capacity to attract and to move its visitors does not exhaust its rhetorical significance. Nor does its extended appeal through media and popular culture reproduction. We will argue here that the Vietnam Veterans Memorial is an instance of an emergent discourse within the cultural rhetoric of public commemorative monuments. Specifically we will claim that it is a prototype of postmodern memorializing, perhaps among the first of its kind, but certainly one of the most visible.

Our principal aim is not to advance a generic typology of postmodern architecture or even of postmodern commemorative monuments. The potential of such a project would be limited by the fact that we deal centrally with only one case. Furthermore, any encounter with postmodern discourses problematizes the very notion of a genre.[6] Rather, by contextualizing the Vietnam Veterans Memorial within the conflicts between modernists and postmodernists over the "built environment," we hope to contribute sensibly to the critical conversation about how the Memorial "works" rhetorically, as well as about a postmodern criticism in rhetoric.[7] Specifically, we will argue that a reading of the Vietnam Veterans Memorial as a postmodern commemorative text contributes to our understanding of it as a multivocal rhetoric, highlights and helps to account for differences among other critical accounts of the Memorial, firmly establishes the political character of the Memorial's rhetoric, and helps to explain its peculiar power to evoke response. Moreover, such a consideration suggests that the Vietnam Veterans Memorial has established at least tentatively the conditions for a postmodern monumentality.

We will begin with a general discussion of the differences between the discourses of modernist and postmodern architecture, as a context for understanding the rhetoric of what we call postmodern memorializing. Following that, we will describe how the Vietnam Veterans Memorial appropriates the rhetoric of postmodern architecture for its unique acts of memorializing.[8] We will conclude with a discussion of the rhetorical, cultural, and political significance of this emergent postmodern discourse of memorializing.

### ▨ THE CONTESTATION OF METANARRATIVES: MODERNIST AND POSTMODERN ARCHITECTURE

Postmodernism is a many-faceted "ism," whether it is articulated with literature, criticism, feminist theory, the graphic and performing arts, popular culture production, or architecture. But perhaps the most encompassing and intuitively appealing description of postmodernism is Lyotard's; he designates the postmodern as "incredulity towards metanarratives" (*Postmodern Condition,* xxiv). While Lyotard's definition is by his own admission extremely simplified, it does serve an orienting function in the midst (not necessarily the center) of the strategic dislocations and disjunctions that constitute the postmodern. Lyotard's concern is with the displacement of legitimating discourses (metanarratives) to which other discourses are submitted for judgment.[9] These metanarratives are problematized by postmodernism for various reasons, but one principal concern stands out, at least for Lyotard. Because of their status as legitimating discourses, metanarratives rigidify norms and patterns of thought, and they "terrorize" the non-normalized:

> By terror I mean the efficiency gained by eliminating or threatening to eliminate, a player from the language game one shares with him. He is silenced or consents, not because he has been refuted, but because his ability to participate has been threatened (there are many ways to prevent someone from playing)" (*Postmodern Condition* 63–4).

The postmodern constitutes a refutation or dislocation of the legitimating capacity of these metanarratives. The central mission of postmodernism, if there is one, appears to be to reveal the non-necessity of what appears to be necessary.[10]

The postmodern, thus, seeks a disruption of the "normalized." This stance is exemplified perhaps more clearly in architecture than in other arts, for the modernist movement in architecture was explicitly and thoroughly committed to a metanarrative of social transformation through progress, in the form of technological innovation, universal rationality, and corporate power.[11]

### Modern Architecture

McLeod describes the principle of the modern movement in architecture as a "messianic faith in the new" (19). Progress was the driving objective, and it entailed a deliberate break with history, as Fisher, et al. suggest:

> For one of the fundamentals of modernist thinking has been . . . to see the architecture of the past not as a source but as an enemy of the new. Modernity in the twentieth century had no intention of compounding the supposed error made in the nineteenth, that of using historical architectural styles as models for all architectural thought. Modernism represented a rejection of history (8).

The architecture of modernism was to be "purged of every intentional historic or symbolic contamination" (Portoghesi 4), because of its commitment to the new and for fear that historical reference or mannerism might interfere with the efficiency and functioning of a structure (Broadbent 120).

The goal was, according to Jencks, to design "neutral buildings which have a 'zero degree' of historical association" (*Language,* 20).

Rather than constituting an art form, modernist architecture was to signify the twentieth century's achievements and dominance of technological innovation, rationality, and corporate power. The beauty of architecture would lie not in its form or style but in its function (Connor 67). Technological progress would constitute the aesthetic and provide the solution to social ills (McLeod 19). Modern architecture would insure a rational society by ordering the physical space of the social world in such a way as to invite (or demand) a functionalism and efficiency modeled on the factory (Connor 76; Jencks, *Language* 31). As Moriarty describes it, "Ostensibly freed of history, the Modernist celebration of the future could be characterized by a faith in social and aesthetic progress . . . the Modernist program of the Bauhaus, Mies and Gropius, C.I.A.M. and Corbusier mapped a utopian vision onto a rational program for a rational society" (2).[12]

With the rationalization of the social world as their goal, modernist architects sought a perfect, universal style of simplicity. As Hattenhauer suggests, "Modernists believed that they were beyond cultural relativity. They believed that their structures would mirror natural laws, not block them with cultural conventions" (75). Hence the frequent designation of modernist architecture as "the International Style." Because their forms were supposedly timeless and universal, they transcended national and historical boundaries. In fact, the notion of a "style" is not quite accurate to describe modernist architecture, for as Portoghesi points out, "a style by its very nature can be substituted by another which follows. Instead it [modernism] was seen as something beyond style, the definitive fulfillment of a program which cannot change . . ." (4).[13] Modernist architecture's prototype was "the box," typically massive and frequently calling attention to itself only by its size and display of its own structural elements such as pipes and girders; these typically were its only ornaments (Jencks, *Language* 13; Connor 77).

The "purity," "essence," and "unity" attempted by the modernists has been criticized roundly; their structures are frequently characterized as "desolate," anonymous, and "mute" (Fisher et al. 7; McLeod 34).[14] Modernism's economies of scale have led to its description as "cheapskate." Modernist architects' seeming inattention to "context," or the urban fabric in which their buildings are situated, has driven critics to suggest, as Jencks does, that such construction is "dropped unceremoniously, like an urban bomb" (*Language* 125–6). Moreover, the status of the architect as an artist ultimately conflicted with the modernist ideal of simplicity and efficiency as art. Holenstein suggests that the modernist architect needed to be an expert in organizational efficiency rather than an artist. Connor elaborates the conflict, arguing that the impersonality of the modernist program was a fundamental contradiction of the idea of architecture as an art with "heroic individual vision and expression—architecture as the 'pure creation of the mind' as Le Corbusier put it" (73).[15]

Nor have critics been alone in commenting on modernism's shortcomings. McLeod points to the "popular dissatisfaction with corporate skyscrapers and public housing projects" that argued for architects "to recognize emotional and social needs" of their clientele (29).

## Postmodern Reactions

Both the ideology and the "style" of modernism have been placed at issue by postmodern architecture. Although there are numerous brands of postmodern architecture, particular features arise frequently enough so that they might be considered characteristic. Most generally, the postmodern architectural project must be seen as political, as a deliberate dissolution of the utopian metanarrative of modernism and frequently of metanarrativity in general.[16] Postmodern architecture symbolically undercuts modernism's progressivist faith in the new and its valorization of rationality, technology, and corporatism, all of which objectify and dehumanize the social sphere and the individuals who inhabit it. Moreover, postmodern architecture formally and symbolically questions the value of metanarrativity at large. Its refusal of a single, signature style and its reliance on multiple, sometimes conflicting, genres defy reference to singular standards of judgment. In so doing, it removes the legitimating grounds for the valorization or normalization of any particular architectural rhetoric.

Postmodernists, furthermore, insist upon restoring architecture's "voice." Jencks describes architecture as "a form of social discourse," offering choices among alternatives, and being able to either acknowledge or disguise its "partisan nature" (*Architecture Today* 15). Postmodern architects are quite explicitly interested in their art as a rhetoric, as a partisan and meaningful language.[17] They are particularly concerned with restoring to architecture what it lost in modernist manifestation—all aspects of its language save the syntactic. Modernist architecture's signs were almost purely self-referential and limited by a closed system of "legitimate" signifiers. Modernism jettisoned the symbolic and rhetorical dimensions of its language, as Connor acknowledges in describing a modernist building, as "pure sign, which does not refer to anything outside itself . . ." (70). Modernism, according to Hattenhauer, attempted to "exclude all semantic content, all connotation" (76).

By contrast, Stern argues that:

> Traditional post-modernism recognizes both the discursive and expressive meaning of formal language. It recognizes the language of form as communicating sign as well as infra-referential symbol: that is to say, it deals with both physical and associational experience, with the work of art as act of "presentation" and "representation" ("Doubles" 86).

Postmodern architecture restores the symbolic dimension to architecture, and its proponents recognize, as well, the actional and political character of architectural language. Jencks suggests that, "architecture really is a verb, an *action*" (*Language* 104), that the presence of a structure is itself a message. Portoghesi argues that the postmodernist reaction "restores 'the word' to architecture, through the reappropriation of metaphor and symbol and the capacity of shape itself to evoke not just abstract ideas, but also forms which accord with the taste and sensibility of the people" (29). Jencks goes so far as to suggest that, "the term 'Post-Modern' has to be . . . used more precisely to cover, in general, only those designers who are aware of architecture as a *language* . . ." (*Language* 6).[18] The "language" of postmodern architecture is disruptive; it displaces the tendencies of its modernist counterpart by: 1) a refusal of unities or universals, 2) attention to and use of context, and 3) an interrogative, critical stance.

McLeod describes postmodern architecture as a *refusal of universal models* and as a corresponding embrace of pluralistic objectives (19). The rejection of universals and espousal of pluralism are formulated in a number of ways in architectural structures, perhaps the most common of which is a melding of incompatible symbols, forms, styles, and textures within a particular structure. This strategy, frequently referred to as the characteristic postmodern "pastiche," "collage," or "eclecticism," results in a symbolic fragmentation of unity (Connor 72; Foster 127; Harvey 82). Connor describes this as a "movement from univalence to 'multivalence' " (72), an active cultivation of the "symbolic contamination" that modernism sought to eliminate (Portoghesi 4).

Another important gesture in postmodernism's espousal of pluralism is its integration of the historical. "Where modernist architecture seemed to celebrate its absolute break with the past in its rigorous purging of all archaism," Connor explains, "postmodernism shows a new willingness to retrieve and engage with historical styles and techniques" (74). Postmodern architecture "cites" or "quotes" historical motifs as part of its eclectic and pluralistic rhetoric.

Postmodern architecture frequently incorporates regional characteristics and ornament as well as historical forms to achieve this pluralism. The vernacularization of architecture involves the use of particular materials, forms, and styles found in the locale of a building as a counter to the culturally sterile modernist concrete box design. Occasionally, "regionalisms" are imported, that is borrowed from one locale for integration in another.[19] Ornament also is sometimes incorporated, almost gratuitously, for interest or to reassert the symbolic and aesthetic functions of architecture (Jencks, *Language* 142).

While these strategies of eclecticism, historicism, regionalism, and ornament are clearly disruptive of modernist purity, modernist statements are not wholly eliminated from postmodern architecture. Modernist themes are freely incorporated as parts or aspects of a structure. Fisher, et al. suggest that, "A major part of this rediscovered architectural language consists in playing off the contrasts between a modern form . . . and a historical reference" (8). Jencks concurs, arguing that postmodernism "includes" modernist style "as a potential approach." He points to the work of Venturi, Stern, and Moore, whom he describes as "hard-core" postmodernists and whose work quotes modernist design (*Language* 7). Portoghesi describes one purpose of this "citation" of modernism, in his description of the New York Five:[20] "Forms which had symbolized a hope to change the world are used to demonstrate the fact that it cannot change . . ." (88). Not all citations of modernism are so strongly anti-utopian; some are simply ironic or humorous elements that distance the postmodern structure from its thoroughly modernist predecessor.

By juxtaposing historical, vernacular, ornamental, and even modernist themes, postmodern architecture eschews the simplicity, symmetry, and unity of modernism as well as the possibility of a governing or legitimating universal. Equally important, postmodern architecture *interacts with its contexts* in a definitive manner. Connor explains:

> [T]he language of architecture, as well as depending upon internal relationships of difference, is itself part of a much larger field of intersecting language and communication structures. . . . Where, for LeCorbusier, an architectural construction was to be seen in the rigorously reduced terms of its own lines, surfaces, and masses, for Jencks these abstractions are always placed in signifying contexts. What is more, the codes which are used to understand or interpret the abstract forms of architecture are not fixed or unchanging, since they always derive from and reflect the multiple contexts in which any work of architecture is experienced and 'read' (72).

He continues, suggesting that, "for many champions of postmodernism, architecture always consists precisely in the relationships to what is not itself" (72–3). These relationships drawn in postmodernism emphasize the character of a structure with regard to its surroundings as well as its "personability."

In contrast to Jencks' description of modernist building as the dropping of an urban bomb, postmodern architecture takes into account its natural and built environment; it is "carefully set in its context" (*Language* 126). He characterizes one development as "sympathetic" to its natural setting (*Language* 126). Stern emphasizes the importance of contextualization within the built environment as well:

> Buildings which relate to surrounding buildings have more power than those which don't relate to them (what was once called "common courtesy" could also be called "contextual integration"). . . . Architecture is "story telling" or a communicative art. . . . [S]ingle buildings—no matter how distant from other pieces of architecture—are part of a cultural and physical context and we, as architects, are compelled to recognize these connections in our theories and in

the combination of forms which we establish in that which we too casually call "design" (qtd. by Portoghesi 88).

Stern's concern is an important one, for he suggests that buildings collaborate in a sense to produce their "story"; a structure articulates with its cultural and physical contexts in communicating.[21]

Postmodern architects also differ from their modernist counterparts in their concern for the physical and psychological comfort of people who use or inhabit their buildings. Rather than attempting to adapt people to buildings as modernists tended to do, postmodernists make efforts to adapt buildings to people. The goal is to make buildings appealing to the senses, directing a "constant attention to tight space, to touchable close-grained details [that] adds up to a consistent bodily experience" ( Jencks, *Language* 117).[22] Some postmodernists even have turned toward a populist, anti–*avant-garde* collaborative design program with clients or communities. Instead of imposing design solutions on their clients, clients or users "co-author" structures. The result, says Jencks, are buildings that "show a complexity and richness of meaning, a delicate pluralism, that usually takes years to achieve" (*Language* 105–6).

In addition to its refusal of universals and its contextual gestures toward its surroundings and users, postmodern architecture is characterized by an *interrogative, critical stance.* As Jencks points out, "Not only does [architecture] express the values (and land values) of a society, but also its ideologies, hopes, fears, religion, social structure, and metaphysics. It may represent these facts and ideas or betray them . . ." (*Architecture Today* 178). Portoghesi puts the case somewhat differently, in his suggestion that the rhetorical tendency displayed by postmodern architecture "allows architecture to criticize and dissent as well as accept . . ." (29). This critical function provides commentary not merely on technical architectural concerns but on larger social issues as well. Postmodernism's critical position is rarely assertive; it seeks to "raise, if not answer," questions ( Jencks, *Language* 138). Nonetheless, as Connor argues, "postmodern architectural theory gives its object, the postmodern building itself, the status of a kind of theory, or critical reflection on itself . . ." and on its physical and cultural environment (78).

## Implications for Criticism

The character of postmodern architecture suggests particular critical assumptions. Providing more than a litany of characteristics to identify, this characterization of postmodern architecture implies elements of an appropriate critical stance. As Connor puts it, postmodern architecture allows "into its own form something of the multiplicity of ways of reading it, or, in a sense, reading itself in advance" (72). Perhaps most obviously, the postmodernists' effort to reincorporate symbolic and advocative meaning in their structures suggests the legitimacy in general of rhetorical readings of these structures. However, the manner of such a reading is circumscribed by the peculiarities of postmodern architecture. Postmodernism's refusal of unities invites multivalent readings. The goal is not to locate *the* message but the multiple, frequently conflicting, messages. To attempt a unified, centered reading, thus, is to miss the point.

Postmodern architecture's contextualism—its sensitivity to its environment and users—also invites a particular critical focus. Foster correctly recognizes the importance of approaching postmodern architecture as a "text" rather than as a "work" (129). This distinction was formulated most clearly by Barthes, who suggested that, "the work is a fragment of substance, occupying a . . . space . . ." ("From Work" 156). "[T]he work can be seen" and is tangible ("From Work" 157). By contrast, the text "can cut across the work, several works" ("From Work" 157). It is a "multidimensional space in which a variety of writings . . . blend and clash. The text is a tissue of quotations drawn from innumerable centres of culture" ("Death" 146). The appropriate model for modernist structures is the "work," for this type of architecture seeks a unity of its own without reference to elements outside itself. By contrast, postmodern architecture draws from outside the structure itself to form the character of the structure. Postmodern architecture is composed of its building in relationship to what the building is not, its "outside" or its "other." The "text," because it problematizes the boundaries of "inside" and "outside," or "work" and "context," is a more appropriate model for understanding postmodern architecture. The "other," what might be understood as the physical or cultural context of a building in the "work" model, becomes an integral and inseparable part of the architectural "text."[23] The postmodern structure's "references" to its surroundings and its "citation" of regional and historical motifs are inscribed in that structure. Thus, the critic must take account of a structure's relation to the physical environment, cultural situation, and use, for all of these are as much a part of the "text" as the building itself.[24]

"Authorship" also is problematized in "reading" postmodern architecture. That is so not only because some postmodern structures are "authored" or designed by collectives, but also because the "text" model implies a displacement of authorship. In the case of a collectively designed building or development, "authorship" as a unifying principle or as an interpretive precept fails. No unity arises from collective design; in fact, plurality is cultivated. And authorial intent is of negligible value in interpreting a "design" that may incorporate as many intentions as there are collaborative designers.

The authorship principle is displaced, though, even in critical engagement with non-collaborative projects. To consider architecture as "text" is to recognize that no single individual "creates" that text, for it is a reiteration and weaving together of multiple quotations, forms, and gestures, many of which exist apart from the intervention of an "author" or architect. Thus, while architects can and certainly do voice their intentions, the critic must consider their statements as merely part of the architectural text, not as an interpretive foundation upon which to build a reading.

The interrogative, critical posture of postmodern architecture suggests that the critic be particularly attentive to the political character of an architectural text. Postmodern architecture is an attempt to "speak" not only to architects about technical architectural matters, but also to viewers and users of buildings about substantive socio-cultural matters. It questions and critiques ideas as well as architectural forms. To assume that postmodern structures are composed solely of building techniques or that they are merely reflections of a culture, therefore, would be inappropriate. They frequently question and critique the norms and values of a culture.

The strategic difficulty of a postmodern text imposes an additional requirement on the "reader" or critic. Although describing the reading of postmodern writings and not of architecture, Bannet's discussion is useful. She suggests that such difficult writings:

> are designed to . . . make the reader look *at* them and to work at them, actively involving him in their construction or recreation. As Barthes points out, the difficulty and indeterminacy of such texts prevents the reader from consuming them at a gulp and throwing them away. The reader cannot simply glance through [such] a . . . text, extract a discursive message and shelve the book. He must come back to the text again and again; he must brood on it; he must relate to it as a puzzle or a game, in which he participates by deciphering the allusions, by reconstructing the relations between parts, by seeking the significations which govern the form (8–9).

Postmodern architectural structures invite the same kind of care and thoughtfulness in reading that a postmodern thinker's writings do. They are "difficult," strewn with allusions, frequently lacking in a structural or conceptual unity, and cryptic in the extreme. Their rhetoric requires more than a glance; it demands engagement.

The critical posture of postmodern architecture raises a final concern peculiar to analyzing public commemorative monuments. It places at issue the conditions of possibility for a postmodern "monumentality," a problem that has plagued architects of both modern and postmodern ilk.[25] Given modernism's insistence on pure rationality and functionalism and on the purgation of history and symbolism, monumentality was rendered virtually inconceivable. As Collins and Collins argue, "The 'international' modern movement made such a point of breaking with history, with historic styles and tradition, that the achievement of monumentality as it had been previously thought of was at first not even considered worthwhile" (15). They conclude that, "the quality of being monumental . . . was considered by the modernists to be rather evil . . ." (19). Even those who considered monumentality to be important "never seemed to know or to agree generally about just what it was and how best to achieve it and still be 'modern'" (Collins and Collins 26).[26]

That exemplars of modernist commemorative monuments are difficult to find reinforces the problematic nature of these questions. Eero Saarinen's "Gateway Arch"—the Jefferson National Expansion Memorial—in St. Louis certainly is the best example of a modernist "non-utilitarian" monument, but there are few others that are notable.[27] The most purely modernist commemorative tendency was that of naming bridges, freeways, and turnpike service areas after prominent individuals.[28] This practice reflects modernism's concern for rationality and functionalism. But, it hardly provides a postmodern architect with stylistic or formal architectural properties to incorporate or to dislodge. Thus, without a clearcut modernist formula for public commemoration, how is a recognizably postmodern commemoration possible?

Public commemorative monuments "sacralize" individuals, places, and ideas, as we have pointed out. Thus, monumentality appears to be beyond the grasp of modernist architecture. For much the same reason, though, the question must be put of postmodern architecture. How, given its presuppositions, is a postmodern monumentality possible? Decisions about whom or what to memorialize appear to require recourse to some principle of who or what is *worthy* of public commemoration. They seem to demand a reliance, in fact, upon a metanarrative. James Ackerman points out the problem: ". . . the whole question of monumentality is the wrong question for now, another holdover from the past we've lost. How can a society like our own, which has no dreams, no confidences, and no faith, deal with monuments or monumentality?" ("Forum" 38).[29] If the postmodern is definitionally "incredulity toward metanarratives," how can a postmodern architectural statement assume or sanction a metanarrative? This problem raises the question again of how public commemoration is possible within the terms and conditions of postmodernism. This concern is vital, but it cannot be resolved in the absence of specific cases. Thus, we turn to an examination of the Vietnam Veterans Memorial for a determination.

## ■ ANALYSIS OF THE VIETNAM VETERANS MEMORIAL

The Vietnam Veterans Memorial consists of three structures: the well-known, black, V-shaped wall, a flagpole, and a statue of three American soldiers. The wall, the original and unanimous choice of the design selection committee, was supplemented later by the flagpole and statue in a compromise. The wall is heavily reliant upon modernist gestures.[30] Its sheer, unadorned surfaces and apparent formal symmetry bespeak a unity of design that seems to deny a link with postmodern architecture.[31] However, other features of the wall, and of the Memorial taken as a whole, justify and even invite such a characterization. A reading of the Memorial as postmodern accommodates and accounts for diverse, sometimes contradictory readings, and it adds to the critical conversation, especially in helping to identify and explain the Memorial's *political* rhetoric. It also helps to account for the Memorial's rhetorical power and its instigation of a new monumentality.

We will describe first the ways in which critical assumptions about textuality and authorship come into play in accounting for the Memorial's rhetoric. Second, we will discuss peculiarly postmodern characteristics of the Memorial that lend support to other critical readings and also help to account for differences in those readings. Third, we will argue, contrary to most critics, that the Vietnam Veterans Memorial assumes a provocative political stance. Fourth, we will describe how the postmodern textual "difficulty" enhances the Memorial's capacity to evoke response. Finally, we will suggest how the Vietnam Veterans Memorial negotiates the problem of postmodern monumentality, essentially relegitimizing monumental architecture in postmodernity.

The critical assumptions implied by the character of postmodern architecture are particularly appropriate to a reading of the Vietnam Veterans Memorial. To approach the monument as an inclusive text is to recognize its peculiar character as two monuments contained in one. Although some critics may choose to treat the Lin wall and the flag and Hart statues as two separate monuments (Morris), or to consider only the wall (Foss), the fact remains that the Memorial is constituted by both. To treat them as separable is to neglect the Memorial's character as culturally constituted and to overlook its nature as itself a political compromise. The antithetical designs of the wall and the statue undercut any possibility of bringing a single warrant to bear for interpretation, and they foreclose a unitary standard of judgment. Their status as parts of the Vietnam Veterans Memorial suggests that multivalent readings are not just possible but that they are necessary. Moreover, they invite a textual reading that places no demands on the unity or consistency of the rhetorical object.

That conclusion is reinforced by the Memorial's character as a site for supplemental rhetorical activity. Items that visitors leave at the Memorial relieve its starkness and alter its symbolic field. These artifacts are collected each day and housed elsewhere, to be replaced with others left by subsequent visitors. The text of the Memorial changes materially over time. Each addition alters the text, for it focuses on a different individual, a different aspect of the war, or a different meaning a visitor has attached to his/her experience of the Memorial. The wall, thus, serves as a repository of more than its own story; it admits within its text the multiple decorations, stories, interpretations, elaborations, and arguments that visitors leave at the site.[32] These supplements question the "completeness" or unity of the Memorial as a work and suggest that it be approached as a text.

Also inviting textual consideration is the wall's mirror-like granite surface, which "quotes" whomever and whatever is within its reflective range. Mirrored consistently in the wall's surface are the Lincoln Memorial and Washington Monument. But the visitors and activities in which they engage (mourning, reuniting, comforting) are also cited in the reflective surface, contributing to what Haines calls the Memorial's "shifting symbolic ground, a fluctuating, constantly renegotiated field" (9).[33]

There can be little doubt that the wall is the focal point of the Memorial. It is more interesting, more unusual, and more inviting than the statue. It has received far more public comment. And even the figures in the statue refer to the wall; their gaze is directed toward it. Nevertheless, it is important to consider the Vietnam Veterans Memorial as it has been socially named and politically constituted—as a monument composed of two principal parts. If we consider the wall as the locus of the rhetorical text, supplemented by the addition of statuary, mementos, and visitors, we will be in a better position to understand the rhetorical stance of the Memorial.[34]

To consider the Vietnam Veterans Memorial as a text is necessarily to problematize its authorship. The Memorial is technically a collectively designed monument, even though the wall and the statue were not the result of a cooperative effort. Even the design of the wall itself, though, must be considered a product of more than one individual's creativity. The criteria for design selection, set by the Vietnam Veterans Memorial Fund, constrained significantly the possibilities for the monument and, in fact, specifically *required* what has become one of the wall's most noteworthy features—the list of names of the dead and missing.[35] Thus, the Vietnam Veterans Memorial Fund must be considered partially responsible for the wall's design; the motivations of more than one individual resulted in the monument's particular character. And, as we will discuss further on, the compromise that led to the supplement of the wall by the statue and flag also was the outcome of a collective effort. Whatever the intent of the Vietnam Veterans Memorial Fund in establishing its criteria, and whatever Maya Lin's and Frederick Hart's design intentions, the compromise that incorporated them all in the Memorial also removed any special interpretive authority from these "authors." Hart's and Lin's designs, when juxtaposed, alter one another's rhetoric substantially, thus restricting the designers' ability as authors to interpret or account for their own work.

To consider the Vietnam Veterans Memorial as a text and to deauthorize its authors is also necessarily to expect multiple, possibly strongly divergent, readings. Starting with the wall as the locus of the Memorial's text, three peculiarly postmodern accents—its displaced symmetry, "regional" citations, and contextualism—begin to explain the Memorial's rhetorical character and also help to account for conflicting claims advanced by other critics.

Although the structural profile of the wall is symmetrical, the sequence of names listed on its surfaces undermines the symmetry. The list of names is chronologically ordered by date of death, but the list begins at the vertex of the angle formed by the two walls, proceeds to the right and begins again on the left wall, ending at the vertex. In order to read the names sequentially one must necessarily divert attention from the wall in the midst of his/her reading, walk the length of the wall, and begin reading again. To accept the symmetry of the wall's structure is to break the sequence; to follow the sequence is necessarily to counter the symmetry.

These agonistic elements of symmetry and sequence help to explain how some critics can arrive at the conclusion that the wall provides a sense of closure while others claim that it denies this sense.[36] To focus on one element or the other, structural symmetry or "narrative" sequence, is to allow for a sense of closure. The symmetrical structure has borders; it designates completion of itself and of the war. It is uninterrupted and whole, perfectly balanced, and finished. The sequence of names, though broken, leads to a sense of closure by bringing "the names of those killed at the beginning and at the end of the war . . . together" (Carlson and Hocking 205). However, the structural symmetry and the sequence of names that can individually produce a sense of closure, countermand one another. Thus, to read the symmetry or the sequence may be to experience a feeling of closure, but to read both together is to be denied that sense.[37]

The wall's regional and contextual motifs also lend credence to a postmodern reading and help to account for some critical disagreements. The wall's formalist character is dispersed in two particular regional, in this case local, designations.[38] First, its polished granite surfaces with inscribed names is reminiscent of a gravestone, a resemblance heightened by the flowers, flags, and other items left by visitors at the Memorial (Griswold 706–7).[39] Second, its collection of names is no different, except in magnitude, from many smaller memorials commemorating sacrifices of locals in a war or in several wars. As Haines suggests, the wall recapitulates these "familiar 'roles of honor' [sic] erected on court house squares following other wars" (4). The wall, thus, presents itself as a local memorial, but one of enormous proportion and sited on "national" territory.[40]

The familiar, local sense of the wall is supplemented by its accommodation of the physical environment and its visitors. The wall is unobtrusive, invisible in fact from the north, for it is built into a rise in the earth. It does not dominate the landscape but respects it. Too, it is accessible to visitors. Unlike many statuary monuments, it is not raised on a base, forcing visitors to gaze always upward. Neither its height nor an official rule prohibits physical contact with the wall. It is, unlike many other monuments, accessible to touch. As Griswold observes of the Memorial, "When people find . . . the name they've been looking for, they touch, even caress it, remembering. One sees this ritual repeated over and over" (709). Many visitors also take with them a rubbing of the name, a special token that the wall gives to them as a remembrance.

These imported localisms and accommodations to the physical and

peopled environment not only reflect characteristics of a postmodern architectural rhetoric; they also help to account for critics' antithetical views
regarding the degree of comfort one feels at the Memorial. The wall has
been described by some as promoting a sense of serenity, security, and
comfort (Foss 333; Haines 7), while for others like Griswold, it "is not a
comforting memorial" (709). Again, conflicting claims are legitimized by
the symbolic gestures of the Memorial. If one reads local sites like cemeteries
and courthouse squares in the wall, the very familiarity of these citations may
provide security or comfort. So too might the "shelter" of the hill into which
the wall is built, or the "personability" of the wall.[41] However, if one reads
the strong reference to death and the magnitude of that reference, the effect
is anything but comforting.

Consideration of other postmodern characteristics of the Vietnam Veterans Memorial, particularly its departure from generic norms, articulation
with its built environment, its encoding of its own history, its symbolic
collage of names, and its actional character, point to the Memorial's function as itself critical and decidedly political. Critics frequently have claimed
that the wall or the Memorial makes no political statement.[42] Some ground
this claim in the criterial stipulation for the design competition, that the
chosen design for the monument would make no political statement (Ehrenhaus, "Silence" 49). Others base their claim on Maya Lin's early insistence that the wall made no political statement (Foss 334).[43] Some argue
that the wall maintains an apolitical character through a studied ambiguity
(Foss 334; Haines 6), or by refusing to answer questions that it raises
(Carlson and Hocking 206; Griswold 711). We will maintain, to the contrary, that the wall itself bears a strongly political statement and that that
statement is reinforced by the wall's relationship to other monuments within
its proximity and to its "other side"—the Hart statue and flag.[44] We will
suggest that the interrogative features of the wall, which have been interpreted as politically ambiguous, do not serve as a means to eschew political
statement. Rather these features constitute the political message; questioning *is* the point, and that point is a thoroughly political one.

The departure of the Vietnam Veterans Memorial's wall from the generic norms of commemorative public monuments has been noted frequently by critics. Foss' description makes the case most emphatically:

> That this memorial is a far cry from the customary warrior's monument is
> immediately evident. . . . We have, then, in the Vietnam Veterans Memorial,
> violation of the conventional form of war memorials. . . . Lacking the clear,
> patriotic sense that emerges from most war memorials, visitors to the Vietnam
> Veterans Memorial are able to bring new kinds of expectations to the work
> (332–3).[45]

The sense of generic violation is intensified by the Memorial's placement in
West Potomac Park. The principal monuments there—the Lincoln Memo-

rial, the Washington Monument, and the Jefferson Memorial—provide a sharp contrast to the Vietnam Veterans Memorial. They are stately and white. They impose upon the landscape and draw attention to themselves by means of their size and emulation of ancient architectural forms. The wall is dwarfed in stature by these monuments, it is black rather than white, and it eschews the *gravitas* of neoclassical construction. In fact, the geometry of the wall reinforces the contrast; its two walls "point" directly to the Washington Monument and the Lincoln Memorial. Moreover, because the wall is built into the ground, it is invisible from the north side (interestingly the direction of the White House).

That the violation of norms and the placement of the wall *can* be read as political is undeniable. The objections that were raised in 1981 were based on those characteristics. Ehrenhaus summarizes:

> For James Watt, former Secretary of the Interior, and a delegation of 27 Republican Congressmen, the design "makes a political statement of shame and dishonor, rather than an expression of national pride." . . . Tom Carhart, a West Point graduate and Vietnam Veteran, is a vocal opponent of the Memorial's design because it violates traditional form. He refers to it as a "black trench" that is "anti-heroic." Its black walls are "the universal color of sorrow and dishonor," and he asks, "Why can't we have something white and traditional and above ground?" ("Silence" 50).[46]

While others claimed in response that the wall's design was apolitical, the wall's contrast with its built environment and its fracturing of generic norms remained unaddressed. The wall is relatively small in stature; it is the color of sorrow, if not shame; and it offers no vainglorious narrative of the virtues and values preserved by the U.S. involvement in the war. Although we do not share the views of Carhart or Watt that the wall resembles a trench, or that it is a symbol of shame or dishonor for veterans, we do concur that it takes a political stance. It does so by virtue of these departures from the norm and the contextual emphasis of those departures.

The generic violations and the contextual emphasis of those violations is not merely incidental to a reading of the wall; these features are vital components of the Memorial's text. A departure from generic norms in rhetoric typically signals either a peculiarity of situation calling for alterations of type and/or the inadequacy of a generic norm to appropriately respond to a situation.[47] Simply put, generic violations typically are not gratuitous. The generic violations in the case of the wall certainly are not; they mark a dissatisfaction with the capacity of the "normal," monumental discourse to adequately commemorate Vietnam veterans. Given the public response to the Vietnam war itself, that should not be surprising. Public commemorative monuments are usually heavily reliant upon a socially-shared sense that those who perished did so for the greater good or for a cause worth pursuing. But this extremely unpopular, by many accounts immoral, war provides nothing like a consensual warrant to authorize valorization of the war dead. That such a premise is clearly lacking, and that that lack *demands* a departure from generic conventions, itself is a political statement. To honor the veterans of the Vietnam war, something besides the derived value or political merit of the war itself is necessary as a premise.

Ironically, the compromise that added the flag and Hart statue intensified the wall's already political character. Represented in the Memorial are two radically different historical accounts of the Vietnam war itself. The wall inscribes names in the order of death, providing a sequential account of U.S. involvement in the war. The temporal sequence is registered and divided by years and by each loss of life. The historical narrative is a chronicle of death. The statue of the three soldiers symbolizes a hypothetical inflection point in time, capturing a "close-up" image of what one scene in Vietnam might have looked like. Rather than representing history as a sequence, the statue encapsulates it synecdochically in its representation of all Vietnam veterans by three particular soldiers. This moment of life contrasts sharply with the wall's narrative of death. The structures taken together inscribe a history, forming a space of cooperative conflict and commenting on each other's statement about the war. Their presence together on the memorial site, in fact, serves as a historical marker for both the contestation of an appropriate commemorative rhetoric for Vietnam veterans (itself a political dispute),[48] and for the historical domestic conflict over the war and its conduct.

The Memorial is a testimony to the conflict that led to the compromise of its own character; it is a historical recapitulation of the battle over the appropriate rhetoric of commemoration. The construction of the wall was given final approval only after a compromise was struck to include the flag and the Hart statue along with the wall. The "nasty fight" leading to the compromise began after Maya Lin's design for the wall had been chosen from among 1421 proposals in the spring of 1981 (Hess 125). Lin's design also had been approved by all requisite authorities—the National Capital Planning Commission, the Commission of Fine Arts, and the Department of the Interior. However, as a response to objections raised by some veterans, congresspersons, and H. Ross Perot, then Interior Secretary Watt "placed a stop order on the Memorial's construction permit" (Gans 325).[49] The stop order was lifted only after the compromise was struck to add the statue and flag.

The three structures are not only symbolic of the conflict over appropriate commemoration; they constitute the actual historical residue of that conflict. Together they mark a historical battle over "what can be said" about the war, a battle that proved too contentious to be resolved in consensus; only a compromise that allowed both voices to be heard allowed the Memorial's construction to proceed.

It is difficult to maintain that this battle and its results are apolitical. At issue in the conflict and in its resulting compromise was what rhetoric about the Vietnam war would be sanctioned by being given public voice. The conflict over appropriate commemoration resulted in a compromise, but it certainly did not resolve the issue. The Memorial represents the conflict itself, and like the conflict, culminates in the two sides being endlessly articulated rather than transcended. The presence together of the wall and the statue allows them to "question" one another's legitimacy indefinitely.

But the tension between the compromise structures does more than comment on the socio-political problem of public commemoration; it designates the domestic conflict over the war itself. As members of the Commission of Fine Arts observed, the battle over appropriate commemoration penetrated to a battle over the appropriateness of the war. The wall does not portray the Vietnam conflict as an event worthy of admiration or its veterans as heroic. The flag and statue add precisely those dimensions of meaning to the memorial site. The inscription at the base of the flag pole "affirms the principles of freedom for which [the Vietnam veterans] fought." And the statue, as Morris notes, depicts the soldiers as heroic:

> Neither speaking of death nor even inviting us to contemplate death, this second memorial encourages only heroism and the silence of heroes. Weary though they may be, these heroes are alive. And that is how we are to remember them: alive and heroic (215).

While the wall chronicles U.S. involvement in the war according to a sequence of death, the statue designates a hypothetical moment of the war by reference to life and courage.

The two views represented by these structures are not compatible, but the compromise renders the site as a trace of the conflict over the war. As Maya Lin suggested, "in a funny sense the compromise . . . brings the memorial closer to the truth. What is memorialized is that people still cannot resolve the war . . ." (qtd. by Gans 328). Even the placement of the structures in relation to one another reinforces her conclusion. Although the soldiers in Hart's statue appear to be gazing at the wall, nothing else connects the wall and the statue. To contemplate one, a visitor must turn his/her back on the other.

The Memorial's political statements in no way detract from its capacity to commemorate Vietnam veterans. If architecture is a verb, as Jencks has suggested, its power as such is nowhere better demonstrated than in the Vietnam Veterans Memorial. Its presence alone acknowledges the veterans, provides them a "space" that recognizes them as a group, and thus renegotiates their status in the culture.[50] The Memorial's existence is one of many cultural signs that the country has recovered from its "trance of collective amnesia" concerning the war (Butterfield 26).[51]

Furthermore, the Memorial emphasizes perhaps more clearly than any monument that has preceded it the worth of the individual. The wall refuses to cede representation of all the war's veterans into a singular, iconic representation. In addition, it makes no attempt to prize the worth of the collective above the value of individual life. The wall is a unity in that it serves as a monument to Vietnam veterans as a unified group, but it also commemorates each of the dead and missing as an individual by its "collaging" of names. Each of the names references a unique individual. Each name insists upon consideration beyond its presence in the midst of the others, for each refers to much more than the collective of which it is a part. Each individual named on the wall had as *one* role in life to be a soldier in Vietnam. But many other aspects of his/her life also are referenced by his/her name; they become a part of the memorial as well, diversifying the apparent unity of the wall's signification. The structural integrity of the wall unifies as a collective those who died or were listed as missing in Vietnam, but the unity disintegrates in the face of the symbolic potency of each name. The wall's inscribed dialectic between individual and collective does not culminate in synthesis; it preserves reference to the veterans as individuals *and* as a group. The Memorial provides a space of recognition and acknowledges Vietnam veterans both as a group and as individuals. In so doing, it allows for legitimate commemoration even in the absence of an expressed valorization of the war effort or outcome.

As a result of the Vietnam Veterans Memorial's conflicting messages, visitors could leave the site with their views fundamentally unaffected, having been reaffirmed in "whatever individual expectations and perspective [they] wish to bring to the memorial . . ." (Foss 334). More likely, though, visitors to the Memorial leave with more than they brought with them, as a result of the Memorial's difficulty as a text. The complexity and agonistic character of the Memorial's rhetoric invite active engagement by the visitor. It seems unlikely that anyone could be unaffected by the opposed views and difficult issues posed by the Memorial. Its rhetoric virtually demands that one either resolve the issues in a tentative or qualified fashion, or that he/she leave with critical and gnawing questions still to consider. In either case, the questions and qualifications *constitute* a major component of the message. Regardless of the stance one may take regarding the Vietnam war or the most appropriate way of commemorating its veterans, the Memorial invites doubt and critical differentiation of issues. Someone who believes that U.S. commitment to the war was justified still sees, like other visitors, the chronicle of death that resulted from that stance. He/she is invited to weigh the cause against the cost. One convinced that the U.S. involvement was wrong or foolish still witnesses each name and the tragedy it represents. He/she is invited to honor the dead, if not the "cause" for which they died. In sum, the Vietnam Veterans Memorial provokes engagement; it is not easily consumed or immediately intelligible. Its rhetoric does not sanction a touristic, consumptive response; it invites an engaged and thoughtful reading.

Also related to the absence of an explicit warrant for valorization in the Memorial is the final question to be addressed here: how a postmodern monumentality is possible. It is important to examine what the Vietnam Veterans Memorial can tell us about what the conditions are of a postmodern monumentality, *how* it is possible given the situational and theoretical problems confronting it. Two conditions for a postmodern monumentality are suggested by the Vietnam Veterans Memorial. It suggests, first, that postmodern monuments eschew metanarrative sanction. Second, while not necessarily foregrounding an explicit confrontation with modernism, the Vietnam Veterans Memorial suggests that the postmodern monument must at least differentiate itself substantially from modernist attempts at memorializing.

It is difficult to imagine a language—of architecture or of any other kind—that can completely divest itself of recourse to the legitimating capacity of metanarrative.[52] That the Vietnam Veterans Memorial approaches that state, however, is almost undeniable. A single "story" about the war or its veterans cannot "contain," account for, or legitimate the rhetorics of both the Hart statue and the Lin wall.[53] Nor can any account of the war encompass, much less do justice to, the individual lives represented by the inscriptions on the wall. If the Memorial does not eschew metanarrative altogether, it certainly does challenge us to find an *adequate* discourse that would authorize and hold together its multiple and disjunctive "stories."

This kind of challenge may prove to be a necessary characteristic of postmodern monumentality. Rather than telling *the* story, it tells multiple stories. Any one of the stories—of victimization, of a just cause for the war, of individual sacrifice—warrants commemoration of the dead. But the stories conflict, refusing easy containment within a single account. Because of the difficulty of the text, then, the monument becomes a site not only of commemoration but also of questioning, perhaps even of incredulity. The problem of contemporary monumentality, long wrestled with by architects and other artists, is transformed from a specialists' debate to a cultural problem; it is not solved but rearticulated. The monument itself declares the postmodern "problem"—the lack of a metadiscourse that legitimates or sanctions another discourse. Such a declaration may prove to be the only possibility for a postmodern monumentality.

Since the modern tendency was to commemorate primarily by naming functional structures, it provides few gestural or thematic architectural signs that can be called into question directly by a postmodern monumentality. However, the existence of the Vietnam Veterans Memorial is already a reaction to such rational functionalism. By its having been conceived and built at all, it abrogates this modernist tendency; it plainly differs in character from the turnpike service area, with the memorial swimming pool, or the memorial student union. It reinvokes the *primary* goal of monumentality: to commemorate. It leave the functionalism of modernism aside, essentially changing the subject. It does not comment on modernist functional memorials; it simply questions them by being and by differing.

The rare modernist "intentional" monument receives essentially the same kind of treatment. It receives no explicit commentary, but its mode of discourse is essentially renounced. A brief encounter with the Jefferson National Expansion Memorial establishes a clear case of contrast with the Vietnam Veterans Memorial. Saarinen's graceful Arch is a study in size, engineering, and technological achievement. While it has come to represent a "gateway to the West," such rhetorical implications were incidental to the design. According to Temko, Saarinen's goal was "to create a monument not only to the Virginian and the nation, but also to the modern age" (18). Temko explains further that, for Saarinen, the "spirit" of the monument was to be its "mechanical" character. It was to be absolutely permanent and comparable as a work to the Washington Monument. Hence its stainless steel frame and enormous height. "[I]ts scale," reports Temko, "is that of the civilized future" (19). Even the shape of the monument was rationalistic:

> Although the first Jefferson Memorial design of 1948 was of partly subjective inspiration, it was also a stroke of rational structural functionalism: a catenary arch which, geometrically, was as predictable as a circle. The steel-plate shell of the G.M. dome and the concrete shell of the M.I.T. auditorium are governed by the same geometric purism, and thus absolutely subject to the laws of what Nervi calls "Building Science" (Temko 42).[54]

The "remarkable engineering feat" of the monument is commented upon at least as much as the pioneering effort that it commemorates (Bricker, et al. 261). The "don't miss" at the Museum of Westward Expansion (under the Arch), according to one tourist guide, is the documentary, *Monument to the Dream* (Charters 421). This half-hour chronicle is not about westward expansion but the building of the Arch.

The Arch and everything associated with it refers primarily to the structure itself, its engineering and its magnificent (modern) accomplishment. Its commemoration, except of itself, however, is strained. As Gass puts it, the Arch is "simple, direct, and grand enough to wrench a WOW! from a clod," but it is also "a logarithm," "a speechless overhang" (140). He continues:

> Beneath the Arch—this quintessentially American symbol of Finnish design . . .—lies history, dead as we desire it to be; so dead indeed that the museum buried there has nothing much to display, and concentrates instead on exhibiting the techniques of exhibition: on layouts, labels, lighting, models and montages . . . everything absolutely up-to-date. History is as dead as God, but there is no history (Gass 142).

The monument is an outstanding example of the modernist rational program. It only nominally refers to anything outside itself. It is a feat of modern technology and a defeat of history. It is a "pure" form, remarkable not because of what it represents or says but because it "stands without inner frame support" (Bricker 261).

The Vietnam Veterans Memorial obviously eschews this brand of monu-mentalizing. It does not represent a great engineering achievement, nor is its construction its message. It references stories from and about the war, and it acknowledges and refers to elements of its historical landscape. It does not command respect for its syntactical elements of size, shape, or structural integrity, but for its symbolic gestures outside itself. The Vietnam Veterans Memorial refuses the modernist program, at least as it is exemplified in Saarinen's prototype and in the "functionalist" memorial. In so doing, it suggests the second possible condition of postmodern monumentality, an abrogation of modernist formulae for commemoration.

## CONCLUSION

In addition to arguing for a type of reading of the Vietnam Veterans Memo-rial that emphasizes its postmodern rhetorical features, this discussion also highlights concern for the rhetoric of public commemorative monuments at large. Furthermore, it brings to the surface a number of assumptive issues that rhetorical critics must address.

That the Vietnam Veterans Memorial incorporates the characteristic features of postmodern architecture itself is significant. The wall *looks* more like a modernist structure than a postmodern one, but any reading that embraces more than its symmetrical silhouette will acknowledge its depar-ture from modernist style and dogma.[55] And, any reading that takes account of both the wall and the statue must dismiss the possibility of reading the Memorial as a modernist "work."

The significance of classification, though, is less important in its own right than its implications for the posture assumed by the critic in reading the monument. Because of its complexity, the Vietnam Veterans Memorial lends itself to a "textual" reading. Because of its multiple "authorship," it reads well in the absence of an "authorized" interpretive grounding from the planners and architects. Its multiplicity argues for numerous readings, but it demands no agreement among them.

The Vietnam Veterans Memorial reflects what is frequently called the "both-and" of postmodern architectural practice, in contrast to the mod-ernist "either-or." In other words, it is inclusive; it does not suggest one reading or the other, but embraces even contradictory interpretations. The Memorial both comforts and refuses to comfort. It both provides closure and denies it. It does not offer a unitary message but multiple and conflict-ing ones. Its "syntactical" elements (for example, color, size, shape, geome-try, placement, material, and inscriptions) do not speak with one voice. These, and the more complex symbolic gestures of symmetry, sequence, regionalism, contextualism, contrast, and reference, speak agonistically. They do not add up to a correct or synthetic interpretation. They offer diverse messages, sanctioning the legitimacy of "both-and."

Though the wall appears at first to be a simple and easily readable structure, it is remarkably complex, even when considered apart from the statue and flag. Its structure and shape give it a unity and self-containedness that are undermined by the presence of thousands of names, the order of the names, the reflective capacity of the polished granite surface, and the mirroring of and gesturing toward other structures. Those already complex features of the wall are complicated further by consideration of the wall together with its counterpart statue and flag; to examine both as parts of the Memorial is to render any unifying reading virtually impossible.

The dual and dialectical expressions of the two "parts" of the Memorial add difficulty to any reading. Most important, they intensify the sense that the Memorial speaks politically. The two components oppose one another in what they say about the war. The opposition defies synthesis. The structures stand as durable, visible representatives of opposing stances, "arguing" their cases against each other without mediation. They *constitute* the outcome of political compromise. Moreover, they vouchsafe the cultural legitimacy of two opposed points of view about the Vietnam war and commemoration of its veterans. The Memorial stands as a commemoration of veterans of the war, *and* as a monument to political struggle.

Since the Vietnam Veterans Memorial was approved and built, numerous "intentional" monuments have been proposed, and some of these have been constructed. As Haines suggests, "Construction of The Wall seems to have started a trend" (18n). Monuments have been proposed to honor Korean war veterans, as well as protesters of the Vietnam war (Haines 18n). Maya Lin was commissioned to design the Civil Rights Memorial in Montgomery, Alabama, which was dedicated in November 1989. A monument to the students killed at Kent State in 1970 also has been built. The NAMES Project International AIDS Memorial Quilt was displayed for the first time in 1987 and continues its memorializing journey throughout the world.[56]

That the Vietnam Veterans Memorial may have begun a new trend in monument building is itself an important contribution, especially in response to modernism's inclination toward "functionalist" memorials. Equally important, however, is the degree to which these new monuments respond to the demands of a postmodern condition. Such an extended subject is well beyond the scope of this paper, but it is worth noting that two of these newer monuments clearly appropriate elements of the Vietnam Veterans Memorial's rhetoric. Fox recognizes the "same combinations" of elements in the Civil Rights Memorial and in the Vietnam Veterans Memorial. And, the AIDS Quilt follows the Vietnam Veterans Memorial in its emphasis on naming the dead. Only additional critical study can bear out the degree and character of influence exerted by the Vietnam Veterans Memorial. But these similarities do suggest that the Memorial may have altered the public commemorative norm for the foreseeable future.

In addition to the concerns raised here about the rhetoric of the Vietnam Veterans Memorial and of public commemorative monuments, several issues more generally pertinent to rhetorical criticism emerge in this analysis. Traditional views of textuality, authorship, and the politics of discourse are all raised as problems.

First is the question of textuality. The frontiers of a discourse are, by some accounts, *never* certain (Foucault, *Archaeology* 23–5). That is, since any discourse is "caught up in a system of references to other books, other texts, other sentences," its boundaries are not certain nor easily identifiable (Foucault, *Archaeology* 23). To assume that a speech or a book or an architectural structure is a "unit," complete unto itself, *is* to assume and to make a crucial, critical *choice;* it is not to recognize an absolute fact. Put another way, a discourse, at least by Foucault's way of thinking, is not an entity given in reality. Its character is a premise of critical argument.

Even if one can assume, in some cases (for example, that of a modernist building), the unity of a work as pregiven in its material form, postmodern discourses seek to problematize that unity. Thus, the distinction between treating rhetoric as a work and as a text becomes tremendously important, if not in the case of all discourse, then at least in the case of postmodern discourses. Postmodern rhetoric recommends a critical practice that considers pregiven material unity irrelevant. To treat a post-modern discourse as a complete or unified structure is to utterly miss the point. The goal of a textual reading is to grasp the multiplicity of any discourse; to constrict or expand the scope of a text is to yield very different readings.

When the material unity of a work is suspended in favor of considering a text, authorship becomes a tertiary consideration. The "fragments" that are treated as part of a text have various sources; they compose a unity drawn by a critic rather than by an author (McGee). Thus, the authority of the speaker, writer, or architect to interpret his/her own *work* is displaced by the critic's reading of a multiple text. The critic takes on the task of defining the range of inclusiveness of his/her object of study. The critic's intervention begins with the construction of the text, not with the selection of a work.

Finally, this discussion questions the wisdom of treating any discourse as if it were apolitical. Jencks' claim, that architecture is a verb, provides the key. If we expand his claim to read, "rhetoric is really a verb or an action," the case becomes clearer. To the extent that a discourse is an action, it impinges upon the meaning, truth value, status, and range of action of other discourses (Foucault, "Subject and Power" 219–21). It exerts force, in other words, within its field of action. The choice to consider politics as a *type* of rhetoric rather than as an aspect of all rhetoric is called seriously into question.

These concerns reinforce similar views expressed by post-structuralist thinkers. Lyotard, Barthes, Foucault, and others, have argued for reconsideration of some of the most taken-for-granted critical assumptions. The assumptions that the "text" is not at issue, that authorship offers unifying and interpretive grounding, and that the political is simply another genre of rhetoric, are raised as questions; their status as assumptions is displaced. But, if these thinkers' arguments are not convincing to rhetorical critics, certainly the character of postmodern discourses must be. These rhetorical events themselves invite reconsideration of the assumptions critics typically make. To accept these traditional assumptions (that the work is a given, that authorship constitutes interpretive authority, and that a genre matrix contains politics within a single category of discourse) is to refuse important elements of critical practice. These assumptions remove the critic's tasks of *forming* a text, of becoming the authorizing voice, and of understanding rhetoric as praxis. In challenging these assumptions, the critic becomes an interventionist rather than a deferential, if expert, spectator.

# ▨ Notes

[1]See Barthes, who argues that, "human space in general (and not only urban space) has always been a signifying space" ("Semiology" 191), and that contact with the majority of monuments is an encounter with the "historical Sacred" ("Eiffel Tower" 241). Also see Curtis, who suggests that, "Monumentality seems to be related to intensity of expression, elemental formal power, dignity, and gravity: In a phrase, it is a matter of lasting presence" (65).

[2]Schwartz notes, for example, the conflict over whom to memorialize iconically in the Capitol building in Washington, D.C. These conflicts during the antebellum period account for the early lack of commemoration of anyone or anything save the "founders" and founding events of the country. Antebellum leaders were unable to come to agreement on legitimate figures for commemoration, and their inability to do so was related to the larger political tensions between North and South. Similarly, Gregory and Lewis remark on the difficulty of establishing agreement on a monument commemorating the students killed at Kent State in May 1970 and upon the ways in which the meaning of the Statue of Liberty was placed at issue. Morris discusses the conflicts over cemetery design and about the difficulty involved in appropriately memorializing George Washington in the nation's capital.

[3]For more on the derivation and symbolic range of the term "monument," see Choay. Morris argues that, "public memorials 'speak' publicly by attempting to shape and possess the affective norms of the present and the future by first shaping and possessing the past. . . . Literal constructions of social reality, memorials 'speak' through cultural form, and their 'speaking' is a signification of the culture(s) to which they belong" (202). Morris suggests not only that public memorials have epideictic and deliberative functions, but also that they provide a rich interpretive source for understanding the cultures that produce them.

[4]The Vietnam Veterans Memorial has been the subject of several critical discussions in rhetoric and communication studies. See: Carlson and Hocking; Ehrenhaus. "Silence;" Ehrenhaus, "Vietnam Veterans Memorial;" Foss; Haines; and Morris. Essays also displaying a particular sensitivity to the rhetorical potential of the Vietnam Veterans Memorial include Gans; and Griswold. Also see Jensen, who argues that both the Vietnam Veterans Memorial and the AIDS Quilt provide opportunity for "creative adjustment" to complex, tragic realities.

[5]The design jury was a group of eight internationally recognized artists and designers selected by the Vietnam Veterans Memorial Fund (VVMF). It was chaired by Grady Clay, editor of *Landscape Architecture.*

[6]See, for example, Hutcheon on the boundary disputes in postmodernism. Also see Rosemarin.

[7]While we intend to demonstrate how the monument reflects the postmodern profile, our primary concern is with how it "speaks" by assuming that profile. Our primary goal is to afford some insight about the unique rhetorical statements of the Vietnam Veterans Memorial. We are not as concerned with whether there is a group of monuments in the world that we could dub as "postmodern monuments" as we are with understanding this one.

Our stance is much like that advocated in Rosemarin's treatment of genre. She argues that genres should be seen as premises of critical practices, not as hypotheses about "reality," and that the value of a generic premise is predicated upon its ability to illuminate a literary (or rhetorical) act.

Interest in a postmodern critical stance in rhetoric has emerged recently with such statements as those by Hart 386–98; and Brock, Scott, and Chesebro 427–500.

[8]What we see as a postmodern commemorative monument does not, and probably cannot, align precisely with postmodern architecture, even in the case of the Vietnam Veterans Memorial. Commemorative monuments present a problematic case for both modernist and postmodern architecture, as we will discuss further on. Thus, our characterization of the Vietnam Veterans Memorial will not fit precisely the characteristics of postmodern architecture considered generally. Since our goal is not to establish the verifiable or falsifiable legitimacy in "reality" of the genre of postmodern memorializing but to comment on the Vietnam Veterans Memorial, we do not see this as a particular problem.

[9]He expands upon this concern in *The Differend.*

[10]Foucault described the work of the intellectual "to describe that-which-is by making it appear as something that might not be, or that might not be as it is. . . . [H]istory serves to show how that-which-is has not always been; i.e., that the things which seem most evident to us are always formed in the confluence of encounters and chances, during the course of a precarious and fragile history. . . , It means that they reside on a base of human practice and human history; and that since these things have been made, they can be unmade, as long as we know how it was that they were made" ("Critical Theory" 36–7). Speaking of Foucault's histories, Flynn describes them as leaving us "with a heightened sense of the contingency of our most prized necessities . . ." (116).

[11]Postmodernism does not oppose all modern architecture. It places itself in opposition to the modernist (International Style) movement in particular. See Stern 75–77, for the distinction. Also see the editor's headnote to Serenyi 181.

[12]"Mies" refers to Mies van der Rohe. C.I.A.M. was the Congrès Internationaux de l'Architecture Moderne. For further discussion of the ideological character of the modernist movement, see Holenstein.

[13]Collins and Collins compare it to Esperanto and to Richards and Ogden's Basic English project (15). Also see Holenstein 52–4; and Wingler 195.

[14]Professional criticism of modernist architecture has been widespread. Among its most well-known criticisms are the following: Blake; Jacobs; Venturi; Venturi, Brown, and Izenour; and Wolfe. Prince Charles' recent assault on the architecture of Great Britain is exemplary of the popular distaste for the International Style.

[15]Connor's reference is to LeCorbusier, *Towards a New Architecture* 218.

[16]The one exception seems to be postmodern "classicism," which remains closer to a norm than do other "brands" of postmodern architecture. For a description of postmodern classicism, see Jencks, *Architecture Today* 292–311.

[17]For examples of others (in addition to architects) who treat architecture as a rhetoric, see: Altman; Eco; Hattenhauer; Mechling and Mechling; Medhurst and Benson 387–8; and Stuart. Medhurst and Benson, in their introduction to a section on "Rhetoric of Architecture," suggest that architects "take on the role of cultural rhetoricians, often expressing the views and values of the society from which they come—occasionally reacting against these traditional views" (387).

[18]Some acknowledge that modernist architecture also was rhetorical, but inadvertently so. See, for example, Jencks, *Language* 50. He seems to imply that architecture cannot not communicate.

[19]For a discussion of "critical regionalism" in architecture, see Frampton.

[20]The "New York Five" are Peter Eisenmann, Michael Graves, John Hejduk, Charles Gwathmey, and Richard Meier.

[21]Also see Venturi, Brown and Izenour.

[22]Also see Connor 75; and Frampton.

[23]For further useful discussion of the distinction between work and text, see LaCapra; and McGee.

[24]This sets our view of a "text" in opposition to that of the so-called "textual critics." See, for example, Leff; and the essays in Leff and Kauffeld.

[25]The entirety of Volume 4 (1984) of the *Harvard Architectural Review* is devoted to the issue of monumentality in the urban environment. Monumentality was the concern of a special issue of *Oppositions* also in the Fall 1982 (Volume 25). The essays in these two journals point to the continuing and serious concern registered about the problem.

[26]They do suggest, however, that modernism found its particular brand of monumentalism but only later in the movement.

[27]A non-utilitarian monument is one that serves no purpose except for commemoration. See Barber; Riegl 21–2; and Forster 2. Giurgola ("Forum" 39) makes a similar distinction, suggesting the possibility of building a monument or "simply using monumentality only in an architectural sense."

[28]Collins and Collins also note that useable structures, like hospitals, schools, and homes, were sometimes considered monumental (28). They suggest further that the Tennessee Valley Authority development was seen as a prototype of modernist monumentality (31). Mayo too notes this "new tradition of commemoration" that grew in importance after World War II; he links it specifically with modernism as well (202–3).

[29]In fact, the editor's introduction to the forum transcript of the Harvard conference suggests that, "The most formidable challenge . . . remained unanswered throughout the day: that our society is too diverse for any symbolic expression in architecture to convey or embody a collective ideal" ("Forum" 37).

[30]Several critics, in fact, have described it as a modern or modernist design, among them: Ehrenhaus, "Silence;" Hess; and Hubbard. Our view is more consistent with Griswold's argument in response to Hubbard, that the Vietnam Veterans Memorial is "erroneously assimilate[d] to modernist architecture whose purpose is not to be *about* anything in the world so much as to *be* a thing in the world." Griswold attributes Hubbard's mistake to a "failure to consider the complex symbolism of the Vietnam Veterans Memorial" (719).

[31]Griswold, despite his rejection of Hubbard's classification of the wall as modernist, still claims that the wall is symmetrical and that there is no tension in its design (20).

[32]For an extensive analysis of a selection of these artifacts, see Carlson and Hocking; also see Ehrenhaus, "Silence" 54.

[33]The use of mirroring surfaces is itself a symptom of the postmodern turn in architecture. Agrest suggests that in her observation that, "The meaning of an architecture of mirrors today is more a symptom of a moment of transition and adjustment than an established

condition in and of itself'' (120). Her discussion also indicates how mirroring serves to reinforce the need for a "textual" reading. She argues that a mirror "*dematerializes* the building, producing other images instead" (119). She continues: "The architecture of object by the use of mirrors paradoxically negates its own objecthood. This is clear particularly if one considers the architecture in context. The presence of the object is subdued by the fact that it attempts to absorb its context; it is object and context at the same time. Permeated by the qualities of its context, the building seems to replace, literally, its style and materials with an illusory image" (129).

[34]This case for changing the boundaries of the rhetorical object for analysis is consistent with McGee's notion that "text construction is now something done more by the consumers than by the producers of discourse" (288).

[35]Actually, the original idea for the inclusion of all the names was Jan Scruggs'. It was later incorporated as a criterion for the design jury by the Vietnam Veterans Memorial Fund. See Fish 1.

The other criteria specified a "reflective and contemplative" design that would "harmonize with its surroundings, especially the neighboring national memorials," and that made "no political statement about the war" ("Vietnam Veterans Memorial").

The Vietnam Veterans Memorial Fund was a non-profit organization that ultimately raised $9 million and secured the parkland site for the Memorial. Site selection was accomplished with the aid of Senators Domenici and Mathias. See Fish 2; and Lang 69. Public Law 96–297 provided the site.

[36]See Carlson and Hocking 205; Ehrenhaus, "Vietnam Veterans Memorial" 64; and Griswold 708.

[37]This is nowhere close to Ehrenhaus' reasoning for his claim that the wall "prevents" closure ("Vietnam Veterans Memorial" 64). However, it provides specific textual evidence for his claim.

[38]Although regionalism and localism are not precisely the same, their effect—structural features that are recognizable and familiar because of their "normal" locale—is similar.

[39]Morris discusses the site's similarity to a "romanticist" style of cemetery design.

[40]Two other national monuments bear this "local" characteristic—the U.S.S. *Arizona* Memorial in Pearl Harbor and the First Division Monument in Washington, D.C. The U.S.S. *Arizona* Memorial displays a white tablet listing the names of the 1,177 crewmen who died on the ship. The base of the First Division Memorial is inscribed with the names of 5,599 men of that division who were killed in World War I. The names of the 4,365 First Division soldiers killed in World War II were added later. See Murfin 106; and Goode 133.

[41]Gans provides another possibility in her anthropomorphic reading (323). She sees the wall as representing a person with arms reaching out in an embrace. Anthropomorphism is a favorite token of some postmodern architects. See Jencks, *Architecture Today* 313.

[42]Rather than assuming a rather disingenous stance on the part of these critics, one that would have them suggesting that an apolitical rhetoric is even conceivable, we assume that they mean specifically that the wall makes no political statement about the Vietnam war. Some make that qualification explicitly; others do not. It is our assumption that no rhetoric is able to eschew politics. This is a position consistent with most postmodern critics, but it is most clearly articulated by Lyotard. He argues that, politics "is not a genre, it is the multiplicity of genres. ... It is, if you will, the state of language" (*The Differend* 138). But, by arguing that the Memorial makes a political statement, we are not merely begging the semantic question of "politics." We will suggest that the Memorial makes a political statement about the war specifically and about commemorative rhetoric generally.

[43]That Maya Lin is hardly a credible source on this issue is not typically considered. For her to claim that her design *did* make a political statement would have been to acknowledge that selection criteria were violated.

⁴⁴No doubt the differences between our view and that of other critics are due in part to divergent critical assumptions. Most of the critics considered here discuss only the wall, and they treat it as a work rather than as the locus of a text. Moreover, some are reliant on the "authors'" statements as interpretive grounding.

⁴⁵Also see Carlson and Hocking 204; Ehrenhaus, "Silence" 48; Ehrenhaus, "Vietnam Veterans Memorial" 54–5; Griswold; and Hess.

It should be noted that, if one considers the whole Memorial, violations of convention are intensified. It is extremely unusual, perhaps unprecedented, for two monuments commemorating the same "event" in different ways to be located on one site.

⁴⁶Ehrenhaus' references are to "Watt Raises Obstacles;" and Carhart.

⁴⁷These are merely differences of emphasis. Both derive from the notion of a "fit" between a situation and the rhetoric that responds to it.

⁴⁸As Morris points out, the Vietnam Veterans Memorial engaged a "cultural conflict over the correct form and function of memorializing" (199).

⁴⁹Perot, a Texas millionaire, had provided seed money for the design competition.

⁵⁰Fox notes the "important statement" made by the "very existence" of a memorial in another case—Montgomery, Alabama's Civil Rights Memorial.

⁵¹Haines remarks on the virtual flood of other cultural products about the Vietnam war: "the struggle over the war's meaning now approaches the size of a major communications industry, including films, recorded music, novels, memoirs, biographies, histories, oral histories, television dramas and documentaries, plays and symposia" (3).

⁵²By using the term "meta*narrative*" throughout, and by suggesting that such discourses are difficult to escape, we do not mean to imply that a narrative is a privileged *state* or characteristic of all discourse. Nor does Lyotard. He is very clear about his designation of narrative as a genre of discourse in *The Differend.*

⁵³Any attempt to contain one or the other or to hold them to the standards of the other would be to commit "terror" in Lyotard's sense, or to victimize the "phrase regimen" of one or the other. The two components of the Memorial constitute a "differend," in Lyotard's terms, "a case of conflict, between (at least) two parties, that cannot be equitably reolved for lack of a rule of judgment applicable to both arguments" (*The Differend* xi).

⁵⁴"Nervi" refers to Pier Luigi Nervi, a modern rationalist architect.

⁵⁵Actually, even a clearly modernist monument (like the Gateway Arch) does not look very much like a modernist building. The simple reason is that monuments frequently do not look like buildings. To argue that the Vietnam Veterans Memorial, or any other monument, is "modernist," therefore, one would have to consider more than its resemblance to typical modernist buildings.

⁵⁶Although it is not an architectural monument, it is an important successor of the Vietnam Veterans Memorial.


# ▓ Works Cited

Agrest, Diana. "Architecture of Mirror/Mirror of Architecture." *Oppositions* 26 (Spring 1984): 119–33.

Altman, Charles F. "The Medieval Marquee: Church Portal Sculpture as Publicity." *Journal of Popular Culture* 14 (1980): 37–46. Rpt. in Medhurst and Benson, 389–99.

Ashabranner, Brent. *Always to Remember: The Story of the Vietnam Veterans Memorial.* New York: Dodd, Mead, 1988.

Bannet, Eve Tavor. *Structuralism and the Logic of Dissent: Barthes, Derrida, Foucault, Lacan.* Urbana: U of Illinois P, 1989.

Barber, Bernard. "Place, Symbol, and Utilitarian Function in War Memorials." *Social Forces* 28 (October 1949): 64–8.

Barthes, Roland. "The Death of the Author." *Image, Music, Text.* Trans. Stephen Heath. New York: Hill and Wang, 1977. 142–8.

Barthes, Roland. "The Eiffel Tower." *A Barthes Reader.* Ed. Susan Sontag. New York: Hill and Wang, 1982. 236–50.

Barthes, Roland. "From Work to Text." *Image, Music, Text.* Trans. Stephen Heath. New York: Hill and Wang, 1977. 155–64.

Barthes, Roland. "Semiology and Urbanism." *The Semiotic Challenge.* Trans. Richard Howard. New York: Hill and Wang, 1988. 191–201.

Blake, Peter. *Form Follows Fiasco: Why Modern Architecture Hasn't Worked.* Boston: Little, Brown, 1977.

Bricker, Charles C., et al. *America's Historic Places: An Illustrated Guide to Our Country's Past.* Ed. Richard L. Scheffel. Pleasantville, NY: Reader's Digest, 1988.

Broadbent, Geoffrey. "The Deep Structures of Architecture." *Signs, Symbols and Architecture.* Ed. Geoffrey Broadbent, Richard Bunt, and Charles Jencks. New York: John Wiley and Sons, 1980. 119–68.

Brock, Bernard L., Robert L. Scott, and James W. Chesebro, eds. *Methods of Rhetorical Criticism: A Twentieth-Century Perspective.* 3d ed. Detroit: Wayne State UP, 1989.

Butterfield, Fox. "The New Vietnam Scholarship." *New York Times Magazine* 13 February 1983. 26–32.

Carhart, Tom. "Insulting Vietnam Vets." *New York Times.* 24 October 1981. 23.

Carlson, A. Cheree, and John E. Hocking. "Strategies of Redemption at the Vietnam Veterans' Memorial." *Western Journal of Speech Communication* 52 (1988): 203–15.

Charters, Mallay B. *Let's Go: The Budget Guide to the USA, 1990.* New York: St. Martin's. 1990.

Choay, François. "Alberti. The Invention of Monumentality and Memory." *Harvard Architectural Review* 4 (1984): 99–105.

Collins, Christiane C., and George R. Collins. "Monumentality: A Critical Matter in Modern Architecture." *Harvard Architectural Review* 4 (1984): 15–35.

Connor, Steven. *Postmodern Culture: An Introduction to Theories of the Contemporary.* Oxford: Basil Blackwell, 1989.

Crook, J. Mordaunt. *The Dilemma of Style: Architectural Ideas From the Picturesque to the Postmodern.* London: John Murray, 1987.

Curtis, William J.R. "Modern Architecture, Monumentality and the Meaning of Institutions: Reflections on Authenticity." *Harvard Architectural Review* 4 (1984): 65–85.

deBlaye, Edouard. *Dollarwise USA, 1989–1990.* Ed. Susan Poole. Trans. Maxwell R. D. Vos. New York: Simon and Schuster, 1989.

Eco, Umberto. "Function and Sign: The Semiotics of Architecture." *Signs, Symbols and Architecture.* Ed. Geoffrey Broadbent, Richard Bunt, and Charles Jencks. New York: John Wiley and Sons, 1980. 11–69.

Ehrenhaus, Peter. "Silence and Symbolic Expression." *Communication Monographs* 55 (1988): 41–57.

Ehrenhaus, Peter. "The Vietnam Veterans Memorial: An Invitation to Argument." *Journal of the American Forensic Association* 25 (1988): 54–64.

Fish, Lydia. *The Last Firebase: A Guide to the Vietnam Veterans Memorial.* Shippenburg, PA: White Mane, 1987.

Fisher, Volker, Andrea Gleiniger-Neumann, Heinrich Klotz, and Hans-Peter Schwartz. *Postmodern Visions: Drawings, Paintings, and Models by Contemporary Architects.* Ed. Heinrich Klotz. Trans. Yehuda Shapiro. New York: Abbeville, 1985.

Flynn, Thomas. "Foucault as Parrhesiast: His Last Course at the Collège de France (1984)." *The Final Foucault.* Ed. James Bernauer and David Rasmussen. Cambridge, MA: MIT Press, 1988. 102–18.

Forster, Kurt W. "Monument/Memory and the Mortality of Architecture." *Oppositions* 25 (Fall 1982): 2–19.

"Forum Transcript: Monumentality and the City, December 12, 1981." Conference held at Harvard Graduate School of Design. *Harvard Architectural Review* 4 (1984): 37–51.

Foss, Sonja K. "Ambiguity as Persuasion: The Vietnam Veterans Memorial." *Communication Quarterly* 34 (1986): 326–40.

Foster, Hal. *Recodings: Art, Spectacle, Cultural Politics.* Seattle: Bay Press, 1985.

Foucault, Michel. *The Archaeology of Knowledge and The Discourse on Language.* Trans. A. M. Sheridan Smith. New York: Harper, 1972.

Foucault, Michel. "Critical Theory/Intellectual History." Trans. Jeremy Harding. *Michel Foucault: Politics, Philosophy, Culture: Interviews and Other Writings, 1977–1984.* Ed. Lawrence D. Kritzman. New York: Routledge, 1988. 17–46.

Foucault, Michel. "The Subject and Power." Afterword to Hubert L. Dreyfus and Paul Rabinow. *Michel Foucault: Beyond Structuralism and Hermeneutics.* 2d ed. Chicago: U of Chicago P, 1983. 208–26.

Fox, Catherine. "No Catharsis in Civil Rights Memorial." *Los Angeles Daily Journal* 10 November 1989. II:1.

Frampton, Kenneth. "Towards a Critical Regionalism: Six Points for an Architecture of Resistance." *The Anti-Aesthetic: Essays on Postmodern Culture.* Ed. Hal Foster. Port Townsend, WA: Bay Press, 1983. 16–30.

Gandelsonas, Mario. "On Reading Architecture." *Progressive Architecture* 53 (March 1972): 68–88.

Gans, Adrienne. "The War and Peace of the Vietnam Memorials." *American Imago* 44 (1987): 315–29.

Gass, William H. "Monumentality/Mentality." *Oppositions* 25 (Fall 1982): 21–51.

Goode, James M. *The Outdoor Sculpture of Washington, D.C.: A Comprehensive Historical Guide.* Washington, D.C.: Smithsonian Institution Press, 1974.

Gregory, Stanford W., Jr., and Jerry M. Lewis. "Symbols of Collective Memory: The Social Process of Memorializing May 4, 1970, at Kent State University." *Symbolic Interaction* 11 (1988): 213–33.

Griswold, Charles L. "The Vietnam Veterans Memorial and the Washington Mall: Philosophical Thoughts on Political Iconography." *Critical Inquiry* 12 (1986): 688–719.

Guillerme, Jacque. "The Idea of Architectural Language: A Critical Inquiry." *Oppositions* 10 (Fall 1977): 21–26.

Haines, Harry W. " 'What Kind of War?': An Analysis of the Vietnam Veterans Memorial." *Critical Studies in Mass Communication* 3 (1986): 1–20.

Hart, Roderick P. *Modern Rhetorical Criticism.* Glenview, IL: Scott, Foresman, 1989.

Harvey, David. *The Condition of Postmodernity: An Enquiry into the Origins of Cultural Change.* Oxford: Basil Blackwell, 1989.

Hattenhauer, Darryl. "The Rhetoric of Architecture: A Semiotic Approach." *Communication Quarterly* 32 (1984): 71–7.

Hess, Elizabeth. "A Tale of Two Memorials." *Art in America* 71 (1983): 121–6.

Holenstein, Elmar. "Exursus: Monofunctionalism in Architecture between the Wars (LeCorbusier and the Bauhaus)." Trans. Diane Nelson. *Oppositions* 24 (Spring 1981): 49–61.

Hutcheon, Linda. *A Poetics of Postmodernism: History, Theory, Fiction.* New York: Routledge, 1988.

Jacobs, Jane. *The Death and Life of Great American Cities.* New York: Random House, 1961.

Jameson, Fredric. "Architecture and the Critique of Ideology." *The Ideologies of Theory: Essays 1971–1986.* Volume 2: *The Syntax of History.* Minneapolis: U of Minnesota P, 1988. 35–60.

Jencks, Charles. *Architecture Today.* London: Academy Editions, 1988.

Jencks, Charles. *The Language of Post-Modern Architecture.* Rev. enlarged ed. London: Academy Editions, 1981.

Jencks, Charles. "Rhetoric and Architecture." *Architectural Association Quarterly* 4 (1972): 4–17.

Jensen, Marvin D. "Making Contact: The Vietnam Veterans Memorial and the NAMES Project Quilt." Paper presented at the Speech Communication Association Convention. New Orleans, LA, November 1988.

LaCapra, Dominick. *Rethinking Intellectual History: Texts, Contexts, Language.* Ithaca: Cornell UP, 1983.

Lang, John S. "A Memorial Wall That Healed Our Wounds." *U.S. News and World Report.* 21 November 1983. 68–70.

LeCorbusier, Henri. *Towards a New Architecture.* Trans. Frederick Etchells. London: John Rodker, 1927.

Leff, Michael. "Textual Criticism: The Legacy of G. P. Mohrmann." *QJS* 72 (1986): 377–89.

Leff, Michael C., and Fred J. Kauffeld, eds. *Texts in Context: Critical Dialogues on Significant Episodes in American Political Rhetoric.* Davis, CA: Hermagoras Press, 1989.

Lyotard, Jean-François. *The Differend: Phrases in Dispute.* Trans. Georges Van Den Abbeele. Minneapolis: U of Minnesota P, 1988.

Lyotard, Jean-François. *The Postmodern Condition: A Report on Knowledge.* Trans. Geoff Bennington and Brian Massumi. Minneapolis: U of Minnesota P, 1984.

Mayo, James M. *War Memorials as Political Landscape: The American Experience and Beyond.* New York: Praeger, 1988.

McGee, Michael Calvin. "Text, Context, and the Fragmentation of Contemporary Culture." *Western Journal of Speech Communication* 54 (1990): 274–89.

McLeod, Mary. "Architecture." *The Postmodern Moment: A Handbook of Contemporary Innovation in the Arts.* Ed. Stanley Trachtenberg. Westport, CT: Greenwood, 1985. 19–52.

Mechling, Elizabeth Walker, and Jay Mechling. "The Sale of Two Cities: A Semiotic Comparison of Disneyland with Marriott's Great America." *Journal of Popular Culture* 37 (1973): 253–63. Rpt. in Medhurst and Benson. 400–13.

Medhurst, Martin J., and Thomas W. Benson, eds. *Rhetorical Dimensions in Media: A Critical Casebook.* Dubuque, IA: Kendall/Hunt, 1984.

Moriarty, Marilyn F. "Perspectives on Postmodern Architecture." In Conference Schedule and Supplement for *Postmodernism and Beyond: Architecture as the Critical Art of Contemporary Culture.* University of California, Irvine. October 26–28, 1989. 1–3.

Morris, Richard. "The Vietnam Veterans Memorial and the Myth of Superiority." In *Cultural Legacies of Vietnam: Uses of the Past in the Present.* Ed. Richard Morris and Peter Ehrenhaus. Norwood, NJ: Ablex, 1990. 199–222.

Murfin, James. *The National Parks of America.* New York: Multimedia, 1989.

Portoghesi, Paolo. *After Modern Architecture.* Trans. Meg Shore. New York: Rizzoli, 1980.

Riegl, Alois. "The Modern Cult of Monuments: Its Character and Its Origin" [1903]. Trans. Kurt W. Forster and Diane Ghirardo. *Oppositions* 25 (Fall 1982): 21–51.

Rosemarin, Adena. *The Power of Genre.* Minneapolis: U of Minnesota P, 1985.

Schwartz, Barry. "The Social Context of Commemoration: A Study in Collective Memory." *Social Forces* 61 (1982): 374–402.

Scruggs, Jan C., and Joel L. Swerdlow. *To Heal a Nation: The Vietnam Veterans Memorial.* New York: Harper, 1985.

Serenyi, Peter. "Mies' New National Gallery: An Essay on Architectural Content." *Harvard Architectural Review* 1 (1980): 181–9.

Stern, Robert. "The Doubles of Post-modern." *Harvard Architectural Review* I (1980): 75–87.

Stuart, Charlotte L. "Architecture in Nazi Germany: A Rhetorical Perspective." *Western Speech* 37 (1973): 253–63.

Temko, Allan. *Eero Saarinen.* New York: George Braziller, 1962.

Venturi, Robert. *Complexity and Contradiction in Architecture* (New York: Museum of Modern Art and Graham Foundation, 1966).

Venturi, Robert, Denise Scott Brown, and Steven Izenour. *Learning from Las Vegas.* Cambridge: MIT Press, 1972.

"Vietnam Veterans Memorial." U.S. National Park Service pamphlet. 1984.

"Watt Raises Obstacles on Vietnam Memorial." *New York Times* 13 January 1982. A12.

Wingler, Hans W. *The Bauhaus.* Cambridge, MA: MIT Press, 1969.

Wolfe, Tom. *From Bauhaus to Our House.* New York: Farrar, Straus and Giroux, 1981.

# CHAPTER 16 ⬜

# THE RHETORIC OF
# AMERICAN FOREIGN POLICY

**Philip Wander**

*In this commentary, Philip Wander describes how a politicized and polemical manuscript about the American government's Vietnam war rhetoric—he calls it "an antiwar speech with footnotes"—collided unsuccessfully with journal editors and reviewers for years. Then after shelving the project for a decade, Wander discovered that it might be "safely" reintroduced as "historical scholarship," rather than as a politicized and polemical statement. Wander's commentary traces the fate of this "reborn" essay.*

## COMMENTARY

In her poem "My Guilt," Maya Angelou talks about the guilt she feels, as a poet, when writing about injustice—slavery, heroes dead and gone, and lynchings. Her guilt lies in the pride she takes from not screaming about what she sees and feels. On the scaffold, the page before her, she takes to dying like a man. She does it to impress the crowd. Her sin, she says, lies in not screaming loud.[1]

Whatever the "Vietnam war" has come to mean, the war was horrifying in 1967. I woke up every morning feeling or knowing that I would feel angry. I took the war personally. My mind was being filled with carnage. Riding my bicycle to work one day, I saw a poster of a small child crying, suffering from burns caused by napalm. It had been pasted on an olive drab U.S. mail box. The color recalled America's glorious past (the Second World War) as well as an over-investment in camouflage paint.

I went to rallies, marches, joined a speaker's bureau at San Jose State where I met "old" and "new leftists" like Robin Brooks (once identified by *Look Magazine* in the late 1950s as one of the most "dangerous" professors in the United States) and David Eakins from history (a well-known and widely respected "new Left" theorist), Bob Gliner from sociology (who has produced several documentaries shown on public television), and Jack Kurzweil from electrical engineering (a leading political organizer in the Bay Area), and a number of students who taught me about the place of passion and organizational skills in politics.

What I learned was that the only way I could continue being a "professor" (that is, teaching) and working toward tenure (that is, becoming a "lifer," a goal I would have scoffed at at the time) was by integrating moral and political commitment into my work. This was not a matter of principle, it was a matter of survival, and it had to do not only with a professional life, but with people fed into a slaughterhouse to slaughter others. These "others" included mothers and babies, grandfathers and aunts who lived thousands of feet below young, high-tech American missionaries who, in a modern, electronic work-a-day-world, flew their "missions" over primitive, non-Christian, underdeveloped peoples.

I decided to go through the *Department of State Bulletin* to determine how this horror had been justified. A few hours every other day, often between classes, I read every speech, letter, toast (I remember John Foster Dulles invoking Buddha), etc., made by government officials about Vietnam or Indochina, from the 1950s up to 1972. What I discovered was that official statements, abstract, ritualized, melted away. What remained was a small child crying. I felt angry, betrayed. I had heard my father's war stories a hundred times (he had served in Germany with the "Black Cat Division," the Thirteenth Armored, during WWII), when Hitler existed and there were camps to liberate.

It was tough to write under these conditions, especially to do scholarly writing about Vietnam. After a presentation at a Western Speech Association meeting during this period, Lloyd Bitzer asked me in all seriousness: "How do you know that the war is wrong?" I answered, "When I was a boy and visited my grandfather on his farm in Iowa, I would have known, looking up in the air, that having bombs dropped on us was wrong." But I remember thinking at the time, "Jesus, what *is* wrong, if dropping bombs on small children, mothers, and grandfathers is not wrong?"

I kept my thoughts to myself. Along with Bitzer and others of our generation, I participated in a system that avoided controversy (or housed it in the "past"), recoiled from feeling, and equated moral and political commitment with a lack of scholarly restraint. Detaching feeling from thought and writing was part of what it meant to be a professional. This calamity was not caused by Bitzer or Wander, but we participated in, reproduced, and were (and are) to some extent defined through it.

During the Vietnam war, we could scream our protest and not be disappeared. To some extent this reminded us that the United States was and is a great place to live. But the same could not be said for the Vietnamese or, for that matter, American soldiers who were fighting and dying in a war in which many of them did not believe. The war, recalling Pericles' Plague Speech, was not about democracy. We were not bringing democracy to Vietnam, any more than the French tried to bring it to Indochina. It was about tyranny (or fascism as we called it), about the domination of another weaker people. Whatever the terms *fascism, Stalinism,* or the *Holocaust* now mean, it was occurring then, but it was proceeding under terms like *duty, patriotism, foreign policy. It had to be stopped!*

The first incarnation of "The Rhetoric of American Foreign Policy" was as an antiwar speech with footnotes. In the same year, Steve Jenkins and I published an essay advocating "worthwhile" scholarship. Encouraged by the response, I sent off a manuscript about the official justification of the war in Vietnam to the *American Quarterly* (replete with quotations from R. G. Collingwood). It was politely rejected. I turned it around, and sent it to *Philosophy and Rhetoric.* Two referees and the editor concurred in their rejection. One of the rejection letters included the following rhetorical question: "What if one stuffed Richard Nixon's speech of 1969 in Wander's face?" The letter was unsigned.

Rejections hurt. My first rejections took a week to shake off. They still take a couple of hours. They hurt, because they open up, if only for a moment, little fissures of self-loathing, fear, feelings of inadequacy as a scholar, a human being, a lover, a son, etc. In such moments, the appeal of Kafka's story about a man slowly becoming a cockroach becomes real. Bluntly stated: Having Nixon's speech stuffed in my face pissed me off.

In relation to "The Rhetoric of American Foreign Policy," however, my metamorphosis had only just begun. I revised and sent the manuscript to the *Quarterly Journal of Speech,* where the editor was my dissertation advisor and friend, Edwin Black. I admired him and his work. Imagine my childish delight then when his referees recommended publishing the manuscript with "minor revisions." Edwin, however, with whom I have had and continue to have many arguments over politics, crossed out the more political/ polemical sentences and paragraphs. He told me to read George Orwell's "The Politics of the English Language" and respond to the comments sent by the referees. I revised, placing the good (that is, the political-polemical) stuff into footnotes. It came back again. Again, without explanation, controversial passages were crossed out. Again I revised, stuffing the "offensive" passages into footnotes. It came back a third time. This time when I sent it back I could not reread the piece. It was rejected.

Wanting father's approval, or mother's love, wanting to be a famous author in "the field," wanting to write about Vietnam (notice the slippage here from the ideals "professed" above) added up. In writing and revising and having my manuscript rejected, I discovered how easy it was to sell out. I had, in fact, tried to sell out. Fortunately for me, no one was buying. I have always been grateful to Edwin for letting me off the hook. He has been kind enough over the years not to remind me of it, though my reputation as a "radical," "Marxist," "ideology critic" (names I have found odd and limiting, though not objectionable) invites a retrospective.

About the essay: I jammed the revisions into a folder, filed it under "foreign policy," and left the field. I started writing media criticism. I took a vow to write what I truly believed in the way that I wanted to say it. The war was over. Ten years later, fumbling through my files for another paper, I unearthed the folder, read the manuscript, and realized that it had now become "historical scholarship." The difference between polemic and history has to do not only with tone ("emotional," "polemical," "un-well-rounded"), but also with timing and, in the case of scholarship, primary research. Words that evoked outrage during the war had cooled. I thought, "Maybe I could rewrite the piece." This was followed by another thought, "But what for? Vietnam is over. Let it rest." Exhuming Vietnam, confronting my manuscript—my "revisions"—was damned painful.

Then, one day in a used book store, I ran across Jean Paul Sartre's indictment of American actions in Vietnam drawn up for the war crimes tribunal set up by Bertrand Russell. What Sartre said and the way he said it surprised me. He opposed the war and wrote the indictment while it was still going on, but there was no stirring moral indictment accompanied by photographs of napalm victims. The United States, Sartre argued, was continuing a policy pursued by France, Belgium, and Great Britain in the nineteenth century, a policy of domination. If a country or a nation wants to dominate a people who do not want to be dominated, it must be prepared to use terror and, if necessary, to kill every man, woman, and child (in effect, to commit genocide), if it is to retain control when collectively challenged.

Thucydides warned against a policy of empire. The Mytilinian debate and the Melian dialogue have to do with "disciplining" a colony and a neutral city-state in the interests of empire. Thucydides made a distinction between a war and an act of domination that I found helpful. War has to do with a violent conflict between two city- or nation-states when the outcome is in doubt; domination has to do with a violent conflict where there is no doubt about the outcome. Slowly it became obvious to me that Vietnam was not unrelated to other historical events. It was no longer history imprisoned in memory or the past.

There was work to do, but I ran into an academic prejudice. It held that events talked about in official statements about foreign policy and how officials in this or other countries responded to them was the stuff to be analyzed. Obvious now, but a breakthrough for me at the time—foreign policy rhetoric is aimed not only at elites, but also at domestic audiences. It certainly affects domestic audiences. President Reagan, during this period, was arguing that a revolution in Nicaragua could spill over into Mexico leading to massive immigration into the United States. Listening to him, I recalled all those thick, red arrows that for thirty years had been curving and hooking into the United States. Each arrow carried in its wake Soviet (and/or Chinese) armies, or millions of refugees into Galveston, New York, Los Angeles, sometimes Seattle, or nuclear missiles.

Nicaragua had no air force or missiles or navy. The Sandinistas were not poisoning coffee. But America paid for "freedom fighters," gave them "humanitarian aid" (to stem the tide of communism), slipped money under the table it turned out, after Congress had drawn a line. America was not fighting a war, it was engaging in domination, but it was domination explained to an audience fearful of a vast, surging "it." This "it" included anything and everything that was "un-American."

At a Speech Communication Association convention in Washington, D.C., I was a critic respondent on a panel organized by and including several people who had been or were speech writers and organizers in significant political campaigns. After listening to their comments, I noted that the word "imperialism" had not been uttered, and furthermore that, regardless of the facts, I did not think they would recommend that any candidate use that word. Afterwards, Bob Shrum, who had been Teddy Kennedy's and George McGovern's speech writer (and who had been an outstanding debater at Georgetown), muttered that the American people were not ready to hear it.

Shrum was correct—that is, correct within a two-party, mass media democracy operating under the shadow of a "Soviet Union." This is part of the joy and the responsibility of "scholarship": saying what ought to be and needs to be said, even when no one is ready to hear it. There is no guarantee that such speech will get into print, but if scholarly discourse can sustain the harsher truths, a small, public platform remains.

There is something else which must be said. "The Rhetoric of American Foreign Policy," with its Aristotelian bent and scholarly flare, reeks of compromise. Strategic, necessary, useful compromise, but in relation to the Philippines, Guatemala, Brazil, Iran, Vietnam, Chile, Nicaragua, Angola, Indonesia, and the millions of men, women, and children of color who have been sacrificed to our "national interest"—I take the history of invasions and the ongoing CIA machinations as the warrant for such morbid conclusions—writing in English may be understood as an offense. On Monday, October 26, 1992, a *New York Times* editorial appeared entitled, "The Mozote Horror, Confirmed." In 1981 American-trained Salvadorian soldiers murdered a thousand men, women, and children in the remote village of Mozote. At the time, just after the story broke, the Reagan administration certified that the Salvadorian government was "making a concerted and significant effort" to promote human rights and end "the indiscriminate torture and murder of its citizens." The finding was necessary for releasing U.S. military aid to El Salvador. Ten years later, the remains of scores of children are being exhumed there.

The unspeakable truths of American foreign policy, the millions of souls sacrificed to make and keep our "sphere of influence," mock the rhetoric of American foreign policy. They also mock "The Rhetoric of American Foreign Policy." The immensity of the horror and the style and tone of the saying of it create an unresolvable tension. W. E. B. Du Bois once commented on this problem. He addressed the problem of race during a period in which lynchings were widespread. His own wife and child had been terrorized during a pogrom in Atlanta. "I realize that the truth of history lies not in the mouths of partisans," he wrote, even as he was pulled toward partisanship, "but rather in the calm Science that sits between. Her cause I seek to serve, and where-ever I fail, I am at least paying Truth the respect of earnest effort." In the conflict between partisan and historian/critic/scientist, between professing and professionalism which occurs in the face of horror, there are moments when scholarship muffles what ought to be screamed.

## ■ Note

¹Angelou, Maya. "My Guilt." *Just Give Me a Cool Drink of Water 'fore I Die.* New York: Bantam Books, 1971. 46.

# The Rhetoric of American Foreign Policy

**Philip Wander**

> It is noble to avenge oneself on one's enemies and not to come to terms
> with them; for requital is just, and the just is noble; and not to surrender is a
> sign of courage. . . . We must also (with ceremonial oratory) take into
> account the nature of the particular audience . . . it is not difficult to praise
> the Athenians to an Athenian audience.
>
> —ARISTOTLE

Like any other body of stock phrases or standardized code of expression, the rhetoric of American foreign policy protects us against reality, that is, against the claim on our attention that any event or fact makes by virtue of its existence. If one were always responsive to such claims, writes Hannah Arendt, one would soon be exhausted, and yet such claims must be kept firmly in mind if one is to remain alert to matters too important to be obscured by language.[1] "Defending the Free World," "protecting our National Security," "weighing our National Interest," "countering the Communist Menace," the language is familiar. It has, over the last half century, set aside whole worlds of fact and contained, when it did not encourage, some of the most disturbing events in American history.

In one sense, the commonplaces of such rhetoric are dictated by the occasions. They are part of a ritual wherein government officials represent foreign policy to the people. If talk about foreign policy is understood as a government's definition of the state's international objectives combined with a plan for reaching them and if policy expresses the needs and wants of the state whose fulfillment the government conceives of as beneficial, then the public justification of policy may or may not have any relation to the deliberation of policy. Ideology, according to one former State Department official in the early 1970's, plays little or no part in actual decisions which are garbed in moral terms to satisfy onlookers.[2]

In another sense, however, it will not do in politics to make too sharp a distinction between the contexts of justification and deliberation. Another student of international relations, Grant Hugo, worries about the tendency in foreign affairs to create a discrepancy between the natural meaning of words and their practical significance. He finds this tendency troubling because the speaker often ends up as misled as the audience, a problem which becomes apparent when a speaker or a government ends up publicly committed to a view of foreign affairs embracing impractical or dangerous policies.[3]

Apart from whether or not government officials try to mislead the public is the larger concern about how their words work. Whatever answer one gives to this question will greatly influence what one decides is an appropriate critical response. If it is assumed, for example, that official statements about foreign policy are supposed to express the thoughts of the speaker or reflect accurately the facts of the situation, criticism will proceed along lines of moral fault. Such criticism favors maxims about distortion and lying. An analysis of the speaking situation which includes institutional arrangements, sanctioned roles, and the existence of vested interests, however, will press beyond the claims of individual morality to understand the political system and its limitations. What I am suggesting is that a full understanding of the rhetoric of American foreign policy must take into account: (1) the ceremonial nature of that rhetoric; (2) its function in domestic politics; and (3) its relation to facts and events beyond the language employed, matters on which the lives of tens of millions, if not the whole of humanity, now depend.

## ■ DOMESTIC POLITICS AND FOREIGN POLICY RHETORIC

Placing rhetoric in relation to real people whose passivity, assent, or action has a bearing on a speaker enables us to get at the pragmatics of political communication. The pivotal term in communication theory is "audience," in political theory "group" or "party." The domestic audience for foreign policy address is in a position to determine whether or not an administrative advocate and his or her party will remain in power. Organized elements within that audience—economic interests, ethnic groups, popular socio-political movements—are in a position directly to influence the outcome of an election. Because America's relations with other governments may be of consequence, for economic, ethnic, or ideological reasons, to such groups, because national elections are determined on the basis of a given party's ability to link such groups into loose coalitions and to appeal to the mass electorate, foreign policy rhetoric takes on meaning in the context of domestic politics which would be lost in an exclusive focus on international relations.

This is not peculiar to the United States. In societies where relatively autonomous and conflicting groups struggle for power, observes Marcel Merel, a French scholar, the facts of international affairs tend to take on the coloring—light or dark—of the society envisioned by those seeking office. Trapped in the contradiction between the demands of their representative function and those of their ambition to acquire power, he writes, the parties often have no choice but to camouflage the facts of international politics under the colors of domestic politics.[4] The "facts" not only reflect the worldview of a particular party and the coalition it represents, but also, if only through negation, the worldview and the "facts" promoted by rival parties and coalitions. It is this dynamic, I think, which explains why the rhetoric of American foreign policy seems, on the face of it, so empty, vague, and misleading.

Whatever attitude one takes toward foreign policy rhetoric, that it is meaningless, misleading, dangerously provocative, or, following Merel, an important buffer between governments and excitable mass electorates; whatever special interests, political groups, or institution one believes, on any given moment, to be most influential in shaping mass opinion, this much is clear.[5] A systematic examination of the rhetoric of American foreign policy will take into consideration a variety of audiences, the relative importance of any given audience within the context of domestic politics, and the ways in which official statements are or are not adapted to them. While the meaning of such rhetoric will not be exhausted in audience analysis—government action does have real and sometimes terrible consequences—any effort to understand or, for that matter, to change policy must take such audiences into account.

While the definition of audience in relation to statements about foreign policy is fairly clear, both in terms of historically identifiable groups and through survey opinion research, what constitutes an "argument" in debates over foreign policy presents a problem. It is tempting to leave the definition of argument operational—it is what we say it is. But argument in the world of affairs is not arbitrary. Foreign policy refers to actions undertaken by a government in relation to other nations. We do not, in this context, talk about propositions in the logical sense of statements about which something is affirmed or denied. And while we may define an argument as that which offers good grounds for supporting a proposal, stressing the facts of the situation, "facts" in foreign affairs even when knowable are so changeable, so responsive to political calculation, so shaped by differing points of view that one is soon driven from precise philosophical or scientific formulations.

The study of argument need not be abandoned because neither logic nor science provides an adequate body of rules for either definition or evaluation. If we are prepared to admit that there are times when formal definitions and technical solutions are not very useful, and assuming that this is one of them, then we may proceed to study argument in context—the historical context in which real people were in fact debating what for them were important issues. We can, therefore, approach debates over foreign policy searching for arguments, grounding the meaning of those arguments in a context of groups or parties engaged in a struggle for political power, articulating that struggle through the ways such groups spell out their interests in an effort to inspire their partisans, attract other groups with whom coalitions might be formed, and recruit from that vast, unorganized aggregate known as the "mass audience." Our definitions of both audience and argument, therefore, are rooted in historical struggle and the ideological conflicts in which they appear.

I have discussed the assumptions underlying ideological criticism for political communication, mass media, and rhetorical theory and criticism elsewhere;[6] I have also explored the worldviews or ideologies of particular movements.[7] What follows is not another theoretical statement or historical study, but a critique of the rhetoric of American foreign policy. It begins with an attempt to isolate a mode of argument employed during the early stages of American involvement in Vietnam, a mode I call "prophetic dualism." The questions here concern the precise form this argument takes, its function in and relation to political coalitions arrayed under, represented, or sought out by the Democratic and Republican parties at the time, and its implications for the formulation and conduct of foreign policy.

The essay then turns to another mode of argument employed in Vietnam, this during a period when decisions were being justified over the number of advisors to be stationed there, and later, whether or not more combat troups were needed, a mode I call "technocratic realism." This argument will also be considered in light of Democratic and Republican political coalitions and the implications it holds for the conduct of foreign policy.

Finally, this essay examines the ground of foreign policy rhetoric, what "prophetic dualism" and "technocratic realism" agree upon, an agreement so fundamental that it has become tacit public knowledge. We will consider this agreement in relation to interests working to influence government policy, whoever is in power, over the expenditure of public funds on the military and the making and enforcing of economic, political, and military commitments.

The debate over American foreign policy, with the pressures of overpopulation, environmental destruction, the development of weapons of terrifying potential, and the depletion of natural resources, will grow more intense. Apart from the arms race, which receives most of the attention, and rightfully so, are problems associated with a projected decline of raw materials—manganese, cobalt, chromium, aluminum, tin, nickel, petroleum, iron, titanium, etc.—necessary for the operation of modern technological societies. With this decline, we can expect more energetic competition between nations over both markets and raw materials. Surveying this prospect, Paul Varg warns against the attractions of "gut nationalism." Domestic politics in the United States and other liberal democracies are not divorced from questions of foreign relations. Foreign policy issues, he notes, have traditionally been used to secure party advantage. But we can no longer afford political partisanship that exploits popular ignorance for the sake of taking office.[8] The dangers are real; the need for debate over our "national interest" obvious.[9] This essay is a preface to such a debate.

## ■ "PROPHETIC DUALISM": THE EISENHOWER-DULLES ADMINISTRATION

On April 6, 1984 at the Georgetown Center for Strategic and International Studies, President Reagan denounced second-guessing in Congress about keeping American forces in Lebanon. "Unfortunately," he complained, "many in Congress seem to believe they are still in the troubled Vietnam era, . . . clearly Congress is less than wholly comfortable with both the need for a military element in foreign policy and its own responsibility to deal with that element."[10] He ended his speech with a discussion of the "lessons" to be learned from Vietnam. He was right; there are lessons to be learned, but not necessarily those he would teach. In the early 1950s, during the Eisenhower-Dulles administration, a prominent and recurring argument supporting American policy in Vietnam concerned America's moral or spiritual superiority. Religious faith, moral insight, a respect for the laws of God formed a set of virtues attributed to the nation which, as we shall see, could be called upon not only to explain why those in power deserved to be there, but also why the United States should engage in certain kinds of action abroad. The argument, as it appears in statements about foreign policy, I shall call "prophetic dualism."

In its perfected form prophetic dualism divides the world into two camps. Between them there is conflict. One side acts in accord with all that is good, decent, and at one with God's will. The other acts in direct opposition. Conflict between them is resolved only through the total victory of one side over the other. Since no guarantee exists that good will triumph, there is no middle ground. Hence neutrality may be treated as a delusion, com promise appeasement, and negotiation a call for surrender.[11]

To appreciate this argument and how it works requires one to go beyond denunciations of moralism to meditate not only on American history and the political situation in which the argument was actually employed, but also on the composition of the group employing it. It is perhaps obvious, but there is, in American history, a religious cast to public discourse.[12] Piety becomes especially thick about the "nation." Only in the United States, writes Sacvan Bercovitch, tracing the metamorphosis of the Puritan "jeremiad" into rhetoric, ideology, and ritual in American culture, has nationalism joined with the Christian meaning of the sacred.[13] However much influenced by Puritanism, the nation underwent an apotheosis during two World Wars. America's "mission," her moral and spiritual superiority, became an official part of the war effort, themes absorbed in and recapitulated in a thousand different ways through popular culture. During these periods of national crisis, patriotism virtually became law, criticism of government policies grounds for censorship, public protest evidence if not of treason then some lesser form of un-Americanism.

With Dwight Eisenhower, commander of the allied armies in Europe, running for the office of president, patriotism, high moral purpose, and the religious tone that went with it became associated with the political coalition supporting the Republican party. The fact that the party was dominated by what E. D. Baltzell calls the "Protestant Establishment,"[14] which has traditionally adopted a posture of moral and social and economic superiority, further encouraged a patriotic and high moral tone. It was, moreover, a tone contrasting the Republican with the Democratic party which, during the late 1940s and early '50s, the "McCarthy period," was being attacked for being soft on Communism, losing China, and harboring traitors.

The attack on the Democratic camp by Senator Joseph McCarthy, with the support of the "old stock" wing of the Republican party led by Senator Robert Taft, made inroads into traditionally Democratic constituencies— Irish Catholics in particular, Catholics and labor in general.[15] Again, a religious, though nondenominational tone, was indicated. Thus, the pro-American, anti-Communist movement McCarthy came to symbolize broadened the Republican coalition, bringing with it a style of discourse— patriotic, moral, and religious—for which Americans had been prepared during the Second World War; it was a style appropriate to a Protestant establishment with fundamentalist followers, since it included, through McCarthy, an attack on the Truman-Hiss-Acheson side of the establishment which excluded poor Protestants as single-mindedly as it did poor Catholics;[16] and it was a style highlighting the "disloyalty" and "un-Americanism" attributed to the recent Democratic administration. In this larger context, "prophetic dualism" constituted a sophisticated ideological apparatus for coping with a "Communist menace" at home and abroad. A domestic division between "fellow travelers" and "loyal Americans" resonated with an international division between the "Free World" and "Atheistic Communism."

To see how this argument worked in the context of foreign policy, one has to turn to concrete examples. Those who sought to justify foreign policy along moral lines include Democrats like Truman and Acheson, but it is principally associated with John Foster Dulles, Secretary of State under Eisenhower. "We have our principles," Dulles declared in a speech before the American Legion, October 10, 1955:

> Our productivity and our power do not rattle haphazardly about the world. They are harnessed to basic moral principles. There is a school of thought that claims that morality and foreign policy do not mix. That never has been, is not, and I pray never will be the American ideal.

With the spiritual, there was a pragmatic reason for framing arguments about moral principles:

Our people can understand, and will support policies which can be explained and understood in moral terms. But policies merely based on carefully calculated expediency could never be explained and would never be understood.[17]

Beyond the domestic audience (the "American people"), however, lay a world of international affairs and the specter of evil.

In an address made before the American Bar Association, August 24, 1955, President Eisenhower fused government and religion in American foreign policy, drawing the contrast between Good and Evil that is the hallmark of prophetic dualism:

The central fact of today's life is the existence in the world of two great philosophies of man and government. They are in contest for the friendship, loyalty, and support of the world's peoples. On the one side, our Nation is ranged with those who seek attainment of human goals through a government of laws administered by men. Those laws are rooted in moral law reflecting a religious faith that man is created in the image of God and that the energy of the free individual is the most dynamic force in human affairs.

The contrast is balanced:

On the other side are those who believe—and many of them with evident sincerity—that human goals can be most surely reached by a government of men who rule by decree. Their decrees are rooted in an ideology which ignores the faith that man is a spiritual being, which establishes the all-powerful state as the principal source of advancement and progress.[18]

As it was articulated during the Eisenhower-Dulles administration, prophetic dualism involved religious faith, the faith of our fathers, the ideals of freedom, individuality, a militant God, and the existence of evil in the world.

The God officially invoked was the God who presided over the founding of America, the God who abhored Atheists and loathed communist slavery. It was the God who had been America's "co-pilot" during World War Two. For the Eisenhower administration, God was not dead. He, and it was most definitely a "He," was a living God, a God to whom government officials, in moments of national crisis, might turn for support. It is also the God of Bible-Belt Protestanism and working-class Catholicism; the God, not surprisingly, of the more authoritarian elements in the body politic and certain personality profiles.[19] But while this God might be located in a particular constituency or in a psychological type, He may, in moments of confusion, terror, or terrible disappointment, be summoned. It is in such moments that a figure, which for the unbeliever counts as a rhetorical convention, may become a source of political influence, a Presence above and beyond what the Enlightenment or "secular humanism" celebrates as the Rule of Reason.

In the context of domestic politics, there are advantages for state managers to be gained from the use of prophetic dualism. Put quite simply: God dampens public debate. How can one argue with God's will when it is clearly expressed? How does one argue over obvious, absolute principles? While a "crisis" may argue for an end to debate, spiritual imperatives close it down. "The government and every leader of a business or profession," Eisenhower declared on May 20, 1954, "must band together to show that the United States is a great organism of free men who put freedom above all other values." Sometimes he thought Patrick Henry might have overstated the case—"Give me liberty or give me death!"—but still, Eisenhower concluded, the statement was true for "our race."[20] There is a synthesis here of nationalism and spiritualism, a way of thinking. Eisenhower does not so much urge a point of view as call on absolute support for an absolute.

I find it difficult, since the great divisions opened up by Vietnam, not to marvel at the serenity with which Eisenhower and Dulles could count on the support of every American. Dulles thought it was a matter of policy following from principle:

> The reality of the matter is that the United States, by every standard of measurement, is the world's greatest power not only materially but spiritually. We have national policies which are clear and sound. They fit a civilization based on religious faith. They are strongly implemented but at a cost we can afford to live with. They have evolved on a nonpartisan basis, and, in broad outlines, they are overwhelmingly backed by our people.[21]

As a form of argument, prophetic dualism calls for overwhelming support—a response appropriate to the world's greatest spiritual power. In the context in which Dulles spoke during the 1950s, there were real obstacles facing those who might have been willing to dissent. These obstacles, now known as "McCarthyism," also favored "nonpartisan" support.[22]

One advantage of prophetic dualism, for those in office, is that it stifles debate; another is that, because it posits a life-and-death struggle, it encourages a heightened dependence on the established order. Conflict is inevitable between Good and Evil. Serious enough in the face of two World Wars, such conflict becomes positively chilling in a nuclear age. Dulles, however, did not draw back from the abyss. There were, he declared in a news conference in 1956, "basic moral values and vital interests for which we stand, and the surest way to avoid war is to let it be known in advance that we are prepared to defend these principles if need be by life itself."[23] Without the will to defend basic principles, thought Dulles, civilization declines; the good, through compromise, intimidation, and weakness, may cease to exist. Writing in *Foreign Affairs*, in 1957, Dulles observed that the United States was not content to reply upon a peace which could be preserved only by a capacity to "destroy vast segments of the human race." Though horrifying, and both Eisenhower and Dulles repeatedly expressed their longings for peace, nuclear war nevertheless remained a "last alternative." The good news, according to Dulles, was that American scientists had developed nuclear weapons that did not involve such widespread harm to humanity.[24]

While it restricts debate and encourages dependence on existing authority, prophetic dualism has serious drawbacks for those in power. Prophetic dualism leaves little room for adaptation or compromise, as was demonstrated following the French defeat in Vietnam. On July 15, 1955, President Eisenhower, on the eve of his departure for the Heads of Government meeting to be held in Geneva to negotiate French withdrawal, addressed the nation over radio and television. The problem facing Eisenhower was not only the political and military realities surrounding the defeat and the need to explain the failure of the "Free World" in its struggle with the "Communist menace," but also, and more importantly, how to explain negotiations with the forces of Evil. How could an American audience, for whom the perfidy of Communist leaders promised deception and lies, accommodate itself to the reality of a Communist victory and a negotiated settlement?

The precedent offered by Korea did not apply. Korea was not a war but a "police action" designed to uphold the law. The conflict had been assigned to a Democratic administration's failure to take a hard-line against Communism. The line in Korea was drawn at the 38th parallel. The line held. The French (i.e., "Free World") defeat in Vietnam, however, represented a complete collapse and withdrawal. Eisenhower, therefore, had to justify what, in the brutal dualities of right-wing American politics, was unjustifiable.

Eisenhower recognized the problem. America's purpose in attending the conference was not a sign of weakness; on the contrary, the willingness of the Free World to participate in negotiation set it apart from the Communist bloc.

> We (the Free World) are not held together by force, but we are held together by this great factor, and it is this: The free world believes, under one religion or another, in a Divine Power. It believes in a Supreme Being. Now this, my friends, is a very great factor for the conciliation and peace at this time because each of these religions—each one of them—has as one of its basic commandments the words—the terminology—that is similar to our Golden Rule. . . . This means that the thinking of those people is based upon ideas of right and justice and mutual self-respect, consideration for the other man. And this means peace, because only in peace can such conceptions as these prevail. This means that the free people of the world hate war, and they want peace and are dedicated to it.

But how does one negotiate with forces not committed to the Golden Rule, committed in fact to its opposite? How can the forces of Light make agreements with the forces of Darkness and hope to survive? Eisenhower's answer is instructive. He transcends, yet does not abandon, the great spiritual struggle.

> Now, it is natural for a people, steeped in a religious civilization, when they come to moments of great importance—maybe even crisis—such as we now

face, to turn to the Divine Power that each has in his own heart, believes in his own heart, for guidance, for wisdom, for some help in doing the thing that is honorable and is right. I have no doubt that tonight, throughout this country, and indeed, throughout the free world, such prayers are ascending.

In a spiritual struggle, communing with one's God not only strengthens the supplicant, but it can also, in the case of an interventionist God, affect the outcome. Thus it was not deliberation, debate, or discussion of the great national issues which became appropriate. It was, instead, the isolating act of prayer, an act which, nevertheless, took on political significance: "Prayer is a mighty force. And this brings me to the thought that through prayer we could also achieve a very definite and practical result at this very moment." The United States could be conciliatory, because it did not seek conquest, tolerant, because it had no wish to impose its way of life on others and, secure, because its representatives were firm in the consciousness of its citizens' "spiritual and material strength and . . . defense of the right."[25]

The dualities embedded in the rhetoric of American foreign policy did not originate with Eisenhower or Dulles, nor can they be explained adequately through a kind of residual Puritanism in American society. And while it is true that such dualities resonate with the millenial beliefs of Fundamentalist Christians and that the Communist Menace has come to stand for the anti-Christ, Fundamentalism prior to the Great War was committed to Pacifism. The militant anti-Communism associated with the Bible Belt does not appear in Fundamentalist literature until 1924–25.[26] What is more, the dualities now so common in talk about foreign policy appear in the rhetoric of many European societies in the first quarter of the 20th century.

Through modern literature, Paul Fussell traces a vision of a bifurcated and hostile world back to the Great War with its hundreds of miles of parallel trenches, orange belts of barbed wire, the stench of decaying flesh, and massive efforts to justify the catastrophe to civilian populations on both sides of the struggle.[27] What we have called prophetic dualism in the rhetoric of American foreign policy during the 1950s neither originated with the Republican party nor with Fundamentalism in this country. While it forms an important element in the worldview of the right-wing in American politics, it must also be understood as part of the cluster of images, themes, grammatical forms, and emotions making up the culture of war in the twentieth century.

### ▨ "TECHNOCRATIC REALISM": THE KENNEDY-JOHNSON ADMINISTRATIONS

For all the charm of Camelot, the poignance of its fall and the eloquence of its court historians, the change from a conservative Republican to a liberal Democratic administration not only failed to lead America away from the abyss, it also seemed, in the early days of the Kennedy administration, to lead even closer to it.[28] This was the period of the Cuban invasion, Berlin crisis, the decision to send troops into Thailand and Vietnam, resumption of atmospheric nuclear tests in response to a Russian breach of an unofficial agreement to halt such testing, and the "Cuban Missile Crisis," which at the time felt like the moment before the final conflagration. Yet there is some basis for associating the end or, perhaps, a beginning of the end of the Cold War with the Kennedy administration.

However the election victory in 1960 is explained—the want of a shave, the return of the Irish, Catholics, and unions to the Democratic party, Chicago theft, etc.—the fact remains that a coalition dominated by labor, racial and ethnic minorities, middle-class professionals, and the intelligentsia, scornful of an America shaped along lines laid down by a Republican God and Protestant fundamentalists, calling for a variety of liberal reforms, took on a much more secular, humanistic, scientific, and negotiable tone than the previous administration.[29] The Faith of our Fathers, though still ritually invoked, gave way to the prospect of a managerial-technocratic revolution and a greater horizon for irony, wit, and compromise.

A measure of the difference in style this coalition allowed, encouraged, and found beneficial may be gleaned from one of the most eloquent speeches ever made by an American official on foreign policy—Kennedy's address on June 10, 1963, at the American University in Washington, D.C. Three months before the signing of the Nuclear Test Ban Treaty, Kennedy announced a major shift in American foreign policy through a frontal assault on Manichean dualities in the articulation of foreign affairs. The way in which he confronted the orthodox patriotism and religiosity associated with the Bible Belt, veterans groups, and the business community in the United States is, in itself, a work of political art. He attacked the dualities associated with the right wing by showing that they were shared by the leaders in the Soviet Union. In doing so, he expressed the hope that what the Russians said did not express what they believed.

> It is discouraging to read a recent authoritative Soviet text on military strategy and find, on page after page, wholly baseless and incredible claims—such as the allegation that "American imperialist circles are preparing to unleash different types of wars . . . that there is a very real threat of preventive war being unleashed by American imperialists against the Soviet Union . . . and that the political aims of the American imperialists are to enslave economically and politically the European and other capitalist countries . . . and to achieve world domination . . . by means of aggressive wars."

Such views were inaccurate, untrue, propagandistic. They were also dangerous, though possibly revealing: "Truly as it was written long ago, 'the wicked flee when no man pursueth.' " The Biblical allusion speaks to those who would frame foreign policy in apocalyptic terms, linking together Soviet propagandists and their American counterparts. The Soviets become less a symbol of evil and more a "warning to the American people not to fall into the same trap as the Soviets, not to see only a distorted and desperate view of the other side, not to see conflict as inevitable, accommodation as impossible, and communication as nothing more than an exchange of threats."

And yet, how are international affairs to be understood, if not through conflict between the Soviet Union and the United States? Answering this question, Kennedy approached the sublime. In order to appreciate this move, however, one must grasp the problem of cold-war dualities here and now. What Kennedy did was to confront the dualism implicit in right-wing rhetoric in the United States and the Soviet Union and deny the implication that either side has to be destroyed:

> Let us not be blind to our differences but let us also direct attention to our common interest and to the means by which these differences can be resolved. And if we cannot end now our differences, at least we can make the world safe for diversity.

What is the basis for a willingness to tolerate Evil or, in Kennedy's words, a "profoundly repugnant" system? Here he offers not merely a rejoinder to traditional dualities, but also a way to transcend them. "In the final analysis," a phrase taking on new life in a nuclear age, "our most basic common link is that all inhabit this planet. We all breathe the same air. We all cherish our children's future. And we are all mortal."[30]

Thus Kennedy offered a rhetorical alternative to the "natural" divisions underlying the Cold War, a critique of a right-wing coalition opposed to any negotiations with the "enemy," and an alternative to the culture of war which had, as a result of two world wars, wormed its way into the deepest recesses of modern consciousness.

A liberal administration might reject the notion that any system can be so evil that its people must be considered as lacking in virtue; yet it must, in the world of affairs, be able to respond to real threats. How can an Administration dedicated to tolerance and accommodation protect American interests in international affairs? The answer lies in the mode of argument I call "technocratic realism." In technocratic realism, negotiation becomes possible over areas of mutual interest—a retreat from the horrors of nuclear war, for example. But while negotiation and compromise become possible, competition between the United States and the Soviet Union over economic, military, and scientific matters would remain keen.

Instead of a Holy War, therefore, technocratic realism looked to peaceful, though vigorous, competition. How does one win such a contest? Not through harsh religious sentiments, but through hard-headed calculation. Addressing a conference on Cold War Education at Tampa, Florida in July, 1963, Roger Hilsman, Assistant Secretary for Far Eastern Affairs, discussed

the "Challenge to Freedom" in Southeast Asia. He denounced the traditional dualities underlying foreign policy rhetoric. They were, he thought,
over-simplified. He detailed a more complex, more "realistic" approach:

> Precision, wisdom, realism: These require the utmost in cool and unemotional
> judgment and what I called earlier cool, deliberate analysis. Tough minds,
> analytical minds, are required to carry this nation through the dangerous era in
> which we live. Our minds must be keen enough to recognize that no situation
> is simple: that untidiness is characteristic of most problems; that there are no
> shortcuts to success, no neat, swift solutions anywhere. Today the critical issues
> we face demand of all of us the capacity to live in a complex world of untidy
> situations and yet do what is required of us with steady nerves and unflinching
> will.[31]

Technocratic realism finds the modern world much too complex for old
time religion. Not the prophet, but rather a skilled, tough expert is what is
needed, one whose mind is unclouded by violent and dangerous emotions;
one who is wise, analytical, precise.

The persona of the technocrat emerged out of the university intellectuals, government bureaucrats, and skilled professionals who formed part of
the coalition which brought the Kennedy administration into power. If
problems in foreign affairs were simple, direct, mere matters of holding to
sure principles, such an expert would not be needed, but the problems were,
in what has become a familiar term, "complex." It is rare, observed U. Alexis
Johnson, in an address delivered at the University of Nebraska in 1963, that
"there are just two sides to a problem or that the issues are black and white
in good Western movie fashion—and the business of carrying out foreign
policy can be complex indeed in this complex world."[32]

Where prophetic dualism took its stand on principle, technocratic realism (Dulles called it "calculated expediency") began with a hard-headed
look at American interests. Such interests, it concluded, were ill-served by
military conflict. Economic competition was infinitely more desirable. Thus
it stressed "efficiency" over "morality," and argued that the affluence of the
Free World evidenced not only its greater humanity, but also its superior
economic and social systems. Dean Rusk, Secretary of State under both
Kennedy and Johnson, characterized the role of the United States in world
affairs as competitive but in economic rather than in military terms:

> The performance of our economic system under the conditions of liberty is itself
> one of the most powerful supports of the simple notions of liberty to which we
> as a nation are dedicated. We need not dwell on our military power; it is so vast
> that the effects of its use are beyond the comprehension of the mind of man.
> It is so vast that we dare not allow themselves to become infuriated.[33]

An economic contest between the Free World and the Communist Bloc
transformed a Holy War into an international game of profit and loss, a
game which, during the boom years of the early 1960s, government officials

could realistically and happily argue that the United States was winning. Within this view of the world, the United States was to encourage prosperity at home and "nation building" abroad, for Communism, so the argument went, held no fascination for prosperous, well-fed peoples. Growth in gross national products did not depend on a belief in God or adherence to the Golden Rule. In place of war and the threat of war, America offered the world technical assistance.

One of the advantages of technocratic realism was that it could be adapted to explain hostile actions in international affairs and justify a more moderate course of action than would otherwise be the case when confronting Evil. Scientifically conducted cost-benefit analyses provided by "experts" could be counted on to reveal the advantages not only to United States, but more importantly to the native populations in "underdeveloped" countries falling within America's "sphere of influence" (terms like "underdeveloped" and "developed" countries, "sphere of influence," and "power vacuum" are part of the vocabulary of "realism" in foreign affairs).[34] American technical assistance in military matters, as a consequence, could be justified through the improved management and superior organization it provided.

Technocratic realism has, from an official point of view, the advantage of doing away with the need to consult those affected by specific policies about their social, political, or economic preferences. Natives are not in the position to make informed judgments. They do not possess the facts. They have no experience in the potential of modern techniques for nation building. The problem, then, for a more advanced society is how most efficiently and effectively to diffuse modern innovations into underdeveloped countries. The appeal to expertise implicit in computer assisted, statistically based calculations of the facts of the situation also raises issues beyond people living in "advanced" societies. Ordinary people, it is assumed, are not equipped to grasp the demands made on American foreign policy, to deliberate issues about which most of the information, for reasons of national security, cannot be made available, or to understand the technical instruments used to select, process, and interpret the data relevant in the formation of government policy.[35]

The rhetoric of technocratic realism, with its commitment to dispassionate, informed, and pragmatic expertise, did not originate with the Kennedy administration any more than prophetic dualism originated with Eisenhower and Dulles. The most immediate and pertinent source for the technocratic intelligentsia—the scholars, intellectuals, and skilled professionals making up part of the Kennedy coalition and who were represented in his administration—grew out of the Progressive Era in the United States. The shift away from public participation in important political matters toward reliance on "expertise" was an explicit part of the Progressive movement. Between 1916 and 1922, during the "Red Scare," academics and business leaders began to lose faith in public debate in this country as a way of solving political problems. They thought it exacerbated class conflict, divided labor and management, and was beset by pressure groups.

The Brookings Institute, the New School for Social Research, the Twentieth Century Fund, and the *New Republic* magazine were originally part of efforts made by corporate liberals to initiate social, political, and economic reforms through increased governmental efficiency and control, through research and recommendations for new policies, and through educating those who would implement these reforms. Thus faith in efficient management, avoiding public controversy and debate, and in developing a more scientific approach to decision making and policy implementation underlying foreign affairs has its origins in the Progressive Era and domestic reforms that inspired and commended American liberalism up to and beyond the New Deal.[36]

Exponents of this tradition in the Kennedy-Johnson administrations articulated America's managerial role in the early stages of Vietnam, a role confined to advisory, logistic, and technical assistance. This approach had had considerable appeal in domestic politics. President Johnson, in his Johns Hopkins speech, April 7, 1965, offered a team of "experts" to design a food program for South Vietnam and a plan to develop the Mekong River region as an inducement to end the war. What he did was to extend his domestic programs, called the "War on Poverty," from the homefront to the Third World. This portion of the speech was meant to placate domestic liberals, while the portion responding to an appeal from seventeen nonaligned "bellweather" nations to begin immediate negotiations was intended to influence correspondents like Walter Lippman.[37]

There were references to atrocities committed by the "enemy," but in the early stages of Vietnam the technocratic ethos predominated. The unwillingness of the "men of the North" to help in fulfilling the unsatisfied wants of the people of the region was, thought Humphrey, unfortunate.[38] "I long for the day," declared President Johnson in July, 1966, "when we and others—whatever their political creed—will turn our joint resources to battle against poverty, ignorance, and disease." This day had not arrived; American expertise and know-how had been thwarted in its attempt to assist others, because, Johnson went on, "some men, in some places, still insist on trying to force their way of life on other peoples."[39]

The ends were given. Like the War on Poverty, the War in Vietnam was being undertaken by those better trained and educated and therefore better able to minister to the needs of the people. There was no need for debate. The only problem lay in eliminating obstacles to enlightened management.

The failure of the Johnson administration to negotiate with the "men from the North" (the official line was that conflict was taking place between two nations, a North and a South Vietnam, and that the North had invaded the South), military reversals, a growing need to mobilize public opinion in the United States for what could no longer be characterized as advisory, logistical, or merely technical assistance, but had become or was about to become an even larger military effort on the part of the United States, led to a change in the rhetoric of American foreign policy. What one sees is the inclusion of another, not unfamiliar, mode of argument. It was displayed as early as August, 1964 in a speech President Johnson made dedicating the Samuel I. Newhouse Communications Center at Syracuse University. His reason for having American troops in Vietnam was the same, he said, as that of Presidents Eisenhower and Kennedy before him—to make certain that the governments of Southeast Asia leave each other alone, resolve their differences peacefully, and devote their talents to better the lives of their peoples by working against poverty, disease, and ignorance. But then, shifting to another mode, Johnson referred to the Gulf of Tonkin and an attack on American warships:

> None can be detached about what has happened there. Aggression—deliberate, willful, and systematic aggression—has unmasked its face to the entire world. The world remembers—the world must never forget—that aggression unchallenged is aggression unleashed. We of the United States have not forgotten. That is why we have answered this aggression with action.[40]

American action in Vietnam was helping the world remember a lesson, a lesson it should have learned during the Second World War about the terrors of systematic and unchecked aggression.

The tendency to treat the other side as the "enemy," the conflict as irreconcilable, and the struggle a Holy War was fully developed in a nationally televised speech the Commander of American forces in Vietnam, General William Westmoreland, gave to a joint session of Congress, April 26, 1967. Within his capabilities, said Westmoreland, the "enemy in Viet Nam is waging total war all day, everyday, everywhere. He believes in force, and his intensification of violence is limited only by his resources and not by any moral inhibitions." Endeavoring to show the support American policy enjoyed in other parts of the world, he listed a number of countries—Korea, Australia, New Zealand, Thailand, and the Philippines who had sent detachments to Vietnam. These countries become rhetorically significant, in Westmoreland's words, a "symbolic reminder that the whole of free Asia opposes Communist expansion."[41]

Despite their logical and seemingly political incompatibility, prophetic dualism and technocratic realism not only can co-exist, elements of each may appear in the same speech.[42] This does not mean that these modes of argument do not speak to different audiences. A prophetic persona coupled with Manichean dualities resonates with the worldview of Christian Fundamentalism, an important constituency in American politics, while a technocratic persona and the secular calculations associated with science and technology relate to the worldview of a managerial-humanist elite, the "new

class" described by Alvin Gouldner.[43] A useful theoretical distinction, however, may obscure what is in fact occurring. Was the emergence of these two
forms of argument during the Johnson administration a logical error, a
blurring of categories? Does it approach something like mixing metaphors?
Not, I think, in politics. If an administration seeks, in the face of a crisis in
foreign affairs, to broaden its constituency, then one may expect arguments
relating to the worldviews of various groups to be employed. Thus the
emergence of prophetic dualism and its growing importance in the rhetoric
of the Johnson administration may be understood as an effort to appease,
neutralize, or enlist the same political constituency appealed to during the
Dulles-Eisenhower years. Once one penetrates the logic of coalition formation, one moves beyond philosophical and literary notions of argument into
the practical demands of political struggle.

This, then, leads to a deeper level wherein foreign policy rhetoric,
apparently trapped in a means-ends dilemma and the vicissitudes of domestic politics, achieves cohesion. To reach this level, however, one must ask
what binds together prophetic dualism and technocratic realism, what renders attacks on them unrealistic, idealistic, an academic exercise. Beneath
isolated and abstracted forms of argument and the demands of political
pluralism is the realization that arguments over foreign policy share a view
of the world, literally "the world," so deep and fundamental as to be called
the "ground" on which foreign policy is debated in this country. It is ground
shared by various administrations, Republican and Democrat. It is ground
so pervasive, so obvious, so free of challenge that, once articulated, one can
but say that such is the nature of foreign policy rhetoric. And yet what we
may be prepared to call "nature" in this matter contains the potential for
destruction.

## ▉ PROPHETIC DUALISM, TECHNOCRATIC REALISM, AND NATIONALISM

The rhetoric of American foreign policy has to do with nations. Nations, in
official statements, are personified. They act morally and immorally. They
use force. They violate one another's rights. The "United States," in the
debate over Vietnam was "obliged," just as any individual is obliged to help
those whose rights are being threatened by brute force, to help the man who
is being forced to defend himself.[44] Both prophetic dualism and technocratic realism agree that nations are the irreducible units in foreign affairs,
that nations are to be understood as people, that they are, literally, actors in
international affairs, and that nations live in a world where, if the freedom
of one nation is threatened, other nations are obliged to help.

Both modes of argument agree that the international community embraces a hierarchical order—there are superior and inferior nations. More-

over they agree that one nation is clearly superior to all the rest, and that is the United States. The "United States," in the rhetoric of American foreign policy, is much more than a geographical designation, an administrative unit, or a large number of people sharing a language, culture, and a history. The United States is the manifestation of Truth, Justice, and Freedom placed on this earth by a God whose purpose it is to make of it an instrument for extending His spiritual and material blessings to the rest of humanity. The ground on which the rhetoric of American foreign policy is situated is the Nation. Its personification as an Actor with a sense of purpose, an important mission in a world of nations, and a moral and spiritual center raising it above all other nations forms the essential story out of which reasons are given in support of foreign policy.

A language which takes nations as its irreducible unit, like any other that trades in vast numbers of people, differs from and will, under certain circumstances, conflict with ways of talking about the world that centers on human beings as individuals. These conflicts become acute when the subject is an action having human suffering as its inevitable consequence. This becomes obvious when what is called "common language" has embedded in it some sense of individual worth, the precepts of "common law," the universalizing inclinations of Human, Natural, or Inalienable Rights. Such language will prove inadequate precisely at the point at which pain and death come to people who have committed no crime, whose guilt has not been established, or whose punishment is out of all proportion to the alleged offense (i.e., having the wrong beliefs, being in the wrong "zone," refusing to obey orders). This is why, in order to avoid getting bogged down in moral concerns, government officials develop a special language to explain policies having to do with people outside the society in whose name policy is being planned and executed.

This situation is not peculiar to American foreign policy. George Orwell pointed to the abstract and facile euphemisms British officials called upon while trying to justify the use of force in Burma in the 1920s and '30s:

> Defenseless villages are bombarded from the air, the inhabitants driven out into the countryside, the cattle machine-gunned, the huts on fire with incendiary bullets, this is called "pacification." Millions of peasants are robbed of their farms and sent trudging along the roads with no more than they can carry: this is called "transfer of the population" or "pacification of the frontiers."[45]

Language dealing with vast numbers of people typed according to race, religion, or nationality obscures the relationship between official policy and human experience. What "national interest" dictates in the Third World may enable one to calculate the effects of a given course of action, but it automatically dehumanizes the people most immediately and profoundly affected.

A similar result occurs when conceiving of national interest in relation to industrialized countries. "Force," for example, as Aldous Huxley noted in 1937, is a dangerously abstract word when applied to the affairs of nations. He demonstrates this point by translating the phrase, "You cannot have international justice, unless you are prepared to impose it by force," into common language.

> You cannot have international justice, unless you are prepared, with a view to imposing a just settlement, to drop thermite, high explosives and vesicants upon the inhabitants of foreign cities and to have thermite, high explosives and vesicants dropped in return upon the inhabitants of your cities.[46]

To contemporary ears, the phrase "thermite high explosives" does not have the impact it did for Huxley and his audience, but the development of nuclear weapons has not had any appreciable effect on the language of foreign policy by virtue of the fact that millions more lives now hang in the balance.

Nuclear weapons are profoundly unsuited for distinguishing between the guilty and the innocent, or for taking into account the distinction between the guilt of individuals and that of peoples. They are, as Robert Oppenheimer noted in 1946, the supreme expression of Total War.[47] And yet when talking about foreign policy, their darkness is often passed over or minimized. In a debate over what America's response should have been in support of the French in Indochina, the moderator, Arthur Krock, asked then Senate minority leader, Mike Mansfield, whether or not he agreed with Senate majority leader William Knowland's solution, which was the use of "massive retaliation." Mansfield demurred. He did not see how it could be applied there with any effect.

> I believe that there is a tremendous deficiency in this massive retaliatory striking arm of ours. It is all right to have these things on paper but . . . where would you drop bombs in Indo-China? There are very few places you could drop them in China except at Mukden or Harbin.

"Massive retaliation" was inappropriate because of the absence of metropolitan areas. Atomic bombs are designed to destroy cities. They would have minimal effect in the jungle area around Dienbeinphu. Mansfield offered another reason for not using atomic weapons.

> I think that many of these people are looking to China today as the champion of the colored races. And they are going to say, "Why, these white folks are taking it out on us. They don't drop atom bombs on white people but they drop them on the Japanese, the Chinese." And I think the revulsion against us would be great.[48]

Nowhere in the debate did either Mansfield or Knowland consider the vast and indiscriminate slaughter of men, women, and children, the charred villages, the human consequences of the use of atomic weapons. Theirs was an analysis of what was in the "national" interest. Even so, their exchange has a kind of clarity, almost innocence, when compared with how policy planners now talk about such matters.

It is in the context of the continued development of nuclear weapons and multi-billion dollar weapons systems and the knowledge that the United States is not secure from attack that more sophisticated ways of talking about the use of "force" have evolved. Dr. Fred Charles Ikle, an official in both the Nixon and Reagan administrations and an authority on nuclear disarmament, claims that arms experts and military planners "insulate themselves from the potential implications of their labors by layers of dehumanizing abstractions and bland metaphors." The term "assured destruction," for example, does not really indicate what is to be destroyed. But then, he goes on in language uncharacteristic of government officials, the term " 'assured genocide' would reveal the truth too starkly."[49]

Even if one chooses to deliberate foreign policy under the aegis of the national interest, and nations will continue to be the building blocks of the international order for some time, the debate over what constitutes America's interests in Third World countries as well as in nuclear armaments remains muddled.[50] The debate is distorted in pluralistic societies by the advantages foreign affairs offer in domestic political struggles. It is further distorted by a willingness on the part of the electorate to allow state managers, aspirants for office, along with their scientific and military "experts" to set the agenda, determine the issues, and select the vocabulary. As a consequence, the debate over foreign policy rarely gets to fundamental issues, such as what will, in the long run, serve our "national interests."

With regard to the Third World, the countries not only in Southeast Asia and Africa, but also in countries like Panama, Chile, Nicaragua, El Salvador, Guatemala, Grenada, etc. making up Central and South America, terms like "military aid," "sphere of influence," "power vacuum," "Communist infiltration," and "counterinsurgency" mystify both the policies being advocated and their human consequence. Moreover, they obscure changes which have taken place over the last few decades in how such terms have been officially employed. The phrase "helping free world nations defend themselves from armed aggression" implies assisting countries to defend themselves from threats posed by other, more powerful, hostile countries. Yet American "aid" has changed, according to Asbjorn Eide, from arms designed to protect countries from external aggression to arms designed to suppress internal uprisings, designed to strengthen the "capacity of the police and the military of the Third World for local control by their own forces, but with equipment and training from the outside."[51] Thus the term "counterinsurgency" refers to the ability of those in power rapidly to deploy troops on a guerilla battlefield at the first sign of native unrest. More than military assistance on the part of the United States, this involves an extended network of military bases, the acquisition of giant transport aircraft, fast supply ships, along with the political resolve to send supplies, "advisors," even combat troops into areas where "freedom" is threatened.

The rhetoric of American foreign policy does not become any less opaque over the issue of nuclear weapons. Alexander Haig, as Secretary of State under Reagan, observed:

> Restraint of the Soviets, reinvigoration of our alliances, a new approach to the Third World, a healthier U.S. economy and a stronger military—these are the signals of our determination to restore leadership in the world.[52]

But what did this mean? "Restraint of the Soviets"—how does this phrase relate the development, threat of development, or use of nuclear weapons? The issue is not clear; nowhere is it more vague than over the conception, development, and use of modern weapon systems, presumably a part of the "stronger military" to which Haig refers.

Public debate over such matters is, when it is not deemed inappropriate, certainly confusing. There is a tendency to assume that the highly technical aspects of a weapons system are beyond the capacity of the ordinary citizen to understand and that, in the interests of "national security," such information ought to be kept secret. And yet, because of the complexity of modern weapon systems, it takes several years before a system can contribute to national security. This means that debates over "defense" will, at certain points, transcend engineering and enter the world of science fiction. Here the hypothetical example becomes pivotal. Frank Barnaby put it precisely: "Since the range of conceivable developments in the opponent's weaponry is more or less unlimited, a case can be made for initiating programs to protect oneself against as many conceivable developments as possible."[53] The rhetorical morass *this* creates he calls the "worst case syndrome;" this is where the development of new weapons systems depends on the degree to which one is animated by fear.

The problem, however, is neither purely psychological nor semantic. The debate over the need for new weapon systems does not begin with a dispassionate, scientific weighing of "data" by certified "experts." It begins in the context, in both the Soviet Union and the United States, of a military-industrial-bureaucratic-professional-political coalition of interests reaping enormous benefits from each new commitment to spend hundreds of billions of dollars on each new system. A "military-industrial complex" is what President Eisenhower called it. In his final address to the nation, on January 17, 1960, he characterized the problem in this way:

> The U.S. has been compelled to create a permanent armament industry of vast proportion and to maintain a defense establishment employing 3.5 million persons and spending huge sums. This conjunction of an immense military establishment and a large industry is new in the American experience. The total influence—economic, political, even spiritual—is felt in every city, every state house, every office of the federal government. We must recognize the imperative

need for this development. Yet we must not fail to comprehend its grave implications.[54]

The unfortunate effect of Eisenhower's warning has been to provide a noun, "military-industrial complex," for a political process. What the "complex" refers to is the existence of a powerful coalition of interests in this society which seeks to influence political decisions in disturbingly predictable ways. At the time Eisenhower spoke, the economies of twenty-two states depended heavily on military spending. In fourteen states military industries made up a significant percentage of total manufacturing employment. Defense assets during this period were greater than the combined wealth of the 100 largest corporations in America. The annual purchases of the Air Force alone were larger in volume than the output of General Motors.[55] The ongoing interests of this coalition are not irrelevant to the forty-four Senators and over two hundred Representatives from such areas.

Translating this into public debate as it now exists, arguments over "defense," the desirability of weapon systems, arms sales to the Third World, the stance taken by the United States in world affairs are, in various ways, shaped by an enormously wealthy and powerful coalition of vested interests. For this coalition, increases in military spending and the continued production and sale of armaments becomes less a matter of disinterested judgment about the nature of nuclear war or the need for social programs than an article of faith, an ideological commitment.[56]

Public debate over strategy tends to be grounded in the assumption that ever more powerful weapons systems (anti-ballistic missiles, B-1 bombers, MX missile system, laser satellites, etc.) *will* be produced and that the real issue has to do with technical feasibility and cost effectiveness. Instead of debate over "first strike capability," "counter-value" versus "counter-strike force," and "genocide" along with their economic, social, political, and moral implications, observes Barnaby, arguments in this country tend to dissolve into a "mass of detail on specific new weapon systems or particular improvements to existing weapons and in equally narrow comparisons with Soviet capabilities."[57] Even as the ethos of "technocratic realism," with its claims on objectivity and expertise, has, for scientists themselves, lost much of its allure,[58] the debate over armaments gets lost in "scientific" shorthand and in accounting mentality invited by the context in which most of these debates take place—the piecemeal review of military spending that occurs when the federal budget is up for consideration.[59]

## ■ SUMMARY

The rhetoric of American foreign policy lends itself to cynical and bitter commentaries on lies, half-truths, and macabre scenarios. Because of this, foreign policy rhetoric's connection with real issues having to do with human suffering may be overlooked. Even when such issues are identified, critics rarely get beyond denouncing the devil-theory underlying "prophetic dualism," the cult of expertise in "technocratic realism," or the humanistic void in "nationalism." Foreign policy, however, reaches beyond what is officially said about it. The task of criticism in our time is to raise real issues and to assist in the creation of publics able to and, in the interests of human survival, willing to rise above parochial concerns. Criticism confronting technique with purpose, euphemism with reality, and silence—the threatened silence of future generations—with speech will not alter the predicament in which we find ourselves; but it will keep the task clearly before us.

## ▉ Notes

¹Hannah Arendt, *The Life of the Mind,* I (New York: Harcourt Brace Jovanovitch, 1978), p. 4.

²Werner Levi, "Ideology, Interests, and Foreign Policy," *International Studies Quarterly,* 14 (1970), 28. Robert P. Newman's review of the deliberations which took place during the Cuban Missile crisis also supports this view: "Foreign Policy: Decision and Argument," *Advances in Argumentation Theory and Research,* ed. J. Robert Cox and Charles Arthur Willard (Carbondale: Southern Illinois University Press, 1982), pp. 318–42.

³Grant Hugo, *Appearance and Reality in International Relations* (New York: Columbia University Press, 1970), p. 19.

⁴Marcel Merel, "Political Parties and Foreign Policy in Pluralist Regimes." *International Social Science Journal,* 30 (1978), 84. He wrote: "(Political parties) promise happiness and security if they eventually reach office or if they remain there a little longer . . . they offer foreign policy to their electors as a 'bonus' " (p. 85). Pluralism is a political term describing a society in which no one group rules; rather, various groups work together to form coalitions. There is serious debate over: (1) the degree to which vested interests (i.e., the corporate state, military-industrial complex, power elite, etc.) have consolidated their hold on the state, and (2) the desirability of greater public participation in government.

⁵Over the last twenty years, there has been a major shift in thinking on this issue in the United States. Seymore Martin Lipset wrote in 1966 that "polls do not make policy so much as follow policy in international affairs . . . the president makes opinion, he does not follow it;" "The President, the Polls and Vietnam," *Trans-Action,* 3 (1966), 20. The gradual but steady decline in support for government policy in Vietnam, despite all official efforts to the contrary, see Hazel Erskin, "The Polls: Is War a Mistake?," *Public Opinion Quarterly,* 34 (1970), 134–50, requires a revision of what used to be conventional wisdom if not in politics then among social scientists. This is the conclusion of William Lunch and Peter Sperlich in "American Public Opinion and the War in Vietnam," *Western Political Quarterly,* 31 (1979), 21–44. Stressing the relationship between foreign policy and domestic issues like energy, employment, and defense, the Brookings Institute recommends new instruments for carrying out foreign policy that will be more effective and responsive to "public" and congressional concerns; Graham Allison and Peter Szanton, "Organizing for the Decade Ahead," *Setting National Priorities: The Next Ten Years* (Washington, D.C.: The Brookings Institution, 1976), pp. 227–70.

⁶See my chapter "Cultural Criticism" in *The Handbook of Political Communication,* ed. Dan Nimmo and Keith R. Sanders (Beverly Hills: Sage, 1982) pp. 497–528; "The Ideological Turn

in Modern Criticisms," *Central States Speech Journal* 34 (1983), 1–18; "The Aesthetic Dimension: A Note on Ideology, Criticism, and Reality," *Argument in Transition: Proceedings of the Third Summer Conference on Argumentation,* ed. David Zarefsky, Malcolm A Sillars, and Jack Rhodes (Annandale, VA: Speech Communication Association, 1983), pp. 159–69; "An Ideological Turn in Rhetorical Theory: The Third Persona," *Central States Speech Journal,* forthcoming Fall 1984.

[7]See my "The John Birch and Martin Luther King Symbols in the Radical Right," *Western Speech,* 35 (1971), 4–14; "Salvation Through Separation: The Image of the Negro in the American Colonization Society," *Quarterly Journal of Speech* 57 (1971), 57–67; "The Savage Child: The Image of the Negro in the Pro-Slavery Movement," *Southern Speech Journal,* 37 (1972), 335–60.

[8]Paul Varg, "Foreign Policy: Past and Future," *Centennial Review,* 21 (1977), 261–72. The dangers associated with industrialized societies trying to secure markets and raw materials has become apparent over the past century. Sartre noted the efforts by "developed" nations to divide the world into "spheres of influence" and subjugate smaller, less developed countries through colonial rule, native chiefs, or heads-of-state. He placed Vietnam in the context of French, German, English, and Italian colonial history; *Between Existentialism and Marxism,* trans. John Mathews (New York: William Morrow and Company, 1974), pp. 67–83. Whatever the differences, there are remarkable similarities between colonial and modern techniques for controlling native populations. See Asjorn Eide, "The Transfer of Arms to Third World Countries and their International Uses," *International Social Science Journal,* 28 (1976), 307–25.

[9]The need for such a debate and a larger sense of "argument" required is addressed by Walter R. Fisher, in "Narration as a Human Communication Paradigm: The Case of Public Moral Argument," *Communication Monographs,* 51 (1984), 1–22.

[10]*The New York Times* (April 7, 1984), 5.

[11]This mode of argument has, by one name or another, attracted the attention of rhetorical theorists. For a history of the ways in which the "enemy" has been characterized, see Robert L. Ivie, "Images of Savagery in American Justifications for War," *Quarterly Journal of Speech,* 47 (1980), 279–94. F. Michael Smith, "Rhetorical Implications of the 'Aggression' Thesis in the Johnson Administration's Vietnam Argumentation," *Central States Speech Journal,* 22 (1972), 217–24 and Richard Cherwitz, "Lyndon Johnson and the 'Crisis' of Tonkin Bay: A President's Justification of War," *Western Journal of Speech Communication,* 42 (1978), 93–104 stress its use in the context of Vietnam. John Cragan and Donald C. Shields summarize this mode under the term "Cold War Drama" and evidence its continuing appeal in "Foreign Policy Communication Dramas: How Mediated Rhetoric Played in Peoria in Campaign '76," *Quarterly Journal of Speech,* 63 (1977), 281–89.

[12]On the connection between religion and politics, see Roderick Hart, *The Political Pulpit* (Purdue University Press, 1974).

[13]Sacvan Bercovitch, *The American Jeremiad* (Madison: University of Wisconsin Press, 1978), p. 176. The classic statement on this issue is Robert Bellah's essay, "Civil Religion in America," *Daedalus,* 96 (1967), 1–21. See also John F. Berens, "The Sanctification of American Nationalism, 1789–1812," *Canadian Review of Studies in Nationalism,* 3 (1976), 172–91; and " 'Like A Prophetic Spirit': Samuel Davies, American Eulogists and the Deification of George Washington," *Quarterly Journal of Speech,* 63 (1977), 290–97.

[14]E. Digby Baltzell, *The Protestant Establishment: Aristocracy and Caste in America* (New York: Random House, 1966). See also Christopher Lasch, "The Foreign Policy Elite/And the War in Vietnam," *The World of Nations* (New York: Vintage Books, 1974), pp. 232–49.

[15]Baltzell, pp. 277–93. For a statistical breakdown of what Joseph McCarthy meant for Republican votes in 1952 and 1956, see Kevin Phillips, *The Emerging Republican Majority* (New York: Anchor Books, 1970), pp. 156–62.

[16]On the appeal of "McCarthyism" to people alienated from the political establishment, growing economic centralization, and impersonal bureaucracies, and how this has been over-

looked in the alarm over McCarthy's attacks on personal freedoms, see Martin Trow, "Small Businessmen, Political Tolerance, and Support for McCarthy," *American Journal of Sociology,* 64 (1959), 270–81.

[17]*Department of State Bulletin* (hereafter *DSB*), 22 (1955), 640–41.

[18]"The Peace We Want," *DSB,* 33 (1955), 375–76.

[19]See F. D. Herzon, J. Kincaid, and V. Dalton, "Personality and Public Opinion: The Case of Authoritarianism, Prejudice and Support for the Korean and Vietnam Wars," *Polity,* 11 (1978), 92–113.

[20]"The Influence of Business on American Freedom," *DSB,* 30 (1954), 837–38.

[21]"The Goal of Foreign Policy," *DSB,* 30 (1954), 894.

[22]The limits "McCarthyism" placed on critical activity in a number of spheres—religion, labor, politics, culture, scholarship, and intellectual activity—are explored in *The Specter: Original Essays on the Cold War and the Origins of McCarthyism,* ed. Robert Griffith and Nathan Theoharis (New York: New Viewpoints, 1974). See especially Norman Markowitz's essay, "A View from the Left: From the Popular Front to Cold War Liberalism," 90–115. Robert P. Newman, in a brilliant essay, anchors McCarthyism in domestic politics through Protestant fundamentalism and the "loss of China" and reveals its ideological utility in the struggle for power between the Republicans and Democrats. See "Lethal Rhetoric: The Selling of the China Myths," *Quarterly Journal of Speech,* 61 (1975) 113–28. Failure in Vietnam, explained President Johnson in private, would make the "loss of China" and "McCarthyism" look like "chickenshit" by comparison; cited in Henry De Weerd, "Strategic Decision Making: Vietnam, 1965–68," *The Yale Review,* 67 (1978), 482.

[23]"News Conference," *DSB,* 34 (1956), 155.

[24]"Challenge and Response in United States Policy," reprinted in *DSB,* 37 (1957), 572.

[25]"To See the Road to Peace," *DSB,* 33 (1955), 133.

[26]See George Marsden, *Fundamentalism in American Culture: The Shaping of Twentieth-Century Evangelicalism* (New York: Oxford University Press, 1980), pp. 206–11.

[27]Paul Fussell, *The Great War and Modern Memory* (New York: Oxford University Press, 1975), pp. 75–113. Robert Ivie notes the use of "binary opposition" in justifying war throughout American history, "Images of Savagery" and Ronald Reid examines it in his study, "New England Rhetoric and the French War, 1754–1760: A Case Study in the Rhetoric of War," *Communication Monographs,* 43 (1976), 259–86. But the "paranoid melodrama" to which Fussell refers is peculiarly modern in its psychological depth and global reach. The "absolutistic" and "totalizing" style characterizing it resonates with two World Wars and the "total" annihilation promised by a Third; it was also, during the Great War, a conscious part of the propaganda campaigns conducted by the parties involved; see Harold Lasswell's chapter on "Satanism" in *Propaganda Technique in World War I* (Cambridge: MIT Press, 1971), pp. 77–101. It may be, however, that the term "savage" provides the 19th century analogue, for while government officials did not press anything like the modern dualities on France, England, or Mexico in the 18th and 19th centuries, certainly not after the initial conflict, "savage" (unless preceded by the word "noble") connotes ferocity and unspeakable cruelty. Used as a noun, as in "Indian savage," it could be and was in fact called upon to justify policies of extermination or what we now call "genocide." See Robert L. Ivie, "The Metaphor of Force in Pro-War Discourse: The Case of 1812," *Quarterly Journal of Speech,* 68 (1982), 240–53.

[28]Between 1961 and mid-1962, the "Kennedy Administration could not lessen Cold War tensions but only intensify them. These policies differed in no important essential from the Eisenhower policies after 1954. The New Administration was only more efficient and determined in carrying them out." Walter LeFeber, *America, Russia, and the Cold War 1945–1971* (New York: John Wiley and Sons, Inc., 1972), p. 227.

[29]See Kevin Phillips, pp. 160–65. In 1960 the Union vote was nearly 2–1 for Kennedy (it had been equally divided between Republicans and Democrats in 1956); 3–1 for Kennedy

among Catholics (it had gone Republican in 1956); professional and managerial support was up 12% in 1960 over 1956. See Fred J. Greenstein, *The American Party System and the American People* (Englewood Cliffs, NJ: Prentice Hall, Inc., 1963), p. 24.

[30]"Toward a Strategy of Peace," *DSB*, 49 (1963), 3–4. Kruschev's visit four years earlier and his call for "peaceful coexistence" anticipated many of the themes in Kennedy's speech. See Khruschev's article, "On Peaceful Coexistence," *Foreign Affairs*, 38 (1959), 1–18. For an insightful analysis of this speech and its domestic and international significance, see Theodore Windt's essay, "Seeking Détente with Superpowers: John F. Kennedy at American University," *Essays in Presidential Rhetoric*, ed. Theodore Windt with Beth Ingold (Dubuque, Iowa: Kendall/ Hunt, 1983), pp. 71–84.

[31]"The Challenge to Freedom in Asia," *DSB*, 49 (1963), 49.

[32]"Address," *DSB*, 49 (1963), 78.

[33]"The Role of the United States in World Affairs," *DSB*, 56 (1967), 770.

[34]Technocratic realism refers to "official" explanations of foreign policy. "Realism" as an alternative to the murderous dualities of the Cold War grew out of the work of professional diplomats, academic experts, and intellectuals. In its critical phrase, before the liberals took power, the position taken by George Kennan, a career diplomat and the major intellectual influence on the articulation of American foreign policy during the late 1940s and '50s, and liberal academics sounded much the same. But the tension was manifest even then. David Riesman and Michael Maccoby called for more realism in foreign affairs, but criticized foreign policy "experts" and the assumption that their "style of rationality" does not suppress important concerns. They questioned the requirement of "technical knowledge" and a "polished" vocabulary for entering into the debate over disarmament. At the same time, they commended the Rand Corporation and the CIA. See "The American Crisis, *The Liberal Papers*, ed. James Roosevelt (New York: Doubleday Anchor, 1962), pp. 13–47. By 1970, humanist critics included those who embraced technocratic realism, those who saw government officials falling away from realism, and those who saw liberalism's reliance on experts and belief in the "system" as fatal. See Grant Hugo, "Cant and Foreign Policy," *Appearance and Reality* (New York: Columbia University Press, 1970), pp. 17–32; Ralph K. White, "Black and White Thinking," *Nobody Wanted War: Misperception in Vietnam and Other Wars* (New York: Doubleday Anchor, 1970), pp. 241–319; and *Power and Consciousness*, ed. C. O'Brien and W. Vanech (New York: New York University Press, 1969); especially Peter Nettl, "Power and the Intellectuals," pp. 15–32, and Noam Chomsky, "Objectivity and Liberal Scholarship," pp. 43–136.

[35]See Fisher, see also my "The Rhetoric of Science," *Western Journal of Speech Communication*, 40 (1976), 226–35.

[36]See David Eakins, "The Origins of Corporate Liberal Policy Research, 1916–1922: The Political-Economic Expert and the Decline of Public Debate," *Building the Organizational Society*, ed. Jerry Israel (New York: The Free Press, 1972), pp. 163–80.

[37]See Kathleen J. Turner, "Press Influence on Presidential Rhetoric: Lyndon Johnson at Johns Hopkins University, April 7, 1965," *Central States Speech Journal*, 33 (1982), 425–36.

[38]"Perspective on Asia," *DSB*, 55 (1966), 6.

[39]"Two Threats to Peace: Hunger and Aggression," *DSB*, 55 (1966), 115.

[40]"Address," *DSB*, 51 (1964), 260–61.

[41]"Report to Congress," *DSB*, 56 (1967), 739–40. The rhetorical escalation represented by a shift to prophetic dualism alarmed some liberals who were prepared to take a "realistic" approach to foreign policy. Thus Reinhold Niebuhr urged that Vietnam be understood as a practical matter of imperial politics and not a holy war between two powerful ideologies. In the tradition of technocratic realism, Niebuhr blamed the problem on the "public:"

The average voter knows little and cares less about these imperial responsibilities, such as assuring the safety of the non-Communist nations on the fringes of Asia, but is moved only by appeals to our democratic idealism, which usually is formed by static anti-Communism. Our engagement in Vietnam has consequently forced the administration to create a series of obvious fictions or myths calculated to obscure the hiatus between our idealism and our hegemonial responsibilities. See "The Social Myths of the 'Cold War,' " *Journal of International Relations,* 21 (1967), 55.

⁴²These two modes do not exhaust the possibilities. Prophetic dualism, for example, is but one way of drawing moral principle into foreign policy. The Bill of Rights, the basis of the Civil Rights and Anti-War movements claiming the right to disobey immoral laws, translated, in the Carter administration, into an international commitment to "Human Rights." Again, though, the move from principle to action clarifying a domestic coalition's worldview proved confusing in international affairs and ill-suited in justifying compromise. "The mindset of those whose experience in foreign affairs was shaped by Vietnam and the civil rights struggle," writes Linda Miller, "has proved inadequate to the task of forming a new consensus. Charges of crisis-coping are leveled at those who plead devotion to 'world order.' " See "Morality in Foreign Policy: A Failed Consensus?," *Daedalus,* 109 (1981), 46. Miller offers a psychological, a formal, and a "complex world" explanation for the failure of the Carter "mindset;" she ignores a Cold War coalition including powerful economic and political interest groups whose appeal expands when official policy eschews the use of force or places limits on our "hegemonial responsibilities." The resurgence of a nationalist-militarist-fundamentalist coalition over the Panama Canal Treaty is a case in point. See Ronald A. Sudol, "The Rhetoric of Strategic Retreat: Carter and the Panama Canal Debate," *Quarterly Journal of Speech,* 65 (1979), 371–91.

⁴³Alvin Gouldner, *The Future of Intellectuals and the Rise of the New Class* (New York: The Seabury Press, 1979).

⁴⁴Johnson, "Two Threats to Peace," pp. 115–16.

⁴⁵George Orwell, "Politics and the English Language," *The Orwell Reader,* introd. Richard Rovere (New York: Harcourt, Brace & World, 1956), p. 363.

⁴⁶Aldous Huxley, "Words and Behavior," *Collected Essays* (New York: Harper & Brothers Publishers, 1958), p. 249.

⁴⁷"The Atom Bomb as a Great Force for Peace," *American Foreign Policy Since 1945,* ed. Robert Divine (Chicago: Quadrangle Books, 1969), p. 33.

⁴⁸William F. Knowland and Mike Mansfield, "Our Policy in the Far East: A Debate," *American Foreign Policy Since 1945,* pp. 107–8. It is, in our time, difficult to fathom the seriousness with which the French defeat was viewed in light of a Communist Monolith; as Knowland declared:

> The loss of Southeast Asia would lead to the loss of the balance of Asia. That might mean the ultimate destruction of Europe based on Lenin's theory that the road to Paris is through Peking. And if we had the entire world pass into the Communist orbit, it would make, in effect, a continental Dienbienphu out of the United States (p. 106).

⁴⁹"Can Nuclear Weapons Last Out the Century," *Foreign Affairs,* 51 (1973), 280–81. Ikle was not arguing for abandoning nuclear weapons, but for directing them not at major population centers but at crucial links in the economic and industrial structure located in less populated areas.

⁵⁰This is the view of Harlan Cleveland, a former diplomat, in his essay, "The Future of International Relations," in *Knowledge and the Future of Man,* ed. W. J. Ong, S. J. (New York: Simon and Schuster, 1968), pp. 73–4.

⁵¹Eide, p. 310.

⁵²Santa Cruz *Sentinel,* May 10, 1981.

⁵³"The Dynamics of World Armaments: An Overview," *International Social Science Journal,* 28 (1976), 253.

[54]Quoted in R. Joseph Monsen, Jr. and Mark W. Cannon's excellent chapter, "The Military Bureaucracy," in *The Makers of Public Policy: American Power Groups and Their Ideologies* (New York: McGraw-Hill Book Company, 1965), pp. 262–63. For a recent debate over the "military-industrial complex," see the exchange between Seymour Melman and Jacques S. Ganster in the *Defense Management Journal*, 15 (1979) 2–13.

[55]Monsen and Cannon, pp. 264–69.

[56]Barnaby, p. 264. The same mechanism, it must be emphasized, exists in the Soviet Union. They feed off one another, each new technological breakthrough, each new idea providing the basis for a "worst case" scenario on the other side.

[57]Barnaby, p. 255.

[58]See Dixon T. Long, "The Changing Role of Science in the Foreign Policy Process," *The Policy Sciences Journal*, 5 (1976), 193–98.

It was not simply that scientific experts came to be associated with American failures in Vietnam, as Irving Louis Horowitz points out. When social scientists developed misgivings about continued escalation, they lacked a constituency with which to resist military and political advisors who were able consistently to isolate and suppress the opposition of scientifically trained experts within the government. This lack of constituency, coupled with the enthusiastic support of other "experts" for the war, for new weapons systems, nuclear arms, etc. has led to a disillusionment with science and scientists as the answer to America's problems. See Horowitz's chapter, "The Pentagon Papers and the Tragedy of American Research," in *Ideology and Utopia in the United States* (New York: Oxford University Press, 1977), pp. 275–91.

[59]Barnaby, p. 255.

# CHAPTER 17 $\boxed{\phantom{xxxxxxxxxxxxxxxxxxx}}$

# REMINISCENCES OF LOS ALAMOS

**Bryan C. Taylor**

*In this commentary, Bryan C. Taylor raises an important issue when he suggests that, as critics, we are never fully aware of or in control of our own inventional processes and practices. Hence, all reflections on our own invention as critics are going to be partial, including his own account of his research in nuclear history. Rather than being purely the inventors of criticism, Taylor suggests, we as critics are also invented by it.*

## COMMENTARY

I have the luxury of writing this essay while actually being *in* Los Alamos, where, in the late summer of 1992, I am studying the Laboratory's Bradbury Science Museum. As I begin, I am working in the museum director's cramped and spartan office. The office is located in a metal trailer wedged into the side of a hill between a metal foundry and a cryogenics lab. A dozen other "temporary structures" surround this one, sprawling testimony to the organization's chronic shortage of office space. The noise from the foundry's machinery is constant and distracting. Overhead, though, silver and purple rainclouds are silently regrouping after a storm. Their shadows fall across the Jemez Mountains that rise to the west, and the tall pines there shift in color from green to black, black to green.

This is my luxury: I can reflect on "inventing" the essay, *"Reminiscences of Los Alamos,"* smack in the middle of its apparent referent. Daily, I travel the same ground where John Manley, Joseph Hirschfelder, and Norris Bradbury talked and worked while *they* invented the atomic bomb between 1943 and 1945. My sense of nuclear history and how I came to it are continually sharpened as a result.

But I am also challenged by writing this here. The wartime Los Alamos

**417**

of those scientists is gone forever. Both the Laboratory and the surrounding town have since grown dramatically, and few of their original structures remain. The community energetically recovers and promotes that history, however, through a variety of images, artifacts, and stories (for example, at the Bradbury Science Museum). This promotion depicts the wartime Los Alamos as if it were a "factual" event whose meaning is self-evident. This unreflective realism is directly opposed to the post-structuralist orientation of the *"Reminiscences"* essay, which asserts that discourse does not refer to a preexisting, "objective" reality. Instead, discourse reflects in its images, metaphors, and silences the cultural construction of humans, their world, and their history *as* meaningful.

In the essay, I examined how the discourse of Los Alamos scientists could, then and now, define the Bomb as a "real," "useful," and consequential object. My commitment to that critical orientation now creates a dilemma. I am surrounded here by representations of wartime Los Alamos. With varying explicitness, they all insist that "something happened," and that I accept its facticity. These forms can be compellingly "real," as when I encountered the office chair belonging to wartime laboratory director Robert Oppenheimer in a warehouse. One arm was slightly more worn than the other, and the hair stood up on the back of my neck. At such times, I lose my detachment about *how* the meaning of such objects is created, and to what ends. They seem naturally *to exist,* and I surrender to them.

Then, at other times, when the employees of the museum argue passionately about the "right" way to present Los Alamos history to visitors, I recover my critical bearings. Yes, something happened at Los Alamos, but the meaning of that event is created through discourse, and is subject to dispute and revision. That dispute is particularly acute in the current post–Cold War climate in which the narratives of Soviet threat and nuclear deterrence that traditionally defined Los Alamos are no longer legitimate, and its scientists must reestablish their worth to the nation.

I outline my current situation to indicate where the *"Reminiscences"* essay has led me. This is the place from which I now try to reconstruct its invention. I believe, in fact, that this is the *only* way that the process of invention can be fully analyzed. I am strongly influenced by critical and "counter-rational" theory that depicts social action as overdetermined (influenced by multiple and conflicting forces), and as "pre-sensical" (with intention and meaning attributed by actors retrospectively). The social act of criticism is no exception. I certainly had *some* preexisting goals and techniques in 1987 for analyzing these three narratives. Convention, in fact, dictated that I articulate them: here, the "theoretical issues" section of the essay functions as a reassurance to the reader that I am in fact a "rational" critic who first derived, and then systematically applied, various "methods" to the selected texts.

This section is partially a fiction, however, fabricated as a concession to the "methodism" that pervades contemporary critical inquiry. That methodism positions the critic as the generative site of invention (he or she "did" it), asserts that such activity is primarily cognitive, and implies that it occurs immediately *prior* to the critical act. Methodism also implies that critic is both relatively conscious and in control of all the forces activated in that practice. In recounting my analysis of the three assumptions, I take issue with these assumptions.

Writing, and thus criticism, I argue, are "embodied" practices. They are always connected to the writer's unique history of pleasure and pain, and are grounded in the psychic traces of bodily experience within institutions (for example, the family, school, church). We write about what we love and what we fear, and although we may efface the fact with our "academic" voice, we invent—and are invented—*from* other places, times, and voices. Not all are cited.

The *"Reminiscences"* essay came from many places. Its immediate context involved my Ph.D. coursework at the University of Utah in critical theory and cultural studies. There, I read and talked and wrote about the relationships between culture, communication, power, and subjectivity. I was strongly affected by discussions that challenged me to see common forms and practices (e.g., conversation) as instrumental to the reproduction of social structure and ideology. I struggled to pay attention to (and sometimes deny) the ways in which I was implicated in that reproduction (e.g., as a university instructor). I was supported and challenged in this process by friends and professors who sought to embody critical theory in their practices (e.g., in promoting diversity and dialogue in the classroom). This education was both painful and exhilarating. The pain came from learning new ways to see and speak about social life as a site of power relations. The exhilaration came from hard-won understanding of those relations. One theme that consistently emerged in these discussions was that criticism should "matter," that it should "make a difference" to a community larger than our academic discipline.

Before I was a graduate student, though, before I moved to Utah, before all this, I was a child. I was a child in a suburban home in Western Massachusetts. I was the child of a mechanical engineer and a homemaker who moved East from Kansas because my father found work in New England's large industrial plants. I have many bodily memories of being that child: the smell of burning leaves in the fall, the taste of chocolate birthday cake, the blur of vacation scenery through the back window of a Dodge van. These were some of my recurring pleasures. But I also endured, as do many children, recurring violence: violence that fell on my body from hands, fists, belts, and, above all, from angry and frightening voices. These were not the only things I knew, but they were important. That violence hurt me and it silenced me. I could not understand it, and it marked me anyway.

One afternoon in 1986 I was browsing in a bookstore by the university and was struck by the pale and melancholy face staring out from the cover of a volume entitled *J. Robert Oppenheimer: Letters and Recollections.* I was vaguely aware that Oppenheimer was a physicist who had worked on the Manhattan Project during World War II and that his reputation was later ruined during the McCarthy era. I bought the book and entered into the world of nuclear weapons (or, to be more precise, formally acknowledged its presence). Oppenheimer's poignant letters to his family and friends between 1918 and 1945 charted the fate of an intellectual within the developing "organization" of nuclear weapons: the amoral and patriotic embrace of "service," the delight in technique, the repression of moral dilemmas.

Since I was taking a seminar on autobiography, I wrote an essay exploring those themes. The seminar professor criticized the essay as commonsensical, and challenged me to see it as the beginning of a long-term study, one that would require extensive research and revision of my ideas. While I was angered by his criticism, it spurred me on. I rewrote the essay again and again, reading extensively about the rich and secret world of wartime Los Alamos. I wanted to understand the environment in which a man of Oppenheimer's poetry and intelligence would come to make nuclear weapons his life's work. It was not that I thought it was somehow inconceivable, but the irony hooked me. It is probably no accident, further, that I pursued the project while living in Utah, where I encountered the lingering anger and bewilderment of "downwinders," residents who had been affected by radioactive fallout from nuclear tests conducted at the Nevada Test Site during the 1950s and 1960s. One statistic summarized their suffering, and I will never forget it: during that period the rate of *childhood* leukemia in Southern Utah doubled.

During this time, I began to work on the project in my dreams. In one, the western horizon of Salt Lake City erupted in blinding nuclear fire. I woke up sweating and shaking, having accessed the nuclear terror that psychologists such as Robert Jay Lifton believe lies buried in the cultural unconscious. In another, Oppenheimer's aging face shimmered before me and spoke: "Leave me alone." In a final dream, I believe we reconciled. We approached each other on a deserted downtown street, and he seemed urgent to speak with me. When we were close, he pulled on my sleeve. He opened his mouth, and a swarm of Monarch butterflies flew out.

In the fall of 1987 I enrolled in a seminar on "counter-rational" organizational theory taught by a visiting professor. This material set me to thinking about Los Alamos—with which I was now fascinated—as an organizational phenomenon: a distinct historical life-world in which speech and writing were used to conceptualize and coordinate human labor, materials and technology. I also was involved at that time in a small study group reading critical theory. I had stumbled across *Reminiscences of Los Alamos* while "shopping" for background material in the university library. As I read, however, it moved on my conceptual grid from "context" to "text." I knew that I wanted to try again to write about nuclear autobiographies, and the critical theory I was reading helped me to see the relationship between personal narrative and social structure anew.

The text held ten separate reminiscences. Three were from women, and I set those apart for a future project that would study the "difference" in gendered Los Alamos voices. Of the other seven, I was drawn to the three selected because they most clearly recalled the "organization" of Los Alamos. I remember the act of writing the essay vividly: my list of "questions" laid beside the text like scalpels; my ambition to "see" patterns beyond what was immediately apparent, and "hear" voices that had been excluded; my involuntary shudder as the "fission" metaphor took shape and clarified the organizational operations of ideology; an accidental encounter with *Nazi Doctors* that made me take a deep breath and up the stakes of the analysis; the silent companionship of a Burmese cat named Grace Jones; endless pots of coffee.

I let that first draft sit for several months while I worked on different projects. I felt that it was good work, however, and presented it a year later at a national conference. The panel members and the audience at my presentation were supportive, and I began to consider submitting the essay for publication. Conventional wisdom in my graduate program held that "having something in print" when I started my job search would improve my chances. That time was approaching, and so—ambitiously—I sent the essay to *the* leading journal in our field. I trembled a bit opening the envelope containing the acknowledgment of its receipt, and then again five weeks later, opening the fatter envelope that I knew contained *the verdict.* I was stunned: the three reviewers of the essay were extremely positive and had strongly recommended its publication. The editor, however, had committed the pages remaining under his editorship, and recommended that I resubmit it to the journal's *new* editor. Verdict deferred, but I was giddy with the near-miss.

The next miss was not near, and it established my belief in the arbitrariness of the journal review process, and the polysemy of texts. As advised, I resubmitted the unchanged essay to the same journal under its new editor. This time, the three reviewers savaged it: I had neither justified the theoretical perspective nor validated it; there were excessive typographical and grammatical "errors" (one reviewer devoted a half-page to correcting my use of the verb "gloss"); and—most egregiously—there was an "offensive" and "excessively political" tone in the analysis. That tone was most evident for the reviewers in a concluding sentence that originally followed a Richard Feynman quote: "It remains for us to think and speak about *it:* this organized violence, both banal and extraordinary, which is imminent—poised to strike at us—and immanent—poised to strike *as* us." One of the previous reviewers had described this passage as "superb."

I take rejection no better than the next author, and I vented anger and indignation, but I also believed that the reviewers had misunderstood the analysis. Their caricatures of the theoretical perspective led me to believe that they were not familiar with it. They simply denied its validity and demanded "more": "Simply to point to the existence of some words or ideas in a discourse does not constitute anything near evidence that other words or ideas are constrained." This comment clarifies two principal burdens of deconstruction: providing an overview of the text for the reader which clarifies its patterned elements so that claims about its absences have foundation, and continually arguing "first principles" of critical theory with more conventional readers.

Undeterred, I sent the article—again *with no changes*—to a regional journal with a reputation for publishing innovative work. This time, I worked with two supportive reviewers who suggested including the paragraph on narrative theory, and who sharpened my use of organizational communications concepts. After the revisions were complete, the journal editor noted that "even ten years ago I do not think you could have drawn the Nazi–Los Alamos parallel without crossing the line between scholarship and journalism." He deleted the essay's final sentence quoted above: "I think it does cross the line."

Let me now summarize two themes in this minor odyssey pertaining to invention. I return in the process to my earlier challenge to conventional understandings of invention: that it is a relatively original and conscious act, performed immediately prior to criticism.

Simply put, my invention of the essay came—at least in part—from a collaborative, irrational, unconscious, historical, and embodied place: from my own "invention" within my family, and then more directly from the discursive milieu of my graduate education. I have come to see more clearly since I wrote the essay that I study nuclear weapons because I am trying to understand the relationships between violence, fear, silence, and discourse. I am drawn to those relationships because they formed an important part of my early world. I believe that in my volcanic unconscious, where repressed experiences are continually converted to metaphors and metonyms, falling blows have reappeared as falling missiles. What I wish to emphasize is that *I did not fully know this when I wrote the essay.* Invention, it would seem, has its own secrets: this one has emerged only recently.

Finally, my experience with the essay's three submissions was sobering, but valuable. It clarified the "open secret" of the review process: Its stunning arbitrariness. I believe that the essay generated wildly divergent reactions because it is "undisciplined": It merges two previously distinct zones of study (nuclear criticism and organizational communication), and it is explicitly political. I learned, however, that I did *not* have to compromise those features to secure the essay's publication. I continue to invent and be invented.

# Reminiscences of Los Alamos:
## Narrative, Critical Theory,
## and the Organizational Subject

Bryan C. Taylor

High atop a mesa in northern New Mexico, five thousand soldiers, scientists, and technicians assembled between 1943 and 1945 to produce the end to World War II and, some hoped, to all war. The site of their labor was the secret Los Alamos Laboratory, part of the United States government's Manhattan Project. The Manhattan Project was unprecedented in scale and in principle as a collaboration between science and the state to produce a weapon of war. To the dismay of many of its laborers, the atomic bomb produced at Los Alamos was not only used with devastating effectiveness against a Japanese enemy, but also appropriated as an enduring instrument of Cold War strategy. Continuously refined since then, the technology of nuclear weapons continues as a deterrent and a bargaining chip in the conduct of superpower foreign policy.

The labor of Los Alamos has been "preserved" in an ongoing cultural dialogue about the moral, political and psychological implications of nuclear weapons.[1] In this paper, I contribute to this dialogue by studying personal narratives about the Los Alamos project from a text entitled, *Reminiscences of Los Alamos, 1943–1945*.[2] I argue for the value of these narratives in illuminating the structure of the nuclear weapons organization and the experience of its members. The text contains recollections by several Los Alamos members about their work and community, assembled from a 1975 series of public lectures. These lectures were organized in the belief "that it would not only be worthwhile for posterity, but extremely interesting for the present generation to hear about the aspirations, fears and activities of those who participated in this watershed. . . ."[3] The narratives are driven by a tension between pride and regret. Their speakers attempt to reconcile the knowledge that the product of their labor ended a war, but now threatens to end the world. "Can we celebrate our successes," Victor Weisskopf has asked elsewhere, "and remain silent about the consequences?"[4] In speaking to the history of our nuclear culture, I believe that these narratives also speak to its future, and to the consequential role of the organization as a "site" where this future is "produced."

■ **THEORETICAL ISSUES: SUBJECTS AND OBJECTS
OF THE NUCLEAR WEAPONS ORGANIZATION**

My study of these narratives combines two fields of critical theory: one
nuclear, the other organizational. Works in both these conventionally separate fields have recently evaluated paradigms that conceptualize their objects of study as "text."[5]

Textualism is widely adopted in nuclear criticism, where nuclear issues
are considered *to be* symbolic issues. "Nuclear weapons," argues Jeff Smith,
"are not autonomous metaphysical ultimates, but historically contingent
products of certain cultural (hence discursive) conditions."[6] French philosopher Jacques Derrida has argued that nuclear weapons and war are "fabu-
lously textual," and exist for us only in a confluence of signifying systems
including protest placards and computer "war games." As a non-event to
date, global nuclear war is essentially narrative and rhetorical, and exists
only in simulations, projections, and the passionate dialogue surrounding
their evaluation.[7] Following from this premise, nuclear critics seek to intervene in the rhetorical production of nuclear "reality" by authorities in order
to relativize, historicize and transform it. "The power of the bomb," notes
David Dowling, "is ruled by the power of the word, and only by the continual
de-construction of the word will we avoid the destruction of the world."[8]
Most works of nuclear criticism have in some way challenged the "normal"
representations of the bomb in Western popular culture, news media, and
foreign policy discourse. Collectively, they have elaborated the term "nukespeak" in describing official discourses that reify and mystify the bomb
within the self-sealing "logic" of nuclear deterrence. The discourses of
deterrence pretend to neutrality and "rationality," and habituate citizens to
the bomb's continual presence.[9] Nuclear critics revise the bomb as an object
of speech and writing that reflect "structures of meaning which masquerade
as revealed truth."[10] One topic recently suggested for such criticism included, "the psychology of arms racers. . . . What do scientists want? What
do soldiers dream?"[11]

Critical theorists of organization, alternately, have invoked the metaphor of "text" to study organizational activity as the symbolic document of
a structured life-world and its communicative reproduction. This metaphor
legitimates the use of hermeneutic methods to unravel the nature and
significance of this activity by focusing on the modes of its production and
interpretation.[12] Organizational activity can be "read" as a text whose "surface structure" (static, conventional patterns of behavior and understanding) reflects traces of determination by "deep structure" (core rules, metaphors and values).[13] The critical elaboration of structure in organizational
speech and writing reconstructs the ways in which subjectivity and social
reality are constructed in the organizational milieu. As John Forester states,
"organizations not only produce goods and services, but also produce and

reproduce their members' knowledge and beliefs, their deference and consent to organizational authority . . . and their attention to a selective range of organizational problems and tasks."[14] In reading the expressions of this process, critics foreground issues of power and domination by focusing on how organizational authorities invite participation in systems of discourse. In a variety of ways, organizational discourses mediate between humans and their labor, and regulate its forms of "management." In reading the organizational text, critics construe issues of "meaning" as issues of "politics," engaging "politics" as forms of practice that determine the expression of human experience and its meaning.

Communication theorists Stanley Deetz and Dennis Mumby have developed a critical project that engages the organization as a "site" of ongoing conflict between multiple "voices" (e.g., of investors, environmentalists, and regulators), all struggling to legitimate their respective interests as *the* principles of organization.[15] Deetz and Mumby draw on Habermas' discussion of "knowledge-producing interests"[16] and "universal pragmatics" to describe how in consequential organizational routines, the representation of competing interests is frequently subject to systematic distortion. Demonstrating a pernicious trend of social modernism, organizations commonly privilege the interests of *technical rationality* (including profit, control, productivity and growth) over *practical* interests which focus on the quality of human relationships and *emancipatory* interests which enable reflective activity. Organizational communication, argue Deetz and Mumby, elevates the interests of particular groups over others (e.g., "owners" over "labor"), and represents those sectional interests as "natural" and "universal."

Deetz contends that organizational critique involves "looking for the story that did not get expressed [in organizational routines], and consider[ing] how interests are lost to expression."[17] This story of alternative and repressed arrangements is written by the critic, who challenges the grammars, vocabularies and networks of typification that constitute the "official" structure of the organization, and that permeate its texts. Following Deetz and Mumby, I use the term "structure" to designate a configuration of power and interests in the organization which works to order the use of symbols and the creation of meaning within its domain. Used in this sense, the term is distinct from "(administrative) structure," the traditional descriptor of hierarchical and reporting relationships in organizations.

These critical projects of "nuclear" and "organizational" textualism are embedded within a broad movement currently reappraising the value of narrative as an object of study in the human sciences.[18] This movement engages narrative as a "site" where ideological operations to construct what is "true," "good," and "possible" for cultural life become apparent. Narratives are ideological, notes Fredric Jameson, in that they function to invent "imaginary or formal 'solutions' to unresolvable social contradictions."[19] Working from this perspective, critics investigate the propositional, plotted and moralizing elements of narrative as formal evidence of how power and authority circulate discursively. As sites of ideological productivity, narratives constrain the meaning that events may have by ordering the possibilities for their representation. Textual theorists often reference the work of Althusser to describe how narratives "interpellate" their consumers into the "subject positions" that they offer, and orient consumers towards particular modes of being and acting in the social world.[20] Contemporary narrative theory includes both a general "incredulity towards meta-narratives"[21] that structure cultural life, and a specific interest in "how particular narratives, or clusters of narratives, might function to enable or constrain behavior within the context of certain ideological meaning formations."[22]

Drawing on these arguments, this essay displays the organizational structure of Los Alamos through a particular form of organizational text: the life history. There is considerable support for interpreting life histories to detail how cultures enable and constrain forms of human experience and action.[23] As the medium of reflective human consciousness, autobiographical language reveals the limited symbolic options that speakers have for assembling and displaying the self, and the worlds that they inhabit. As an "object" of knowledge, autobiographical subjects can only "find" and "talk" the self within existing cultural contexts which order and moralize their lives. The fixed and limited ways in which autobiographies represent these contexts become evidence for critical claims about how ideology and social structure enforce particular meanings over others, and naturalize particular ways of speaking *as* being. Critical theory posits a link between the structure of such narratives and the social structure guiding their production at the level of language. At this level, the critic attends to the "traces" of ideology as an ordering principle for narrative: static patterns of tone and imagery, the assertion of reference to a "natural" or "objective" world, the denial or deferral of contradiction, and attempts to obscure the historically "real" conditions of always contingent meanings.[24]

Applied to organizations, this argument addresses how a particular form of rationality (as a system of shared orientations to practice) operates to structure the experience of organizational members,[25] and how this rationality is subsequently represented in their memoirs. What can these narratives tell us about the dominant symbolism through which potential and entropic human beings are marked and managed as organizational subjects?[26] How do their memoirs "recover" these activities? How do they reveal the authorized positions for speech that characterize the "normal" subject position in organizations?[27]

I focus here on three narratives from the *Reminiscences* text in order to yield some insight into what scientists want and what soldiers dream, and to suggest how at Los Alamos these modes of desire were braided in a structure that authorized a "rational" subject for the first nuclear weapons organization. I have chosen these three narratives because they explicitly engage elements of Los Alamos structure: the ways in which work was organized, conventional ways of speaking about that work, and a collective sense of organizational identity and purpose. The analysis begins with a brief review of the history of the Los Alamos Laboratory as a context for considering its representation in these narratives.

## ▨ THE CONTEXT OF THE NUCLEAR WEAPONS ORGANIZATION

In his recent history, *The Making of the Atomic Bomb*,[28] Richard Rhodes locates the development of Los Alamos and its nuclear purpose within five twentieth-century events and trends:

(1) a revolution in nuclear physics that first modelled the nuclear structure of the atom and then theorized control over its fissioning potential;

(2) the evolution of technologized warfare that refined both 'hardware' (e.g., artillery, poison gas, the machine gun) and 'software,' the bureaucratic methods of state organization that interlocked military markets with industrial producers. This weapons work was aided by the patriotic scientist who believed that he "belong[ed] to the world in times of peace, but to his country in times of war"[29];

(3) the legitimation and escalation of strategic bombing against civilians and cities by enemy air forces. Bombing technology and technique evolved along with military rationales that expanded the definition of permissible victims. This rhetorical "move" produced psychic numbing for strategists, and increased destruction for "the enemy";

(4) the fusion of racist propaganda with the gruesome experience of the U.S. military in its Pacific Island campaigns that encouraged American perception of the Japanese enemy as fanatical and bestial. Dreading the prospect of invading the Japanese mainland, U.S. strategists projected those dehumanizing images onto enemy civilians; and

(5) the rhetoric of "unconditional surrender" drafted in the Potsdam and subsequent U.S. declarations that bitterly divided Japanese military and civilian authorities, and delayed and ambiguated their response. The U.S. administration interpreted this delay as a warrant for the bomb's use, which would galvanize a stubborn enemy, save lives, and shorten the conflict.[30]

The possibility of a nuclear weapon had first been brought to the attention of the Roosevelt administration in 1939, through the efforts of emigre scientists Leo Szilard and Albert Einstein. Haltingly, and with lingering cynicism, the government pursued the project through a succession of administrative bureaus. It received increased priority in 1941, however, following confirmation by scientists in Great Britain of the potential for an explosive chain reaction in uranium, and Japanese "bolt from the blue" at Pearl Harbor.

Los Alamos was originally planned as a means to centralize Manhattan Project labor on the nuclear weapon. Directed by U.S. Army General Leslie S. Groves, the Project was an industry unto itself, establishing enormous production plants for fissionable materials in Hanford, Washington and Oak Ridge, Tennessee. At the University of Chicago's "Metallurgical Laboratory" scientists perfected the chain-reaction process that could liberate explosive energy. Los Alamos, in turn, became a site for integrating theory and experiment, and translating crude designs into an engineered, applied technology. The Laboratory's New Mexico location was selected by its director, the brilliant and eccentric theoretician, J. Robert Oppenheimer, who decided that a remote boy's school satisfied criteria for both aesthetics and security. As the construction of spartan housing and technical facilities commenced, Oppenheimer courted the Allies' best scientific minds, many of whom had fled the anti-Semitic purge of Europe by Nazi Germany. Most answered Oppenheimer's call, enticed by the scientific challenge, the thought of working with the giants in their fields, and the prospect of contributing to the war effort. In spite of their misgivings at building a weapon of unparalleled destruction under military supervision, Oppenheimer noted, "[t]his sense of excitement, of devotion and of patriotism prevailed."[31]

Assembling at Los Alamos in April, 1943, these chemists, physicists and engineers listened to orientation lectures that clarified their purpose and their agenda. Two chemical isotopes, Uranium 235 and Plutonium, were known to be capable of sustaining chain reactions yielding an explosion. The scientists were charged with designing and constructing the devices that would initiate, control, house, and deliver the critical mass of nuclear material. Critical mass could theoretically be assembled by firing two sections of material together (the "gun" method) or by surrounding material with high explosives and detonating them, compressing that mass into criticality ("implosion"). As the couplings between materials and assembly techniques were painstakingly developed, the Laboratory's administrative structure expanded to match personnel and resources to problems. In early 1944, a team of British scientists joined the Laboratory. Among them was the spy Klaus Fuchs, who, escaping detection, passed information about the weapon to Soviet agents and hastened the international arms race.

The scientists labored under intense pressure, believing that Nazi scientists had also accessed prewar research publications and were attempting to construct a nuclear weapon. While the Laboratory remained under nominal civilian control, the surrounding base was administered under intensive military security that enforced isolation, censorship, secrecy, and containment. As a community, Los Alamos endured the squalor and hardships of rapid, unplanned growth: a skyrocketing birth rate, shortages of housing and food, sporadically functioning utilities and muddy, unpaved roads. The scientists' labor culminated out of false starts, dead ends, interpersonal conflicts, and exhaustive calculation in a uranium-gun bomb presumed reliable, and a plutonium-implosion bomb that would be tested—code name 'Trinity'—at a remote site two hundred miles to the south. This nerve-wracking test detonation fused the sand under the bomb's tower into crystals of translucent jade. Its roiling mushroom cloud appeared awesome, fulfilling and ominous to the scientists huddled in trenches and bunkers at the site, and to those looking on from surrounding mountaintops. They had fulfilled their charter in making the weapon, and now awaited its use.

In early August, 1945, crews flying modified B-29 bombers delivered the products of Los Alamos labor upon the cities of Hiroshima and Nagasaki, destroying their infra-structures and incinerating thousands of their inhabitants. News of the bombs' use and subsequent Japanese surrender produced widespread jubilation at Los Alamos, and a more subtle and unfocused anxiety. Following the war, the scientists returned to academe and industry. A few, like Oppenheimer, gravitated towards Washington, where the battle for control of atomic energy was about to be waged. Under post-war administrations, the laboratory itself found sustained purpose in developing nuclear weapons for a Cold War arms race, and continues in that capacity today.[32]

The narrators in *Reminiscences of Los Alamos* draw from these events to position the subjectivity of their narratives. Indeed, editor Lawrence Badash emphasizes in his introduction the value of this subjectivity, compared with more conventional treatments of Los Alamos history: The speakers "give us not a technical or administrative account of the New Mexico achievements, but rather [rare] personal vignettes of the period 1943–1945."[33] Clearly this distinction between "technical" and "personal" speech genres is false and unstable. The speaking subjects of *Reminiscences* are not independent from technical or administrative discourses, and in fact represent the very locus of their productivity. In these narratives, I believe, we find "personal" voices infused with "rational" elements of Los Alamos structure as contexts for their meaning.

In the three narratives themselves, these elements include (a) an implicit metaphor of "fission" which joins the organizational *technology* of Los Alamos with its organizing *technique;* (b) a "rhetoric of measurement" that constrained the meaning of Los Alamos labor and its consequences; and (c) an expression of the technological imperative as a guiding principle for organizational identity and purpose. Throughout my interpretation, I emphasize how these narratives—through what they systematically make present *and* absent—reconstruct the subjects and objects of Los Alamos' organizational practice.

## JOHN H. MANLEY: FISSION AS TECHNOLOGY AND ORGANIZING TECHNIQUE

John H. Manley's narrative, "A New Laboratory is Born,"[34] gives an overview of the complex technological and administrative problems attending Los Alamos growth between 1943 and 1945. Reviewing his own history in the context of these developments, Manley sees a personal, fated "road to Los Alamos"[35] that began with his appointment to Columbia University in the 1930's, and culminated in his service as an administrative aide to Laboratory director Robert Oppenheimer.

At Chicago, Manley recounts, he became interested in the "basic" nuclear physics that would became "applied" in the nuclear weapon. Incrementally, his developing expertise with nuclear accelerator technology advanced his steps "along the road."[36] The identities of Manley's machine, and of himself as its operator, became tightly coupled; when one was pressed into service,.the other followed. "The accelerator sat for awhile [at the Chicago Met Lab] and then in 1943 was dismantled and moved to Los Alamos. So it was drafted, as well as . . . myself."[37] In Chicago, Manley labored to perfect the chain reaction process, studying how differing materials would slow down the catalytic, escaping neutrons from fissioning material. He was subsequently assigned to assist the more theoretical Oppenheimer in perfecting the process "that would really give an explosion."[38]

Manley's interpretation of the atomic bomb proceeds technically and rationally. He represents that object as an assembly of materials whose contingent relations became the bracketed domain of knowledge at Los Alamos.

> The physics of an explosive chain reaction is really very different from the physics of the chain reacting pile . . . the chain reaction for a bomb . . . must go fast and be propagated by fast neutrons, otherwise the reaction time would be so long that the material would simply expand and you'd get a fizzle with no real explosive result. And so a point to remember is that bomb design depends very critically on the fast neutron properties of all materials that are involved in the bomb itself.[39]

As one of the Laboratory's administrators, Manley was also familiar with the "problem of liaison" among early Manhattan Project sections, which, he states, "was a fantastically difficult one."[40] The scientists thus proposed establishing a laboratory that would officially centralize "interchange of ideas on the experimental and theoretical difficulties."[41] Consolidation was attractive to Project Director Groves "not only from the technical," but also "the security point of view" as well. "If he could coop these people up in one place, it would be a lot easier to control their talking."[42]

In this passage, Manley signals the presence of an *implicit* metaphor linking the technology and organizing technique of Los Alamos. While he does not explicitly formulate it as such (as do others; see below), there are strong parallels in this narrative between "fission" as the *process* over which the scientists sought control, and "fission" as an *image* of their laboring process.[43] As the former, "fission" describes how neutrons liberated from bombarded and ruptured neutrons pierce the nuclei of *other* atoms, producing both immense energy and more neutrons. Ideally, the neutrons released will achieve a "self-sustaining" chain reaction. This imagery of "atoms," "energy," and "control" also illuminates the structural conditions under which this labor was organized and managed.

Specifically, while control over the fissioning process of nuclear materials constituted the scientific task at the laboratory, the fissioning of discourse, or the "talking" of Los Alamos members was the concern of administrators, who, like the scientists, were concerned with "control"—with obligation and constraint—over "reactions" within their domain of authority. More specifically, controlling the "talking" of scientists involved containing that process within a monitored, isolated locale where particular models for speaking would be enforced, and which ideally would proliferate as consensual contexts for the bomb and its labor. Fission describes, subsequently, the dialectical process through which Los Alamos members confronted rational and "typificatory schemes"[44] of their labor, and of themselves as laborers, and reproduced these constructs in their discourse. The object of security practices was the "yield" of potentially "exploding" signification by organizational actors in their discourse. In recruitment and administrative procedures, Los Alamos authorities "centralized" rational definitions of the bomb as technical labor, and naturalized them as part of an organizational morphology, as a basis for consensus. At Los Alamos, the "purity of materials" ("are their communists among us?"), the mass of their "critical assembly" ("how many people do we need?"), and the control of their interactions ("should we compartmentalize information?") described the concerns of *both* the scientists and the military authorities.

This imagery surfaces again as Manley reviews the organizing principle of the laboratory and the "thinking" of its scientists in 1942. He describes how their "concerns" were grounded in ". . . difficulties with the science involved . . . We thought if we could get good measurements of nuclear properties it wouldn't be too hard to do the business of getting explosive material together somehow so that it would go bang. But the important questions were how much material could be assembled in one weapon, and how much could that amount of material be reduced by surrounding it with some 'nice stuff.' "[45] This material that he describes would serve to "hold the explosive together for a while so it wouldn't expand too fast and blow itself apart, stopping the reaction," and would also "reflect back neutrons effectively so that those that *might* escape would come back and feed into the chain reaction and you'd get more energy out."[46] The variable speed of assembling sub-critical masses to generate "a bang instead of just a proof,"

Manley emphasizes, was "a tough question which caused us a lot of pain."[47]

Again, this passage invokes a parallel between technological process and the concerns of organizing technique. Organizational culture functions fundamentally to establish common orientations among its members to the symbols of organizational practice, "hold[ing] together" the prolific practice of sense-making by actors. Administration and security at Los Alamos included those practices that constrained the public expression of private experience (e.g., by censoring mail and posting military spies in surrounding towns). Meanings "that might escape" from the mesa needed to be blocked and returned to the ongoing "chain reaction" of rational-technical labor, optimizing its productivity. Institutional authority at Los Alamos functioned to create and maintain definitions for the subjects and objects of organizational practice. Standardized and enforced, these meanings for 'who we are' and 'what we're doing here' fissioned and reproduced, maximizing the energy of pliable, adaptive laborers.

One meaning essential to the Los Alamos "community," Manley emphasizes, was this shared orientation to "task": "Perhaps [Los Alamos] could be called a new civilization colonizing this . . . Plateau. . . . This re-colonization was for a very different purpose than the earlier one. Our task was to pursue a development to resolve a conflict of half the world. To make a new scientific laboratory and a new community was a step in that task."[48]

Manley extends the implicit connection between technological innovation and organizational growth in recounting how the imposition and internal generation of new tasks led to increases in Los Alamos personnel (e.g., for plutonium purification and fabrication and for the design of the ballistic technology for the uranium bomb). During 1945, however, the scientists received a "terrible" and "inescapable . . . shock"[49] in matching their materials to their weapons technology. "Of the two fissile explosives, U-235 and plutonium, we finally had to conclude that a gun [method] just would not assemble plutonium fast enough . . . The choice was to junk the whole discovery . . . and all of the investment in time and effort . . . *unless* somebody could come up with a way of assembling the plutonium material into a weapon that would explode. It was again a Los Alamos challenge to do just that."[50] Physicist Seth Neddermeyer subsequently developed the implosion method of assembling fissionable materials, and contributed in turn to the fissioning of organizational structure: "This too had an extra effect on the manpower situation."[51] The final phase of wartime growth occurred during preparation for the 1945 Trinity test of the implosion weapon, "a tremendous field operation which took lots of people, lots of ingenuity."[52]

Manley confirms the parallel between fissioning as technology and as technique in arguing the laboratory's efficiency for the record: "why was it that Los Alamos was able to accomplish this remarkable task with no *more* people than it had?"[53] It was the adaptability of multitalented personnel, he emphasizes, and their ability to be pressed into new and different service that enabled the organization's success. The professional expertise of Los Alamos scientists also became a fissioning material. Assigned to conduct blast measurements at the Trinity explosion, for example, Manley and his group re-invented themselves as specialists. "Using basic physics principles, reading the literature, nabbing a few experts and talking to the theorists, we became instant blast experts."[54]

As he continues his testimony to security as an organizing technique, Manley reasons that, "the remarkable way in which the purpose of the whole operation was kept from public view seems to me to attest to the fact that people really were cooperative about the necessity for secrecy and approved generally of the way the security operation was run."[55] Manley's claim is contested as an account of history, however, by the early resignation of scientist Edward Condon in anger at oppressive security, and Laura (wife of physicist Enrico) Fermi's statement that the European-born scientists were reminded by the barbed wire and armed patrols of concentration camps.[56] Manley equates the adaptation of Los Alamos subjects to the imposed structure with their endorsement, but they are not the same thing. "[T]he Americans," notes Richard Rhodes, "accepted the fences around their work and their lives as a necessity of war . . . [which] was a manifestation of nationalism, not of science, and such did their duty on the Hill at first appear to be."[57]

Manley also praises the scientific colloquia and meetings which signi-fied Oppenheimer's subversion of military designs for compartment-alization of information. "These discussions brought forth ideas and were excellent morale boosters. I'm sure the work went faster . . . as a result."[58] He presents this subversion of complete military secrecy as a minor victory for the scientific value of free exchange of knowledge. It was also a victory for the rational efficiency of laborers, however, and for the institutionally-designed assembly of subcritical practitioners into a critical laboring mass yielding the energy of their theorizing and experimentation. More tightly coupled within Los Alamos as a result, the scientists were still contained from without, protected by barbed wire and military police from, among other things, alternative ways of making sense of their labor and its pur-pose.

As Earl Shorris notes, the metaphor of laborers as fissioning "atoms" is not a neutral one.[59] It reflects a totalitarian impulse in organizational prac-tice whose logical conclusion is the abolition of human autonomy. Atomized workers are fundamentally *crowded*, both physically and psychologically. They are disciplined by management so that difference, disagreement, slack and uncolonized psyche recede before an enforced commitment to organi-zational goals. In this way, as Los Alamos scientists manipulated matter, they were themselves invited to participate in a rationally biased commitment to technological innovation. Exactly what the discourse of that commitment excluded, I explore in the next narrative.

## ▨ JOSEPH O. HIRSCHFELDER: MIRACLES AND THE RHETORIC OF MEASUREMENT

Joseph O. Hirschfelder signals the celebratory tone of his narrative with its title, "The Scientific and Technological Miracle At Los Alamos."[60] His use of the word "miracle" is somewhat incongruous, conflating a supernatural event with the rational manipulation of matter performed at Los Alamos. Asserting a "miracle at Los Alamos" invokes a transcendental sponsorship for organizational practice that simultaneously inflates—or mystifies—the accountability of human practitioners.

"I believe," Hirschfelder testifies, "in scientific-technological miracles since I saw one performed at Los Alamos during World War II."[61] This statement confirms the narrator's role as witness. The passive verb "performed" again obscures the actors and agency that accomplished the performance. But Hirschfelder soon resolves the uncertainty. "[S]cientists and engineers," cooperative and devoted, working and playing "free of all outside distractions"[62] produced the miracle: "an atomic bomb which creates temperatures . . . 15,000 times as hot as molten iron . . . [and] pressure greater than at the center of the earth . . . while unleashing the tremendous energy stored in the atomic nuclei."[63]

This dubious miracle, the human construction of the supernatural, is depicted by Hirschfelder in the measurement of its function, its performance as an agent of temperature and force. Yet measurement, as a practice producing knowledge of phenomena, conventionally occurs in a context that delimits the meaning which that knowledge may come to have. Specifically, as the 'scientific' analysis and bracketing of systemic behavior and process, measurement can obscure the connected objects of the process. Here, it is a rhetorical figure that deletes the signification, the making present, of those who will experience the consequence of the weapon's energy. This account does not engage those victims who will know, very briefly, those temperatures of a magnitude of molten iron.

Measurement and experiment then, may be understood as signifying practices, as the construction and communication of knowledge within institutional conventions for meaningful expression. Like all signifying practices, measurement is ideological in establishing normative positions for speaking/knowing subjects, the objects of their knowledge, and the meaning of their relations. Objective measurement is ideological in functioning within discursive structures that would mediate objects to the subjects that speak of them, in order to secure those objects for the exercise of power. In truncating—silencing—the human objects of the practice of nuclear weapons, the measurement of nuclear effects becomes a political act. The dead of Hiroshima and Nagasaki were thus silenced by definition, left "without voice or civil rights or recourse."[64] Hirschfelder's account signals the function of scientific measurement—a routine practice at Los Alamos—in accomplishing that silence in advance, a pre-emptive strike of exclusive signification.

Hirschfelder proceeds in the narrative to recall the "tremendous task" of producing fissionable materials which "required a great scientific and engineering effort."[65] The development of the bomb's technology became the principle of organizational growth at Los Alamos: "The idea was that as each new problem developed, experts were recruited to solve that problem."[66]

After completing his first assignment to develop ballistics theory for the Uranium "gun" assembly, Hirschfelder headed a group given the problem "of determining all of the effects of an atomic bomb which would take place after the nuclear fissions had occurred."[67] He blithely confirms that the rational definition of "effects" as an issue of empirical measurement was consensual: "Many of the weapon effect problems were completely unfamiliar to me and I was most grateful for the unselfish help which we received from many people. Wouldn't it be wonderful if we could all work together in this manner for peaceful instead of military objectives?"[68] Echoing Manley's earlier account, Hirschfelder confirms that "fission" characterized both the Laboratory's technology and its structuration: "By the time that the atom bomb was tested . . . Los Alamos was three deep in experts and tensions were so high that if the atomic bomb had not functioned, there would have been a much greater explosion between the scientists."[69]

Hirschfelder and his team pursued, nonetheless, "the large number of seemingly unrelated problems . . . [in] predict[ing] the radioactive fallout"[70] from the impending Trinity test. Their findings were also generalized for subsequent military use. Consistently in Hirschfelder's narrative, these "problems" and "effects" derive their meaning from the context of professional authority, and an intertextual system of institutional knowledge:

> 1) First, we had to study the formation of the ball of fire. This involved aerodynamics, including the radiative transport of energy, and for this we studied Chandrasekhar's astrophysics treatise on the dynamics of nebulae. . . .
> 2) The second problem was the rise of the fire ball and the generation of winds along the ground . . . Sir Geoffrey I. Taylor, the world's greatest authority on turbulent and convective aerodynamics, helped us with this problem. . . .
> 4) If the bomb were detonated within a half-mile of the ground, the air currents sweeping along the ground pick up dirt, rocks and assorted debris . . . To learn how wind picks up debris from the ground, we studied Department of Agriculture soil conservation reports and Bagnard's treatise, *"The Physics of the Blown Sand"*. . . .[71]

These examples suggest how the formulation of weapons problems and effects at Los Alamos was embedded in a structure promoting measurement as an official and desirable narrative for nuclear explosion. Because it was analytic and reductive, however, that narrative incompletely represented the process, and constrained the signification of human experience as its outcome. Humans, as a result, are only implicit here as the brief inhabitants of fireballs and the eventual consumers of radioactive "debris." The primary fate considered in this context is that of "the radioactive materials."[72] Humans do eventually figure in Hirschfelder's account, but ironically, as the population within the Trinity test area that the scientists were trying, through their research, to *avoid* harming: "At the Alamogordo bomb test this [the inverse relationship between altitude and fallout accumulation] was important because most of the people in the area lived on hilltops, so they were not in danger."[73] The populations subsequently to be put at risk are absent. This narrative glosses the utility of "effects" studied at Trinity for the annihilation of human life.

When they tracked the dispersing radioactive fallout from the Trinity test blast, Hirschfelder and his companion confronted two witnesses of the explosion: a mule ("his jaws were wide open, his tongue hanging down, and he was completely paralyzed"), and an elderly storeowner (" 'You boys must have been up to something this morning. The sun came up in the West and went on down again' ").[74] The dazed mule has disappeared when they return; the storeowner suffers acceptable exposure to fallout. Inevitably, Hirschfelder and his companion confront themselves as the radioactive objects of Los Alamos practice, scrubbing themselves "with lots of soap and repeated rinsing and chang[ing] into clean clothes."[75] Their car was sufficiently radioactive to later distort Geiger counter readings upon its return to Los Alamos. An anxious U.S. Army officer, ordered to return them to Albuquerque, first asked them to sit in the front of his car with the driver, and then hailed a jeep to take them to their destination.

Overall, in reconstructing organizational meanings for the "effects" of the atomic bomb, this account selectively considers the objects of those effects. The objects are inanimate, or if animate, surviving; the narrator even confronts himself as an object of the effect of the observed upon the observer. But this narrative does not imagine, *even in retrospect*, the future when the objects of these effects were the living, and then the dead, whose presence was disallowed in the ideological, signifying practices of measurement. Having previously stated that "it takes a genius to figure out the consequences"[76] of a scientific discovery, Hirschfelder's narrative now seems ironic. "Frankly, I am quite amazed at the success that we had in predicting the effects of the atom bomb. I would say that we didn't miss a single effect. . . . I went through in considerable detail the kind of thoroughness that one had to have in order to make these predictions . . . We have the theoretical ability; we have the computing machines. . . ."[77]

The concrete "effects" of the weapon on the communities of Hiroshima and Nagasaki—death, desolation, burns, radiation poisoning, starvation, thirst, a legacy of birth defects[78]—form the "unconscious" material of Hirschfelder's narrative.[79] They are historically and materially real events, but are systematically excluded from this professional and technically informed reminiscence. Hirschfelder's account suggests a hegemonic conception of the bomb which was rhetorically derived from a structure that excluded the representation of human victims. This deep structure is also evident in the technical, "official" history of Los Alamos, compiled by David Hawkins shortly following the war. It describes how in "the summer and fall of 1943, the shock wave produced in air by the explosion, the optimum explosion height, and *the effects on* [its] *diffraction by obstacles such as buildings* . . . were investigated" [emphasis added].[80] In a stunning inversion of moral perspective, potentially human "obstacles" were seen as affecting the blast wave, but not vice versa. For any number of reasons, as this next narrative suggests, it was easier to think about the technological challenge of the weapons.

## NORRIS BRADBURY: THE NECESSITY OF NUCLEAR INNOVATION

Norris Bradbury's narrative, "Los Alamos—The First 25 Years,"[81] extends the wartime portrait of the Laboratory offered by other voices in the *Reminiscences* text. Bradbury successfully directed the Trinity test and the assembly of the implosion bomb for use on Nagasaki and was then appointed to succeed Robert Oppenheimer as Laboratory Director in 1945. Thirty years later, he reflected upon the laboratory's post-war development as a strategic instrument of nuclear weapons research for superpower policy. Bradbury's narrative emphasizes the continuity of a technological imperative that established one rationale for scientific labor in weapons development: that it realized what was potential, and therefore inevitable, in the manipulation of natural phenomena. "If you are a scientist," Robert Oppenheimer had consoled laboratory members in 1945, "you cannot stop such a thing."[82] The scientific pursuit of "knowledge," relentless and rational, coupled at Los Alamos with a nationalistic ideology construing that knowledge as best possessed by the United States. Bradbury's narrative details how this combination of professionalism and nationalism persisted as a potent myth for Los Alamos labor.

Although agreeing to accept the assignment only temporarily, Bradbury stayed on as Laboratory director for twenty-five years, "and I have never had the slightest regret of the decision I made or the task I undertook."[83] In 1945 that task involved winding down the wartime labor of four thousand personnel and contemplating the future. Organizational streamlining was initially simplified by the mass defection of Los Alamos staff to an admiring military-industrial complex, seeded for growth: "Everybody wanted out. Science in the war years had been a *fantastic* thing . . . It had invented the proximity fuse for anti-aircraft warfare; it had invented radar, and had invented the atomic bomb . . . [T]he public reaction and the Washington reaction was that scientists were wonderful. Physics, chemistry and mathematics were going to come in for enormous growth."[84]

Amid this "chaotic . . . exodus,"[85] however, the Laboratory was directed by the U.S. military to measure the effects of fission weapons being tested in the Bikini Islands of the Pacific Ocean. Bradbury interpreted the task as the catalyst for innovation in measurement technology: ". . . the instrumentation problem was beyond belief; the logistics were fantastic."[86] In spite, or because of this trial, Los Alamos reestablished its identity in service: ". . . at least Bikini gave us an objective, a challenge, and there's nothing like a task to pull yourself together. So we did."[87]

Additionally, Bradbury had to steer between competing visions of nuclear energy as military and civilian interests grappled for its control. Los Alamos was popularly characterized at that time as both "a monument of man's inhumanity to man," and as an essential industry when "bigger and better bombs were the obvious order of the day."[88] Although Bradbury asserted the necessity of individualism ("I had to have some beliefs of my own"[89]), his construal of the organization's purpose accommodated the military desire for weapons innovation. Bradbury accepted what was technologically possible as ideologically necessary, and an agenda of tasks emerged: "It was well known that there were lots of things that had to be done, or certainly ought to be done, in terms of better utilization of materials, better yield to weight ratios. There is a basic problem of any device: it has to be delivered; it is no good in your cellar. Its size and its weight interact directly with . . . the delivery technology. Those things had to be done. Other little bits and pieces . . . that we knew about but simply hadn't had time to explore, were staring at us from behind the scenes, among them . . . the possibility of bringing about the fusion reaction in deuterium . . . the so-called [hydrogen] 'super-bomb.' "[90] For Bradbury, the technological imperative of realizing possible innovations combined with nationalism to establish an organizational purpose: "So I felt that these were the sorts of things that had to be done and this country had to do them. I simply . . . do not share the feeling that if you don't do something nobody else will."[91]

Curiously, Bradbury juxtaposes this recollection of Los Alamos' growth with a brief fantasy of its demise, which (he muses) has been prevented only by the deterrent value of its product in international relations.

No one makes nuclear weapons or bombs of any sort with any desire to use them. There is no pleasure in using them. In fact, one makes them with a profound desire . . . never to *want* to use them, never to find a *need* to use them. The whole object of the nuclear weapons business has been to put itself out of business. . . . And yet, if you asked me in 1945, would we still be making bombs 25 years later, I would have said I don't think so. . . . But we're still at it . . . , I simply do not want this country ever to be in a position of coming to a[n arms negotiation] conference table on the weak side.[92]

Conflating the voices of strategist and scientist, Bradbury professes ambivalent wonder at a monolithic arms race, and articulates the paradox of weapons-work in the age of deterrence.

Bradbury's laboratory subsequently resolved to "get at" innovations in fission weapons and reestablish a "broad foundation . . . of fundamental nuclear research."[93] That reorganization expanded and specialized work assignments, which were nonetheless still "related to . . . our major objective, which at that time of course had to be weapons."[94] The possibility of constructing a thermonuclear weapon dictated the Laboratory's basic research as one among "our major application efforts."[95] Bradbury contrasts the 1949 Soviet test of a fission weapon with the earlier Los Alamos effort and argues that the American project was technically more ambitious. American detonations of the bomb, he concludes, should be interpreted as evidence of how an imminent technology was valiantly liberated from the realm of the possible. In contrast, "They [the Soviets] knew it *could* be done, which we did *not* know. The great thing that Alamogordo said, and that Hiroshima and Nagasaki said, was that a nuclear explosion was possible. Up to that time one couldn't see . . . why it shouldn't be possible, but it was a regime of temperatures and pressures and behavior that one had never seen in an experimental laboratory before."[96] Similarly, by perfecting the fusion weapon the Laboratory would, ironically, "re-establish our lead over the Russians—until they catch up with us again. . . ."[97]

This argument for superpower vigilance and "mirroring" voiced here by Bradbury also swayed President Harry Truman in his brief deliberation over authorizing the H-Bomb's development. It was opposed but not defeated at the time by a proposal from physicists Enrico Fermi and Isador Rabi for a bilateral moratorium on thermonuclear weapons testing. Recurring proposals for test bans of imminent technologies have conventionally been defeated by exaggerated and simplistic representations of the Soviet threat to U.S. national security.[98] Yet in their moral acuity and persistence, these oppositional voices form a prior "utterance" to which Bradbury's argument gains meaning implicitly as a reply.[99] The muted questions of "why not stop now?", and "when and how will we stop, if ever?" circulating in nuclear culture have historically shadowed the bomb's seemingly infinite and inevitable evolution.

But energized by the prospect of restoring American nuclear advantage, Bradbury proceeded to implement the research program, discounting "gross exaggeration[s]" from alarmists who argued "that we had done wrong by the world in developing the fission bomb and that we shouldn't do this again," and from a military believing that without the hydrogen weapon "the world is going to come crashing down around our ears."[100] Daunted by these voices, and by the weapon's theoretical complexity, Bradbury struggled to establish "how this could be a coherent, logical, reasonable program that didn't fritter away effort in useless and failing experiments."[101]

It is interesting to linger on Bradbury's response to this problem. Specifically, he preferred to design a "reasonable" program that would counter the extremist voices, both moralizing and militaristic. What is reasonable, presumably, is that which counters extremism. This recourse to reason, however, produced a decision—to proceed with development of the hydrogen weapon—which served the military interest. This discourse about the decision-making process evokes the argument of Frankfurt School critic Max Horkheimer that "reason," in its modern and arguably debased form, is commonly used as a warrant in order to sustain the authority of conservative interests already in place.[102] In other words, what is "reasonable" (as Bradbury construes it within the "logic" of nuclear deterrence) is that which sustains the innovation and proliferation of nuclear weapons as programs of Los Alamos labor. The conclusion is internally consistent, but does not reflect on the contingencies of its initial premise: namely, that it is necessary to keep building.

The eventual success of the thermonuclear weapon, Bradbury continues, resulted from scientist Stanislaw Ulam's theoretical breakthrough, which was itself dependent upon the fissioning quality of Los Alamos personnel. "This constant interplay between people, each one coming up with an unworkable idea, let's say, but fertilizing an idea in somebody else's mind is terribly important."[103]

Subsequently assembled and detonated, the prototype hydrogen weapon was also interpreted by Bradbury as a sign—like its fission counterpart—of support for unceasing proliferation: "[It] was technically an enormous success. Physically, it was a totally useless device, but it showed very clearly in what direction we had to go to make a weapon, and that was done very rapidly in the following years."[104] That process of development, however, led the Laboratory staff to confront the limits of innovation and the consequence of that impasse: ". . . we faced another sort of crucial question. Here we had another jump. We had gone from chemical, pre–World War II explosives to nuclear explosions by 1945, a thousand times more effective. We'd now gone from a few kilotons to megatons, another factor of a thousand. No one saw or sees any way to go another factor of a thousand . . . So you don't really care if the bomb's much bigger than you have now. You wouldn't know quite what to do with them."[105]

In addition, wartime espionage had ensured that "the Russians were eventually going to get it."[106] Recalling how he learned of an imminent breakthrough by British scientists in mastering the weapon's technology, Bradbury confirms the symbiosis between the technological imperative and nationalism: "It would have happened anyway, and I'm glad that we did it first."[107] This rationale, for Bradbury, silenced moral concern and, along with the bureaucratic imperative, confirmed the Laboratory's identity in its service. "Nobody *likes* atomic bombs . . . we all hate them. But it has to be done and it had to be done. Much as I look forward some day to an international agreement which banishes the damned things, I didn't want my laboratory to wake up some morning and find it was out of a job. Twenty years or more could be spent refining, modifying, making better, doing all kinds of things with fusion type weapons, making them more effective death carriers."[108]

The "whole new set of technical problems"[109] arising from this formulation subsequently received priority, but Bradbury also moved to diversify the Laboratory's research during the 1960's into the study of nuclear medicine and reactor design. Currently, these programs constitute more than forty percent of the Laboratory's labor. But as its Director noted in 1982, "our major activity remains weapons research and development, both nuclear and nonnuclear."[110] The Los Alamos worldview, as articulated by Bradbury, continues.

Throughout, Bradbury's account braids the ideology of nationalism with the technological imperative to form a rationale—and to define a laboring subject—for Los Alamos nuclear weapons production. His closing traces that trajectory beyond his tenure as its director to relentless future iterations. Accounting for the construction of a nuclear particle accelerator at the Laboratory, Bradbury explains: "It's not for bombs, it's not for energy, it's just plain good physics, and the argument for doing plain good nuclear physics has to be what it always has. You've got to look under every stone and see what might be there. . . . You simply cannot let the country leave stones unturned. There may not be anything there, but suppose there is. You'd better find it."[111]

That argument summarizes the history of organizational purpose at Los Alamos.

## ■ CONCLUSION: ORGANIZATIONAL TEXTUALITY, CRITICAL CONSCIENCE

What, then, can personal narratives contribute to the understanding of organizational structure? *Reminiscences of Los Alamos* presents "sites of signifying practice [and] forms of social productivity,"[112] where "the structures that enable and constrain . . . thoughts and actions become palpable."[113] The reflective stance of Los Alamos scientists, adopted in their narratives, suggests the local, rational schemes for meaning and action that structured their routines.

John Manley's account highlights the organizational monitoring and control of the "fissioning" potential for meaning and labor within the lab's membership. Joseph Hirschfelder's account suggests that a normative rhetoric of measurement operated in the organization to constrain the signification of human victims. Norris Bradbury's account illuminates the hegemonic imperatives of nationalism and technological innovation that sustain Los Alamos today as a center for weapons research and development. In my interpretation of these accounts, I have attempted to show how the "personal" narratives of organizational members are infused with patterns, images and references that suggest the productivity of organizational structure in ordering the meaning that they attribute to their working experience. I have explored Los Alamos as an organizational site where meanings of the utmost consequence were made and negotiated. I have considered the ways in which those processes constitute the "how" of the "what" in these narratives, mediating the subjects of Los Alamos labor and their objects. I have represented these organizational actors as language-users, spinning (and spun in) structural webs of signification. Out of these arguments, an image of the organizational reality of Los Alamos emerges for consideration and reflection.[114]

A recently published text offers, by way of comparison, one option for this reflection: *The Nazi Doctors,* by psychologist Robert Jay Lifton.[115] Lifton's analysis of interviews with the professionals and technicians who staffed Nazi concentration camps complements the recollections of Los Alamos scientists in obvious ways. Both texts recall the same war-torn period. Both describe organizational technologies producing mass death. Less obviously, they also describe how symbolic fields can be normatively organized to enable technologized killing.

Nazi authorities, Lifton argues, gradually redefined the practice of medicine and its objects. State-appointed medical bureaucrats, devoted to Nazi programs of eugenics, isolated and excluded dissenters from those programs while empowering doctors who participated. Nazi rhetoric established a class of subhuman, largely Jewish, objects who were excluded from the Hippocratic obligation and imbued with utility for completing state-legitimated "research." Drawing on the surplus value of signifiers such as "doctor," "research" and "subject," the Nazi state reconstructed connections between these and related signifiers to produce the paradoxical practice of killing (the undesirable) *as* healing (the diseased body of the state).[116] The professionals on whom all death-technology depends, notes Lifton, "have a special capacity for doubling. In them a prior, humane self can be joined by a 'professional self' willing to ally itself with a destructive project, with harming or even killing others."[117] Embedded in a completely technicized environment bureaucratically dividing the labor of genocide, the Nazi doctors applied their wisdom:

> The gas chambers were sufficient, you see, that was no problem. But the burning, right? The ovens broke down. And they (the corpses) had to be burned in a big heap . . . The problem is really a large technical difficulty. There was not too much room, so first one thought one would have to take small piles . . . Well, . . . that would have to be tried out . . . And then everyone contributed his knowledge of physics, about what might possibly be done differently. If you do it with ditches around them, then the air comes up from below and wooden

planks underneath and gasoline on top—or gasoline underneath and wood in between—these were the problems. Well the solution was not to let the fire die. And maintain the cooperation between the gas chamber and the crematorium. When (the fire) reached a certain intensity, then it was just right—but then you could not get to it, so it was still too hot, etc. Those were the problems.[118]

"Those were the problems": echoes of Joseph Hirschfelder and the technical definition of task that evacuates all humanity from its object. I suggest this connection between Nazi doctors and Los Alamos scientists to establish how the management of signifying practices by organizational members is a precondition for producing the technologies of mass death.[119] The responsibility for liberating the obscured object of these practices, nuclear and otherwise, is a moral one. It falls—however reluctantly—to the activist and the critic to engage the texts of organized life which work to level all differences among their subjects, and which accomplish the complete and final silence of their objects. In the absence of the critical voice, this story by Los Alamos scientist Richard Feynman suggests, the haunting voice of the repressed returns only to a few, and always too late.

> After the thing went off [at Hiroshima], there was tremendous excitement at Los Alamos. Everybody had parties, we all ran around. I sat on the end of a jeep and beat drums and so on. But one man I remember, Bob Wilson, was just sitting there and moping.
> I said, "What are you moping about?"
> He said, "It's a terrible thing that we made."
> . . . You see, what happened to me—what happened to the rest of us—is we *started* for a good reason, then you're working very hard to accomplish something and it's a pleasure, it's excitement. And you stop thinking, you know; you just *stop*. So Bob Wilson was the only one who was still thinking about it, at that moment.[120]

# ▪ Notes

[1]For discussions of cultural reactions to nuclear science in general and Los Alamos in particular, see Paul Boyer, *By the Bomb's Early Light: American Thought and Culture at the Dawn of the Atomic Age* (New York: Pantheon Books, 1985); Paul Brians, *Nuclear Holocausts: Atomic War in Fiction, 1895–1984* (Kent, OH: Kent State University Press, 1987); and Spencer R. Weart, *Nuclear Fear: A History of Images* (Cambridge: Harvard University Press, 1988).

[2]*Reminiscences of Los Alamos; 1943–1945,* ed. Lawrence Badash, Joseph O. Hirschfelder and Herbert P. Broida (Boston: D. Reidel Publishing Co., 1980).

[3]*Reminiscences,* "Preface," ix.

[4]Victor F. Weisskopf, "Looking Back on Los Alamos," in *Assessing the Nuclear Age: Selections From the Bulletin of the Atomic Scientists,* ed. L. Ackland and S. McGuire (Chicago: Educational Foundation for Nuclear Science, 1986), 25.

[5]For appraisal of the current influence of textualism in communication study, see: George Cheney and Phillip K. Tompkins, "On the Facts of the Text as the Basis of Human Communica-

tion Research," and Mary S. Strine, "Constructing Texts and Making Inferences: Some Reflections on Textual Reality Construction in Human Communication Research," in *Communication Yearbook 11*, ed. James A. Anderson (Newbury Park, CA: Sage, 1988).

⁶Jeff Smith, *Unthinking the Unthinkable: Nuclear Weapons and Western Culture* (Bloomington: University of Indiana Press, 1989), 21.

⁷Jacques Derrida, "No Apocalypse, Not Now (full speed ahead, seven missiles, seven missives)," *Diacritics, 14* (1984): 20–31. If Derrida is correct, then the validity of nuclear criticism is also thrown open to vexing questions; see J. Solomon Fisher, *Discourse and Reference in the Nuclear Age* (Norman: University of Oklahoma Press, 1988).

⁸David Dowling, *Fictions of Nuclear Disaster* (Iowa City: University of Iowa Press, 1987), ch. 7.

⁹*Nukespeak: The Media and the Bomb*, ed. Crispin Aubrey (London: Comedia Publishing Group, 1982); *Language and the Nuclear Arms Debate: Nukespeak Today*, ed. Paul Chilton (Dover, NH: Francis Pinter, 1985); "The Rhetoric of Nukespeak," *Communication Monographs, 56* (1989): 253–272; Carol Cohn, "Sex and Death in the Rational World of Defense Intellectuals," *Signs, 12* (1987): 687–718.

¹⁰David Cratis Williams, "Nuclear Criticism: In Pursuit of a Politically Enabling Deconstructive Voice," *Journal of the American Forensic Association, 24* (1988): 193–205.

¹¹"Proposal for a *Diacritics* Colloquium on Nuclear Criticism," *Diacritics, 14* (1984): 2–3.

¹²Gareth Morgan, "Paradigms, Metaphors and Puzzle-Solving in Organization Theory," *Administrative Science Quarterly, 25* (1980): 605–622; Stanley A. Deetz, "Critical Interpretive Research in Organizational Communication," *Western Journal of Speech Communication, 46* (1982): 131–149.

¹³Stanley A. Deetz and Astrid Kersten, "Critical Models of Interpretive Research" in Linda L. Putnam and Michael E. Pacanowsky (eds.), *Communication and Organizations: An Interpretive Approach* (Beverly Hills, CA: Sage, 1983); Charles Conrad and Mary Ryan, "Power, Praxis and Self in Organizational Communication Theory," in *Organizational Communication: Traditional Themes and New Directions*, ed. R. McPhee and P. Tompkins (Beverly Hills: Sage, 1985), 235–257.

¹⁴John Forester, "Critical Theory and Organizational Analysis," *Beyond Method: Strategies for Social Research*, ed. G. Morgan (Beverly Hills, CA: Sage, 1983), 240–42.

¹⁵Stanley Deetz and Dennis K. Mumby, "Power, Discourse and the Workplace: Reclaiming the Critical Tradition in Communication Studies in Organizations," forthcoming in *Communication Yearbook 13*, ed. J. Anderson (Newbury Park, CA: Sage, 1990); Dennis K. Mumby, "The Political Function of Narrative in Organizations," *Communication Monographs, 54* (1987): 113–127, and *Communication and Power in Organizations: Discourse, Ideology and Domination*, ed. Dennis K. Mumby (Norwood, N.J.: Ablex, 1988). See also Gareth Morgan, *Images of Organization* (Beverly Hills, CA: Sage, 1986), ch. 6.

¹⁶Jurgen Habermas, *Knowledge and Human Interests*, trans. J. Shapiro (Boston: Beacon Press, 1971); Mumby, *Communication and Power*, ch. 3.

¹⁷Stanley A. Deetz, "Ethical Considerations in Cultural Research in Organizations," *Organizational Culture*, ed. Peter J. Frost, Larry F. Moore, Meryl Reis Louis, Craig C. Lundberg, and Joanne Martin (Beverly Hills, CA: Sage, 1985), 253–269.

¹⁸See Hayden White, "The Value of Narrativity in the Representation of Reality," *Critical Inquiry, 7* (1980): 5–27; Wallace Martin, *Recent Theories of Narrative*, (Ithaca: Cornell University Press, 1986). For discussions of the relationship between representation and ideology, see Michael J. Shapiro, *The Politics of Representation: Writing Practices in Biography, Photography and Policy Analysis* (Madison, WI: University of Wisconsin Press, 1988); Richard Harvey Brown, *Society as Text: Essays on Rhetoric, Reason and Reality* (Chicago: University of Chicago Press, 1987).

[19]Fredric Jameson, *The Political Unconscious: Narrative as a Socially Symbolic Act* (Ithaca: Cornell University Press, 1981), 79.

[20]Stuart Hall, "Signification, Representation, Ideology: Althusser and the Post-Structuralist Debates," *Critical Studies in Mass Communication*, 2 (1985): 91–114; Kaja Silverman, *The Subject of Semiotics* (New York: Oxford University Press, 1983).

[21]Jean-Francois Lyotard, *The Post-Modern Condition: A Report On Knowledge* (Minneapolis: University of Minnesota Press, 1984).

[22]Mumby, "Political Functions," 124.

[23]Gareth R. Jones, "Life History Methodology," in *Beyond Method*; Kenneth Plummer, *Documents of Life: An Introduction to the Problems and Literature of a Humanistic Method* (London, George Allen and Unwin, 1983); Janet V. Gunn, *Autobiography: Toward a Poetics of Experience* (Philadelphia: University of Pennsylvania Press, 1982); Lawrence C. Watson and Maria-Barbara Watson-Franke, *Interpreting Life Histories: An Anthropological Inquiry* (New Brunswick, NJ: Rutgers University Press, 1985); and M. M. J. Fischer, "Ethnicity and the Post-Modern Arts of Memory," *Writing Culture: The Poetics and Politics of Ethnography*, ed. James Clifford and George Marcus (Berkeley: University of California Press, 1986).

[24]See Catherine Belsey, *Critical Practice* (New York: Methuen, 1980); Lennard J. Davis, *Resisting Novels: Ideology and Fiction* (New York: Methuen, 1987), ch. 2; and Janet Wolff, *The Social Production of Art* (New York: St. Martin's Press, 1981).

[25]J. Kenneth Benson, "Organizations: A Dialectical View," *Administrative Science Quarterly*, 22 (1977): 1–21.

[26]See Michel Foucault, "Afterword: The Subject and Power," *Michel Foucault: Beyond Structuralism and Hermeneutics*, ed. Herbert L. Dreyfus and Paul Rainbow (Chicago: The University of Chicago Press, 1982), 208–229.

[27]The "materialist theory" of language, which conceptualizes the speaking subject as ideologically produced in the fixing of relations between signifiers is elaborated in Rosiland Coward and John Ellis, *Language and Materialism: Developments in Semiology and the Theory of the Subject* (Boston: Routledge and Kegan Paul, 1977).

[28]Richard Rhodes, *The Making of the Atomic Bomb* (New York: Simon and Schuster, 1986).

[29]Rhodes 95.

[30]See James W. Hikins, "The Rhetoric of 'Unconditional Surrender' and the Decision to Drop the Atomic Bomb," *Quarterly Journal of Speech*, 69 (1983): 379–400.

[31]Rhodes 452.

[32]Complete accounts of Los Alamos history are contained in Rhodes, chs. 14–19, James W. Kunetka, *City of Fire: Los Alamos and the Atomic Age, 1943–1945* (Albuquerque: University of New Mexico Press, 1979) and Ferenc Morton Szasz, *The Day the Sun Rose Twice: The Story of the Trinity Site Nuclear Explosion, July 16, 1945* (Albuquerque: University of New Mexico Press, 1984).

[33]*Reminiscences*, xx.

[34]John H. Manley, "A New Laboratory is Born," in *Reminiscences*, 21–40.

[35]Manley 21.

[36]Manley 22.

[37]Manley 22.

[38]Manley 24.

[39]Manley 24.

[40]Manley 25.

[41]Manley 25.

[42]Manley 26.

[43]For a discussion of the issues surrounding the discovery of metaphors by researchers in organizational discourse, see Stanley Deetz, "Metaphors and the Discursive Production and Reproduction of Organization," *Organization—Communication: Emerging Perspectives, I,* ed. L. Thayer (Norwood, N.J.: Ablex, 1986), 168–182.

[44]Peter L. Berger and Thomas Luckmann, *The Social Construction of Reality: A Treatise in the Sociology of Knowledge* (Garden City, NY: Anchor Books, 1967).

[45]Manley 27.

[46]Manley 27.

[47]Manley 27.

[48]Manley 32.

[49]Manley 33.

[50]Manley 33.

[51]Manley 34.

[52]Manley 34.

[53]Manley 34.

[54]Manley 35.

[55]Manley 35.

[56]Laura Fermi, "The Fermis' Path to Los Alamos," in *Reminiscences*, 89–104.

[57]Rhodes 464.

[58]Manley 35.

[59]Earl Shorris, *Scenes From Corporate Life: The Politics of Middle Management* (New York: Penguin Books, 1984).

[60]Joseph O. Hirschfelder, "The Scientific and Technological Miracle at Los Alamos," in *Reminiscences*, 67–88.

[61]Hirschfelder 67.

[62]Hirschfelder 67.

[63]Hirschfelder 67.

[64]Rhodes 715.

[65]Hirschfelder 70.

[66]Hirschfelder 72.

[67]Hirschfelder 72.

[68]Hirschfelder 72–73.

[69]Hirschfelder 73.

[70]Hirschfelder 73.

[71]Hirschfelder 73–74.

[72]Hirschfelder 74.

[73]Hirschfelder 74.

[74]Hirschfelder 77.

[75]Hirschfelder 78.

[76]Hirschfelder 67, citing Isaac Asimov.

[77]Hirschfelder 83. This comment occurs in the transcripts of the audience discussion following Hirschfelder's prepared address.

[78]Rhodes 732–734.

[79]See Belsey, and Jameson for discussions of History and the unconscious material of culture as the objects of ideological constraint in narrative.

[80] *Project Y: The Los Alamos Story, Part I: Toward Trinity,* by David Hawkins, *Part II: Beyond Trinity,* by Edith C. Truslow and Ralph Carlisle Smith (Los Angeles: Tomash Publishers, 1983), 88.

[81] Norris Bradbury, "Los Alamos—The First 25 Years," *Reminiscences,* 161–176.

[82] J. Robert Oppenheimer, "Speech to the Association of Los Alamos Scientists," [ironic acronym: "ALAS"], *Robert Oppenheimer: Letters and Recollections,* ed. Alice K. Smith and Charles Weiner (Cambridge, MA: Harvard University Press, 1980), 317.

[83] Bradbury 161.

[84] Bradbury 162.

[85] Bradbury 162.

[86] Bradbury 162.

[87] Bradbury 163.

[88] Bradbury 163.

[89] Bradbury 164.

[90] Bradbury 164.

[91] Bradbury 164.

[92] Bradbury 164–165.

[93] Bradbury 166.

[94] Bradbury 166.

[95] Bradbury 166.

[96] Bradbury 167.

[97] Bradbury 168.

[98] See McGeorge Bundy's discussion of the "neglected alternative" in *Danger and Survival: Choices About the Bomb in the First Fifty Years* (New York: Random House, 1988), 214–229.

[99] See V. N. Volosinov, "Appendix I: Discourse in Life and Discourse in Art (Concerning Sociological Poetics)," *Freudianism: A Marxist Critique,* trans. I. R. Titunik (New York: Academic Press, 1976), 92–116.

[100] Bradbury 168.

[101] Bradbury 168.

[102] Max Horkheimer, "The End of Reason," in Andrew Arato and Eike Gebhardt (eds.), *The Essential Frankfurt School Reader* (New York: Continuum, 1982), 26–48.

[103] Bradbury 169.

[104] Bradbury 169.

[105] Bradbury 169.

[106] Bradbury 169.

[107] Bradbury 170.

[108] Bradbury 170.

[109] Bradbury 170.

[110] "Preface," *Project Y,* x.

[111] Bradbury 175.

[112] Strine 495.

[113] Robert Scholes, *Textual Power: Literary Theory and the Teaching of English* (New Haven: Yale University Press, 1985), xi. Cited in Strine, 494.

[114] This goal is advocated by Linda Smircich in "Studying Organizations as Cultures," in Morgan, *Beyond Method,* 160–172; and Louis R. Pondy and Ian I. Mitroff, "Beyond the Open Systems Model of Organizations," *Research in Organizational Behavior, 1* (1979).

[115]Robert Jay Lifton, *The Nazi Doctors: Medical Killing and the Psychology of Genocide* (New York: Basic Books, 1986). Lifton is also the collector of another set of relevant voices, *Death in Life: Survivors of Hiroshima* (New York: Random House, 1967). Those narratives of living and dying within the nuclear blast are used powerfully by Rhodes, 716–734, to reveal what had been repressed in technical and strategic discourses.

[116]See the analysis of *Nazi Doctors* contained in Peter K. Manning, "The Ethnographic Conceit," *Journal of Contemporary Ethnography, 16* (1987): 49–68.

[117]*Nazi Doctors* 464.

[118]*Nazi Doctors* 177.

[119]While it is deliberately provocative, I make this connection with some care. I do not mean to imply that Los Alamos scientists—some of whom were unaware due to secrecy that they were working on a bomb, and most of whom believed that they were saving the Free World—are identical to Nazi doctors. The nuclear scientists and technicians of the Manhattan Project were in fact a conflicted group. Some members of the Chicago Met Lab, with more time on their hands for reflection as their work wound up, organized a petition against the bomb's use on populations. Others led the post-war fight for international control of atomic energy. But at Los Alamos, there was less slack, and the work went on uninterrupted, ceded to military control. As Paul Boyer notes, "perhaps after the passage of four decades, we are ready for a more comprehensive understanding of the moral disintegration wrought by World War II—an understanding that will at least consider in the same context (without necessarily equating) the atomic bomb and the gas chamber." *Bomb's Early Light,* 226.

[120]Richard Feynman, "Los Alamos From Below," *Reminiscences,* 132.

# CONTRIBUTORS

**Thomas W. Benson** is Edwin Erle Sparks Professor of Speech Communication at the Pennsylvania State University.

**Carole Blair** is associate professor of rhetoric and communication at the University of California at Davis.

**Barry Brummett** is professor and chair of communication at the University of Wisconsin at Milwaukee.

**Maurice Charland** is associate professor of communication studies at Concordia University.

**Gary A. Copeland** is associate professor of telecommunication and film at the University of Alabama.

**Bonnie J. Dow** is assistant professor of communication at North Dakota State University.

**Thomas S. Frentz** is associate professor of communication at the University of Arkansas.

**Roderick P. Hart** is F. A. Liddell Professor of Speech Communication at the University of Texas at Austin.

**Robert L. Ivie** is professor and chair of speech communication and theater arts at Indiana University.

**Marsha S. Jeppeson** is a consultant in Sacramento, California.

**Michael C. Leff** is professor of communication studies at Northwestern University.

**Elizabeth Walker Mechling** is dean of the School of Communications at the California State University at Fullerton.

**Jay Mechling** is professor of American studies at the University of California at Davis.

**William L. Nothstine** is a writer living in Portland, Oregon.

**Michael M. Osborn** is professor of theatre and communication arts at Memphis State University.

**Enrico Pucci, Jr.,** is a doctoral candidate in speech communication at the Pennsylvania State University.

**Janice Hocker Rushing** is associate professor of communication at the University of Arkansas.

**449**

**Martha Solomon** is professor of speech communication at the University of Maryland.

**Bryan C. Taylor** is assistant professor of speech communication and theater arts at Texas A&M University.

**Philip Wander** is professor of communication studies at San Jose State University.

# ACKNOWLEDGMENTS

**Bonnie J. Dow,** "Hegemony, Feminist Criticism, and *The Mary Tyler Moore Show.*" From *Critical Studies in Mass Communication,* vol. 7, 1990, pp. 261–274. Copyright by the Speech Communication Association; reprinted by permission of the publisher.

**Elizabeth Walker Mechling and Jay Mechling,** "The Campaign for Civil Defense and the Struggle to Naturalize the Bomb." From *Western Journal of Speech Communication,* vol. 55, 1991, pp. 105–133. Copyrighted by the Western States Communication Association. Reprinted by permission of the publisher.

**Janice Hocker Rushing and Thomas S. Frentz,** "The Frankenstein Myth in Contemporary Cinema." From *Critical Studies in Mass Communication,* vol. 6, March 1989, pp. 61–80. Copyright by the Speech Communication Association; reprinted by permission of the publisher.

**Thomas W. Benson,** "The Rhetorical Structure of Frederick Wiseman's *Primate.*" From *Quarterly Journal of Speech,* vol. 71, 1985, pp. 204–217. Copyright by the Speech Communication Association; reprinted by permission of the publisher.

**Maurice Charland,** "Constitutive Rhetoric: The Case of the *Peuple Québécois.*" From *Quarterly Journal of Speech,* vol. 73, 1987, pp. 133–150. Copyright by the Speech Communication Association; reprinted by permission of the publisher.

**Robert L. Ivie,** "The Metaphor of Force in Prowar Discourse: The Case of 1812." From *Quarterly Journal of Speech,* vol. 68, 1982, pp. 240–253. Copyright by the Speech Communication Association; reprinted by permission of the publisher.

**Barry Brummett,** "Premillennial Apocalyptic as a Rhetorical Genre." From *Central States Speech Journal,* vol. 35, 1984, pp. 84–93. Copyright by the Central States Communication Association; reprinted by permission of the publisher.

**Martha Solomon,** "The Rhetoric of Dehumanization: An Analysis of Medical Reports of the Tuskegee Syphilis Project." From *Western Journal of Speech Communication,* vol. 49, 1985, pp. 233–247. Copyrighted by the Western States Communication Association. Reprinted by permission of the publisher.

**Michael C. Leff,** "Redemptive Identification: Cicero's Catilinarian Orations." In G. P. Mohrmann, Charles J. Stewart, and Donovan J. Ochs (Eds.), *Explorations in Rhetorical Criticism* (University Park, PA: Penn State Press, 1973), pp. 158–177. Copyright by the Pennsylvania State University. Reprinted by permission of the publisher.

**Carole Blair, Marsha S. Jeppeson, and Enrico Pucci, Jr.** "Public Memorializing in Postmodernity: The Vietnam Veterans Memorial as Prototype." From *Quarterly Journal of Speech,* vol. 77, 1991, pp. 263–288. Copyright by the Speech Communication Association; reprinted by permission of the publisher.

**Philip Wander,** "The Rhetoric of American Foreign Policy." From *Quarterly Journal of Speech,* vol. 70, 1984, pp. 339–361. Copyright by the Speech Communication Association; reprinted by permission of the publisher.

**Bryan C. Taylor,** *"Reminiscences of Los Alamos:* Narrative, Critical Theory, and the Organizational Subject." From *Western Journal of Speech Communication,* vol. 54, Summer 1990, pp. 395–419. Copyrighted by the Western States Communication Association. Reprinted by permission of the publisher.